America

SECOND EDITION

America

Volume 1: to 1877

A History of the United States

Norman K. Risjord

University of Wisconsin

Prentice Hall, Englewood Cliffs, New Jersey 07632

Library of Congress Cataloging-in-Publication Data

Risjord, Norman K.
    America, a history of the United States.

    Includes bibliographies and index.
    Contents: v. 1. To 1877 — v. 2. Since 1865
    1. United States—History. I. Title.
E178.1.R59 1988   973   87-25745
ISBN 0-13-025156-9 (v. 1)
ISBN 0-13-025198-4 (v. 2)

Editorial/production supervision: Marjorie Shustak
Cover and interior design: Lee Cohen
Manufacturing buyer: Ed O'Dougherty
Photo research: Lorinda Morris-Nantz/Kay Dellosa
Cover art: John Caspar Wild, "Cincinnati" (Cincinnati Historical Society)

For Bill Kestle, in memoriam—
he brought teachers and books together

America: A History of the United States,
Volume 1: to 1877, Norman K. Risjord

 © 1988, 1985 by Prentice-Hall, Inc.
A Division of Simon & Schuster
Englewood Cliffs, New Jersey 07632

Printed in the United States of America

10 9 8 7 6 5 4 3 2 1

ISBN 0-13-025156-9

Prentice-Hall International (UK) Limited, *London*
Prentice-Hall of Australia Pty. Limited, *Sydney*
Prentice-Hall Canada Inc., *Toronto*
Prentice-Hall Hispanoamericana, S.A., *Mexico*
Prentice-Hall of India Private Limited, *New Delhi*
Prentice-Hall of Japan, Inc., *Tokyo*
Simon & Schuster Asia Pte. Ltd., *Singapore*
Editora Prentice-Hall do Brasil, Ltda., *Rio de Janeiro*

CONTENTS

v

4

BRITAIN'S ATLANTIC COMMUNITY **77**

5

WAR AND THE BONDS OF EMPIRE **96**

6

FLINTLOCK AND QUILL: Winning Independence **124**

7

E PLURIBUS UNUM: 1776–1788 **149**

8

INVENTING A NATION: 1789–1805 **173**

9

THE RISING EMPIRE: 1805–1829   203

10

THE AGE OF JACKSON: 1829–1844   288

11

A PEOPLE IN MOTION   267

16

BITTER REUNION:
1865–1877   **419**

THE DECLARATION
OF INDEPENDENCE   **447**

THE CONSTITUTION
OF THE
UNITED STATES:
And What It
Means Today   **449**

PRESIDENTIAL
ELECTIONS   **467**

INDEX   **471**

CLIO'S FOCUS

PREFACE

A single-authored textbook spanning the whole of American history is an awesome undertaking. Some might even think it presumptuous. My justification—excuse, if you will—is twenty-five years of teaching the American Survey course. One develops, over that span of time, a sense of organization and a facility for explanation. These qualities were tested before a wider audience through broadcasts on the Wisconsin Educational Radio Network in 1965–1966, 1972–1973, 1982–1983, and 1987–1988. I have also benefited enormously from association with many graduate teaching assistants. Vigilant and sometimes critical, they have induced me to keep abreast of current scholarship. For these reasons it proved easier to cover the ground from Columbus to Reagan than I had anticipated.

This is a traditional piece of history, in the sense that it is chronologically organized and focuses to a large extent on public affairs. This, to be sure, reflects the emphasis and approach of my own teaching. But it will also be of value to the more experimental teacher. With a textbook that supplies the nuts and bolts of history, the teacher can afford to spend class time on areas of special interest or questions of historical interpretation. I feel, moreover, that the main purpose of the introductory survey of American history is to provide students with a rudimentary factual base, while entertaining them enough to encourage further study. It is my hope that this book accomplishes that dual purpose.

In this second edition the text has been expanded by about 10 percent. Most of the added material is in the field of social history. This is in part a response to readers who felt more attention ought to be given to this area of history, but it also reflects the thrust of recent scholarship. Some of the most exciting new discoveries have been in the field of women's studies and the family. These, as well as other important contributions of the past five years, I have tried to incorporate in this edition.

An author incurs many obligations in writing a book, and space permits the acknowledgment of only a few. My wife Connie played the role of historical novice, demanding clarification and explanation of many things that historians tend to take for granted. I am also deeply indebted to the unsung heroes of the profession, those who review and critique manuscripts. Their exacting standards, tempered by fairness and empathy, are a credit to the profession. They are, for this edition, John Snetsinger, California Polytech University; J. Carroll Moody, Northern Illinois University; Thomas E. Siefert, Indiana State University; James E. Sargent, Virginia Western Community College; Louis W. Potts, University of Missouri; Bruce J. Dierenfield, Canisius College; and Peter Wallenstein, Virginia Polytechnic Institute & State University.

My editors at Prentice Hall, especially Steve Dalphin and Marjorie Borden Shustak, did a splendid job of guiding the work through the various stages of production. My contact with Prentice Hall was made through Bill Kestle, Prentice Hall sales representative for Wisconsin and a friend of twenty years. Bill died while the first edition was in production. To his memory it is respectfully dedicated.

Norman K. Risjord

1

THE CLASH
OF CULTURES

America was "discovered" at least three times. Christopher Columbus's discovery in 1492, less than five hundred years ago, is only the most recent and best known. Before him, by another five hundred years, had come the Norsemen. And before them, by several thousand years, had come the Indians.

The Norse, or Vikings, had found their way across the Atlantic in the course of the ninth and tenth centuries. From their Scandinavian homeland, they had crossed to the Orkney Islands north of Scotland and leaped from there to Iceland and Greenland. They planted colonies as they went and used each as a base for further exploration.

Some time around the year A.D. 1000, Viking captain Lief Ericson sailed along the coast of North America, perhaps as far south as New England. Shortly thereafter came settlers. The Norse sagas, a mixture of folklore and history, speak of an expedition of 160 men and women, together with some livestock, that came in two ships. During their second winter, the sagas record, the settlers were driven back to Greenland by "Skraelings," Indians who had come to trade and stayed to fight. In recent years archeologists have unearthed the remains of a Norse settlement on the north coast of Newfoundland, though there is no way of knowing whether it is the one mentioned in the sagas. The cabin foundations are unmistakably Viking in design, but there are disappointingly few artifacts. This fact in itself may be significant. If the settlers were driven away by Indians, they at least had time to pack. Nor are there signs of battle; the colony was simply abandoned after a few years.

⊔ The Indian Discovery

The Skraelings whom the Vikings encountered were, of course, the descendants of the first discoverers of America. Their ancestors had come to America from the west, crossing from Siberia some fifteen to twenty thousand years ago, toward the end of the Ice Age. The Wisconsin glacier, so called because of its dramatic impact on the landscape of the upper Middle West, had packed into its icy mass so much of the earth's water that the sea level had fallen by six hundred feet. That had opened a land bridge hundreds of miles wide between Alaska and Siberia. Nomadic hunters drifted across, skirted the north shore of Alaska to the Mackenzie River, and followed that magnificent stream south into central Canada and the Great Plains. Other bands hugged the western coastline, passing into present-day Oregon through mountains kept ice-free by the warm Japanese current in the Pacific Ocean. How long all this took is hard to say, but in Oregon, California, and New Mexico, bone fragments and spearheads have been found that date back nine thousand years.

Those who followed the Canadian rivers into the heart of the continent fanned out south of the Great Lakes into the eastern woodlands. These people were hunters and gatherers; it would be many centuries before they developed the art of planting crops. The Indians who settled in the northern forests lived in cone-shaped *tipis* made of birchbark; those in the warmer southern regions built oval or oblong wigwams made of saplings, bark, bulrushes, or even grass woven into mats. Villages, widely scattered, were composed of extended families, or clans, and clans that spoke the same language formed tribes. Because the forebears of the eastern woodland tribes had arrived in America at about the same time, their languages were similar. Modern-day archeologists refer to them as Algonkian, a name derived from the Algonquin tribe, which ruled the forests between the St. Lawrence River and the Atlantic coast at the time the Europeans arrived.

(*Chapter opening photo*) Mesa Verde, Colorado—a relic of the Pueblo Indian culture that flourished in the American Southwest 1,000 years ago.

The movement of peoples across the Alaskan land bridge went on for thousands of years, and so did their southward drift. Those who followed the Pacific coastline eventually entered what is now California, Mexico, and Central America. Roaming bands met, intermingled, and exchanged knowledge. Later arrivals were equipped with bows and arrows, weapons that revolutionized the art of hunting. In the warm, humid Southwest* some enterprising people discovered edible plants that were the forerunners of corn and squash and nurtured them to improve yields. The art of cultivation, in turn, changed living habits, for it encouraged people to settle down and thus led to the growth of larger communities. Technological developments also afforded security and leisure, which encouraged intellectual and artistic pursuits.

MAYAN CULTURE

In the Isthmus of Central America, the Mayans built a brilliant civilization a thousand years before Columbus. Giant temples for their gods and pyramids for the dead suggest the importance of religious beliefs. Furthermore, the Mayan notion of an afterlife, of spirits that existed beyond the realm of sight and sound and touch, was a powerful idea that took the thoughts of men and women away from the day-to-day gathering of food. The building of temples required an army of workers. Cities sprang up around these construction projects, and people were fed by food growers in the hinterland. Specialization of work encouraged trade, and prosperity fostered art and science. A thousand years before the Spaniards came, the Mayans had a civilization equal to any in the world. Among its achievements were the development of paper, the invention of the numer-

ical concept of zero, and the use of a solar calendar.

THE MOUND BUILDERS

About A.D. 600 or 700, when the Mayan civilization was in its glory, a new people moved into central North America and settled in the lower Mississippi valley. Having come from the north, perhaps directly from Asia, they either brought with them or acquired by indirect contact with the Mayans (whose culture influenced the entire perimeter of the Gulf of Mexico) the custom of collecting the bones of their dead and burying them under mounds. These mounds, the largest of which resembled Mayan pyramids, are to be found throughout southeastern North America. Crop cultivation, which the Mound Builders either developed themselves or borrowed from neighbors, contributed to the rise of large communities. The Mound Builders used iron implements, made a distinctive though rather crude pottery, and wore clothing of woven fabric.

The Mound Builders' prosperity aroused envy among their more primitive neighbors, and envy led to conflict. To shield themselves, the Mound Builders built outposts, among them Cahokia, near the mouth of the Illinois River. Through such outlying settlements, Mississippean culture filtered into the northern woodlands and influenced the tribes living there. The effigy mounds—heaps of dirt shaped to resemble animals—that dot the Great Lakes region are thought to be the result of this influence. Such cultural imperialism only delayed the inevitable, however. Just as Rome had fallen to its primitive and jealous neighbors a thousand years before, the Mound Builders were under attack and on the decline when Columbus reached America.

As the Mound Builders grew weaker, alien tribes—comparatively recent arrivals in North America—moved in among them. Most of these newcomers spoke a common

---

* The famous Petrified Forest of Arizona indicates that the American Southwest and northern Mexico had abundant rainfall five to ten thousand years ago.

Shiloh National Military Park and Cemetery, Shiloh, Tennessee.

Effigy pipe. Found along the banks of the Tennessee River, this pipe made of red bauxite may be one of the relics of the Mound-Builder culture.

language, which anthropologists have labeled Muskogean, after the largest of the tribes, the Muskogi, or Creek. The newcomers absorbed as much of the Mississippean culture as they destroyed. They learned how to farm; they settled into a comparatively sedentary village life; and they even built some mounds of their own. They progressed fairly rapidly in the art of "civilization," as white Europeans defined it. Centuries later, white settlers would call them the civilized tribes.

COMING OF THE IROQUOIS

Close upon the Muskogean migration and mixing with it was the movement of another people, the Iroquois. Theirs was the last migration into the woodlands east of the Mississippi River, where they found much of the land staked out, if not fully occupied. They pushed the Algonkian tribes out of the way, fought when they

had to, settled where they could. At the Appalachian barrier, the Iroquois stream split. One branch, made up of Cherokees and Tuscaroras, headed south to live among their distant relatives the Muskogeans. The remainder pushed into the lush land of green hills and crystal lakes south and east of Lake Ontario.

The Iroquois were corn planters and village dwellers as far back as we can trace them. Whether they acquired this living style from contact with the southern tribes or developed it on their own we cannot say. They built houses in the fashion of the southern Indians but also developed a unique adaptation, the long house, so called because it was fifty to one hundred feet in length. Fashioned of saplings and elm bark, the long house sheltered eight to ten families separated from one another only by cooking fires. White missionaries who stayed among the Iroquois remembered the long house principally for its smoke, dogs, and noise.

Iroquois women tended the fields, while the men busied themselves with hunting and war. Enamored of combat, the Iroquois fought their Algonkian-speaking neighbors, and they fought one another. Because men were often absent, Iroquois society came to be organized along female lines. Women owned the land and governed the household. Families grouped into clans by maternal relationships. Men sat on the tribal councils because most of the decision making involved peace or war, but the delegates were often chosen by clan matriarchs.

The Iroquois fared badly in their hostile environment until, say their legends, they stopped fighting one another and formed the League of the Great Peace. Tribal legends give the honor for this milestone, which occurred in about 1570, to Hiawatha. Blending diplomacy and religious mysticism, Hiawatha persuaded his people to form not only a security pact, but a political union. Hiawatha's confederacy had mostly ceremonial functions at first, but

Indian life. The domed house made of bark, woven mats, thatch, or hides was characteristic of the Indians of the northern woodlands. In the Algonquian languages it was called a *wigwam.*

Courtesy, American Museum of Natural History, New York.

gradually it hardened into a sophisticated governmental system, one unique among North American Indians. The League of Five Nations, as the English called it, was managed by fifty delegates who met every summer at the central council fire of the Onondagua. Representation was proportionate to size, with the Onondagua providing fourteen delegates and the other league members, the Cayuga, the Mohawk, the Oneida, and the Seneca, sending somewhat fewer. Nominated by the female heads of each clan and approved by their tribes, delegates reached their decisions in private and then voted as a unit in the assembly. The system bred strength, cohesion, and morale. By the time Europeans landed on the northern coast of the continent, the Iroquois were a force with which to be reckoned.

THE PLAINS INDIANS

The first peoples who had followed the receding glaciers had found the Great Plains lush and teeming with wildlife. But later, when the climate turned dry and the animals disappeared, the plains hunters sought new food sources. About the time the Vikings began roaming the Atlantic, tribes were once again drifting into the western grasslands. The clans were either a branch of the Mississippean culture or were influenced by it. They lived in villages, in houses made of prairie sod; grew corn, squash, and beans; and had enough leisure time to fashion elaborately decorated pottery. Some, such as the Mandan of the upper Missouri River, were as far advanced in agricultural practices as any of the "civilized tribes." Two language stocks, Siouan and Caddoan, bound these clans together, and both were closely related to Iroquoian. It is possible that all three language groups arrived on the continent together.

The grassland tribes hunted deer and small game. They had no way of overcoming the buffalo except to set the prairie on fire and drive them into traps or over cliffs. In the seventeenth century the Spanish introduced horses into the Southwest,

Indians stalking buffalo. Although this painting was done by George Catlin (1796–1872) in the 1830s, it depicts one of the methods that Indians used to hunt buffalo before horses were introduced to the New World.

Courtesy, American Museum of Natural History, New York.

and the Indian way of life was drastically changed. Hunters became more mobile and warriors more versatile. The Plains Indians abandoned their sedentary life and took to following the buffalo on horseback. Buffalo meat and skin provided all their basic needs. They abandoned their lavishly decorated implements and their insulated earthen houses and began living in portable *tipis* of buffalo skin. By their standards they were wealthy, and their wealth attracted other wandering hunters. Blackfoot, Arapaho, Cheyenne, and Crow moved out of the eastern woodlands and onto the plains. Last came the mighty Teton Dakota, or Sioux, who trekked out of the Minnesota lake country to take up the nomad life in 1775, the year the American Revolution began.

In the Southwest, meanwhile, another cultural interaction was occurring among Indian peoples, a clash that was still in progress when the Spanish penetrated the region. From the first migrations, people had settled in the area of present-day New Mexico and Arizona. Some had stayed on even after the climate turned dry and the

game disappeared. They were an agricultural people who raised a primitive form of corn as early as 1000 B.C., the earliest record we have of this important crop. They spoke a language known as Uto-Aztecan, a name that also reveals the tremendous geographical span of their culture: Among their descendants were the Ute and Comanche tribes of Utah and Colorado; the Taos, Hopi, Pima, and Zuni of New Mexico and Arizona; and the Aztecs of central Mexico.

The culture of the Corn Growers flourished at about the same time as that of the Mound Builders to the east, and it declined for much the same reason. Some time around A.D. 900, their villages (*pueblos* in Spanish) became increasingly elaborate. Terraced apartment houses made of adobe brick housed hundreds of people. Some houses were built into the sides of cliffs to protect people against the weather and to improve their defense capabilities. The Pueblo people had a varied agriculture; they grew corn, beans, squash, cotton, and tobacco. Their pottery was exquisitely shaped and finely decorated, and they wove clothing and blankets from their cotton. Their religious worship included elaborate ceremonies, most of them devoted to the life-giver, rain.

APACHES AND NAVAJOS

About A.D. 1200, newcomers, primitive nomads from the north, moved into the Southwest, and the great pueblos were abandoned one by one. Some, such as the magnificent cliff dwellings at Chaco Canyon, New Mexico, can still be seen today, ghostly reminders of vanished glory. The Pueblo clans called these newcomers *apaches*, which meant "strangers" or "enemies," and one particular group was called *apaches de navahu*, "enemies of the cultivated fields." These people, as they evolved, eventually subdivided into the Apache and Navajo tribes. They came at first as nomads might, in small groups; and although not a military threat, they were troublesome when they stole corn or kidnapped women. Agricultural societies are almost defenseless against such marauders, as the Mound Builders, the Romans, and even the ancient peoples of Mesopotamia might attest.

The *apaches* were hunters from the forested mountains to the north. They wore skins, subsisted on whatever was available (Navajo tales speak of eating birds and lizards), and lived in houses made of sticks and bark. They were too busy surviving to concoct myth and ceremony. But they were quick to learn. While destroying the Pueblo culture, they also absorbed it. The Navajo built pueblos of their own, though not elaborate apartment complexes; they learned how to farm and even to irrigate

The Taos, New Mexico, pueblo as it is today. A pueblo such as this contained about 200 people. Each family occupied a single room, though it might possess other rooms for storage of grain or religious rites. In pre-Columbian times, the lower story had no windows so the entire structure could be more easily defended. The lower rooms were entered by a ladder through a hatchway in the roof.

dry lands (a technique developed by the Pimans, an ancient tribe of what is now Arizona). This acculturation was in process when the Spanish appeared in Mexico. Indeed, some of the nomads, given the name *Apache,* were still filtering down from the north. They were in no way prepared to accept Spanish ways or Spanish rule. Nowhere on the continent was the clash of European and Indian cultures more bloody or more long-lasting than on the southwestern borderlands.

⊔ The Awakening of Europe

The Indians discovered America, and the Norse rediscovered it. But neither event had any impact on the rest of humanity. To have an impact, discoveries must be exploited. Colonies and trade routes must follow discovery, and western Europe in the age of the Vikings lacked the technology to develop them. Europeans did not have the navigational instruments to reach lands beyond the horizon, and their ships were not designed for ocean voyages. Since ancient times, vessels had been propelled by oars; sails were used only when the wind was blowing in the right direction. It was possible to row across the Atlantic, as the Vikings had demonstrated, but not with a cargo of gold or grain. The colonization of the New World waited upon technology.

About the time that the great Pueblo and Mississippean cultures in America went into decline, Europe experienced a cultural rebirth. Beginning in Italy in the twelfth century, an artistic and intellectual awakening known as the Renaissance spread slowly across Europe. Scholars discovered the mathematical and astronomical works of the ancient Greeks and Arabs (both of whom knew the world was round); mapmakers began charting the seas. One adventurous trader, Marco Polo, followed caravan routes across Asia until he reached the throne of the Great Khan in China.

For centuries, people had been preoccupied with religion and life after death; with the Renaissance came a fascination with the here and now. Men and women became more concerned with earthly life, more curious about the world around them. Concern for the material things of life inspired a search for wealth. Geographical knowledge and trade went hand in hand. The lure of knowledge and wealth inspired Prince Henry the Navigator of Portugal, who invited mapmakers and explorers to his court in the early 1400s. Financed by Henry, Portuguese navigators probed the coast of Africa south to the Gulf of Guinea. From bases there, the Portuguese developed a profitable trade in gold and ivory with the kingdoms of central Africa. And curiosity paid dividends. In 1488, Bartholomew Diaz reached the southern tip of Africa, which later adventurers would name the Cape of Good Hope. A decade later, Vasco da Gama ventured around the Cape, crossed the Indian Ocean, and docked at Calicut in India. He returned with a shipload of silks and spices. Europe's trade with the Orient—India, China, and the Spice Islands (the East Indies or Indonesia today)—had for centuries been funneled through the trade routes of the Middle East. Arab and Persian merchants crossed the Indian Ocean on the monsoon winds, and they brought back the silks and spices of the East. These goods were carried overland to the shores of the Mediterranean, where they were picked up by Italian merchants for distribution throughout Europe. Da Gama's voyage around Africa offered at last an opportunity to break the Arab-Italian stranglehold on this trade. Before long, the Portuguese were making regular runs to India and the Spice Islands. Profits from this trade, together with the import of gold and ivory from Africa, made Lisbon, for a time, the commercial center of Europe.

The Price of Spice

The exploration of Africa and the discovery of America resulted from the European search for a route to the Spice Islands of the East. Spices helped to preserve food in an age when refrigeration was unknown, and they enhanced its taste. A few surviving mercantile records from the later Middle Ages show why traders went so eagerly in search of the source. German records from 1393 show a pound of nutmeg being exchanged for seven oxen. Elsewhere a pound of saffron could be traded for a horse, a pound of ginger for a sheep, and two pounds of mace for a cow. At such exchange rates, it is little wonder that India, Malaya, and the East Indies held Europe's attention long after America and the West Indies were discovered.

The growth of trade was made possible by the development of a new style of ship, the carrack, which depended on sails rather than oars. Although clumsy in appearance and difficult to sail, the carrack was an immense improvement over the oar-driven galley and an innovation that in time enabled Europeans not only to discover but also to exploit the unknown. Improvements in navigational techniques also appeared. For instance, the Portuguese discovered that as they approached the equator, the noonday sun stood higher and higher, until at last it was directly overhead. When they went even farther south, the sun reversed itself. Through calculation of the distance of the sun above the horizon, they found that they could tell how far they were north or south of the equator, a position known as *latitude*. In addition, the Portuguese navigators were alert to changes in the prevailing winds, and they put their discoveries to good use. In Portugal, as in all of western Europe, the winds and weather usually came from the west. Off the coast of Africa, however, they came from the opposite direction, the southeast, and near the equator there was hardly any wind at all. This knowledge, invaluable to captains of sailing ships, must have spread rapidly, for it is fairly certain that Columbus knew of wind belts. When he set out for the Orient, he sailed not west but south to the Portuguese Azores, where he picked up food, water, and an easterly wind. Merchants who used these easterly breezes in the following century to reach the Caribbean and Central America named them the trade winds.

⊔ Conquistadors and Missionaries: The Spanish in America

Portugal's dominant position in world trade naturally excited envy, but there were few in Europe who could do much about it. Northern Europe from England to Germany was a patchwork of baronies, too weak and divided to undertake anything except excursions to the Holy Land. Portugal's neighbor Spain, on the other hand, was in a somewhat better position. The marriage of Ferdinand and Isabella in 1489 united the principalities of Castille and Aragon into a kingdom. In 1492, the joint sovereigns expelled the last of the Moors, Islamic invaders who had conquered the country seven hundred years before. Ferdinand and Isabella were looking for new worlds to conquer when Christopher Columbus knocked on their palace door.

CLIO'S FOCUS: On Clio

In Greek mythology the nine muses were the daughters of Zeus and Mnemosyne (Memory). Zeus, king of the gods, assigned them to preside over song and memory. Each was assigned to some department of human knowledge or skill, such as astronomy, epic poetry, lyre-playing, or classical music. Clio, whose name meant "fame" or "renown" in Greek, was responsible for proclaiming deeds of renown. She was thus the muse of history.

Since knowledge then was instilled in human memory and conveyed through the generations in song and verse, the muses were gifted poets and musicians. They were often called upon to judge musical contests among men or between gods and men. On one occasion they themselves were challenged to a lyre-playing contest by a group of mortals. They not only won, but they turned the losers into blackbirds as punishment for having insulted gods with a challenge.

Clio had perhaps the most difficult assignment of all the muses because humankind does not always profit by history. It perversely ignores the past or misinterprets its meaning, even when the past is recorded in song and verse by a goddess. This paradox led the Greeks to coin the pun: "Can Clio do more than amuse?" In brief essays accompanying each chapter of this book, we have focused, in Clio's name, on some little-known facets of history in the hope that our tale will amuse as well as instruct. We trust that Clio will accept the challenge gracefully.

VOYAGES OF COLUMBUS

An Italian from the busy seaport of Genoa, Columbus was already familiar with the western seas. He had visited ports in northern Europe and had even ventured as far as Iceland in the company of fishermen. There he may well have heard tales of lands farther to the west. Was the West another route to the fabulous East? Columbus spent several years trying to get financing for a voyage into the western sea to find out. In 1486 he sought the backing of the Spanish court without success, but when he returned in 1492, the situation in Spain had changed. Columbus's proposal offered Ferdinand and Isabella a way to break the Arab-Italian monopoly on the spice trade, and the price was relatively low—three small carracks and a few months' supplies. Nor were the Spanish monarchs distressed when he returned from that first voyage in 1492 with nothing to show for his efforts but a few hapless natives whom he called Indians in the mistaken belief that he had found the Indies. Ferdinand and Isabella financed another voyage in 1493, and two more after that.

In his four voyages, Columbus discovered and named most of the tropical islands of the West Indies and probed the coast of South America from the mouth of the Orinoco River to the Bay of Honduras. Although he found neither silks nor spices nor Asians, he stubbornly insisted until his death in 1506 that he had reached the Orient. By then, of course, navigators

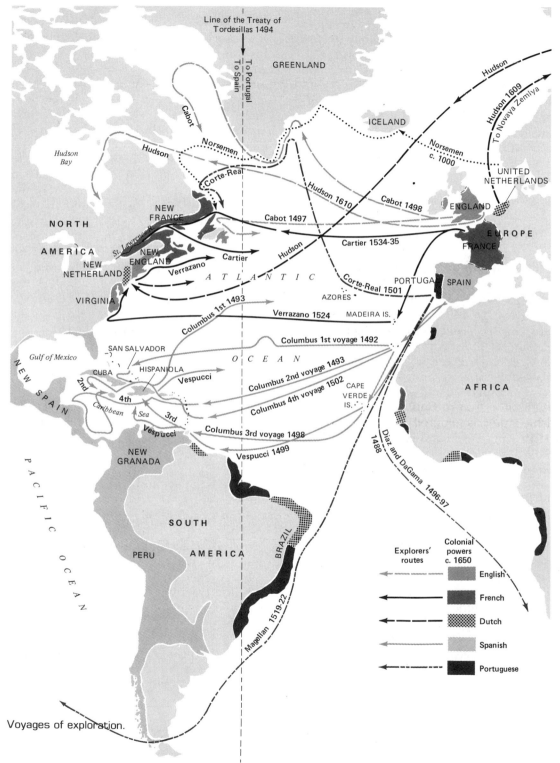

Voyages of exploration.

and their patrons knew better. In 1499, contrary winds blew a Portuguese ship from Africa to Brazil, and its captain had claimed the new land for his country. Two years later, Amerigo Vespucci, an Italian adventurer who sailed in the service of Portugal, explored the coast of Brazil and returned with the claim that it was indeed a new world. A cartographer honored Vespucci by giving his name to the new continent: America.

SPANISH EXPLORATION

Without waiting to find out whether Columbus was right or wrong, Ferdinand and Isabella moved swiftly to capitalize on his discovery. In 1493 they established a colony on the island Columbus had named Espanola ("little Spain," Santo Domingo today). Using the gentle Arawak Indians as slaves, the Spanish mined what gold there was on Espanola, and when that gave out they moved on to Cuba and Puerto Rico, which they conquered in 1509–1511. In 1512 King Ferdinand commissioned Juan Ponce de Leon to explore an island described by Indians as lying to the north and west of Cuba. Sailing in the spring of 1513, de Leon made landfall in the vicinity of the city that later became St. Augustine. The day was Easter Sunday, a holiday the Spanish called Easter of Flowers (*pascua florida*), so de Leon named his new possession Florida. He provoked a fight with Indians every time he stepped ashore, and so learned little about the new land; he followed the coastline south to the keys and north to Pensacola Bay and returned without ever realizing that the land he had found was not an island.

That same year, other explorers made significant discoveries. Balboa added to the growing fund of knowledge by crossing the Isthmus of Panama to its western edge and viewing for the first time the Pacific Ocean, or as the Spanish called it, the South Sea.* Six years later, Ferdinand Magellan battled his way around the southern tip of South America and sailed into the South Sea. He established a new route to the Spice Islands, though it proved to be longer and more difficult than the Portuguese route around the tip of Africa. Magellan was killed in the Philippines in a skirmish with natives, but his lieutenant made it back to Spain with a cargo of spice that more than paid for the expedition. Completion of the voyage also marked the first circumnavigation of the globe (1519–1522). During those same years, Hernando Cortez conquered the Aztec Empire in central Mexico and found a treasure in precious metals greater than anyone had dreamed. A few years later, from 1525 to 1533, Francisco Pizarro worked south from Panama through the mountains of Ecuador and Peru and uncovered the ancient civilization of the Incas. By trickery, deceit, and outright murder he overcame their resistance, stole their riches, and turned them into slaves. For more than two centuries the Spanish exploited the gold and silver mines of Mexico and Peru and sent the treasure by convoy across the Gulf of Mexico to Cuba, then up the straits between Florida and the Bahamas and home via the prevailing westerlies. Madrid replaced Lisbon as the power center of Europe.

The conquests of Cortez and Pizarro centered Spanish attention on the southern continent. The land mass to the north, still vaguely known as Florida, remained shrouded in mystery, although imaginative mapmakers linked it to Mexico. In 1528, Pánfilo de Narváez set out to determine if there was gold to the north as well. He landed on the western coast of Florida and spent three months wandering through a jungle of palmetto and long-leaf pine,

---

* The reason is that from Panama, the Pacific appears to be to the south. Moreover, the only access to it was by the southern route around Cape Horn.

searching for treasure. By the time he returned to the coast, his ships had given him up for lost and returned to Cuba. The nearest Spanish settlement was in Mexico, so Narváez and his men built rafts and began paddling westward along the coast. All perished at sea, except four who were washed up on the coast of Texas. Among these were Cabeza de Vaca and an African, Estevanico. For eight years this pair wandered across mountains and deserts, passing from tribe to tribe, and eventually reached lower California. They found no treasure, but returned to Mexico City with tales of fabulous cities to the north.

In 1537, the year de Vaca returned to Spain with his fantastic tale, the king appointed Hernando de Soto governor of Cuba and Florida. De Soto had participated in the conquest and plunder of Peru, an exploit that had made him wealthy. He clearly hoped that the northern continent held similar riches. As a condition of the appointment, the king demanded a share in the findings, although de Soto had to finance an expedition himself. De Soto landed in Tampa Bay in May 1539 at the head of a band of conquistadors. He carried no tools for colonization and few supplies—only weapons and collars and chains for making captives into slaves. His tactics were crude but simple: He attacked every Indian settlement he encountered, even those that received him hospitably.

De Soto marched across the Southeast from Florida to the Mississippi River, leaving a trail of blood and tears, and all he had to show for his effort was a box of pretty stones collected from the Indians. He did discover the Mississippi, but the Spanish crown did not recognize the significance of the event. After de Soto died of

Early impressions of Florida. This map, drawn in 1564, is the first known drawing of America's trees. Palms, pines, and live oaks with Spanish moss are clearly discernible. The vessels, with gunports below deck, are the latest model galleons.

New York Public Library Picture Collection.

a fever in 1542, in what is now Louisiana, his men made their way to Mexico in makeshift rafts. In those same years (1539–1542), a similar expedition, led by Francisco Coronado, was mounted from Mexico City. Coronado went in search of the fabulous cities mentioned by Cabeza de Vaca. He found only the ruins of the Pueblo culture and vast herds of buffalo in a sea of grass. Dismissing the continent as bereft of riches, no Spaniard ventured again into its interior.

THE SPANISH EMPIRE

By 1542, the year Coronado returned emptyhanded, the boundaries of Spain's empire were marked. Spain claimed the West Indies, the lands bordering the Caribbean Sea and the Gulf of Mexico, and the western coast of South America as far south as Chile. Presiding over this domain was Charles V, the grandson of Ferdinand and Isabella, who, by virtue of his mother's marriage into the Hapsburg family of Austria, was also Holy Roman Emperor. His dominions stretched from Vienna to Peru, from the Baltic Sea to the Mediterranean, and west to the South Pacific. It was the greatest empire the world had ever known.

By 1542, the administrative framework for the empire was also in place. In 1503, while Columbus was still trying to prove he had found the Orient, Spain had created the Casa de Contratación (House of Trade) to control the trade of the New World and collect revenues for the crown. In 1524, the king established the Council for the Indies as the administrative head of the empire. Viceroys in the New World carried out the council's orders: the Viceroyalty of New Spain governed Mexico and the Caribbean; the Viceroyalty of Peru handled the west coast of South America. The structure was highly centralized and

effective; it lasted without serious disruption for almost three hundred years.

The Spanish Empire was a royal enterprise from the outset. The king controlled its expansion and monopolized its profits. Adventurers and dissidents like those who pioneered the British Empire a century later were not allowed in New Spain. Indeed, Spain sent over few colonists of any kind. Soldiers and viceroys served their terms and returned home. Although they occasionally intermarried with the native population, persons of mixed blood were few. Spain did not send colonists to America; instead, it made colonists of the people who were already there. This involved introducing them to European customs, to the Spanish language, and to the Roman Catholic Church. In this way Spain was able to control the native peoples and profit from their labor.

The *encomienda* was the first step in this process of acculturation. The *encomienda* was a tract of land that, together with its inhabitants, was granted to a Spanish colonist. The grantee—the *encomiendero*—was expected to control, educate, and Christianize the natives, and in return he received the profits of their labor. Although humane in concept, the system was susceptible to exploitation: Some *encomiendas* were little more than slave plantations. Church leaders recognized this early and sent a stream of protests back to Spain, and gradually the concept of the *encomienda* was abandoned.

In the seventeenth century, missions became the chief instrument of Spanish colonization. The missions, which were staffed by soldiers and priests, were self-contained communities in which Spanish-style churches, schools, factories, and gardens were established. They were quite successful in parts of America where the native inhabitants were well settled, community-minded, and accustomed to agriculture. Over time, the cultural exchange

THE CLASH OF CULTURES / **15**

produced a new being, the Hispanic American—Spanish in speech, Roman Catholic in religion, yet vitally American in custom and manner.

On the borderlands, the mission system was less successful. The colonization of Florida began in 1565 with the founding of St. Augustine, but little was done thereafter. Florida contained no resources of use to the Spanish, and its native population was generally hostile. Its only value was strategic. Florida commanded the Bahama Strait, principal artery for Spanish gold shipments. In the eighteenth century, Spanish Jesuits established some missions in the province, but they remained beleaguered outposts with no lasting impact on the Indian population.

In the Southwest, the Spanish successfully colonized the Pueblo Indians, often by converting their villages into missions, but they had little luck among the newly arrived Navajos and Apaches. San Antonio in Texas and Santa Fe in New Mexico marked the northern limit of the mission frontier. On the eve of the American Revolution, Franciscan friars set up missions in Alta, California, but by then the days of Spain's American empire were numbered. The closed hierarchies and rigid castes of the Spanish could not withstand the subversive influence of the republican ideology spread by the American and French revolutions.

⊔ The Expansion of England

By the middle of the sixteenth century, the empire of Charles V was beginning to crumble. In eastern Europe he faced chronic warfare with the Turks, who had swept across the Balkans and periodically threatened to attack his capital, Vienna. In western Europe he ran up against a religious upheaval begun by Martin Luther

in 1517. This effort to reform the Church of Rome, called the Protestant Reformation, began in Germany and spread quickly into Switzerland, France, and the Netherlands, leaving in its wake turmoil and war. Exhausted by his burdens, Charles ultimately retired to a monastery. His unwieldy empire was broken up. His son Philip inherited Spain and its New World dominions; he also inherited a crisis in the Low Countries, provinces brought into the Spanish orbit through the Hapsburg connection. In the Netherlands the spread of Protestantism reinforced hostility to alien rule. The revolution that broke out in 1572 led to a long and deadly war. The Dutch war for independence, in turn, helped precipitate a conflict between England and Spain, and that clash of strategic, economic, and religious interests changed the whole future of America.

England had developed a strong government with a respected ruler about the time Spain did. The Wars of the Roses, a bloody civil clash, came to an end in 1485 when Henry Tudor won the crown by battle and pronounced himself King Henry VII. Henry's claim to the throne by right of birth was rather shaky, but there was no one to dispute him, as all potential rivals had died in the fighting. So, in fact, had nearly every titled aristocrat in the realm. Henry and his descendants created a new ruling class by awarding lands and titles to friends, relatives, and political servants. It was the dawn of modern England.

ENGLISH EXPLORATION

In England as in Spain, the new unity led to thoughts of imperial expansion. In 1490 John Cabot (Giovanni Caboto), a Genoese like Columbus, settled in the bustling west country seaport of Bristol. Cabot too had been touring the capitals of Europe trying to secure backing for an effort to reach the Orient by sea. The enterprising merchants of Bristol agreed to finance his venture, and Cabot set out in May 1497 in a small vessel with a crew of eighteen. A month later he landed in the vicinity of Cape Breton Island and then sailed south along what he described as a "barren shore" of a "wooded coast" for several hundred miles. He returned to an enthusiastic reception, for the English recognized the significance of a discovery far to the north of any Columbus had made and of Spanish control. Henry himself granted "To hym that found the new isle" the sum of 10 pounds, a pittance that underscored Henry's reputation for stinginess more than it raised Cabot's standard of living.

When Henry the Miser died in 1509, he bequeathed a handsome fortune to his son, who became Henry VIII. That fun-loving gentleman soon squandered it, but not all on wine and women: He began the construction of a navy to further England's expansion. In 1533 Henry broke with the Roman pope and declared himself to be the head of the Church in England, the first step in a series of changes that brought the Protestant Reformation to England. It also pitted England against Spain, whose ruler Philip II was Europe's staunchest defender of Catholicism. The rivalry became open war in the reign of Henry's daughter, Elizabeth I (1558–1603).

THE AGE OF ELIZABETH

Both Protestant and anti-Spanish, Elizabeth sent money to the Dutch to aid in their revolution and unleashed her "sea dogs" on the Spanish Main. Sir Francis Drake, the most famous of these semi-official pirates, plundered Spanish bases in the Caribbean and even captured the gold storehouse at Cartagena. In 1578, Drake boldly sailed around Cape Horn into the Pacific, which had until then been a Spanish lake. He captured several treasure ships off the coast of Peru, sailed north along the coast of California, evidently looking for a northerly route around the New World, and then headed for China. Continuing on around the world, he docked in London in 1580, with his ship, the *Golden Hind,* jammed to the gunwales with gold. Among Drake's financial backers was the queen herself, and Elizabeth's profit alone was more than a quarter of a million pounds.

This surge of activity abroad signified a quickening of the pace of life in England. Commerce was flourishing as a result of the peace and law the Tudors had brought to the countryside. Money had replaced barter, and prices rose steadily. Arts and literature reflected the vibrant themes of the Renaissance. This was the age of the brilliant dramatists and poets Christopher Marlowe, William Shakespeare, and Ben Jonson. It was also the era of the two Richard Hakluyts, father and son, who put their literary talents at the service of the empire. The elder Hakluyt systematically collected all the accounts of New World exploration and published them in 1582 under the title *Divers Voyages Touching the Discovery of America*. It was both history and propaganda, informing the insular English people of Spain's success and piquing their pride. Two years later he published *A Discourse Concerning Western Planting*, which was a candid plea for empire. Hakluyt stressed the value of colonies as the sources of exotic products that England otherwise had to buy from Spain, as outlets for English manufactured goods, as a boon to English shipping, and as a vent for England's surplus population.

Elizabeth, well in advance of her people as great leaders must be, had already authorized a plantation* in America. In 1578

---

* *Plantation* originally meant "colony," the planting of people. In the American South it came to mean the large estates or farms on which crops like cotton and tobacco were grown.

Radio Times Hulton Picture Library.

Queen Elizabeth in her prime.

problem of supplying such an outpost proved more difficult than Raleigh had supposed, and when Sir Francis Drake arrived the following year, the colonists returned home with him.

Among those involved in this first English venture was John White, an artist who made watercolor sketches showing the daily life of the southern coastal Indians on the eve of English colonization. In 1587 White returned to Roanoke Island, this time as governor. Accompanying him was his daughter, Elinor, wife of Ananias Dare. A month after landing, Elinor gave birth to Virginia Dare, the first English child born in America. When his granddaughter was only nine days old, White returned to

she issued a patent** to Sir Humphrey Gilbert, a "sea dog" who had spent years trying to find a northwest passage around the New World similar to what the Spanish had found at Cape Horn. Gilbert managed to land about two hundred men on the coast of Newfoundland in 1583, but the landscape and the climate proved too forbidding. The settlement was abandoned, and Gilbert perished at sea on the return trip. Elizabeth then transferred the patent to Gilbert's half-brother, Sir Walter Raleigh. In 1585 Raleigh sent over a shipload of colonists, who followed the trade wind route favored by the Spanish and landed on the Carolina capes. Inside the capes, where shallow water afforded protection from Spanish warships, Raleigh's colonists made camp on a tiny spit of land the Indians called Roanoke Island. The island was too barren for agriculture, but Raleigh's purpose in any case was trade—either with the Indians or with the Orient, if and when the northwest passage was found. The

** *Patent* at the time referred to the exclusive right to a tract of land to be developed for profit; later it came to mean the exclusive rights to an invention.

Indians fishing at the seacoast. Among the watercolor sketches of Indians done by John White at Roanoke Island is this portrayal of fishing methods. The cagelike device in the background is a fish trap. Indians in the dugout canoe are cooking fish, an occupation that was not as dangerous as it seems because the dugout itself was fashioned from a log by burning and scraping.

New York Public Library.

England to get provisions for the colony. War prevented him from ever seeing her again.

Angered by Elizabeth's intervention in the Netherlands as well as by her attacks on its treasure ships, Spain sent an armada against England in 1588. The Spanish Armada was deflected by Elizabeth's ships in the English Channel and smashed by storms in the North Sea, but the ensuing war dominated the rest of Elizabeth's reign. John White was unable to return to Roanoke until 1590, and then he found nothing. The colonists had vanished, leaving only the word CROATOAN carved on a tree. Since there was no sign of violence, the phrase apparently referred to a new locale where the colonists had gone. White did not have time to search; the colonists and young Virginia Dare were never seen again.

Raleigh's "lost colony" indicated that the English still had much to learn about the art of colonization. Settlement required better organization and management, and, above all, more capital than a single man could muster. The English had time to digest these lessons, for the war with Spain prevented further colonization efforts for more than a decade.

THE FOUNDING OF VIRGINIA, 1607–1624

Elizabeth died in 1603, and with her ended the Tudor line. Her successor was a distant cousin, James Stuart, king of Scotland, who became James I of England. His succession placed England and Scotland under the same crown, although it would be another century before the two achieved a political union. The end of the war with Spain a year later released English capital and energy for a new try at colonization.

There were two sets of adventurers with proposals ready: One was centered in Plymouth, the other in London. Each had formed itself into a joint stock company. This was a relatively new kind of business organization, one better suited than past forms to the risks of colonization. As the name suggests, it was a corporate body with independent life, and it obtained its capital by selling shares of stock. Unlike a partnership, the joint stock company pooled the risk capital of many investors, and its existence was not dependent on the life span of its owners. It had one other crucial advantage—limited liability. This meant that the owners (the shareholders) were not personally liable for the debts of the company. If it went under, the most they would lose was their investment. This feature enabled joint stock companies to undertake risky adventures that might reap profits only in the long run, such as colonies in the wilderness. It proved an extremely useful device. All the early English colonies in Virginia and New England were established by these business corporations.

James I incorporated the two sets of investors and gave them permission to establish two settlements in North America, then known among the English as Virginia, in honor of Elizabeth, the Virgin Queen. The Plymouth outfit succeeded in establishing a settlement near the mouth of the Kennebec River (in present-day Maine), but it failed after a year, the victim of a harsh climate, hostile Indians, and factional quarreling. The London adventurers fared somewhat better. In December 1606, they sent out 140 men and 4 boys in three small ships under the command of an experienced navigator, Captain Christopher Newport. The fleet followed the familiar southern route, sailed past barren Roanoke Island, and entered the mouth of Chesapeake Bay. It sailed up a broad river for about thirty miles, far enough inland to afford ample warning of Spanish attack. (Although there was peace with Spain, the Spanish still claimed nearly all of the New World by virtue of a papal grant of 1494.) Choosing an island that afforded some protection from Indian attack, the English established a village on May 13, 1607, naming it, as well as the river, after King James.

Jamestown. Jamestown was the first permanent English settlement in America, but its fate was much in doubt for some years. The colonists themselves were partly to blame for their difficulties, but so were the London investors. Those sent over were of two classes—gentlemen, including a number of professional soldiers, and commoners. The commoners had neither mechanical skills nor knowledge of farming. Worse still, they would not work without leadership. The gentry considered physical labor, whether building a fort or plowing a field, beneath their dignity. In the end, both went hungry.

The government of the colony was unwieldy and unworkable. The charter set up a Council of Twelve to manage the settlement but gave it no clear powers. Its president proved weak and indecisive; the members spent their time at intrigue. Captain John Smith, the one colonist with leadership potential, was removed from the council after quarreling with the president. A man of humble origins who had made his fortune fighting Turks in the army of the emperor, Smith was regarded as an insolent upstart by his aristocratic colleagues.

The London investors had conceived of Jamestown as a trading outpost to be supplied by the mother country; there was no point, they felt, in sending people across the ocean to grow corn or other crops. Nor did they consider that as intruders the colonists would be in real danger of Indian attack. Consequently they ordered the settlers to spend their time searching for gold and other items for export: John Smith passed much of the first year exploring the estuaries of Chesapeake Bay. The merchant-adventurers had failed to recognize that time spent in crop raising and fort building would have been time well spent:

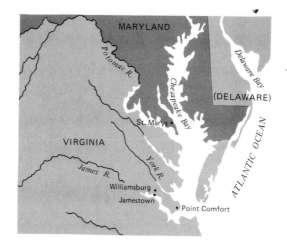

Virginia.

Farming would have provided food for the colonists in the event that the supply ships from England were delayed, and fortifications would have furnished some protection against the Indians.

When Captain Newport returned with supplies after a six-month absence, he found only two councillors alive and at liberty. The rest had died of disease, been executed for treason, or were in jail. In September 1608, Smith returned from a tour of Chesapeake Bay with a boatload of corn obtained in trade with the Indians, and the council rewarded him by electing him president. Smith promptly set the colonists to work planting corn and building a fort. Smith maintained amicable relations with the Indians, principally through his friendship with Pocahontas, the eleven-year-old daughter of Powhatan, the Indian ruler of eastern Virginia.* Smith saved the colony from disaster, but his heavy-handed

---

* The English often applied the European titles "king" or "emperor" to the leaders of Indian tribes. In Powhatan's case they were not far wrong, for he had made himself master of the territory between the Potomac River and the Dismal Swamp, exacting tribute and obedience from the tribes in that region.

methods kindled opposition. Faced with mutiny, he resigned in the summer of 1609 and took the first ship home. It was well for him that he did. Nine-tenths of those he left behind perished during the following winter.

Virginia's Charter of 1609.

Earlier that year, the London investors had obtained a new charter from the king that incorporated them as the London Company and had defined the boundaries of the Jamestown colony as extending 200 miles north and south of Point Comfort (the mouth of the James River). Westward, Virginia was to extend as far as the Pacific. The sea-to-sea grant might seem extravagant until one considers that no one then knew how wide the continent was—Balboa had reached the Pacific after a march of less than a hundred miles. Seeking to rem-

Sketch of a Virginia/Carolina Indian village. Note the planted fields and tidy walkways.

The British Library.

edy the earlier flaws in Virginia's government, the Charter of 1609 provided a single governor with nearly absolute power. The company named Thomas West, Lord De La Warr, governor for life. When it turned out that he was not quite prepared to take up his duties, Sir Thomas Gates, a professional soldier, was appointed interim governor.

With its new charter, the London Company sent to Virginia a fleet of nine ships with 400 colonists, including the first women. But ill fortune continued to plague the colony. Heavy storms scattered the expedition, and Gates was shipwrecked on Bermuda (thus accidentally adding that island to the English empire.) The remaining ships straggled into Jamestown during the autumn, their passengers sick and hungry, their supplies ruined. Jamestown, barely able to feed itself, was not in the least prepared for the new arrivals. To add to its troubles, Smith's departure unleashed the Indians, who had been held in check by his shrewd diplomacy. With Powhatan's angry warriors roaming the woods, the settlers could neither hunt nor fish. The winter of 1609–1610 was known ever after as the starving time. When provisions gave out, the colonists ate horses, dogs, rats, snakes, lizards, and each other. By spring the population was reduced from 500 to 60. Deputy Governor Gates, on the other hand, spent a comparatively pleasant winter on Bermuda, occupying himself and his crew with the construction of a new vessel out of the shipwreck. He sailed into the mouth of the James in May 1610. Horrified at the disaster he found, he prepared to abandon the colony. Before that happened, however, Lord De La Warr arrived from England with more colonists and supplies. Jamestown was saved.

La Warr returned to England a year later because of ill health, and his deputies, Sir Thomas Gates and Sir Thomas Dale, governed the colony by turns until 1618. Professional soldiers both, they instilled discipline in the population. Regulations known as Dale's Laws exacted severe punishment for swearing, gambling, and failing to attend church. The governors also encouraged work by renting out parcels of land to individuals. To end the Indian hostilities, they kidnapped Pocahontas, hoping to ransom her for peace. Powhatan refused to negotiate under duress, and stalemate resulted. Despite the deceit that had attended her capture, Pocahontas learned English and became converted to Christianity. When a young planter, John Rolfe, asked for her hand in marriage, she agreed. So, luckily, did her father. The marriage in 1612 brought peace to the Virginia woods, at least for the moment.

That same year the enterprising Rolfe developed a new method of curing Indian tobacco to make it a bit less harsh. He simultaneously arranged to import tobacco seeds from the Spanish West Indies, which were the source of a tobacco that was lighter, milder, and "sweet scented." Rolfe shipped the first hogshead to England in 1617, where it was received enthusiastically. Spanish West Indian planters had changed the habits of Europe. Tobacco use—whether smoking, chewing, or sniffing—had become a fad, at least among the upper classes. The import of Spanish tobacco cost England an estimated £200,000 a year. To have its own domestic source was a national advantage. It also enabled the London Company to recoup some of its investment, and, most important, it provided Virginia with an economic foundation on which to build a colony.

Ironically, prosperity increased the discontent in Virginia. No longer worried about survival, the planters chafed under the arbitrary rule of their military governors. Every ship carried to London a pouchful of complaint letters. The London Company, meanwhile, was having difficulties of its own. The colonization efforts had drained it of resources; and the tobacco imports were too small to be of much im-

mediate help. The company survived from day to day only by staging public lotteries. In 1618 the company sent over a new governor, Sir George Yeardley, with a plan that was intended to solve these problems.

The Instructions of 1618. The plan, known as the Instructions of 1618, fundamentally altered the political and social structure of Virginia. It addressed these matters:

Representative government. Governor Yeardley suspended Dale's Laws and summoned a representative assembly. Each of the ten settlements ("boroughs," "hundreds," and "particular plantations") was allowed to send two delegates to the assembly, and all adult males participated in the election. The assembly assumed full power of legislation, although its acts were subject to the approval of the company. The first representative assembly in America* met in Jamestown on July 30, 1619.

Private property. Colonists who had been transported to Virginia at company expense had been obligated to work as servants of the company for a period of years and to obtain food and supplies from the community storehouse. The system had discouraged initiative and had added to the colony's troubles. Yeardley, on instructions from the company, offered 100 acres of land to each male who had transported himself to Virginia, and a like amount to each company servant on the completion of his term.

Inducement to immigration. Yeardley was also instructed to use land as an inducement to bring newcomers to Virginia. He offered 50 acres to each person who paid his own way to Virginia, and another 50 acres (both sums later raised to 100) for every individual, including family members, whom he brought with him. The grant was called a *headright*, meaning that it was the right to a tract of land for each "head" transported to Virginia. Note that it was only the right to use land;

---

* Bermuda, which was placed under the jurisdiction of the London Company by a new charter of 1612, obtained the first representative assembly in the New World in 1616.

it did not involve ownership. The company retained title to the land and planned to collect quit rents (so called because a monetary payment released, or "quit," the renter of other obligations, among them military service). Through rent revenues from an ever-expanding population, the company hoped to get some return on its investment.

Despite these reforms, the company's troubles were far from over. Rents, like tobacco receipts, were a long-range proposition, and the company remained desperately short of ready cash. Its lotteries became such a public nuisance that Parliament abolished them in 1621. The company also faced increasing opposition from the king. James had never liked tobacco; he permitted its import only because it brought revenue into the royal treasury. The mortality statistics from Virginia gave the king additional ammunition. Three fourths of all the persons who had been sent to Virginia had died within a short time after their arrival. Something seemed desperately wrong. James naturally felt that both the morals of the matter and the revenue would be improved if he took the colony into his own hands. He needed only an excuse, and the Indians provided that.

The Massacre of 1622.   As long as he lived, Powhatan kept the peace he had promised upon the marriage of his daughter Pocahontas. But after his death, the Indians, angered by white encroachment on their lands, made elaborate plans to wipe out the colony. They struck in March 1622, overrunning every settlement outside Jamestown and killing an estimated 350 whites, or about one fourth of the population. The massacre of 1622 was another tragic episode in the centuries-long clash of cultures. It was also the death knell of the London Company. King James promptly instituted court proceedings seeking to revoke the company's charter, and in 1624 he made the colony his own

personal property. Virginia became a royal colony.

VIRGINIA AS A ROYAL COLONY

The change from corporate to royal colony meant little to Virginia's government and even less to its population. The planters continued to owe quit rents; the only difference was that after 1624 they paid them to the king. The king took over the company's tobacco monopoly and forbade the colonists to sell their crop anywhere but in England.

The assembly, consisting of the governor and his appointed advisors, or council, and of elected representatives, continued to meet after 1624. Governor and council were appointed by the king on the recommendations of the royal Privy Council in London. By mid-century, the interests of the elected representatives, or burgesses, were removed enough that they began meeting separately from governor and council. In 1643 county courts were established. Presiding over these were justices of the peace appointed by the governor. In addition to petty lawsuits, the county courts handled the routine of local government—road and bridge repair, licensing of taverns, and care of the poor.

Virginia in the seventeenth century viewed itself as a transplanted England. The Protestant Church of England was established by law. County government mirrored English local government. The assembly, with its council and burgesses, resembled Parliament. Indeed, toward the end of the century, the burgesses strenuously asserted the rights that had made the English House of Commons a political power: freedom of speech on the floor, immunity from arrest while in session, and above all, the power to raise and spend money—the power of the purse.

CLIO'S FOCUS: Sovereigns of the Sea

The basic form of the modern sailing ship—keel, hull, sails, and rigging—had been developed by the time Columbus sailed the Atlantic. Yet much remained to be done. Indeed, the discovery of America prompted a revolution in ship design that transformed the ungainly cargo carriers of the Mediterranean into sleek mistresses of the seven seas.

The carracks used by Columbus and other explorers were stubby, top-heavy vessels of Italian design. Built to carry cargo, they were nearly as wide as they were long, and they pitched alarmingly with every roll of the sea. A carrack had three masts—fore, main, and mizzen—each made from a single piece of wood. The two forward masts carried large square sails. The mizzen carried a lanteen or triangular sail, which was more effective than square sails when pointing into the wind.

In time of war, kings bought or leased vessels from merchants and then mounted platforms (castles) on them for soldiers. On the bowsprit of every carrack was a grappling hook to hold an enemy ship fast while the soldiers boarded. So naval combat was essentially infantry combat. By 1500 the castles contained cannon and were permanent features of the carrack. Cannon could not be mounted below deck because water would have rushed in the gunports, so badly did the carracks dip with the sea.

The Italian designs were imitated and improved on by shipbuilders all over Europe. By the 1490s both the French and the English were building vessels designed more for war than for commerce. They carried rows of cannon amidships, though still above deck. England's King Henry VII built several of these vessels, which he rented to merchants when they were not needed for military service.

In 1514 Henry VIII ordered the construction of a vessel intended exclusively for war. Fully in character, he demanded that it be the world's biggest and finest. He named it the *Henry Grace a Dieu*, and a magnificent craft it was! It had four masts, each mounted with three sails: main, royal, and topgallant. Each mast was made of three pieces of wood, locked by notching and lashed by ropes. It carried 184 pieces of ordnance and had a displacement of 1,500 tons. (Tonnage was reckoned not by weight, but by volume, one *tun* being a cask of wine.) Another innovation that became standard on warships was the head, a platform that protruded from the bow. In battle it was used for boarding the enemy; the rest of the time it doubled as the ship's toilet (which is still today called the "head" by sailors). Essentially an overgrown carrack, the *Grace a Dieu* must have handled like a floating warehouse, plodding and tippy. With great pomp, Henry VIII rode her across the English Channel in 1519 to negotiate with the French king on the famous Field of the Cloth of Gold—but he refused to come home in her. The *Grace a Dieu*, the first ship of the English navy, served until the reign of Elizabeth.

In the middle of the sixteenth century, Italian builders developed a new type of vessel, the galleon. As the name suggests, it was a derivative of the long, slender galley that had plied the Mediterranean since the time of the Phoenicians. The galleon was three times as long as it was wide, a dimension that gave it both seaworthiness and carrying capacity. The castles were lowered to make it less topheavy, and a row of gunports stretched along the side from bow to stern. It carried a complement of marines for boarding and hand-to-hand combat, but it was designed to fight primarily with cannon. Spain, whose far-flung empire required an up-to-date navy, was among the first to adopt the new design, but Spanish shipbuilders did not do justice to it. Unable to make the joints fit well, they added braces and planking. As a result, Spanish galleons were slow and clumsy, and even with their added braces they came apart under pressure of wind and waves. The English were late in developing the galleon style, and many of the ships Elizabeth sent against the Spanish Armada in 1588 were obsolete. The galleons they did have, however, were quick, maneuverable, and well-manned. English seamanship, more than English technology, defeated the Armada.

The galleon completed the revolution in ship design that had begun with the carrack. Further changes were mostly a matter of size and technological refinement. By the middle of the seventeenth century, ships of more than a hundred guns were built.

But the standard line-of-battle ship was a "74," with three masts, all square-rigged, and three gun decks. Refinements in steering were a bit slower in coming. Galleys and Viking ships were steered by a tiller attached to the side. Carracks and galleons had tillers mounted on the stern. The wheel replaced the tiller early in the eighteenth century.

A variety of devices were used to reduce the friction between wood and water. The Italians coated the bottom of the hull with lead, which functioned also as ballast. Dutch shipbuilders used tallow, and the English experimented with tallow and hair. It was the mid-eighteenth century before anyone thought of copper sheathing, which both increased speed and inhibited barnacles.

After 1800, American designers raked the masts (leaned them backward) so they could hold more sail, flattened the bottom to cut water resistance, and lengthened the fore-and-aft ratio to 5 to 1. A vessel with these features was called a *clipper*. It was the ultimate wooden sailing ship. Yet extraordinary as these famous vessels were, they could have been sailed by Sir Francis Drake or any Elizabethan familiar with the galleon.

Virginia flourished after 1624. Thousands accepted the headright offer and crossed the Atlantic in search of opportunity. Those who could not afford the passage contracted to work as servants for a period of years to planters who paid their costs. Such "indentured servants" were the colony's labor force until they were replaced, after mid-century, by black slaves. Virginia remained until the revolution the largest and richest of England's American colonies.

Thus, after a fitful start, the English began to build their own empire in the New World. Their presence, however, added a new dimension to the clash of cultures that had been going on since the voyages of Columbus. To the conflict of Indian and European would be added the political and religious rivalries among Europeans themselves. This clash would remain one of the dominant themes of American colonial history.

SUMMARY

European visitors to America found civilizations and peoples living in harmony with their environment. Except for some inhabitants of the southern Rockies, who had preceded the Europeans by only a few hundred years, the native American population had migrated from Asia and established itself in the New World ten to twenty thousand years before the arrival of Columbus. The Spanish and the English exploited the Indians when they submitted, and slaughtered them when they resisted. The French and the Dutch were more tolerant, but they too contributed to the decimation of the native population. European germs killed more Indians than European bullets did. And the last page in the tragedy of the Indian peoples was not written until 1890, four hundred years after the first voyage of Columbus.

For nearly three of those four hundred years, European cultures also clashed with one another, warring, proselytizing, trading, and scheming. The two American continents were gradually subdivided by claim and conquest into colonies, each reflecting its distinctive Spanish, Portuguese, English, French, or Dutch cultural heritage. Those cultural distinctions would survive political independence and outlast the four-hundred-year history of the trans-Atlantic frontier.

READING SUGGESTIONS

The starting point for any study of American Indians is the work of the anthropologist A. L. Kroeber, *Cultural and Natural Areas of Native North America* (1939). More recent and briefer is the work of Smithsonian historian Wilcomb E. Washburn, *The Indian in America* (1975). Agronomist Howard S. Russell's *Indian New England before the Mayflower* (1980) focuses on food, but it also covers other aspects of Indian life.

Alfred W. Crosby's *The Columbian Exchange* (1972) looks at the biological consequences of the discovery of America, notably the exchange of deadly diseases between the Old World and the New. William Cronon, in *Changes in the Land* (1984), points out that the Indians, by planting and burning, substantially altered the American landscape long before the Europeans arrived.

The works of Samuel Eliot Morison remain the most vivid and lively account of the age of exploration. His two-volume biography of Columbus, *Admiral of the Ocean Sea* (1942) has been condensed and reissued as *Christopher Columbus, Mariner* (1956). Morison's other masterworks include *The European Discovery of America: The Northern Voyages*, A.D. *500–1600* (1971), and *The*

European Discovery of America: The Southern Voyages, A.D. 1492–1616 (1974). G. J. Marcus's *The Conquest of the North Atlantic* (1981) is the story of the Viking voyages by an author who equals Morison's knowledge of navigation and seamanship.

Lyle N. McAlister's *Spain and Portugal in the*

New World, 1492–1700 (1984) is an excellent treatment of Latin American colonization. *Ralegh's Lost Colony* (1981) by David N. Durant is brief, readable, and contains useful maps. Alden T. Vaughn's *American Genesis, Captain John Smith and the Founding of Virginia* (1975) is the best and most recent study of that colony.

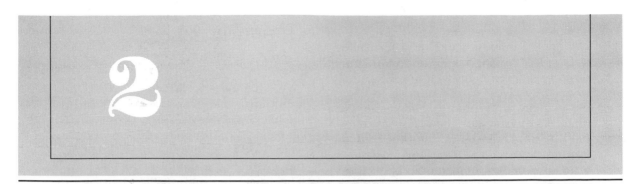

2

Courtesy of the Pilgrim Society, Plymouth, Massachusetts.

AMERICA, THE
PLANTING GROUND

There was no grand design, no master plan in the formation of England's New World empire in the seventeenth century. England's rulers regarded North America as their personal property, but they had neither the time, the energy, nor the resources to exploit it. Imperial affairs drew their attention only rarely, and then their decisions were governed more by political favoritism than by imperial blueprint. As a result, the empire grew haphazardly, taking first one turn and then another as promoters, planners, and politicians by turn gained access to the royal ear.

The first New Englanders hoped to erect a godly kingdom, one especially protected by their creator, like the biblical Zion of the ancient Israelites. Theirs was to be a community of the righteous, preserved from sin by its wilderness isolation, yet serving by its very perfection as a model for the spiritual regeneration of all mankind. Others came to America with less lofty motives. The first settlers of Maryland and Pennsylvania sought refuge from religious persecution. Many of those who went to New York and the Carolinas were fortune hunters dreaming of princely estates where they could live on the labor of others.

Idealism, ambition, humanitarianism, and patriotism forged an empire diverse, often unruly, yet strong and prosperous. By the end of the seventeenth century, the English colonies were attracting migrants from central Europe and were developing trade relations with exotic lands such as Africa and the Indies. The colonies had also by then become a pawn in the great chess game of European diplomacy. The king had to reassert the control he had surrendered to adventurers. The New World empire could by 1700 no longer be a royal afterthought.

⊔Purifying Church and Society

"Wee shall be as a Citty upon a Hill," Massachusetts Governor John Winthrop prophesied. "The eies of all people are upon us." The founders of New England were God's empire builders, creating a model society, a blueprint for all people. The place that might best profit by their example, Winthrop and his fellows believed, was the corrupt and decadent land of England from which they had fled. The New Englanders were Puritans. They knew themselves to be pure, and they expected purity in the church and state that governed them.

THE PROTESTANT REFORMATION

The impulse that fashioned New England had its roots a century earlier in a small university town in Germany. There, in 1517, Martin Luther, a Catholic priest and part-time professor, boldly questioned some of the practices of his church. Priests were selling pardons to sinners, he complained; bishops were growing rich by holding multiple offices. Luther won support among reformers who felt that the Church of Rome and its servants had become too wrapped up in the affairs of this world, too little concerned with the hereafter. As Luther's reform movement spread, the Church organized a countermovement, founding the Society of Jesus (Jesuits) to lead it. Kings and princes became involved, and before long armies were on the move. The Protestant Reformation engulfed Europe in religious wars for the better part of a century.

So combustible was this mixture of religion, politics, and diplomacy that its flames

(*Chapter opening photo*) "Signing the Mayflower Compact" by Percy Moran. A nineteenth-century artist's conception of that historic moment.

soon spread across the Channel to England. The first two Tudors, Henry VII (1485–1509) and Henry VIII (1509–1547), were devoutly Catholic, politically pragmatic, and pro-Spanish. But they were also the members of a new dynasty that had won the crown on the field of battle. They needed time to establish their legitimacy. To counter France, England's traditional enemy, Henry VII allied himself with Spain, sealing the alliance by marrying his son, Henry VIII, to Catherine of Aragon, daughter of Ferdinand and Isabella.

The marriage was not a fruitful one. In twenty years Catherine bore a single child—a daughter, Mary. A succession of stillbirths in the 1520s indicated that she might not be able to have more, and Henry became concerned for the future of the Tudor line. England had had a queen only once before, and her accession had led to civil war. Henry wanted to pass the crown to a son. He asked the pope to annul his marriage to Catherine in order that he might remarry. When the pope denied his request, Henry broke with the Church of Rome, declared himself head of the Church of England, and granted himself the divorce. His second wife, Anne Boleyn, gave birth to another girl, who was named Elizabeth. Henry saved himself the trouble of another divorce and simply had Anne beheaded. A third wife at last gave him the son he desired. In his will he decreed that the crown would pass first to Edward, then to Mary, and finally to Elizabeth.

Henry's break was with the pope, not the Church. He retained all the Roman Catholic ceremonies, including the Latin mass. But under his son, Edward VI, Protestants imbued with Martin Luther's teachings gained influence. They wrote a Book of Common Prayer so that services could be in English, and they restricted the number of offices bishops could hold. Edward died young, and under his half sister Mary, England lurched back into the Roman Catholic fold. Mary was half Spanish and all Catholic, and she was married to Philip of Spain, leader of the Counterreformation. Under her brief rule, a few Protestants were burned for heresy; hundreds of others fled to the European continent.

THE CHURCH OF ENGLAND

When Mary died childless in 1558, Elizabeth inherited the throne. Elizabeth was necessarily a Protestant, and with her blessing Parliament established the Church of England by law. Elizabeth's religious settlement was essentially a compromise. The Church of England retained many of the Catholic forms and ceremonies, as well as the Catholic hierarchy of bishops and archbishops. The principal changes were that the queen, rather than the pope, was the head of the church and that the mass was recited in English, rather than in Latin.

Compromises often make purists unhappy, and the Church of England had its share of critics. More extreme Protestants, especially those who had exiled themselves on the Continent during the reign of Mary, wanted to rid the English church of its "relics of popery." They objected to symbolic gestures, such as kneeling at communion and making the sign of the cross. They wanted to strip church service of its ritual and to focus instead on the sermon, in which a learned minister explained passages from the Bible. Some even wished to do away with the bishops and archbishops and return to the church of the Apostles, in which each congregation ran its own affairs. In short, they wished to "purify" the Church of England by ridding it of the remnants of Catholicism; hence they were known as Puritans.

The Puritans also had some theological reservations about the Anglican Church. England's Protestant exiles had absorbed the ideas of John Calvin, a Swiss theologian whose religious beliefs had altered the course of the Reformation. (French Huguenot, German Reformed, Dutch Reformed, and Scottish Presbyterian churches were all Calvinist.) Calvin's theology was derived from the premise that by his very nature, God was omnipotent and omniscient. Being omnipotent, or all-powerful, God alone determined the population of heaven—that is, who the saints would be. People entered heaven after death not because of anything they did on this earth, but through God's grace alone. A person who felt assured of grace (that is, a "visible saint") naturally led an upright life, but his or her righteousness did not "earn" salvation. That came only through the free gift of God, or the Covenant of Grace, as the Puritans called it.

God's other attribute, omniscience, or all-knowingness, meant that he must have known at the beginning of time who his saints were. At the moment God created order out of chaos, affirmed Calvin, he knew what the population of heaven would be on Judgment Day. Were it otherwise, he would not be all-knowing. It followed,

John Calvin.

then, that certain persons were destined even before they were born to go to heaven after they died. They had no choice in the matter. Their destiny was the free and arbitrary choice of God. This concept of predestination was at the heart of the Puritan theology.

SEPARATISTS AND PILGRIMS

Puritans naturally believed that they were among those "elected" by God, and as "visible saints," they objected to the all-inclusive nature of the English church. By act of Parliament, all subjects of the queen were members of the church, the evil as well as the good. Saintly Puritans thus found themselves kneeling at the communion table alongside sinners. Finding this intolerable, a few of the more extreme Puritans began holding separate church services. From this grew the idea of a separate church altogether, one confined to saints. Such a church was against the law, of course, but some Puritans felt that the law itself, or at least the political meddling that inspired it, was a source of pollution. Church membership ought to be voluntary, they felt, and each congregation of believers ought to run its own affairs. Because they dissociated themselves from the official church and espoused total separation of church and state, this body of extreme Puritans earned the name Separatists. Separatists were a small minority among Puritans, but because of their radical views they attracted considerable attention.

Elizabeth ignored the Puritans' call for reform, but she could not ignore the Separatists. Their notion that religion ought to be free of state regulation threatened the political system itself. Elizabeth's government hounded the Separatists, breaking up their meetings and arresting their leaders. A few were even hanged for treason. Moderate Puritanism flourished, but the Separatists remained a tiny, fugitive sect. Some Separatists, discouraged by the growing persecution, went into exile. Holland, prosperous and religiously tolerant after winning its independence from Spain, attracted a number of them. One congregation of Separatists appeared in Amsterdam and another in the university community of Leyden. After a time, some of the exiles, already referring to themselves as "pilgrims," became discontented with Holland: Persecution had hardened their faith and bound them to one another, but in relaxed and worldly Holland their zeal faded. Fearing that their children would be corrupted and lose their faith, Separatist leaders looked for an alternative. The American wilderness seemed an ideal environment for a community of the righteous. It was hostile enough to bind people together and innocent enough to keep them pure.

The outbreak of war in Europe in 1618 hastened the Pilgrims' plans. The Netherlands was likely to come under attack, either from its old nemesis, Spain, or its mighty neighbor, France. (All three were eventually involved in what became known as the Thirty Years' War.) Pilgrim leaders applied to Edwin Sandys, the treasurer of the London Company, for permission to settle in Virginia. Sandys was delighted with the idea of an industrious, upright folk settling in his colony, especially at their own expense. With financial backing from English merchants, the Pilgrims formed a joint stock company to finance the venture.

At the last minute, the Amsterdam congregation, terrified at the prospects of a long, hard trans-Atlantic passage and the untamed wilderness that would be their new home, lost heart and elected not to go. William Bradford and William Brewster, both of the Leyden group, led the remainder, forty strong, to Southampton, England, where they were to take ship for America. To fill the ship and secure their investment, the merchant adventurers re-

cruited additional colonists in London, bringing the total to 102. Bradford and his fellows were not happy with this dilution of their mission, but there was little they could do. The vessel the company hired, the *Mayflower*, was a "sweet" ship (one having previously been involved in the wine trade) that had an unfortunate tendency to leak. After a couple of false starts, in September 1620 the shipload of "saints" and "strangers" plunged into the vast Atlantic.

⊔ New England

When in 1614 John Smith sailed the coast of North America, mapping its headlands and inlets, he named the stretch of coastline to the north of Virginia *New England*. The *Mayflower* voyagers had a copy of Smith's map to guide them. In reality, the Pilgrims' announced plans of settling in Virginia may have been a ruse to gain financial backing and allay the suspicions of English authorities, for once at sea, they headed for New England. Virginia, after all, offered them little. It was an extension of English society, where the Church of England was established by law. To make a success of their holy experiment, the Pilgrims had to plant themselves on a virgin shore. What the "strangers" thought of this change in plans went unrecorded.

THE PLYMOUTH PLANTATION

The *Mayflower* voyagers landed in the New World on November 9, 1620. A brief survey of the area revealed that they were on a long, narrow sand spit that would later be given the name Cape Cod. They spent the next few weeks poking along the coast, looking for a suitable town site, and finally selected a small estuary John Smith had labeled *Plymouth* on his map. Before landing at Plymouth, the Pilgrims drafted an

The Mayflower Compact, November 11, 1620

IN The Name of God, Amen. We, whose names are underwritten, the Loyal Subjects of our dread Sovereign Lord King *James*, by the Grace of God, of *Great Britain*, *France*, and *Ireland*, King, *Defender of the Faith*, &c. Having undertaken for the Glory of God, and Advancement of the Christian Faith, and the Honour of our King and Country, a Voyage to plant the first colony in the northern Parts of Virginia; Do by these Presents, solemnly and mutually in the Presence of God and one another, covenant and combine ourselves together into a civil Body Politick, for our better Ordering and Preservation, and Furtherance of the Ends aforesaid; And by Virtue hereof do enact, constitute and frame, such just and equal Laws, Ordinances, Acts, Constitutions, and Offices, from time to time, as shall be thought most meet and convenient for the general Good of the Colony; unto which we promise all due Submission and Obedience. In Witness whereof we have hereunto subscribed our names at *Cape Cod*, the eleventh of *November*, in the Reign of our Sovereign Lord King *James* of England, *France*, and *Ireland*, the eighteenth and of *Scotland*, the fifty-fourth. *Anno Domini*, 1620.

Message without words. In 1621, the Narragansett Indians sent Governor Bradford of Plymouth a snakeskin containing arrows. Taking this as a declaration of war, Governor Bradford returned the snakeskin with powder and shot in it. Evidently impressed by this escalation of technology, the Indians did not attack.

MESSAGE WITHOUT WORDS

New York Public Library Picture Collection.

agreement on government. Since they were outside the jurisdiction of Virginia, they felt it necessary to establish a "civil body politic" among themselves. By the Mayflower Compact, a governor and assembly, elected annually, were to pass laws for the general good of the colony. The compact was signed by every adult male on the ship, including some who had come as servants at the expense of others. Religiously democratic because they believed that all saints were equal, the Pilgrims were also politically democratic. Yet, true to their faith, they kept the two spheres separate. No minister ever had political influence at Plymouth. Indeed, for some years the colony did not even have a minister. The *Mayflower* passengers then chose John Carver as governor. When he died a few months later, they replaced him with William Bradford. So able and popular was Bradford that he was reelected annually for almost thirty years.

The Pilgrims had time to build only a few huts of sticks chinked with mud before winter snows set in. Most families spent the winter on the *Mayflower*. There was hardship and hunger that winter, and nearly half of them died. But spring brought new hope—and their first Indian visitors. The coastal Indians of New England had been decimated by smallpox just three years earlier, probably from contact with itinerant European fishermen. This catastrophe was good fortune for the Plymouth settlers, for it allowed them to establish themselves without serious objection from the native inhabitants. Indeed, the site they selected was an abandoned Indian village, so the land was clear and ready for planting. Their only neighbors, an English-speaking pair named Samoset and Squanto, introduced them to the nearest organized tribe, and a lively trade in beaver pelts soon developed. When a relief ship arrived in the summer of 1621 with supplies and more colonists, the Pilgrims loaded it with furs for sale in England. Be-

fore long, their fur trade reached into the Connecticut River valley, and there were Pilgrim trading posts as far south as Narragansett Bay. In 1627, the Pilgrims bought out their London investors and carried the charter of their joint stock company to Plymouth. This action prevented the king from revoking the charter and taking control, as he had done in Virginia.

The Pilgrims experienced some hungry times, but they did not suffer the trials that beset early Jamestown. The Pilgrims had better leadership than the first Virginians, they were more highly motivated and more industrious, and they maintained better relations with the Indians. Most important of all, they had found a means of supporting themselves by exporting furs and fish. The Pilgrims' one failing was that they never obtained legal title to their land: They were the first American squatters. In 1691, the king incorporated them into Massachusetts, and the Plymouth colony disappeared in all but legend.

THE MASSACHUSETTS BAY COLONY

The Puritans, more willing to compromise than the Separatists, had been content to work for reform from within the Church of England. In the time of Elizabeth they formed a small but vocal bloc in Parliament, but Elizabeth kept them isolated. Under James I, the contention between the English crown and Parliament became more serious. James prided himself on his literary talents, having written essays on a variety of topics from tobacco to witchcraft, but he lacked common sense: "The wisest fool in Christendom," his enemies called him. As if to taunt Parliament, James claimed to rule by divine right, asserting that he derived his authority directly from God, to whom alone he was responsible. His opponents, among them many Puritans, could not agree. Even a king is under the law, said they; he could not do anything he wanted. He could not, for instance, imprison or hang Englishmen without the due process of a court trial. James did just that, and he began by imprisoning his critics. James died in 1625; his son Charles succeeded him and quickly revealed that he would carry on the family tradition. His solution to parliamentary criticism was to govern without Parliament, an arrangement maintained for almost ten years.

The controversy over the nature and meaning of the English constitution drowned out for a time the religious quarrel between king and Puritans. Then, in the late 1620s, Charles I resurrected the religious issue. The king's newly appointed archbishop of Canterbury began systematically rooting Puritan ministers out of the church. Faced with religious as well as political persecution, Puritans began thinking of escape. Their thoughts naturally turned to North America, where the flourishing Plymouth Colony presented a ready model. In 1628, a group of Puritans visited a Pilgrim outpost on Cape Ann and thought it a good site for a colony. Returning to England, they formed the Massachusetts Bay Company with help from sympathetic London merchants. They even obtained a charter for their company from the king and the grant of land in New England, although it is unlikely the king fully understood the nature of their enterprise.

In fact, the king probably did not even read the charter. If he had, he would surely have discovered a curious omission. The charter did not specify the residence of the company, so presumably it could situate its "home office" anywhere. Emigrating Puritans quickly took advantage of the omission. Meeting at Cambridge, England, in August 1629, a band of emigrants headed by John Winthrop voted to take the charter to America with them. The company agreed with the idea; stockholders who did not want to leave England sold out to emigrants. The effect of the Cambridge Agreement was to transform a commercial enterprise into a religious experiment. A company became a colony; its government rested on the consent of the governed. And if the king became suspicious, he had no charter at hand to tear up.

Winthrop, elected governor, led the "great migration" to Massachusetts Bay in the spring of 1630. Seventeen vessels, carrying about 2,000 people and ample supplies, tools, seeds, and livestock, made the crossing that year. The migrants of 1630 were too numerous for the tiny fort on Cape Ann, so they moved south to the Charles River (which they graciously named after the king) and founded Boston. They purchased corn from Plymouth and got through the first winter comfortably. More settlers arrived in the spring, and the number increased steadily thereafter. By 1643, when the migration ceased because of the outbreak of civil war in England, the Massachusetts Bay Colony was the home of some 16,000 people scattered in twenty-two towns.

The Puritans had more in mind than mere escape from English persecution; they planned a community led by saints that would reflect God's will, a community that would merit his special blessing. Considering themselves a "chosen people" like the Israelites of the Old Testament, they planned a new Zion in the American wilderness. The covenant with God, an agreement in which the people would follow the path of righteousness, and God would in turn keep special watch over them, was the cornerstone of the Massachusetts Bay Colony.

The Puritans desired a godly community, as had the Pilgrims at Plymouth, but they were not Separatists. The Puritans made no particular distinction between affairs of state and affairs of church. Governor Winthrop and his assistants were elected, but only members of the church were allowed to vote. To become a church

Southern New England, ca. 1640.

member, one had to give evidence of sanctity—testimony of a profound religious experience, for instance. Magistrates enforced the law, punishing both civil crimes (such as theft) and religious crimes (such as heresy). The magistrates were not ministers, however, no minister ever held a political position in the Bible Commonwealth.

Puritans worked within the Church of England as long as they remained in the mother country, but they rejected the English church in the New World. They had no bishops and wanted none. Each congregation selected its own minister and governed its own affairs. Dissent was not tolerated, however. Magistrates banished from

CLIO'S FOCUS: John Winthrop

John Winthrop, the elected governor of the company and colony of Massachusetts Bay, represented the Puritans' curious blend of conscience and conservatism. A landowner and attorney, well-connected socially, Winthrop was a man of affairs, not a religious recluse. Yet he was an intensely pious man who saw God's hand in every human event. He joined the Massachusetts Bay emigration after having been dismissed from a government post for his religious beliefs. But it was not political harrassment that drove him from his native land; it was his feeling that England and its church had become hopelessly corrupt. In Massachusetts he saw the opportunity to create a new society under divine guidance.

Certain he was working under God's approving eye, Winthrop was a self-assured, energetic, and skillful governor. He was an English gentleman with a habit of command and a disdain for the mob. For some years, in fact, he and a handful of assistants made all the laws and regulations for the colony. Only under threat of rebellion, in 1643, did Winthrop finally permit elections. Even then, he and his assistants reserved the ballot for members of the church.

John Winthrop.

New York Public Library Picture Collection.

Winthrop was no democrat. He wished to elevate people spiritually, not socially or economically. The community he helped to found in America never lived up to his moral expectations, but it grew marvelously in wealth and material abundance, in part as the result of Winthrop's practical leadership. Such ironies were not unusual in the founding of America.

the colony those who wished to worship in different ways. If they returned, they were whipped and sent away again. There was no room for discord in God's community: Religious dissidents could have the rest of the continent.

Congregation and town were congruent, at least in the beginning. The town, usually five miles square, was both political subdivision and living arrangement. All were expected to live in the village under the watchful eye of the minister. Farmers rode to their outlying fields to plant or harvest. In the center of the village, adjacent to the "common," was the meetinghouse, which served as both church and town hall.

The Puritan ideal, the community of true believers living and working in harmony, was in fact too rigid to withstand the stresses of time and circumstance for long. By the mid-1630s, many settlers who went to Massachusetts were searching for profit, not salvation. Most were law-abiding citizens, but they lacked the faith that would qualify them for church membership. Some did not bother to attend church at all. Thus, within a few years congregation and community were no longer one. Ministers railed at backsliders, but they were never able to reestablish the fervor and unity of the first arrivals. As Massachusetts society became more wealthy and more worldly, the Congregational Church shrank in importance. In 1662, the clergy sought to counter this by adopting the Half-Way Covenant. By this agreement, the children of church members, who themselves had not qualified for member-

ship, could have their own children baptized in the church. That compromise gave third-generation New World Puritans a partial church membership, though they could not participate in all church functions. It also broadened the church and gave it a greater role in shaping the destiny of the colony.

FOUNDING OF RHODE ISLAND

Religious indifference was a long-term threat to the Bible Commonwealth. Of more immediate concern in the 1630s were schisms within the church that kept Massachusetts in turmoil through the first decade of its existence. Banished nonconformists founded and populated neighboring Rhode Island.

Roger Williams, the founder of Rhode Island, was a Puritan minister who came to New England in 1631 at the invitation of the Salem congregation. Williams had already drifted into Separatism. Although he felt personally assured of salvation, he worried constantly about the possibility of becoming tainted by contact with the imperfect world about him. One obvious source of evil was the connection between church and state. Unless the government itself was always in the hands of saints— an unlikely prospect at best—the church would find itself regulated by sinners. Such views would have found a friendly audience in Plymouth; in the Bay Colony they were heretical. Separation of church and state struck at the very heart of the Bible Commonwealth. Called to account by the magistrates in Boston, Williams boldly told them they had no authority over his congregation. They promptly banished him from the colony. In the late fall of 1635, Williams and a few friends trekked overland to the shores of Narragansett Bay. There they built some huts and formed a community, which they called Providence. The following spring, some of Williams's Salem congregation joined him. Two years later, other exiles appeared in the Narragansett country. These were the followers of Anne Hutchinson.

THE ANTINOMIAN CONTROVERSY

Anne Hutchinson, a devout and bold woman who had been among the first arrivals in the colony, also worried about impurities in her church. The matter that concerned her most was the inclusion of people who were not truly saints. It was an old problem. How was the church to distinguish between those who truly possessed God's grace and those who were hypocrites assuming an air of grace? To admit individuals to the church simply because they behaved well was to admit under a Covenant of Works rather than a Covenant of Grace. And a Covenant of Works was inconsistent with the sovereign power of God. If God was truly sovereign and all-powerful, Puritans reasoned, only he chose who entered heaven, and the reasons for his choice were known only to him. God's choice would be limited, and thus his sovereign power reduced, if he was obliged to accept into heaven people who had done some good deeds on this earth.

Most Puritan clergy agreed with this line of reasoning, but Anne Hutchinson carried the logic a step farther: Were the clergy themselves in grace, or were they simply the most glib hypocrites of all? Did a saint even need a minister? For that matter, did

a saint need laws of any kind? Laws, after all, were made for sinners, not for saints. How far Anne Hutchinson pursued this line of reasoning is not clear, but she did carry her cause far enough to alarm the Bay Colony authorities. Such questions had been raised before. There was even a name for the heresy: antinomianism (*anti*, against, and the Greek *nomos*, meaning law). In 1638 Hutchinson was tried, convicted, and banished from the colony. Along with her husband, her children, and a few friends, she settled on Aquidneck Island in Narragansett Bay, where the group founded the communities that were later to become Portsmouth and Newport.

The Narragansett pioneers were squatters without formal government or land patent, but the outbreak of civil war in 1642 between the English king and a Puritan-controlled Parliament gave Roger Williams an opportunity to win a measure of legitimacy. He journeyed to London and secured from Parliament a charter for the colony of Rhode Island and Providence Plantations. The charter provided for an elected governor and assembly—creating, in essence, a republic within the empire. That the charter made no mention of religion signaled the triumph of the Separatist principles among English Puritans, who by this time called themselves Independents. Williams agreed that church and state should be separate, and Rhode Island thus became the first government in Christendom to practice the principle of religious freedom. The climate of freedom soon attracted persecuted minorities, notably Jews and Quakers. Taking advantage of Rhode Island's magnificent harbors, these industrious folk turned the colony into a bustling trading center.

THE FOUNDING OF CONNECTICUT

The exodus to Rhode Island reflected fractures in the Puritans' religious ideals; the movement of colonists to Connecticut resulted in part from stresses within the rigid town system. In 1635, Reverend Thomas Hooker, pastor of Newtown Cambridge Church, petitioned the Massachusetts General Court for permission to move his congregation to the Connecticut River valley. Among the reasons he gave for desiring such a move were that there were "insufficient lands" to pasture cattle in the Newtown area and that Massachusetts towns in general were too close together. The town system had advantages—notably in community solidarity and defense—but it did not adapt easily to change. Once the town lands were taken up, there was little room for newcomers and little opportunity for the second and third generations. For many the West was an alternative, an escape. The availability of land on the frontier may, in fact, have prolonged the traditional New England town.

Both the Massachusetts Bay and the Plymouth colonies sent exploring parties into the interior. They returned with reports of fertile valley land and access to the sea by way of the mighty Connecticut River. Both colonies were also aware that the Dutch on Manhattan had claims in Connecticut. As a result, the Massachusetts Bay authorities granted Thomas Hooker's request to move, lest the valley be occupied by others. In May 1636, Hooker's flock, numbering about one hundred, established a settlement on the site of modern Hartford. Other towns and congregations followed, establishing towns along the river. Massachusetts at first tried to govern these frontier communities, but in 1637 they set up an assembly of their own.

In 1639, the "river towns" drafted the Fundamental Orders of Connecticut, which has been described as America's first written constitution. The preamble made no reference to the king; power emanated from the people. The document authorized a governor, six assistants, and deputies from each town, all of whom were to be elected annually. The governor had to be

New England gravestone. Carved headstones were the Puritans' earliest art form. The deaths-head and wings depicted death and salvation. Both became highly stylized as the stonecarvers perfected their art.

New York Public Library Picture Collection.

a member of the Congregational Church, but church membership was not a requirement for voting. Indeed, the only requirement was residence ("all that are admitted inhabitants in the several towns"). The governments of Connecticut and Rhode Island were thus the most democratic in the world at that time.

Connecticut did not embrace religious freedom, however. The Puritans who moved into the valley had no quarrel with the church as it was established in Massachusetts. Nor, except for wanting more breathing room, did they quarrel with the town system. Their society became an extension of Massachusetts. In 1638, when two Puritan zealots, Theophilus Eaton and John Davenport, arrived in New England to found a godly community of their own, they chose Connecticut rather than Massachusetts. Their settlement, New Haven, remained a citadel of Congregational orthodoxy for the next two centuries.

Governed by elected representatives, largely independent of royal authority, Connecticut and Rhode Island were odd fellows in the English empire. Connecticut, like Rhode Island, had obtained a charter from Parliament during the English civil war. Both charters were confirmed by the king after royal authority was reestablished in 1660. By keeping a low profile, both colonies retained their unique forms of government until the revolution. Indeed, so content were they that they changed nothing with independence. Connecticut settlers did not write a state constitution until 1818, and Rhode Islanders did not get around to it until 1842.

⊔ Proprietary Plantations

The English civil war (1642–1649), culminating in the execution of King Charles I and the establishment of a republic, interrupted English colonization. When the monarchy was restored in 1660 in the person of Charles II, the colonizing process

was resumed. Within a few years there were English settlements sprinkled along the North American coast from New Hampshire to the Carolinas. The new grants differed from those given the earlier New England colonists, however. The king had become suspicious of private companies that secreted their charters aboard ship and blossomed into self-governing republics in the New World. By granting a land patent to a single person or a small group, the king expected to exert more control over the new colonies.

BALTIMORE'S MARYLAND

This concept of proprietorship was first tried by Charles I when in 1632 he issued a patent to Cecil Calvert, Lord Baltimore, a Roman Catholic and personal friend. The colony was named Maryland in honor of the English queen, Henrietta Maria, who was a French-born Roman Catholic. Baltimore, in fact, intended his colony to be a refuge for Roman Catholics, a persecuted minority in England. The patent gave Baltimore complete control of the colony, including appointment of its governor. But the proprietor was responsible to the king, who retained ultimate ownership. The arrangement was in fact feudal: Baltimore held Maryland in the way a medieval knight held his lands. As an expression of his obligation to the king, Baltimore paid him a "rent" of two Indian arrowheads a year.

From the royal point of view, it was a nice arrangement. Someone else would undertake the burden and expense of taming the wilderness, but the king would retain ultimate control. Baltimore recouped his investment by collecting rents from the people he sent to Maryland. The Baltimore family received about £10,000 sterling a year from Maryland until the revolution.

Maryland was carved out of Virginia. Baltimore's patent extended from the south bank of the Potomac River northward to the fortieth parallel of latitude (roughly present-day Philadelphia). Westward it extended to the "first fountain" of the Potomac. In 1683, Baltimore sent over the first group of settlers, Roman Catholics, and they established themselves on the St. Mary's River, a small tributary of the Potomac. They purchased food and seed from Virginia and began growing tobacco. Lord Baltimore also adopted Virginia's headright system to encourage immigrants. He offered 100 acres of land to every settler who financed his own passage and the same amount to each person he brought with him. It was not an outright gift, for Baltimore collected annual quit rents on the land, but it was attractive enough so that land-hungry opportunists of various faiths soon outnumbered the Roman Catholics.

To protect the Roman Catholic minority, Lord Baltimore decreed religious toleration for Maryland in 1634. The grant was not one of total religious freedom, for the Church of England was established by law, as in Virginia; but other faiths were tolerated. Maryland even attracted a small Puritan element. The colony, like Rhode Island, thus offered a unique combination of freedom and opportunity. Immigrants poured in, and Maryland flourished. The king, too, was delighted. During the 1650s, when no monarch occupied the English throne, Maryland and Virginia had both remained loyal to the crown, while New England had sided with Parliament and its leader, Oliver Cromwell. When Charles II assumed the throne in 1660, he used the Maryland proprietary colony as a model for all future colonial grants.

NEW NETHERLAND

Before resuming the process of planting English colonists in America, King Charles felt obliged to tidy the map. In the middle of the English settlements in North America lay the Dutch colony of New Nether-

land. Established by the Dutch West India Company in 1624, New Netherland extended from the Delaware River north to Connecticut. Although the colony enjoyed a profitable fur trade, it could not be described as flourishing. Most of its inhabitants were not Dutch at all, but Flemings and Walloons (Belgians today). Prosperous and politically stable, the Dutch had not been inclined to leave home. As a result, their control of their colony was tenuous at best, and they weakened their hold further in appointing unpopular, dictatorial governors.

In 1664 Charles II granted New Netherland as a proprietary colony to his brother, James, Duke of York, on condition that James conquer it. When James sailed an English squadron into the mouth of the Hudson River, the Dutch colony surrendered without firing a shot: The inhabitants saw no difference worth fighting about between Dutch rule and English. James named the province New York, after himself, and confirmed all Dutch land titles. He thus solidified his position, because some of the most powerful men in the colony (patroons) had princely estates in the Hudson River valley. But his action also perpetuated the class divisions within the colony. Social unrest and revolution were James's legacy.

THE CAROLINAS

While eliminating the Dutch Empire from North America, Charles II simultaneously extended English holdings southward toward Spanish Florida. In 1663, Charles established a new proprietary colony to the south of Virginia, which he named Carolina. The Carolina grant went to eight men to whom the king had political and financial obligations. Important personages all, they had no intention of moving to their colony. Nor, in fact, did they plan to invest funds in it. They expected people already in America to move into the colony, attracted by headrights. Few did, in part because land was so readily available elsewhere. Development, accordingly, was painfully slow.

By 1670 a few pioneers drifted south from Virginia and clustered around Albemarle Sound (North Carolina). They sent their hogs and cattle into the woods to forage, planted fields of corn, and sent a little tobacco to market in Virginia. Because of Albemarle's shallow harbors and its sandy barrier, known as the Outer Banks, they never developed much ocean commerce. About the same time, emigrants from the West Indies built the village of Charleston on a neck of land between the Ashley and Cooper rivers. Blessed with a fine harbor, Charleston quickly became a trading center. Deerskins, obtained in trade with the Indians, were its principal export until about 1700, when rice was introduced into the area. Rice was a highly profitable crop, but it could be grown only by those with capital to invest because it required dams, levees, and other water-control devices. As a result, people with money made money, and the Carolina low country became, like New York, a land of the very rich and the very poor.

The two Carolina settlements, differing in interests and outlook, soon went different ways. The Albemarle settlement evolved into North Carolina; Charleston and its environs became South Carolina. By 1700 each had its own governor and assembly. The proprietors divided the grant among themselves for purposes of land sales and rent collection. They remained essentially speculators who contributed nothing to the maintenance of government. They ignored the colonists' repeated requests for protection against Indians, Spaniards from Florida, and pirates who infested the islands along the coast. The Carolinas thus represented the proprietary system at its worst. After a bloody Indian uprising in 1715, followed by the pirate Blackbeard's bold blockade of Charleston, the Carolinas asked the king to make them royal colonies. The king gradually bought out the proprietors, and by 1744 both Carolinas were royal colonies.

PENNSYLVANIA AND NEW JERSEY

In contrast to New York and Carolina, which were essentially commercial enterprises, Pennsylvania and New Jersey, the last of the proprietary colonies granted by Charles II, were religious havens. They were settled by members of the Society of Friends, or Quakers.

Believing that they possessed an "inner light," a speck of divinity, the Quakers saw no need for church formalities. One person was as good as another, and no one needed clerical aid in communicating with God or in understanding the Bible. Quaker meetinghouses were as stark as their faith, shorn of everything but bare benches, where Friends sat in silence until some member was moved to speak. Meetings were held several times a week and twice on Sunday. Between services, Quakers were expected to live their faith in their daily routine.

The Quakers' religious devotion was bothersome. Quakers invaded pub and pulpit preaching the "inner light." They even ventured into Puritan Massachusetts, only to be whipped and sent to Rhode Island. Taking the Bible literally, they refused to swear oaths or fight wars. This made them seem subversive to a government that insisted on a loyalty oath for every office. Committed to equality, they refused to doff their hats to aristocrats on the street. That made them seem rebellious. They dressed plainly, worked hard, and often made money. With wealth and social standing, they came to resent the political restrictions on them. Before long, they sought a refuge of their own.

Their attention fell first upon New Jersey. The land between the Hudson and the Delaware rivers had originally been claimed by the Dutch; it thus had fallen to James of York when he conquered New Netherland. James had subgranted New Jersey to two proprietors, but he had given them the right only to sell land; government came from New York. The proprietors divided New Jersey, one taking the eastern half and one the western half. In 1675, a group of Quakers purchased West New Jersey from its proprietor, expecting to turn it into a religious haven. Hundreds of Quakers moved to the province and built farms. They did not like being governed from New York, however; they wanted a province of their own.

William Penn, one of the leaders in the New Jersey enterprise, went to the king with a proposal. Penn's father, Admiral William Penn, was a war hero to whom the king felt both personal and political obligation. Penn asked the king for a proprietary grant in America and, incredible though it seems in view of his religious persuasion, received one. Pennsylvania ("Penn's woods") was sandwiched between New York and Maryland, extending west from the Delaware River five degrees of longitude (roughly to present-day Pittsburgh). King Charles did not trouble himself with cartographic details, and Pennsylvania's boundaries as a result overlapped on the south with the grant earlier given to Maryland. The two colonies fought over the boundary for many years before it was finally surveyed in 1767 by Mason and Dixon. In the meantime, Penn, with the assent of the king, carved another proprietary colony, Delaware, out of the grant originally given to Lord Baltimore. Pennsylvania and Delaware both remained in the hands of the Penn family until the American Revolution.

Penn's Frame of Government. The charter of 1681, modeled on Baltimore's proprietary colony, gave Penn total authority over the colony, subject only to the scrutiny of imperial tax collectors. Penn, true to his Quaker principles, was prepared to share power with his colonists. In 1682, he issued his Frame of Government, which established a governor's council and an assembly, both elected by the adult males in the colony. He also decreed religious freedom. Quakers, like Separatists, believed that a link between church and state defiled the church. Experience proved that Penn was a little too generous in his dispersion of power, and in 1702 he secured a new charter that reduced the size of the assembly and added to the powers of the governor. Even with these modifications, however, Pennsylvania ranked with Rhode Island as the freest, most democratic political system in the world.

Penn himself led the first party of Quaker emigrants in 1682. They sailed into Delaware Bay and proceeded up the Delaware River some miles to a point where the Schuylkill River entered from the west. There, while the colonists struggled to erect crude huts and lean-tos, Penn, with characteristic optimism, sketched a plan for an entire city. He named it Philadelphia; it was the world's first planned urban development. Quakers streamed into the colony over the next few years, their exit from England hastened by new political and religious upheavals. Merchants settled in Philadelphia; farmers took up the rich bottom lands of the Delaware Valley.

Like Roger Williams, Penn believed in paying the Indians for their land. His agents, however, had fewer scruples and bigger appetites. They reimbursed the Indians when they had to, tricked them when they could, and resorted to force when all else failed. Penn's own private secretary, after persuading the Indians to sell as much land along the Delaware as a person could walk around in a day, hired Indian runners to do his "walking" for him.

The Coming of the Non-English. When the Quaker stream dwindled, Penn began advertising his colony. He wrote pamphlets extolling Pennsylvania's political and religious freedom and its mild cli-

New York Public Library Picture Collection.

Penn's Treaty with the Indians, 1683. This famous painting by Benjamin West was an allegory of peace. Penn's
purchase of land from the Indians was widely cited as
an example of Quaker honesty. It is allegedly the only
treaty between whites and Indians that was never broken. Not all Quakers were as scrupulous as Penn, however. Some years later the Indians agreed to sell to
James Logan, Penn's private secretary, as much land
as he could walk around in a stated time. Logan cleared
a path through the woods and hired a relay team of runners to make the "walking purchase."

mate and fertile soil. He blanketed the British Isles with his writings and had them
translated into French, Dutch, and German for distribution elsewhere in Europe.
Penn's brochures found a ready audience
in the Palatinate, a small section of Germany along the Rhine that had been a battleground for centuries. Pietists, ultra-Prot-
estants who believed, as the Quakers did,
that religion was an integral part of one's
daily life, were among the first to come.
Francis David Pastorius, an old friend of
Penn, led his flock out of the Rhineland
in the 1680s and founded the village of
Germantown near Philadelphia. Moravians came in the 1690s and founded Bethle-
hem farther up the Delaware River. The
exodus fed upon itself, as the initial emigrants sent home glowing descriptions of
Pennsylvania's favorable climate and topography, both similar to those of western
Germany. The wars of the French king
Louis XIV added to the distress in the
Rhineland, and when the wars ended in
1713, the trans-Atlantic trickle of humanity
became a flood. The Palatines occupied the
remaining land in the Delaware Valley and
pushed westward into the lush Susquehanna Valley.

Close upon the heels of the Germans

British North America, 1750.

came the Scots-Irish. These were Scottish Protestants who had colonized northern Ireland in the early part of the seventeenth century. King James I had initiated the Scots-Irish colonization movement in Ireland in an effort to impose a Protestant ruling class that would help England keep Ireland under control. But hard times in the linen industry and changes in agricultural patterns induced the Scots-Irish to relocate in the early eighteenth century. Finding New England hostile to newcomers and the South too hot and unhealthy, they settled in Pennsylvania. The Scots-Irish filtered in among the German settlements, establishing communities of their own. Scots-Irish and Germans leapfrogged one another westward, following the Juniata River into the Cumberland Valley, and traversing the pathway southwest into Maryland and Virginia.

Germans and Scots-Irish were the first significant element of non-English in the American colonies. They were the first test of the American "melting pot," the advance guard of two centuries of European emigration. Philadelphia, the gateway to the West, prospered and grew; by 1750 it was the largest city in the New World.

⊔ Imperial Authority and Colonists' Rights: The First Contest

The Massachusetts Bay Colony was barely five years old when King Charles I decided he had made a mistake in giving it a charter. The Puritans ignored royal directives and would not allow members of the Church of England to vote or hold office. Most annoying of all, they extended their territorial claims northward into New Hampshire and Maine, thereby ignoring the boundaries outlined by the king when he issued the charter of 1629. In 1635 Charles initiated steps to have the colony's charter annulled by an English court. The

Puritans delayed a decision for years by ignoring writs and summonses. When a court finally ordered them to surrender their charter, they refused and began fortifying Boston harbor against possible military retaliation. Charles's battles with Parliament in the 1640s distracted him and saved Massachusetts for the time being. Nonetheless, there was a growing feeling among Londoners that the colonies should be brought under closer supervision.

THE NAVIGATION ACTS

The Puritan Parliament that governed England after deposing Charles I shared this concern. In 1651, Parliament adopted a Navigation Act to regulate the commerce of the empire. The act provided that all goods shipped between England and the colonies had to be carried in English or colonial vessels. The act was aimed primarily at Dutch merchants, and its enforcement triggered the First Anglo-Dutch War (1652–1654).

When the monarchy was restored in 1660, Parliament reenacted the Navigation Act and three years later extended its authority. The Staple Act of 1663 "enumerated" prime colonial products—tobacco, lumber, fish—and prohibited the colonists from shipping them anywhere but to the mother country.

The purpose of these acts was to integrate the empire and to make it self-sufficient. Colonies and mother country were to complement one another economically. England provided financial services and manufactured goods; colonies supplied the raw materials. To prevent the colonies from competing with England, regulations were passed in the seventeenth and eighteenth centuries that prohibited the colonies from exporting finished products, such as ironware, textiles, or beaver hats. Colonial staples, on the other hand, possessed a monopoly in England; that is,

English merchants could not purchase any of the "enumerated" products elsewhere. Like most governmental efforts to regulate the economy, the Navigation Acts benefited a few and burdened many. South Carolina rice planters benefited from their monopoly in the English market, and they profited from parliamentary subsidy on indigo, a plant used to make blue dyes for cloth. Virginia tobacco planters and New England fishermen, on the other hand, disliked the Navigation Acts because the laws prevented them from marketing their products on the continent of Europe.

MERCANTILISM

The theory underlying the Navigation Acts, mercantilism, rested on the assumption that international trade was a "zero-sum game," that one nation's gain was another's loss. The object of the game was a favorable balance of trade, obtained by selling more than one purchased. The favorable balance brought gold into the royal coffers, and gold meant power. Thus the government regulated merchants to assure a favorable trading position. The American colonies fit into the English scheme by providing products that England might otherwise have to purchase from rival nations: Lumber from its American colonies freed England from dependence on Sweden; Virginia tobacco and Carolina rice relieved England from having to purchase these products from Spain.

Mercantilism, like most theories, worked better on paper than in practice. To enforce his trade regulations, King Charles II had to create new imperial machinery. The empire he inherited, after all, had arisen without any grand design. His royal predecessors had issued charters and patents as it suited their pocketbooks and their political aims. Religious refugees and land-hungry opportunists had founded America, and neither had paid much attention

to royal directives. Under Charles II, the Privy Council undertook the supervision of the empire and appointed committees of its own members to deal with colonial problems as they arose. In 1675 it formed a standing committee, the Lords of Trade, and in 1696 this body was reformed into a permanent supervisory agency, the Board of Trade and Plantations. Until the American Revolution, the Board of Trade was the heart of imperial administration. It drafted instructions for the royal governors, and it reviewed the laws of colonial assemblies.

The enlarged imperial presence—reflected both in the Navigation Acts and in the evolution of administrative machinery—led the colonists to reconsider their own position in the empire. What rights did they have as transplanted Englishmen? Were they totally at the mercy of the English Parliament and the Privy Council? Since they had no representation in either of those bodies, what means did they have to protect themselves? This concern surfaced first in Virginia during the 1670s in an incident known as Bacon's Rebellion.

BACON'S REBELLION

Virginia's governor, Sir William Berkeley, was intellectually akin to his royal master, Charles II. He had little use for representative government and considered the assembly a nuisance. Through bribery and patronage he shaped the assembly to his liking and then congealed it by refusing to hold elections. A small circle of the governor's favorites managed the colony. In 1670 the assembly imposed a property qualification on the right to vote, hoping to ensure that Virginia would be governed only by the "better sort," if and when the governor permitted an election.

Economic hard times aggravated the situation. By 1660, Virginia produced more tobacco than Englishmen could use, and prices fell. The Staple Act, which prevented Virginians from selling their tobacco in continental Europe, was a further complication. Even Governor Berkeley admitted that the Navigation Acts were "mighty and destructive" to Virginia's economy: He wanted Virginians to extend their activities into new fields, but the Privy Council discouraged such diversification, for the customs duties on tobacco netted the English government £100,000 a year. In 1673, Parliament even placed a duty on the shipment of tobacco to other colonies. Virginians understandably felt trapped.

In 1673 Charles added to their worries. He granted the southern part of Virginia to two English aristocrats to whom he apparently felt some obligation. The grant included the right to collect all rents and taxes in the area. In addition, while in exile Charles had made a proprietary grant of the Northern Neck (between the Rappahannock and the Potomac rivers) to Lord Culpeper. Neither grant included authority to govern, but the omission was small comfort. What rights did they have, Virginians wondered, if the king could simply grant away their lands on a royal whim?

In 1674, the Virginia assembly sent three agents to London bearing a proposal for a new charter. Ever since James I had revoked the colony's charter a half century before, Virginia had been without a frame of government. The draft for a new charter revealed the trend of American thought. It asserted that colonists ought to possess "the same liberties and privileges as Englishmen in England," and among these liberties were the guarantee of no further proprietary grants, the reinstatement of the colonial assembly's authority, and the guarantee that taxes would not be imposed without the consent of the people and their assembly. The Lords of Trade gave their approval to the new charter for Virginia, but the king himself quashed it. Charles had other plans for America, and they did not involve a definition of colonial rights. It may not have mattered, for the anger of Virginians had by then reached the flash point.

Indian raids triggered an uprising. Susquehanna Indians, driven south by the Iroquois, began raiding the frontier. When Governor Berkeley refused to act, frontier vigilantes took matters into their own hands and banded together in self-defense. They found a ready leader in young, impetuous Nathaniel Bacon, who through family connections was a member of the governor's council, although he had resided in the Virginia colony only two years. In 1676 he led his band in search of the marauders, and finding none, massacred a village of peaceful Indians. That deed made him a hero, at least among frontiersmen, whose families had been menaced by Indians.

The governor deprived Bacon of his seat on the council and issued a writ for the election of a new assembly to counter the popular discontent. To the governor's distress, Bacon was elected to the House of Burgesses. The new assembly, meeting in the summer of 1676, approved a dozen laws (known as Bacon's Laws, although Nathaniel Bacon had no hand in drafting them) designed to limit the power of the gentry and enhance the role of the populace. One statute prohibited members of the council from holding any other office, and another ordered that the parish vestries, which were organs of local government, be popularly elected. The property qualification of 1670 was repealed, so that every white adult male was allowed to vote. Frightened by the popular uproar, Governor Berkeley reluctantly approved Bacon's Laws and even gave Bacon a military commission to fight the Indians. Bacon turned on the governor instead, and, after a brief and bloodless skirmish, sent him fleeing across Chesapeake Bay to the Eastern Shore. Bacon then fell ill of a fever and died. The governor returned and hanged Bacon's followers; a new assembly repealed

New York Public Library Picture Collection.

The burning of Jamestown, 1676.

his laws. Nothing came of the rebellion except a legacy of resistance to royal authority.

That same year, 1676, King Charles II did grant the Virginians a new charter, but it was not framed as a concession to their demands. The charter confirmed their land titles except in the Northern Neck, but it contained no mention of their rights. Charles, in fact, had decided that colonists did *not* possess the rights of Englishmen; they were totally subject to royal fiat. And his desire of the moment, as he turned his attention from Virginia to other colonies, was greater control, not less.

THE DOMINION OF NEW ENGLAND

Massachusetts was still the king's biggest headache. Not daunted in the least by the efforts of Charles I to revoke their charter,

Bay Colony leaders violated the Navigation Acts, ignored the Lords of Trade, and stubbornly asserted their claims to New Hampshire and Maine. Their transgressions were brought to royal attention by the reports of Edward Randolph, an energetic customs collector sent to the colonies by the Privy Council. Influenced in large part by Randolph's reports, the Court of the King's Bench in 1677 declared that Massachusetts had claim to neither New Hampshire nor Maine. Two years later, New Hampshire (populated mostly by emigrants from Massachusetts) became a royal colony. Massachusetts, however, held on to Maine by secretly buying out the heirs of an early proprietor.

In 1684, another English court annulled the Massachusetts charter altogether. The action was part of a comprehensive plan to streamline the colonial empire. The king planned to consolidate all the New England colonies into a single dominion. Such an organization would enable the colonies to pool their resources for defense (New England had barely survived a major Indian uprising, King Philip's War, in 1675–1676) and would allow imperial authorities to exert closer supervision. Charles died before he completed formation of the dominion, but his successor, James II, carried it through. James even added to the Dominion of New England his own proprietary colonies of New York and New Jersey. In 1686 he sent Sir Edmund Andros to Boston as governor-general of the dominion. Ruling together with an appointed council but without an assembly, Andros had the authority to make laws, impose taxes, and administer justice. A professional soldier, he expected to muster the New Englanders as he would one of the king's regiments.

Within little more than a year, Andros alienated everyone in Massachusetts— farmers, merchants, and clergy. He imposed taxes without summoning an assembly; he called land titles into question and collected quit rents. He abolished town meetings, enforced the trade regulations, and ordered toleration for members of the Anglican Church. Boston was soon seething with hatred for the "tyrant Andros" and the customs collector, the "evil genius" Randolph. In 1688, Increase Mather, the president of Harvard College and the leading cleric in the colony, slipped out of Boston and took ship for England to present the colony's grievances to the king. James rejected his pleas, but fortunately for Mather and for New England, the king's own tenure was near an end.

THE "GLORIOUS REVOLUTION"

In England, James II had done a similar job of alienating landed gentry, city merchants, and the clergy. With characteristic Stuart disdain for representative government, he dispensed with Parliament and suspended laws that did not suit him. Worst of all in the minds of many was the fact that he was a Roman Catholic, the first to occupy the throne since "Bloody Mary." The English tolerated James for a time because they anticipated a Protestant succession: James's elder daughter, Mary, was a Protestant, and she was wedded to a Protestant, William of Orange, the ruler of Holland. But then, in June 1688, James's second wife gave birth to a boy, an event that raised the specter of a Catholic succession. A parliamentary delegation visited William of Orange and invited him to come to England to rule jointly with his wife. William agreed and crossed the North Sea in November 1688, blown, so it was said, by a "Protestant wind." James fled to Paris, Parliament offered the throne jointly to William and Mary, and the Glorious Revolution was complete.

When news of the revolution reached Boston in April 1689, the populace rose up, clapped Governor Andros in jail, and proclaimed their loyalty to the new sovereigns. Increase Mather, acting on cue, applied to the king for a new charter, and William, flattered by his promises of loyalty, agreed. He was not willing to restore the Puritan oligarchy to power, however. The charter he signed in 1691 was in fact a compromise. It joined Massachusetts Bay, Plymouth, and Maine into the royal colony of Massachusetts. The king would appoint the governor, but both the council, which doubled as the upper house, and the lower house, or House of Representatives, were to be elected. Rather than religious persuasion, a predetermined level of landholding was the qualification for voting and officeholding, and thus the Puritans lost their political monopoly. They did, however, win a bill of rights, drafted by Increase Mather and his son Cotton, which was appended to the charter. It was the first recognition by an English monarch that the colonists possessed at least some of the rights of Englishmen.

That was the most William III would concede, however. In other respects he reasserted the Stuart policy of enhancing imperial control. When New York experienced a revolution similar to Boston's, William dispatched a naval squadron to suppress it and had the rebel leader, Jacob Leisler, hanged for treason. He created the Board of Trade in 1696, and in 1702 he eliminated one more proprietary colony by converting New Jersey into a royal colony.

THE EMPIRE IN 1700

Thus, although the issue of imperial authority versus colonial rights had not been resolved by 1700, the colonies and the mother country had at least found a means of coexisting. The imperial machinery was largely in place. The only addition after 1700 was a ministerial post for the colonies, called the Secretary of State for the Southern Department (replaced in 1768 by the

Colonial Secretary). An imperial bureaucracy was also evident by 1700, staffed by men who were more tactful, if less able, than the abrasive Edward Randolph. The colonies for their part had won a considerable degree of self-government by 1700. Although the rights of transplanted English people remained undefined except in the case of Massachusetts, their assembly members had become self-confident spokesmen for their interests. Modeling themselves on the English House of Commons, the assemblies had won such elementary privileges as freedom of speech in debate, freedom from arrest while in session, and the right to determine, through seating, their own membership. Most had also won the right to levy taxes and appropriate money. And the representatives knew well—from the experience of Parliament in its battles with the crown—that the power of the purse was the key to all other legislative powers.

This tacit understanding held for more than half a century. Under it, the colonies slowly matured. Colonial leaders gained experience in the art of government and developed a better insight into their rights and interests. When the understanding was broken by Parliament in the 1760s, the colonies moved swiftly in the direction of total independence.

SUMMARY

Religion was the motivating factor in the founding of seven of England's colonies in the seventeenth century. The Separatists in Plymouth (1620) and the Puritans in Massachusetts Bay (1630) intended their colonies to be refuges from persecution and models for the regeneration of humankind. Connecticut (1636) and New Hampshire (1622, 1639) were offshoots of Massachusetts Bay. Rhode Island (1635), an offshoot of another kind, was populated by religious dissidents from Massachusetts. Maryland (1632) was intended as a refuge for Roman Catholics, Pennsylvania (1682) as a refuge for Quakers. In all seven colonies, religion soon yielded to economics as new immigrants arrived in search of land and opportunity. Puritans maintained control in the New England colonies, except for Rhode Island, but elsewhere the religious refugees soon found themselves in a minority. Social diversity in Pennsylvania, Maryland, and Rhode Island led to the first experiments in religious toleration.

Two colonies owed their origins to military strategy. England seized New York from the Dutch in 1664 to eliminate an imperial rival, and it established Georgia in 1732 as a buffer against Indians and Spaniards. In the remaining colonies—the Carolinas (1663) and New Jersey (1665)—profit was the principal motive. King Charles II and his brother, James of York, granted these colonies to English grandees in payment of political and financial debts. All three suffered varying degrees of neglect until finally taken back and made into royal colonies.

After allowing the Massachusetts Bay Company a remarkably liberal and open-ended charter in 1629, the English crown seemed to awaken to the potential as well as the responsibilities of empire. It spent the rest of the century trying to establish its authority over an increasingly complex, profitable, and unruly empire. Proprietorships, navigation acts, the Dominion of New England, and the Board of Trade were among the devices used. Ultimately, all but five colonies (three proprietary and two corporate) were recovered by the crown. The colonists resisted with subterfuge and occasionally with violence, but by 1700 a working balance was achieved. The balance lasted for more than half a century, during which the colonies slowly and steadily matured socially, economically, and politically.

READING SUGGESTIONS

The classic treatment of Puritan thought is Perry Miller's two-volume *New England Mind* (*The Seventeenth Century*, 1939; *From Colony to Province*, 1953). Most students will probably prefer the shorter and less lofty treatments by Alan Simpson, *Puritanism in Old and New England* (1955) and Edmund S. Morgan, *Visible Saints* (1963). George F. Willison's *Saints and Strangers* (1945) is an entertaining history of the Plymouth colony. John Demos's *A Little Commonwealth: Family Life in Plymouth Colony* (1970) is a pioneer work in colonial social history. For further information on the Bay colony's schismatics, Anne Hutchinson and Roger Williams, consult Emery Battis, *Saints and Sectaries* (1962), and Edmund Morgan's biography of Williams.

Histories of the later colonies include these: Thomas J. Condon, *New York Beginnings* (1968); Wesley F. Craven, *New Jersey and the English Colonization of North America* (1964); Gary B. Nash, *Quakers and Politics . . . 1681–1726* (1968); Wesley F. Craven, *White, Red, and Black* (1971); Hugh T. Lefler and Albert R. Newsome, *North Carolina* (1954); and M. Eugene Sirmans, *Colonial South Carolina.*

Bernard Bailyn, *The New England Merchants in the Seventeenth Century* (1955), traces the growth of a commercial economy in New England, and David Lovejoy, *The Glorious Revolution in America* (1972), describes American resistance to the efforts of the Stuart Monarchy to gain greater administrative and economic control of the empire. Richard R. Johnson, *Adjustment to Empire: The New England Colonies, 1675–1715* (1981), shows how imperial authority and colonial rights became accommodated to one another by the end of the seventeenth century.

3

New York Public Library Picture Collection

THE AMERICAN:
New Man, New Woman

What first struck travelers who visited colonial America was that there were no monuments and no ruins. In Britain one could hardly travel a day's journey without chancing upon a stone circle erected by Druids, a road laid out by Romans, or a castle built by some medieval baron. In America there was nothing like this. All was new. And when anything became worn out, it was usually torn down and replaced. America had no past; it was a land without a history. The newness conditioned its people. Having cast aside much of the cultural baggage brought over from Europe, they were inventive, inquisitive, open to new ideas and new ways of doing things. They were free without having, as yet, a philosophy of freedom.

Novelty and freshness were everywhere, in part because the virgin continent had not yet been defiled. To sailors everywhere, the seagull is a sign that land is near. To those approaching North America, the first sign of land was a fragrance—the fresh smell of pine trees, which some captains swore they could detect 180 miles out to sea. Landfall only reinforced the traveler's sense of primitive virginity. A ship making its way to Philadelphia, the most common port of entry, wound up the Delaware River for miles through stands of hardwood and pine, broken by an occasional clearing. Philadelphia, a city of 30,000 by 1760, was as large as Bristol or Edinburgh, and second in size only to London itself, yet it was dwarfed by its awesome environment. The approach to New York conveyed a similar impression, as an incoming vessel slipped past the barren dunes and wind-blown thickets of Long Island and through the narrows that separated it from forest-shrouded Staten Island. Perched on the tip of Manhattan Island, New York in 1760 was a pleasant port of 20,000, still very much Dutch in appearance, and showing little sign of its future growth and greatness.

A sense of the pristine and the primitive was the first thing that struck the European upon arriving in America. Growth was the second impression; signs of it were everywhere. Fields were being cleared, buildings erected, entire cities laid out with utter confidence in the future. The population numbered about two million in 1760, and it was doubling itself every twenty-five years. The immigration spurt of Germans and Scots-Irish was partly responsible, but so was the American tendency toward large families. In a rural society where labor was scarce, children were an economic asset. Infant mortality was high by modern standards (a quarter of all newborns failed to survive childhood), but it was lower than in Europe. The reason may be the dispersal of population: Water was less easily polluted, epidemics were less disastrous.

⊔A Wilderness Civilization

The population still clung to the seacoast in 1760. Western pioneers had barely reached the first range of Appalachian highlands. In New England, the advance guard was pushing north along the Connecticut River into southern New Hampshire and Vermont. In New York, the fierce Iroquois prevented any population movement west of Albany and Schenectady. The farthest inland settlements were in the Cumberland and Shenandoah valleys of Pennsylvania and Virginia, and even those were less than 200 miles from the sea. One intrepid Virginian, Dr. Thomas Walker, crossed the ridges of southwestern Virginia in 1750 and discovered the Cumberland Gap, but no one retraced that path until the eve of the revolution.

Cities contained less than 10 percent of

(*Chapter opening photo*) Benjamin Franklin holding a copy of his Almanack.

the total population in 1760, but they had an influence disproportionate to their size. Third in size behind Philadelphia and New York was Boston, at 16,000 people and growing scarcely at all. Charleston, South Carolina, and Newport, Rhode Island, each with a population of about 7,500, were the only other urban centers that might rate being called cities. Steady growth inspired pride and a desire for civic improvement. Philadelphia claimed the first fire department, the first public library, and the first hospital in America—all the result of the civic enterprise of its foremost citizen, Benjamin Franklin. Charleston had the best musical society and most active theater on the continent. The main streets of the cities were paved by mid-century, either with cobblestones or with squared blocks that had come into port as ships' ballast. Philadelphia's streets were lighted with oil lamps and guarded by a force of constables. Every city had at least one newspaper; Philadelphia had six (two in German), as many as could be found in the great city of London.

CREATED UNEQUAL?

American society was new and, by comparison with Europe, formless, but it was not entirely without European influences. Americans shared the European presumption of social inequality. They lacked the rigid feudal structure of Europe, which placed peasants at one end of the social scale and aristocrats at the other, but they habitually referred to "upper orders" and "lower orders." In America there was no aristocracy with inherited lands, titles, and privileges, but wealthy Americans modeled themselves on the English upper class and considered themselves a gentry. To be a gentleman or gentlewoman required more than riches, although money was essential. Inherited wealth was more a sign of status than was new money, and dress, manners, speech, and education were important.

In the seventeenth century, colonial governments often enforced inequality. In 1651, the Massachusetts General Court expressed its "utter detestation that men and women of mean condition, education, and calling should take upon them the garb of gentlemen by wearing of gold or silver lace, or buttons or points at their knees, or walk in great boots, or [that] women of the same rank . . . wear silk or tiffany hoods or scarfs." In 1653, two Newberry, Massachusetts, women were brought before the magistrates for wearing silk scarfs, but they were released when they proved that their husbands were worth £200 each. In the course of the seventeenth century, Connecticut punished thirty young men for wearing silk or sporting unacceptably long hair.

Such regulations withered in the eighteenth century as the concept of personal rights and legal equality slowly crystallized, but rank and status still counted by custom. In New England churches, a seating committee assigned pews, giving the best to families of wealth and rank. In the Anglican churches the vestries performed this task. Occupations were perceived in terms of social status, just as they are today. Planters, merchants, lawyers, and physicians were of "the better sort"; day laborers, tenant farmers, and teachers ranked at the other end of the spectrum, only a cut above the servants. In the South, gentlemen held the title *esquire*, even in official records. George Washington, one of the few privileged to use *esquire*, almost always followed his signature with it.

Improved living conditions and the accumulation of wealth by all segments of American society blurred the European-born notions of social class. By current estimate, the American economy advanced at the rate of 0.6 percent a year between 1660 and 1774, compared with a rate of approximately 0.5 percent a year for Britain. Such steady growth spelled opportunity for nearly all. During that same time period,

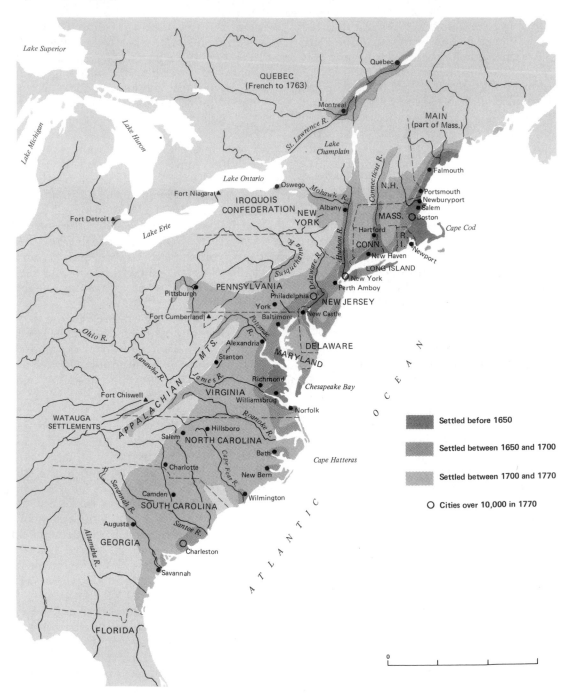

Colonial settlement, 1650–1770.

annual income per capita rose from $550 to $800 (in 1980 dollars). Such an income provided adequate food and housing, though few luxuries. There was inequality, to be sure, and it probably increased in the course of the eighteenth century. The rich got richer, but the poor improved their lot as well.

In 1774, at the end of the colonial period, the richest 10 percent of colonists possessed 50 percent of the total wealth of the colonies. In 1962 (the most recent date for which such figures are available), the richest 10 percent held about 60 percent of the wealth. At the other end of the scale, the poorest half owned 2 percent of the physical wealth in 1774 and 3 percent in 1962. In sum, American society on the eve of the Revolution appeared, in terms of the distribution of wealth, very much as it does today.

This, however, is almost all that can be said in a general way of American society in the mid-eighteenth century. There were enormous regional variations and even diversity from colony to colony. There was great regional inequality in terms of wealth. Southerners had more physical assets than northerners, and if southern slave property is counted as wealth, the South was twice as wealthy as the North on the eve of the Revolution. Within the South, too, there was greater inequality, as the gap between rich planters and poor white farmers widened steadily over time. The ways in which people lived and earned a living varied with every colony, and even within each colony there was great diversity—between town and country, settled seaboard and primitive frontier. The differentiation was in fact increasing as society became more complex, occupations more specialized, and trade more diversified. The greatest differences, however, were between northern colonies and southern and between the seaboard settlements, both northern and southern, and the frontier. Let us, then, examine colonial American

within this framework—northern society, southern society, and frontier life.

⊔Life and Work in the Northern Colonies

ECONOMIC LIFE

Nine out of every ten American families in 1750 made their living by farming. And the majority of these could best be described as subsistence or semi-subsistence farmers. The farm family fashioned nearly everything it needed to subsist, with a small surplus—beef, cheese, apple brandy—for market. In 1787, an elderly farmer proudly, and perhaps nostalgically, recorded what his life had been like:

> At this time my farm gave me and my whole family a good living on the produce of it, and left me one year with one hundred and fifty silver dollars, for I never spent more than ten dollars a year which was for salt, nails, and the like. Nothing to eat, drink or wear was bought, as my farm provided it all.

The farm and, it might be added, the busy hands of his wife and children.

One cannot speak of an "average" farm because wealth depended on one's age. In New England, a young farmer just getting started might possess only 20 or 30 acres, which was barely enough to provide subsistence. By the time he reached middle age, he would have increased his holdings to 100 acres or more. In old age his holding declined to 60 or 80 acres as he provided for his children. Rarely on any family farm was more than 40 acres under cultivation. This was not the result of laziness, but of primitive technology. The wooden plow, which had undergone little improvement in five hundred years, clung so to the soil that two or three horses were required to pull it. Even then, a farmer could plow

Land Tenure and the Wilderness

Tenure was the method by which land was held, whether through ownership or rental. In medieval Europe, only the crown and the church owned land. All others, whether aristocrats or peasants, held their "fees" under some sort of obligation paid in the form of service, rent, or symbolic gesture. (Lord Baltimore, for instance, furnished the king with two arrowheads as symbolic rent for his colony of Maryland.) There were often restrictions (entails) on what a landholder could do with his property, and if he died without heirs, the land usually reverted to the crown.

"Free and common socage" was the tenure by which most of England's yeomen farmers held their land, which meant that the only obligation they owed was to attend the courts of the manorial lords. When royal courts replaced manorial courts, even this obligation evaporated, and by the seventeenth century such unencumbered possession was called a freehold. A freehold could be sold, broken up, or passed on to an heir. The charters of the New England colonies specified that land tenure was to be by freehold. The imposition of quit rents in Pennsylvania and the southern colonies was a technical encumbrance, but many farmers simply "squatted" on their lands without bothering to obtain title or pay rent. In Maryland, the proprietors' effort to set up a manorial system failed. As a result, only New York had a sizable class of tenant farmers (perhaps 6,000 by 1750), and even there, resistance to the exactions of landlords (known locally as "rent wars") kept the colony in turmoil for years.

Nothing was more important in the shaping of American society than the freehold land tenure. Because it was common, it was democratic. Because it was independent of obligation, it encouraged independence of thought and action.

---

only an acre a day. In the relatively short growing season of the northern colonies, the plowing, planting, weeding, and harvesting of 10 or 12 acres was as much as a man could handle. Children might add to acreage but not to income, for they consumed almost as much as they produced. Hired help was out of the question, except for comparatively wealthy commercial farmers. With land cheap and abundant, rare was the man willing to work for another. Wages, by European standards, were therefore exorbitant.

The shortage of labor also shaped to a large extent the strategy of the northern farmer in exploiting the remainder of his acreage. To prepare a field for wheat or corn required weeks of cutting and stump-pulling. Timber, by contrast, was a standing crop, ready for harvest; it needed only to be cut and worked. In New England, until the end of the seventeenth century, lumber was the subsistence farmer's principal cash crop; grain was grown only for family consumption. The cutover lands, instead of being cultivated, were turned into pasture. By the mid-eighteenth century, cattle raising was the small farmer's principal source of cash.

Commercial farming involved fewer

people and more income. Commercial farming meant production for a market, whether it was fruits and vegetables sent to a nearby city, or beef, pork, and flour shipped to Europe. Good soil was one determinant of commercial agriculture; the other was accessibility to market. Commercial farmers either resided close to urban centers or reached them easily by navigable waterways. Overland traffic was slow and expensive. In 1750, eastern Massachusetts, seaboard Connecticut, the lower Hudson River valley in New York, and the lower Delaware valley in Pennsylvania and New Jersey were regions of commercial farming. The income generated by farm exports, in turn, encouraged class stratification and occupational diversity in these regions. Isolated hamlets, such as Groton, Connecticut, Burlington, New Jersey, and Lancaster, Pennsylvania, blossomed into small cities in the latter half of the eighteenth century, as they acquired shopkeepers and artisans, lawyers and physicians—the service occupations needed for a re-

gional economy entering the first stages of modernization.

By the eve of the American Revolution, a commercial farming area such as Lancaster County, Pennsylvania might have a third of its taxable population engaged in nonagricultural pursuits. High income and new enterprises, in turn, helped create the relatively high level of savings and investment needed for the development of manufacturing. The counties along the lower Delaware River in Pennsylvania and New Jersey boasted by 1750 what one traveler described as "the best iron works in the country," a glass factory, and numerous sawmills and flour mills. Pig iron, a crude metal that had to be reworked into utensils, had become one of the area's staple exports. Manufacturing was in its infancy; nearly all was done in the home or in the shops of self-employed artisans. But in Pennsylvania and New Jersey, and to a lesser extent in Massachusetts and Connecticut, there were portents of future smokestacks.

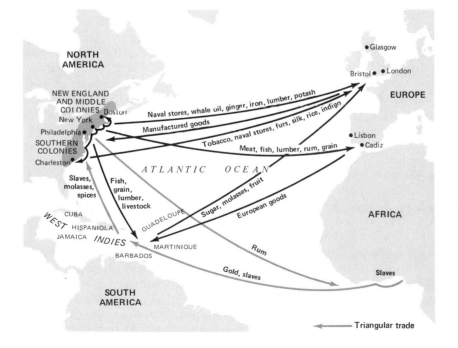

Throughout the seventeenth century, the trade of the northern colonies was, like their agriculture, a matter of bare subsistence. They imported capital goods, such as plows and cows, and they exported principally lumber and fish, products that required relatively small amounts of capital and labor. In 1750, lumber and fish were still the main exports of the northern colonies, though by that date flour, beef, rum, and iron were part of the sales package. Accompanying the growing variety of goods was a new diversification of markets. After 1700, the British sugar islands in the West Indies—Jamaica, Barbados, St. Kitts—had become important trading partners of the mainland colonies. The price of sugar in Europe—and hence its profitability in the West Indies—had begun to fall by 1750, but in the interim, the sugar planters profited by the millions in sterling through their trade with Britain. A third of this income went to the North American colonies in exchange for flour, fish, meat, and lumber; The remainder was distributed among the cost of acquiring new slaves, transportation costs, and personal profit. John Adams, like many New Englanders, saw providence in profit, and expressed it thus: "The commerce of the West Indies is a part of the American system of commerce. They can neither do without us, nor we without them. The Creator has placed us upon the globe in such a situation that we have occasion for each other."

West Indian sugar had changed the eating habits of the Western world. Before the New World was discovered, sugar, chiefly in the form of honey, was found only on the tables of kings and princes. Cane sugar, produced on Caribbean islands governed by England, France, and the Netherlands, or Spain and on portions of Portuguese Brazil, was inexpensive enough to appease the palates and rot the teeth of the common people. Such was the seemingly insatiable demand for sugar that West Indian planters found it profitable to import food from the North American mainland and devote all their land and labor to the cane. They also found it more profitable to work their slaves to death than to give them leisure and time for procreation. As a result, sugar and slaves became the base of a "triangle trade" that came to be dominated by the merchants of Boston, Newport, New York, and Philadelphia.

The "Triangle Trade." The trade, was in fact, a collection of overlapping "triangles," the points of which were North America, Britain, Spain-Portugal, the Guinea coast of Africa, and the West Indies. The islands shipped sugar, molasses, and, most important, bills of exchange (money) to the mainland colonies. British America sent the bills of exchange to Britain to pay for British manufactured goods that it imported. It also sent rum, which New Englanders distilled from West Indian molasses, together with manufactured hardware, to Africa to exchange for slaves, which were then taken to the West Indies to exchange for more sugar and molasses.

These linkages generated a self-sustaining economic growth. The earnings of overseas merchants were distributed among artisans, shopkeepers, and farmers in the hinterland in exchange for their goods and services. "Surplus" income was often reinvested. By 1750, American-built ships dominated the Atlantic trade. The career of Thomas Hancock of Boston is illustrative. He was born in 1703, the third son of a Congregational minister. His two older brothers were sent to Harvard, then a seminary for Congregational preachers; Thomas was apprenticed at the age of fourteen to a bookseller. At the end of his seven-year indenture, he opened his own business and made a "good" marriage to the daughter of an established merchant. Ambition and family connections soon produced a fortune. Within a few years he was trading molasses for fish in Newfoundland, importing Dutch tea via the West Indies, and building a fleet of his own. By 1737 he was wealthy enough to build a mansion on Beacon Hill. His son John emblazoned the family name on the Declaration of Independence.

The Colonial Craftsman. The growth of the seaboard cities and the appearance of inland marketing centers encouraged the rise of a "middle class" of specialized artisans. From the earliest settlements in New England, one out of five male immigrants was a skilled craftsman, and many brought with them the tools of their trade. These people contributed to the growth of the economy by fashioning the ships and barrels used in the West Indies trade, and they contributed to their communities by making and repairing things that others could not, from houses to horseshoes. Every village crossroads needed a blacksmith, a miller, a carpenter, and perhaps a wagonmaker. As the community grew, there would appear a shoemaker, a tailor, and a cooper. The house carpenter might make use of a mason to do his stonework and a glazier for his windows. In a growing coastal community, the shipbuilder would establish a ropewalk and employ the services of a sailmaker.

The least skilled and poorest of the colonial craftsmen were the shoemakers, tailors, and weavers, in part because they competed with women working without wages in the home. These occupations were usually held by young men who moved on to more lucrative trades as they grew older. They also usually worked without helpers. Artisans of higher status acquired apprentices to help them. These were usually local boys whose families were too poor (perhaps because of the early death of a father) to help them become established. In return for his labor, the apprentice was given room and board and training in a craft.

The most prosperous of colonial craftsmen were the smiths and the millers. Each occupation required start up capital, a shop or mill, and tools and equipment. Each craftsman also possessed skills that their neighbors lacked and could not do without. In addition to shoeing horses, the smiths manufactured and repaired the many iron utensils used in the kitchen and hearth. Millers were often the commercial link between the rural village and the outer world. If a village had an export surplus, it was usually flour or lumber, and each product had to go through a milling process. A mill was so important to a community's growth that towns frequently offered concessions in the form of land, a monopoly, and relief from taxation for anyone who would start one. A single structure often produced both flour and lumber. The flowing water that moved a grindstone in the harvest season pushed a saw blade at other times of the year. Because of the profits to be made, many of a colony's richest men, whether merchants, lawyers, or planters, erected mills on streams they owned and hired laborers to operate them.

FROM PURITANS TO YANKEES

Aboard the vessel that had brought the Puritans to Massachusetts in 1630, Governor John Winthrop had told the company that they must be "knitt together in this worke as one man." The Puritan community was a reflection of Puritan religious beliefs. Civil and church authority worked together to enforce uniformity of belief and to punish errant behavior. Community leaders regulated every detail of human life in their efforts to make New England towns models of piety, decorum, and social harmony. The wilderness, the dark and evil world beyond the clearings in which Indians lurked, was an added incentive to preserve cohesive communities through the seventeenth century.

The model, nevertheless, barely survived the first generation of Puritans. As population increased and the wilderness receded, settlers moved into the vacant lands between villages and established farms. Most of these pioneers were hardworking and righteous, but they were no longer under the close scrutiny of the village minister. And they were usually quite content to let town affairs be managed by a small village elite. Thus, by the end of the seventeenth century, the Puritan community had become the New England village, held together by economic and occupational relationships, rather than by a covenant with God. Even so, the two landmarks of the village—the church and the courthouse—symbolized the continuing

Mrs. Elizabeth Freake and Baby Mary, by an unknown artist (ca. 1674). Children were looked upon, and treated, as miniature adults.

Worcester Art Museum.

strength of the old values, piety and order.

The educational system was the main agency for transmitting these values from one generation to the next. Americans in the eighteenth century, not only in New England but elsewhere, had no concept of childhood. Children were viewed—and treated—as small adults. In family portraits of the time, children appear somber and bewigged, wearing the same clothes as their parents, only smaller. The education of children was thus simply a matter of training them to shoulder their adult responsibilities. In New England, this meant curbing their natural passions (each newborn being, the Puritans believed, was fettered with Adam's "original sin" until saved by God's grace) and instilling discipline. The first was accomplished by a liberal use of a birch rod; the second was the province of the *New England Primer*. The most widely used book in colonial America, the *Primer* was a reader with a message. Much of the work was cast in the form of a catechism, a series of questions and answers that distilled the community's orthodox beliefs. Children committed these to memory long before they understood the meaning of the words. The catechism stressed the importance of obedience, submission to authority, and the control of aggressive impulses.

Paradoxically, the preservation of the Puritan value set—that is, its very success in governing the mind of New England— helped to fracture community harmony. Disciplined, industrious people, where opportunities are abundant, are usually successful, and success bred wealth. In all but the most stagnant New England towns in the eighteenth century, the gap between rich and poor widened. In Northampton, Massachusetts, for instance, the upper 10 percent of property owners controlled a fourth of the taxable wealth in 1676; by 1750, they owned a third. Over the same span of years, the proportion owned by the bottom third of the taxpayers remained the same, about 10 percent. Successful artisans and merchants went faithfully to church, and they accepted unquestioningly the values instilled in them in youth. But religious commitment—the concept of life as preparation for afterlife—was increasingly rare. By the mid-eighteenth century, the Puritan had been transformed into the stern and frugal Yankee, a competitive buzzsaw precisely because he believed God to be on his side.

The Gospel of Work. A similar transformation occurred in eighteenth-century Philadelphia. The Society of Friends, itself a form of Puritanism, likewise stressed virtues of piety, frugality, and austere simplicity, a formula that proved, as in New England, to have its material rewards. The Quakers' reputation for honesty and faithfulness also made them successful merchants because customers flocked to do business with them. The Quakers' creed discouraged ostentation but not the acquisition of wealth. William Penn himself advised his children that diligence was "the Way to Wealth" and that frugality was the best and easiest "Way to be Rich" because "A Penny sav'd is a Penny got."

A third of a century later, in 1754, Benjamin Franklin used Penn's phrase "The Way to Wealth" as a title for an essay that summarized in everyday English this special blend of religion and capitalism. Bred in Boston and educated in Philadelphia's school of experience, Franklin was the archetype of the new man, the American. Through his almanac, published under the pseudonym Poor Richard, Franklin had distilled the Puritan ethic in unforgettable maxims, the best of which he inserted in "The Way to Wealth." The values he celebrated were distinctively American, stressing self-reliance ("Tis hard for an empty bag to stand upright"), equality ("Kings and bears worry their keepers"), thrift ("Waste not, want not"), and industry ("Lost time is never found again"). To the classic Christian virtues of faith, hope, and

charity, middle-class northerners, in effect, had added a new set of values. As an ethical system it was unbeatable, for the reward for virtue was not in the hereafter but in the here and now—in the form of wealth and success. It amounted to a new Testament, a Gospel of Work, and Franklin was its apostle. It was a fitting ethic for a new, self-made society.

It was fitting at least, for men. It is doubtful that Franklin's success ethic had much appeal for women. Women in the eighteenth century remained fettered by centuries-old laws and customs. Under the English common law, a female was the ward of the most closely related male—her husband if she was married, or the nearest relative if she was not. Only through him could she own property, enter into contracts, or sue for damages. Among the wealthy, and even among the middle classes, marriages were arranged by parents, usually to achieve some family goal of wealth, power, or prestige. Since divorce was practially impossible in the Church of England, a woman might be trapped for life if the bargain was a bad one.

There is some evidence, however, that American women did benefit from the newness of America, which put a premium on the worth of the individual. Colonial courts were more willing than English courts to recognize a woman's right to own property and to enter into contracts. In Plymouth colony, a will that disinherited a wife was commonly set aside if she could demonstrate that she had contributed to the husband's estate by her own diligence and industry. Similarly, Plymouth courts recognized the validity of premarital contracts made by women concerning the disposition of their property after marriage. Widows often drove hard bargains upon entering into second marriages because they were valuable mates; a second husband was entitled by law to the use or rent from any property a woman inherited from her first husband. One Massachusetts woman demanded that her suitor keep a coach and horses for her in return. Most secured the right to dispose of their inherited property by last will and testament.

Colonial laws required husbands to support their families and whipped those who deserted. In New England, law forbade husbands and wives from striking one another, and some courts punished spouses for abusing each another verbally. After hearing evidence on the conduct of one neglectful husband, a Massachusetts court gave specific instructions for his future behavior, ordering that he "bee admonish't for his cruelty and unkindness to his wife, and that hee forthwith provide Suitable meate drinke and apparrell for his said wife for future . . . or allow her five Shillings per weeke." Divorce was also somewhat easier in America than in Europe, where it was exclusively the province of the church. In New England, divorce cases were handled by civil authorities, and courts generally considered adultery or desertion valid grounds for divorce.

No one in colonial America questioned the view that a woman's place was in the home. Her job was to use, as wisely and as frugally as possible, her husband's earnings to supply the needs of the family. She turned the flour into bread, the wool and flax into clothing, the feathers into bedding. These responsibilities required a certain amount of managerial ability; but no matter how much a woman possessed, she was subject to her husband's authority. Her function was "to guid the house &c. not guid the Husband," declared one minister in a sermon. That same cleric expressed the typical male's estimate of women's intellectual capabilities when he exhorted each husband to instruct his wife in religion but "to make it easy to her." Nevertheless, some women did enter occupations, among them printing and medicine. In northern cities where many husbands went to sea

Weaving, among the chores of the household.

The Bettman Archive, Inc.

and so were absent much of the time, some women managed retail stores. On smaller farms, women played a crucial economic role, for it was they who fashioned the family's necessities, from clothing to soap. Their contributions may have enhanced their status as family decision makers, but the evidence on this point is sketchy. American women, in sum, were probably better off than those in Europe. But both still had a long way to go.

⊔ The South and Slavery

In contrast to the northern colonies, where semi-subsistence farming was the rule, the coastal regions of the South were given to commercial farming. Its cash crops were the great export staples—tobacco in Maryland and Virginia, rice and (after about 1750) indigo* in South Carolina. These areas—Tidewater Maryland and Virginia, Albermarle Sound in North Carolina, and low-country South Carolina—had a high proportion of landless whites, perhaps 30 percent of the taxables, and concentration of property in the hands of the few. It was an overwhelmingly rural society. In 1750 only Charleston, South Carolina, could be termed a city. Richmond, Virginia, was less than twenty years old; Baltimore, Maryland, and Raleigh, North Carolina, had yet to be founded. Only about 6 percent of all whites could be termed artisans, merchants, or professionals; the remainder worked the land as planters, overseers, or tenant farmers.

Northern and southern colonies began to show sharp differences in the seven-

teenth century. Religious and cultural attitudes were one obvious reason, but another, less obvious, reason was the death rate. New England received a massive infusion of 20,000 immigrants in the decade of the 1630s and almost none thereafter. The English civil war of the 1640s interrupted the flow of immigrants, and when normality was restored in the 1660s, the flourishing tobacco colonies on the Chesapeake seemed more attractive. For the next twenty years, restless Englishmen seeking farms of their own streamed into Maryland and Virginia. From the 1680s onward, the transatlantic flood poured into Pennsylvania and the Carolinas.

Even without substantial immigration after 1640, the New England population had quadrupled by 1700. In the Chesapeake, by contrast, over 100,000 immigrants had arrived in the course of the century, yet the total population in 1700 was no more than 70,000. The major explanation for this extraordinary discrepancy is disease, its presence or absence. There were almost no epidemics in seventeenth-century New England. As a result, individuals who survived the common childhood diseases could expect to live at least to the age of sixty. Women thus had additional childbearing years; some were still bearing children when they were grandmothers. By contrast, the low and marshy Chesapeake was a land of death. Malaria lurked in the swamps; drinking water carried deadly typhoid bacteria. Those who survived these assaults commonly fell victim to pneumonia or influenza. A youth of twenty-one who survived the "seasoning" of a year's residence in the Chesapeake climate could expect to live to age forty or forty-five—but no more.

High mortality slowed the growth of the Chesapeake economy and delayed the appearance of a wealthly class. Men died before they had a chance to add significantly to their estates, and their orphaned children were usually too young to take over.

---

* Indigo, a weed whose juices made a blue dye much in demand in Europe, was introduced into South Carolina by Eliza Pinckney, who managed a plantation of her own, in addition to mothering two of South Carolina's most distinguished revolutionary leaders, Thomas Pinckney and Charles Coatsworth Pinckney.

Widows almost invariably remarried, and stepfathers took over the estate. The constant breakup of families delayed the development of a European-style gentry class in which an inheritance and the prestige that went with it was passed from father to son.

Indentured Servants. High mortality created a severe labor shortage that forced Chesapeake planters to import servants. That was the most striking difference between the southern colonies and the northern—unfree labor. Slavery existed in all the British-American colonies until the revolution, but it never became an important source of labor in the North. The reason, essentially, was the climate. The northern growing season was comparatively short, and winter snows prevented farmers from employing slaves in clearing land or mending fences. An idle slave was a financial drain. For northern farmers, slavery was simply not profitable. Slaves were employed in some northern shipyards and occasionally in the shops of craftsmen, but they were chiefly used as domestic servants.

In the South, by contrast, the production of labor-intensive staples, such as tobacco and rice,* was profitable only with unfree labor. Until near the end of the seventeenth century, white indentured servants were the main source of southern plantation labor. Indentured servants, migrants principally from the British Isles and Germany, were people too poor to finance their own passage to America. Accordingly, they entered into a bond, or indenture, by which they agreed to work off the cost of their journey. The indentures specified the time of service, usually four to seven years. Transportation companies sold these bonds to planters in need of labor. Such servants went to all the colonies, but only in the South were they a central feature of the labor system.

As chattel property, indentured servants could be bought and sold, rented out, or passed on by inheritance. They did, however, have certain legal rights. They had access to courts, they could sue and be sued, and they had the right to own property. Although servants were subject to physical punishment, usually whipping, an excessively brutal master might be deprived of his servant by a court. Masters were also obliged by law to provide them with "sufficient" food and clothing, and most indentures specified that masters were to provide, at the expiration of a servant's term, enough clothes, tools, or money to enable the servant to get a start in life. Maryland even provided each one with fifty acres of land. There was no social stigma on former servants; they were expected to blend into the community. But how many actually succeeded is questionable. One rather depressing estimate is that only two out of ten developed a comfortable living as farmers or artisans. The remainder either died prematurely, drifted onto the frontier, returned to Europe, or joined the ranks of landless "poor whites."

Although indentured servants were commonly employed in artisans' shops in the northern colonies, in the South they were mostly confined to the hoe and ax. This probably also included women, who constituted about a quarter of all indentured servants. The English disapproved of field work for women, and there is some evidence that female servants resisted being "put into the ground." But most had little choice. They were owned by small planters who had few domestic duties to be performed. Large planters, who did have "domestic employments," usually preferred to use black slaves.

THE ORIGINS OF SLAVERY

Black Africans had been in the Chesapeake since 1619, when a Dutch vessel brought a cargo of them into Jamestown. The first

---

* A fieldhand could tend only about five acres of tobacco or rice in a year.

arrivals seem to have been treated as indentured servants, but by the 1640s, Virginia courts recognized that certain persons were in lifetime bondage. In the 1660s, the Virginia assembly passed an act making slavery inheritable, the status of the child depending on the status of the mother. Even so, as late as 1670 slaves made up less than 5 percent of Virginia's population and were outnumbered at least three to one by indentured servants. To that date also, most slaves in the Chesapeake had come from the West Indies, having been cast off, due to age or infirmity, by the sugar planters. In 1672, King Charles II chartered the Royal African Company, bestowing on it a monopoly of the slave trade in the English empire. By 1698, when the monopoly was terminated, slaves in Virginia and Maryland represented a fifth of the population and a majority of the work force. The monopoly was ended in response to the demand of West Indian planters for more and cheaper slaves, a recognition, as one black historian, with bitter irony, has put it, that "the right of a free trade in slaves was . . . a fundamental and natural right of Englishmen." Free enterprise worked its marvels. The slave population doubled in the next decade, and it doubled

again every decade thereafter until near the middle of the eighteenth century.

The reasons that southern planters shifted from white servants to black slaves is still subject to debate. English laborers, one historian has argued, were inefficient, subject to illness in the hot southern climate, and unruly, whereas Africans were more resistant to diseases and accustomed to the backbreaking labor of tilling the soil. This explanation has not satisfied other historians, who wonder, in view of the intricacies of tobacco culture, why planters would prefer Africans, who knew nothing of tobacco growing and who had to be taught the language before they could be taught the art. These scholars point to servant prices. By the end of the seventeenth century, fewer English poor wished to come to America—a result, apparently, of better conditions in England. Those who did come accordingly commanded a higher price for their indentures, so for large planters with capital and organization, African slaves were more profitable. Large planters led the way in switching from servants to slaves, and small planters eventually followed suit.

The Africans had begun by enslaving one another. Even before America was dis-

A nineteenth-century artist's conception of the interior of a slave ship.

National Maritime Museum, Greenwich, London.

covered, the kingdoms of western Africa commonly made slaves of captives taken in their wars with one another. These slaves were often sold to merchant-peddlers, who plied the trade routes of the Sahara, and were sold again on the shores of the Mediterranean to Greek, Roman, or Egyptian masters. The sale of captives to European ship captains for transfer to the New World was an extension of the system, but it was an extension that differed in kind and in scale. The kidnapping and sale of Africans to work the plantations of the New World involved a degradation and a risk of death unknown in any earlier form of slavery. By the early eighteenth century, the insatiable demand for slaves, not only in the sugar islands but in the mainland colonies, had become a principal cause of warfare among African kingdoms, and slave-hunting expeditions ranged far into the interior.

Mungo Park, a Scottish trader, described a "coffle," or train of captives that he marched with for 550 miles across Africa at the end of the eighteenth century. It consisted of 73 men, women, and children strung together by leather thongs tied around their necks. Some tried to commit suicide on the journey; others died of exhaustion. At the coast they were paraded naked for examination by ships' surgeons. The elderly, the diseased, and the infirm who were lucky enough to be rejected probably remained enslaved in Africa. Those who passed muster were branded with hot irons and held in pens until they numbered enough for a ship's cargo. They were then ferried in canoes to the tiny wooden slavers lying at anchor in the harbor. Aboard ship they were packed in layers between the decks, so close together they could barely move, there to undergo the month-long voyage to the New World and probable early death.

Each step in this process, each calculated indignity, was intended to demoralize, terrify, and ultimately subdue the captive by reducing him or her to bewildered docility. Rarely did it succeed. Out of fear and desperation, many captives committed suicide by leaping overboard from the ships before they could be chained. Some escaped during the voyage. More than fifty black mutinies are recorded in the slave trade. They continued to resist even after they had been landed and sold. "A new negro," wrote a traveler in Virginia in 1740, "if he must be broke, either from obstinancy, or, which I am more apt to suppose, from greatness of soul, will require more hard discipline than a young spaniel. You would be surprised at their perseverance; let a hundred men show him how to hoe, or drive a wheelbarrow, and he'll take the one by the bottom and the other by the wheel; and they often die before they can be conquered."

Slave revolts, though not common, occurred often enough to keep the white population in constant apprehensiveness. Virginia and South Carolina, which had the largest slave population, rumbled with conspiracies throughout the early decades of the eighteenth century. In 1739, a major uprising occurred on the Stono River in South Carolina, after the governor of Spanish Florida, as a war measure, offered freedom to slaves who escaped to St. Augustine. Some eighty blacks from low-country rice plantations broke into a warehouse that stored guns and ammunition, stole some of both, and started south to Florida. South Carolina militia pursued them and, in a pitched battle, killed about half and captured the remainder.

As the slave population grew, colonial assemblies began passing laws to keep it under control. In 1705, Virginia codified its various regulations, and the colony's slave code quickly became a model for other colonies. It prohibited slaves from leaving their plantations without written permission and authorized whites to form slave patrols to police the roads and check slaves' passes. Slaves were forbidden to own dogs or weapons and could not congregate in groups of three or more, except at work or during authorized festivities. Some colonies prohibited owners from inflicting excessive punishment, but in general the slaves' only protection against brutality was their masters' self-interest.

FREE BLACKS

Unlike any slave system in history, New World slavery rested on racism. Blacks were systematically brutalized as part of the method of enslaving them, but they were enslaved in the first place because white Europeans and British-Americans regarded the peoples of Africa as subhuman. Slavery rested on racial bias and in turn fostered it. The importance of race can be seen in the treatment of free blacks. Every colony had a few. Some were descendants of the first black indentured servants, but most were beneficiaries of private manumission (that is, a planter's act of freeing his slaves, usually in his will). All colonies permitted owners to free their slaves if they wished, but this allowance was gradually restricted. An act passed in Virginia in 1723 provided that slaves could be freed only with the approval of the governor and council. Free blacks were targets of prejudice and objects of suspicion. Whites correctly viewed them as a potential threat to the system because they were a living reminder that it was possible to be both black and free. Rightly or not, whites blamed free blacks for inspiring slave resistance, and as the slave codes increased in severity, so did the restrictions on free blacks. In 1705 Virginia denied to blacks, mulattos, and Indians the rights to hold public office and to testify in court. In 1723 these same groups were deprived of the right to vote. South Carolina required free blacks to leave the colony. Nearly all colonies, whether in the North or the South, forbade interracial marriage. A final indication of prevailing attitudes among whites in the colonial era was that there was practically no criticism of slavery. Only Quakers and Moravians, consistent with their notions of human equality, voiced any objections. Nearly everyone else simply accepted the institution as something rooted in nature and sanctioned by history.

AN AFRO-AMERICAN CULTURE

Vicious though it was, slavery in the mainland colonies of British America differed in one crucial respect from slavery in the West Indies: mortality. Blacks brought from Africa had a far better chance of survival in the mainland colonies than in the Sugar Islands. Some time early in the eighteenth century, perhaps about 1720, the birth rate began to exceed the death rate, and thereafter the black population increased naturally. By the time of the revolution, about 250,000 Africans had been brought into the colonies, and the black population numbered about 500,000.

The natural increase in the black population did not equal that of the white population, but given the low survival rates of slaves in the West Indies and in Portuguese Brazil, it was remarkable nonetheless. The reasons are a matter of conjecture. Mainland plantations, especially in the tobacco country, were more widely dispersed than in the sugar islands, thus inhibiting the spread of disease. Tobacco was also less profitable than sugar, so tobacco planters imported a higher proportion of less-expensive female slaves, creating a sex ratio that encouraged the development of family life. Planters, in fact, encouraged childbirth because it added to the labor supply. Most planters also allowed young children to remain with their mothers, thereby beginning the process of family formation.

Blacks imported from Africa came from different cultural backgrounds, but they shared a belief in the importance of family and kinship. African society was structured on kinship relations, and in America the slave family became the repository of Afro-American culture. Marital unions, though not recognized by law and rarely by white planters, were formal and usually enduring. Fathers were usually not allowed to reside with their children, but even if they were sent to some distant plantation or farm,* the kinship ties remained. Uncles or cousins took up their childrearing duties. Through the family, African traditions were preserved and passed on, though within the bounds of what the white masterclass would tolerate. Music, dance, games, folktales, taboos, and superstitions were among the cultural survivals of the African past, though each was modified in the American environment. The result was the gradual emergence of an Afro-American culture, a world view that was neither African nor American but a blend of both. And for many it was a psychological fortress in the brutal world of slavery.

THE SOUTHERN STYLE OF LIVING

Class distinctions were more evident in the seaboard South than elsewhere in the American colonies. This was evident in the gap between rich and poor—10 percent of the men owned 40 percent of the wealth—and it was evident in the deference the wealthy commanded. In his late years, one Virginian vividly recalled his youthful feelings when, as a propertyless schoolmaster, he received a visit from the local grandee:

---

* A farm, to Virginians, was a patch of land without a domicile. Slaves, usually under an overseer, worked the land in the growing season and returned to the plantation in the winter.

When I viewed him riding up, I never beheld such a display of pride arising from his deportment, attitude, and jesture; he rode a lofty, elegant horse, . . . his countenance appeared to me as bold and daring as satan himself, and with a commanding authority [he] called upon me, if I were there to come out, which I accordingly did, with a fearful and timorous heart.

As important as the man in that portrait was the horse. It was often said in the eighteenth century that Virginians would go five miles to catch a horse in order to ride one mile. Being mounted on a "lofty, elegant horse" was part of the gentleman's self-presentation, a source of inner pride and outer command.

Cavalier was the word for horseman, but in Virginia it had a special meaning: It referred to the mounted aristocrats who supported the king against Puritans and Parliament in the seventeenth-century English civil war. Legend had it that the followers of the king fled to Virginia and Maryland upon the triumph of the Puritan leader Oliver Cromwell, and there in the king's "old dominion" they fathered a New World aristocracy. Though widely believed by Virginians, this version of history was pure myth. The gentry of Maryland and Virginia were a home-grown product that gained their position atop society through hard work and good tobacco prices. Yet, like most myths, the cavalier legend influenced behavior. The southern gentry modeled themselves on the English aristocracy and its code: Dress, manners, a devotion to honor, and a habit of command distinguished the southern gentleman. Wealth and family pedigree were important but not essential. George Washington was one of many self-made gentlemen.

The chief differences in living style between the wealthy and the lower orders were two. Among the wealthy, there was a clear separation of the planter's family from the people on the plantation, a clear distinction between master and servants, and the wealthy had more commodious houses. The gentry lived in houses of five to twelve rooms, each with its own function—kitchen, hall (living room), dining room, and bedrooms. In the houses of lesser planters, containing only two or three rooms, there was no such distinction; living, cooking, and sleeping quarters, particularly among large families, overlapped. In the one-room houses of the very poor, the overlapping must have verged on chaos. Within the house, the best index of wealth and comfort was the bed. This was usually the biggest single item of household expense. Even an ordinary bed cost as much as a horse; the elegant structures of the wealthy, with feather quilts, high posts for air circulation, and curtains to keep out insects, cost as much as a prime field hand. The poor, as well as the servants of the wealthy, slept on hammocks or on the floor on ticks stuffed with cattails or rushes.

The styles of work and living of southern women also varied with degrees of wealth, but as with the menfolk, with no great gap in standards. Except perhaps among the mercantile elite of Charleston, there was no "leisure class." Like her husband, the wife of a wealthy planter had to have managerial talents, for she was in charge of the household, which meant overseeing the duties of servants, planning meals for a daily throng, and keeping accounts. Women, except among the poor, were not expected to work in the fields, but in households without servants they tended a garden, managed the dairy, and raised poultry. In a rural economy, where the home was the place of business, women performed valuable economic functions which, though they did not confer much status, commanded respect. The speed with which people who had lost their mates remarried testified to the economic, as well as emotional, interdependence of the sexes.

Paralleling the transition from Puritan to Yankee in the northern colonies was the appearance of a "southern mentality" in the plantation colonies. Hard work, self-reliance, and independence were as much revered among southerners of the middle classes as they were in the North, but they were virtues born of the wilderness environment and rural isolation, not the church and the community. The southerner lived in isolation; community was an occasion, not an institution. Community was a Sabbath, when friends met at church, a court day when suits were settled and horses swapped, or an election when everyone got drunk at the expense of the candidates.

The northerner was restless; the southerner was almost nomadic. Having more tillable land, the southern colonist wasted it with even greater profligacy. He lived with his eye on the horizon, clearing, tilling, and abandoning the soil, ever pushing his way westward. His fences, made of pine split into rails, were movable from one plot to the next. Even his house, made of split green wood, was disposable. The wood warped and cracked as it aged, and within a few years it rotted, by which time the southerner was ready to move on.

Benjamin Franklin, with his stress on the value of time, labor, and pennywise savings, was an American archetype, but so was the restive Virginian, with his hand on the whip and his eye on the main chance. And it is difficult to say which contributed more to the American experience. After all, while New Englanders were still exploring the mysteries of salvation, the Virginians were exploring Kentucky.

⊔Life on the Frontier

The third region of colonial America, the frontier, stretched from the hardwood forests of Maine and New Hampshire to the long-leaf pine woods of Carolina and Georgia. Its westward limit in 1750 was the

Transporting hogsheads of tobacco to a merchant's wharf for shipment to Britain.

Rare Book Division, The New York Public Library, Astor, Lenox, and Tilden Foundations.

CLIO'S FOCUS: Colonial Dining and Wining

Massachusetts Governor John Winthrop imported a fork from England in 1633. It arrived in a leather case of its own, together with a matching knife and bodkin. It was a treasured object, and properly so. Winthrop's was probably the first fork ever brought to America. Forks were scarcely known, even in England. They had been invented in Italy in the previous century, and travelers were just beginning to introduce them into northern Europe. They did not become common in America until the eve of the revolution.

People ate with spoons out of a wooden bowl called a trenchard. Among the wealthy, each diner had one of his own; among the poor, the bowl was placed in the center of the table for each to dip with spoon or fingers. Without a fork it was difficult to cut meat at the table, so colonial recipes usually called for finely chopped meat in a soup, stew, or ragout. Fresh meat was rare anyway, except during the autumn "killing time." Meat was preserved by drying or salting; to be rendered edible, it had to be heated in water. Soup or stew was the end product. The most common vegetables, at least among the poor, were New World species—squash and pumpkins in the north, sweet potatoes in the south.

Dinners usually began with pudding, which was simply boiled meal, sometimes sweetened with maple sugar. In England, hasty pudding was made by cooking wheat cereal or oatmeal in milk; in America, the dish was more often made with corn.

The pudding apparently replaced bread in the afternoon or evening meal. Bread was more often eaten at breakfast. Wheat bread was rare until the eighteenth century because the available strains of wheat did not ripen well in the cool northern climate. Rye was more easily grown, and a blend of rye flour and corn meal made a bread called "rye-an'-injun."

Europeans used water for bathing, not drinking. They knew nothing of germs or pollution, but they did know that water brought "agues" and "fevers," which today might be identified as typhus or typhoid. Hence the English and Dutch drank ale or beer; the French and Spanish drank wine. Beer was also the common method of preserving water on long ocean voyages. The Pilgrims were still drinking beer from the *Mayflower* months after they landed at Plymouth. In America, where pollution was less a problem, transplanted Europeans gradually became acquainted with the virtues of water. Governor Winthrop, who seems to have been something of a culinary adventurer, ordered water to be the standard beverage in his household.

Milk was the common drink at breakfast until tea became popular in the eighteenth century. Americans were unacquainted with coffee until after the revolution, when they began trading in the Mediterranean and Africa. In colonial times, the favorite nonalcoholic beverage was undoubtedly apple cider. The first settlers brought apple trees and grafts from England. The trees flourished in every colony, north and south, and when properly stored, the fruit stayed fresh for months. In the northern colonies apples were the only fresh fruit available in the winter. Nearly every rural household had a cider mill, usually built on a hillside, so wagons could unload apples at the top and take away barrels of cider at the lower level. When allowed to stand a few days, cider "hardened," as natural yeasts turned its sugar to alcohol. The resulting drink was lighter and drier than the cider and slightly fizzy. John Adams was a lifelong advocate of temperance, but every morning he drank a tankard of hard cider as soon as he got out of bed.

A Sunday dinner menu in the Adams household on the eve of the revolution reveals the changes that took place in colonial eating habits in the century and a half after Governor Winthrop purchased a fork. The first course was a pudding of Indian meal, molasses, and butter. Then came a course of veal and bacon, followed by neck of mutton and vegetables. The meat was sliced at table with the aid of a fork and eaten from flat plates rather than bowls. Among such gentry as the Adamses, the use of fingers was probably already taboo. In Europe the fork had helped promote rules of dining etiquette, and the changes were being felt in America. In rural areas, however, and on the frontier, spoon, trenchard, and stew were seen well into the nineteenth century.

A wilderness farm. Trees were girdled to kill them so as to provide light for the first year's crop. When the trees fell they were burned for potash.

Yale University Art Gallery, The Mabel Brady Garvan Collection.

Allegheny Mountains. There was no discernible line of settlement, no boundary between civilization and savagery. The frontier, rather, was a few scattered patches of sunlit clearings where red men and white tended a few hills of corn while keeping a wary eye on one another.

Farming on the frontier was almost purely subsistence, except for those families fortunate enough to have access to navigable water. Farm products, except for distilled spirits, could not be transported overland because freight charges were pro-

hibitive. For those with access to water, the cash crop varied. New England frontiersmen sent lumber and firewood to the seaboard. In western Pennsylvania, pioneers burned their excess wood in great pits, made a mild lye of the ashes, called potash, and sold that to soapmakers. In the Carolina backwoods, pine logs burned slowly in pits yielded pitch and tar that was sold to shipbuilders to patch the seams of wooden vessels.

There were few class distinctions on the frontier, if only because all was new. Farms were small, except in the Virginia Piedmont,* and the amount of cultivated land tinier yet. Clearing the land was so laborious and time-consuming that there were few opportunities on the frontier to get rich. In Virginia, eastern planters led the way onto the Piedmont frontier, laying claim to huge tracts of land in order to ensure themselves future tobacco land. But few of them settled in the wilderness to live.

Because land was cheap on the frontier, nearly everyone was a landowner. Four out of five families owned their farms, and those who did not simply squatted on the land of others without paying rent. George Washington, who received extensive tracts on the frontier as a reward for his military services, was driven to distraction by ten-

ants who failed to pay rent, and he periodically toured his holdings to roust squatters. The result was the rough equality of common poverty, but the equality dissolved as population and development brought diversity and specialization. Taverns and trading posts sprouted where horsepaths crossed, a smithy, a schoolteacher, and a minister settled nearby, to be followed by a lawyer, a physician, and ultimately a merchant with eastern connections. It was a developmental process that the seaboard settlements had gone through a generation or two before. The frontier did not make American society permanently equal or democratic, but it did, so long as it lasted, afford an opportunity for American society to reconstitute itself anew.

SUMMARY

Few of the people who came to America in the seventeenth century expected to sever their ties with England. Even the Puritans, who left to escape corruption and persecution, retained English habits, English styles of building, and English law. The Virginians consciously modeled themselves on the English gentry and adopted the English church, English forms of local government, and English jurisprudence.

Nevertheless, as the colonies matured they became more distinctively American in

economic interest and in identity. The most important factor shaping this American identity was the novelty and spaciousness of the American environment. Novelty placed a premium on ingenuity and inventiveness; space placed a premium on labor. For the imaginative and the energetic, opportunity was often there. Even in the seventeenth century there was a fluidity to American society, a value placed on individual worth, that was not present in Europe. In his classic essay *The Way to Wealth*, Benjamin Franklin distilled the set of values—self-reliance, thrift, and industry—that would become the American creed.

Because of the shortage of labor, wages were generally higher than in Europe, but not all segments of the American population benefited. American women were better off legally than their European coun-

---

* Each of the southern colonies had three subregions—the Tidewater, which was the coastal plain where rivers were affected by ocean tides; the Piedmont, which stretched from the falls of the rivers (inland market towns, Alexandria, Richmond, Petersburg, Fayetteville, were located on this "fall line") to the mountains; and third, the Appalachian highlands, which began in Virginia and North Carolina with the Blue Ridge.

terparts, and they probably had more opportunity for gainful pursuits. But they remained snared in the web of restraints imposed on women by law and custom. And the shortage of labor, which went far to enhance the worth and freedom of whites, ironically brought about the enslavement of blacks. Southern tobacco and rice planters, finding white labor, whether free or indentured, too expensive, turned to slavery in the last decades of the seventeenth century. Slavery and capitalism evolved together as planters poured their profits into enlarging their labor force.

Slavery and the plantation system shaped the southern mentality. The courtly attention to manners and honor, borrowed from the English gentlemanly code, blended with capitalistic acquisitiveness. Benjamin Franklin, with his emphasis on the value of time, labor, and pennywise saving, was the archetypical Yankee. The restless Virginian, with his hand on the whip and his eye on the main chance, was yet another form of that new being, the American.

READING SUGGESTIONS

Daniel J. Boorstin's *The Americans: The Colonial Experience* (1958) is a thought-provoking answer to the question, "What is this new man, the American?" Kenneth A. Lockridge, *New England Town: Dedham . . .*, (1970), and Richard Bushman, *From Puritan to Yankee* (1967), describe the process at the community level. Bernard Bailyn, *The New England Merchants in the Seventeenth Century* (1955), discusses the development of American commerce; and Carl Bridenbaugh, *Cities in the Wilderness* (1938), describes the rise of cities.

Jackson T. Main's *Society and Economy in Colonial Connecticut* (1985) uses probate records to obtain a profile of the wealth and status of Connecticut's people in the eighteenth century. His portrait of a prosperous, "steady" people may apply to New England generally.

Edmund S. Morgan, *The Puritan Family* (1944), is a classic, but it should be supplemented with Laurel Thatcher Ulrich, *Image and Reality in the Lives of Women in Northern New England, 1650–1750* (1982), a sensitive re-creation of life on the colonial frontier. Carl Degler, *At Odds* (1980), is an imaginative reinterpretation

of the roles of women and families in America from colonial times to the twentieth century.

Edwin L. Perkins, *The Economy of Colonial America* (1980), is a brief overview. Alice Hanson Jones, *Wealth of a Nation To Be* (1980), provides extensive data on American wealth on the eve of the Revolution, together with a comparison with Europe of that time and America of today, but it is not a book to be undertaken by the casual reader.

Thad Tate's *The Chesapeake in the Seventeenth Century* (1981) traces the rise of the plantation system. David W. Galenson, *White Servitude in Colonial America: An Economic Analysis* (1981), and Winthrop Jordan, *White over Black* (1968), depict the economic and psychological reasons for the origin of slavery. Edmund S. Morgan, *American Slavery, American Freedom: The Ordeal of Colonial Virginia* (1975), offers a slightly different interpretation. Morgan also discusses the appearance of a southern temperament, supplementing the old but still useful study by Louis B. Wright, *First Gentlemen of Virginia* (1940).

4

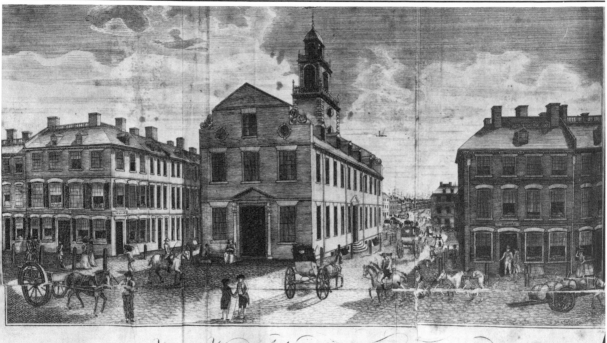

A S.W. View of the STATE HOUSE in BOSTON.

BRITAIN'S ATLANTIC COMMUNITY

It has been said that the only culture in colonial America was *agri*culture. There was more wit than truth in this, for by the middle decades of the eighteenth century, the colonies were alive with political and religious discourse, scientific inquiry, and artistic endeavor. Prior to that intellectual renaissance, however, the American mind was dull indeed. The number of creative individuals in the first half of the eighteenth century could be counted on one hand. The vast majority of Americans seemed preoccupied with material comforts, bustling about their daily tasks, drawing their intellectual sustenance from newspapers and their sense of direction from Sunday sermons.

How had it happened? Why was there no patience with the sublime and the esthetic in early America? Among the founders of New England and Virginia were men and women of intense intellectual energy. John Smith in Virginia and William Bradford in Plymouth even possessed rare literary talent. But when these vigorous minds died or departed, later colonists were unable to generate an independent cultural life. Harvard College, founded with great expectations in 1636, degenerated into a provincial seminary for training Congregational ministers. The most widely read piece of literature in the seventeenth century, Michael Wigglesworth's *Day of Doom* (1662), was a poetic digest of Puritan theology designed to make it easy for children to learn and remember. Why was early America so intellectually barren?

Benjamin Franklin blamed the dearth of American books and paintings on the wilderness environment. Americans, he felt, were too busy chopping, plowing, and building to devote time to the finer arts. There was a kernel of truth to this, for the preoccupation with elementary comfort, the social flux as people cleared land, harvested crops, and then moved on, hindered the development of an esthetic consciousness. So too did the high death rate that persisted throughout the seventeenth century. Broken families and orphaned children are unlikely vehicles for transmitting an esthetic tradition; as a result, by the end of the seventeenth century the American colonies were a cultural backwater, a distorted and pale reflection of England's creative civilization in the "golden age" of Queen Anne.

⊔Intellectual Bridges

Scientific inquiry was the only landmark in America's dreary intellectual landscape at the turn of the century. The principal reason for this was the activities of the Royal Society, which had been founded in London in 1662 for the purpose of collecting and studying information from all over the world. By enlisting correspondents in America and occasionally electing distinguished colonists to their ranks, the members of the Royal Society stimulated a good deal of scientific investigation, speculation, and report.

SCIENCE

The first colonist chosen to join the Royal Society was John Winthrop, Jr., son of the founder of the Massachusetts Bay Colony and himself the perennially elected governor of Connecticut. Winthrop's interests ranged from medicine to metallurgy. This good Puritan saw no conflict between science and religious belief; indeed, he viewed science as a means of improving the lot of humankind while it abided fleetingly in this life. In Virginia, wealthy and worldly William Byrd II, who was anything but a Puritan, shared Governor Winthrop's

(*Chapter opening photo*) Eighteenth-century Boston.

scientific curiosity. He too was elected to the Royal Society before the seventeenth century was out, on the strength of an essay entitled "An Account of a Negro Boy That is Dappled in Several Places of His Body with White Spots." Byrd was also concerned with the practical applications of science, especially where it benefited him. Among his contributions to the Royal Society's publications was an essay on the healthful and life-giving qualities of Virginia tobacco.

A Boston cleric, son and grandson of Puritan ministers, Cotton Mather was a bridge of another kind. Where Byrd and Winthrop spanned the Atlantic intellectual community, Mather strode the time gap between the medieval world of divine governance and the modern world of science and inquiry. His first important writing was a detailed account of his experimental efforts to cure a thirteen-year-old witch who had become possessed by the Devil. In 1689, at the age of twenty-six, he played a major role in the overthrow of the Dominion of New England, drafting a declaration that both justified the removal of the governor and called for a restoration of popular rights and liberties.

Mather's greatest work, the *Magnalia Christi Americana* (1702), was an extended (850-page) sermon, a denunciation of wealth and worldliness of the sort that had spewed forth from Congregational pulpits for half a century. But it was also good history, as Mather conscientiously recorded an impartial record of New England's past. To Mather, the history of Massachusetts was a cycle of progress, backsliding, divine vengeance, reaffirmation of faith, and renewed progress. Mather made no distinction between religion and history, nor did he see a gap between religion and science. His father, Increase Mather, president of Harvard, was one of the first Congregational clerics to endorse the Copernican theory that the world revolved around the sun. Cotton

New York Public Library Picture Collection.

Cotton Mather. This is a 1727 mezzotint engraving by Peter Pelham. Engravings were reproductions of painted portraits. Since there were then no portrait painters in Boston, Pelham had to make both portrait and engraving. This is the earliest American mezzotint.

Mather believed that the sheer immensity of the universe, together with its rich variety, required a divine creator. Nothing less could have done it. That there were laws of nature, such as Isaac Newton's law of gravity, proved only that God had seen fit to create a rational universe. But it did not mean that God was bound by those laws. He could always intervene, thought Mather, when a miracle seemed required.

The death of Cotton Mather's wife of smallpox in 1713 turned his scientific curiosity to the field of medicine. It was well known that those who survived a case of smallpox* were immune, but only the strong and otherwise healthy survived. When Mather asked his black servant whether he had ever had smallpox, the man replied "yes and no." He explained that in his native Guinea he had been given a small dose of the disease which "would

---

* So named to distinguish it from the "great pox," or syphillis, both diseases being characterized by skin pustules, or "pocks."

forever preserve him from it." The man referred, of course, to inoculation and indicated that it was common practice in his part of Africa. Mather stored the information, and when a smallpox epidemic broke out in Boston in 1721 he suggested to the town physicians that they give inoculations. Only one, Dr. Zabdiel Boylston, was bold enough to try it. He eventually inoculated 242 persons, only 6 of whom died, a mortality rate of 2.5 percent. The mortality in the city as a whole was nearly 15 percent. Realizing the significance of these statistics, Mather sent them to a friend in the Royal Society for publication. That in itself may have been the most important result of the affair: It was the first use of probability statistics in the field of medicine, and it encouraged further inoculation experiments in Britain and elsewhere in the colonies. Despite such efforts, Cotton Mather lived in a society that was still more medieval than modern, and his efforts to transcend his world only left him socially isolated, an object of ridicule rather than admiration.

EDUCATIONAL INTERCHANGE

Even so, by the time Cotton Mather died in 1728 there were stirrings of intellectual activity abroad in the colonies, as they came to share in the Western world's intellectual renaissance, known as the Enlightenment. Americans who went to Britain for education and professional training absorbed the new ideas and carried them home. William Byrd II, who crossed the Atlantic eight times, was one of the first of these itinerant savants, and the contacts he made in London provided him with lifelong intellectual sustenance. As the century wore on, the number of Americans journeying to the mother country increased. By 1776, more than five hundred young Americans had been sent to Britain for schooling. Edin-

burgh attracted more than any other university, partly because living costs in Scotland were cheaper and because its medical faculty had an international reputation. Most Americans went to Britain to study either medicine or the law.

Americans also had a natural affinity for Scotland. It was a provincial culture, like that of the American colonies, yet it was experiencing a cultural awakening that paced the Western world in the fields of science, medicine, architecture, and painting. Scots, in turn, had an affinity for Americans. Well educated but often penniless, Scots found employment in the southern colonies, where public schools were nonexistent, tutoring the sons and daughters of the planter-gentry. Scots also staffed the colonial colleges. John Witherspoon, who left a Presbyterian pulpit in Scotland in 1768 to become president of the College of New Jersey at Princeton, breathed life into that newly founded institution. Among his alumni was James Madison. At the College of William and Mary in Virginia, William Small introduced Thomas Jefferson to the Newtonian universe and instilled in the young Virginian a lifelong interest in mathematics and physics.

Scots also had a great influence on the development of American medicine. Most American physicians gained their knowledge of medicine by serving a brief apprenticeship to a practicing doctor. Of the 3,500 persons practicing medicine on the eve of the revolution, only about 200 had medical degrees. Most of these were obtained at the University of Edinburgh. Not until 1766, when the first medical school opened in Philadelphia, did the colonies possess facilities for formal medical training.

Professional training, it must be noted, was a mixed blessing. European medicine was fettered with dogma, such as the notion that disease resulted from an imbalance in the body "humors." In the mid-eighteenth century, European medicine adhered to the theories of a Dutch physi-

Library of Congress.

Harvard College
in 1726.

cian Hermann Boerhaave, who described the human body as a hydraulic mechanism full of pumps and pipes. Fever (the most common symptom of illness), he explained, was the heat generated by friction as blood pushed its way past some blockage in the system. The remedy for this "tension" was usually bleeding the patient. This prescription did provide some symptomatic relief, for loss of blood often lowers body temperature, but its effect was to weaken the patient further. American practitioners, unaware of these arcane theories, were more inclined to let nature take its course. They used medicines derived from local herbs and often prescribed such common-sense remedies as rest and fresh air. This approach at least had the advantage of doing a minimum of harm to the patient. Significantly, an Edinburgh-trained physician, Benjamin Rush, introduced the technique of bleeding to America, and colonial physicians quickly accepted it as the latest scien-

tific advance. Bleeding* persisted in the New World long after European doctors had abandoned the practice. Among those whose deaths were hastened by bleeding were George Washington and Rush himself.

London, rather than Edinburgh, was the mecca for American lawyers. Attorneys, like physicians, learned their craft through apprenticeship. Those who wished more formal training attended the Inns of Court in London. The curriculum at the Inns was not demanding; wealth and social grace were the key to advancement. Of the two hundred Americans who attended the Inns in the colonial period, most returned home without bothering to complete the three- to five-year course. If they returned with only the rudiments of the English common

---

* The most common method was to place leeches on the bedridden patient. Physicians were colloquially, often sarcastically, referred to as "leeches."

law, they nonetheless bore with them the latest currents of European thought. Thomas Jefferson, whose own legal training was at the College of William and Mary, advised young attorneys to study "physics, ethics, religion, natural law, belle lettres, criticism, rhetoric, and oratory," in addition to the law. Such a curriculum prepared a young man for public service as well as private practice. Public attitudes recorded the progress of the profession. In the seventeenth century, lawyers were objects of suspicion; they were thought to be practitioners of the obscure, using strange-sounding words to protect the rich and cheat the poor. Colonies as disparate as Plymouth and Georgia prohibited lawyers in their early days. By the end of the colonial period, lawyers had achieved an influence in colonial society far out of proportion to their numbers. Nearly one-half of the signers of the Declaration of Independence and three-fifths of those who signed the federal Constitution had some formal legal training.

By mid-century, the Atlantic exchange was infusing new energy into the colonial colleges. The first colleges had been founded primarily for the training of clergy. Harvard (1636) and Yale (1701) were Congregational seminaries. The College of William and Mary in Virginia (1693) was supported by the Anglican Church, though for many years it was little more than a reformatory for the teenaged sons of the gentry. Latin and Greek dominated the curriculum, with a bit of Hebrew added in the New England schools for better study of the Bible. A gift of English books to Yale in 1714 brought the scientific discoveries of Sir Isaac Newton to the colonies. Thereafter, natural philosophy (science) became part of the curriculum, but Newton's ideas were usually taught from the books of his pious popularizers.

In 1753, Benjamin Franklin, who thought the ancient languages were not the most valuable equipment for an agricul-

tural or commercial people, helped to found the New World's first secular school, the College of Philadelphia. The curriculum devised by Franklin focused on modern languages, mathematics, and science. The emphasis on practical skills caught the attention of Philadelphia's merchants, who subscribed four thousand pounds as an endowment. Franklin's choice as provost of the college, William Smith, proved to Franklin's dismay* to be a strong Anglican, but he was also an influential teacher. He introduced the scions of Philadelphia's merchants to the latest currents of European thought. He also encouraged them to present plays and poems of their own on public occasions. For a short time, Smith even published a magazine devoted to the literary efforts of his young friends. His most famous student was Francis Hopkinson—poet, essayist, and musician—whose song "Hail Columbia!" would serve as the country's unofficial national anthem through the nineteenth century.

The Scottish connection, so important in the field of medicine, was central to the collegiate revival as well. In 1766, the College of New Jersey (Princeton), which had been founded by Presbyterian evangelists twenty years before, invited a Scot, John Witherspoon, to be its president. Witherspoon introduced Americans to the Scottish Common Sense philosophy, which rejected metaphysical subtleties* and taught that knowledge was derived from simple perception of observable data. Such teachings, especially when spiced with memorable maxims drawn from the great English Whig writers, blended with the preconceptions of Americans and made Witherspoon

---

* At the outset of the Revolution, Franklin's allies ousted Smith and renamed the school the University of Pennsylvania.

* The most influential metaphysician of the day was another Scot, David Hume, who argued that the human mind itself was but a theater of passing impressions in which cause and effect relationships were nothing more than repetition and habit.

the most popular educator of his day. Among the students filling their notebooks with Witherspoon's principles of moral philosophy was a young Virginian, James Madison.

THE ARTISTIC COMMUNITY

In science, medicine, the law, and education, the Atlantic intellectual bridge was essentially a one-way street—European ideas and practices flowed westward, providing challenge and stimulus to American intellectual life. The artistic exchange was more nearly equal. Europe provided tradition and technique; America provided much of the talent. When Benjamin Franklin complained that "our geniuses all go to Europe," he probably had in mind American painters. He ultimately found this a source of pride. In 1783 Franklin boasted: "In England at present, the best History Painter, West; the best Portrait Painter, Copley; and the best Landscape Painter, Taylor, at Bath, are all Americans." Painters gravitated to Europe in order to acquaint themselves with the style and techniques of the old masters. The best often remained because they found patrons among the aristocracy and a ready appreciation for competent work. Even so, there

Benjamin West's *Death of Wolfe* (1771). This work revolutionized painting. British artists commonly chose classical subjects and clothed their heroes in Roman togas. West chose a current event—the conqueror of New France dying in his moment of triumph—and clothed the cast in contemporary garb. The London artistic community condemned the painting until King George III ordered a replica for his private quarters. A blend of news and patriotism, the *Death of Wolfe* was the first painting that pleased both prince and commoner.

The National Gallery of Canada, Ottawa. Gift of the Duke of Westminster, 1918.

was talent enough to go around. No generation of Americans has produced artists that excelled the genius of Benjamin West, John Singleton Copley, and Gilbert Stuart.

Pennsylvania-born Benjamin West was the center of the "American school" in London. Friends sent him to Europe in 1760 to study the Renaissance masters, and after some years in Italy he settled in London. West arrived in Europe just as neoclassicism was coming into vogue. The classical revival, which would influence western art and architecture for the next half century and more, was inspired by archeologists' discovery of the remains of Pompeii and Herculaneum, buried under volcanic ash since A.D. 79. European architects found elegance in the mathematical proportions of Greek and Roman buildings. European painters began depicting great events from classical history. Some pronounced history to be the only subject worthy of painting. Feeling the classical current even in Pennsylvania, West experimented with *Death of Socrates*. William Smith, provost of the College of Philadelphia, saw the painting and urged West to go to Rome.

In England, West portrayed both classical events and Bible stories, for these were the subjects that earned commissions from the English aristocracy. But as his reputation grew, his thoughts turned increasingly to his native land, which he was never to see again. Abandoning classical topics, though not the classical style, he began painting scenes from the American past. His masterpieces—*Penn's Treaty with the Indians* and *The Death of Wolfe* (1771)—started a vogue of historical painting. West welcomed aspiring young Americans to his London studio and gave them advice and instruction. Among West's protégés were Charles Willson Peale and Jonathan Trum-

John Singleton Copley's *Boy with a Squirrel* (1766). Copley sent the painting to Benjamin West in London for exhibition, but the accompanying letter identifying himself was lost. West recognized that the painting was American because the boy was holding a flying squirrel, an animal unknown in Europe. He exhibited it, and it won instant acclaim. But it took two years before the painter was properly identified.

Courtesy, Museum of Fine Arts.

CLIO'S FOCUS: An American Style in Building

Colonial architecture, like the colonial economy, was dependent on England. American designers used English handbooks and followed English models. In designing the Redwood Library in Newport, for example, Peter Harrison copied the façade from one book, the doorway from another, and the interior from a third.

English architects, in turn, followed the lead of a sixteenth-century Italian, Andrea Palladio, who had revived the classical forms of ancient Greece and Rome. Palladio applied columns for decoration, using them to set off doors and windows, or to hold up porticos (porches) whose only function was to show off the columns. English architects went even further; they devised huge, ornate columns that dominated the building. Peter Harrison followed this Palladian style in the Redwood Library, but he also gave the structure a personality of its own. By using plain, undecorated Doric columns in his portico, Harrison recalled the elegance of ancient Greece rather than the imperial splendor of Rome or modern Britain. He built with wood, and his windows were as austere as those of a Congregational meetinghouse. The result was a structure that was peculiarly American, even New England, in inspiration.

The Redwood Library, Newport, Rhode Island.

Photo by John T. Hopf, Courtesy of Newport County Chamber of Commerce.

Peter Harrison was a merchant who dabbled in architecture; Thomas Jefferson, a lawyer by training, dabbled in everything. Architecture was among his many interests, and he too relied on English handbooks. The idea for his plantation home, Monticello, may well have come from one of the handbooks published by an English architect, Lord Burlington. There is a marked resemblance between Monticello and Burlington's Chiswick House in London. Chiswick House was the city dwelling of a landed aristocrat, and everything about it bespeaks aristocratic splendor, from columned portico to roofline statuary. The stairway was as difficult to ascend as the ladder of English society.

In adapting Burlington's design, Jefferson made some significant changes. He all but eliminated the stairway, and he cut the height of the building in half. By placing the first floor half underground (outbuildings such as stables, kitchen, pantry, and wine cellar were similarly recessed to keep them from detracting from the house), he made the house appear to be only a story and a half. He replaced the statuary with a simple balustrade more reminiscent of classical Rome than Palladian Italy. Through such changes, Jefferson translated the elegant idiom of the English aristocracy into a simple yet dignified style that fitted a Virginia country squire. Like Harrison's library, Monticello had a distinctively American flavor.

bull, both of whom returned home to portray the heroes and events of the American Revolution.

The best portrait artist of prerevolutionary America was John Singleton Copley. A native of Boston, Copley earned a modest living delineating the profiles of his wealthy townsmen. His most famous picture, *Boy with a Squirrel*, was exhibited in London in 1766 by a ship captain with a discriminating eye, and it won him immediate recognition. Benjamin West offered advice on improving his style and urged him to come to Europe. Although Copley denounced America as a cultural desert, he delayed a visit to London until 1774. Even then, he went less to gain instruction than to escape the violence of the approaching revolution. He never returned.

Rhode Island's Gilbert Stuart also journeyed to London on the eve of the revolution. West was so impressed with the young man's talent that he offered him free room, board, and lessons. Specializing in portrai-

ture, Stuart developed a distinctive style of his own, one that emphasized color and texture rather than line. He opened a studio of his own and was an immediate success. Britain's King George III and France's Louis XVI both sat for him. His lifestyle exceeded his income, however, and in 1792 he returned to America with the intent of recouping his fortune by painting and selling replicas of George Washington. The American president obligingly sat for two portraits (the first being a failure), and the result was the "Athenaeum" portrait, the head on an unfinished canvas that remains the accepted likeness of Washington. Stuart ultimately settled in Boston, and for the next thirty years he was the dominant figure in American art.

Music. When, in 1763, Sally Franklin attempted to find samples of American music to send to a friend in Europe and uncovered only "a few Airs," her father, Benjamin, reminded her that "Music is a new art with us." Franklin was referring to secular music, of course, but even in the churches music was used cautiously in early America. New England Puritans frowned on music-making as time wasted. In their church services, they allowed the singing only of the Psalms of David—and then only because David had sung them to his God. The Anglican Church, on the other hand, was more lenient. Organ music and hymns were an important part of its services. Southerners accordingly were more tolerant of secular music. On court days, when planters gathered at their county courthouses to vote, pursue litigation, or swap horses, there was always a good deal of merrymaking. Traveling musicians and actors planned their itineraries around such occasions. In 1762, residents of Charleston founded the St. Cecilia Society, the oldest musical society in America. It engaged professional musicians by the season for its fortnightly concerts, thus providing the first steady work for that itinerant craft. By that date, instrumental music had become acceptable even in Puritanical Boston, and concerts were periodically staged in all the northern cities. Even so, they failed to encourage prophets of cultural progress like Benjamin Franklin. Most were simply social gatherings followed by dancing. One New Yorker complained in 1764 after attending a concert that "nothing is heard during the whole performance, but laughing and talking very loud, squawling, overturning the benches," all of which he attributed to young women trying to make themselves seen.

Theater. The dramatic arts also suffered from the puritanical attitudes of Americans. Actors, like painters and musicians, were itinerants, who shuttled among the urban centers, timing their schedules to coincide with public events like the Annapolis racing season or the opening of the Virginia assembly. Producers tried to overcome public suspicion of the theater by advertising their performances as "moral dialogues." Shakespeare's *Othello*, for instance, was billed as a "moral dialogue in five parts." Plays commonly started at 6:00 P.M., so that a spectator might "go home at a sober hour, and reflect upon what he has seen, before he retires to rest."

Williamsburg boasted a theater as early as 1752, and one was built in New York the following year. Eight years later New York acquired a second one, with a capacity for 350 spectators. To that point no American play had been produced. Theaters carried only English drama, with Shakespeare being the most popular. The first American drama to be professionally performed on an American stage was Thomas Godfrey's *The Prince of Parthia*. A blank-verse tragedy in five acts, the plot was borrowed in bits from *King Lear, Macbeth,* and *Othello*. Written in 1765 at the outset of the political controversy that would lead to revolution, the play was loaded with Whiggish politics, wherein kings were "tyrants" who regarded their people as "common rubbish." Over the next decade the theater was frequently used as a forum for political satire, and that, no doubt, helped render it respectable.

⊔The Age of Reason

The imposing shadow of one man, English mathematician and physicist Sir Isaac Newton, fell across eighteenth-century thought. His *Principia Mathematica* (1686) was a mathematical demonstration that the force of gravity, which operated to hold objects on earth, was what kept the moon in orbit. By projection it could be assumed that the same force kept the planets in orbit around the sun. Not only did Newton's discovery solve the mystery of the solar system, but it suggested that the entire universe was governed by scientific laws. These laws were susceptible to experimental test and could be uncovered by ordinary human beings. And what a revelation that was! It swept away the world of the Middle Ages, full of mysteries, spiritual wonders, and divine miracles. The universe Newton projected was simple, uniform, governed by law, and capable of being understood by the finite minds of humans. As a proud English poet phrased it, "God said, 'Let Newton be!' and all was light."

The modern scientific revolution was in fact already under way when Newton announced his discovery, but the implications of Newton's laws inspired wide-ranging inquiry. Naturalists found that gases and fluids behaved in systematic ways and devised laws to explain them. Scientists began collecting and classifying plants and animals. In Sweden, Carolus Linnaeus established the science of botany by classifying plants according to their reproductive patterns. With the help of London merchant Peter Collinson,* Linnaeus established a trans-Atlantic network of amateur botanists who collected specimens for him. Among these was a Charleston, South Carolina physician, Alexander Garden, whose efforts Linnaeus commemorated by giving his name to the gardenia.

French thinkers gave birth to the modern discipline of economics by discovering that even human commerce followed certain mathematically defined principles, such as the "laws" of supply and demand. They became known as Physiocrats because they postulated a natural order for human affairs, much like the natural order that governed the motions of the planets. Because commerce was governed by natural laws, the Physiocrats argued that goods would flow more smoothly, and hence more profitably, if allowed to follow their

natural channels without governmental interference. Capsulated in the phrase *laissez faire*, this thesis was the first important challenge to the centuries-old dogma of mercantilism. In 1776 the Scot Adam Smith put the theory into English in his *Wealth of Nations*, and this work, in turn, became the foundation for the Anglo-American philosophy of free enterprise.

The common denominator in this ferment was a faith in human reason. Nothing, it seemed, was beyond the human mind. Newton himself promoted this faith by developing the principles of differential calculus, which permitted natural phenomena to be explained, or predicted, through mathematical equations (the method was independently developed by the German philosopher Leibnitz). Thus, the first half of the eighteenth century is commonly referred to as the Age of Reason, or the Enlightenment.

Rationalism could also be applied to the principles of government. John Locke, a friend of Newton, deduced a system of government in the way one might work out a theorem of Euclidean geometry. His *Treatises on Civil Government* (1691) were a rationale for the Glorious Revolution of 1688. His argument began by postulating a social condition that preceded government, which he called the state of nature. In such a primitive society every person enjoyed certain fundamental rights, among them the rights to life, liberty, and property. When society grew more complex and people felt the need for law and order, they entered into a social contract that formed a government. There were, in a sense, two contracts—one an agreement among the people to form a government, the other an agreement between the people and an assigned ruler. The latter gave the ruler power to govern, while the people retained the rights they had earlier possessed. Thus, if a ruler violated those rights—for instance, by hanging, imprisoning, or fining individuals without due process of law—

---

* Collinson also provided Benjamin Franklin with the apparatus needed for his electrical experiments, which culminated with the famous kite experiment in which Franklin established that lightning was a form of electricity.

John Locke.

New York Public Library Picture Collection.

the contract was broken and the people had the right to rebel.

The contract that Locke envisioned was between English king and English aristocracy, not between king and common people. The central dynamic of Locke's government was the balance of power between king and Parliament, not between king and people. His thesis became a rationale for the English Whigs, the political party that had opposed the pretensions of the Stuart dynasty in the latter half of the seventeenth century. The Whigs had fought the notion that a king ruled by divine right and could do whatever he wished; they had engineered the Revolution of 1688. The Whigs were a party of landed grandees and London merchants. The struggle that Locke elevated into a philosophy was between king and aristocracy, crown and Parliament. Whigs resisted the king, but they were not defenders of the common people.

Partial though it was as a philosophy of freedom, whiggery had its uses. Adapted by Americans, the Whig view provided the colonial gentry with a rationale for resisting the authority of imperial governors. Virginians, smarting from the harsh repression of Bacon's Rebellion, found in whiggery a code of gentlemanly resistance. Sir Edward Coke, the great English jurist who had resurrected the long-forgotten Magna Carta in his efforts to limit the powers of King James I early in the seventeenth century, became an American hero. Coke was influential because his writings were used as texts by American lawyers. Of the English jurist, Thomas Jefferson observed: "A sounder Whig never wrote, nor one with profounder learning in the orthodox doctrines of British liberties. Our lawyers were then all Whigs."

Political rationalism had implications that extended far beyond Lockean whiggery. The French philosopher Voltaire suggested that all institutions that could not be rationally justified ought to be swept away. Among such illogical and unjustified institutions Voltaire placed the monarchy and the state-connected church. Jean-Jacques Rousseau, a Swiss political theorist, argued that humankind might eliminate all evil and corruption inherited from the past and start civilization afresh with a new social contract.

JOHN LOCKE AND THOMAS JEFFERSON

A student at the College of William and Mary in the 1750s, when such heady notions were sweeping America, Thomas Jefferson was heir both to Virginia whiggery and Lockean rationalism. His Declaration of Independence, which heralded the American Revolution in 1776, was an exquisite summation of the political ideals of the Enlightenment. Believing, with Locke, that government could be deduced like a Euclidean theorem, Jefferson began the Declaration with a series of "self-evident" truths: that "all men are created equal," that they are "endowed by their creator," not by any earthly authority, "with certain unalienable rights; that among these are life, liberty, and the pursuit of happiness." (*Property*, the word employed by Locke, Jefferson considered too narrow; people might have other aims in life than wealth.)

"To secure these rights governments are instituted among men," Jefferson's logic proceeded, expressing a concept that was a radical departure from Locke. The purpose of government, Jefferson was saying, is not to glorify the monarch, nor expand territory, nor to muster armies and navies. The object of government is simply to preserve rights that the people possessed before the government was created. How is this ensured? By "deriving their just powers from the consent of the governed." With that innovation, Jefferson figuratively stood Locke on his head. The central dynamic in Locke's concept was the relationship between king and aristocracy (or Parliament). The people were not actively involved; they simply stood by and had rights. In Jefferson's construct, the governed are the source of authority; the ruler is only their agent. In one sweep of the quill Jefferson not only destroyed the theory that kings ruled by divine right, he destroyed Lockean Whiggery as well. It has been said, with justice, that all of American history has been an effort to explore the radical implications of the Declaration of Independence.

REASON AND RELIGION: DEISM

Neither Newton nor Locke saw any inconsistency between science and religious belief. Locke thought that "the works of Nature everywhere sufficiently evidence a deity." Like his Boston contemporary Cotton Mather, Locke thought that the rich variety and splendid order of the universe could have been achieved only by a divine creator. Other rationalists, without questioning the divine creation, used the same argument to question commonly held Christian beliefs. After all, if God could be understood from reading the "book of nature," what need was there for Scripture? What need was there for a church, for that matter? If God created this orderly, rational universe, in which certain principles worked always and everywhere, he had no need to interfere in its operation. Indeed, he dared not, for a revelation or a miracle (the parting of the Red Sea for Moses, for instance) was by its very nature unreasonable and contrary to God's own laws. Rationalists, whether studying anthills or the heavens, agreed that nature revealed a deity, but it was a deity much different in substance from the God of the Puritans, the Anglicans, the Roman Catholics, or the Jews. The God of nature was simply a First Cause, a sublime architect, "a Fabricator," as Jefferson put it, "of all things from matter and motion." This line of thinking was called *deism*. Deists likened God's role in the universe to that of a watchmaker who put the pieces together, wound up the mechanism, and then let it tick along on its own.

Deism was not a religious sect or a church; it was a way of looking at the world. Thomas Jefferson was an Anglican and a deist. John Adams was a Congregationalist and a deist. Benjamin Franklin contributed money to every church in Philadelphia; he too was a deist. Deism appealed to the educated in both Europe and America, but its chill rationalism had little appeal to the poor and the uneducated, who preferred a more personal, more emotional religious experience. Rationalists dismissed religious fervor as *enthusiasm*, but it had its appeal. Indeed, it is one of the paradoxes of the age that in the heyday of the Enlightenment, the middle decades of the eighteenth century, a vast, intensely emotional religious revival swept both Britain and America. In Britain it was known as the Methodist movement; in America it was called the Great Awakening.

⎵The Great Awakening

The revival sprang up in several places almost simultaneously, but it had a common root. It was a reaction against the staid formality into which most churches had fallen. The Church of England, on both sides of the Atlantic, was a hollow shell. In Virginia and Maryland, nearly half of the parishes had no minister at all. In those churches that were occupied, services were short and perfunctory, viewed by the parishioners more as a social occasion than one of moral uplift. In New England, the Congregational clergy reflected the genial tolerance of the age of reason and exalted the worth of human activity, rather than God's grace.

Pietist sects, Moravians and Mennonites, who had migrated to America at the turn of the century seeking freedom from persecution, helped to inspire the revival. The pietists made religion an element of their daily lives. Their beliefs governed dress, living habits, modes of work. Their piety and rectitude impressed even those who had no wish to join them. In 1735, John Wesley, an Anglican minister on his way to Georgia to convert Indians, experienced a spiritual rebirth when he encountered a collection of Moravians on shipboard. He saw that through the personal emotional experience of conversion, the lives of individuals could be altered. He returned to Britain, where his earlier efforts to enliven the Anglican Church had been derided as "methodism," and together with his brother Charles (best known for his hymns), he started a religious revival among Britain's lower classes. Pollinated in Georgia, the Methodist movement flowered in Britain and then showered its seeds upon every part of the imperial community.

Moravians who settled in Pennsylvania also influenced the neighboring Lutheran and Presbyterian churches in much the same way. The Presbyterian church was brought to America by the Scots-Irish who flooded into Pennsylvania in the early decades of the eighteenth century. It was rooted in Calvinism, like the Congregational churches of New England, but in a century of isolation in hostile Ireland, Presbyterian services had degenerated into an icy formality. In 1726, the Reverend William Tennent, seeking to put life into the church, established a "log college" in the Raritan Valley of northern New Jersey for the training of young evangelists. The most famous graduate of the school was his son, Gilbert Tennent, who carried the torch of religious awakening from the Middle Colonies to New England. The Tennents focused their sermons on the simple themes of sin, guilt, and redemption. Their technique was to convince an assembled multitude of its guilt, of the extent to which it had fallen away from the example of its forebears, and then hold forth the promise of redemption through conversion, good works, and an upright life.

In New England, about the same time, the Congregational clergy was searching for ways to overcome apathy and indifference. The only way to reach the hearts of the apathetic, some ministers concluded, was to humiliate and frighten them by depicting the hopelessness of the human condition and the horrors of damnation. Beginning in 1735 Jonathan Edwards, a master of this technique, led his Northampton, Massachusetts, congregation in a revival of piety such as New England had not seen since the founding generation. As conversions multiplied and church membership increased, Edwards came close to replicating the Puritan model, where congregation of saints and village community were one and the same.

It is easier to describe the phenomenal success of the revival than to explain it. Calvinist clergy has been condemming the

Sinners in the Hands of an Angry God

The appeal of the evangelist was an emotional one. That made it more powerful, for who could deny it? Who dared to? Imagine the impact of the following sermon on a congregation of New England townspeople, perched uncomfortably on hard wooden benches in a half-timbered edifice whose only adornment was whitewash on the walls. The minister thundering his jeremiad is the best-educated, most respected member of the community.

> The wrath of God is like great waters that are dammed for the present; they increase more and more, and rise higher and higher, till an outlet is given; and the longer the stream is stopped, the more rapid and mighty is its course, when once it is let loose. It is true that judgment against your evil works has not been executed hitherto; the floods of God's vengeance had been withheld; but your guilt in the meantime is constantly increasing, and you are every day treasuring up more wrath; the waters are constantly rising, and waxing more and more mighty; and there is nothing but the mere pleasure of God that holds the waters back. . . .
>
> Thus all you that never passed under a great change of heart, by the mighty power of the Spirit of God upon your souls; all you that were never born again, and made new creatures, and raised from being dead in sin, to a state of new, and before altogether unexperienced light and life, are in the hands of an angry God. . . .
>
> The God that holds you over the pit of hell, much as one holds a spider, or some loathsome insect over the fire, abhors you, and is dreadfully provoked: his wrath towards you burns like fire; he looks upon you as worthy of nothing else, but to be cast into the fire; he is of purer eyes than to bear to have you in his sight; you are ten thousand times more abominable in his eyes than the most hateful venomous serpent is in ours. . . .

So loudly did the terrified assemblage moan and wail that the minister had to halt his delivery. With his hands clasped behind his back and his eyes fixed on the end of the church bellrope, he waited for the noise to subside. At last, he relented:

> Therefore, let everyone that is out of Christ, now awake and fly from the wrath to come. The wrath of Almighty God is now undoubtedly hanging over a great part of this Congregation: Let everyone fly out of Sodom: "Haste and escape for your lives, look not behind you, escape to the mountain, lest you be consumed."

Source: Jonathan Edwards, "Sinners in the Hands of an Angry God," 1741.

worldliness of the their congregations for more than a century. Why the sudden success in the 1730s? Some historians have suggested that there were social and economic factors at work, conditioning people to receive the evangelists' message. Disease and death may have been one factor. An epidemic of diptheria had recently swept through the colonies, killing some 20,000 people, most of them children. The 1730s were also a time of economic slump, as trade faltered and prices fell. Changes in sexual mores as intimate villages blossomed into inland marketing centers and seaports grew into cities may also have been a factor. Perhaps people saw in the combination of

Fogg Art Museum, Harvard University.

George Whitefield. This painting is probably by New England artist Joseph Badger, whose style was primitive, simple, and direct. Here he managed to convey a figure who was at once cross-eyed and commanding.

disaster and declining morality the approach of doomsday and sought to make their peace with God.*

As if to draw together these loose threads of revival, George Whitefield landed on American shores in 1739. An Episcopal clergyman converted by the Wesleys, Whitefield landed in the southern colonies and began a triumphant tour northward. A brilliant orator "who could make Hell so vivid that one could locate it on an atlas," Whitefield was a new breed of preacher who shunned the closely reasoned theology favored for generations by orthodox clerics. Instead he wept and

---

* The combination of disaster (world war) and immorality is a central theme of the Jehovah's Witnesses, one of the most energetic of today's Pentecostal churches.

roared, he prayed and begged, demanding a faith that was experienced with passion. In the summer of 1740, Whitefield blazed into New England, jamming the churches with the wondering and the penitent and speaking at huge open-air meetings. In Northampton Edwards welcomed him joyously and wept throughout his sermon. After more than a year of astonishing success, Whitefield sailed home from New York.

The uproar gradually subsided, although currents of religious enthusiasm rippled through American society for the rest of the century. Church membership increased for a time and then fell away. Both Presbyterian and Congregational churches were left bitterly divided between orthodox "old lights" and evangelical "new lights." In New England, new light Congregationalists contemplated anew the ancient question that had so troubled Roger Williams and the Separatists—how to distinguish between true converts and glib hypocrites. They finally hit upon the idea of adult baptism as a means of cleansing past sins and symbolizing spiritual rebirth. With this concept was born the Baptist church. Following Whitefield's example, the Baptists sent itinerants on the road to spread their gospel. These horseback evangelists had spectacular success on the southern frontier, an area that had been largely ignored by the established Anglican church. Presbyterians and, after the revolution, Methodists followed their example, leaving in their wake a reservoir of piety that characterizes the Appalachian highlands even today.

REVIVALISM AND THE SOCIAL ORDER

Like early Christianity, evangelical religion appealed to the down and out. Conversion was an equalizing experience; a convert, bolstered by the warm glow of inner light, could look upon as "equals" even those who pretended to be his "betters." Conversion also offered an escape from the harsh realities of daily existence—disease, debt, hunger, and sudden death. Converts found themselves in a close-knit, supportive community, often publicly sealed by a rite such as adult baptism. This was especially true in the southern colonies, where class differences were firmly drawn and the upper classes regarded religious enthusiasm as undignified.

In New England, rich as well as poor fell under the spell of the revival. The Puritans had always had ambiguous feelings about wealth. They accepted it when earned and held wealthy people in high esteem. But they also saw that it could lead to greed, luxury, and conflicts with authority. A pious merchant who accepted a cargo of illicit goods from the West Indies might tell himself that British trade regulations were unreasonable, but he also knew that he had broken the law to turn a profit. He knew too that when such base impulses gripped his soul, no amount of outward piety and rectitude would help. Whitefield and other evangelists told him precisely that, and then offered a release—a spiritual rebirth that converted misery into joy.

But the revivalists undermined the social order nonetheless, because they called into question existing law and authority, which stood allied with religious orthodoxy. Evangelists stressed that salvation did not come from the mere observance of the law; it required a personal relationship with God. Christ's authority, said Jonathan Edwards, nullified earthly authority. It was a concept not far from Anne Hutchinson's antinomianism, and it had the same revolutionary implications. Converts, confident in the awareness of divine favor, might well refuse to submit to a social order that seemed alien. An early sign of such rebellion was the Baptists' refusal to pay religious taxes whose proceeds went to the established Congregational church in New England. The controversy went on for years until finally drowned in the greater din of the revolution. When the revolution came, Baptists, Methodists, and other new lights were in the forefront of the movement to take away the privileges of the established churches and separate religion from government altogether. Some new lights, such as the physician-reformer Benjamin Rush of Philadelphia, considered the revolution an opportunity to cleanse American society generally, to purge such evils as liquor and slavery. Rush and his compatriots were not successful, but the connection between evangelical religion and reform persisted well into the nineteenth century.

SUMMARY

Even as the American colonies matured socially and economically, they remained cultural dependents of Britain. Of American art and literature in the seventeenth century there was almost none. John Winthrop, Jr., and Cotton Mather in New England and William Byrd in Virginia made scientific and historical contributions to the Atlantic exchange, but these men stand out precisely because they were rarities. The first American colleges, Harvard and William and Mary, hardly rated the name. For university training, especially in the fields of law and medicine, Americans went to England or Scotland.

In the early decades of the eighteenth century, ideas associated with the Enlightenment filtered across the Atlantic and stimulated a surge of scientific and artistic activity. The scientific revolution that had begun with the discoveries of Copernicus, Galileo, and Newton led to the application of the scientific method and scientific reasoning in fields as diverse as politics and religion. The closely reasoned political treatises of John Locke were standard reading for educated Americans; the right to "liberty and property" was the watchword of the day. Some even considered the radical notion—expressed in its starkest form by the French *philosophes*—that every human institution which could not be rationally justified (monarchy? aristocracy? state-affiliated church?) deserved to be swept away.

While some Americans worshipped reason in the mid-eighteenth century, others rediscovered God. An evangelical revival, kindled in isolated parts of New England and the middle colonies in the 1730s, swept the seaboard in a firestorm of enthusiasm in the 1740s. The Great Awakening faded almost as suddenly as it had arisen, but it left two enduring faiths, Methodist and Baptist, and a lasting imprint on American Protestantism.

READING SUGGESTIONS

Michael Kraus, *The Atlantic Civilization: Eighteenth Century Origins* (1949), is still the best introduction to colonial culture. Daniel Boorstin, *The Americans: The Colonial Experience* (1958), offers some shrewd insights on the beginnings of the professions, especially law and medicine. Lawrence A. Cremin, *American Education: The Colonial Experience, 1607–1783* (1970), is comprehensive and detailed. Bernard Bailyn analyzes the social function of education in *Education in the Forming of American Society* (1960).

Kenneth Silverman's, *A Cultural History of the American Revolution, 1763–1789* (1976) examines the remarkable flowering of American painting, music, literature, and theater in the revolutionary era. Henry F. May, *The Enlightenment in America* (1976), distinguishes between a "moderate Enlightenment," which proved attractive to many Americans, and a "radical Enlightenment," which caused political divisions among Americans after the Revolution.

Biographies of people who made important contributions to colonial life and thought include: Richard S. Dunn, *Puritans and Yankees: The Winthrop Dynasty of New England, 1630–1717*

(1962); Robert Middlekauf, *The Mathers: Three Generations of Puritan Intellectuals, 1596–1728* (1971); and Carl Van Doren, *Benjamin Franklin*. Dumas Malone, *Jefferson the Virginian* (1948), details the impact of the Enlightenment on one American college, William and Mary, and on its most distinguished alumnus.

J. M. Bumsted and John F. Van de Wetering, *What Must I Do To Be Saved?* (1976), is a good, brief introduction to the Great Awakening. The founding of the Baptist church in America is traced in William G. McLoughlin's biography of Isaac Backus (1967). Paul Conkin's *Puritans and Pragmatists* (1974) contains a lucid summary of Jonathan Edwards's complex thought. James Henretta, *Evolution of American Society, 1700–1815* (1973), in a brief discussion of the Great Awakening, suggests some of its social and economic causes. Rhys Isaac, *The Transformation of Virginia, 1740–1790* (1982), details some of its social consequences. David O. Lovejoy, *Religious Enthusiasm in the New World* (1985), places it in the broader context of early American revivalism.

5

WAR AND THE BONDS
OF EMPIRE

When William of Orange, ruler of the Netherlands, accepted the crown of England in 1688, he was not simply adding a new country to his collection; he was also forging an alliance. William's tiny homeland was being menaced by powerful, aggressive France under the direction of King Louis XIV. Louis had outlined a plan to extend France to its "natural frontiers," the Alps and the Rhine River. In the course of the 1680s, Louis annexed part of the Netherlands (Belgium), conquered Alsace, and laid waste the Rhineland. To resist French expansion, William and various German principalities formed an alliance, which they called the League of Augsburg. William accepted the English crown in order to bring England into the league. France had already declared war on the Netherlands in 1688; England joined the war in 1689. That conflict was the first in a series of wars that embroiled England and France for the next century. The conflict inevitably spilled over into the New World, setting English and French colonists at one another. Indeed, as the years passed, imperial control of North America became the principal aim of the conflict.

⊔French Canada and British America

Long preoccupied with European affairs and beset by internal religious disputes, France was slow in awakening to the possibilities of New World empire. Between 1534 and 1543, Jacques Cartier had explored the American coast from the Gulf of St. Lawrence to New England, thereby establishing a French claim; but nothing further was done until 1603, when Henry IV, first of France's Bourbon kings, chartered a joint stock company. In 1608, a year after the English founded Jamestown, Samuel de Champlain founded the settlement of Quebec on the St. Lawrence River. Quebec, like Jamestown, was intended as a post for trade with the Indians and as a way station on the route to the Orient, if a northwest passage were ever found.

Champlain sealed his trade relations with the Algonkian-speaking tribes of the St. Lawrence valley by siding with them in warfare against their ancient foe, the Iroquois. The Iroquois responded with bloody attacks on French settlements that slowed the growth of the colony. At the time of Champlain's death in 1635, the settlement at Quebec numbered only about 200 soldiers and fur traders. Even after the French reached a truce with the Iroquois in the 1640s, the colony grew slowly. Because the company that governed the colony monopolized the fur trade, the colonists were left with few opportunities to get ahead, and other potential immigrants were thus discouraged from making the long journey from France. New France remained a group of tiny settlements huddled along the St. Lawrence River. Its colonists grew enough crops to feed themselves, but never enough for export.

Although New France was small and weak, its soldiers and missionaries penetrated deep into the interior of the continent. In 1634, Jean Nicollet followed the Ottawa River westward to the upper Great Lakes, penetrating as far as a Menominee Indian village on the site of what would later be known as Green Bay, on Lake Michigan. By 1670, the Jesuits had missions at Sault Ste. Marie and Green Bay. In 1673, Father Jacques Marquette, a Jesuit, and Louis Joliet, a soldier, set out from the mission at Green Bay to investigate Indian stories of a gigantic waterway in the heart of the continent. They reached the Mississippi by way of the Fox and Wisconsin rivers and followed the great waterway as far south as the junction with the Arkan-

---

(Chapter opening photo) The Boston tea party, as seen by a contemporary artist.

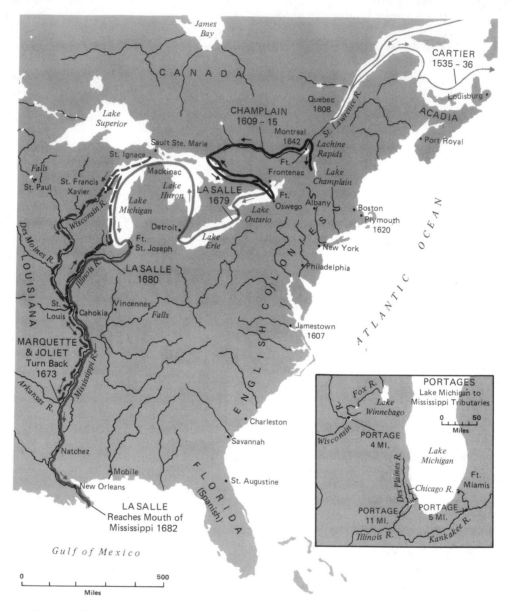

The French in North America.

sas River. At that point they realized that the Mississippi flowed into the Gulf of Mexico and, fearing capture by the Spanish, turned back. On the homeward journey they entered the Illinois River, crossed over into the upper reaches of the Chicago River, and followed the shore of Lake Michigan back to Green Bay. A decade later, in 1682, Robert Cavalier, Sieur de la Salle, traced the Mississippi all the way to the Gulf of Mexico. At the point of land where the river spilled into the gulf he erected a mighty cross, claimed the entire valley for France, and named the area Louisiana in honor of the king.

Since the tributaries of the Mississippi— notably the Ohio River, the Tennessee, and the Cumberland—originated in the Appalachian Mountains, La Salle's audacious claim placed New France figuratively at the "back door" of the English colonies. Indeed, it overlapped some of the western claims of the Pennsylvania, Virginia, and Carolina colonies. Thus, when the War of the League of Augsburg blazed in Europe only six years later, the flames inevitably spread to the American frontier.

A HALF-CENTURY
OF CONFLICT, 1689–1754

The American colonists, with little understanding of European rivalries, called the War of the League of Augsburg (1689– 1697) simply King William's War. Although the fighting in this conflict was largely confined to Europe, the French did unleash their Indian allies on the American frontier. A joint French and Indian force conducted a particularly grisly raid on Schenectady, New York, in 1690. Other-

Rare Book Division, The New York Public Library, Astor, Lenox and Tilden Foundations.

Edward Teach (1680?–1718). The period from 1689 to 1713, when Europe was distracted by war, was the golden age of piracy. Edward Teach—Blackbeard—was the most feared of all. He was a walking arsenal of guns and knives. Lighted matches stuck under his hat gave off a sulphurous odor and gave his face a satanic glow.

LaSalle Claims a Continent

On that day, the realm of France received on parchment a stupendous accession. The fertile plains of Texas; the vast basin of the Mississippi, from its frozen northern springs to the sultry borders of the Gulf; from the woody ridges of the Alleghenies to the bare peaks of the Rocky Mountains—a region of savannahs and forests, suncracked deserts, and grassy prairies, watered by a thousand rivers, ranged by a thousand warlike tribes, passed beneath the sceptre of the Sultan of Versailles; and all by virtue of a feeble human voice, inaudible at half a mile.

Source: Francis Parkman, describing LaSalle's claim to the Mississippi, April 9, 1682.

wise the war was a standoff, and the Peace of Ryswick (1697) called for a mutual restoration of conquests.

Both sides considered the truce to be temporary, and the French used the lull to strengthen their hold on La Salle's vast claim. In 1699 they established a mission at Cahokia on the Mississippi River, opposite the mouth of the Missouri. They erected forts at the Straits of Mackinac in the following year and at Detroit the year after that. In 1702 the French also put a garrison on Mobile Bay. These efforts ensured that the next war would see more fighting in North America.

The War of the Spanish Succession (1702–1713) (Queen Anne's War in America) originated, as its name suggests, in the question of who would control Spain and its vast American empire. The heir to the throne of Spain was a young grandson of Louis XIV, and England felt it could not allow the treasure of the Spanish Main to fall into the hands of the French monarch. Again the main theater of fighting was Europe, where the brilliant English general, John Churchill, Duke of Marlborough, administered the French army its first defeats in nearly a century. But there was also more military activity in the colonies than in the previous war. In 1710 a British colonial force captured French Acadia, renaming it Nova Scotia. By the Peace of Utrecht (1713), Britain (England and Scotland had been formally united into Great Britain in 1707) obtained Nova Scotia, Newfoundland, and Hudson Bay, as well as the fortress of Gibraltar at the southern tip of Spain.

The settlement at Utrecht brought peace to Europe for some years. In the interim, the British colonies grew in wealth and population, while the French staked new territorial claims. In 1718 the French

The surrender of Fort Louisburg, 1758.

New York Public Library Picture Collection.

founded a settlement at New Orleans to reinforce their claim to the lower Mississippi, and two years later they constructed Fort Louisburg on Cape Breton Island to protect the sea approaches to the St. Lawrence. In the succeeding decade the French moved into the Indian country south of the Great Lakes and established an outpost at Vincennes on the lower Wabash River.

FOUNDING OF GEORGIA

France had lost part of its North American empire at Utrecht, but the French royal family (the Bourbons) was allowed to occupy the throne of Spain. This resulted in a working alliance between France and Spain that menaced British interests in America. The French at New Orleans and Mobile and the Spanish at Pensacola and St. Augustine systematically began to encourage the Indians to raid the Carolina frontier. Britain countered this by founding a new colony in the South, Georgia. The settlement would solidify British claims in the region and serve as a buffer for the rich, rice-growing colony of South Carolina.

The agent for this extension of Britain's strategic interests was James Oglethorpe, a member of Parliament with a humanitarian concern for the plight of Britain's poor. Envisioning America as a haven for the penniless, Oglethorpe and several friends petitioned the British government for a new proprietary colony. The petition coincided with the ministry's strategic needs, and a charter for Georgia (named after King George II) was issued in 1732. The charter was modeled on earlier proprietary grants but had provisions designed to ensure greater royal control. Oglethorpe and his associates were to settle Georgia and govern it, but after twenty-one years it was to revert to the king as a royal colony. Thus the king allowed humanitarians to expand his empire, while ensuring that the empire ultimately would remain his.

As a humanitarian venture, Georgia was a failure. Oglethorpe burdened the colony with excessive regulations. He limited the size of farms to 50 acres; he prohibited liquor, slaves, and "that other scourge of mankind," lawyers. He advertised to attract the English poor, but since he never provided transportation money, few ever went to the colony. Georgia, in fact, was settled in the same way as other southern colonies—by a few religious pietists and a lot of adventurers, who chafed at Oglethorpe's regulations. The trustees of Georgia who had remained in England eventually became discouraged by the bickering in the colony. They summoned Oglethorpe home and asked the king to take charge of the colony ahead of schedule. The king did so in 1752. Thereafter, Georgians acquired slaves, began growing rice and cotton in the fashion of South Carolina, and prospered.

In the meantime, Britain and France had once again come to blows. The War of the Austrian Succession (1740–1748)—King George's War to the colonists—originated in the militant expansionism of a relative newcomer on the European scene, the kingdom of Prussia (forerunner of modern Germany). France sided with Prussia, Britain with Austria, and the two imperial rivals carried their conflict to North America. The high point of the war was the seizure in 1745 of Fort Louisburg by an army of New Englanders. When Britain returned the post to France at the end of the war in exchange for concessions in India, New Englanders were outraged. Imperial warfare was beginning to loosen the bonds of empire.

Even so, both Britain and France emerged from the war with a heightened sensitivity to the importance of North America. Both considered the Peace of Aix-la-Chapelle, signed in 1748, a mere truce. Anticipating renewal of the conflict,

CLIO'S FOCUS: Scalping—Who Started It?

Who originated scalping—the white man or the Indian? The traditional view, popularized by Hollywood movies, was that "savage" Indians scalped "civilized" whites as part of their resistance to the "taming" of the continent. In the 1960s and 1970s, adherents of the Indian rights movement began offering another version. Whites, they said, had long been accustomed to cutting off parts of their victims' bodies in European wars; they taught the savage practice to the innocent Indians. This version, which served both Indian activism and white guilt feelings, appeared several times on television and in prominent news magazines during the 1970s, and despite doubts expressed by some historians, it has become a fixture in current American lore.

As evidence for the new version, proponents usually point to the scalp bounties offered by colonial governments. But this is a slender reed on which to perch an argument. It is true that colonial governments did pay both white soldiers and Indians for Indian scalps, but it does not follow that the Europeans taught the Indians *how* to scalp each other.

On the other hand, there is sound evidence for the traditional view that the Indians started it. There are, for instance, the journals of early explorers who saw Indian cultures in their original state, uninfluenced by contact with whites. Many reported instances of scalping. In 1540, two of Hernando De Soto's men were killed by Apalachee Indians, who removed their scalps with "great ease" and carried them off "as evidence of their deed." In 1609 Samuel de Champlain's Algonkian allies scalped their Iroquois captives and presented the trophies to Champlain with the request that they be given to the French king. In Virginia, Captain John Smith reported that Powhatan showed all visitors a row of scalps hanging on a line between two trees, intending, thought Smith, "to half conquer them by this spectacle of his terrible cruelty." The early explorers also described the ritualistic treatment accorded scalps after they were removed. Scalps were carefully dried, stretched on hoops, and painted. They were then carried around on long poles, worn as necklaces, or incorporated in a dance.

All this suggests that the practice of scalping was firmly embedded in Indian religious and social rituals long before Europeans reached the New World. The languages of the eastern woodland Indians are rich in specific expressions referring to the scalp and the act of taking it. European languages, by contrast, did not even have a word for it. In describing what they saw, early explorers stretched for words that would convey meaning to European readers. Champlain used the French word *tête* (head), but that proved too ambiguous; other writers used combinations of words that conveyed an image of skin and hair. The English word *scalp* originally referred to the crown of the head, and it did not come into common usage as a description of the Indian practice until King Philip's War in 1675.

Europeans in the sixteenth and seventeenth centuries commonly removed parts of the body, such as fingers or ears, as battle trophies, and few American colonists showed any moral revulsion to scalping. In fact, it was popular among frontiersmen because it offered an avenue for revenge for their own losses. Political leaders, moreover, found the offer of scalp bounties an inexpensive way of seeming to take the offensive when wars were not going well. But there is no evidence that any colonist would have been able to teach the Indians anything on this subject that they did not already know.

both maneuvered for position. In 1749 King George issued a charter to a group of prominent Virginians who had formed the Ohio Company. He granted them a sizable tract of land along the south bank of the Ohio River (present-day West Virginia) and authorized them to settle it. The king and his ministers were thus extending the policy they had begun in Georgia—using American land hunger to further Britain's imperial interests. The Ohio Company employed Christopher Gist, an Indian trader, to blaze a trail from the upper Potomac to the Monongahela River.

The French, meanwhile, moved south of the lakes, building a string of forts between Lake Erie and the Ohio River. Alarmed, the Ohio Company in 1753 Gist and 21-year-old George Washington (the half-brother of one of the shareholders in the company) to discover what the French had in mind. The pair returned through winter snows with the news that the French considered all the western rivers to be theirs. A glance at the map showed Virginia's governor, Robert Dinwiddie, that the most strategic site, and likely meeting point for the two advancing empires, was the forks where the Allegheny and Monongahela rivers joined to form the Ohio. Whoever controlled that controlled the West. In the spring of 1754, Dinwiddie sent Washington and Gist across the mountains again, this time with a de-

tachment of soldiers and instructions to build a fort at the junction. When they arrived at the Monongahela, Gist's Indian scouts informed them that they were too late. The French had reached the forks the

Pennsylvania-Virginia frontier, 1754–1756.

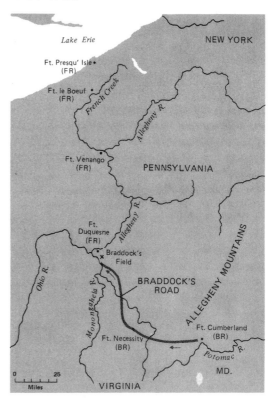

previous winter and had erected Fort Duquesne. Washington put up a small palisade of his own, naming it Fort Necessity, and then went scouting for more information. The French learned of his presence and sent out a detachment to investigate. With the help of Gist and his Indian friends, Washington ambushed the French party, killing the young lieutenant who led it. Angered, the French came out in force, surrounded Washington at Fort Necessity, and compelled him to surrender. They made him sign a confession that he was guilty of "assassination," and then, in the gentlemanly fashion of eighteenth-century warfare, they let him return to Virginia with his men. The escapade was, in fact, the first shot in a new war. This time it began in North America, and it would be fought for empire.

THE GREAT WAR
FOR EMPIRE, 1754—1763

At the very moment in June 1754 that Washington and the French were exchanging shots, delegates from the northern colonies were assembling at Albany, New York, for a meeting with the Iroquois. The meeting had been suggested by the Board of Trade in anticipation of renewed warfare. Board members wanted the help of the Iroquois, who were considered the best warriors on the continent. The Iroquois refused a formal alliance with the colonists, but the conference at least secured their friendly neutrality. The skillful diplomacy of the Iroquois, and their ability to play one white "invader" off against another, enabled them to resist the pressures of the advancing white frontier until well after the revolution. Other coastal tribes were either decimated by war and disease (Indians were peculiarly susceptible to lung diseases such as pneumonia and tuberculosis) or were pushed westward across the mountains.

It had occurred to a number of delegates chosen to attend the Albany Congress that as the first intercolonial meeting, it might be a good place to discuss greater political and military cooperation among the colonies. Several delegates arrived with plans, but the only one discussed was that put forth by Benjamin Franklin. His scheme, known as the Albany Plan of Union, recommended a president-general for all the colonies, appointed by the crown, and an intercolonial legislature elected by the various assemblies. The conference approved the plan, but it met with a chilly reception in the colonial assemblies, who were jealous of their own hard-won powers.

In the aftermath of Washington's defeat, Virginia called upon the mother country for help. Although war had not yet been formally declared, Britain sent two regiments of regulars to the colonies under the command of General Edward Braddock. Arriving in the spring of 1755, Braddock marched up the Ohio Company's trail into the Monongahela Valley and was ambushed by French and Indians just eight miles from Fort Duquesne. Braddock fell in the first volley, and his army fled in panic. The debacle left the frontier exposed to Indian raids from Maine to Virginia.

Before declaring war in 1756, Britain entered into a new alliance, one that ultimately dictated its military strategy. Britain's new friend was Frederick the Great, King of Prussia and the finest general in Europe. The alliance between Britain and Prussia threw the rest of Europe (Austria, Russia, and ultimately Spain) into the arms of France. The man who saw opportunity in this grand rearrangement was William Pitt, who became Britain's prime minister in 1757. A brilliant orator who would appear in the House of Commons dressed in black velvet trimmed with white lace, Pitt had a vision of imperial glory. For a half-century, Britain had been fighting to

"Join or Die" was America's first political cartoon, printed and probably drawn by Benjamin Franklin. It was intended to promote the plan of union which he presented to the Albany Conference in 1754. In succeeding years it became a symbol of colonial unity against British transgression.

preserve the balance of power in Europe. Let Frederick handle that, Pitt argued. Britain's true interests lay in America. It must be a war for empire!

Pitt's strategy of concentrating Britain's military resources on the conquest of Canada soon paid off. In 1758, General John Forbes built a new road to the Ohio across Pennsylvania* and seized Fort Duquesne. The following year General James Wolfe sailed up the St. Lawrence and seized Quebec after a battle on the Plains of Abraham outside the city. And in 1760, Lord Jeffrey Amherst, having descended on Montreal

by way of Lake Champlain, accepted the surrender of French Canada.

The war had quickly become enormously expensive. King George III, upon inheriting the throne in 1760, dismissed Pitt and opened secret peace talks with France. Frederick of Prussia, who had staved off assaults from French, Austrians, and Russians for four years, was left to the mercy of his enemies. Before the fighting stopped, however, Britain seized the French islands in the West Indies; and when Spain made the mistake of entering the war on the side of France, Britain grabbed two of its colonies, Cuba and the Philippines.

By the Peace of Paris of 1763, Britain retained Canada and Louisiana east of the Mississippi and returned to France the

---

* After the revolution, Forbes's Road became a major route for westward migration. Today, having been somewhat improved, it is known as the Pennsylvania Turnpike.

The Wars for Empire			
European War	American Name	Dates	Peace Settlement
War of the League of Augsburg	King William's War	1689–1697	Ryswick
War of the Spanish Succession	Queen Anne's War	1702–1713	Utrecht
War of the Austrian Succession	King George's War	1740–1748	Aix-la-Chapelle
Seven Years' War	French and Indian War	1756–1763	Paris

West Indian Sugar Islands. Britain gave Cuba and the Philippines back to Spain in exchange for Florida; in compensation for the loss of Florida, Spain received from France the part of Louisiana that lay west of the Mississippi. The French empire in North America was no more. Britain and Spain were the sole proprietors of the continent—if one overlooks the claims of the principal residents, the Indians. The British Empire was at its zenith. It was also about to come apart.

⊔ War and the Bonds of Empire, 1760–1763

The half-century of imperial conflict in some ways strengthened the ties between Britain and its colonies. Each needed the military assistance of the other. When differences did arise, military necessity made compromise essential. So amicable was the relationship on the whole that colonists later viewed those years with some nostalgia. Well they might, for in this period of "salutary neglect,"** the colonial assemblies expanded their powers and heightened their self-confidence. Often it was the planning, fighting, and financing of war that enabled them to do so. British officials clung to the mercantilist notion that colonies were dependencies that existed solely for the benefit of the mother country. Yet when they examined their empire after the fighting ceased in 1760, they found a substantial gap between imperial theory and imperial practice. The colonists governed their own affairs with only incidental—and often ineffectual—imperial control.

MONEY AND COMMERCE

Colonial politics turned on the relationship between the governor and the lower house of the assembly. The one represented imperial authority, the other represented the people. The assemblies derived their authority from popular consent, expressed both through frequent elections (held annually in most colonies) and through suffrage qualifications that were low enough to permit a majority of white males to vote. By the end of the seventeenth century, most assemblies had won the right to levy taxes and appropriate the revenue—the crucial power of the purse—and in the early decades of the eighteenth century they wielded this power against the governors. Governors were dependent for their salaries on assembly appropriations in every colony but Virginia, where the gover-

---

** On the eve of the revolution, when the colonists were resisting the British government's taxes and regulations, they looked back with nostalgia on the early decades of the century, when they had prospered through neglect.

North America in 1763.

nor was paid out of an export tax on tobacco. The assemblies frequently used this as a bargaining tool, and when a governor refused to compromise, he went unpaid.

The assemblies extended the power of the purse to include the printing of money, especially in wartime. Massachusetts, which had issued the first American coins, the pine tree shillings of the 1670s, had pioneered the use of paper money. In 1690, as a matter of wartime finance, the Massachusetts General Court had authorized the issuance of bills of credit, paper IOUs that the colony expected to redeem after the war. Other colonies had followed suit, and in the military emergency Britain had dared not object. The bills had not been declared legal tender for the payment of debts; that is, people had not been required by law to accept them. But the colonial governments had accepted them in the payment of taxes. (This, in fact, was the way they were retired from circulation when the military emergency passed.) As a result, the notes held their value as they passed from hand to hand. British merchants were leary of colonial paper, however, and at their insistence the Board of Trade instructed governors to veto further issues.

The colonists, however, had found paper money useful even in times of peace. They were chronically short of money because whatever gold or silver came into their hands (usually through trade with the West Indies) was sent to Britain to pay debts. Throughout the prerevolutionary years, Americans, especially New Englanders, purchased more from the mother country than they were able to sell to it. This situation forced them to trade with the Spanish, French, and Dutch islands of the West Indies in order to obtain coin that was acceptable to British merchants (the dollar, or piece of eight, was a Spanish gold coin). But they were still in need of some medium for domestic exchange, and paper currency suited fine.

In the skirmishing between governor and assembly, the salary and paper money questions often became intertwined. A prolonged controversy arose in the 1720s, when a governor had been appointed in Massachusetts with instructions to extract a permanent income from the assembly. The assembly replied with a one-year salary grant. When the governor rejected it, the assembly offered him a five-year grant, but as an amendment to a bill authorizing more paper money, and with the governor's salary to be paid in paper. When the governor rejected this proposal, he went unpaid until he left the colony in 1730. In the following decade New Hampshire refused to pay its governor when he vetoed

a paper money bill, and the poor gentleman went without salary for five years. The Rhode Island colony, in which the governor was popularly elected, had fewer difficulties. In fact, it was an example of the maxim that liberty requires restraint. By 1750 the colony was foundering in half a million British pounds worth of paper money, and merchants outside Rhode Island would not accept its currency. In 1751 Parliament passed a Currency Act that prohibited the New England colonies from making paper legal tender and declared that new issues had to be redeemed through taxes in two years.

Another area of dispute was colonial commerce. The colonists had long been inclined to ignore customs regulations. Most of the smuggling involved the French Sugar Islands—Santo Domingo, Guadaloupe, and Martinique. The French government subsidized the raising of sugar cane, but it barred the import of rum and molasses into France in order to protect its brandy industry. These by-products of sugar refining could be purchased by Americans much more cheaply in the French islands than in the British islands. The New England rum industry as a result was built on French molasses; and rum sales were one of New England's few money earners. In 1733, at the instigation of the British West Indian planters, Parliament had passed the Molasses Act, which placed a high tariff on the import of foreign sugar and molasses. Faced with ruin, New Englanders had simply ignored the law, and Britain had made no effort to enforce it. Indeed, evasion of regulations generally had become the fashion, made easy by corrupt officials and friendly juries.

RIGHTS AND AUTHORITY

Writs of Assistance. Not even war halted the illicit trade; in fact, it may have encouraged it because higher risks meant higher prices. British efforts to halt smuggling during the French and Indian War provoked a dispute that revealed how loose the bonds of empire had become. In the late seventeenth century, Parliament had authorized the use of writs of assistance—warrants that enabled customs collectors to summon sheriffs and other peace officers to assist them in the search for smuggled goods. The writs were not ordinary search warrants, for they did not specify the object of the search. They were general warrants that allowed officials to rummage through a vessel or a warehouse looking for anything that might be illegal.

The writs were not used in the colonies until the French and Indian War, when the Massachusetts Superior Court began issuing them to customs collectors in order to halt trade with the French Sugar Islands. The death of King George II in 1760 voided all existing writs, and a band of Massachusetts politicians decided to fight their reissuance. They employed a young attorney, James Otis, Jr., who startled the superior court with the argument that the rights of citizens (in this case, their right of privacy) stemmed from natural law as well as from the British Constitution, and that an act of Parliament contrary to either the Constitution or natural law was void.

Otis's thesis was as potent as it was novel. For a century, English Whigs had been contending that the powers of the crown were limited; but no one had thought to question the powers of Parliament. The Constitution Otis invoked was not a single document; it was a collection of laws and judicial precedents dating back to Magna Carta (1215) designed to protect Englishmen from arbitrary actions by the crown. If Parliament too was to be bound by the Constitution or by rights that stemmed from natural law, as Otis suggested, what was the extent of its powers? Did people have certain basic rights that no government could infringe upon? The implications of Otis's argument were revolution-

ary, but he did not take it that far. Nor did others at the time. The court ruled against Otis, and the controversy subsided rather quickly. The constitutional point, however, was not forgotten.

The Parson's Cause. A parallel dispute—and one that received much more publicity—arose in Virginia during the French and Indian War. This one involved paper money. In Virginia, tobacco was money; warehouse certificates representing stored tobacco circulated as currency. When the tobacco crop failed and prices rose, a debt measured in pounds of tobacco could become an onerous burden. That is precisely what happened in 1758. The Virginia assembly responded with a debtor relief measure known as the Two Penny Act. This allowed debts, taxes, and wages, customarily paid in tobacco, to be settled at the rate of two pennies for each pound of tobacco due. Since the market price was four to six pence per pound, the act effectively cut debt obligations by one half to two thirds. Among the losers were the clergy, who were paid in tobacco.

The British Privy Council subsequently declared the Two Penny Act void, and the clergy sued for back pay. Among the suits was that of Reverend James Maury of Hanover County. The court ruled in favor of the clergyman; the only question before the jury was the amount of damages. Young Patrick Henry, newly admitted to the bar and hired at the last minute by the defense, proceeded with the radical argument that the king and Privy Council had no authority to disallow an act passed by a colonial legislature, and that by so doing the king "forfeits all rights to his subjects' obedience." The jury awarded Maury a single penny in damages. The Parson's Cause, as the case came to be known, was another alarm signal that the empire was coming unraveled. London officials might well have paid it more attention, for it marked Patrick Henry as a radical willing to question the very basis of their authority.

The Proclamation of 1763. Indian policy was another source of friction between colonists and mother country as the French war drew to a close. The British had agreed to protect the Iroquois against future white encroachment in order to secure their support in the war. When the Cherokees hit the warpath in 1759, similar promises were made to them. After the French surrendered, the British army found itself patrolling the frontier to protect the Indians from colonial rum runners, traders, and land speculators. In 1761, the ministry ordered that all land grants in Indian territory must have crown approval. Some of the king's ministers felt that the only permanent solution was to turn the West into a huge Indian reservation. They reasoned that, by keeping the two races apart, the likelihood of conflict and hence the costs of defense would be reduced. A secondary benefit was that colonists confined to the seaboard would be easier to control. The ministry was considering this proposal when an Indian uprising forced them to act.

In the spring of 1763 followers of the Ottawa chief Pontiac simultaneously attacked several western outposts in a superbly organized effort involving many tribes. Every stockade west of Niagara, except Detroit, fell before the Indian onslaught. In the east, Fort Pitt (formerly Fort Duquesne) was under siege for weeks. Three relief expeditions sent to Detroit were chopped to pieces by Pontiac before his alliance fell apart and he abandoned the siege in early 1764. Sporadic fighting continued for two more years before Pontiac finally signed a peace treaty.

In October 1763, King George III issued a proclamation prohibiting the colonists from settling west of the Appalachian ridge, from Maine to Georgia. Traders in the western reservation had to get special licenses to do business with the Indians. Colonists were offended at the limitation, even though there was still considerable land available east of the mountains. The proclamation of 1763 was especially resented by the Virginia and Pennsylvania speculators who had claims in the west as a result of earlier Indian treaties. The proclamation did not cause open resistance, but it was an irritant—one of a growing number.

⊔ British Challenge and Colonial Response, 1764–1770

George Grenville, who as head of the Treasury was the king's chief minister at the end of the French and Indian War, faced two urgent problems: a staggering war debt and a vast array of new imperial commitments. Britain's national debt had doubled during the war. The annual interest charge alone was £2 million, an amount nearly equal to the normal peacetime revenue. In addition, Grenville felt obliged to maintain military garrisons in Britain's new possessions from Quebec to Florida, lest the French and Spanish move back in. With all these obligations, it was certain that British taxes would remain high; it seemed only fair that American colonists share some of the burden. To this point they had made no direct contribution to the maintenance of Britain's army and navy.

Collecting money from Americans was no easy task. The imperial tax collection machinery had become rusty from salutary neglect. One report given Grenville estimated that £700,000 worth of foreign goods were smuggled into the colonies annually and that New England alone consumed 4 million gallons of French molasses on which no duty was paid. Before new taxes were imposed, it was clear that the customs service had to be overhauled. Hence the twin horns of Grenville's "new" imperial policy: (1) to reinforce and reinvigorate the machinery of colonial administration and (2) through taxes, to force the colonists to contribute to the cost of empire. The policy was hardly new; British rulers had pursued those goals, with varying success, for a century. What was new was the political reality of colonial self-rule.

The colonists perceived Grenville's policy as a challenge to their hard-won right to govern themselves. Their response, mild at first and moderate in tone, became increasingly radical in tone and violent in action. Eventually, many Americans became convinced that Britain's goal was nothing less than to enslave them. "This radical change in the principles, opinions, sentiments, and affections of the people," John Adams later wrote, "was the real American Revolution."

THE REVENUE ACT OF 1764

In 1765, Parliament approved the first of Grenville's reforms, the Plantation Act, commonly referred to in the colonies as the Sugar Act. Aimed primarily at smuggling, the act laid down a rigid code of procedures for ships entering and leaving American harbors. It also established at Halifax, Nova Scotia, a vice admiralty court for the trial of offenders. Functioning without a jury, an admiralty court, it was hoped, would be more likely to secure convictions. Similar courts were later set up in all the principal colonial ports. Finally—and from the American point of view most important—the act reduced the tariff on foreign sugar and molasses from 6 shillings to 3. The lowered duty, it was thought, would discourage smuggling and thus yield a rev-

enue to the crown. But it also changed the nature of the duty from a trade regulation (an effort to exclude foreign molasses) to a tax. Therein lay the trouble. The colonists had long submitted to Parliament's trade regulations (Navigation Acts), but never before had Parliament levied taxes on them. Taxes had long been the province of the colonial assemblies. The power of the purse, it will be remembered, was the foundation of many of the assemblies' other powers. To the colonists, taxation and self-rule were closely linked.

The colonial response was instant and forceful. Within a year, eight assemblies adopted resolutions of protest. Early protests went to the Board of Trade; later ones were sent directly to Parliament. Rhode Island pointed out that the molasses duty would ruin its rum industry, disrupt the slave trade, and prevent the colony from buying British goods. New York and Virginia both protested the injustice of being taxed by a body in which they had no voice, the British Parliament. It was a fundamental principle of the British Constitution, said the Virginia assembly, "that the people are not subjected to any taxes but such as are laid on them by their own consent, or by those who are legally appointed to represent them."

This was a new point of contention in the developing imperial debate—the relationship between taxation and representation. The members of the British House of Commons were elected by counties and boroughs, but they did not directly represent the people who chose them. They were not required to reside in the community that elected them, and they would have rejected any effort by their constituents to tell them how to vote. Instead, each member of the Commons thought of himself as virtually representing every British subject, and he voted, supposedly, with the interests of the entire empire in mind.

This British concept of virtual representation—that is, place, rather than people—made no sense to the colonists,* for in most colonies delegates were required to reside in the community they represented. New England towns frequently instructed their representatives on how to vote, and in all colonies, assemblymen felt that their votes reflected the will of their constituents. This assumption was at the root of the assemblies' self-confidence. Americans regarded the theory of virtual representation as sophistry at best, and at worst, as an effort to impose Parliament's authority in place of the colonial assemblies. As a Rhode Island newspaper expressed it: "It is really a piece of mockery to tell us that a country, detached from Britain, by an ocean of immense breadth, and which is so extensive and populous, should be represented by the British members, or that we have any interest [influence] in the house of commons."

THE STAMP ACT

By the time the colonial protests arrived in London, Parliament was giving its final approval to the next item in Grenville's program, the Stamp Act. This brought forth one element that was missing in the 1764 colonial protest—violence. The act levied a tax on colonial legal documents, newspapers, almanacs, playing cards, and dice. The tax was collected by the sale of stamps, which were to be affixed to the

taxed items, and the act provided for the appointment of stamp distributors in every colony. The act passed the House of Commons by a wide margin, apparently as a show of unity in the face of colonial protest. The king's ministers clearly understood its implications. The author of the Stamp Act called it "the great measure of the session . . . on account of the important point it establishes, the right of Parliament to lay an internal tax on the colonies."

The colonial reaction was predictable. A French statesman of the eighteenth century once remarked, "The art of taxation consists of plucking the maximum number of feathers from the goose with the minimum of squawking." The Stamp Act plucked the most sensitive, articulate portions of the colonial goose—lawyers and journalists—for it was their documents chiefly that had to bear the stamps. A loud squawk was inevitable, and it came swiftly. Even before the act was passed, seven colonies filed petitions of protest with king and Parliament. The battle lines were drawn.

The text of the Stamp Act arrived in the colonies in April 1765; the law was to go into effect on the first of November. In May, the lawyer Patrick Henry arrived in Williamsburg to take his seat in Virginia's House of Burgesses; it was his first political office. The session was nearly over; two thirds of the members had gone home when Henry rose to present a set of seven resolutions. Four of his proposals firmly restated the position that Virginia had taken the previous year in regard to taxation and representation. A fifth resolution, passed by a narrow margin and repealed the next day, boldly declared that anyone supporting Parliament's position ought to be considered a traitor. All five resolves were reprinted in northern newspapers. Henry's fiery rhetoric helped to escalate the intensity of the colonial protest.

In Boston, a group of shopkeepers and artisans, among them Samuel Adams, call-

---

* No colony apportioned representation by population, although in Massachusetts, Boston had four representatives while the other towns had two. In the southern colonies, where representation was by counties, populous counties were subdivided, thus creating additional representation as population increased. The United States House of Representatives, whose members are elected by arbitrarily drawn population districts, was a new departure in the concept of representation.

The Whig Version of History

When George Grenville introduced the subject of a stamp tax in the British House of Commons, he pointed out that it was only reasonable that the colonies should share some of their burden of their own defense. In the debate that followed, no one denied that Parliament had the right to tax the colonies or that it was proper for them to contribute. The most ardent defenders of America argued only that the colonies should be allowed to tax themselves. Charles Townshend expressed the prevailing sentiment when he asked with rhetorical flourish: "Will these Americans, children planted by our care, nourished up by our indulgence until they are grown to a degree of strength and opulence, and protected by our arms, will they grudge to contribute their mite to relieve us from the heavy weight of that burden which we lie under?"

Colonel Isaac Barre, who had been a soldier in America during the French war, responded with words that made him an instant hero in the colonies. He provided the colonists with both a label—"Sons of Liberty"—and a sense of historical mission.

> They planted by your care? No! Your oppressions planted 'em in America. They fled from your tyranny to a then uncultivated and unhospitable country where they exposed themselves to almost all the hardships to which human nature is liable, and among others to the cruelties of a savage foe, the most subtle, and I take upon me to say, the most formidable of any people upon the face of God's earth. . . .
>
> They nourished by *your* indulgence? They grew by your neglect of 'em. As soon as you began to care about 'em, that care was exercised in sending persons to rule over 'em, in one department and another, who were perhaps the deputies of deputies to some member of this house, sent to spy out their liberty, to misrepresent their actions and to prey upon 'em; men whose behaviour on many occasions has caused the blood of those sons of liberty to recoil within them; men promoted to the highest seats of justice; some who to my knowledge were glad by going to a foreign country to escape being brought to the bar of a court of justice in their own.
>
> They protected by *your* arms? They have nobly taken up arms in your defence, have exerted a valour amidst their constant and laborious industry for the defense of a country, whose frontier while drenched in blood, its interior parts have yielded all its little savings to your emolument. And believe me, remember I this day told you so, that same spirit of freedom which actuated that people at first, will accompany them still.

ing itself the Loyal Nine, met to consider how to prevent the act from taking effect as scheduled. Their solution was to turn to political purposes the popular love of violence. Rioting was common in colonial Boston; artisans and laborers staged an anti-Catholic free-for-all every Guy Fawkes Day (November 5). The Loyal Nine simply made arrangements with artisan leaders fa-

miliar with organized riots to instill some fear into Andrew Oliver, the designated stamp distributor. On August 14, the collector's office was badly damaged; he resigned the next day. Two weeks later, the mob wrecked the houses of an Admiralty court official, a customs official, and finally of Lieutenant Governor Thomas Hutchinson himself. Similar riots led to the resignations of stamp distributors in other colonies. By November, when the Stamp Act was to take effect, it was all but dead.

Colonial merchants, though somewhat alarmed by the lower-class violence, nevertheless did their part to resist the act by making nonimportation agreements—in effect, a boycott of British goods. This sort of retaliation struck British merchants in their pocketbooks, and they in turn began to pressure Parliament for repeal of the Stamp Act. Before Parliament could act, America took the first step toward intercolonial union—the Stamp Act Congress.

As early as June 1765, Massachusetts had suggested an intercolonial congress to draft a coordinated response, and in October, twenty-seven delegates from nine colonies met in New York. The congress drafted a statement that summarized the colonial interpretation of the English Constitution and the empire. The colonies, it said, owed "all due subordination" to Parliament, but that meant only a general superintending power, such as the right to regulate trade. Governmental actions that affected the daily lives of Americans, among them taxation, were the province of the colonial assemblies.

By midwinter, "popular" leaders, as they called themselves, appeared in several colonies to provide leadership and organization for the resistance movement—Samuel Adams in Boston, Isaac Sears in New York, Charles Thomson in Philadelphia, Christopher Gadsden in South Carolina. Their followers took the name Sons of Liberty, a phrase coined by Colonel Isaac Barre, one of the few pro-American members of Parliament. Shopkeepers and tradesmen were at the core of the Sons of Liberty. Merchants and lawyers, the professionals most affected by the Stamp Act, participated at first, but they were soon distressed by the violence and dropped out, even though the popular leaders worked hard to keep the violence carefully under control. Govern-

ment, as embodied in the king and his agents the governors, was never threatened; Americans objected only to the policies of the king's ministers. Resistance was not yet revolution.

In the spring of 1766, Parliament, persuaded that the losses in American trade due to the boycott exceeded the value of the taxes collected, repealed the Stamp Act. It coupled the repeal with a face-saving Declaratory Act which stated that Parliament had power, if it wished to exercise it, to legislate for the colonies "in all cases whatsoever." Among those instrumental in securing repeal of the Stamp Act was Benjamin Franklin, who had been sent to London as an agent for Pennsylvania. In testimony before a committee of the House of Commons, Franklin distinguished between external and internal taxation. It was the latter, such as the Stamp Act, that caused trouble. External taxes, in the form of customs duties, Franklin suggested, were within the powers of Parliament.

THE TOWNSHEND TAXES

Charles Townshend, a new head of the Treasury, decided to test this thesis. At his instigation, Parliament in 1767 imposed customs duties on a variety of goods imported by the colonies—paint, tea, glass, paper, lead, and some luxury items. As if to ensure colonial opposition, the act stated that it was intended to defray the costs of civil government in America. In other words, some of the proceeds of the act were earmarked for the salaries of colonial governors and judges, who had previously been dependent on the assemblies for their pay. The act thus challenged directly the authority of the colonial assemblies, for the threat to withhold salary was one of the few levers the assemblies had against their governors. The taxes, moreover, were avowedly for revenue purposes; customs duties in the past (the molasses tax, for instance) had been levied to influence colonial trade patterns.

The colonial response this time was less violent but more organized. Merchants, the group most burdened by the taxes, formed agreements not to import British goods until the taxes were repealed. Economic coercion of this sort, the colonists hoped, would injure British exporters and put pressure on Parliament. The Sons of Liberty took it upon themselves to enforce the nonimportation agreements by publishing the names of those who cheated.

Franklin's distinction between internal and external taxation was largely his own. Colonial assemblies made no such distinction in their petitions. Their view was that there was no power of taxation without representation. Despite Parliament's theory of "virtual representation," the colonists saw that they had no real influence on its decisions. They saw too that Parliament's true voting constituency in Britain approved large tax levies on America because they lessened Britain's own tax burden. The colonists concluded, in short, that Parliament had no power to levy taxes of any kind on America. This new—and, in the British view, more radical—colonial position was outlined by John Dickinson, one of Franklin's rivals in Pennsylvania politics, in his *Letters from a Farmer in Pennsylvania* (1768).

THE BOSTON MASSACRE

By 1768, officials charged with collecting taxes in smoldering Boston were openly threatened on the streets; they finally fled for safety to a fort in Boston harbor. In the House of Representatives, Samuel Adams, who had been elected a delegate in 1766, was made clerk, a position that allowed him to author or edit all petitions and correspondence. At Adams's sugges-

tion, the House ordered a gallery installed from which the populace could view the proceedings. Adams then packed the gallery with his own followers.

To restore order, four British regiments were sent to Boston from Halifax. Adams threatened to oppose the army at the water's edge, but the troops landed without incident. Their presence, however, increased tensions. The Sons of Liberty taunted them on the streets. Because they were poorly paid, the redcoats eagerly sought part-time jobs in the city, and the competition increased the friction between soldiers and city laborers. Fights were frequent. On March 1, 1770, a pitched battle between ropemakers and soldiers height-

Paul Revere's engraving of the Boston Massacre was more propaganda than art. He depicts the British soldiers smiling with sadistic pleasure as they fire into the hapless crowd. A verse beneath the picture interprets their expressions:

. . . fierce Barbarians grinning o'er their Prey, Approve the Carnage and enjoy the Day.

The Metropolitan Museum of Art.

ened tensions further. On the next day, Boston's streets were spattered with handbills warning of a military takeover by the British. On the evening of March 5, a crowd gathered around a British sentry and began showering him with ice and snowballs. A corporal's guard of six soldiers went to his rescue. The crowd grew larger and more nasty. Church bells began ringing all over town. One soldier, felled by a piece of brick, came up shooting. Other shots rang out, and five citizens of Boston fell to the street, four dead at the scene and another mortally wounded. All were tradesmen, typical members of the Sons of Liberty. Among them was Crispus Attucks, a ropemaker by trade, who thus became the first black martyr to the Revolution.

Governor Hutchinson put an end to the violence by moving courageously into the mob and ordering the arrest of the soldiers. Samuel Adams and other radicals tried to capitalize on "the bloody business in King Street" with angry speeches, but in fact tensions eased rather quickly. The soldiers shrewdly hired Samuel's cousin, John Adams, as defense counsel. Though a member of Samuel Adams's circle, John undertook the defense on the ground that, as an attorney, he was obliged to defend anyone until proven guilty.* A jury, packed with persons loyal to the crown, some said, convicted only two of the soldiers, and these received the comparatively light punishment of a branding on the hand.

By one of those odd coincidences of history, Parliament repealed most of the Townshend duties on the same day as the Boston Massacre. It was a gesture of conciliation, although Parliament kept the duty on tea in order to save face and retain the principle of taxation. The colonists ignored the gesture because they did not pay taxes on tea anyway. Because Dutch tea was considerably cheaper than British tea, it ranked with molasses as a favorite item for smugglers. Brought in illicitly, Dutch tea escaped all duties; Parliament's levy was an idle gesture. Tensions eased, and the boycott of British goods was quietly ended.

The Boston Massacre ended the first phase of the revolutionary movement. What began as a constitutional protest had by 1770 escalated into open hostilities culminating in five deaths. The events of 1765–1770 revealed the dilemma Samuel Adams and other popular leaders faced. To make themselves heard, they had to resort to violence. Yet violence frightened the moderate majority, the middle-class merchants and shopkeepers whose support was needed for success. The dilemma was never fully resolved; because of further British blunders, it did not have to be.

⊔ The Path to Revolution, 1770–1775

The next few years were, by comparison, fairly calm. In Boston, Samuel Adams seemed isolated and lonely. Even his friend and financial benefactor John Hancock deserted him in 1771, running for a seat in the assembly as an ally of the governor. James Otis, whose conduct had become worrisomely erratic, went irrecoverably insane. The Popular party, as the radicals had come to call themselves, was a shambles.

THE COMMITTEES OF CORRESPONDENCE

Undaunted, Adams resolved to strengthen his organization. In 1771 he proposed that committees of correspondence be set up in the various Massachusetts towns, an idea

---

* Some suspect that John Adams's appointment as defense counsel was contrived by Samuel Adams and the Loyal Nine, in whose interest it might have been not to have a defense attorney who might have probed too deeply into the underlying causes of the massacre.

that might have originated with James Otis's sister Mercy, the wife of the Plymouth lawyer James Warren. Although removed from the Boston scene, Mercy Warren had kept in close contact with the Adams circle. She had even lent her pen to the cause by writing plays that satirized British officials. The problem Mercy Warren and other radicals in towns outside Boston faced was coordinating their efforts. The idea of committees of correspondence—a network of standing committees for exchanging ideas, coordinating plans, and reinforcing one another—was a natural solution that caught on quickly. By 1772 the communications network stretched throughout Massachusetts.

The need to extend the network throughout the colonies was soon apparent. Although there were no major confrontations in the years immediately following the Boston Massacre, there were running disputes with the British authorities in nearly every colony. The assemblies of Georgia and South Carolina dueled intermittently with their governors. North Carolina experienced a full-scale uprising of backwoodsmen that the governor finally suppressed in the open battle of Alamance, 1771. In the spring of 1772, Rhode Islanders captured and burned a British warship, the *Gaspee*, which had been irritatingly vigorous in searching for smugglers. Learning of the *Gaspee* incident, the Virginia House of Burgesses set up a committee of correspondence and suggested that other colonies do the same. By the end of 1773, the intercolonial network was in place.

Adams's apparatus would not have survived for long, however, without another confrontation; nothing is quite so tiresome as a rebel without a cause. Fortunately for Adams and other popular leaders, the British soon provided them with one. The business cycle took a downward turn in 1772, and among the British companies facing bankruptcy was the poorly managed East India Company. The company was responsible for governing the portions of India under British control, and it had a monopoly over British Far Eastern trade. The company's principal staple was tea, which it shipped to Britain. It sold little tea in the colonies because Americans found it cheaper to buy smuggled tea from the Dutch.

Parliament set out to reorganize the insolvent company in the spring of 1773, and company officials requested that they be given a means of dumping their surplus tea on the American market. Parliament obligingly approved a measure, the East India Act, that authorized the company to sell its tea in the colonies through its own agents. By using its own agents, the company could bypass colonial middlemen and thus compete in price with Dutch tea. In the House of Commons, the opposition suggested that removing the tax on tea, a relic of the Townshend duties, might be a simpler way to end smuggling and to increase legitimate sales in the colonies. Lord North, the king's chief minister since 1770, rejected the idea. North had been selected by the king because of his loyalty to the crown, and he faithfully reflected the royal view that the colonists had been coddled too much. Proceeds from the tea tax had enabled him to pay governors' salaries in certain of the colonies, thereby relieving them from dependence on legislative handouts. North was unwilling to give up the leverage thus gained, especially since it might appear to be another concession to the Americans. Thus the East India Act became another political challenge. Colonists saw it as a transparent attempt to bribe them out of their liberties with cheap tea.

THE BOSTON TEA PARTY

In New York and Philadelphia, there was organized opposition even before the tea ships arrived. In both cities, the Sons of

Liberty pressured the consignees to resign from the company. Thus there was no one to whom the tea could be delivered. In Boston, however, it was a different story. Lieutenant Governor Hutchinson had suffered a decade of abuse from popular leaders. His house had been ransacked; his private correspondence had been stolen and published. When the first tea ship, the *Dartmouth*, beat its way into Boston Harbor on November 28, 1773, Hutchinson saw his opportunity for revenge. Customs regulations required a ship captain to pay duties on his cargo within twenty days. If he failed to do so, the cargo could be confiscated by crown officials. With the governor's backing, the merchant consignees, one of whom was the governor's son, stood firm. They would accept the tea. Thus the governor had only to enforce the law, and one way or another, the tea would be unloaded. Once unloaded, it was certain to be sold.

Boston's popular leaders called a mass meeting at Faneuil Hall, and five thousand people appeared, testimony to the effectiveness of Adams's communications network. The majority agreed that the tea would not be landed and appointed a committee to guard the ship. Both sides were gambling; unfortunately, the governor held the better hand. As the days passed, Bostonians learned that tea consignees in New York and Philadelphia had resigned. If Bostonians yielded and allowed the *Dartmouth* to be unloaded, they would be jeered the length of the continent. On the evening of December 16, 1773, with the confiscation deadline coming up the next day, another mass meeting was held; so many attended that it had to be adjourned to the Old South Church. After some inconclusive discussion, Samuel Adams announced that he was going home to "set down and make myself as easy as I can, for this meeting can do nothing further to save the country." His pronouncement evidently was a signal, for the crowd immediately poured out of the hall and swept down to the wharf. There a band of men disguised

as Indians (apparently a symbolic reference to New York, where "Mohawks" had frightened the tea consignee into resigning), went aboard the *Dartmouth*. Within three hours, 342 chests of tea, worth about £10,000, were dumped into the Boston harbor.

The Boston Tea Party was a calculated risk. Such open vandalism might well have alienated moderates and left the popular leaders more isolated than ever. The perpetrators evidently expected the British government to react with a new provocation, and it did. Parliament was furious. Even friends of America thought that the colonists had gone too far. Lord North prepared a series of coercive acts, and Parliament approved them without a murmur of opposition. The purpose of the acts was to punish Boston and reestablish royal authority throughout Massachusetts. A Boston Port Act prohibited vessels from entering or leaving the port of Boston, except to carry food and fuel, until the town paid for the tea. The Massachusetts Government Act revised the colony's charter to strengthen the powers of the royal governor. The council thereafter was to be appointed by the governor instead of by the delegates to the lower house; juries were to be chosen by sheriffs, rather than by popular elections; and no town meetings could be held without the governor's consent. Governor Hutchinson departed for England that year, and the ministry replaced him with General Thomas Gage, the commander of the troops occupying Boston. The changes, in effect, placed Massachusetts under military rule. A third measure, the Administration of Justice Act, allowed the governor to remove to another colonial court or to England the trial of any magistrate or customs collector who might be sued for trying to enforce the acts of Parliament. A final act, the Quartering Act, made colonial authorities responsible for finding barracks for royal troops that might be sent into a colony.

A month after these punitive measures

were sent off to the colonies, Parliament passed the Quebec Act. This act extended the boundaries of Quebec southward to the Ohio River, thereby giving Canada jurisdiction over the trans-Appalachian Indian reserve. The act also promised toleration for French Roman Catholics and guaranteed the Catholic clergy "their accustomed Dues and Rights." The Quebec Act was, for its time, an enlightened piece of legislation. It was doubtless an important factor in keeping Canada loyal to the empire after other colonies rebelled. Yet American colonists inevitably linked it with the Coercive Acts; they felt it too was a form of punishment. New Englanders were particularly incensed because the act's concessions to

"Taking the Pledge." This British cartoon, entitled "A Society of Patriotic Ladies at Edenton in North Carolina," was published in London in March 1775. It ridiculed the role of women in the American nonimportation movement. The women are emptying their tea canisters and signing a pledge that they will not drink tea or wear clothes manufactured in England.

Metropolitan Museum of Art, New York.

Catholics placed the pope, their ancient foe, at their back door.

The Coercive Acts—or Intolerable Acts, as Americans commonly called them— united the colonists as never before. Shocked by the brutal treatment of Bostonians, towns everywhere sent messages of sympathy and donations of food and fuel. For thousands of Americans, a gift to Boston was their first personal commitment to resist British authority. The Massachusetts Government Act was the ultimate challenge to colonial self-rule. If Parliament could give the governor of one colony virtually dictatorial powers, it could do so in another. If Massachusetts had no rights, the rights of no colony were secure. By midsummer 1774, General Gage was complaining: "This province is supported and abetted by others beyond the conception of most people, and foreseen by none." By autumn he was recommending that the Coercive Acts be suspended unless he was given additional troops to enforce them.

THE FIRST CONTINENTAL CONGRESS

Committees of correspondence had been discussing the idea of an intercolonial congress for more than a year. In May 1774, the Virginia House of Burgesses took up the idea, and when the governor dissolved the assembly, it gathered at the Raleigh Tavern a few blocks away to give its approval. The Massachusetts House, meeting behind locked doors so that the governor could not dissolve it, approved resolutions drafted by Samuel Adams suggesting a congress at Philadelphia on September 1, 1774. All the colonies, except for remote and ill-informed Georgia, agreed, and during the summer informal groups—committees of correspondence, provincial congresses, even mass meetings—went about the business of selecting delegates.

The First Continental Congress was not as united as its promoters had hoped. Massachusetts, which sent John Adams and Samuel Adams, and Virginia, represented by Patrick Henry and Richard Henry Lee among others, were clearly the most radical colonies. Delegates from the middle colonies, among them Joseph Galloway and John Dickinson of Pennsylvania, were decidedly moderate. The two sides differed in both ideology and tactics. In their view of the empire, the radicals had come to deny that Parliament had any authority over the colonies, and they wanted the colonists to arm themselves to resist the Intolerable Acts. Moderates, fearful of mob rule and social chaos, did not want to sever the imperial tie unless there was an intercolonial government to replace it. Adopting this view, Pennsylvania's Joseph Galloway, a one-time political ally of Benjamin Franklin, proposed an intercolonial legislature with power to levy taxes and appoint royal officials. The congress rejected the idea because it took powers away from the individual colonies.

The two sides were about evenly balanced in numbers, but the radicals had the upper hand because they were better organized. This was evident when Galloway offered the Pennsylvania assembly house as a meeting place. The congress chose instead Carpenter's Hall, the home of one of the city's radical guilds. It then selected as its secretary Charles Thomson, the leader of the local Sons of Liberty and a man whom John Adams trumpeted as "the Sam Adams of Philadelphia." The congress was then ready to consider an agenda, and with perfect timing Paul Revere, a courier for the Boston committee of correspondence, rode into town with a set of resolutions in his saddlebags. Adopted by a popular meeting in Massachusetts, the Suffolk Resolves denounced the Intolerable Acts and suggested the colonists arm for their self-defense. The Resolves focused the debate, and the congress, when it approved them, effectively committed itself to a radical stand. The congress concluded by drafting a Declaration of Rights and Grievances that went beyond the issue of taxation and denied Parliament any power of legislation over the internal affairs of the colonies. Congress backed its protest by setting up a Continental Association to block the importation of British goods. It authorized committees of safety in every colony to enforce the stoppage. If Parliament did not yield by the following January, the congress threatened to halt colonial exports as well. With that, the congress adjourned until May 1775.

During the winter of 1774–1775, royal authority slowly deteriorated. When colonial governors dissolved the assemblies to silence their protests, the lower houses reformed themselves into conventions or provincial congresses and continued to govern as before. In every village and county, committees of safety sprang up to enforce the Continental Association. The congress, in authorizing the association, had taken the first step toward the exercise of governmental power. The association effectively forced all colonists to choose sides. Resistance to British rule no longer was voluntary; it had become compulsory by decision of the majority. Elected committees and congresses filled the vacuum left by the collapse of royal authority.

New England was an armed camp that winter. Militia paraded on every village common; towns stockpiled arms and gunpowder. The British army controlled Boston and nothing else; whenever the British set foot in the countryside to seize an arms cache or break up a town meeting, the militia mustered to meet them. So quickly could these colonial volunteers move in response to an alarm that some called them Minutemen. At this point, Parliament considered making concessions to the colonists but decided against the idea. The North ministry was convinced that it was facing only a small group of troublemakers in Massachusetts. This kind of misperception had been at the root of British errors from the beginning. In the spring of 1775, the colonial secretary commanded General Gage to move into the countryside, confiscate the arms stockpiles, and reestablish British authority. Gage's attempt to carry out the order triggered the American Revolution.

The Coming of the Revolution

British Challenges to American Self-Government	American Responses
Revenue Act (Sugar Act), 1764: Customs duty on molasses; vice admiralty courts	Newspapers essays and pamphlets denying Parliament's right to tax for revenue purposes
Stamp Act, 1765: Excise on goods produced within the colonies	"No taxation without representation"; riots that prevent enforcement; formation of Sons of Liberty; Stamp Act Congress
Repeal of Stamp Act; passage of Declaratory Act, 1766	Popular leaders improve their organizations
Townshend Taxes, 1767: Customs duties with proceeds earmarked for payment of governors' salaries	John Dickinson's *Letters from a Farmer in Pennsylvania*; nonimportation agreements; harrassment of customs collectors in Boston
British army landing in Boston to protect customs officials, 1768	Boston Massacre, March 1770
Repeal of Townshend taxes, except for tax on tea	Improved organization: committees of correspondence
East India Company Act (Tea Act), 1770	Tea parties in Boston, New York, and Philadelphia
Intolerable (Coercive) Acts, 1774: Revoked Massachusetts Charter; closed port of Boston; quartering of troops; transportation of offenders to England for trial	First Continental Congress: Declaration of grievances; Continental Association prohibiting trade

SUMMARY

The French empire in North America was both far-flung and flimsy. French explorers, fur traders, and missionaries staked an early claim to the Great Lakes and the Mississippi Valley (Louisiana), but the colony never became densely populated or economically stable. French territorial claims nevertheless provoked a confrontation with the English, and between 1689 and 1763 the two fought a series of wars for empire, a struggle for the control of North America.

Neither Britain nor France seemed at first to realize the imperial stake in the struggle. In the first two wars—the League of Augsburg (1689–1697) and the War of the Spanish Succession (1702–1713)—the imperial contest was secondary to dynastic rivalries between the Bourbons and the Hapsburgs. Gradually, however, imperial ambitions came to dominate. At the end of the War of the Spanish Succession, Britain demanded and received the cession of Newfoundland, Nova Scotia, and the lands bordering Hudson Bay. In the War of the Austrian Succession (1740–1748), a British and colonial force captured Fort Louisburg, guarding the entry to the St. Lawrence River, but Britain returned the fort at the end of the war. In the climactic Seven Years War (French and Indian War, 1756–1763), Britain conquered New France and obtained Canada and Louisiana east of the Mississippi, as well as Florida (from Spain). The great war for empire, however, loosened the bonds of empire. By removing the French threat to the American colonies, it reduced their dependence on Britain. When the British after the war undertook to reorganize the imperial administrative machinery and imposed taxes to make the Americans pay for their own defense, the colonies reacted violently. A series of political blunders by the British, coupled with ever more extreme colonial rhetoric, triggered the series of events that led to revolution. Parliament retreated several times in the face of colonial resistance, repealing the Stamp Act in 1766 and the Townshend taxes in 1770. But after the Boston Tea Party (1773)—a destructive protest against a tax that was more symbol than burden—Parliament reacted angrily. It passed a series of Coercive Acts (1774) designed to punish Boston and Massachusetts. Among them was an act suspending the Massachusetts charter and placing the colony under military rule. Viewing the elimination of civil government in one colony as a threat to all, the colonial assemblies sent delegates to a Continental Congress, which met in Philadelphia in September 1774. The congress sent a Declaration of Grievances to the king, backed it with an embargo on trade, and authorized the colonists to arm for defense. During the winter of 1774–1775, New England turned itself into an armed camp, and neither colonies nor imperial government made any serious effort to resolve their differences. A British effort to seize a colonial arms cache at Lexington and Concord in April 1775 provoked the American Revolution.

READING SUGGESTIONS

Francis Parkman's dramatically written classics, *Count Frontenac and New France under Louis XIV* (1877), *A Half Century of Conflict* (1892), and *Montcalm and Wolfe* (1884), still repay the reader. A briefer summary of the imperial warfare is Howard H. Peckham's *The Colonial Wars, 1689–1762* (1964). Patricia Dillon Woods, *French-Indian Relations on the Southern Frontier, 1699–1762* (1980), combines traditional military history with anthropological studies of Indian life.

The literature on the coming of revolution is rich and growing. Broad overviews of the subject include E. James Ferguson, *The American Revolution: A General History, 1763–1790* (1974), and Norman K. Risjord, *Forging the American Republic, 1760–1815* (1973). Risjord's *Representative Americans: The Revolutionary Generation* (1979) is a biographical approach to the subject. Merrill Jensen, *The Founding of a Nation* (1968), is the most comprehensive treatment of the chain of events leading to the Revolution.

The role of cities and urban mobs is the subject of several excellent books: Gary B. Nash,

The Urban Crucible: Social Change, Political Consciousness, and the Origins of the American Revolution (1979); Pauline Maier, *From Resistance to Revolution* (1972); and Dick Hoerder, *Crowd Action in Revolutionary Massachusetts, 1765–1780* (1977).

Bernard Bailyn's *The Origins of American Politics* (1968) is a brilliant essay on the revolutionary mind, and his award-winning biography, *The Ordeal of Thomas Hutchinson* (1974), is an excellent excursion into the Loyalist mentality.

6

View of The ATTACK on BUNKER'S HILL, with the
Burning of CHARLES TOWN, June 17, 1775.

BOSTON

CHARLES TOWN

FLINTLOCK AND QUILL:
Winning Independence

eneral Thomas Gage, British commander in Boston, told London authorities he needed 20,000 troops to bring New England under control. What he got in the spring of 1776 he didn't need—three more generals (William Howe, John Burgoyne, and Henry Clinton) and orders to find and arrest the leaders of the opposition. The opportunity to seize the opposition leaders soon presented itself. Spies informed him that the American colonists had a huge arms cache at Concord, some 18 miles to the west of Boston, and that the rebel leaders Samuel Adams and John Hancock were staying in nearby Lexington. A quick thrust into the interior might win Gage everything he wanted and break the back of colonial resistance.

Preparations for such a march could not be easily hidden, however, and by April 18 all of Boston seemed aware of the British plans. Patriot leaders guessed that Lexington and Concord were the British targets, and that evening two express riders, Paul Revere and William Dawes, set out by different routes to alert the countryside. Both fell into the hands of British patrols, but a third rider, Dr. Samuel Prescott, carried the alarm to Concord.

The British force of 700 light infantry crossed the Charles River during the night, and an advance guard of 60 arrived in Lexington at dawn. Greeting them were about 70 Minutemen, drawn up in two ragged lines on Lexington Green. The British commander ordered them to lay down their arms and disperse. Before they could comply, shots rang out, and the British platoon fired a volley. By the time the British commander regained control of his men, 8 Americans lay dead and 10 more were wounded. The British marched off to Concord, where they engaged in another skirmish and suffered their first casualties. Americans, this time, had fired back.

Finding no munitions in Concord, the British started home around noon. By then thousands of Minutemen were pouring in from neighboring towns, taking up positions along the road. The British ran an 18-mile gauntlet of musket fire on their return to Boston, suffering 273 casualties. "O! What a glorious morning is this!" exclaimed Samuel Adams as he and John Hancock prepared to depart for Philadelphia and the Second Continental Congress. On the horizon was the prospect of a free, continental republic, an asylum for humankind.

⌐ The Odds of Victory

The contest, at first glance, seemed an unequal one. Britain, with 9 million people, outnumbered America three to one. Britain's imperial dominion stretched from Ireland to India. The empire had industrial technology, vast financial resources, a highly trained army, and a navy that ruled the seas. Americans had few arms, little money, ill-trained militia, and no ships.

Yet the disparity was more apparent than real. Britain did have economic resources and the capacity to mobilize them through a sophisticated banking system, but fighting a war across 3,000 miles of ocean stretched those resources to the limit. In the end the British quit not because they were defeated on the field of battle, but because the economic price of winning was too high. Their army, moreover, though well trained and well equipped, was quite small. Britain had never maintained a large standing army; the wooden walls of its navy were its first line of defense. Nor, in the absence of conscription, was there any large pool of manpower on which to draw. As a result, early in the war the North ministry had to hire

---

(Chapter opening photo) The Battle of Bunker Hill and the British burning of Charlestown, June 1775.

125

German professionals. The province of Hesse-Cassel alone provided so many that Americans referred to all German mercenaries as Hessians.

A mercenary army involved special problems. Morale was low, desertion was high, and discipline was ferocious. An army of mercenaries had to move in lock step, and there was little latitude for individual initiative or heroism. Much of the sluggishness that characterized British movements during the war was not the fault of British generals, but rather the nature of an eighteenth-century European army. America's citizen-soldiers, though ill trained and poorly armed, had incentives of a different sort. Enlisted for periods of three or six months, they came and went as they pleased, particularly in the seasons of spring planting and fall harvest. Yet in an emergency they seemed almost to spring from the soil, and by sheer weight of numbers they could turn a battle, as General Burgoyne discovered at Saratoga.

The vast distances in America and the lack of strategic population centers encouraged amateur warfare. In Europe the capture of a capital city—Paris, Berlin, Vienna—was sufficient to end a war. In America the seizure of Philadelphia meant nothing; indeed, many had never heard of the city. The Continental Congress, far

from being wedded to its quarters, simply set up shop in the village of York, Pennsylvania. The distances meant also that American commanders could retreat endlessly without yielding anything. British generals, such as Burgoyne in New York and Cornwallis in the Carolinas, tramped hundreds of miles only to find that in the end they controlled nothing but the soil under their feet, while a hostile wilderness closed in behind them. The huge expanse of America and the price of conquering it were what ultimately gave Americans the victory.

⊔Washington Takes Command: Boston to Trenton

By June there were about 10,000 armed farmers surrounding Boston in a loose siege under the direction of the Massachusetts Council of War. On June 16, the council ordered the fortification of Bunker Hill on the Charlestown peninsula just north of Boston. Working frantically through the night, the militia threw up earthworks on Bunker Hill and on Breed's Hill, which was closer yet to the harbor (although the whole exercise was futile, since they lacked artillery to menace British shipping). Perched on the hills, and dangerously exposed, the American detachment, only 1,500 strong, was tactically worthless. General Gage let his ships bombard them for a while and then decided on a land attack.

The attack force of 2,400 was commanded by Sir William Howe. Howe first tried a flank attack, which failed. He then sent his redcoated lines straight up the hill toward the American breastwork. Twice the line fell back under withering fire before it finally climbed over the top and sent the Americans fleeing across the neck. The victory cost the British 1,000 casualties, a fourth of them killed on the spot. Ameri-

Boston and vicinity, 1775–1776.

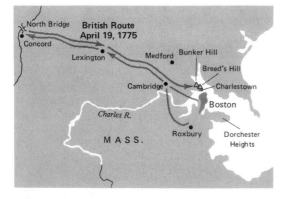

can losses were 140 killed and 271 wounded. For the British, it was the bloodiest battle of the war.

The battle of Breed's Hill, fought on June 17, 1775, taught each side a lesson. It taught British commanders that Americans would fight, especially from cover. It taught the Massachusetts Council of War that it could not battle the British Empire alone. The council asked the Continental Congress to take charge of the war, and in July that body created the first regiments of Continental regulars, riflemen from Virginia and Maryland. Congress also named a commander-in-chief, choosing one of its own members, George Washington, a delegate from Virginia.

The choice of Washington was essentially a political one—he came from the right state. A Virginian as commander would stop the whispers that it was New England's fight and would encourage military enlistment in the South. Furthermore, that Washington was reputed to be one of the wealthiest men in America might appease conservatives, who feared the "rabble" more than they feared the king. The British also changed commanders, replacing Gage with Sir William Howe. The ministry was pondering several plans for reconciliation, and Howe was thought to be a more convincing agent for peace than the detested Gage.

Washington took command of what amounted to a siege of the city of Boston. Lacking the strength to attack the British in the city, he could only watch and wait. During the autumn his army melted away, as New England's citizen-soldiers went home to bring in the harvest. The departures at least eased his problems of supply, for he was critically short of food, clothing, and tents. At one point during the winter, Washington, the besieger, had fewer men than Howe, the besieged.

In February 1776, Washington received some welcome reinforcement—cannons— which had been dragged through the win-

Courtesy of Fort Ticonderoga and the Joseph Dixon Crucible Company.

"The Noble Train of Artillery," by Thomas Lowell, shows Americans dragging Ticonderoga's guns across New England on sleds to Washington's army.

ter snows of New England on sleds from Fort Ticonderoga on Lake Champlain. The fort had been captured in the early days of fighting by Ethan Allen, leader of a band of frontiersmen known as the Green Mountain Boys, and by Benedict Arnold, a Connecticut merchant turned general. Washington mounted the artillery on Dorchester Heights, just to the south of Boston, a site that gave him command of the harbor. The British evacuated on March 17 and sailed to Halifax, Nova Scotia, for rest and recuperation.

AN ASYLUM FOR MANKIND

As the conflict intensified, the absurdity of fighting *against* the empire to preserve their rights *within* the empire gradually dawned upon Americans. In January 1776, a pamphlet published in Philadelphia, entitled *Common Sense*, boldly advocated political independence. The author was Thomas Paine, a recent emigrant from Britain whom Benjamin Franklin had encouraged to come to America. A natural propagandist, Paine put the argument for independence in language everyone could understand. He pointed out how odd it was for a continent to be ruled by an island. With heavy-handed sarcasm, he traced the history of the English monarchy to demonstrate the absurdity of choosing rulers by heredity. Paine not only wanted independence; he wanted a republic. And in breathtaking prose he affirmed the American mission in the world:

> O! ye that love mankind! Ye that dare oppose not only the tyranny but the tyrant, stand forth! Every spot of the world is overrun with oppression. Freedom hath been hunted round the globe. Asia and Africa have long expelled her. Europe regards her like a stranger, and England hath given her warning to depart. O! receive the fugitive, and prepare in time an asylum for mankind.

In April 1776, the North Carolina Provincial Congress approved a resolution favoring independence; other assemblies in the South and in New England followed suit. The middle colonies were more hesitant. On June 7, 1776, Richard Henry Lee of Virginia rose in the Continental Congress to offer a resolution "that these United Colonies are, and of right ought to be, free and independent states." Lee's resolution also called for the forming of "foreign alliances" and a "plan of confederation." While delegates from the middle colonies awaited instructions from their assemblies, the congress appointed a committee that included Thomas Jefferson, John Adams, and Benjamin Franklin to draft a declaration. The committee asked Jefferson, who had already demonstrated a flair with the quill, to undertake a rough draft.

The opening sentence of the Declaration of Independence reflected the results of a decade and a half of imperial controversy. "When in the course of human events," Jefferson began, "it becomes necessary for one people to dissolve the political bands which have connected them with another . . ." The British were "another" people. The revolution of mind and heart had already taken place.

Jefferson then launched into the rationale for political revolution. Government, he explained, originated in the need to protect humanity's fundamental rights, and when it failed in that obligation, it was the duty of the people to alter or abolish it. The remainder of the Declaration was a long list of British misdeeds. Some of these were genuine American grievances, others half-truths (for example, the accusation that Britain imposed slavery on the colonies) inserted for their shock appeal. Jefferson directed his indictment not at Parliament, whose authority over America he had long since denied, but at the king, the ruler of the empire and the last tie between colonies and mother country. "And for the support of this Declaration," Jefferson concluded, "with a firm reliance on the protection of divine Providence, we mutually pledge to each other our Lives, our Fortunes, and our sacred Honor."

On July 2, the Congress passed Lee's resolution, and two days later it approved, with only minor changes, Jefferson's draft. New York, whose provincial congress agonized over the issue, gave its approval five days later, making its passage unanimous. Americans had a new war aim: independence. On July 2, 1776, the day that the Continental Congress approved Richard Henry Lee's resolution, a British fleet bearing Howe's army sailed into New York harbor. It was an instant reminder that proclaiming independence was only the first step; independence now had to be won. Howe had spent the spring in Nova Scotia, recuperating and rebuilding his army. The British ministry, abandoning for the moment further thoughts of conciliation, sent him 9,000 Hessian mercenaries. The force that Howe disembarked onto Staten Island totaled some 30,000 in all.

But Washington had anticipated the move. New York was centrally located, offering the British a base from which to range far into the American interior. It had the finest natural harbor on the Atlantic coast, and its population was rumored to be loyal to the crown, or at least neutral. Washington began moving his troops as soon as the British left Boston. The site he chose for the defense of New York was a rise of land called Brooklyn Heights at the western end of Long Island. He dug in, hoping to turn the action into another Breed's Hill.

Howe crossed over to Long Island in mid-August. Instead of a frontal attack on Washington, he sent his ablest lieutenant, Lord Cornwallis, on a wide flank attack that caught Washington utterly by surprise. The Battle of Long Island on August 27, 1776, was an American rout. Both armies rested for two days, and then Washington escaped, rowing with his army across to Manhattan at night past the British ships lying in the East River. When Howe landed on Manhattan on September 15, the American troops guarding the beach panicked and fled, and Washington retreated northward through Harlem to White Plains.

Cornwallis then attacked the American forts guarding the Hudson River midway up Manhattan Island. Washington, unsure

Washington crossing the Delaware. This famous painting was done in 1848 by Emanuel Leutze, who had grown up in America but returned to his native Germany at the age of 22. He painted it in Dusseldorf, using German students as models. One humorist has suggested that the painting ought to be titled "Washington Crossing the Rhine."

New York Public Library Picture Collection.

of his next move, crossed to the New Jersey side of the river in a hesitant effort to relieve one of the forts. Cornwallis turned and started after Washington, who fled west across New Jersey. Arriving at the Delaware River on December 1, Washington seized all the available boats and crossed to the safety of Pennsylvania.

Cornwallis was ready to call it quits for the year: The campaigning season was over, and it was time for winter quarters. Armies rarely campaigned in winter because of poor road conditions and the lack of forage for horses. Cornwallis installed 1,300 Hessians at Trenton as an advance base from which the British expected to descend on Philadelphia the following year. He set up supply bases at Princeton and New Brunswick and returned to New York for a winter round of festivities with New York's loyalists.

Washington, however, was in desperate straits. Large segments of his army were still in White Plains, New York; the force with him had melted to 5,000 in the race across New Jersey, and the enlistments of many of those expired at the end of the year. At this critical juncture, Thomas Paine sharpened his quill and put it once more to service. His pamphlet *The Crisis* appeared in mid-December. "These are the times that try men's soul's," Paine warned:

> The summer soldier and the sunshine patriot will, in this crisis, shrink from the service of his country; but he that stands it now, deserves the love and thanks of man and woman. Tyranny, like Hell, is not easily conquered; yet we have this consolation with us that the harder the conflict, the more glorious the triumph.

The ink on Paine's appeal was scarcely dry when Pennsylvania militia, aroused by the threat to their homes, flocked to Washington's camp. With a reinforced army, Washington decided to attack. On the night of December 25 he slipped across the Delaware River and descended on Trenton,

capturing the entire garrison with scarcely a shot. He then returned to Pennsylvania with his prisoners. When word of the Trenton raid reached New York, Cornwallis rushed out, assembling an army as he went. Washington boldly recrossed the river, and while Cornwallis dashed down one road toward Trenton, Washington took another and fell on Princeton. Washington burned the supply base and retired north to the hill country near Morristown, satisfied at last to go into winter quarters.

Since Washington's presence at Morristown was still a menace to the British supply line, Cornwallis evacuated his forward bases and returned to New York. In a brilliant campaign of ten days, Washington had undone everything the British had accomplished since August. General Howe was back where he started—in control of New York City and little else. Next time, he would go to Philadelphia by sea.

⊔1777: Turning Point

With a little imagination, one could see a gallows in a drawing of the number seven, and to have three of them in one year seemed ominous indeed to Americans mindful of the fate of revolutionaries who fail. Had they been privy to British plans as that year opened, their concern would have deepened. The Colonial Secretary, Lord George Germain, concocted for the first time a comprehensive plan for reducing the colonies to submission. The strategy grew out of the American failure to win over the "fourteenth colony," Canada.

Early in the revolution, Congress had authorized a two-pronged assault on Canada. One force, led by General Richard Montgomery, struck toward Montreal by way of Lake Champlain. The other, commanded by Benedict Arnold, descended on Quebec by way of the Kennebec River in Maine. For heroism and hardship, the American venture into Canada is unsur-

The Saratoga Campaign, 1777.

passed in the annals of warfare. But it failed, largely because most Canadians remained loyal to Britain. In a final assault on Quebec on New Year's Eve, 1775, Montgomery was killed, Arnold wounded, and General Dan Morgan, commander of the Virginia riflemen, captured. In the course of 1776 the British and Canadians chased the ragged American army back up the St. Lawrence River to Lake Champlain.

General John Burgoyne, who had accompanied the British force that drove the Americans from Canada, returned to London in the winter of 1776–1777 to secure support for a new British strategy. He wanted to lead an invasion of New York by way of Lake Champlain with a fresh army of 6,000. Following the Hudson River south, Burgoyne would link up with the British army in New York, thereby severing the colonies in two. Colonial Secretary Germain agreed, and he also approved General Howe's proposal to descend on Philadelphia in 1777. The British strategy

presented a dismal prospect for Americans in 1777.

Burgoyne's thrust through the heart of New York, together with Howe's capture of Philadelphia, might well have broken the Americans. Even so the British scheme had flaws, not least of which was the failure to take into account American conditions—the vast stretches of landscape and the undetected legions of citizen-soldiers. Burgoyne's march was the dramatic pinnacle of the war. He had to be stopped, yet there was no organized force in his way. Washington felt obliged to follow Howe south to Philadelphia. The drama, moreover, was played against the superb backdrop of the Adirondack Mountains, tinged with autumn reds as the action reached a climax. The principal was "Gentleman Johnny" Burgoyne, a haughty aristocrat and shrewd tactician, accompanied by some disciplined regulars, assorted Canadians and Indians, and a baggage train filled with the general's spare uniforms and choice wines. Opposing him was a ragged, untrained assemblage of New England and New York farmers—a "rabble in arms," sneered Burgoyne.

Getting under way in June 1777, Burgoyne swept down Lake Champlain, captured Ticonderoga, and moved into the Hudson River Valley. As he proceeded, the alarm sounded across New England, and thousands of flintlock-bearing farmers converged on Albany. New Hampshire and Vermont militiamen filtered behind Burgoyne and harassed his supply line. Congress appointed General Horatio Gates to command, a nomination that unfortunately overlooked the claim to the position that Benedict Arnold rightfully had. Gates stationed his army on Bemis Heights, a high ground adjacent to the Hudson River that overlooked the open expanse of Freeman's Farm. Burgoyne appeared in mid-September, and an opening skirmish of September 19 ended inconclusively, largely because Gates refused to leave his hill.

In the following days Burgoyne built

New York Public Library Picture Collection.

Women at war. The journals kept by soldiers on Benedict Arnold's march to Quebec talk of two women, the wives of soldiers, who accompanied the expedition and shared its hardships. This nineteenth-century re-creation has them helping to push boats up the Kennebec.

earthworks for protection while the American commanders, Gates and Arnold, quarreled about tactics. Arnold wanted to attack and was so insistent that he was relieved of his command. On October 7 the British opened the second battle of Freeman's Farm with a flanking movement. Virginia riflemen moved to counteract it, and there was a momentary stalemate until Arnold flashed onto the field on a great brown horse. "Follow me, boys!" he yelled, "and we'll have them all in Hell by nightfall!" The American army streamed down the hill and slammed into the British earthworks, capturing one of them. Arnold was wounded in the leg in the melee.* Burgoyne retired to a prearranged defensive position, and ten days later, at the nearby

village of Saratoga, he surrendered his entire army.

Howe's campaign fared somewhat better. To avoid crossing New Jersey, which had proved disastrous the previous year, Howe proceeded to Philadelphia by sea. He sailed in July 1777, leaving Sir Henry Clinton in command of New York. Suspecting Howe's intent, Washington moved south, leaving enough troops behind to keep Clinton bottled in New York. Howe landed in Chesapeake Bay, defeated Washington at Brandywine on September 11 by using the same flanking tactics that had worked so well on Long Island, and slipped into Philadelphia. In October, Washington attempted to reenact his Trenton success with a surprise raid on a British outpost at Germantown. But the attack failed, the victim of poor timing and bad luck. Washington then retired some 25 miles west to Valley Forge and went into winter quarters.

---

* There is a monument to Benedict Arnold's leg today on the Saratoga battlefield. It was the patriot part of him; the rest turned traitor.

Benjamin Franklin, serving as American envoy to France, maintained a bold front when he learned that Howe had taken Philadelphia, the American capital. "I beg your pardon, sir," was his reply. "Philadelphia has taken Howe." In truth, that proved to be the case. Howe controlled nothing but the city; he was as isolated as Burgoyne was in upstate New York. The following year the British army evacuated the city and returned to New York.

THE REVOLUTION BECOMES A WORLD WAR

Congress early in the war had recognized the need for foreign aid and saw in France, Britain's old imperial rival, a likely benefac-

tor. In 1776, Congress sent to Paris a three-man delegation—Benjamin Franklin, Silas Deane, and Arthur Lee—to seek money and munitions. French Foreign Minister Vergennes, eager to embarrass Britain, agreed to furnish secret aid, but until he had some evidence of the Americans' staying power, he refused to commit France openly to the American cause. When the news of Saratoga reached Paris, Vergennes offered a formal military alliance, and Franklin accepted. France declared war on Britain in May 1778. Spain, France's traditional family ally, entered the war a year later on France's promise that Spain might recover Florida and Gibraltar. Spain fought only as an ally of France, however. Suspicious of American republicanism, it declined any association with the United

Molly Pitcher. Her real name was Mary Hays, and she was a water carrier at the Battle of Monmouth, which was fought on a blistering summer day in June 1778. Legend has it that when her husband was wounded she took his place at the cannon.

The Bettmann Archive, Inc.

States. The British, angered at the Dutch willingness to trade with Americans, declared war on the Netherlands in 1780. By then the revolution had become a world war.

From the outset, a steady stream of European professional soldiers had come to America to offer their services. Some gave Washington no end of trouble because they demanded military commands that placed them above American officers, a situation that produced resentment and led to a number of resignations. But many valuable services were provided by the Europeans, among them the Polish cavalry tactician Casimir Pulaski, fortifications engineer Thaddeus Kosciusko, and the young French aristocrat Marquis de Lafayette, whom Washington came to regard as his best lieutenant.

Another such foreign officer appeared at Washington's winter camp at Valley Forge. He identified himself as Baron von Steuben, a general in the armies of Frederick the Great of Prussia. Although he exaggerated his rank (he was a captain) and his title (he had none), he made a good impression on Washington because he asked for nothing but to be helpful. Washington was impressed enough to make him inspector general and to ask him to train his army. Von Steuben's task was not easy, since Americans did not take kindly to military discipline, but he eased them into it with colorful expressions and considerable profanity, all in a mixture of French and German. Each day's lesson, written out laboriously in French, was translated into English and printed on the army's lone press. He taught the soldiers the musket drill for systematic loading and firing; he taught them how to march in step to avoid straggling; and he showed them how to deploy from marching column to line of battle. In von Steuben's hands, Washington's continentals became a European-style professional army, and they never lost again in the open field of battle.

THE WAR MOVES TO THE SOUTH, 1778–1781

General Howe turned over his command to Sir Henry Clinton in 1778 and headed for home. Clinton, who had never approved the Philadelphia venture, moved the British army back to New York that summer, fighting an inconclusive battle with Washington at Monmouth, New Jersey, on the way. Thereafter the war in the north subsided into a siege of New York, the tedium relieved only by Benedict Arnold's attempt to betray West Point in 1780. Arnold's plot failed; he escaped to British lines, and his confederate, Major John André, was caught and executed as a British spy.

Clinton's new objective was the south, and the shift was overdue. The southern colonies had been far more valuable to the British than the northern because they produced staples—tobacco, rice, indigo—that Britain needed. In the Carolinas, moreover, there were a large number of newly arrived Scots who were known to be loyal and waiting for an opportunity to help Britain. North Carolina loyalists had taken up arms in 1776 and were decisively defeated at Moore's Creek Bridge. The British had made an unsuccessful feint at Charleston in 1776; Clinton now resolved on a full-scale campaign. The British landed at Savannah in December 1778 and quickly made themselves masters of Georgia. After a year of maneuvering through the swamps of low-country South Carolina, they trapped an American army in Charleston and forced its surrender. This surrender of 5,000 men was the greatest American defeat of the war (and the largest in any foreign war until Bataan in 1942).

Feeling his campaign completed, Clinton left Cornwallis in command and returned to New York. Congress created a new army in the south and named Horatio Gates its commander. Cornwallis smashed

Southern campaigns, 1780–1781.

that army at Camden in August 1780 and set up a chain of garrison posts to keep South Carolina under control. Congress then asked Washington to designate a new commander, and Washington selected the best man he had, Nathanael Greene of Rhode Island, a bookseller before the war.

Through the early months of 1781, Greene played cat-and-mouse with Cornwallis through the pine woods of North Carolina. Whenever Cornwallis came close to trapping him, Greene skipped into Virginia. Cornwallis became convinced that he could not hope to hold the Carolinas under

subjection without crushing Virginia. Serene and untouched by war, Virginia was a reservoir of men and supplies for the American armies. In April 1781, Cornwallis started north into Virginia. Instead of tracking him, Greene headed for South Carolina to recapture the outposts Cornwallis had left behind.

Unfortunately for Virginia, Greene's action left it helpless. Its plight was worsened by the presence of a British naval squadron in Chesapeake Bay commanded by the zealous turncoat Benedict Arnold, who was burning and plundering at will. Washing-

Metropolitan Museum of Art, New York.

"I have not yet begun to fight." This was the famous reply of Captain John Paul Jones when the British captain asked him to surrender. The battle between Jones's *Bon Homme Richard* (named after Benjamin Franklin's pseudonym "Poor Richard") and the British warship *Serapis* took place on September 23, 1779, off the coast of France. Jones went on to win after a three-hour fight. After the British surrendered, Jones transferred his crew from the *Richard*, which was a sinking inferno, and sailed the *Serapis* into a French port.

ton sent Lafayette with a few regiments to keep an eye on the British commander, but Lafayette was not strong enough to offer battle. After a summer's rampage, Cornwallis retired to Yorktown on the York River to await supplies and reinforcements from New York. Lafayette settled in Williamsburg and wrote Washington to suggest that they might have Cornwallis trapped if Washington brought the main army south quickly. Lafayette's letter coincided with a note to Washington from French Admiral de Grasse saying the French fleet would be in American waters that autumn. Washington asked the French to proceed to the Chesapeake and quickly marched his own army south, leaving a token force around New York. Within two weeks, the combined French and American armies had Cornwallis under siege. The French warships turned back the British relief squadron in a pitched bat-

tle off the Capes, and after losing several redoubts to the encroaching allies, Cornwallis surrendered on October 19, 1781. The fighting was over.

⊔ The Path to Peace

The Continental Congress had originally instructed Benjamin Franklin and his cohorts in Paris to secure financial aid from France, but not a military alliance. There were those who had been not at all happy when Franklin had violated his instructions and signed the treaty of alliance. Purists such as Samuel Adams and Thomas Paine had fretted about the corrupting influence of a decadent European monarchy.* As a

---

* In fact, the only bit of European corruption the French introduced to America was the practice of dueling with pistols. In America, it evolved into the frontier gunfight.

result, Congress delayed sending further instructions to Franklin concerning American aims in a peace settlement.

Forced to mark time, Franklin moved to the Parisian suburb of Passy, pursued a romance or two, tinkered with his electrical experiments, became fascinated with hot-air balloons, and developed a stock answer to all queries concerning peace. Peace would be easy, he would say; the British need merely concede independence. Reconciliation and friendship were something else. Americans had suffered much injury; they deserved recompense. The cession of Canada and Florida would do nicely, he would suggest, eyes twinkling through bifocals, his latest invention.

CRISES AT HOME, BARGAINING ABROAD

Congress, in fact, was too preoccupied with other problems to give much thought to peace. Most pressing among these by 1780 was money. Congress had financed the war in the way the colonies had earlier financed the French wars—by issuing paper money. States had also issued paper money of their own. The various currencies were accepted at first, but as the printing presses continued to crank, the value of the money declined. By the end of 1779, the economy was awash in a sea of paper. The situation was desperate enough to set Tom Paine to work on another "Crisis" essay.

In the emergency, new leaders surfaced in Congress. "Nationalists" is as good a description of them as any, because for some years they had been searching for ways to strengthen the powers of Congress. The group included conservatives, among them John Jay and Robert R. Livingston of New York, who had dragged their feet on independence in 1776. These men had wanted to create a strong federal government *before* declaring independence to prevent any possibility of social disorder. The most important member of this contingent was Robert Morris, a wealthy Philadelphia merchant who during the war had received and distributed French arms and other supplies sent to America.

The nationalist program was threefold. First, to restore public faith in government paper, they issued new bills and offered to exchange them for the old at the ratio of forty old dollars for one new. Second, they persuaded Congress to set up the Office of Finance, with Morris as secretary. And third, they had Congress charter a bank, the Bank of North America, which would loan the government money and help finance the war. Morris, who had a better credit rating than the government, even issued bills of his own. The program worked, and the money crisis eased.

A further reform enacted by the nationalists in Congress was the creation of the Office of Foreign Affairs, with Robert R. Livingston as secretary. The initial task of this forerunner of the Department of State was to negotiate a peace settlement. The military situation in 1780 was not bright, and the nationalists were less mistrustful of France than some earlier leaders of Congress had been (Samuel Adams retired in 1779). So Benjamin Franklin was instructed to follow the lead of France—let the French get what they could for America at the peace table. Franklin realized that this was a prescription for disaster. The French might secure American independence, but they would not win much territory. It was not in France's interest to create an American colossus. Vergennes might even demand the return of Louisiana as the price for French support. So Franklin resolved to ignore the French when the opportunity came to talk peace—which Washington's victory at Yorktown presented. The North ministry resigned in the spring of 1782. Franklin knew the new British colonial secretary and wrote to him; the secretary sent a secret agent to Paris. Franklin summoned John Adams, who was in the Hague, and John Jay, who was in Madrid, to join the talks.

New York Public Library Picture Collection.

Surrender of Cornwallis. This painting by Jonathan Trumbull was sketched shortly after the Revolution but not completed until 1820. It was commissioned by Congress to decorate the capitol, which had to be rebuilt after the British burned the building in 1814. Trumbull served as aide-de-camp to Washington early in the Revolution and studied in London under Benjamin West after the war.

A preliminary agreement was reached in November 1782. The British agreed to American independence and promised to evacuate their armies. The boundaries of the new nation would extend north to the Great Lakes (the New England border was sketched on a rough and inaccurate map), west to the Mississippi River, and south to Florida (the thirty-first parallel of latitude). Securing the Great Lakes and the Mississippi was a major diplomatic achievement. In 1778, George Rogers Clark had led a force of 175 frontiersmen into the Illinois country and captured the British-held outposts of Vincennes on the Wabash River and Kaskaskia on the Mississippi. When a British raiding party from Detroit recap-

tured Vincennes, Clark crossed southern Illinois in the dead of winter to clear the British out once again. It was a gallant effort, but the British still held Detroit and other posts on the Great Lakes at the end of the war. Franklin's diplomacy finished what Clark had started.

The Anglo-American negotiators left a number of thorny issues for future settlement. Americans, especially Virginians, owed a substantial amount of money to British merchants. Franklin resisted any promise of repayment; in the end, the treaty stipulated only that the states would open their courts to British lawsuits. Merchants would have to recover their own debts. Loyalists were another difficulty, because the states had confiscated the property of those who had fled to Canada or to Britain. British negotiators demanded that the property be restored or the loyalists be paid for it. Franklin skirted this issue because the states had sold much of the property to finance the war. In the end, the treaty merely prohibited the states from further seizures.

The Peace of Paris, 1783. Once the preliminary articles were signed, the American commissioners sent Franklin to inform Vergennes. It was a delicate mission, since under the alliance Franklin and Vergennes had signed in 1778, each side had agreed not to make peace without the other. Vergennes, who had an extensive spy network,

North America in 1783.

- English
- French
- Spanish
- United States

already knew of the double-cross, and he greeted Franklin with chilly formality. Franklin shrewdly pointed out that it would be harmful if the British thought there was a rift in the Franco-American alliance. The French and the Americans must keep up a show of unity at the public peace conference. Vergennes agreed and cautiously asked how this might be achieved. Franklin, with straight face, suggested that another loan of about 6 million livres would surely do it.* And so the packet vessel that carried the terms of the Anglo-American accord also carried French gold for the empty coffers of the Continental Congress.

The Anglo-American articles were ultimately incorporated into the world settlement, the Treaty of Paris, signed on September 3, 1783. In this agreement Britain ceded to Spain the territory south of the thirty-first parallel—East Florida, which had been Spanish before 1763, and West Florida, the Gulf Coast from Mobile to New Orleans, which had been part of French Louisiana. Britain retained Canada, and Russia owned Alaska. The rest of North America was divided between the United States and Spain.

⊔ The Revolution Within: Democratic Change

"The American war is over," wrote Philadelphia physician Benjamin Rush shortly after the fighting stopped. "But this is far from being the case with the American revolution. On the contrary, nothing but the first act of the great drama is closed." Patriots such as Rush felt they were engaged

---

* The French livre was about equal in value to the Spanish dollar, or piece of eight. The latter coin, which became common in America as a result of the West Indies trade, ultimately became the American unit of currency.

in something far more significant than a simple colonial rebellion, that their revolution was the first step in the regeneration of all humanity. They considered themselves something new on the world scene— a society of free propertyowners, equal before the law and equal in the eyes of one another. They perceived Europe as an inherently corrupt society in which feudal oligarchies, governments controlled by a small faction of persons or families, lorded over the landless, ignorant masses. "In monarchies," declared David Ramsey, patriot-historian of South Carolina, "favor is the source of preferment; but, in our new forms of government, no one can command the suffrages of the people, unless by his superior merit and capacity." At the heart of this "new form of government" was the "man of virtue," the disinterested citizen who labored for the common weal and not for private interest.

The implications of this ideology were radical indeed, but not all of them were immediately evident. The revolution reordered American society in many ways, but it also left much of the old. The revolution was indeed only the first act in the great drama of American democracy.

The Revolution and Social Status.

Among the changes wrought by the revolution were those in the social composition of government. Each of the colonies had been governed by a narrow elite of merchants and landowners. In Virginia, for instance, the same three men had occupied the key posts of treasurer, attorney general, and speaker of the house for nearly twenty years before the revolution. Many officials had fled at the outset of the revolution, although by no means all, and the "popular" leaders who replaced them were men of smaller fortune and lesser social status. The new state governments were sprinkled with farmers, shopkeepers, and tradesmen, even though most leadership positions continued to be occupied by the wealthy, the genteel, and the educated.

The revolution also affected the composition of American society. An estimated half-million Americans (20 percent) remained loyal to Great Britain after independence. Those with governmental positions lost their offices; those who had fought with the British or had fled abroad lost their property. Some sixty to eighty thousand loyalists had gone to Canada or Great Britain during the war, and their departure had created opportunities for others. In New York and New England, a disproportionate number were merchants or professionals, and although many of these returned from exile after the war, few recovered their wealth and status. Not all loyalists were wealthy. In the south, most were small farmers, many of them recent emigrants from Scotland. Nevertheless, the departure or disgrace of a substantial segment of the population caused some rearrangement of the American social structure.

The Revolution and the Land.

The revolution also brought some modest changes in landholding. Most families in prerevolutionary America had owned land or town houses, but there had also been huge chunks of land set aside for the privileged few. In New York and Maryland substantial numbers of tenant farmers worked the estates of the wealthy. During the revolution, the New England states seized forest preserves that had been set aside for the crown, the proprietary states grabbed the holdings of the Penn and Calvert families, and all the states confiscated property to finance the war. Much of it ended up in the hands of wealthy men who had the money to purchase it. Many of these speculators, however, broke the great estates into smaller parcels and resold them as soon as they could. Thus the revolution produced considerable redistribution of land

and led to some tentative steps toward agrarian democracy.

Economic Impact of the Revolution.

The revolution meant economic opportunity for many Americans. Both armies had to be fed. French (who arrived in 1780) and British troops regularly paid for their supplies in gold or silver coin. The farmers of southern New England, New York, and New Jersey, where troops were stationed throughout the war, prospered handsomely. Wartime demand for uniforms, boots, tents, blankets, and guns created new prospects for American artisans. A familiar example is teenage Eli Whitney, famed for his later invention of the cotton gin, developing a nail manufacturing business on his father's farm when the supply of European nails was cut off by the war.

For others the war was a financial disaster. The American economy, especially in the southern colonies, was dependent on foreign trade. British warships in the Chesapeake and British occupation of Charleston destroyed southern commerce in the last years of the war. Tobacco and rice rotted on the wharves while planters struggled to feed their slave labor force. The fighting, which in parts of the South amounted to a civil war of American against American, also caused widespread destruction. And independence itself was a mixed blessing. In 1783, the British government issued an order in council prohibiting American trade with the islands of the British West Indies. Understandably enough, the British felt that once Americans had fled the empire, they were not entitled to its privileges. This Navigation Act was particularly hard on New England, where the exchange of lumber and fish for Caribbean sugar and rum was an economic mainstay. A simple statistic tells the tale. By one recent estimate the per capita product in 1774 was $804 (in 1980 dollars). In 1790 that same output was $437. These figures are only estimates, but if they are anywhere near accurate, the revolution cut the standard of living for most Americans nearly in half. It is generally reckoned that Americans did not regain the living standard of the early 1770s until the end of the century. Ironically, the prosperity then was due primarily to a new outbreak of fighting between Britain and France, which opened new trade outlets for Americans in the West Indies and Europe.

The Revolution and Slavery.

Blacks benefited from the revolution more than any other group, in part because they had the most to gain. Colonial Americans had taken slavery for granted, viewing it as part of the natural order of things. Revolutionary Americans wondered if slavery was incompatible with the notion of human equality. Many began to view it as an aberration, a "peculiar institution" that, even if it were to be preserved, would have to be justified and defended. The first abolition society, founded in Philadelphia on the eve of the revolution, was Quaker in inspiration. Its secretary, Dr. Benjamin Rush, although not a Quaker, was a deeply religious man who viewed the revolution as an opportunity to cleanse American society of its impurities. Revolutionary idealism added a secular dimension to antislavery. In 1785 the first secular antislavery society was organized in New York; by 1790 there were antislavery societies in every state except the Carolinas and Georgia, although their membership was small.

During and after the revolution, every northern state either abolished slavery or adopted a program of gradual emancipation. Vermont led the way in 1777 with a constitutional provision abolishing slavery. Massachusetts appended a Bill of Rights to its 1780 Constitution containing the statement that all men are born free. Quock Walker, a Boston slave, appealed to the state supreme court, contending that

The Revolution and Slavery

In 1783, Nathaniel Jennison was indicted by a Massachusetts court for criminal assault on Quock Walker, a black. Jennison's defense was that he was entitled to beat Walker because Walker was his slave. This required the state's Supreme Judicial Court to rule on the legality of slavery under the Massachusetts constitution of 1780.

> . . . But whatever sentiments have formerly prevailed in this particular or slid in upon us by the example of others, a different idea has taken place with the people of America, more favorable to the natural rights of mankind, and to that natural, innate desire of liberty, which with Heaven (without regard to color, complexion, or shape of noses-features) has inspired all the human race. And upon this ground our Constitution of Government, by which the people of this Commonwealth have solemnly bound themselves, sets out with declaring that all men are born free and equal—and that every subject is entitled to liberty, and to have it guarded by the laws, as well as life and property—and in short is totally repugnant to the idea of being born slaves. This being the case, I think the idea of slavery is inconsistent with our own conduct and Constitution; and there can be no such thing as perpetual servitude of a rational creature, unless his liberty is forfeited by some criminal conduct. . . .

Source: Chief Justice Cushing, *Walker v. Jennison*, 1783.

the clause ended slavery in Massachusetts, and the court agreed. Connecticut, Rhode Island, and the middle states adopted programs of gradual emancipation. Most provided for the freeing of slave children when they reached a certain age. New York's program was so gradual that there were still a few slaves in the state as late as the 1820s.

Every southern state except South Carolina and Georgia prohibited the further import of blacks from Africa, a move that reflected both humanitarianism and the selfish desire to maintain the domestic price of slaves. But only Virginia moved against the institution of slavery. Virginia passed a law permitting private manumission and required that all slaves brought into the state be freed within one year. All states except South Carolina and Georgia had offered freedom to any slave who enlisted in the revolutionary army, and thousands had accepted. But the biggest instrument of emancipation had been the British army. Southerners estimated that the British had taken as many as 25,000 slaves from their plantations during the war. Since most of these had subsequently been set free (some, in fact, had been repatriated to Africa), it seems likely that they had been runaways who had fled into British camps in search of freedom. Southerners denied this idea and demanded compensation. Virginians used these losses as an excuse to delay payment of prewar debts owed to British merchants, thus complicating British-American relations in the postwar period.

THE REVOLUTION WITHIN: LIBERAL REFORM

The American Revolution, some have observed, was the first in a series of "liberal" revolutions that rocked the Western world between 1776 and 1848. Among the similar uprisings were the French Revolution

CLIO'S FOCUS: Daughters of the Revolution

In colonial America, a young girl grew up in a very narrow world. While her brothers went away to school, or traveled to market towns to learn a trade, she rarely went farther than the nearest neighbors. She was expected to marry and bear children, and her youth was devoted to preparation for this destiny. An endless round of household chores with little or no education inevitably meant a life of dullness and drudgery. Women accepted this routine, with a joyless fatalism, as an obligation conferred by birth—or, as one put it, "a part of the curse denounced upon Eve." Even the occupations of single women (nearly all of whom were widows) reflected the focus on domesticity. They were spinsters or seamstresses, they kept inns or boardinghouses, they specialized in dressmaking or midwifery. Those who swerved from the norm, by managing a print shop or a plantation, were nearly always carrying on the business of a deceased husband. Abigail Adams, who had a high sense of her personal worth, was a rarity. Most women deprecated themselves (one described her letters as "insipid scribbles") and their "humble duties."

The revolution was an awakening for women, just as it was for the masses of humble men who participated in riots or joined the Sons of Liberty. The boycott of British goods, which was one of the principal weapons against British transgression, launched the household into the center of politics. Nonimportation could not work unless women altered their buying and consumption habits while increasing their homespun production. Politicians and public printers recognized this and made candid appeals for support. The keeper of home and hearth commanded a new respect.

Women responded with patriotic zeal. They even organized a Daughters of Liberty to coordinate the boycott. Although short-lived, it was the first multiple-branched women's association. The revolution heightened women's interest in politics and diplomacy. Those fortunate enough to read and write perused newspapers and plied their husbands for information.

During the war, military recruitment created labor shortages in some areas, and women moved out of the household to fill the vacuum. Abigail Adams, while her husband was absent in Philadelphia, took over supervision of their farm, though she knew little of horticulture. "I believe I could gather corn and husk it," she confessed to John, "but I should make a poor figure at digging potatoes." Nevertheless, when her husband returned from the congressional session, he found the fields plowed and manured for spring planting, and the pasture fertilized with seaweed brought up from the beach. Abigail had hired help, rented an extra horse from her father, paid the yearly taxes, and even purchased an extra parcel of land on her own initiative. Her neighbors had fared as well, Abigail reported, in the absence of menfolk. They were even prepared to defend themselves. If General Howe, after evacuating Boston, returned to Massachusetts, Abigail predicted: "An army of women would oppose him." She assured her husband: "We possess a spirit that will not be conquered. If our men are drawn off and we should be attacked, you would find a race of Amazons in America."

Women had a chance to do just that when the British invaded the South in 1779–1780. After the fall of Charleston, South Carolina's fighting men took to the woods to fight as guerrillas, and the state government was in disarray. Women had to manage plantations, control the slave labor force, and keep the community functioning. Eliza Wilkinson, a resident of the sea islands, recalled after the war that when the British occupied South Carolina, "None were greater politicians than the several knots of ladies, who met together. All trifling discourse of fashions, and such low chat was thrown by, and we commenced perfect statesmen." New-found independence and broad responsibility were a heady combination. Eliza Wilkinson at least thought the wartime performance of women entitled them to political rights. Rebuffed, she exploded to a friend: "I won't have it thought that because we are the weaker sex as to *bodily* strength, . . . we are capable of nothing more than minding the dairy, visiting the poultry-house, and all such domestic concerns. . . . They won't even allow us the liberty of thought, and that is all I want. . . . Surely we may have sense enough to give our opinions to commend or discommend such actions as we may approve or disapprove; without being reminded of our spinning and household affairs as the only matters we are capable of thinking or speaking of with justness and propriety."

One woman, Mary Willing Byrd of Virginia, couched her appeal for equal rights in the same rhetoric that patriots had used against Britain. She proclaimed: "As a female, as the parent of eight children, as a virtuous citizen, as a friend to my Country . . . I have paid my taxes and have not been Personally or Virtually represented. My property is taken from me and I have no redress."

One state did experiment with women's suffrage after the war. The New Jersey constitution of 1776 gave the vote to "all free inhabitants," a grant that appeared to enfranchise free blacks as well as women. The phrase was probably a legislative oversight. Had the enfranchisement of blacks and women been intentional, there would have been more legislative debate and newspaper commentary. Nonetheless, both blacks and women who possessed the requisite amount of property availed themselves of the opportunity. In 1790 the state legislature acknowledged the practice by adopting an election law that referred to voters as "he or she." In 1797 Federalist women, voting in a bloc, were the decisive factor in the defeat of a Jeffersonian candidate for Congress. The Jeffersonian got his revenge a decade later when he guided through the legislature a law that disenfranchised both women and blacks. Thus ended the new nation's most interesting experiment in democracy.

Outside of New Jersey, there was little impulse during or after the revolution to alter the laws and customs that chained women to husbands and households. Even so, the self-respect won during the war revealed itself in subtle ways. The birth rate declined fairly dramatically in the postwar years, as women sought to free themselves from the debilitating round of pregnancy, childbirth, nursing, and new pregnancy. Divorce, another sign of female liberation, also increased quite dramatically in the postwar years—or at least it did in those states historians have had an opportunity to examine.

In 1791 there appeared in the *Columbian Magazine* a remarkable essay called "On the Supposed Superiority of the Masculine Understanding." The author, who signed herself simply "A Lady," presented for the first time in print the argument, central to feminism, that men and women were of equal mental capacities, that the supposed inferiority of women was due to defects in their education, deprecatory social customs, and legal discrimination. The essay was the opening salvo in the nineteenth-century women's rights movement, a full year ahead of the better-known *Vindication of the Rights of Woman* (1792) by the English radical Mary Wollstonecraft.

The feminist awakening, of course, was confined to a tiny minority of women, and it had little immediate impact on American thought or custom. Republican political thought stressed the importance of a virtuous citizenry, and women, as the traditional repositories of virtue, were accorded a central role in the process. But be it noted that the inculcation of virtue in children was simply an extension of women's traditional domestic duties. Commentators on the status and role of women in the republic assumed that women's destiny was to marry and have children and that the educational system ought to train girls for that goal. Women enhanced their self-respect during the revolution, and the household gained new significance in American political thought. But the long-run result was not true liberation but rather the nineteenth century's glorification of women's domestic role. The revolution laid a foundation for women's rights, but only that; the structure had yet to be built.

of 1789, the Latin American revolutions of 1810–1820, and the various European revolutions of 1820, 1830, and 1848. These liberal revolutions were generally middle class in origin; they led to the formation of republics, or at least constitutional monarchies; and they were liberal, or capitalistic, in economic philosophy.

Liberalism was rooted in the eighteenth-century Enlightenment. It sprang from the rationalist concept that human institutions ought to accord with reason, that things need not be accepted merely because they had been handed down from the past. Liberal revolutions thus commonly unleash a host of reformers who scrutinize the social skeleton, seeking ways of making government, religious bodies, educational systems, and law codes more comprehensible, more just, and more humane.

In America, the preeminent liberal reformer was Thomas Jefferson, who saw in the revolution the opportunity to restructure Virginia. In 1776, while serving in Congress, Jefferson had drafted for Virginia a state constitution containing a number of radical innovations, among them the idea of furnishing every household with 50 acres of land to make propertyholding universal. His draft, unfortunately, had been ignored by the Virginia convention, which preferred instead a more conservative rewriting of the colonial charter. Three years later, Jefferson served on an assembly committee that undertook a total overhaul of the state's law code. Jefferson thought the laws ought to be simplified and clarified so that they could be read and understood by all. He also wanted to eliminate such feudal relics as primogeniture (the passing of an estate only to the eldest son) and entail (restrictions that prevented the breakup of landed estates). Finally, he thought that the law ought to be more humane. Colonial Virginia had more than twenty crimes that rated the death penalty; Jefferson would have reduced the number to two, murder and treason. Not all of Jefferson's proposals won approval, although most were pushed through by James Madison after Jefferson was named American envoy to France in the 1780s. Nonetheless, his program served as a model for other states. Nearly all revised their law codes to eliminate penalties that maimed and to reduce the number of capital crimes.

Educational reform was also on Jefferson's agenda. In 1779 he presented the assembly with a comprehensive plan for publicly financed education for all children, male and female. Girls would not receive formal training beyond the elementary level in Jefferson's scheme, but for boys he provided a pyramid of educational advancement, at the peak of which was instruction at the College of William and Mary. The system was selective ("raking geniuses from the rubbish," as Jefferson put it) and was designed to provide trained leadership for a democratic society.

The Virginia assembly ignored Jefferson's education plan, but other states did make progress in the field. Five had constitutional provisions that made the state responsible for supervising education. Several states used the proceeds from the sale of loyalist property to set up school systems, but only Connecticut had a publicly

Virginia's Statute for Religious Freedom

As early as 1777 Thomas Jefferson, as a member of the Virginia assembly, drafted a bill to disestablish the Church of England in Virginia. Although the bill had the support of Presbyterians, Baptists, and Methodists, it took ten years to pass in what Jefferson characterized as "the severest contest in which I have ever been engaged." The bill was finally pushed through the assembly by James Madison after Jefferson had departed as American envoy to France. Informed of its passage, Jefferson exulted that Virginia's was "the first Legislature who has had the courage to declare that the reason of man may be trusted with the formation of his own opinions." Jefferson counted authorship of this measure, along with the Declaration of Independence and the founding of the University of Virginia, as the most important contributions of his life.

Be it enacted by the General Assembly, that no man shall be compelled to frequent or support any religious worship, place or ministry whatsoever, nor shall be enforced, restrained, molested, or burthened in his body or goods, nor shall otherwise suffer on account of his religious opinions or belief; but that all men shall be free to profess, and by argument to maintain, their opinion in matters of religion, and that the same shall in no wise diminish, enlarge, or affect their civil capacities. . . .

Source: Virginia, An Act for Establishing Religious Freedom, 1786.

financed system that was free and open to all. Higher education also expanded rapidly after the revolution. North Carolina opened the first state university in 1789, and by 1800 the nine colonial colleges tripled to twenty-seven.

Liberal revolutions were commonly anticlerical because the church was often seen as a pillar of the old order. In America the many churches that came into being after the Great Awakening provided additional incentive for disestablishment, or the separation of church and state. Presbyterians, Baptists, and Methodists engaged in bitter theological disputes, but they could all agree that no one church ought to have the support of government. As a result, the Church of England, which was the state church in New York and in the south, was disestablished everywhere during or shortly after the revolution. New England's state-connected Congregational Church fared somewhat better, however. New Hampshire, Massachusetts, and Connecticut retained their Congregational establishments for a generation after the war.

Although the church-state relationship was severed outside New England, no states except Rhode Island and Virginia achieved total religious freedom. Most Americans nevertheless felt that theirs was a Protestant country. New York, New Jersey, and the Carolinas banned Catholics and Jews from officeholding. Pennsylvania required that its officeholders believe in the divine inspiration of both Old and New Testaments, and Delaware required a belief in the Trinity. Virginia alone passed a statute committing itself to religious freedom, and again the author was Jefferson. The Statute for Religious Freedom (1786) guaranteed not only the right to believe but, equally important, the right to disbelieve.

The social revolution that accompanied the War for Independence, in summary, was limited in scope. Merchants and landowners were still in the seats of power. A few avenues of opportunity had been opened for the "lower orders" of society, but in a static preindustrial economy, opportunities were not many. Some slaves had been freed, but the vast majority of Afro-Americans remained in bondage, and their condition was soon to worsen, as southern agriculture turned to cotton. Nonetheless, American society was more liberal and more democratic after the revolution than before. A commitment to social progress had been made, and it was a foundation on which later generations could build.

SUMMARY

In its military aspects, the American Revolution was essentially a guerrilla war, though the term itself was not coined until some years later. In attempting to suppress the rebellion, Britain faced difficulties that have since become recognized as characteristic of such warfare—poor communications (the campaign of 1777), extended supply lines (Burgoyne, Cornwallis), isolated outposts that invited attack (Ticonderoga, Trenton, Germantown, Ninety-Six), and the sudden mobilization of masses of hostile farmers (Bunker Hill, Saratoga, King's Mountain). General George Washington, slow to comprehend the novelty of the military situation, trained his troops by European rules. While his men learned the art of war, Washington suffered a series of defeats (Long Island, Brandywine, Germantown), but he eventually earned a draw

(Monmouth) and a final victory (Yorktown). The latter was made possible by the aid of the French army and navy, which had been drawn into the war by a treaty of alliance (1778) negotiated by Benjamin Franklin.

At the peace table, the American negotiators won more territory than their armies had on the battlefield. The new republic embraced the eastern half of the continent south of the St. Lawrence River and the Great Lakes and east of the Mississippi. On its southern flank, the province of Florida was ceded by Britain to Spain.

The social changes that accompanied the revolution were neither violent nor far-reaching. The poorer elements of society, largely ignored by colonial officials, found themselves with new influence because of their role in the revolutionary movement.

But only Pennsylvania sought to give them the vote. Women too emerged with heightened consciousness of their importance, though they also remained without political power. Blacks likewise improved their condition, at least in the North, where the states undertook either immediate or gradual programs of emancipation.

Some land changed hands as Loyalist and crown estates were confiscated, broken up, and sold, but the wealthy remained firmly in control of the economic and social order. The revolution did present an opportunity, however, for liberal rationalists, such as Thomas Jefferson, to reform legal codes, improve education, and separate church from states. Though limited, the social revolution that accompanied the War for Independence was a foundation on which later generations could build.

READING SUGGESTIONS

The best military account of the American Revolution is Don Higgenbotham, *The War of American Independence* (1971), but Douglas S. Freeman's seven-volume biography of George Washington (volumes 4 and 5 of which deal with the revolution) also makes lively reading. The classic summary of the revolution within is J. Franklin Jameson, *The American Revolution Considered as a Social Movement* (1925), though Jameson's work has been updated by Jackson Turner Main, *The Sovereign States, 1775–1783* (1973). The ideology of the revolution has been explored by Gordon Wood in *The Creation of the American Republic, 1776–1787* (1969), although Linda Kerber argues in *Women of the Republic* (1980) that to understand the ideology of the revolution, one must understand its impact on women. Mary Beth Norton's *Liberty's Daughters: The Revolutionary Experience of American Women, 1750–1800* (1980) is also indispensable.

John J. McCusker and Russell R. Menard, *The Economy of British America, 1607–1789* (1985) is a treasurehouse of information, with some particularly interesting conclusions concerning the economic impact of the revolution, but it is not to be picked up for light reading. The impact of the revolution on blacks has been explored by Benjamin Quarles in *The Negro in the American Revolution* (1961), by Arthur Zilversmit in *The First Emancipation: The Abolition of Slavery in the North* (1967), and by D. L. Robinson in *Slavery in the Structure of American Politics, 1765–1820* (1971). The relationship between the revolution and American art and literature has recently been examined in two fine books: Kenneth Silverman, *A Cultural History of the American Revolution, 1763–1789* (1979), and Joseph J. Ellis, *After the Revolution: Profiles of Early American Culture* (1979). Jonathan R. Dull's *A Diplomatic History of the American Revolution* (1985) is a brief synthesis aimed at the general reader.

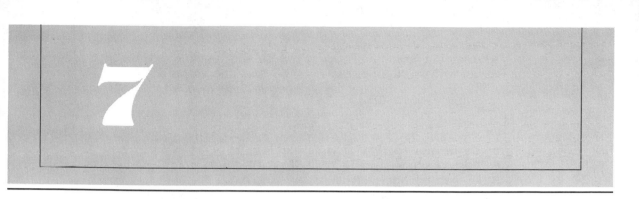

7

The Bettmann Archives.

E PLURIBUS UNUM:
1776–1788

The most remarkable feature of the American Revolution was the ease with which Americans slipped into independence. Except for the fighting on the battlefield, there was comparatively little violence. A few loyalists were tarred and feathered, but not one was executed or imprisoned for any length of time. The American Revolution, in short, was the most orderly of all modern revolutions. Part of the reason was the dominance of the middle class in American society. The colonies were not ruled by the feudal castes that inspired mass executions in the later French and Russian revolutions. The orderliness also rested on a common agreement on political ends: Americans assumed from the outset that theirs was more than a colonial uprising against empire; it was a republican revolution against monarchy.

The republican ideology itself was more presumed than discussed. No great political treatise emerged from the revolution, perhaps because none was needed. Even the Declaration of Independence, so its author later confessed, was nothing more than a compendium of generally accepted ideas. Americans entered the revolution with a fully formed concept of republicanism. The century-long contention between the colonial assemblies and imperial authority transformed the Whiggery of John Locke into a republican ideology. Lockean theory had centered on the balance of power between crown and Parliament. The colonial experience had involved contests between governors and assemblies.

As a result, the emerging republican ideology was hostile to executive power. Americans mistrusted executives, whether governors or presidents, as would-be kings. Legislators, in contrast, were seen as defenders of popular liberties, simultaneously strengthened and harnessed by close association with their constituents.

And, at bottom, the constituency, from which the republic derived its authority, was made up of propertyowners and taxpayers, free men who, ideally, could balance their own interests with the common good. The need to fill the governmental vacuum created by the collapse of royal authority in 1775–1776 presented an early opportunity to put theory into practice.

⊔Fourteen Republics*

It was almost inevitable that Americans would put their constitutions in written form. The English constitution was "unwritten" only in the sense that it was not codified; it was in fact a collection of documents from Magna Carta to the Bill of Rights. Each of these documents aimed to limit governmental power and define the rights of Englishmen. Americans, moreover, had long considered their written charters as bastions against royal tyranny and guarantors of their rights. Thus, as royal authority disintegrated in the winter of 1775–1776, the state provincial congresses began planning conventions to draft constitutions that would outline the state governments and define their powers.

The idea of a constitutional convention, on the other hand, was new—or at least largely untested. Such a convention functioned as a constituent authority, a First Cause in government; that is, it met exclusively for the purpose of creating a government and then was dissolved. It was the voice of the governed forming an elementary social contract. As a result, the docu-

---

* The original thirteen states plus Vermont, which freed itself from the claims of New York and New Hampshire, drafted a constitution in 1777, and entered the union in 1791.

(*Chapter opening photo*) Alexander Hamilton, by portrait artist John Trumbull.

ment it created was graced with higher authority. It was a fundamental law that could not be easily changed. A constitution provided a framework within which a lower order of law, legislative statutes, could meet the changing needs of the community. The constitutional convention also solved an elemental problem facing all revolutionaries—legitimacy—because it derived its constituent authority from the governed themselves.

STATE CONSTITUTIONS

Most of the state constitutions were drafted in 1776 and 1777, although Massachusetts delayed until 1780, and Connecticut and Rhode Island, content with their colonial charters, did not bother with constitutions until many years after the revolution. Not all states held conventions; in some, the pressures of war obliged the assemblies to undertake the task. In all cases, however, the constitutions in one way or another were submitted to the people for approval. Usually the ratifying electorate was broadened to include not just propertyowners but all white adult males. In one state, New Jersey, free black men and white women participated as well.

Although innovative, the constitutions bore the stamp of experience. For a century and more, the assemblies had been the bulwark of colonial rights because their members had considered themselves the agents of the people. The revolutionary constitutions gave the assemblies the central role in governing; in many states they even chose the governor and the judges. The governor, in the past the symbol of royal authority, became a mere figurehead. Governors were usually elected annually, limited in the number of times they could be reelected, and subject to impeachment. Pennsylvania abolished the position of governor altogether, substituting an elected executive council. The upper house of the legislature, which in colonial times doubled as an executive council, also lost status. Pennsylvania, Vermont, and Georgia did away with the upper house altogether.

Representation in the assemblies of the new states also reflected the colonial experience. Every state constitution required that assembly members be residents of the towns, counties, or districts they represented. Parliament had never imposed a residence requirement on its members; indeed nonresidence was the basis for the theory of "virtual representation" by which Parliament had presumed to tax the colonies. In the seventeenth century, several colonial assemblies had instituted a residence requirement, and they had found that it enhanced their authority. Colonial delegates stood tall in the public trust precisely because they were selected at county

Patrick Henry. Like his fellow radical, Samuel Adams, Henry was more effective in starting revolutions than in building governments.

New York Public Library Picture Collection.

polls and town meetings and were subject thereafter to local instruction.

Several revolutionary state constitutions flirted with the more radical notion that delegates might represent people rather than places. Colonial assemblies, like the English House of Commons, represented a state's counties and towns. In 1780 Massachusetts broke with this tradition by assigning representatives to districts whose boundaries were determined by the number of people they included. Five states even provided for a periodic adjustment of representation to reflect population changes. By these measures Americans ensured that their republics would also be democracies.

Neither Whig theory nor colonial experience, on the other hand, provided any clear guidelines as to the role of the people in the day-to-day operation of government. As a result, the degree of democracy worked into the constitutional mechanism varied from state to state. South Carolina, Maryland, and New York were easily the most conservative. In the South Carolina Provincial Congress, low-country planters waited until back-country members went home for the winter and hastily drew up a constitution that ensured their hold on the state. In South Carolina's government, as outlined by the framers of the state constitution, the people's role was limited to electing members of the lower house, and voters were forced to choose among members of the elite because delegates were required to possess 500 acres or £1000 in personal property. Maryland and New York placed similar property requirements on officeholding. Maryland tried to insulate its upper house from popular influence by having senators chosen by electors, who were in turn chosen by voters.

Pennsylvania, Georgia, North Carolina, and Vermont all drafted fairly democratic constitutions. Pennsylvania's was the most radical and experimental of all. It gave the vote to all adult male taxpayers and their adult sons, instituting virtually universal manhood suffrage. The general assembly was elected annually, and no member could serve more than four years out of seven. The purpose of this limitation on service was to prevent the formation of a governmental elite divorced from the citizenry. To encourage active popular participation in the legislative process, the Pennsylvania constitution also provided that sessions be open to the public, that votes and proceedings be published weekly, and that all bills be printed for the people's consideration prior to their last reading. An executive council of twelve men chosen every three years by the voters was provided for; its members had no special qualifications other than a belief in the Bible. This council did not participate in lawmaking; its main duty was to appoint judges and other state officials. Judges were limited to seven-year terms and could be removed at any time by the assembly. All in all, it is hard to see how Pennsylvania's farmers could have done anything more to ensure popular control of the government. An early draft even included a provision for the breakup of great landed estates on the theory that disparities in wealth are inimical to democracy. This radical notion was later deleted, however.

Finally, each of the constitutions contained a guarantee of rights, focusing principally on legal rights that ensured speedy and fair court trials. Nine states appended Declarations of Rights to their constitutions; the others incorporated guarantees directly into the texts. Considerable variation and numerous omissions were evident, for the concept of a list, or "bill," of rights was still evolving. Virginia's declaration, which was imitated by several other states, did not even include freedom of speech, and its statement on religious toleration was inconclusive. The declarations were nevertheless a distillation of colonial experience, and an enduring legacy. They stated the fundamental American commitment that government is limited, strictly so when it confronts the rights of citizens.

THE ARTICLES OF CONFEDERATION

In the First Continental Congress, Joseph Galloway, an ally of Benjamin Franklin and who was later to become a loyalist, suggested a plan of colonial union as a way of restoring harmony with Britain. Galloway's proposal was in many ways similar to the plan Franklin had proposed at the Albany Congress twenty years before. It envisioned a crown-appointed president-general for the colonies and a grand council selected by the colonial assemblies. It differed from Franklin's plan principally in that the consent of both Parliament and the colonial grand council was needed before any measure affecting the colonies became law.

Although conservatives, among them John Jay of New York and Edward Rutledge of South Carolina, had given the Galloway plan strong support, Congress had never approved it. Those who endorsed the Galloway plan were among those who stalled on independence in the Second Continental Congress. They wanted to establish an American union before they shucked the imperial union, fearing that a lapse in governmental authority might invite anarchy and mob rule. To alleviate such fears, Richard Henry Lee's independence resolution of June 7, 1776, included the proposal "that a plan of confederation be prepared and transmitted to the respective colonies for their consideration and approbation." As soon as independence was approved, John Dickinson of Pennsylvania submitted a rough draft for the Articles of Confederation, but it was not until November 1777 that Congress approved them. It was another four years before all thirteen states approved the Articles. The final holdout was Maryland, whose assem-

bly demanded that Virginia cede its vast western land claims to Congress first. On the basis of its colonial charter, Virginia claimed Kentucky and the entire region between the Ohio River and the Great Lakes. Marylanders had bought lands in the Ohio Valley and thought they might get better treatment if Congress, rather than Virginia, governed the West. Virginia ceded its claims in 1781, and Maryland signed.

The authority of the confederation that the Articles created did not go far beyond the power of the existing Congress. The Articles authorized neither an executive nor a judicial branch of government. Congress was given power to conduct foreign relations, to coin money, to regulate Indian affairs, and to settle disputes among states. It did not have the power to tax or to regulate trade. It was expected to subsist on financial contributions from the states. Each state had one vote in Congress; the states retained the ordinary powers and duties of government.

At the same time, the Articles did envision a continental union. They prohibited the states from conducting foreign relations and from making war. The Articles also barred the states from discriminating against the citizens or products of other states and from inhibiting interstate travel. The confederation created by the Articles seems weak when compared to the federal union established by the Constitution in 1787, but viewed in its own time, it was as strong as any confederation that had ever been created.

The weakness of the Articles was not immediately apparent. There was little criticism of the provisions during the war, and except in the realm of taxation, there was no effort to add to the powers of Congress. What made the government appear weak after the war was not so much the unequal distribution of power between Congress and states as Congress's fundamental inefficiency, which stemmed in part from the absence of an executive who could offer some imaginative leadership. Congress filled the executive void with committees. John Adams, a glutton for work, served on no less than eighty committees during the war. But committees were no substitute for a single decision maker. "There is as much intrigue in this State House as in the Vatican," complained John Jay, "but as little secrecy as in a boarding-school."

The inefficiency resulted also from absenteeism. In a misguided effort to promote rotation in office, the Articles stipulated that no delegate could serve more than three years out of six. In fact, delegates came and went much more frequently than that. The revolutionary leaders were amateurs; politics was not a career. Most served because they felt a public obligation and left office as soon as they found it convenient to do so. Samuel Adams and James Madison spent nearly all their lives in public service, but they were exceptions. Congressional service was especially burdensome because it necessitated absence from home or plantation for long periods of time and at great expense. As a result, turnover was high among delegates and absenteeism even higher. At times during the mid-1780s, Congress could not even muster a quorum to conduct business.

So acute were the problems that through the 1780s the members of Congress seemed unable to reach a decision on any important point. For a time, it seemed, they could not even decide where they would meet. A mutiny of Pennsylvania troops in 1783 sent members fleeing ingloriously to Princeton, New Jersey, a move that proved unsatisfactory: The town was so small that many delegates could find no living quarters (James Madison had to share a bed with another Virginia delegate). They subsequently held sessions in Annapolis, Maryland, and Trenton, New Jersey, before settling in New York in late 1784. Referring to the postwar fascination with hot-air balloons, one newspaper wit

suggested that Congress ought to attach itself to one so that it could supervise the country from above and "pop down" into a state whenever its services were needed.

ACHIEVEMENTS UNDER THE CONFEDERATION

Although the target of national ridicule by the mid-1780s, the Confederation Congress did manage a few achievements. The structure set up in 1780–1781, for instance, with secretaries of finance, foreign affairs, and war, provided the country with a rudimentary federal bureaucracy. Secretary of Finance Robert Morris, who held office until 1784, was chronically short of funds because states lagged in their contributions, but he did negotiate loans from Dutch bankers that kept the government functioning. Robert R. Livingston, the secretary of foreign affairs, reached a trade agreement with the Dutch in 1782, and his successor, John Jay, signed a similar treaty with the French in 1786. As a result of these agreements, American exports to both Europe and the West Indies rose steadily through the 1780s. The executive offices, in short, afforded valuable experience in the art of governing a continental republic. Significantly, these three offices formed the president's cabinet when the federal government was established in 1789.

By far the most considerable achievement of the confederation was the establishment of a national land policy and a system of territorial government. Both would endure into the twentieth century. The state cessions of western land claims in the early 1780s endowed Congress with an empire north and west of the Ohio River. South of the Ohio, Virginia retained its hold on Kentucky until it became a state in 1792; North Carolina governed Tennessee until it was ceded to Congress in 1789; and Georgia claimed title, although a dubious one, to Alabama and Mississippi. The wilderness empire bounded by the Ohio River, the Great Lakes, and the Mississippi River presented Congress with three tasks. The land had to be surveyed for sale; government had to be installed; and the Indians had to be pacified. The Confederation Congress accomplished the first two; President Washington was left with the burden of ongoing Indian warfare when the federal government was set up.

The Northwest Ordinance of 1785 provided for the subdivision of the West into salable units. Adopting New England's method of settlement by well-defined towns, Congress ordered the West divided into squares. Beginning at the point where the Ohio River emerges from Pennsylvania, east-west ("base") lines and north-south ("range") lines were to be marked out at 6-mile intervals. The 36-square-mile units thus formed were called townships. Within each township, surveyors would mark out another grid of 36 sections, each containing 640 acres. Every inch of land could thus be precisely identified by its location within a township. Title disputes and overlapping claims, which so troubled the southern frontier, where each pioneer surveyed his own farm, would be avoided. The ordinance listed a price of $1 per acre for land sales; the minimum purchase was 640 acres. The ordinance also reserved section 16 in each township for the maintenance of public schools, an initial step toward federal aid to education.

The ordinance of 1785 set up guidelines for the surveying of all the American West. Because of it, western state boundaries today generally are in accordance with surveyors' lines rather than features of the landscape. The surveying process was slow, however: By 1800 only the first seven ranges of southeastern Ohio were surveyed, and settlers were "squatting" on unsurveyed lands to the west. Few pioneers had the $640 required for a minimum purchase of land, so most of the land went to

middlemen, who broke it into smaller parcels and offered it on credit. Congress, ever thirsty for money, soon became impatient with its own system. Within two years it was deeding million-acre tracts in Ohio to speculators with ready cash. To encourage settlement and promote land sales, these speculators in turn pressed Congress to tackle the second of its obligations—territorial government. This Congress fulfilled in the Northwest Ordinance of 1787.

The ordinance provided a government for the "Territory North West of the River Ohio" and outlined the stages by which a wilderness community might evolve to statehood. In the initial stage, the territorial government consisted of a governor, a secretary, and three judges, all appointed by Congress. The second stage began when the "colony" contained 5,000 adult males. At that point, the voters could elect a territorial legislature, which in turn could send a nonvoting representative to Congress. Governor and judges, however, would continue to be responsible to Congress. When the population of the district reached 60,000, it could frame a constitution and apply for statehood. When Congress approved the constitution, the territory would be admitted to the Union "on an equal footing with the original States." Not less than three nor more than five states might be formed from the entire area.

The terms of the ordinance revealed the influence of eastern speculators and delayed western self-government—and hence potential assaults on the speculators' interests—more or less indefinitely (Ohio, the first state carved out of the region, was not admitted to the Union until 1803; Wisconsin, the last, did not achieve statehood until 1848). The ordinance also ensured that the seaboard would retain control of Congress by making western states few and large (Jefferson, in a 1784 ordinance that was never adopted, had suggested carving ten states out of the Northwest).

Despite the questionable motives of its

Western land cessions, 1781–1802.

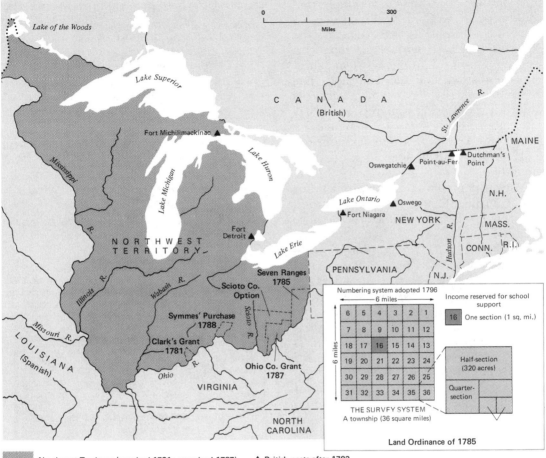

0 300
Miles

Lake of the Woods

Lake Superior

C A N A D A
(British)

Fort Michilimackinac ▲

Lake Huron

Lake Michigan

St. Lawrence R.

MAINE

Oswegatchie Point-au-Fer ▲ Dutchman's
▲   ▲   Point

Lake Ontario   ▲ Oswego
▲ Fort Niagara

N.H.

NEW YORK

Mississippi R.

Fort
Detroit

N O R T H W E S T
T E R R I T O R Y

Lake Erie

PENNSYLVANIA

Hudson R.

MASS.

CONN. R.I.

N.J.

Illinois R.

Wabash R.

Scioto R.

Seven Ranges
1785

Scioto Co.
Option

Symmes' Purchase
1788

Missouri R.

L O U I S I A N A
(Spanish)

Clark's Grant
1781

Ohio R.

Ohio Co. Grant
1787

VIRGINIA

NORTH
CAROLINA

Numbering system adopted 1796
— 6 miles —

6	5	4	3	2	1
7	8	9	10	11	12
18	17	16	15	14	13
19	20	21	22	23	24
30	29	28	27	26	25
31	32	33	34	35	36

6 miles

Income reserved for school
support

16 One section (1 sq. mi.)

Half-section
(320 acres)

Quarter-
section

THE SURVEY SYSTEM
A township (36 square miles)

Land Ordinance of 1785

▨ Northwest Territory (acquired 1781; organized 1787)   ▲ British posts after 1783

Northwest Ordinance of 1787 and Land Ordinance of 1785.

authors, the Northwest Ordinance of 1787 contained a number of enlightened features. It provided for gradual statehood. Although the territorial government established by the ordinance was essentially imperial in nature, built into it was the first opportunity in history for "colonies" to become the equal of the "mother country." The ordinance also provided an extensive bill of rights (including freedom of speech and religion, right to trial by jury, and freedom from arbitrary arrest) for the Northwest Territory and prohibited slavery throughout the region. By setting up effec-

tive government for the area, it helped hold the union together. And by establishing the procedure for achieving statehood, it enabled the republic to spread from sea to sea. It was easily the most important and far-reaching accomplishment of the Confederation Congress.

YEARS OF TRIAL, 1783–1786

At the very moment in July 1787 that the Northwest Ordinance cleared Congress, a convention was meeting in Philadelphia to draft the blueprint for a government that would replace the Confederation Congress altogether. Despite its achievements, the Congress had not been able to cope with pressing postwar problems—demobilization, depression, and social turmoil. The chain of adversity was not necessarily its fault, but it did bring Congress into disrepute. Reformers at first attempted to amend the Articles of Confederation, but by 1787 they had decided to scrap them altogether.

Postwar demobilization is a problem for any government, and the Confederation Congress faced special difficulties because it lacked money even to pay the army. From 1779 to 1781, a succession of mutinies wracked Washington's winter quarters at Morristown, New Jersey, as soldiers demanded back pay. The mutinies ended only when Washington executed some ringleaders. The states pacified their troops with promises of land, and Congress agreed to postwar pensions of half-pay for five years. Discontent then flared up among the officer corps. In the spring of 1783, a number of anonymously written essays circulated through Washington's headquarters at Newburgh, New York, demanding lifetime pensions at full pay for officers. If this were not granted, the addressees suggested, the army might move on Congress itself. Washington defused the crisis by persuading the officers to let him present their demands to Congress, and Congress responded by granting half-pay for life. But the specter of military rule lingered for years, especially as the nation staggered through a morass of economic and social turmoil that seemed to bring it ever closer to anarchy.

Depression was at the root of the difficulties. It began late in 1784 and continued for the next two years. A shortage of money was the principal symptom, if not the cause. British goods flooded the American market when the fighting ceased, and

Americans hastened to buy. What little gold and silver there was in the country flowed back to Britain in payment. The states aggravated the problem by retiring their paper money after the war, principally by accepting it in taxes. It was sound fiscal policy for the time, but it worsened the money shortage. British trade policy was also a factor. An order in council (that is, a directive from the British ministry) of 1783 excluded the United States from trade with the British West Indies on the not unreasonable theory that, having left the empire, the United States was no longer entitled to its trading privileges.

Rhode Island paper money. Observe that each note was numbered and signed, but observe also that there is no provision for its redemption in gold or silver. Nine pence would have bought a bottle of whisky or a good meal in a tavern.

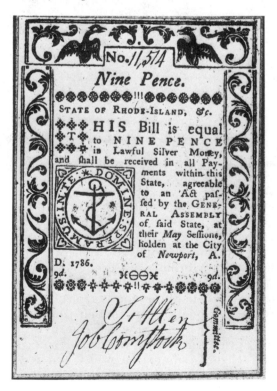

The action hit New England especially hard because West Indian trade was its chief source of foreign currency. Without money people could not buy, and the economy slipped into depression.

Several states responded by issuing paper money. Others made commodities such as tobacco and deerskins the equivalent of money, a practice that gave rise to the expression *buckskin* or *buck* as a synonym for the dollar. Merchants and creditors fretted about such debt relief measures. They had loaned money in hard coin; they did not want to be paid back in depreciated paper.

As it turned out, the merchants themselves determined the value of the currency. In those states in which the issue of paper money was limited and merchants accepted it, the money held its value. But in those states in which merchants undermined it by raising prices, it depreciated. Rhode Island, long accustomed to wallowing in worthless paper, had the worst experience. There the legislature was ultimately obliged to make its paper legal tender in order to force merchants to take it. The merchants responded by closing their shops and fleeing to Boston with debtors, so rumors told, hard on their heels trying to pay.

Paper money—or rather the lack of it—in one instance led to the most serious social upheaval of the period, Shays's Rebellion. In the summer of 1786, a bill for the issuance of paper money was set before the Massachusetts legislature, but that merchant-dominated body adjourned without taking action. At popular meetings in several towns, citizens protested. During the autumn, mobs of angry farmers disrupted court proceedings in four towns across the state. The poor unleashed their fury on the courts because the law, through foreclosure and other debt-collection devices, was in their eyes the instrument of the wealthy. In September, a worried governor called out 600 militiamen to protect the state supreme court, then meeting at Springfield. A mob led by Daniel Shays, a bankrupt farmer and former army captain, dispersed the troops and disbanded the court.

When the governor declared Shays and his followers outlaws, the farmers decided to live up to the name. The various bands planned a joint assault on the federal arsenal at Springfield to seize munitions. Once properly armed, they expected to move on the legislature in Boston. The governor, verging on panic, ordered General Benjamin Lincoln and 4,000 militiamen (paid by private subscription because the treasury was empty) to relieve the arsenal. Lincoln routed the Shaysites in February 1787 and captured a handful of rebel leaders.

Recognizing the movement for what it was, a protest against injustice rather than a threat to governmental authority, the legislature offered amnesty to those who had participated in the "rebellion," excepting only Shays and three other leaders. Shaysites in fact won control of the assembly in elections held later in 1787 and then enacted a number of reforms that limited judicial seizure of property for debt. The uprising had nevertheless sent a shiver of fear the length of the seaboard. Congress greeted the emergency by authorizing a force of 1,340 men, ostensibly to fight Indians since Congress lacked the authority to suppress domestic violence. Thomas Jefferson, almost alone among American statesmen, kept his head. "A little rebellion, now and then, is a good thing," he reflected, because it would keep politicians alert to popular grievances. "The tree of liberty must be refreshed from time to time with the blood of patriots and tyrants. It is its natural manure." Jefferson could afford to be philosophical: He was in Paris, 3,000 miles from Massachusetts. Those closer to the scene saw only further evidence of a drift toward anarchy.

⊔ Toward a Stronger Union

Efforts to strengthen the Articles of Confederation began almost as soon as they were ratified. In 1781, Robert Morris, as part of his finance program, recommended that Congress be given the power to levy customs duties. Such a move required an amendment to the Articles of Confederation, and amendments required the approval of all thirteen states. Congress proposed an amendment giving itself power to collect customs duties, but the amendment died when Rhode Island refused to agree to it. A revised amendment was submitted to the states in 1783, and this time New York objected. In that year Congress also asked for power to regulate trade so that it could retaliate against the British for excluding American vessels from the West Indies.

That amendment was still under consideration by the states when James Madison ended a three-year stint in Congress and returned to Virginia. He was convinced that Congress had to be given more powers, and trade regulation was a promising avenue of reform. In 1785, with Washington's support, Madison induced the Virginia assembly to appoint commissioners to meet with Marylanders to discuss navigation on the Potomac River and in Chesapeake Bay. Washington invited the commissioners to meet at Mount Vernon, his home, and the group compiled a series of recommendations on trade for the consideration of the Maryland and Virginia assemblies. While the Virginia House of Delegates debated these proposals in the winter of 1785, someone suggested that the House issue an invitation to all the states to attend a convention to discuss commerce in Annapolis the following September. The assembly agreed. Even those who, like Patrick Henry, were content with the Articles of Confederation saw no harm in such

The Pennsylvania Academy of the Fine Arts. Presented by Mr. R. Patterson, Joseph and Sarah Harrison Collection.

A growing national spirit. Charles Willson Peale specialized in painting the likenesses of the heroes of the Revolution (he painted Washington four times). In 1786 he purchased a museum in Philadelphia in which to display his paintings. It was a candid appeal to American patriotism, and it brought Peale a lifetime's income. In this painting, "The Artist in His Museum" (1822) (then located in Independence Hall), he proudly displayed the museum as it was in its prime. The paintings of heroes line the wall on the upper left.

meetings. Madison, in fact, had come to see great potential in them: A convention might be able to draft a new frame of government altogether.

Twelve delegates, representing New York, New Jersey, Delaware, Pennsylvania, and Virginia, gathered in Annapolis on September 11, 1786. The Maryland assembly, although sympathetic to constitutional reform, refused to attend because it did not want to embarrass Congress. Finding

CLIO'S FOCUS: James Madison: Father of the Constitution

Of all the founding fathers, James Madison played the most important role in the framing of the American Constitution, yet he is also the most enigmatic. There is little in his life that would explain his strong federalism. He had no military experience, such as colored the views of Washington and Hamilton. He lacked the interstate and international mercantile connections that some Federalists had, and he never suffered indignities at the hands of a mob. He owned land and slaves, as Washington did, but he was far from a wealthy man. Indeed, the pay of a public servant was an important source of support throughout much of his life. All of the founding fathers acted out of concern for the public interest, or at least thought they did. With Madison there is not even a hint of private interest. Madison's writings were among the most profound of his age, but his motive may have been nothing more than a simple feeling that the federation was untidy. A drifting government and a turbulent populace violated his sense of order and propriety.

Madison was a diminutive man, short and slight of build, "no bigger," someone said, "than half a piece of soap." To his friends he was "Jemmy." He was a wretched public speaker. In public meetings, the clerk sometimes had to omit part of his speech because Madison spoke so softly he could not be heard. In his youth he suffered from chronic ill health. He pushed himself so hard in school that he suffered a physical breakdown. He did not serve in the revolutionary army because he was subject to periodic fits, which Madison himself diagnosed as epilepsy. Yet his was perhaps the most profound intellect of all the nation's founders.

He entered Princeton in 1769 at the age of nineteen and compressed three years of college work into two. The president of the college, Dr. John Witherspoon, a Scot who would later become a revolutionary activist and signer of the Declaration of Independence, took personal charge of the young scholar, introducing him to the latest currents of European thought. After leaving Princeton, Madison began the study of law, but not with any intent to practice. He focused on legal history and the study of political systems. He seems from the beginning to have envisioned a career as a statesman and public servant.

The formation of Virginia's state government in 1776 offered him the opportunity. He sought and won election to the assembly and instantly plunged into the debate over Virginia's Declaration of Rights. The Declaration (a forerunner of the U.S. Bill of Rights) did not go far enough, Madison thought, in securing religious freedom. It merely promised toleration, while retaining the connection between the government and the Church of England. Madison lost this battle, but in the course of it he found an ally in Thomas Jefferson. The friendship and collaboration between the two would become one of the enduring themes of the young republic.

Their initial association was brief, however. In 1777, Madison was not reelected to the House of Delegates because he refused to treat the voters to rum punch, as was the custom in Virginia. (Washington's first election to the House of Burgesses in 1758 had cost him 160 gallons of rum, beer, and hard cider, which worked out to roughly a quart and a half per voter.) Madison regarded the practice as inconsistent with the principles of a republic. The voters showed their concern for principle by replacing him with a local tavernkeeper.

The legislature recognized his worth, however. In 1780 it sent him to Congress, where he quickly joined forces with Alexander Hamilton, James Wilson, and other nationalists who were seeking to expand the powers of the central government. When his term expired in 1783, Madison returned to Virginia, convinced that a complete overhaul of the confederacy was necessary. Characteristically, he immersed himself in the history of constitution-making, asking Jefferson (who had replaced him in Congress) to send to him from New York "whatever may throw light on the general constitution and droit public of the several confederacies which have existed."

In April 1784, Madison secured election to the Virginia House of Delegates. The record is silent as to whether he treated the voters to rum punch, but Madison's silence itself suggests that he might have yielded on this minor point of principle. Before the assembly opened, Madison sought a meeting with George Mason, author of the Declaration of Rights and elder statesman of Virginia politics. The two reached agreement on a range of issues—passage of the statute for religious freedom, blocking the issues of state paper money, and approval of amendments adding to the powers of Congress. Their adversary on all three issues was the formidable Patrick Henry. Over the next three years, Madison, through organization and effort, secured nearly everything he wanted. The experience brought into being a federal "party" in Virginia, and it matured Madison's thought. By 1787, Madison had seen the connection between the need to enhance federal powers and the need to restrict the vices of the states and the people. This synthesis, reinforced by his study of past confederacies, made Madison the intellectual leader of those who would frame the U.S. Constitution.

themselves in general agreement on the need for change, the Annapolis delegates quickly adopted a resolution drafted by Alexander Hamilton of New York proposing yet another convention to meet in Philadelphia in May 1787 to consider commerce and "such other purposes" as public affairs might require. The conference then abruptly adjourned, and its members scattered; a North Carolina delegate who arrived the next day found they had all left town. Delegates to the convention from Massachusetts, New Hampshire, and Rhode Island were in fact still on the way.

The Annapolis men, not sure of their strength in the country, clearly wished to avoid protracted debate. In the nine-month interval before they reassembled at Philadelphia, events might add to their support.

FRAMING THE CONSTITUTION

Twelve states responded to the Annapolis Convention's call and sent delegates to Philadelphia in May–June 1787 (the self-appointed outcast was Rhode Island).

About half of the fifty-five men who ultimately took part in the proceedings were individuals of ordinary talents, but several states made an effort to send their best. The Virginia delegation boasted such luminaries as Washington, Madison, George Mason, and the state's governor, Edmund Randolph. Pennsylvania's contingent included Benjamin Franklin and Robert Morris; South Carolina sent its usual assortment of Rutledges and Pinckneys. Notable absentees were Jefferson, who was in France; John Adams, who was in England; and Richard Henry Lee and Patrick Henry, both of whom had been nominated by Virginia but refused to attend. Lee apparently did not comprehend the importance of the meeting; Henry, a defender of state's rights and the status quo, later explained, "I smelt a rat."

Although a majority of the delegates were nationalists interested in reforming the government, they represented a broad cross section of political and regional interests. The selection of delegates did not generate important controversy in any state. The convention seemed to result from a general feeling, even among those who supported the Confederation, that something had to be done to breathe life into the central government. Had the state assemblies anticipated the results of the convention they would surely have been less agreeable, for what happened at Philadelphia was nothing less than a revolution.

Alone among the delegates, James Madison had recognized the importance of advance preparation. The convention's mandate was ill defined, and few delegates had a clear notion of what form a proper government ought to take. Thus the man with the agenda was certain to guide the proceedings. Madison had spent the previous winter studying history and political theory, and he arrived in Philadelphia with a plan in hand, a plan so bold in the changes it proposed that it instantly commanded attention.

At the outset, the delegates made two important decisions. The first was to conduct their business in secret. Their rationale was that the meeting would thus be a genuine forum for the exchange of ideas. Men would be free to change their minds without accusations of inconsistency, and potential opponents of a new constitution would be deprived of ammunition until it was all over. The second procedural decision was to retain the system of voting by states, the position of each state to be determined by a poll of its delegation. However, to avoid the veto power that had strangled the efforts to amend the Articles, the delegates agreed that major decisions needed the approval of only nine states and that minor decisions required a simple majority. With these housekeeping matters settled and George Washington installed as presiding officer, the convention was ready for business.

After Governor Randolph, the head of the Virginia delegation, "opened the main business" with a speech detailing the defects in the Confederation, he submitted James Madison's proposals, which became known as the Virginia Plan. Madison envisioned a federal government of three branches: executive, legislative, and judicial. The legislative branch was to be composed of two houses with voting in each apportioned by population, a feature that served the interest of Virginia and the other large states. Both the executive and the legislative branch would have broad powers of governing, and therein lay the boldness of the scheme. Madison expected to turn the Confederation inside out, resting critical powers with the federal government rather than with the states.

The convention discussed the Virginia Plan for two weeks, and a revealing division appeared. The delegates from the larger states, who favored proportional voting and centralized power, favored the scheme; those from the small states, who wanted equal representation and limited power, disliked it. On June 15, William Paterson of New Jersey offered an alternative set of proposals on behalf of the small states. The New Jersey Plan was essentially a revised version of the Articles of Confederation with added powers for Congress. With only New York, New Jersey, and Delaware backing it, this idea was voted down, and the wrangling continued.

In early July the convention reached a compromise. Voting was made proportional to population in the first house (which the Committee on Detail later named the House of Representatives) and equal in the other house (later named the Senate). To satisfy the large states, the first house was given primary power over revenue measures. Delegates from the small states, with their interests protected by the compromise, shed their fears, and the remaining features of the Virginia Plan were approved in short order. The main battle thereafter was a dispute between northern and southern states as to whether the southern states were entitled to count slaves as population for the purposes of representation. The delegates finally reached a compromise that allowed these states to count three-fifths of their slaves in calculating the representation.

The Federal Convention. Thomas Rossiter (1818–1871) portrayed Washington presiding over the final day of the convention. Behind him is a tapestry featuring a sunburst design. On that final day Benjamin Franklin was heard to remark that he had wondered throughout the proceedings whether the tapestry represented a rising or a setting sun. But he added, now that the Constitution was completed, "I have the happiness to know that it is a rising and not a setting sun."

New York Public Library Picture Collection.

The result of these compromises was a unique governmental structure, blessed with extensive powers and yet curiously self-limited. Congress had ample powers to govern effectively. It had power to tax, to appropriate money for the general welfare, to declare war and raise armies, to coin and borrow money, and to regulate trade. Yet as broad as these powers were, the very listing of them limited them. Congress had *these* powers, *and none other*.

The powers conferred on the president were even more remarkable. Americans had very little experience with elected governors, and their colonial experience had taught that executive power was often arbitrary. Nevertheless, the federal convention made the president the commander-in-chief of the armed forces, gave him extensive powers of appointment and dismissal, and allowed him to veto measures passed by Congress. But the convention also subjected the president to controls. His appointments had to be approved by the Senate. His vetoes could be overridden by two thirds of the members of each house of Congress. And for very grave misdeeds he could be impeached and removed from office, although such an extreme measure was made difficult by the requirement that he be convicted of a crime by two-thirds of the Senate.

A third institution shared in this separation of powers—the judiciary. The members of the convention, most of whom were lawyers, favored federal judges who were experienced in the law and given office for life to ensure their independence. But they also realized that many Americans—the great majority in rural areas—distrusted courts of law and considered them the agents of the rich and powerful. Many state constitutions had left the selection of judges to the legislature rather than to the governor in the hope of retaining greater popular control over the court system. The federal convention solved the problem thus: The Constitution gave the president

the power to appoint federal judges, but only with the consent of the Senate; and judges were granted tenure for life pending good behavior. But the framers of the Constitution were silent as to the number of federal courts and their powers of jurisdiction. They left these matters up to Congress, and hence posterity.

"If men were angels," Madison would write later in *The Federalist*, a series of essays designed to win popular support for the Constitution, "no government was necessary." Yet precisely because humans were fallible, to entrust them with authority was to risk the abuse of it. The solution, said Madison, was this: "You must first enable the government to control the governed; and in the next place oblige it to control itself." This, although the members of the convention did not fully comprehend it in the summer of 1787, was what the Constitution achieved. It conferred broad powers on each branch of government and then ensured against abuse by giving each branch a veto of sorts over the others. Congress passed laws, but the president could veto them. The president appointed officials and negotiated treaties; the Senate had to approve them. Congress had the power to raise and support armies; the president commanded them. The president appointed the justices of the Supreme Court; Congress determined their number and jurisdiction. By this system of checks and balances, ambition was made to counterbalance ambition, all for the common good. Following the Watergate crisis of the early 1970s, after President Richard Nixon's claim of extraordinary powers was checked by Congress and the courts, Senator Hugh Scott of Pennsylvania addressed a letter to James Madison, saying simply: "Dear Mr. Madison: It worked."

The constitutional compromises also added a new dimension to the concept of federalism—that is, the sharing of power between central government and states. In this realm also Americans had little experience. The imperial contest had been a matter of either-or: Either Parliament ruled the empire, or the colonies governed themselves. Under the Articles of Confederation, the basic powers of government (taxation and trade) had rested with the states. Under the federal Constitution, the branches of the federal government—executive, legislative, judicial—had extensive powers, but they were specifically enumerated. By implication, made explicit by the tenth amendment of the Bill of Rights, all other powers were retained by the states and by the people. Today these residual powers are called the police powers, meaning the power of states and municipalities to carry out the day-to-day functions of government, those concerned with the health, safety, welfare, and morals of the citizenry.

AN ECONOMIC DOCUMENT

Having agreed on the general framework of the federal government, the delegates filled in the details during August 1787. At this point too they inserted some provisions that reflected their own conservative social and economic views. As lawyers, merchants, and landowners, they had been alarmed by the debtor relief measures passed by various state legislatures in the 1780s. They had also been badly frightened by Shays's Rebellion in Massachusetts. So they tacked provisions onto the Constitution that forbade the states to issue paper money or to pass any law that interfered with private contracts. The Constitution also gave the federal government power, at the request of a state, to suppress "domestic violence."

Not all the delegates approved of the terms of the developing Constitution. Several, who felt that too much power was being conferred on a new and untried government, voiced their disagreement and left for home. Others departed for per-

sonal reasons. Of the fifty-five delegates sent to the convention, only forty-one remained when printed copies of the Constitution were handed out on September 12. At that juncture came the most dramatic protest of all. George Mason, the author of Virginia's Declaration of Rights and the self-designated guardian of civil liberties, took the floor to object to the absence of a bill of rights. The delegates had created a powerful engine of government, he reminded them; it would be well to add guarantees of popular rights. Madison replied that the powers given the federal government, although extensive, were specific and thus limited. Congress had not been delegated the power to abridge freedom of speech or press or any other right; guarantees were unnecessary. Weary delegates agreed, and Mason was shouted down. When the moment for signing came, on September 17, Mason, joined by Edmund Randolph of Virginia and Elbridge Gerry of Massachusetts, refused to add their names to the Constitution. It was the opening shot in the battle for ratification, because the absence of a bill of rights became a rallying point for the opponents of the Constitution.

⊔ The Struggle over Ratification

Because they had worked in secrecy and had far exceeded the authority given them, the framers of the Constitution knew that they had to submit their final draft to the people for approval. They hoped to avoid the petty rivalries that had frustrated earlier efforts to alter the Articles of Confederation. The Constitution specified that it was to be ratified not by state legislatures, but by specially elected ratifying conventions, where presumably it would be the only order of business. The Constitution further provided that it would go into effect when nine of the thirteen states gave approval.

Publication of the text of the Constitution generated a torrent of pamphlets and essays, some criticizing and some defending the document. The pent-up emotions of a generation repulsed by tyranny and obsessed with liberty flowed into print. Opponents pointed to the elitist features of the Constitution and predicted that its vast powers would lead to tyranny. The Constitution itself answered many of these dire predictions. It had previously been assumed that the people's choices for government were limited to a loose confederation of democratic states or a powerful national body controlled by an elite. The Constitution demonstrated that something in between was possible. The powers it conferred were enumerated, not endless, and the state governments would continue to play an important role. The Constitution itself helped to shape the distinction between a *federation* of states and a *confederation*. Supporters of the Constitution paraded this feature by calling themselves Federalists; that left their opponents with the unimaginative and unappealing label of Antifederalists.

The Federalists. The most thoughtful of the essays were those that appeared in the New York press under the pseudonym "Publius" and that were ultimately collected as *The Federalist Papers*. The authors of these essays were principally Madison and Hamilton; John Jay also contributed a few. Most of the essays provided a line-by-line elucidation of the Constitution, but a few, especially those by Madison, sought to rest the Constitution on a theoretical framework. And the theory Madison devised was as novel and original as the document he sought to defend.

Political theorists since Aristotle had been preoccupied with the balance of interests among the one (king), the few (aristocracy), and the many. English Whig theory revolved around the same distinctions, formalizing them with a social contract. America's state constitutions authorized two-house legislatures on a similar theory: The lower houses, declared such theorists as John Adams, were the democratic element in the government; the upper houses were the province of the wealthy and the well-born.

In America, as Madison well knew, this dualism bore no relation to reality. In the 1780s the American states, with one or two exceptions, were totally in the hands of the people. The members of the upper houses, on the average, had no more wealth or social standing than the members of the lower houses. In fact, as Madison explained in *Federalist* Number 10, American politics was a jumble of conflicting interests: rich versus poor, religious versus secular, landed versus mercantile, educated versus unskilled. The problem, as Madison diagnosed it, was that special interest groups had been able to win control of certain states in the 1780s—debtor-farmers in Rhode Island and North Carolina, merchants in Massachusetts—and that these groups had imposed a tyranny of their own as they rode roughshod over the rights of others.

Madison's remedy was to expand the arena of politics, and he argued that the Constitution did just that. In a continental arena, each special interest would be only one of many. Federal statesmen, free of ties with any interest group, could be expected to work for the welfare of all. Although there is no evidence that Madison had read Adam Smith's *Wealth of Nations*, his argument was quite reminiscent of that economist's metaphor of the "invisible hand"—the idea that private selfishness through free competition promotes the public good.

The Bandwagon Effect. The choice of party names was prophetic. Federalists had more than a party label; they had a design for government, a proposal to defend. Antifederalists disliked what they saw but could not agree on an alternative. Many Antifederalists recognized that the Articles of Confederation needed amending; they merely felt that the Constitution went too far. Federalists had the initiative, and that was the secret to their success.

Delaware, a small state that could not hope to survive as an independent entity should the Union dissolve, was the first to ratify the Constitution. Pennsylvania followed. Pennsylvania Federalists already had a party organization fashioned in opposition to the state's democratic constitution of 1776. Forcefully dragging several members into the hall in order to achieve an assembly quorum on the last day of the session, they pushed through a resolution calling for a ratifying convention to meet on November 21. They then mounted an intensive newspaper propaganda campaign while the opposition was trying to collect itself. Federalists won the election by a two-thirds majority and pushed the Constitution through the ratifying convention in three weeks.

New Jersey, Georgia, and Connecticut were the next states to ratify; the first two did so by unanimous votes. Like Delaware, all three were small and comparatively weak. New Jersey and Connecticut were sandwiched between large, commercially powerful neighbors, who would surely dominate them if the Union should fail. Georgia was menaced by Indians on one border and Spaniards on another. By January 1788, five of the necessary nine states

The Eleventh Pillar. This cartoon celebrated the ratification of the Constitution by New York, the eleventh state to do so. Eleven pillars, it contends, make a sound foundation for "The Federal Edifice," and it expresses the hope that North Carolina and Rhode Island will soon join.

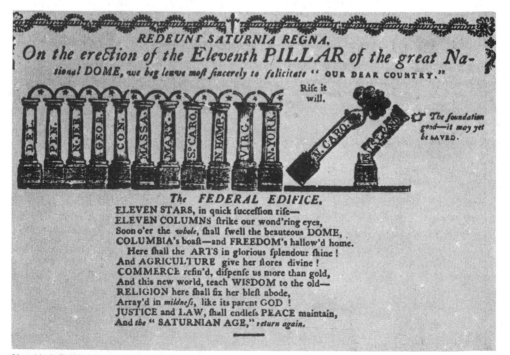

REDEUNT SATURNIA REGNA.

On the erection of the Eleventh PILLAR of the great National DOME, we beg leave most sincerely to felicitate " OUR DEAR COUNTRY."

Rise it will.

DEL. / PEN. / N. JER. / GEOR. / CON. / MASSA. / MARY. / S° CARO. / N. HAMP. / VIRG. / N. YORK.

N. CARO. / R. ISLAND.

☞ The foundation good—it may yet be SAVED.

The FEDERAL EDIFICE.

ELEVEN STARS, in quick succession rise—
ELEVEN COLUMNS strike our wond'ring eyes,
Soon o'er the *whole*, shall swell the beauteous DOME,
COLUMBIA's boast—and FREEDOM's hallow'd home.
Here shall the ARTS in glorious splendour shine !
And AGRICULTURE give her stores divine !
COMMERCE refin'd, dispense us more than gold,
And this new world, teach WISDOM to the old—
RELIGION here shall fix her blest abode,
Array'd in *mildness*, like its parent GOD !
JUSTICE and LAW, shall endless PEACE maintain,
And *the* " SATURNIAN AGE," *return again*.

New York Public Library Picture Collection.

were aboard the federal ship of state, and every state except Rhode Island had scheduled a convention.

In February, Massachusetts gave its approval after a protracted fight. Seaboard merchants and lawyers generally favored the Constitution; western Shaysites opposed it. Many of the approximately three hundred delegates, however, were uncommitted; open to persuasion, they were looking for leadership to the aging heroes Samuel Adams and John Hancock. Adams had misgivings about the Constitution but announced his approval after a meeting of the Sons of Liberty, headed by Paul Revere, voted for it. Federalists brought Hancock around by hinting that, if Virginia failed to ratify, Washington could not be president. The office then would likely go to a New Englander, and no one had a better claim than Hancock. Massachusetts ratified, 187 to 168. In April and May 1788, Maryland and South Carolina gave their approval, each by better than two-to-one majorities. Each state was dominated by a merchant-planter elite, although in Maryland even small farmers of the upper Potomac basin voted in favor of the Constitution. In June, New Hampshire ratified, and the Constitution stood approved.

The Federal Union, however, still had two gaping holes—New York and Virginia—and each was evenly divided. In Virginia the Piedmont area and the counties south of the James River, Patrick Henry's turf, were generally opposed to the Constitution. The Shenandoah Valley and the counties composing present-day West Virginia were solidly in favor of it. Westerners wanted federal help against Ohio Valley Indians.

In the convention, Patrick Henry and George Mason were a formidable Antifederalist alliance, although the Federalists could muster Washington, Madison, Randolph (who had had another change of heart), and the young Richmond attorney John Marshall. Hoping to win over those who were still wavering, Madison announced on the convention floor that he would work for a bill of rights if the Constitution were approved. The announcement, dramatic though it was, swayed very few; neither did the reams of oratory that followed. Nearly all the delegates were committed in advance through promises to the voters. The convention approved the Constitution in July 1788 by a vote of 89 to 79. In New York, the city and its environs favored the Constitution, while the rural parts of the state generally opposed it. Its convention ratified a few days after Virginia did, but by the slim margin of 30 to 27. There the promise of a bill of rights was an important factor, along with the threat that New York City would secede from the state if the state failed to join the Union. Two states remained. North Carolina's convention met that summer, and after some debate it voted to adjourn without taking action. Rhode Island ignored the entire affair. Both states joined the Union belatedly after Congress threatened to treat them as foreigners in matters of taxation and trade.

The social and geographical patterns of the vote on the Constitution suggest that most voters viewed the Constitution in light of their own interests. Merchants, professional men, former army officers, and river valley landowners generally favored the new government, as did the mechanics and tradesmen of the cities. Large landowners residing in the interior, remote from lines of communication, were inclined to oppose the Constitution; so were most small farmers, except those living in areas of Indian danger.

Many influences worked on the electorate in 1787–1788, just as Madison had anticipated. Yet once the votes were cast, the lines were drawn with remarkable firmness. That is because the election turned on an issue rather than on personalities. The delegates to the ratifying conventions were not "virtual" representatives, free to

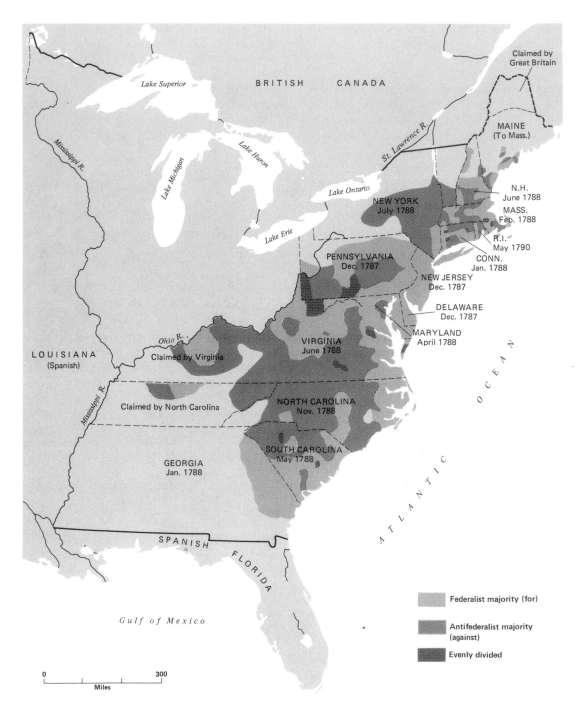

Ratification of the Constitution.

vote their consciences. They stood for an idea; they were bound by their promises to the voters. In like vein, the political entities that appeared during the ratification debate, Federalists and Antifederalists, distinguished themselves from each other by ideologies rather than by personalities and interests. The Constitution not only created a new government; it made possible a national politics, a politics dominated by party organizations confronting one another on a variety of issues, notably taxation, trade, and foreign policy.

SUMMARY

The Declaration of Independence inspired a flurry of state constitution making. Some states summoned special conventions for the purpose, but in most the legislature undertook the task. Every state, however, provided for popular ratification of the document, a recognition that a constitution was a "higher law," one resting on the constituent authority of the people themselves.

The most striking feature of the revolutionary state constitutions was their similarity to the colonial charters. The colonists had not objected to their colonial governments: They had objected to parliamentary intrusions on those governments, as well as the lack of adequate safeguards for individual rights. Once the imperial connection was broken, a charter was easily converted into a constitution. Significantly, every state appended to its constitution a declaration of rights.

The other feature common to the revolutionary constitutions was legislative supremacy. Governors had been the symbols of royal authority, and the executive branch remained under suspicion until long after the revolution. In most states governors were mere figureheads; key appointment powers remained with the assemblies. Only in Massachusetts and New York, states dominated by coalitions of merchants, lawyers, and landowners, were governors given effective powers. These states, along with South Carolina, were also the most resistant to democratic demands from the "lower orders." Elsewhere the states expanded participation in the political process by reducing property qualifications for voting and officeholding, although only the state of Pennsylvania went so far as to give all male taxpayers the right to vote.

Conservatives, who had dragged their feet on independence for fear that the sudden elimination of royal authority would lead to mob rule, were responsible for the drafting of the Articles of Confederation. Diluted by Congress, the Articles did not create the strong, effective government its sponsors desired. They were, in effect, little more than a confirmation of the existing system. They authorized neither an executive nor a judiciary. Congress had power to conduct foreign relations, coin money, regulate Indian affairs, and settle disputes among states. But it lacked the power to tax or to regulate trade. As a result, it staggered through the postwar years in chronic insolvency.

The confederation, which went into effect in 1781, boasted some achievements. A financial crisis late in the war induced Congress to establish some executive departments—an Office of Foreign Affairs and an Office of Finance, departments which would, after the establishment of the federal government, form the nucleus of the president's cabinet. The confederation also had a good record in foreign affairs. It entered into an important commercial agreement with France in 1786, and it obtained sizable loans from Dutch bankers. Finally, Congress laid the foundation for the territorial system in the West. The Northwest Ordinance of 1785 provided for the rectangular survey of the West, and the Ordinance of 1787 set up the stages by which a wilderness became a state.

In most other respects, however, the government appeared to flounder. The nation's most serious problems—depression, debtor relief and religious controversies, social upheaval—were not of Congress's making, but they alerted many, especially among the wealthy, to the need for stronger, more effective government. By 1786 such men were calling themselves Federalists. They attempted first to amend the Articles. Failing in that, they initiated a series of conventions to discuss more far-reaching revision. Their efforts culminated in the summoning of a federal convention in Philadelphia in the summer of 1787. There some fifty-five men, nearly all Federalists, drafted the federal Constitution, making the document public in September 1787. A furious debate ensued, but one by one, beginning with the smaller and weaker states, state ratifying conventions gave their approval. The Constitution went into effect in June 1788, when the requisite number of states had given their approval. Whether this parchment could be converted into an effective government, however, remained to be seen.

READING SUGGESTIONS

For the evolution of a republican ideology in the American Revolution, see Gordon S. Wood, *The Creation of the American Republic, 1776–1787* (1969). The best analyses of the revolutionary state constitutions are Elisha P. Douglass, *Rebels and Democrats* (1957), Jackson T. Main, *The Sovereign States, 1775–1783* (1973), and J. R. Pole, *Political Representation in England and the Origins of the American Republic* (1973).

The best overview of the confederation period is Forrest McDonald, *E Pluribus Unum: The Formation of the American Republic, 1776–1790* (1965), although Merrill Jensen's classic *The New Nation* (1950) remains the standard authority on the 1780s. Recent quantitative studies of the workings of the Continental Congress are H. James Henderson, *Party Politics in the Continental Congress* (1974), and Jack N. Rakove, *The Beginnings of National Politics: An Interpretive History of the Continental Congress* (1979). State politics in the 1780s are exhaustively—and exhaustingly—treated by Jackson T. Main in *Political Parties before the Constitution* (1973), and Norman K. Risjord in *Chesapeake Politics, 1780–1800* (1978).

The scholarly warfare over Charles Beard's *An Economic Interpretation of the Constitution of the United States* (1913) has largely subsided. For the most recent analysis of the relationship between economic interests and attitudes toward the Constitution, see Risjord, *Chesapeake Politics.* Several recent writers have stressed psychological and ideological factors in the drafting of the Constitution, among them Frederick Marks, *Independence on Trial: Foreign Affairs and the Making of the Constitution* (1973) and John F. Berens, *Providence and Patriotism in Early America* (1979). The best descriptions of the ratification process are Forrest McDonald, *We the People* (1958) and Jackson T. Main, *The Antifederalists* (1961). Forrest McDonald's *Novus Ordo Seclorum* (1985) is the long-awaited sequel to *We the People.*

8

INVENTING A NATION:
1789–1805

here was an undercurrent of apprehensiveness in the politics of the early republic. Gone by 1789 was the boastful optimism of '76, when John Adams declared that the American Revolution was "the most complete, unexpected, and remarkable, of any in the history of nations." In its place was anxiety—fear that the republic was drifting into monarchy or anarchy, fear of a military takeover, fear of foreign intervention. Periodic uprisings, such as Shays's Rebellion, did nothing to allay the trepidation, nor did the violent rhetoric that accompanied the beginnings of political parties. Few men in 1789 truly expected the Constitution to long endure. But endure it did, principally because the Federalists showed extraordinary managerial talent in organizing a government.

By 1800 it was clear to all that the Constitution would prevail. Political disputes by then involved not the form of government, but the policies it would pursue. Defeated at the polls in that year, the Federalists turned over power to a new set of leaders with different interests and different views. Such a peaceful transition was rare in its time—and is still, even in our own.

⊔From Constitution to Working Government

Despite their overwhelming victory in the ratification process, the Federalists were still "running scared" when they approached the first congressional election in the winter of 1788–1789. "A considerable effort will be made to procure the election of Antifederalists to the first Congress," fretted Washington, "to undo all that has been done." Federalists need not

have worried. The results indicated that even those voters who had opposed the Constitution were willing to give it a try. In the first House of Representatives there were only half a dozen Antifederalists, most of them from Patrick Henry's part of Virginia. In the Senate there were only two, both from Virginia. The Henryites in the Virginia assembly deprived Madison of a seat in the Senate, so he secured election to the House instead. The electoral college met in February 1789 and chose Washington president, as expected. John Adams, second highest in the balloting, became vice president.

The First Congress gathered in New York in March 1789 and marked time awaiting the president. Washington, busy with his affairs at Mount Vernon, was late in arriving, and in the interval Congress wrangled over titles. John Adams, who presided over the Senate, wondered how to address the chief executive, volunteering the thought that "Mr. President" was not dignified enough. Federalist senators suggested "His Excellency" or "His Elective Highness," nonsense that prompted one Antifederalist to dub Adams "His Rotundity." Beneath the surface hilarity, however, lay an undercurrent of party tension. The inauguration took place on April 30, and Washington's garb—a dark suit of American manufacture adorned with an elegant dress sword—bespoke his desire to retain republican simplicity while commanding respect for the office.

The government's first need was revenue. In May, Madison, who assumed the role of Federalist floor leader in the House, introduced a bill levying customs duties on imports. The general level of rates was 5 percent of the value of the article, but a protective duty of 50 percent (high enough to discourage imports) was placed on a few products, such as steel and cloth, to encourage their domestic manufacture.

(*Chapter opening photo*) George Washington taking the oath of office, 1789.

⊔ Fleshing Out the Executive Branch

Congress next turned to the task of fleshing out the constitutional outlines for the executive and judiciary. The three executive departments that had been formed in the last years of the revolution were reshaped into the state, treasury, and war departments. As secretary of state, Washington appointed Thomas Jefferson, who had been serving as minister to France since 1784. To head the treasury, the president named 32-year-old Alexander Hamilton, an experienced financier who had helped organize the Bank of New York in the mid-1780s. Washington's former artillery commander, Henry Knox, had been managing the war department for some years; he and his staff were simply brought into the new government.

The judiciary caused Congress more trouble. Courts had come under attack in a number of states during the depression years; an added layer of federal judges was certain to arouse suspicion. The constitutional convention evaded the problem by placing in Article III a vaguely worded authorization vesting the judicial power of

The columned building at the end of the street in this water color sketch was originally New York's City Hall. It was the seat of the Continental Congress for a time, and after the Constitution was approved it became the first capitol of the federal government. Under its columned portico Washington was inaugurated President, April 30, 1789. (The new government went into effect on March 4, but last-minute details at Mount Vernon and celebrations along the route delayed the first President's arrival in New York until the end of April.) The "widow's walks" on the tops of the houses bespoke New York's seafaring history. The stepped gables on the house fronts were reminders of the city's Dutch ancestry.

New York Public Library

the United States in "one Supreme Court, and in such inferior Courts as the Congress may from time to time ordain and establish." Even so, this provision was a major target of Antifederalists in the ratification debate. Federal courts, Antifederalists argued, would be remote, inaccessible to the poor, and chiefly of value to merchants in collecting debts.

Congress, after an extended debate, worked out a compromise. The Judiciary Act of 1789 authorized a Supreme Court of six members (the current number, nine, was not set until after the Civil War) and a hierarchy of circuit and district courts. This satisfied the demands of nationalists for a uniform federal system of justice. In a bow to Antifederalist fears, however, Congress limited the jurisdiction of the federal courts to cases arising out of the Constitution, laws, or treaties of the United States. In short, ordinary civil and criminal jurisdiction was left to the state courts.

BILL OF RIGHTS

Having brought the government into being, Congress turned its attention back to the constitutional blueprint. The absence of a Bill of Rights had been the subject of criticism during the ratification debate, and it had been a rallying cry for Antifederalists. A people that had just concluded a war in defense of their rights was naturally concerned that those rights be forever guaranteed. Nearly every state convention suggested amendments to the Constitution, and a couple approved the Constitution only after the Federalists promised to add a bill of rights.

Madison, a foe of a bill of rights when George Mason first proposed it at Philadelphia, was nevertheless one of the first to recognize the political advantages in the idea. Amendments that guaranteed such obvious freedoms as speech, press, and religion would not seriously hamper the new

government, yet they would cut the ground from under the Antifederalists. Madison took it upon himself to collect and codify the more than two hundred amendments proposed by the ratifying conventions, and early in the summer he introduced seventeen to the House of Representatives. Congress cut the number to twelve, and the states over the next two years gave their approval to ten. (Among those eliminated were an amendment excusing conscientious objectors from military service, one that continually enlarged the House of Representatives as population increased, and one that stipulated that a pay increase voted by one Congress could not go into effect until the next Congress, so there would be an election in between—all a measure of Madison's progressivism and foresight.)

Only the first eight amendments are specifically concerned with rights. The Ninth Amendment was a catchall, a guarantee of undefined rights beyond those listed in the first eight amendments.* The Tenth Amendment, which specified that all powers not delegated to Congress are retained by the states and the people, is simply an affirmation of federalism.

The Bill of Rights did not attain constitutional significance until the twentieth century, when the federal government became large enough and powerful enough to invade the lives of citizens. (The Supreme Court did not have occasion to examine the meaning of free speech, for instance, until 1919.) Madison himself tended to disparage the amendments, calling them a mere "paper barrier" against the passions of the multitude. Yet they did have short-run political impact. Criticism

---

* It has been seldom invoked, although the Supreme Court did refer to it in 1962 when it overturned a state law that prohibited the sale of birth control devices, thereby establishing a right that evidently had not occurred to the Founding Fathers.

of the Constitution subsided; Antifederalism was dead.

HAMILTON'S FISCAL SYSTEM

After a busy summer, members of Congress departed for home in September 1789, leaving one crucial problem unresolved—the public credit. Now that the government had revenue, it was important that it pay off its debts so it could borrow money in the future. The matter was not as simple as it appeared. The various paper securities issued by the war department, by the office of finance, and by Congress itself during the revolution had depreciated considerably in the 1780s, and much

When Washington married the widowed Martha Custis in January 1759, he found himself the stepfather of her two children, John Parke Custis (Jackie), age 3, and Martha Parke Custis (Patsy), age 2. These were the only children they ever had. Martha was a possessive, indulgent mother who showered the children with gifts from their infancy. George felt for the children less a parent's devotion than a stepfather's sense of responsibility. Determined to be "generous and attentive," Washington closely supervised the childrens' education. Both, alas, proved uneducable. Patsy, an epileptic, died in a fit at age 12; and Jackie grew into a spoiled, indolent young man who secretly cheated his stepfather whenever he had the opportunity. After sitting out most of the Revolution, he attended Washington's camp at Yorktown, caught a fever, and died. He left two children, George Washington Parke Custis (Little Washington) and Eleanor Parke Custis (Nelly), whom the Washingtons took in and raised at Mount Vernon. They appear in this painting by Edward Savage, *The Washington Family,* done shortly after Washington became President. Most family portraits of the 18th century have a rigid formality about them, in part because children were portrayed as miniature adults. Savage, however, captured in this scene an appealing sense of family warmth.

The John Carter Brown Library, Brown University.

of the debt had fallen into the hands of merchant-speculators. If those notes were paid off at face value, the speculators would get a hefty windfall. Aware of the political ramifications, Congress dumped the problem into the lap of the new secretary of the treasury, Alexander Hamilton, with a resolution asking him to prepare recommendations.

Hamilton labored hard through the autumn, and when Congress returned to New York in January, he was ready with a report on the public credit. Hamilton's proposal was simple, courageous, and politically explosive. He proposed to redeem the wartime securities at their face value by offering to exchange them for government bonds. These bonds, to be issued by the treasury, would bear an interest of 4 percent and would be paid off from government tax receipts over a period of fifty years. Such bonds could be expected to hold their value, and the government's credit would be restored. Beside the government, the chief beneficiaries of Hamilton's scheme were the wealthy, for it was they who held the wartime securities. Hamilton considered this an additional advantage. Wealth to him meant power, and to have the most powerful element in society tied to the government by self-interest would ensure the durability of the Federalist new order. In Congress, Madison spoke up for those who did not benefit by the plan—planters, farmers, and tradesmen. These were the people saddled with taxes that Hamilton would channel into the pockets of northern merchants. The House of Representatives overrode his objections and approved Hamilton's funding system by a lopsided majority. Madison's opposition, nevertheless, was the first crack in Federalist ranks.

The second feature of Hamilton's report created more opposition. In addition to funding the national debt, Hamilton proposed that the federal government assume the debts incurred by the states in fighting the war. The debts were incurred in the common cause, he argued; it was only just that they be borne by all. Under this plan, creditors of the states would be tied to the federal treasury, thereby strengthening federal authority at the expense of the states. Madison was again on his feet in opposition, and this time he got more support. The southern states had borne the brunt of the fighting in the last years of the war; their governments had been disrupted, their accounts were in disarray. The confederation finance office had routinely rejected southern claims for compensation after the war because they were not in proper order. Southern congressmen feared that if the federal government suddenly assumed state debts, most of the federal payments would go to the tidy accountants of the North. Southerners, with help from Pennsylvania, managed to defeat assumption of state debts on three successive roll calls in the spring of 1790.

THE BEGINNING OF POLITICAL PARTIES

The alliance with Pennsylvania was a fine thread in the web of intrigue that marked the beginning of political parties. No one, except New Yorkers and New Englanders, was content with the location of the nation's capital in New York. Southerners considered it too distant from home, too fever-ridden in summer, and too frigid in winter. Madison was particularly offended by the city's coarse amorality, as merchant-speculators crowded the House galleries to salute the Hamiltonian scheme. Pennsylvanians naturally wanted to return the capital to Philadelphia. Southerners preferred a site on the Potomac, but they were willing to bargain. Southerners and Pennsylvanians had a working alliance that involved both the capital and state debts when Thomas Jefferson arrived in town to take up his duties as secretary of state.

The Library Company of Philadelphia

"Indians Being Shown Philadelphia" commemorates a 1793 visit to the nation's capital of a delegation of western Indians. The Speaker of the House of Representatives himself escorted the Indians around the city.

Jefferson later claimed that Hamilton initiated things by coming to him with a plea for help, and Jefferson agreed to hold a dinner party to bring the various elements together. Whether in fact a deal was worked out over a bottle of Jefferson's favorite Madeira cannot be told, but somehow that summer a compromise was achieved. The capital was moved to Philadelphia, where it was to remain for ten years while a new capital was built on a site of Washington's choosing. The Treasury switched its policy and began accepting southern debt claims, and in Congress enough votes were switched to allow passage of assumption of state debts. The Pennsylvanians doubtless thought that in ten years' time the capital would be permanently fixed in Philadelphia. If they felt betrayed when Washington chose instead a ten-mile square of land straddling the Potomac and suspiciously close to Mount Vernon, they were gentlemanly enough

not to show it. The Virginians won not only the capital; due to the relaxed regulations, they were also the chief beneficiaries of assumption of state debts.

When Congress reconvened in December 1790, Hamilton was ready with two more papers, a second report on the public credit and a report on a national bank. In the first of these he proposed additional taxes to pay off the debt he had amassed, and Congress responded with the excise of 1791, which placed duties on various goods—mostly luxuries, such as whiskey— produced within the country. The excise ultimately produced a taxpayer rebellion (the Whiskey Rebellion, in 1794), but there was little immediate opposition because Madison, among others, had long favored a tax on luxuries to keep the republic lean and virtuous. The proposal for a national bank caused more difficulty, for such an institution would solidify the alliance between government and northern mer-

The Whiskey Rebellion. In this drawing, whiskey rebels have tarred and feathered a federal tax collector and are riding him out of town on a rail, while the mob cheers.

chants. The Bank of the United States, as it came to be called, was to serve as the agent of the Treasury in the collection and disbursement of funds. Its notes were accepted by the government as legal tender, and they were intended to function as a national currency. The government was to own one fifth of the shares of stock, and the president would appoint one fifth of the board of directors.

When the bank charter came before Congress in February 1791, Madison was again in the forefront of opposition. He had long favored strong, effective government, but he disliked the prospect of a government wedded to northern merchants. He rested his argument, however, on broader ground, pointing out that Congress lacked the authority to create a bank, since the chartering of corporations was not among its delegated powers. Congress approved the charter anyway, but Madison's argument did raise some doubts in Washington's mind. He decided to seek the opinion of his cabinet, treating that body for the first time as a group of advisers. Jefferson followed Madison's lead and claimed that the bank was unconstitutional. Hamilton ingeniously turned the constitu-

tional argument on its head. At the end of the list of delegated powers granted Congress in Article I, Section 8, he pointed out, is authority to pass all laws "necessary and proper" to carry out its powers. Among the delegated powers, Hamilton continued, is power to coin money, collect taxes, and pay debts; surely a bank was a "necessary and proper" agent for carrying out these assignments. Hamilton, in effect, was suggesting that buried in the specifically delegated powers of Congress were certain "implied powers" that gave Congress latitude and flexibility in meeting the needs of the nation. The argument convinced Washington, and he signed the bank charter into law.

The split between Jefferson and Hamilton reflected the widening rift in Federalist ranks. The break that had begun with Madison in Congress now extended to the president's cabinet. And the dispute had become an ideological one. Hamilton stood for the expansion of federal authority and liberal use of presidential powers; Jefferson and Madison preferred a narrow interpretation of the Constitution and a strict accounting of governmental powers. By the end of 1791, Jefferson and Madison were referring to themselves as "republicans" or the "republican interest." It was a shrewd choice of name, for it implied that their opponents were covert monarchists, subverting the government by their careless use of executive powers. The label also gave the opposition an identity; a party system was beginning to form.

Through 1792, President Washington remained aloof from the party contest, and both sides supported his reelection. Republicans concentrated their fire on Vice President Adams, whose political writings seemed to endorse the principle of executive authority. Adams too won reelection, but several states gave their vice presidential electoral votes to New York's Antifederalist Governor George Clinton, and Virginia threw its to the aging revolutionary Samuel Adams.

Republicans took their case to the people in pamphlets and newspaper essays. In mid-1791 Jefferson and Madison persuaded Philip Freneau, a poet-journalist from New Jersey, to start an anti-Hamilton newspaper in Philadelphia, the *National Gazette*. But despite Freneau's strenuous efforts, the public was not much involved in the party contest. Hamiltonian finance was simply too dry a text for partisan sermonizing. Foreign affairs was another story: A republican revolution in France and the outbreak of war in Europe sparked an intense debate concerning American policy. The European war, a match between British monarchy and French republicanism, provided party propagandists with symbols familiar to every voter. Within a year, every county courthouse was the scene of intense partisan debate. Grassroots organization would complete the formation of the first party system.

⊔ Foreign Policy and Party Politics

News of the outbreak of war in Europe reached Philadelphia in early April of 1793. Washington immediately summoned his cabinet to consider America's alternatives. The alliance with France, signed by Benjamin Franklin in 1778, was still in effect. The alliance did not oblige the United States to enter the war, but it did require it to help defend the French West Indies if attacked. That they would be attacked was highly likely. For half a century the British navy had made a practice of seizing French sugar islands at the first hint of war.

The cabinet split along familiar lines. Hamilton leaned toward Britain in the conflict, on the realistic ground that the former mother country was still America's principal trading partner. The success of his financial system depended to a large extent on peaceful trade and foreign credit. Jefferson, on the other hand, was more sympathetic to France. He had been in Paris in the heady days of 1789 when the populace overran the Bastille and a convention undertook to limit the powers of the king. Republican France, Jefferson felt, was a natural friend and ally in a world full of monarchies. Neither Jefferson nor Hamilton wanted to enter the war, and Washington eventually compromised their views in a proclamation warning Americans not to engage in hostile activities.

CITIZEN GENET

The very day that Washington's Neutrality Proclamation was issued—April 20, 1793—an emissary of the French republic, Edmond Genet, landed in Charleston, South Carolina. Charleston was not a common port of embarcation, and Genet later claimed that his ship was forced into the harbor by adverse winds. More likely it was a political wind, for Genet well knew that the southern states were predominantly Jeffersonian and pro-French. Even South Carolina Federalists, mindful of French aid in the revolution, welcomed him enthusiastically.

Genet's instructions were to secure an American commitment to live up to the terms of the 1778 alliance and, if possible, to enlist American ships as French privateers. A privateer was a warship that preyed upon enemy commerce for its own profit. Possession of a letter of marque, issued by a government at war, distinguished it from a common pirate. Impressed with his welcome, Genet issued letters of marque and French flags to several Charleston ship captains and started north toward Philadelphia. Republicans organized banquets and receptions at every stop along the way.

Word of Genet's activities preceded him, and he got a frosty reception from Washington. Secretary of State Jefferson was cordial but firm. American seaports were not to be turned into French naval bases, he informed the Frenchman; there were to be no more privateers. Genet, having mistaken southern hospitality for political passion, concluded that the administration was out of touch with the people. He went to the press with his story, accusing Washington of being an enemy of France. Worse, he commissioned another privateer, *La Petite Democrat*, right in the nation's capital. The vessel slipped into Delaware Bay before Jefferson could stop it. Chagrined, Jefferson sent an account of Genet's antics to the French government, confident that the French would recall their wayward emissary. But the cycle of French revolutionary politics had brought a new government to power, and a message recalling Genet was already on the way. The new government was controlled by extremist Jacobins,* who were already indulging in the bloodbath known as the Reign of Terror. Rather than face the guillotine, Genet decided to remain in America. He settled in New York and married a daughter of Governor George Clinton.

---

* Jacobins, so named because they met secretly in a convent built by Jacobin friars in Paris, were a club of radical revolutionaries who wanted to eliminate the French aristocracy.

Through all this the Republican press, led by Freneau, lavished praise on Genet, identifying its own cause with that of the French. Jefferson soon realized that Genet was political poison, but the damage was done. When Genet publicly criticized Washington, the public rallied to the president. In sudden disfavor, Republicans fell silent and regrouped. They were soon presented with an opportunity to recover. By the winter of 1793–1794, the nation was involved in another diplomatic confrontation—this time with Great Britain.

TROUBLE WITH BRITAIN

Britain's grant of American independence in 1783, as Benjamin Franklin predicted, brought peace but not friendship between the two nations. Britain excluded American vessels from the West Indian colonies, refused to discuss a trade agreement, and did not even maintain a fully accredited minister in the United States until 1791. Most galling of all to Americans, the British violated the peace agreement by maintaining military garrisons on American soil, notably in the northwest posts along the Great Lakes—Oswego, Niagara, Detroit, and Michillimackinac (in the straits between Lake Michigan and Lake Huron). Britain justified the trespass on the grounds that Americans too had violated the treaty by refusing to pay their prewar debts. Most of these were debts owed by southern planters to British merchants. Southerners demanded that Britain first reimburse them for slaves carried off during the war. The round of claims and counterclaims only deepened the mutual distrust.

Indian warfare after 1790 called new attention to the British presence in the Northwest. There was sporadic fighting along the Ohio River throughout the 1780s, and it intensified when war veterans with land warrants established Marietta on the north bank of the river in 1788. There

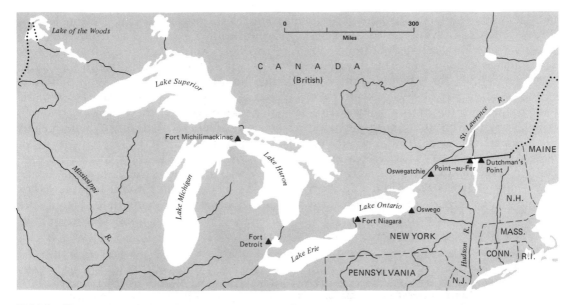

British military posts after 1783.

Indian wars in the Northwest, 1790–1795.

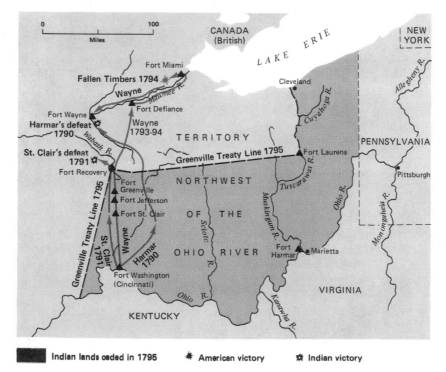

■ Indian lands ceded in 1795   ✴ American victory   ✹ Indian victory

had been no legitimate Indian cessions north of the Ohio River, and Indian resistance to white encroachment stiffened. In 1790 an expedition sent by President Washington into the Miami country of western Ohio suffered heavy casualties and managed only to burn a few Indian cornfields. The following year another expedition under General Arthur St. Clair suffered the worst defeat in the history of the frontier at the hands of Miamis and Shawnees—more than 900 dead and wounded.

Americans suspected that British Indian agents, stationed at Detroit and Fort Malden (at the mouth of the Detroit River), were supplying arms to the Indians. Their suspicions were confirmed when the British in 1793 boldly moved south into Ohio and built a fort (Fort Miami) on the Maumee River (near present-day Toledo). In that same year a new American commander, General Anthony Wayne, began building a string of forts of his own, as he drove into the heart of Miami country. He erected Fort Greenville near the headwaters of the Miami River, Fort Recovery at the site of St. Clair's defeat, and Fort Defiance at the junction of the Auglaize

Federalist architecture. The Massachusetts State House, designed by Charles Bulfinch, was completed in 1797. Bulfinch's design relied heavily on the work of the Scottish architect, Robert Adam, who lent grandeur to his public buildings by the use of ponderous arches and columns and balustrades as decoration. This form of design became known as the "federal style," both because it coincided with the beginnings of the federal government and because it was much favored in Federalist New England.

Greater Boston Convention and Tourist Bureau.

and the Maumee. On August 20, 1794, Wayne decisively defeated the Miamis in the Battle of Fallen Timbers and sent them scurrying to the British for help. Fearful of provoking a new Anglo-American war, the British commander at Fort Miami closed his gates to the Indians and shortly thereafter retired to Detroit. In the summer of 1795, Wayne forced a mass meeting of Indian delegates from all the northwestern tribes to sign the Treaty of Greenville, in which they ceded all but the northwest corner of Ohio.

Paralleling the border warfare in 1793–1794 was an Anglo-American confrontation on the high seas. When the war with France began, Britain threw up a naval blockade that sought to cut the French off from their colonies in the West Indies. When the French opened their colonies to American vessels as a means of evading the blockade, Britain countered by invoking the "rule of 1756." Instituted during the French and Indian War, this regulation declared that a trade illegal in time of peace was illegal in time of war. Since France did not allow American traders in its empire in peacetime, it could not, said the British, do so in wartime. The irony of the regulation was that Britain was seeking to enforce French navigation acts the French did not want enforced. Adding churlishness to malevolence, the British did not inform Americans of the new regulation. The Royal

Republican architecture. Thomas Jefferson rejected the ornate architecture of the former mother country. He thought that simpler, classical forms of design were more suitable for a republic. As secretary of state, Jefferson was in charge of the construction of the nation's capital, and he saw to it that the architectural flavor of Washington, D.C., was Roman. The University of Virginia (1817), portrayed in this lithograph, was Jefferson's final architectural statement. Its centerpiece was a Roman rotunda, built in precise mathematical proportions, facing two rows of pavilions, each representing a different Greek order.

Courtesy Old Print Shop, New York.

Navy simply seized every American vessel it encountered carrying French goods, more than two hundred in all.

THE JAY TREATY

When news of these British seizures arrived in Philadelphia in the spring of 1794, Madison proposed that Congress cut off all trade with Great Britain. Federalists immediately objected. Their mercantile clients were making enough profit out of the neutral trade to compensate for a few losses, and they did not want to antagonize Britain, the country's principal trading partner. In the end, Congress compromised on a thirty-day embargo. To prevent a further deterioration in Anglo-American relations, Federalists pressed Washington to send a special emissary to Britain. Washington agreed, and selected John Jay. The choice underscored the importance Washington attached to the mission. Jay was Chief Justice of the Supreme Court, and he had served as secretary of foreign affairs in the Confederation.

Jay, through no fault of his own, arrived in London at the wrong time. Britain was supreme on the sea, its allies were closing in on Paris, and the French were tearing themselves apart in a Reign of Terror. The ministry of William Pitt desired peace but was not disposed to grant concessions. To get a dialogue started, Jay dropped any notion of securing a statement of America's neutral rights—which meant, in effect, an acceptance of the British position on blockades, searches, and seizures.

The treaty signed in November 1794 created an international commission to supervise the payment of American debts, and the British agreed to surrender the northwest posts by June 1796. A commercial agreement made each the "most favored nation" in trading with the other (which prevented special favors from being granted to a third party) and gave Ameri-cans limited trading privileges in India and the British West Indies. Given Jay's lack of bargaining leverage, the settlement was probably the best that could be obtained. The British certainly considered it generous; Pitt had to defend himself in the House of Commons against charges of being pro-American. The treaty did usher in a decade of Anglo-American goodwill, and in the atmosphere of friendship Americans gained trading privileges in the West Indies far beyond the limited provisions of the treaty. The commercial benefits of Jay's diplomacy were reflected in the booming economy the Jeffersonians inherited after 1800.

The problem with the treaty was its short-run political impact. Southerners immediately noted that most of the British concessions benefited the North (surrender of forts and trading concessions), while the American concessions meant that they would have to pay their debts. Jefferson and Madison were particularly offended at the treaty's failure to define neutral rights, which left the United States humiliatingly subject to the whims of British naval officers. The provision for commercial equality actually worsened the situation because it deprived America of its one shield, commercial retaliation such as the embargo on trade that Madison had been pushing in Congress.

Aware of its political implications, the Senate voted to keep the treaty secret until it was ratified. Inevitably it leaked to the Republican press, which exploded in indignation. Crowds assembled on village greens and in county courthouses to sign mass petitions addressed to the president. Shrieked one Republican editor: "Damn John Jay! Damn anyone who won't damn John Jay! Damn anyone who doesn't sit up all night with a candle in his window damning John Jay!" Jay himself ruefully observed that he could have found his way across the country at night by the light of his burning effigies.

The initial uproar was spontaneous, but politicians soon gained control of the demonstrations and turned them to party advantage. The meetings frequently named committees to maintain contact with party leaders and disseminate party views. Republicans had the initial advantage in organization because of the unpopularity of the treaty, but Federalists were quick to react with meetings and committees of their own. The Jay Treaty completed the polarization of the country. By the time Washington left office, scarcely a voter was not committed to a party.

PINCKNEY'S TREATY

Europeans were forced to guess the contents of the Jay Treaty, since the Washington administration refused to disclose its provisions. But it was widely assumed that the treaty amounted to an Anglo-American alliance. This produced a mixed reaction. The French were furious and the Spanish were terrified. Spain had been seduced into the war by British diplomacy but felt uncomfortable in the British embrace. France was Spain's traditional companion. By 1795, moreover, the French were beginning to win. A new government, the Directory, had restored order in Paris with the help of a fast-rising Corsican soldier, Napoleon Bonaparte. The Netherlands had fallen under French control; Prussia and other German states had quit the war. The Spanish Bourbons, ever timid, and despite the wealth of their empire, chronically insolvent, wished for peace.

The Spanish hesitated to desert the British, however, without first pacifying Brit-

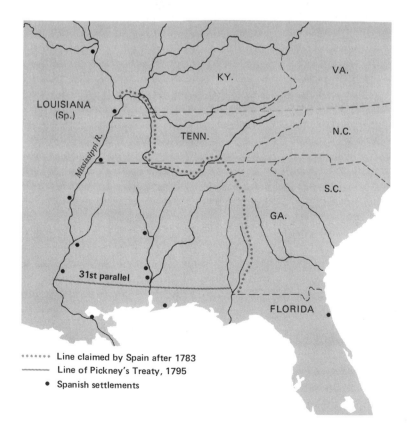

······· Line claimed by Spain after 1783
——— Line of Pickney's Treaty, 1795
• Spanish settlements

ain's seeming ally, the United States. And there were a number of disputes to be resolved. After the American Revolution, Spain, fearful of American expansionism, had tried to create a buffer between its exposed imperial flank in Florida and Louisiana and the United States. During the 1780s, Spain laid claim to the southwest as far as the Tennessee River, provided arms and supplies to the warlike Creeks, encouraged separatist movements in Kentucky and Tennessee, and closed the lower Mississippi to American traffic. These activities kept the area in turmoil and stalled the growth of Georgia and Tennessee.

In October 1795, Spanish premier Prince Godoy (who described himself as "the prince of peace") summoned the American minister in Madrid, Thomas Pinckney, to the royal palace of San Lorenzo. Anxious to mend Spain's New World fences, Godoy agreed to Pinckney's every demand. Spain settled on the thirty-first parallel as the northern boundary of Florida and agreed to open the port of New Orleans to American shippers for a period of three years. The Treaty of San Lorenzo (commonly known as Pinckney's Treaty) was thus a diplomatic triumph for the United States. But it also gave Godoy the leverage he needed to switch sides. Within a year, Spain was in military alliance with France.

By then France was on the brink of war with the United States. The French entanglement dominated Washington's last year in office and the four years of his successor, John Adams.

⊔ John Adams's Presidency

Washington's troubles with the French began with the Genet mission, which offended him, and the Reign of Terror, which horrified him. Democratic Societies, which appeared in a number of cities and towns in the wake of the Genet mission, worried him. The societies were pro-French in sympathy and Jeffersonian in politics, and most were quite short-lived. But Washington compared them to the Jacobin clubs of France and fretted that the societies were the agencies of French subversion. These concerns also made Washington, who had remained aloof from the Jefferson-Hamilton squabble through his first term, more of a party president. Fear that the Republicans were tools of the French, together with Republican newspaper criticism of his foreign policy, drove him into the ranks of Federalists. This was most evident in his cabinet appointments.

Jefferson, uncomfortable with the cabinet tension he himself had helped to create, resigned his post at the State Department at the end of 1793, and Hamilton, citing financial hardship, followed a year later. Washington named moderate Edmund Randolph to succeed Jefferson, but when he resigned after only a year, Washington turned to an arch-Federalist, Timothy Pickering of Massachusetts. To the Treasury, Washington named Oliver Wolcott, a protégé of Hamilton's from Connecticut. When aging Henry Knox left the War Department, Washington replaced him with Maryland Federalist James McHenry, whose partisan vigor compensated in part for a fuzzy mind.

WASHINGTON'S FAREWELL

In a farewell address in September 1796, Washington warned against partisanship, especially of the sort that associated with British or French interests. He also recommended that Americans "steer clear of permanent alliances with any portion of the foreign world." Since Europe was frequently involved in warfare, Washington thought it best that Americans confine themselves to trade and avoid military commitments. Ironically, the Jay Treaty was being read in France as precisely what Washington warned against—an Anglo-American alliance. And Washington's refusal to disclose the terms of the treaty did nothing to dispel French fears. The result was a French overreaction that clouded the election of 1796 and troubled the administration of Washington's successor, John Adams.

Both parties made formal nominations in 1796, and they did it by caucus of party members in Congress. The caucus, a meeting at which party policy and candidates were decided upon and a recent addition to the party apparatus, would remain the standard vehicle for presidential nominations until the 1820s. The Federalists named Adams and Thomas Pinckney, the latter having returned victoriously from Spain. Republicans chose Jefferson and New York Senator Aaron Burr. Adams won the election by 71 electoral votes to Jefferson's 68. Under the rules set up by the Constitution, Jefferson, by coming in second, became vice president. It was to be an uneasy four years for both men.

The Clash of Ideologies. Americans of both political persuasions had a low regard for human nature. Because human nature was frail, it was generally agreed, republics were frail. These feelings produced, according to one historian "a peculiarly volatile and crisis-ridden ideology, one with little resilience, little margin for error, little tradition of success behind it, and one that was vulnerable both psychologically and historically." Republicans and Federalists concurred that greed and corruption were the nemesis of the republic; they disagreed, however, about its cause and cure. Republicans blamed the Hamiltonian system, with its crass appeal to self-interest, and they denounced as degenerate the speculation in paper wealth that it fostered. The Jeffersonians had no objection to business activities. Indeed, their in-

sistence on separating the functions of business and government foreshadowed the age of laissez faire with its accompanying spurt of economic growth. What troubled the Jeffersonians instead was that government favors were going to a favored few. They worried that this privileged elite might come to dominate the government and undermine the republic.

Federalist apprehensions were even more complex. Many Federalists, especially in New England (which would dominate the party after 1800), believed that religious faith was the key to human virtue. The future of the republic thus depended on a religious citizenry. For nearly a century, the Calvinist clergy had witnessed the seemingly steady decline of religious commitment. Religious rationalism (deism) and worldly ostentation seemed to go hand in hand. By the 1790s there were so many ominous portents abroad that armageddon seemed at hand. With the French Revolution came a new interest in the writings of French rationalists, such as Voltaire, who rejected religion altogether as either harmful or irrelevant. The 1795 publication of Tom Paine's *Age of Reason,* a distillation of the religious skepticism of the French Enlightenment, was a terrible shock. Paine was not only irreligious; he was popular. Worse yet, he coupled political radicalism with religious rationalism. For a clergy accustomed to law, order, and "steady habits," this was alarming indeed.

It was easy enough for them to link the Jeffersonian Republicans with this insidious French influence. The Republicans were strongest in the South, a land of irreligious and luxury-loving nabobs, and in the cosmopolitan cities like New York and Philadelphia. In the Democratic Societies, which had sprung up in the wake of the Genet mission, Federalists even saw the advance agents of French subversion. These secret clubs were not only pro-French and Jeffersonian; some even embraced such radical causes as women's rights, penal reform, and free public education. Thus Federalist apprehensions by the beginning of John Adams's presidency were verging on paranoia. Some, such as Timothy Dwight, president of Yale and widely known as the "Protestant Pope of New England," believed there was an international conspiracy afoot aimed at the United States. A war scare with France brought these xenophobic fears to the surface.

THE QUASI-WAR WITH FRANCE

In France, the idealism that had characterized the early years of its revolution had degenerated into a rather nasty imperialism. French armies had overrun the Netherlands, western Germany, and northern Italy. The French had set up republican governments in those areas, which were little more than satellites of the Directory in Paris. After Spain switched sides and Austria purchased peace by surrendering Belgium to France in 1797, Britain was left standing alone.

Perceiving the United States to be an ally of Britain's, France then turned on the American republic. A decree of March 1797 (coinciding with Adams's inauguration) authorized the seizure of American vessels found carrying British goods. By June, some 316 ships were confiscated in the West Indies. Secretary of State Pickering thought the seizures a cause for war, but Adams decided on a final effort at negotiation. To aid Charles C. Pinckney, whom Washington had sent to Paris, Adams sent John Marshall, a young Virginia Federalist, and Elbridge Gerry of Massachusetts. When the three American commissioners gathered in Paris in the fall of 1797, they found French foreign minister Talleyrand uncommunicative. They were preparing to return home when three French agents, subsequently described in the American report as X, Y, and Z, appeared at their chambers. These agents suggested that the wheels of diplomacy might be greased with a gift to the Directory of $250,000 and an official loan to the French government of $12 million. The Americans disliked the idea of a bribe, though they knew such things were standard in European diplomacy, and they objected outright to the loan because it would have compromised American neutrality. That, of course, was precisely what Talleyrand wanted. He hoped to undo the Jay Treaty, tie America to France, and leave Britain isolated.

When it became apparent that Talleyrand would not modify his demands, Marshall and Pinckney sent a blistering note to President Adams describing the humiliating treatment they had received and started home. Gerry stayed on in hope of reaching a settlement. When President Adams published the XYZ dispatches in the spring of 1798, the public reacted with outrage. Newspapers shrieked "Millions for defense, but not one cent for tribute!" Congress girded for war. It increased the regular army to 10,000 and authorized the president to enlist a "provisional army" of 50,000. It created a Department of the Navy to administer the half-dozen warships that had been under construction since 1794, and it permitted privateers to capture French armed vessels. It did not declare war, however, principally because the president never requested it. Fighting was confined to a couple of naval engagements in the West Indies, as the fledgling American navy chased the French out of the New World.

THE "REIGN OF WITCHES"

After completing preparations for a military contest with the French foe abroad, the Federalists turned on their domestic enemies. The function of political parties was not yet fully understood, and Federalists tended to view any opposition as divisive. They worried too, as Washington had, about the spread of the French revolutionary ideology. Some feared the Jeffersonians were disciples of Jacobinism. What alarmed Federalists most was an influx in the late 1790s of immigrants with either radical or pro-French ideas.

The radical turn in the French Revolution after the king was executed in 1793 forced many moderates to flee. Perhaps as many as 15,000 made their way to the United States. Although not Jacobins, as Federalists feared, they continued to identify with their native France, and most supported the Jeffersonian party in America. Another source of French refugees was the Caribbean island of Santo Domingo, where an upheaval that began as a slave uprising and ended in civil war sent some 10,000 Creoles, mulattoes, and white planters fleeing to America. The majority landed in Norfolk and Baltimore, adding fuel to Federalist fears of Jacobinism in those Republican cities. A third source of potentially subversive immigrants was Ireland, where an uprising against British rule was crushed in 1798. Although there was no spurt of Irish refugees, the arrival in America of several of the most prominent Irish patriots worried Federalists. Federalists who already believed there was an international conspiracy afoot saw added danger in this insidious influx of foreigners. The war scare gave them an opportunity for an assault on aliens and other subversives.

The Jeffersonian minority in Congress resisted the military preparations as unnecessary. Indeed, they regarded the entire XYZ affair as a Federalist plot to keep themselves in power. On the other hand, they had no objection to the regulation of enemy aliens. A bill giving the president power to deport citizens of a country with which the United States was at war slipped through Congress with little opposition. Republicans became alarmed, however, when Federalists introduced a bill giving

the president authority to deport any alien he saw fit. That seemed politically motivated, as well as conferring on the president a potentially dangerous power. Republicans also objected to a Naturalization Act that extended the waiting period for an alien to become a naturalized citizen (and hence obtain the right to vote) from five to fourteen years.

After cutting at the fringes of Republican support, the Federalists in July 1798 struck directly with a Sedition Act that made it a crime to publish anything of a false, malicious, or scandalous nature against the president, the cabinet, or the Congress (but not the vice president, who was fair mark for any sort of slander). The measure did include certain procedural safeguards—trial by jury and proof of both falsehood and malicious intent—but Federalist judges ignored or evaded these restrictions.

The Sedition Act was transparently political. It bore an expiration date of 1800, which meant that it was designed to muzzle criticism during the presidential election. Its enforcement was likewise slanted. Not a single Federalist was brought to trial, although Federalist papers were at least as abusive as the Jeffersonian sheets. In the end twenty-five newspaper editors were arrested, seventeen indicted, and ten convicted. It was not a "reign of terror" in the French style, but Jefferson's characterization—a "reign of witches"—was not far off the mark.

THE TRANSIT OF POWER

In public disfavor because of their supposed French connection and a minority in Congress, the Republicans could do little but vote "no" to every Federalist proposal. Early in the decade, when resisting the grand designs of Alexander Hamilton, the Republicans had developed a theory of limited government through strict construction of the Constitution. The bitter experience of 1798 brought their philosophy into sharper focus: They would be suspicious ever after of armies, navies, taxes, banks, bonded debts, and the exercise of presidential power.

In the late summer of 1798, a worried quartet of Republican leaders met at Monticello, Jefferson's home. Present were Jefferson and Madison, John Breckinridge of Kentucky, a former Virginian and ally of Madison's, and Wilson Cary Nicholas, a trusted friend of Jefferson's. The Alien and Sedition Acts were clearly unconstitutional, in their view, but what could be done about them? Judicial review was a possibility. State courts in the past had occasionally ruled on the constitutionality of legislation, and lawyers generally assumed that federal courts could do the same. Yet in actuality, there was little chance that the Federalist-dominated Supreme Court would listen sympathetically to a Republican appeal.

The strategy agreed upon at Monticello was to draft resolutions for submission to two reliably Republican state legislatures. That at least would call attention to the Federalist repression and stir public debate. Jefferson prepared one set of resolutions, which Breckinridge agreed to take to the Kentucky assembly, and Madison drafted some for Virginia's. Similar in their constitutional concept, the Virginia and Kentucky resolutions represented the first extended statement of the doctrine of states' rights. Jefferson and Madison maintained that the Constitution was a compact among the states that delegated certain specific powers to a federal authority. The federal government, as a result, was simply the agent of the states, set up to handle certain mutual problems. The states retained ultimate sovereignty. The states thus had the right to determine when the federal government exceeded its authority and the option to seek "measures of redress." The resolutions went on to demonstrate that the alien and sedition laws were unconstitutional usurpations of power. Jefferson's resolutions boldly declared the Federalist laws "null and void"; Madison, more temperate by nature, simply asserted Virginia's right to "interpose" for the protection of its citizens against federal tyranny.

As a philosophy of limited government, the Virginia and Kentucky Resolutions provided a philosophical foundation for the Republican party, but their political impact was marginal. Several state legislatures discussed them, but not one responded favorably. The Federalist acts were ostensibly directed against aliens and subversives, and Americans seldom rally to the defense of those two groups. More important in undermining Federalist popularity were the image of militarism and the burden of taxes that resulted from the war preparations. A split in party ranks also hampered Federalists as they prepared for the pivotal election of 1800.

President Adams had triggered the war scare when he published the XYZ dispatches by calling on Congress to shore up national defenses. Before long, he had second thoughts. He considered the alien and sedition laws unnecessary, though he was unwilling to veto them. To his credit, however, he deported not a single alien. Enforcement of the sedition act he left to Federalist prosecutors and the courts. Nor was Adams enthusiastic about the army, since the possibility of French invasion was remote. He was slow in issuing recruiting orders, and consequently the ranks were never filled. When Adams invited Washington to come out of retirement to command the army, Washington insisted that Hamilton be named inspector general. Adams reluctantly agreed, but thereafter lost interest in the army altogether. By the end of 1798 a schism in Federalist ranks was apparent. "High" Federalists, which included all the president's cabinet, favored a formal declaration of war and looked to Hamilton for guidance. Moderates, promi-

CLIO'S FOCUS: The Constitution in Brick and Marble

Americans were accustomed to converting wilderness into cities, but Washington, D.C., was something new. Never before, in America or in Europe, had a city been created for the sole purpose of housing a government. Conceived by many of the same men who wrote the Constitution, Washington, D.C., reflected the aspirations of the nation's founders. President Washington commissioned a French engineer, Pierre Charles L'Enfant, to design the city. L'Enfant modeled his street plan on that of the French royal city of Versailles, with diagonal streets radiating from the capitol superimposed upon a grid of right-angle intersections.

The most striking feature of the city, nevertheless, was not the street plan but the placement of buildings. On the highest point of land, L'Enfant situated the capitol, whose wings housed the two branches of Congress. A mile and a half away, down Pennsylvania Avenue, stood the executive mansion. Grouped around it were the executive departments—State, Treasury, and War. Designed by James Hoban, the president's house was overly large for a private residence. Its size was intended to lend esteem to the presidency.

At a third point, about equidistant from executive mansion and capitol, was the Supreme Court building. The triangular relationship was a physical representation of the separation of powers within the government. The city was a brick and marble rendition of the Constitution.

Washington, D.C., also reflected the republican ideology of the Founding Fathers. The site was militarily indefensible and without commercial importance. The city was therefore dependent for support on the larger community it governed. It could not control its own destiny; the consent of the governed was, for those placed in authority, a physical necessity. They survived by commanding popular respect, not military force.

Begun in 1791, the capital city was far from finished when the government offices moved there from Philadelphia in 1799, the last year of John Adams's presidency. The Supreme Court had to take temporary quarters in the basement of the capitol. The House of Representatives had only a partial roof. The president's house was so open and drafty that John and Abigail Adams had to keep a fire lit in every room. Pennsylvania Avenue was a dirt trail through the woods where congressmen hunted grouse in their spare time. "A malarial hamlet," sneered one foreign diplomat. But like the republic for which it stood, Washington, D.C., had a magnificent future.

nent among whom was John Marshall, adhered to Adams.

In publishing the XYZ dispatches, Adams had proclaimed that he would not send another envoy to France without advance assurances that he would be received in a proper manner. By early 1799, Adams had evidence that the French were prepared to meet this condition. Talleyrand had been surprised and alarmed at the belligerence of the American response. He was accustomed to "shaking down" the governments of Europe without rippling the surface of diplomatic niceties. The Directory had its hands full with Great Britain, whose navy had recently smashed both the French and Spanish fleets in the Mediterranean. It did not need an American war. Elbridge Gerry returned home with word of Talleyrand's change of heart. William Vans Murray, American minister to the Netherlands, conveyed Talleyrand's formal assurances. Adams responded with a new three-man commission, including Murray, who was already on the scene. Departure of the other commissioners was delayed, however, by Secretary of State Pickering, who refused to sign their marching orders. Adams had to intervene personally to get his peace commission afloat. Then he fired Pickering and, for good measure, Secretary of War McHenry, both of whom were more loyal to Hamilton than to Adams. The new secretary of state was John Marshall.

For once, the timing of the American peace effort was right. By the time the commissioners arrived in Paris in early 1800, there had been another turnover in the turbulent French republic. General Napoleon Bonaparte made himself First Consul in a coup d'état (a military takeover), and he was already nursing plans for a restoration of the French Empire in the New World. (He obtained Louisiana from Spain later that year.) To do this, he needed friendly relations with the United States. The Convention of 1800 terminated the

alliance of 1778 and the American commitment to defend the French West Indies. Napoleon refused to pay for the vessels France had seized, but he did agree to a new reciprocal trade agreement.

Late in his life, John Adams considered the peace settlement with France his finest moment, and rightly so. His initiative ended a dangerous crisis, and it did so at considerable political cost. With peace, the public zeal that had bolstered the Federalists subsided; voters began to worry about the cost of patriotism in terms of debts and taxes. The peace initiative, moreover, left Adams's own party hopelessly divided. Some of the High Federalists were even prepared to work openly for Adams's defeat.

THE ELECTION OF 1800

Hamilton kept his head throughout the French crisis, even counseling moderation to warhawks such as Pickering. But he overworked himself in trying to rebuild the army and lost his sense of perspective. When the Federalist caucus nominated Adams and Charles Coatsworth Pinckney in 1800, Hamilton concocted a frenzied scheme for slipping Pinckney into the presidency in place of Adams. The plot turned on the constitutional means of choosing president and vice president by first- and second-place votes in the electoral college. Hamilton would have all Federalist electors vote for Pinckney, while throwing away a few Adams ballots to ensure that he came in second. In view of the Republican challenge, the whole idea had an air of unreality. To further the plot, Hamilton published a critique of Adams's presidency. Republicans gleefully republished it, noting that if what the Federalists said about one another was true, Jefferson ought to be president.

The Republican caucus, adhering to the Virginia–New York alliance forged in

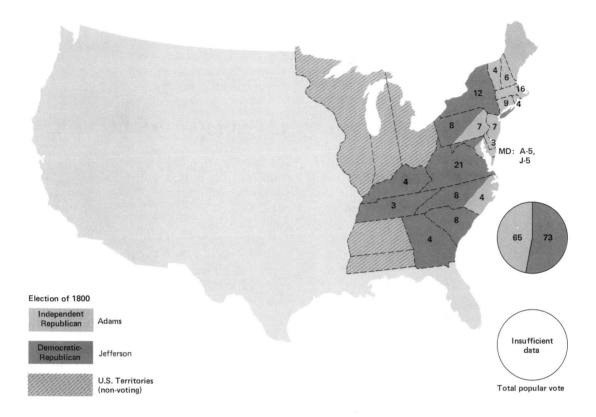

Election of 1800

Independent Republican — Adams

Democratic-Republican — Jefferson

U.S. Territories (non-voting)

Insufficient data

Total popular vote

MD: A-5, J-5

1796, renominated Jefferson and Burr. The election was remarkably close. A glance at the electoral map suggests that, despite the clash of ideology, the biggest factor was sectionalism. New England and most of the middle states adhered to Adams; the South was Jefferson country. The election turned on New York, where the Republicans' smooth-running organization secured early control of the legislature and hence the state's electoral delegation. Republicans emerged with 73 electors to the Federalists' 65.

So rigid was Republican unity that when the electoral college met in early 1801, every Jeffersonian elector cast one vote for Jefferson and one for Burr. The tie, under the Constitution, had to be resolved by the House of Representatives voting by states, with each having one vote. Ironically, the House that would choose between the two Republicans was Federalist controlled, being a "lame duck" session* of the Congress elected in 1798. Federalists decided to take advantage of this momentary opportunity by supporting Burr in the hope that he would feel obliged, once in office, to retain Federalist policies and Federalist office-holders. Burr did nothing to discourage the intrigue.

The House began balloting on February 16, 1801, just three weeks before the inauguration. With sixteen states in the Union,

---

* A *lame duck* is a politician who serves out a term after having been defeated for reelection. A lame duck session is a session of Congress that takes place after an election but prior to an inauguration.

nine was the requisite majority. Jefferson received the vote of eight states, Burr seven, and one was divided. The ratio held firm through thirty-five ballots over the next week. Embarrassed by the lack of fair play and fearing irreparable damage to the Union, moderate Federalists broke the deadlock. After receiving indirect assurances from Jefferson that he intended nothing revolutionary, a few moderates switched votes or cast blanks. Jefferson won ten to four, two divided. Jefferson was president, and Burr, though nominally vice president, was politically dead.

Hamilton's wild intrigue before the election and the Republican embarrassment afterward convinced all that the system needed modifying. A constitutional amendment, the twelfth, provided that nominees for the offices of president and vice president be specifically designated. The amendment clearly relied on political parties to serve as nominating clearing-houses. Indirectly, parties were incorporated into the Constitution. So accepted were they by then that this revolutionary change occasioned no public comment. George Washington, in his first inaugural address, had referred to the American republic as a "great experiment," and the phrase itself expressed both the rosy potential of the Constitution and Federalist anxiety over the future of the republic. Yet by their efforts Federalists had made the experiment work. By 1800 the republic was internationally respected, internally stable, eyed covetously by international investors, and boasting an annual budget surplus.

Even so, the most enduring legacy of the Federalists may have been their peaceful surrender of power. The parties simply changed roles. The smooth transit of power evidenced a remarkable degree of sophistication for so young a nation, and stood in favorable contrast with contemporary France. There the emergence of Napoleon first as military leader and then as self-proclaimed emperor was more in accord with the historic fate of republics—the Rome that had succumbed to Caesar, for instance, or the English Commonwealth that had yielded to Cromwell in the seventeenth century.

⊔ Jeffersonian Liberalism

At twelve noon on March 4, 1801, a tall, lanky, sandy-haired Virginian stepped out of his boardinghouse in Washington, D.C., and walked up New Jersey Avenue and into the capitol building to be sworn in as president of the United States. Dressed in a well-tailored but unadorned coat and breeches, Thomas Jefferson was indistinguishable from the small throng of friends and well-wishers who accompanied him. Inside the capitol were Aaron Burr, already sworn in as vice president, and John Marshall, who had been elevated to the post of Chief Justice only a few weeks before. The entire ceremony was over in minutes. Its simplicity befitted the man and the moment. "The changes of administration," a Washington lady noted in her diary, "which in every government and in every age have most generally been epochs of confusion, villainy and bloodshed, in this our happy country take place without any species of distraction, or disorder."

Jefferson himself wanted nothing more than stability and domestic tranquillity. "We have called by different names brethren of the same principle," he said in his inaugural address. "We are all republicans: We are all federalists." The statement was a deliberate effort to soothe the passion that had torn the country in the French crisis; it was a reminder that Americans, while differing at times on means, were in accord on fundamentals. Implicit in the transfer of power, nonetheless, was a profound change in attitude. Jefferson's inaugural address set forth the principles of the new order. In foreign policy he promised "peace, commerce, and honest friendship with all nations—entangling alliances with none." The principle was not much different from Washington's farewell plea, but it was one that had yet to be put fully into practice. Jefferson also promised "the support of the State governments in all their rights, as the most competent administrations for our domestic concerns and the surest bulwarks against anti-republican tendencies." Specifically he guaranteed "freedom of religion, freedom of press, freedom of person." These, said Jefferson, are not the tenets of party, they are the pillars of the republic. They are the source of the nation's strength. "If there be any among us," he continued, alluding to the distemper of 1798, "who would wish to dissolve this Union or to change its republican form, let them stand undisturbed as monuments of the safety with which error of opinion may be tolerated where reason is left free to combat it." Addressing himself specifically to the Federalist preoccupation with law and order, Jefferson declared:

> I know, indeed, that some honest men fear that a republican government cannot be strong; that this government is not strong enough. . . . I believe this, the strongest government on earth. I believe it is the only one where every man, at the call of the laws, would fly to the standard of the law, and would meet invasions of the public order as his own personal concern. Sometimes it is said that man cannot be trusted with the government of himself. Can he, then, be trusted with the government of others? Or have we found angels in the form of kings to govern him? Let history answer this question.

Therein lay the Jeffersonian persuasion. Federalists, reflecting Old World notions, had supposed that the durability of the government rested on armies and navies, the rich and well-born, the pomp and pageantry of office. Jefferson turned the idea around. The true strength of a nation, he was saying, is a public-spirited, virtuous citizenry. The government would endure as long as it held the affection of its people.

And that affection, Jefferson concluded, is best secured by "a wise and frugal government, which shall restrain men from injuring one another, which shall leave them otherwise free to regulate their own pursuits of industry and improvement, and shall not take from the mouth of labor the bread it has earned." Liberalism,* seeping into American thought since the revolution, became with Jefferson an American creed.

GALLATIN AT THE TREASURY

The task of dismantling the Federalist system and lightening the burdens on the people fell to Secretary of the Treasury Albert Gallatin. Indeed, Gallatin's policies were as central to the Jeffersonian system as Hamilton's had been to the Federalists'. Swiss by birth and Pennsylvanian by choice, Gallatin had served in Congress during the formative years of the Republican party. He had established himself as Hamilton's principal antagonist, being one of the few Republicans able to do battle head to head in the arena of public finance. At Gallatin's instigation, the House of Representatives had established the Ways and Means Committee in an effort to wrest fiscal policy from the grip of the executive.

Gallatin brought to the Treasury in 1801 the Republican premise that debts and taxes were an evil that diverted capital from productive enterprise. Republicans had argued for a decade that a national debt was a blessing only to bankers and speculators

---

* Liberalism, derived from "liberal" and "liberty," meant freedom from government. In political terms, liberalism refers to a government that has few officeholders, a low budget, and light taxes. In an economic sense, liberalism means the absence of government regulations—that is, free enterprise. In the twentieth century the term has come to mean the use of government to promote the public welfare, by, for instance, regulating big business.

dealing in public paper. Reversing the usual order, in which debts were paid after the Treasury's other obligations were met, Gallatin made debt retirement his central concern. He proposed to use three fourths of the government's annual income to pay off the national debt. He also proposed eliminating the hated Federalist excises, notably the whiskey tax that had caused an uprising in his native Pennsylvania in 1794. A "wise and frugal government" could subsist on customs duties alone—that and the sale of lands taken from Indians.

The assault on debts and taxes left Gallatin with little more than $2 million a year for the ordinary functions of government. That invited a third attack, on the size of government. Little could be done to cut the number of civil employees, for the Fed-

Jefferson as president. This portrait was painted by Rembrandt Peale, son of Charles Willson Peale, in 1805.

Courtesy of The New-York Historical Society, New York City.

eralists had not wasted money there. The Washington establishment numbered only 96 people, and there were only about 1,200 federal employees in the entire nation, most of them customs collectors. The navy, however, was an inviting target. It was conventional Republican wisdom that navies, by their mere existence, invited war. At Gallatin's order, the navy was dismantled and its ships sold, except for the six frigates completed in 1799–1800. The army, which never quite attained the 50,000 authorized by Congress in 1798, was cut to 3,000—enough, Gallatin estimated, to man the forts on the western frontier. Neither Jefferson nor Gallatin worried much about coastal defense. Adequate fortifications, given the nation's extended coastline, were beyond its means; less-than-adequate forts were a waste of money. Better to rely in any case on "peace, commerce, and honest friendship with all nations."

Devoting 75 percent of the federal budget to paying off the national debt would, in our own day, be a prescription for disaster. That Gallatin managed it was a measure of the insignificance of the federal government in his time. In truth, his estimates were conservative. Despite the reduction in taxes, Treasury receipts increased dramatically during his tenure, largely because of trade expansion and rising land sales. Indeed, as early as 1806 Gallatin foresaw a time when the government would be out of debt and showing a mounting surplus. He went to Jefferson with the problem, though it was scarcely a troublesome one. The logical solution was to eliminate taxes altogether; Jefferson instead instructed him to investigate ways of spending the surplus on a nationwide system of public roads and canals. That two such devotees of limited government could even consider a vast federal public works program was a measure of their flexibility and their pragmatism. Unfortunately, this experiment in using government funds for national development never came about.

Foreign crises and trade restrictions diminished the government's revenue, and the War of 1812 blasted Gallatin's debt retirement agenda. Not until 1835 did the government again face the prospect of being debt-free.

THE PRACTICAL PRESIDENT

Pragmatism, like liberalism, was a hallmark of the Jefferson presidency. Federalists had accused Jefferson of being variously a dreamer and a doctrinaire, but he was neither. He was by nature a compromiser, even an opportunist. His one flirtation with political philosophy, the doctrine of states' rights that he set forth in the Kentucky Resolutions, he abandoned in order to purchase Louisiana in 1803. He had stormed against the Bank of the United States for a decade, yet when Gallatin suggested that the bank performed useful services for the Treasury, Jefferson agreed to let it be. They decided only to sell the government's shares of stock in order to sever the official connection between bank and Treasury. The bank served Republicans loyally for a decade until Congress, more wedded to the "principles of '98" than Jefferson, refused to renew its charter in 1811.

Jefferson's flexibility and his aversion to conflict were evident in his appointment policies. The Federalists boldly challenged him. In the last weeks of Adams's administration, the Federalist lame duck Congress adopted a new judiciary act that expanded the number of federal courts, authorized new circuit court judges, and provided justices of the peace for the District of Columbia. Adams had hastened to fill the new posts with Federalists; rumor had it that he was up till midnight on March 3 making assignments. It was a spectacular departure from the rules of fair play, and Republicans were understandably furious. Jefferson worried that the Federalists, having been defeated at the polls, were fortifying themselves within the judiciary.

He was not, however, willing to evict Federalists from office en masse. Most officeholders were honest civil servants; Jefferson could not bring himself to dismiss them simply to reward his own followers. In the end, he removed only the "midnight appointments" (a category extended to all executive appointments made after December 12, 1800, the date on which Adams knew he had been defeated), and officials guilty of negligence or misconduct. The compromise satisfied neither disgruntled Federalists nor hungry Republicans, but it was the fairest solution Jefferson could see. Most of the "midnight appointments" automatically lost their jobs when Congress, at Jefferson's request, repealed the Judiciary Act of 1801. The repeal sparked a torrid debate in Congress. Federalists claimed that Congress did not have the constitutional power to abolish courts and predicted the repeal would be overturned by the Supreme Court. Republicans, mindful that the Court was in the hands of Federalists, denied that it had any jurisdiction over acts of Congress. Shortly thereafter John Marshall responded with a ringing affirmation of judicial review which, far from resolving the controversy, intensified Republican mistrust of the judiciary.

MARBURY V. MADISON

The case of *Marbury* v. *Madison* (1803) originated in the "midnight appointments." William Marbury was a Maryland Federalist Adams named as a justice of the peace for the District of Columbia. His commission was signed but undelivered when the new administration took office. James Madison, whose duties as secretary of state included administration of the District of Columbia, found it, and on Jefferson's instruction did not deliver it. Marbury thereupon sued for a court order requiring

Madison to surrender the commission. The Judiciary Act of 1789 permitted the Supreme Court to take original jurisdiction in suits against executive officers of Madison's rank, so Marbury started at the top. Marshall dismissed the suit for lack of jurisdiction, holding that Congress lacked the constitutional power to give the Court jurisdiction of this sort. Marshall went on to assert that if he had possessed jurisdiction (if Marbury had worked his way up through the federal courts on appeal), he had full power to issue directives to the president and members of his cabinet.

Though weak in its legal reasoning, Marshall's decision was a brilliant political stroke, for it established the Court's supremacy over both the legislative and the executive branches of the government. It established the principle of judicial review. And he let the Republicans win the case. What could Jefferson say? That he was above the law and not subject to the courts? Marshall had snared him with his own philosophy of limited government.

Marshall's thrust was the more galling because, in the view of Republicans, he was himself a "midnight appointment," having been placed on the Supreme Court by Adams in January 1801. He had been duly confirmed by the Senate, however, and there was no way to be rid of him except by impeachment. Jefferson was bitter enough to try just that, but the process had first to be tested. The Senate first removed a district judge, who was guilty mostly of alcoholism, and then Republicans went after Supreme Court Justice Samuel Chase,

Chief Justice John Marshall.

Library of Congress.

a violent Federalist who had conducted some of the sedition trials of 1799 with gross partiality. At Jefferson's suggestion, Republican leaders steered an impeachment resolution through the House of Representatives, and Chase was tried before the Senate in the spring of 1805. For removal from office, the Constitution requires that the impeached official be convicted of "a high crime or a misdemeanor," and House leaders lacked evidence that Chase was anything more than injudicious. Chase's acquittal ended any thought of ousting Marshall. It ended, in fact, the whole controversy over courts and appointments. By 1805, Jefferson had become preoccupied instead with foreign affairs.

In 1804 Jefferson won reelection by a resounding margin; he carried every state but two, Connecticut and Delaware. Federalists in Congress, having lost control of their former stronghold, New England, were reduced to a tiny minority. The parties, Jefferson exulted to a friend, were "almost wholly melted into one." His prediction that the Federalist party would vanish proved premature, but the election was a strong public endorsement of the Jeffersonian system.

Even so, it should be remembered that Jefferson had taken over a strong, respected, solvent governmental structure in 1801. The Federalists had built well in their twelve years in office. It was to Jefferson's credit that he only trimmed their system; he did not overthrow it. But Jefferson's modifications were nonetheless significant: He committed the nation to liberalism and democracy, and that legacy endures.

SUMMARY

The Federalists entered office in 1789 in an atmosphere dark with apprehensiveness, and they left office twelve years later under a cloud of defeat. Yet during their tenure they did better than they themselves realized. The federal government existed only on paper in 1789; it was a stable, respected organism in 1801. The executive departments were in place (the president's cabinet remained unchanged until 1849), and the Supreme Court was staffed with some of the nation's leading lawyers. American credit, shaky in 1789, was as good as that of any nation in the world a decade later.

Perhaps most important of all, the Federalists had kept the country at peace in a world at war. They managed to cling to neutrality despite severe prodding from the European belligerents, Britain and France. And neutrality had paid dividends. It enabled American ship captains to penetrate the closed European empires, opening new markets in the islands of the West Indies. Territorially, it had enabled Washington to win concessions from Spain that settled the nation's southern boundary and opened the Mississippi River to American traffic.

The Jeffersonian Republicans objected not so much to the Federalists' deeds as to their methods. The Federalists achieved political and financial stability by allying with the northern merchant class. This tactic, together with the Federalists' verbal disparagement of the poor, led the Jeffersonians to fear that the republic had fallen into the clutches of a monied aristocracy, one that might prefer a monarchy if it found a king. The Jeffersonian opposition was southern at first, and predominantly rural, but gradually it spread its influence into the North and into the cities. During John Adams's administration, the Federalists contributed to their own downfall by imposing unpopular taxes and repressive legislation. Even so, Jefferson won the presidency in 1800 by the slim margin of eight electoral votes.

Jefferson as president did not attempt to unravel the Federalist system. He engaged in a running fight with Federalists, such as John Marshall, who had entrenched themselves in the judiciary, but otherwise he sought to stop the party warfare. Denounced by the opposition in 1800 as a philosopher and a dreamer, Jefferson proved to be a preeminent pragmatist, whose commonsense management of the government attracted many moderate Federalists. So successful was he in undermining the Federalist ideology and absorbing their personnel that the Federalist party never returned to power. Yet the nation itself was the winner, for the peaceful transition of 1800 from Federalists to Republicans was proof of the young republic's political maturity.

READING SUGGESTIONS

A readable overview of this period is Adrienne Koch's *Jefferson and Madison: The Great Collaboration* (1950). Noble E. Cunningham, Jr., *The Jeffersonian Republicans: The Formation of Party Organization, 1789–1801* (1957), is the seminal work on the beginnings of political parties, resting on the thesis that there is a clear break between the contest over the Constitution and the party battles of the 1790s. Alfred F. Young, *The Democratic Republicans of New York: The Origins, 1763–1797* (1967), and Norman K. Risjord, *Chesapeake Politics, 1780–1800* (1978), find more continuity from the 1780s to the 1790s. Rudolph Bell, *Party and Faction in American Politics: The House of Representatives, 1789–1801* (1974), is a quantitative approach to the question of the origins of parties, though H. James Henderson comes to different and more persuasive conclusions in "Quantitative Approaches to Party Formation in the U.S. Congress," *William and Mary Quarterly* (1973), 307–34.

The best studies of Federalist ideology are Gerald Stourzh, *Alexander Hamilton and the Idea of Republican Government* (1970), and James M. Banner, *To the Hartford Convention* (1970). Good explorations of Jeffersonian ideology include Lance Banning, *The Jeffersonian Persuasion* (1978), and Robert Shalhope, *John Taylor of Caroline* (1980).

On Jefferson's presidency, the best overviews are Marshall Smelser, *The Democratic Republic, 1800–1815* (1968), and Merrill Peterson's splendid biography, *Thomas Jefferson and the New Nation* (1970). Richard Hofstadter's *The Idea of a Party System: The Rise of Legitimate Opposition in the United States, 1780–1840* (1969) traces the concept of party through the first half-century of the republic. Noble E. Cunningham, Jr., *The Process of Government under Jefferson* (1978), examines Jefferson's administrative abilities as president, and Richard Ellis, *The Jeffersonian Crisis: Courts and Politics in the Young Republic* (1971), explores the struggle over the judiciary, while placing it in the larger context of political and social change.

A good introduction to foreign affairs in this period is Felix Gilbert's imaginative reconstruction of American attitudes toward Europe, *To the Farewell Address* (1961), titled *The Origins of American Foreign Policy* in the paperback version. Paul A. Varg, *Foreign Policy of the Founding Fathers* (1963), is a good overview. Alexander De Conde, *Entangling Alliance* (1958) and *The Quasi War* (1966), traces Franco-American relations. Anglo-American relations in this period can be followed through Jerald A. Combs, *The Jay Treaty* (1973), and Bradford Perkins, *The First Rapprochement: England and the United States, 1795–1805* (1955).

9

THE RISING EMPIRE:
1805–1829

A converted merchant vessel, with cannon lashed awkwardly on the deck, was all the United States Navy had. The vessels that had so effectively molested British commerce during the revolution had been sold when the war ended. New warships, authorized by Congress in the 1790s, were still being built. The first of them would not be launched until later that year, 1798. In the meantime, the *Philadelphia,* donated to the U.S. government by the merchants of that city, would have to do.

The merchants had become angered by a French warship that was harrassing their shipping in Delaware Bay. Stephen Decatur, commanding the *Philadelphia,* went in search of the Frenchman. Spotting his quarry, Decatur aimed his ship and let fly a broadside of metal that raked the French vessel from stem to stern. Taken by surprise, the French captain struck his colors. When Decatur went aboard, the Frenchman cried: "Why have you fired upon the French flag? I know of no war between our countries!" "The French have been making war on us for a long time," Decatur replied, referring to the French seizures that had led to the quasi-war. "Now we are defending ourselves." An American boarding party took control of the French ship, intending to incorporate it into the American navy (thereby doubling the navy in size). The French captain watched the American flag run up the mast of his ship and said gloomily, "I wish she had been sunk." Replied Decatur: "She would have been if you had stood on board and fought her."

Underlying that exchange was a new American spirit, a new sort of pride. It was more than simple patriotism; it was *nationalism,* a self-confident national identity. Americans had been searching for a national identity since the revolution. Painters such as Charles Willson Peale and Jonathan Trumbull had self-consciously created a heritage in color by painting the battles and leaders of the revolution. Connecticut schoolmaster Noah Webster had sought to define an American language in his blue-backed *American Spelling Book,* and by 1798 he was contemplating a dictionary of American English. Webster felt that a national culture required a common language. He promoted a uniformity of spelling and a common grammar. His *American Reader* sought to instill patriotism with passages on the battles and heroes of the Revolution. His dictionary, when finally completed in 1828, included words of American origin, such as tomato, corn, prairie, and rattlesnake. It also incorporated some of Webster's spelling reforms, such as dropping the *u* from *favour* and *labour* and reversing the *re* in *centre* and *theatre*—changes that distinguish American from British spelling still today.

It was all but inevitable that this self-conscious search for identity would be felt in politics and diplomacy. The creation of the federal union was itself a form of nationalism. Federalists in 1787 had argued that adoption of the Constitution would help win the nation respect abroad. The success of the Washington administration in driving back British incursions in the Northwest and Spanish pretensions in the Southwest bore them out. As national pride deepened, so did sensitivity to national honor. In 1798, President Adams, with full support from the public, took the nation to the brink of war in response to French treatment of American envoys. Decatur's exchange with the French officer in Delaware Bay reflected the confidence with which Americans faced the challenge of power. Nor was Decatur's an idle boast; in the naval engagements of the quasi-war, Americans defeated and captured two French warships and seized more than eighty armed merchant vessels as prizes.

(*Chapter opening photo*) Raising the American flag in New Orleans after Jefferson's purchase of Louisiana from France.

The Jeffersonians proved equally sensitive to national honor and even more eager than the Federalists to expand the national frontiers. Jefferson and his successors, Madison, Monroe, and John Quincy Adams, doubled the size of the nation by conquest and purchase, staked a claim to the Pacific Coast, and cast an umbrella of diplomatic protection over Latin America. Under the Jeffersonians, nation-building yielded subtly to empire-building.

⊔ An Empire for Liberty

Foreign affairs in Jefferson's presidency was the province of Secretary of State James Madison, though neither he nor Jefferson regarded it as a separate sphere. Years of collaboration had put the two in perfect tune; they worked together in friendship, intimacy, and trust. Madison was by nature more temperate than Jefferson, more disposed to compromise, and his pragmatism was evident in the administration's policy. The posture of defenseless passivity with which the Republicans entered office was soon scrapped. President and secretary of state alike yielded to the responsibilities of power, pursuing what they felt to be the nation's interest with little sentiment and less ideology. In a hostile world the nation's interest might even require a resort to force; they yielded to that necessity as well.

John Adams, after four tempestuous years, managed to bequeath to the Republicans a relatively serene diplomatic landscape. The dispute with the French was ended; relations with Britain were excellent. During the quasi-war the Royal Navy had even convoyed American vessels on the Atlantic to protect them from the French. The one trouble spot was more an annoyance than a danger. The pasha of Tripoli, in the Mediterranean, was demanding additional tribute.

The Muslim city-states on the Barbary Coast of North Africa—Algiers, Tunis, and Tripoli—made a living preying on the commerce of the Mediterranean. The world's maritime powers bought them off with annual tribute and the Washington administration had followed the practice, although Congress authorized the construction of six frigates in 1794 to protect American commerce. Toward the end of Adam's administration, the pasha of Tripoli became unhappy with the tribute he received and threatened war. Jefferson had always considered the tribute a humiliating form of blackmail. He wondered if a show of force in the Mediterranean might silence the Muslim leader. Gallatin's budgetary scalpel had spared the six frigates built by the Federalists—what better place to employ several of them than the Mediterranean? On May 15, 1801, Jefferson's newly formed cabinet made its first foreign policy decision—it voted to send a squadron to the Mediterranean. By the time it arrived, the pasha of Tripoli had plunged ahead with a formal declaration of hostilities. Jefferson found himself in a remote but annoying little war that dragged on for four years. He eventually sent over a sizable squadron that blockaded the port and forced a treaty on Tripoli which ended the tribute.

THE LOUISIANA PURCHASE

Before the administration fully made up its mind on the amount of force to apply in the Mediterranean, it was distracted by a new crisis with France. Even before Napoleon came to power, France's imperial zest had spread from Europe to the New World. In 1795 the French government persuaded Spain to cede it the Spanish half of the island of Santo Domingo, evidently intending to make it the center of a revived French West Indian empire. In 1800 Napoleon went one step further. By the Treaty of San Ildefonso he induced the

Spanish to return Louisiana, which the French had been forced to surrender in 1763. Spain apparently feared that the British might seize New Orleans and so "loaned" the colony to France, which was better able to defend it. Whether Napoleon considered the colony a loan or a gift he never said.

Both parties to the transfer, however, realized that the United States would take exception to it. Having a weak military power such as Spain at America's back door was one thing; having Napoleon there was quite another. Accordingly, they agreed to keep the retrocession secret until France could occupy Louisiana with sufficient force to hold it. In the meantime the Spanish flag would continue to fly over New Orleans; Spanish customs officials would continue to process American boatmen.

The secret naturally leaked out, as secrets usually did in the spy-drenched courts of Europe, and within a year Rufus King, American minister in London, reported the transfer to Jefferson. Jefferson's initial response was mild. Do nothing, he told his minister in Paris, Robert R. Livingston, that would "unnecessarily irritate our future neighbors," so long as the French kept open the Mississippi to American traffic. Napoleon, however, had other plans. In 1801 he sent an army across the Atlantic with instructions first to suppress a slave rebellion in Santo Domingo that had resulted in the creation of a republic governed by Toussaint L'Ouverture. With that accomplished, the French general, Leclerc, was to proceed to New Orleans and assume control of Louisiana.

Apprised of this threat, Jefferson dropped the mask of conciliation. He wrote Livingston an open letter, which he intended the French to see. France, said the president, was America's natural friend, but even a friend would not be allowed on the lower Mississippi. "There is on the globe one single spot, the possessor of which is our natural and habitual enemy.

It is New Orleans, through which the produce of three eighths of our territory must pass to market. . . . The day that France takes possession of New Orleans . . . seals the union of two nations who in conjunction can maintain exclusive possession of the ocean. From that moment we must marry ourselves to the British fleet and nation." With the threat of an Anglo-American alliance in his pocket, Livingston was instructed to purchase, if possible, the "island" of New Orleans and the Gulf Coast eastward to Mobile Bay (a strip south of the thirty-first parallel known as West Florida).

A lull in the European war, the Peace of Amiens, deprived Jefferson's threat of a British alliance of some of its force. But in October 1802, fate presented him a new opportunity. Spanish officials closed the port of New Orleans to American traffic. The West roared with anger; buckskin-clad Tennesseans threatened to march on New Orleans. While Congress discussed a declaration of war, Jefferson named a special emissary, James Monroe, to reinforce Livingston in Paris. Madison drafted the instructions: Purchase New Orleans and West Florida, offering, if necessary, as much as $10 million. Failing that, secure at least an opening of the Mississippi. Failing both, cross the channel and begin negotiations for a military alliance with the British. On the day before Monroe arrived in Paris, in April 1803, Napoleon's finance minister summoned Livingston and offered to sell not just New Orleans but all of Louisiana for $15 million.

Napoleon's plans for a New World empire had been vanquished by mosquitoes. General Leclerc succeeded by treachery in capturing Toussaint L'Ouverture and in momentarily suppressing the black revolt, but his army was decimated by yellow fever. By the spring of 1803, the mosquito-borne plague had taken the lives of 24,000 Frenchmen, including that of Leclerc himself. With no army to occupy New Orleans,

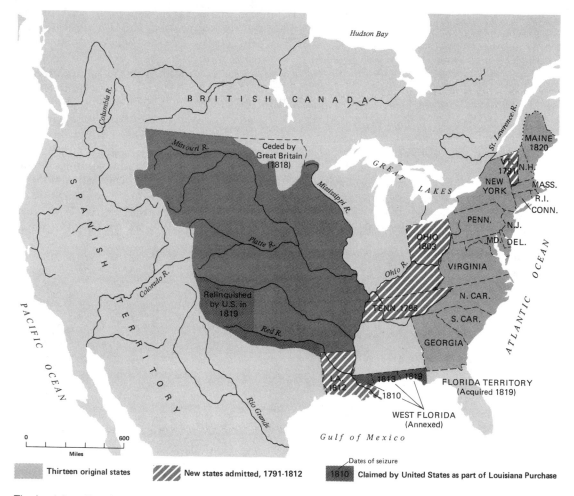

The Louisiana Purchase and new states, 1791–1812.

Napoleon could not hope to hold it. Besides, he was planning new military campaigns in Europe, and he needed money. The sale of all Louisiana was logical enough; without New Orleans, the French had no access to the interior. Monroe and Livingston leapt at the offer, although the price was 50 percent more than they had been authorized to pay. They arranged financing through Dutch bankers and signed the treaty of purchase on April 30, 1803.

LEWIS AND CLARK

Jefferson was, of course, delighted with the purchase, which doubled the size of the nation. An "empire for liberty," he called it. Ever interested in the West, Jefferson had laid plans for exploring the region even before Monroe and Livingston bought it. He asked two Virginia friends and neighbors, Meriwether Lewis and William Clark, to lead an exploration party up the Missouri River and across the Continental Divide to the Pacific. The purchase gave legitimacy to the enterprise, and Lewis and Clark pushed off from St. Louis in the spring of 1804. They spent one winter on the upper Missouri with the hospitable Mandan Indians and a second at the mouth of the Columbia River, returning in 1806 with priceless data concerning the landscape, mineral wealth, and inhabitants of the trans-Mississippi West.

The acquisition of Louisiana did not solve the problem of western trade outlets. It gave the United States control of the Mississippi, but there were other rivers that flowed into the gulf through West Florida.

The agricultural development of Alabama and Mississippi depended on winning title to the Gulf Coast, especially Mobile Bay. Monroe and Livingston, who had been instructed to buy the Gulf Coast and bought the Great Plains instead, were quite aware of this. They asked Talleyrand, who negotiated the purchase for Napoleon, whether Louisiana included West Florida, and the foreign minister had replied simply and enigmatically: "Gentlemen, you have made a good bargain. I trust you will make the most of it." Monroe and Livingston accordingly claimed they had purchased West Florida. Jefferson and Madison agreed,

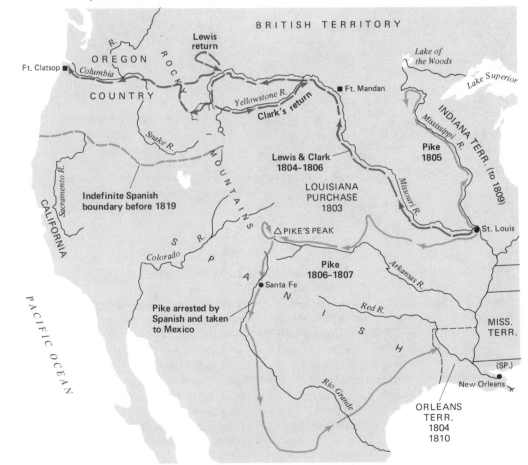

American explorations of the Far West.

though they coupled the claim with periodic offers to buy West Florida from Spain.

Spain, incensed at the French betrayal, denied that the purchase was legitimate and rejected American pretensions to West Florida. By 1805 the dispute had the United States and Spain at the edge of war. In that year, Napoleon, ever short of funds and never averse to selling Spanish real estate, offered to procure West Florida for the United States for a fee. Jefferson actually accepted the offer, but Napoleon was too busy devouring eastern Europe to consummate the deal. West Florida, in fact, was acquired by itinerant Americans who settled in the territory, grew restless under Spanish rule, rebelled in 1810, and declared independence. James Madison, president at the time, sent troops into Baton Rouge and Mobile on the theory that the place had been American all along.

The West Florida controversy, meantime, provided a cover for a wild scheme to dismember the republic—the Burr conspiracy. Aaron Burr, Jefferson's vice president, was politically suspect after the electoral tie of 1800. In 1804 he completed his ruin by killing Alexander Hamilton in a duel. When he left the vice presidency in 1805, Burr toured the West, sounding out the possibilities of separation and a western confederacy. The conspiracy had no chance of success, for westerners were genuinely loyal to the Union, and the British, who might have given it fleeting success, refused to become involved. Well informed by agents whom he had sent west to track Burr's activities, Jefferson ordered the arrest of the conspirators. Burr, who had made his way down the Ohio and the Mississippi with two boatloads of armed men, was picked up by the army in January 1807. He was taken to Richmond, Virginia, to be tried for treason in the federal circuit court, with Justice John Marshall presiding. It was a curious trial. The president, who had watched the conspiracy unfold with detached equanimity, switched roles

and did everything he could to secure a conviction. Justice Marshall, a cousin of Jefferson's and a bitter enemy, seemed more interested in embarrassing the president than in advancing justice. The result was more productive than either deserved. Marshall, pointing out that the Constitution itself defined the crime and required an "overt act," threw out much of the prosecution testimony concerning Burr's behavior. As a result, Burr was acquitted. Posterity was the winner, for treason, as John Marshall defined it, could not become a political weapon to be used by the "ins" against the "outs."

⊔Free Trade and Sailors' Rights

The goodwill that had attended Anglo-American relations since the Jay Treaty evaporated during Jefferson's second term as president. Britain and the United States once more came into conflict on the high seas and in the northwest borderlands. The contention distracted Jefferson in his last years in office, dominated the presidency of his successor, Madison, and ultimately led to the War of 1812. It all began with the renewal of the war in Europe in 1803. Napoleon had planned an invasion of Britain, but that dream vanished when Lord Nelson destroyed the combined French and Spanish fleets off Cape Trafalgar in October 1805. Turning his army eastward, Napoleon pounced upon Britain's allies, and in successive battlefield victories he knocked Austria, Prussia, and Russia out of the war.

By 1807, Britain stood once more alone, while Napoleon made himself master of the Continent from the Baltic Sea to the Mediterranean. The result was deadlock. One was lord of the land, the other sovereign of the sea, and neither could reach the other. The war thus became one of attrition, as each sought to starve the other into submission. By orders in council, beginning in 1806, Britain extended its blockade to include the whole northwest coast of Europe from Denmark to Brittany. Napoleon countered with a Continental System that excluded Britain from its traditional markets on the Continent (notably the Netherlands). To prevent the British from penetrating his enclosure by shipping goods in neutral vessels, Napoleon issued a decree from Berlin in 1806 that ordered the seizure of any neutral vessel that stopped in Britain before coming to a continental port. The British ministry replied with an order in council of November 1807 which required all neutral vessels destined for a continental port to stop in Britain first. Napoleon countered with a Milan Decree which ordered the seizure of any neutral vessel that even submitted to a British search on the high seas. Caught in the middle of this economic squeeze was the neutral United States, whose merchants made tidy profits trading with both sides.

American vessels were swept off the Atlantic by the hundreds, their cargoes sold, and their crews left to make their way home as best they could. The French seized as many as the British did, but from the beginning American anger was directed principally at the British. French seizures occurred in French ports, and a ship in port is subject to the dictates of its host, however unreasonable they might be. British seizures, on the other hand, took place on the high seas and they were, in the American view, contrary to international law.

International law was, at the dawn of the nineteenth century, still in its infancy. Few legal principles were generally accepted. Nonetheless, the United States and other maritime nations maintained that a neutral flag flying at the masthead made both ship and its cargo neutral, regardless of who owned either (a concept that newspapers turned into the slogan "free ships make free goods"). Such vessels, Americans claimed, could proceed even through a blockade, such as that which Britain maintained on Europe. Britain rejected such arguments and insisted on searching each American vessel to determine whether its cargo contained contraband of war or enemy property, either of which made the entire ship liable to seizure.

Americans also objected to the very nature of the British blockade, and in this they were on somewhat firmer ground. A blockade, most students of international jurisprudence agreed, meant the investment of an enemy port (that is, placing ships outside an enemy port). The interception and inspection of neutrals had to take place reasonably close to the blockaded coast. The British, unfortunately, could not conform to that rule. The Royal Navy did not have enough ships to invest every port on the northwestern coast of Europe. Instead, they developed the practice of stopping and searching neutral vessels whenever they encountered them on the high seas. A few British captains brazenly situated themselves on the American coast, where they monitored vessels emerging from American seaports. Secretary of State Madison denounced this practice as a "paper blockade" in violation of international understanding. The daily humiliation kindled American resentment.

British writers, in the rare moments when they felt the need to justify their government's policies, argued that their nation was fighting for survival, that in such conditions the niceties of international law must stand aside. The argument was not without merit, especially as the true dimensions of Napoleon's appetite for conquest became apparent. But the British, unfortunately, did not hold to that elevated rationale. Their motives in some cases were as selfish as Napoleon's. One such instance was the resurrection in 1805 of the "rule of 1756," by which they sought to restrict American trade in the French West Indies. There was no military justification for the seizures that resulted, since most of the American vessels were carrying French sugar and molasses. The British purpose, in fact, was to take over that trade for themselves. They worried that the United States was becoming the world's carrier.

That concern, at least, was justified. American merchants had moved into the shipping vacuum created by the war, and their returns were enormous. Indeed, so profitable was it to carry the goods of others around the empires of others that if one ship in two escaped confiscation, the American owners were ahead. Northern merchants accordingly bore the seizure of their vessels with silent composure. The British regulations pinched Americans' pride, not their purses.

Another indignity Americans suffered was impressment. This primitive form of military conscription had been practiced by the Royal Navy for a century. In wartime, "press gangs" roamed the streets of British

seaports, literally kidnapping men for His Majesty's service. As a result, morale was low in the British navy and mutinies were common. Conditions were so bad that whenever a British warship put into an American port for food and water, a good proportion of the crew "went over the side." Many ended up in the American merchant service, where pay and living conditions were better. The British regarded them as deserters; the Americans considered them immigrants.

To recover their deserters, British ship captains, whenever they stopped an American vessel to inspect the cargo, mustered the crew and "pressed" into British service anyone who could not prove he was an American. As a result, many Americans (perhaps 10,000 by 1811) found themselves in the Royal Navy alongside British deserters. Thus the insult of British inspection was compounded by the injury to American citizens. No particular incident

Impressment. In this artist's vision a British officer surveys a glum American crew, while the American merchant looks on in helpless anger.

New York Public Library Picture Collection.

of impressment was enough to start a war, but it was a continuing source of friction. Significantly, when President Madison asked Congress to declare war in June 1812, he listed impressment as reason number one.

THE CHESAPEAKE AFFAIR

Impressment involved merchant vessels and merchant seamen, but one incident involving an armed vessel of the United States Navy triggered the chain of events that led to war. In response to the British ship seizures, Jefferson ordered the refitting of some of the warships he had inherited from the Adams administration. Among these was the 38-gun frigate *Chesapeake*, which was reserviced in the port of Norfolk, Virginia, in the spring of 1807. When the *Chesapeake* put to sea in June, it was hailed by the British frigate *Leopard*, one of a squadron of British vessels that patrolled the mouth of Chesapeake Bay. The British demanded to board and search for deserters, and when the American commander refused, the *Leopard* opened fire, killing three and wounding eighteen before the American vessel could strike its colors. The British boarded, arrested four alleged deserters (three of whom turned out to be Americans previously impressed into British service), and sailed off, leaving the *Chesapeake* to limp back into Norfolk.

Impressment from a navy ship, executed by force, was more than insult; it was an act of war. A cascade of rage swept the length of the continent. Newspapers screamed for action. President Jefferson, had he called Congress into session instantly, could have secured a declaration of war without difficulty. Instead, he played for time—time to secure redress, should Britain prove willing to recall the admiral responsible and offer apologies, time in which to try commercial coercion, which had worked before the revolution, time, if war proved unavoidable, to prepare.

EMBARGO AND NONINTERCOURSE

When Congress convened in special session in October 1807, Jefferson asked it to prepare for war by enlarging the army and navy, and he requested an embargo on American shipping. The embargo had two purposes: By halting American shipping and the export of American goods, it would pinch both Britain and France and perhaps force both European belligerents to recognize American rights. Second, it would ensure that the vast American merchant fleet and the 40,000 seamen that manned it were at home and available in the event of war. Congress approved the embargo in December. It was, in effect, a self-imposed blockade, for it prohibited American vessels from sailing to foreign ports and foreign vessels from taking on cargo in American ports.

Congress gave only half-hearted support to Jefferson's requests for military preparations, however. Republican congressmen mistrusted the army and viewed apprehensively the taxes it would entail. As the months drifted by, the war threat lessened and American shipping got safely home, thus eliminating some of the rationale for the embargo. Jefferson began to stress the coercive aspect of the embargo—the effort to secure a recognition of American rights without resorting to force. Commercial retaliation, Jefferson came to hope, might become a weapon for peace-loving peoples everywhere. And it nearly succeeded. Within a year there were food riots in English cities, and the textile mills of the north country were standing idle for lack of American cotton. In time, Britain would yield. The ministry rescinded the orders in council in June 1812, in part because of the economic privation caused by America's refusal to trade. But by then the embargo itself had long since been repealed.

The United States could not wait indefinitely for Britain to yield because it too suffered by the embargo. Farm surpluses, normally sent to Europe, rotted on the wharves next to idle ships that rotted at the moorings. The economy came to a standstill because even trade within the country was affected. The nation had few roads and fewer bridges; interstate traffic normally went by sea. Even this coastal trade had to be prohibited, lest some enterprising seafarer skip off to the West Indies or southern Europe with a boatload of fish, lumber, or farm produce.

Jefferson had announced his decision to retire even before the embargo was passed, but the growing unpopularity of the experiment nonetheless clouded his last year in office. The Republican caucus in February 1808 dutifully nominated Madison to replace him, and it renominated as vice president George Clinton of New York, who had been serving in that post since 1805. Beneath this show of regularity, however, there was considerable dissension within the Republican party. The embargo, by contrast, reinvigorated the Federalists. Charles Coatsworth Pinckney, nominee of the Federalist caucus, lost the presidential contest to Madison, but Federalists recovered a number of seats in the congressional election. The election results doomed the embargo. With brief debate, Congress repealed the embargo, the repeal to take effect on Jefferson's last day in office, March 3, 1809.

Unwilling to submit entirely to the edicts of the warring powers of Europe, Congress replaced the embargo with a less stringent form of commercial retaliation, a Nonintercourse Act. This measure cut off trade with Britain and France only, allowing American vessels to ply the rest of the world. Designed as a bargaining lever, the act authorized the president to restore commercial relations with either Britain or France, should one agree to revoke its impediments to neutral commerce. A year later Congress, still shying from the extreme alternatives, war or submission, turned nonintercourse inside out in an effort to encourage bargaining. Macon's Bill Number Two (1810) repealed all previous restrictions, thereby opening American ports to all. Then it authorized the president, should either Britain or France come to terms, to cut off trade with the other. Napoleon, seeing advantage in the offer, promptly announced that his decrees were revoked insofar as they affected Americans. The move was utterly cynical, as he soon after issued a new secret decree broadening the grounds for seizure of neutral vessels. President Madison, less cynical but equally opportunistic, seized the bargaining lever. He warned the British, and when they refused to bend (pointing out, correctly, that Napoleon was still seizing American ships), Madison announced that there would be no further trade with Britain after February 1, 1811. That action at least narrowed the field of possible military opponents to one.

The congressional election that winter revealed the public frustration. A third of the House of Representatives lost their seats, and the newcomers were generally younger men impatient with Jeffersonian pacifism. Ablest among them were Henry Clay and John C. Calhoun, figures who would dominate the next generation of American politics. Clay, from Kentucky, and Calhoun, from South Carolina, reflected the growing anger of South and West, an anger that could be quenched only by war. Before long, this band of energetic young men earned the nickname War Hawks.

INDIAN WARFARE IN THE NORTHWEST

By the time the new Congress assembled in the fall of 1811, the War Hawks had additional cause for anger—British meddling among the Indians of the Northwest. The great Shawnee leader Tecumseh had put together an alliance of the northwestern tribes aimed at preventing further land sales to the American government. The result was stalemate that endured for two years. British Indian agents at Fort Malden gave Tecumseh verbal encouragement and some supplies, but they were not eager for war. They realized that war would lead to the destruction of the Indians and leave Canada exposed to the voracious land hunger of Americans.

In the fall of 1811, Tecumseh traveled south in an effort to extend his alliance, and William Henry Harrison, governor of the Indiana Territory, seized the opportunity to attack. He led an army of Kentucky and Indiana militia northward along the Wabash River to the Prophet's town near the mouth of Tippecanoe Creek. The Prophet, Tecumseh's younger brother, was a mystic with wide influence among the Indians of the region. Harrison camped a few miles from the Indian village on the night of November 5. The Prophet attacked at dawn, fought furiously for a couple of hours, and then mysteriously disappeared. Harrison waited two days for another attack and then moved into the deserted Indian village. He found there cartons of British-made muskets—proof of what the Americans had suspected all along, that the British were the secret force behind Tecumseh. Transgression on the high seas and trespass in the Northwest were once more akin, as in 1794.

The new Congress met on the same day as the battle of Tippecanoe, November 6, 1811. Henry Clay, who had previously served in the Senate, was elected Speaker on his first day in the House, and he used his appointive power to load the important committees with War Hawks. Congress began girding the country for war, a tedious process because Federalists fought the War Hawks every step of the way. The administration did what it could to encourage military preparations. In April of 1812, Madison proposed an embargo to keep American shipping in port, and on June 1 he sent Congress a formal request for a declaration of war. The reasons cited by the president were impressment, the orders in council, and intrigue among Indians of the Northwest. All were incursions on the nation's sovereignty that threatened to reduce America to the status of a British tributary. In President Madison's mind, and to most Republicans, it was a "second war for independence."

The House approved the declaration, 79 to 49, the Senate by 19 to 13. The votes followed the sectional alignment evident since the time of the embargo. South and West were nearly unanimous for war. New England opposed it; the Middle States were divided. It was also a party war. Nearly all Republicans voted for war; every Federalist in Congress voted against it. Republicans feared that the republic itself was in danger if the government could not somehow answer the humiliation heaped upon it by the European powers. Federalists feared that the administration had gone too far, that by declaring war on Britain it was in danger of becoming a satellite of Napoleon. The war vindicated neither; wars frequently have consequences unanticipated by those who begin them.

This particular war began and ended with more irony than usual. The British ministry suspended the orders in council in June 1812, and the ship bearing this news passed the ship carrying the American declaration of war in mid-Atlantic. The revocation eliminated a major sore point and opened the possibility for a peaceful resolution of other American grievances.

CLIO'S FOCUS: Tecumseh: The Greatest Indian

When Tecumseh was only seven years old, white hunters killed his father because he had refused to carry a deer for them. Tecumseh bore a hatred for Anglo-Americans the rest of his life. He avoided the white man's evil habits of smoking and drinking; he would never don their clothing. He would not even allow his picture to be painted, for painting, he felt, was a white man's craft.

His father was a Shawnee, a tribe that had migrated from the South to Ohio. His mother was a Creek, a southern tribe that had once been neighbors of the Shawnee. Tecumseh had relatives in Alabama, Missouri, and Indiana, whom he visited with his mother. Out of his travels came a vision of a continental Indian confederation.

As a young warrior, he fought the white intrusion into the Ohio Valley after the Revolution. Tecumseh's view was that the Great Spirit had made the world in halves. Whites had their half in the East; Indians should be left in possession of the West. In practice, he might have settled for the Ohio River as a boundary, but white population movement in the 1790s made even that impractical.

In the 1790s, Tecumseh was the chief scout for the Indian alliance that fought the armies sent into Ohio by President Washington. When General Anthony Wayne forced the Indians to cede most of Ohio following the Battle of Fallen Timbers, Tecumseh refused to sign the treaty. He was the only important leader to do so. His intransigence made him the spokesman for the Indians of the Northwest. Indian leadership had never been a matter of birth or station; it was granted to those who had courage, strength, and the gift of persuasion. From his youth, Tecumseh had demonstrated all three. He became, by 1800, a defender of Indian rights, a skilled orator who was particularly effective because of his command of history. Defending Indians in courts of law, he overwhelmed his opponents with his knowledge of Indian treaties—when they had been signed, what they had promised, and when the whites had broken them.

The Indians who signed General Wayne's Treaty of Greenville were under the impression that the boundary line established by it would be permanent. Within a short time, whites were pressing for additional cessions. The most insistent was William Henry Harrison, who became governor of the newly created Indiana Territory in 1800. Establishing himself at Vincennes, on the lower Wabash River, Harrison was determined to open his territory to white settlement. Over the next few years he obtained one cession after another that sliced away at Indian holdings. He used every device imaginable. He took advantage of tribal rivalries and conflicting claims, sometimes obtaining a cession by a tribe that did not even own the land. He bribed minor leaders into ceding the lands of an entire tribe. He dispensed whiskey by the barrelful when all else failed.

At the heart of the conflict was a cultural misunderstanding over the nature and use of land. President Jefferson, who supported Governor Harrison's aggressive policies, hoped and expected that the Indians could be assimilated into American society. He even thought that intermarriage would eventually eliminate Indian identity. He wanted to make the Indians into farmers and absorb them into Anglo-American culture, much like immigrants.

Tecumseh was appalled at such a vision. His men were hunters and fighters, who left the tending of corn fields to their women. He regarded fields and fences as chains of bondage. Pushing a plow across a field in order to grow corn for market was a form of slavery. Tecumseh thought that land was like air or water; it was there for all to use. His followers knew no boundaries; they roamed the landscape in search of food to eat or furs to sell. Tecumseh asked nothing of the white man, except to be left alone. And that could never be. He was overwhelmed by a westward push that had three hundred years of momentum behind it.

With help from his messianic brother, The Prophet, Tecumseh forged a league of tribes to resist further land sales. Harrison simply stepped around him and sought out weaker, more susceptible Indian leaders. At Fort Wayne in 1809, through a combination of bribes, threats, and whiskey, Harrison obtained the cession of the central third of Indiana. Tecumseh, with war-bedecked retinue, journeyed to Vincennes to warn the governor personally that white occupation of the cession would mean war. That produced a stalemate which lasted for two years. In 1811, Tecumseh journeyed to Tennessee to persuade the southern tribes to join his alliance. Harrison took advantage of his absence to attack and destroy his headquarters at Tippecanoe. That action threw Tecumseh into an alliance with the British when war broke out in 1812. He was killed during the war in the battle of the Thames, and his dream of an Indian confederation, independent of both the British and American empires, died with him. He was the victim of a conflict of cultures in which there could be no justice, only tragedy.

Had the news arrived prior to the American declaration of war, Madison might have been willing to negotiate. Coming as it did after war was declared, Madison felt obliged to continue the fight in vindication of his other war aims. That meant, essentially, a war to end impressment, since the Indian problem, as Madison well knew, was caused more by American injustice than by British intrigue. And impressment, rendered obsolete by the termination of the Napoleonic War, was not even mentioned in the Anglo-American peace agreement.

⊔ The War of 1812

Divided against itself and ill-prepared for a fight, the United States fared badly in the first year of the war. President Madison had little talent for military planning, and his generals had even less. No one seems to have considered the obvious tactic—a consolidation of American forces for a thrust at Montreal by way of the Lake Champlain invasion route. This would have taken the war onto British soil, forced the British Canadians on the defensive, and cut them off from their Indian allies in the West. Instead, Madison left his armies spread out and his generals on their own initiative.

At Detroit, General William Hull led an army of 2,000 across the river into upper Canada, where he issued a proclamation inviting the Canadians to partake of the blessings of American liberty. Then, learning that Tecumseh's warriors had captured Fort Michimillimackinac at the straits to the north, he hastily retraced his steps. The Indians surrounded Detroit and massacred a relief force coming north from Ohio. In mid-August General Isaac Brock arrived to take command of a British-Canadian force of 700. He built an artillery battery

The *Constitution* and the *Guerriere*. In the first naval engagement of the war, August 20, 1812, "Old Ironsides" reduced the British frigate *Guerriere* to a floating hulk in thirty minutes.

New York Public Library Picture Collection.

on the Canadian side of the river, aimed it at Detroit, and invited Hull to surrender, hinting all the while that if he had to take the fort by storm, he might not be able to control his ferocious allies. Without further ado, Hull surrendered.

In October 1812, the American army hesitantly crossed the Niagara River and fought an inconclusive battle with the British-Canadians on Queenston Heights. The battle cost the life of the ablest of the British-Canadian commanders, Isaac Brock. Lacking reinforcements (because New York militia refused to fight outside their state), the American army, feeling isolated and exposed, withdrew to its side of the river. Another effort to cross the Niagara late that year ended when the commanding general, having got half his army positioned in boats, ordered them disembarked so they could eat lunch. When his second in command accused him of cowardice, he called off the invasion and challenged his subordinate to a duel. So ended the campaign of 1812.

Meanwhile, the tiny American navy gave a good account of itself in the summer and autumn of 1812. The nation entered the war with seven frigates (all but one built during the Adams administration) and a handful of brigs and sloops. The frigates were oversized for their class, carrying more guns and a larger crew than the British frigates. Thus in single-ship duels the Americans had a substantial advantage, but the speed and thoroughness with which they smashed their foes suggest also a superiority in gunnery. In August 1812, the *Constitution* encountered the *Guerriere* just off New York harbor and reduced the British ship to a sinking hulk, without masts or rudder, in thirty minutes. In October, the *United States,* commanded by Stephen Decatur, a hero of the War with Tripoli, defeated the *Macedonian* with superior seamanship. Decatur's cannon were lighter than his foe's but of longer range, so he skillfully avoided a closing and pounded the British ship into submission from a distance.

In a dozen ship-to-ship duels around the world, the Americans won all but one. The single loss was the 38-gun *Chesapeake,* which succumbed to the British frigate *Shannon* in an hour-long fight off Boston in early 1813. The one result of the encounter was a motto for the United States Navy. Mortally wounded, James Lawrence, commander of the *Chesapeake,* issued his last order: "Don't give up the ship. Fight her till she sinks." From mid-1813 until the end of the war, a British blockade kept the American navy in port. American privateers prowled the seas, however, capturing hundreds of British merchantmen. British vessels were not safe even in the English Channel and the Irish Sea. One American captain managed to insert a notice in London newspapers announcing a blockade of the British Isles. The property losses caused a sizable jump in British insurance rates, but the British war effort was not materially affected.

A senseless raid that resulted in the destruction of York (Toronto), capital of Upper Canada, was the principal action on the Niagara-Ontario front in 1813. In the West, however, the picture brightened. So long as Tecumseh's warriors ruled the forests, any expedition sent to recover Detroit had to proceed by water. That meant winning naval control of Lake Erie. At the beginning of 1813, a small British squadron controlled the lake. In March 1813, Master Commandant Oliver Hazard Perry arrived at Presque Isle (present-day Erie), Pennsylvania, with orders to construct a fleet that could challenge the British. In September he sailed out on the lake, and the two squadrons met on September 10 at Put-in Bay (Sandusky, Ohio). Perry, who daringly left his own damaged vessel in the middle of the battle and rowed to a fresh ship, won a narrow victory.

Northern campaigns, 1812–1814.

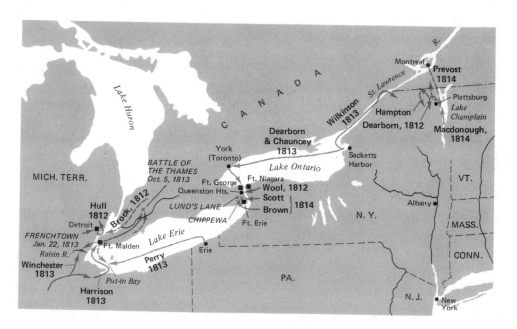

"We have met the enemy and they are ours," Perry wrote to General William Henry Harrison, who was poised on the Ohio shore with an invasion army. Perry ferried Harrison's army across the lake to Canada. Henry Proctor, Britain's timorous commander in the West, abandoned Detroit and Malden (to the disgust of Tecumseh) and retreated east along the Thames River. At Tecumseh's insistence Proctor at last put up a stand in a woods along the bank of the river, some fifty miles east of Detroit. Harrison attacked on October 5, and in an hour of fierce combat he smashed the British-Canadian line and scattered the Indians. Tecumseh was killed, his confederacy demolished, and the Northwest restored to American control.

The defeat of Napoleon freed British forces for a concentrated effort on America in 1814. Napoleon's disastrous Russian campaign in 1812 encouraged Austria and Prussia to reenter the war, and the combined armies of Western Europe finally smashed him at Leipzig in 1813. He was placed in exile on the island of Elba in the Mediterranean. With thousands of red-coated veterans free for American service, Britain planned two major campaigns in 1814. One army was to thrust south along Lake Champlain into New York, while another landed at New Orleans and seized Louisiana. The American government meantime was to be distracted by an amphibious force operating in Chesapeake Bay. Peace talks opened that summer at the neutral site of Ghent, Belgium, and the British delegates, anticipating victory on the battlefield, demanded the cession of whatever lands their armies conquered. The American delegates marked time, awaiting the military outcome.

CAMPAIGN OF 1814

Americans had plans of their own that summer for the Niagara front, and their armies got under way before the British

The Battle of Lake Erie. This painting commemorates the boldness of Oliver Hazard Perry, who changed ships in the middle of the battle. The banner Perry carries bears Lawrence's famous words, "Don't give up the ship!"

New York Public Library Picture Collection.

strategy unfolded. The Madison administration, having suffered through a flock of incompetent generals, found at last in Jacob Brown a man who could fight. Adored by his men, Brown shaped the volunteer army into a disciplined legion. Crossing the river in early July, Brown met an army of British regulars and Canadian militia at Chippewa Creek, within earshot of Niagara Falls. On July 5, 1814, Brown attacked in professional European style. Both sides suffered heavy casualties, but the British retired from the field leaving Brown with a technical victory. The exclamation of the surprised British General Phineas Riall, "Those are Regulars, by God!" told the story.* The cry still reverberates in the halls of the United States Military Academy, which also commemorates the gray uniforms worn at the Battle of Chippewa.

Two weeks later the armies resumed the contest at Lundy's Lane. Again, two lines of infantry seventy yards apart fought muzzle to muzzle until darkness shrouded the field. It was a standoff, with each side suffering more than 900 casualties, but again the Americans were left with the field and a technical victory. In need of rest and reinforcements, Brown retired to Fort Erie. The river proved his undoing. Reinforcements could not get across, a revitalized British-Canadian force laid siege to the fort, and he ultimately surrendered. The war on the Niagara ended in bloody stalemate.

In August 1814, action shifted to the Chesapeake theater. British Admiral Sir George Cockburn had controlled the bay since mid-1813, entertaining himself by raiding towns along the Virginia coast and burning plantations. Reinforced with an army of veterans from the European war,

Cockburn decided to capture Washington, D.C., in August. To sail up the Potomac would alert the capital's defenses, so Cockburn instead landed his troops on the Patuxent River for an overland march on Washington. Encountering an ill-trained assortment of Maryland and Virginia militia near Bladensburg on the edge of the District of Columbia, Cockburn let fly a barrage of Congreve rockets—novel, noisy, but relatively harmless weapons. The American militia, having never seen such a device, fled from the field, sweeping along President Madison and his cabinet, who had come to watch the battle. The British occupied Washington for three days, and then retired to their ships after burning the capitol and several public buildings.

Cockburn then sailed to Baltimore and bombarded Fort McHenry, which guarded the harbor. The fort held out, saving the city. The only notable result was the poem

Jackson's southern campaign, 1813–1815.

Gulf of Mexico

---

* Regulars were professional soldiers, and most of the American army was made up of short-term volunteers.

written by Francis Scott Key, a Maryland lawyer who had gone aboard the British flagship to appeal for the release of several hostages. His poem, put to the music of an English drinking song, "Anacreon in Heaven," became, by act of Congress in 1931, the national anthem.

In September 1814, British military plans began at last to unfold. The Governor-General of Canada, Sir George Prevost, led a magnificent army of 15,000 veterans up the St. John's River to Lake Champlain and laid siege to the town of Plattsburgh, New York. Because of the mountains, British supplies had to move by water; hence the key to the campaign was naval control of the lake. Recognizing this, both sides had spent the summer feverishly building ships. Lieutenant Thomas Macdonough, in charge of the American effort, anchored his squadron in Plattsburg Bay to await the coming of the British. The British arrived on September 11, paired off with Macdonough's ships, and likewise dropped anchor. The battle, unique in naval warfare for having been fought at anchor, was an American victory. Prevost abandoned his siege and returned to Montreal. The Battle of Lake Champlain precluded any British territorial claims in that area.

BATTLE OF NEW ORLEANS

There was still Louisiana, the third British objective. A fresh army of 9,000 redcoats left Europe for the Gulf of Mexico in the fall of 1814. Commanding in the Southwest was a general of the Tennessee militia, Andrew Jackson, elected to his post in the democratic fashion of the West and utterly without battlefield experience. Jackson had taken up arms in the spring of 1814 to suppress an uprising of Creek Indians, which he did in bloody fashion at the Battle of Horseshoe Bend (March 27, 1814). He spent the summer extracting land cessions

from the southern tribes, and in the autumn, hearing rumors of an impending British attack, headed for Mobile Bay. Inspired by Jackson's energy and determination, the defenders of Mobile turned back a British probe at Fort Bowyer. With that front secure, Jackson dashed for New Orleans, arriving with his lanky band of Tennessee and Kentucky volunteers on the second of December. To thicken his ranks, Jackson recruited two regiments of free blacks in New Orleans. To obtain expertise in the handling of his artillery, Jackson persuaded the pirates of Louisiana's Gulf Coast and their leader, Jean Lafitte, to join him.

The British appeared in mid-December, and Jackson erected a defense line of cotton bales along a drainage ditch a few miles south of New Orleans. After some preliminary skirmishes, the British launched their main infantry attack on January 8, 1815, and Jackson's gunners cut them to pieces. When the day ended, more than 2,000 redcoats, including their commanding general, lay dead on the field. In the general's torn and bloody pocket was a commission as governor of the colony of Louisiana. Blacks, pirates, and Tennessee volunteers had turned aside another British intrusion. Jackson's losses were seven killed and six wounded.

New England Federalists had opposed the war from the beginning because they felt Madison had been duped by Napoleon. In their view, the war with Britain effectively made the United States an ally of hated France. In December 1814, Federalist delegates from the New England states met at Hartford, Connecticut, to discuss ways of resisting the war. A few Federalists hoped and many Republicans feared that the Hartford Convention would recommend New England's secession from the Union. The majority of Federalists were not prepared for so radical a step, however; and the convention contented itself with a list of seven proposed constitutional

Isaac Delgado Museum of Art.

The Battle of New Orleans. Jackson's army is lined up behind a drainage ditch and parapet of cotton bales. The British attack across the open expanse of Chamonet farm.

amendments. The first, and most important, would have repealed the three-fifths compromise in the Constitution, by which southerners had been able to count three fifths of their slaves for purposes of representation in Congress. New England Federalists attributed their own decline to the disproportionate power this compromise had given the South. Other amendments were aimed at reducing the influence of the West (by requiring a two-thirds vote in Congress for the admission of new states) and the power of Virginia (by prohibiting the election of a president from the same state in successive terms). In the nation's capital, the Federalist proposals excited only scorn, for by the time they arrived, the war had ended.

THE TREATY OF GHENT

When Napoleon invaded Russia in the summer of 1812, the czar, anxious for a 100 percent British effort against France, offered to mediate the Anglo-American war. John Quincy Adams, son of the second president and American minister to St. Petersburg, transmitted the offer to Madison. The president, reeling from the disasters of 1812, promptly accepted. To conduct the negotiations, Madison named a strong and broadly representative commission. In addition to Adams, the president sent his trusted servant, Albert Gallatin; western War Hawk Henry Clay; Delaware Federalist James A. Bayard; and a lawyer, Richard Rush.

The negotiations, transferred from St. Petersburg to the neutral ground of Ghent, Belgium, dragged on for a year because the British demanded not only any territory their armies might occupy, but an Indian buffer state in the Northwest. By the fall of 1814, it was clear that, with the possible exception of New Orleans, British armies would occupy nothing more than they held at the beginning of the conflict, and Tecumseh's death reduced the idea of an Indian buffer state to an empty dream. The commissioners quickly came to terms, and the treaty signed on December 24, 1814, simply confirmed the stalemate. Nothing was said of American neutral rights or the impressment of seamen. Both issues had been rendered irrelevant by the end of the European conflict. Neither side demanded territory; they simply agreed to stop fighting.

The Treaty of Ghent was a victory for common sense. Neither side felt victimized, and after the war relations between the two countries were more cordial than ever. Within a few years they settled disputes involving the Newfoundland fisheries and ownership of the Pacific Northwest. They also signed an agreement limiting the number of warships on the Great Lakes—the first arms limitation agreement in history. It was, all in all, a satisfactory ending to a frustrating war.

⊔ An Era of Good Feelings and Ill Temper

The Battle of New Orleans was a national baptism. It purged the memories of humiliation, defeat, ineptitude, and surrender that had brought on the war and attended its early days. It cleansed the sins of the past and inspired a new faith, a new self-confidence. Doubts that the republic might not endure vanished. The republic had survived its ordeal by fire; Americans looked to the future with cheer.

Jackson's victory did more than instill confidence; it inspired a creed, a national mythology. Lying dead on the field at New Orleans were the disciplined professionals of Europe, the minions of kings and generals. Victorious behind their rude rampart of cotton bales was an assortment of armed civilians, farmers fresh from the plow, proud of their fighting qualities and their marksmanship, scornful of professionalism and discipline. Such at least was the picture branded on the national consciousness. The battle brought into focus the image Americans had of themselves—spontaneous, self-reliant individuals, blessed by God and nature, and destined for future glory.

From this taproot of national pride grew a new variety of nationalism. Gone was the Jeffersonian fear of power; replacing it was a new concern that the government be made to work better, that power be wielded to some useful end. It was, in truth, Federalism in a new guise. Its spokesmen, however, were new-generation Republicans—indeed, the very men who had led the nation into war, Henry Clay and John C. Calhoun. The Federalist party, far from benefiting from the nationalist mood, continued to wither. The Federalists' opposition to the war, culminating in the Hartford Convention of 1814, marked them with the stigma of disloyalty. In the presidential election of 1816 the party mustered enough strength to nominate Rufus King, and then collapsed.

The dissolution of the Federalists left the nation under the one-party governance of the Republicans for a decade after the war. There were many who welcomed the respite from political tensions. In 1817, Boston's *Columbian Sentinel*, a Federalist sheet that had bitterly denounced the war, surveyed the political landscape and hailed an Era of Good Feelings, an interlude without party warfare. James Monroe, elected president in 1816 to succeed Madison, was temperamentally suited to an era of political charity. His view of the presidency was like Washington's. He considered himself an independent arbiter, a national leader who was above parties. One of his first acts was a visit to previously hostile New England. Not since Washington had a president toured the country, and Monroe's excursion was attended by a steady outpouring of applause. Monroe was a genial man who had devoted his life to public service; as president, he welcomed a time of "good feelings."

He was also the last of a breed, and his time was passing. He was the last of the revolutionary generation, the last president to wear the eighteenth-century garb of knee breeches, silk stockings, and buckled shoes. The age of gentlemanliness and reason in which Monroe had been born was yielding to a democratic age that by comparison seemed coarse and aggressive. Toward the end of Monroe's term, the postwar plans for national betterment succumbed to a moody, defensive regionalism. Good feelings gave way to bad temper; unity was fractured by schism. And from the turmoil emerged a new two-party system.

REPAIRING
THE NATIONAL FABRIC

The war experience revealed some flaws in the national fabric. The difficulties of moving armies and keeping them supplied demonstrated the need for interstate roads and canals. The vexations of wartime finance showed the value of the Bank of the United States, whose charter Congress had allowed to expire in 1811. And when the war ended, a deluge of cheap British goods threatened the survival of the American manufacturers who had sprung up behind the protective wall of embargo and war.

Solving the problem of finance was Congress's first priority. In January 1816, Calhoun introduced a bill to charter a second bank of the United States. Like the first bank, Calhoun's offspring was to be in existence for twenty years and to function as an arm of the Treasury in the collection and disbursement of funds. It could establish branches anywhere it wished, and its notes were to serve as a national currency. The government would subscribe one-fifth of the capital; the president would appoint one-fifth of the directors. In exchange for its privileges, the bank was to give the government a bonus of $1,500,000. The bank charter swept through Congress with token opposition from Federalists, whose objections were not against banks as such, but against Republican banks, and from unreconstructed Republicans, among them John Randolph.

Next on the agenda was a tariff to shield American manufacturers from foreign competition. Henry Clay took this in hand and guided through Congress a duty of 25 percent on textiles and a few other products. The duty was not high and the list of goods was short, but the act was significant nonetheless. It was Congress's first attempt to subsidize American business through tax policy. Once established, the principle could be extended indefinitely.

The construction of a federally financed network of roads and canals was the final objective of the postwar nationalists. It was also the most controversial. People living on the seaboard already had a road system, and they objected to being taxed for the construction of facilities in the West. An appropriation bill squeaked through Congress in early 1817, but President Madison, exerting his power for the last time on his final day in office, vetoed it. The construction of roads and canals, said the president in the tone of a schoolmaster, was not among the delegated powers of Congress. Having yielded on one constitutionally dubious item—the bank, which he had opposed strenuously a quarter-century before—Madison clearly felt that it was time to halt the stretching of the Constitution, the document he had done so much to create.

There were indeed echoes of Federalism in the nationalist program of Clay and Calhoun. The second bank was a resurrection of Hamilton's institution, and the use of federal power to encourage industrial development had been anticipated by Hamilton's 1792 report on manufactures. Federalists could have supported Clay and Calhoun with perfect ideological consistency, but few did. Provincialism and sour partisanship held them back; but so tiny was the Federalist remnant after 1816 that it scarcely mattered. There was, however, one exception: Chief Justice John Marshall seemed to sense after 1815 that his turn had come.

THE MARSHALL COURT

Little was heard from Marshall after the war over the judiciary during Jefferson's first term. Except for the Burr trial, Marshall seemed content to bide his time and wait for the Jeffersonian wind to abate.

The postwar climate of nationalism gave him his opportunity. The other justices by then were Jefferson-Madison appointees, but Marshall managed to hold together, by force of personality and strength of intellect, a nationalist majority. Two decisions in 1819 served to announce Marshall's new position. *McCulloch* v. *Maryland* involved a test of the constitutionality of the newly established Bank of the United States. Maryland was opposed to the bank and sought to keep it out of the state by placing a tax on its notes. McCulloch, cash-

ier of the bank's Baltimore branch, refused to pay the tax; Maryland filed suit, and the case wound its way to the Supreme Court. Marshall, mindful of the constitutional dispute between Jefferson and Hamilton over the bank in 1791, seized the opportunity to give a judicial blessing to the concept of "implied powers." Indeed, Marshall went far beyond Hamilton by asserting that the federal government was not confined at all to specifically delegated powers—it was entitled to use any means to secure a legitimate end, unless the means was specifically prohibited by the Constitution. That, of course, turned the concept of strict construction inside out. Having affirmed the constitutionality of the bank, Marshall pushed on to the conclusion that the Maryland tax was unconstitutional. "The power to tax is the power to destroy," he averred, and a state cannot be allowed to destroy a legitimate arm of the federal government. For the first time, a state law was held invalid as contrary to an "implied" power of Congress. It was more than a century before the Court again conceded the latitude of federal power that John Marshall envisioned in 1819.

The other case involved Dartmouth College, a private corporation chartered by the state of New Hampshire. After the war, the legislature attempted to amend the charter and bring the college under public control. The trustees resisted, and the case of *Dartmouth College* v. *Woodward* resulted. For counsel, the trustees employed Daniel Webster, an alumnus of the college and an influential Federalist in Congress. Arguing that a charter, once granted, cannot be altered, Webster concluded with the plea: "It is, sir, a small college. And yet there are those who love it." Marshall, though also an alumnus of a small college (William and Mary), was more impressed with Webster's argument than his emotion. A charter, he agreed, was a contract, and the federal Constitution prohibited the states from "abridging the obligations of contracts."

The effect of this decision was to enshrine property rights and sanctify contracts. In the long term, Marshall's conservatism created a climate that encouraged saving, investment, and economic development. In the short run, he gave judicial blessing to monopoly, because many of the companies chartered by the states were given, by the terms of their charters, exclusive business rights in their area. When the implications of this became clear, public resentment exploded into an antimonopoly movement that eventually destroyed the monopoly Marshall himself had legitimized, the Bank of the United States.

Five years later, a conflict over a steamboat monopoly presented Marshall with an opportunity to interpret another critical feature of the Constitution—the commerce power. The case of *Gibbons* v. *Ogden* (1824) involved a monopoly of the steamboat traffic on the Hudson River, which the state of New York had granted to Robert Fulton, inventor of the steamboat. Marshall held the monopoly to be invalid on the grounds that New York had no authority to regulate an interstate waterway. The regulation of interstate commerce, said Marshall, was exclusively the province of Congress. The short-run effect of this decision was to free river and coastal traffic from the fetters of monopoly and to encourage the competitive development of western transportation. The long-term effect was to confer on Congress important regulatory authority that it could exert whenever it saw the need. So broad was Marshall's definition of commerce ("any species of intercourse" among states) that it included railroads, automobiles, pipelines, telegraphy, telephones, and tourists—"species," in short, that had not even been invented in 1824.

By the time Marshall died in 1835, the Constitution was a very different instrument from that which the federal convention had written. It was broad in scope, elastic in definition, and able to meet the changing needs of a rapidly growing society. And by putting the law at the service of business enterprise, Marshall had made the law an instrument of that growth.

SOLDIER AND DIPLOMAT: NATIONALIST EXPANSION

The patriotic spirit that gripped the country after 1815 infused foreign as well as domestic policy. John Quincy Adams, Monroe's secretary of state, was a nationalist at heart. In 1803, he was the only Federalist in Congress who supported the

Our Country . . . Right or Wrong

Naval war hero Stephen Decatur was given a dinner in his honor by the citizens of Norfolk, Virginia, in April 1816. He afterwards proposed the famous toast: "Our country! In her intercourse with foreign nations may she always be in the right; but our country, right or wrong!" The toast became a favorite among patriots, but it inspired misgivings too. In May 1846, at the outset of the Mexican War, Kentucky Congressman John J. Crittenden declared: "I hope to find my country in the right; however, I will stand by her, right or wrong." In 1872 Senator Carl Schurz, a German immigrant and a liberal reformer, put it another way: "Our country, right or wrong! When right to be kept right; when wrong to be put right!"

Louisiana Purchase. In 1808, he broke with his party to support the Jefferson-Madison policy of commercial retaliation, and President Madison thereafter made him minister to Russia. After participating in the peace negotiations at Ghent, Adams was made minister to Great Britain. There he worked hard to supplement the peace treaty by resolving remaining differences over fisheries and boundaries until Monroe summoned him to the State Department in 1817.

The British, anxious to keep open the American market for their goods, were amenable to negotiation. In 1817, Richard Rush, acting secretary of state pending Adams's arrival, signed an agreement with British minister Charles Bagot providing for the limitation of warships on the Great Lakes. The following year, Adams negotiated a convention that opened the coasts of Labrador and Newfoundland to American fishermen, established the forty-ninth parallel as the American-Canadian boundary from Lake of the Woods to the Rocky Mountains, and provided for the joint occupation of the territory west of the Rockies (vaguely described as "Oregon"). The joint occupation, renewable after ten years, shelved a sterile diplomatic controversy over the ownership of the Pacific Northwest and left the question of title to be resolved by settlement of the area. Adams, fully aware of the restlessness of Americans, knew which side had the advantage there.

No sooner had Adams finished extracting all he could from the British than General Andrew Jackson presented him with an opportunity to wrest some territory from the hands of Spain. Jackson had been placed in command of the army's Southern Department after the war. The only problem he confronted was Indians. The Seminoles, residents of Spanish Florida, made a habit of raiding the Georgia-Alabama frontier and stealing slaves and horses. Spain, by the terms of Pinckney's Treaty

(1795), was obliged to control the Florida Indians, but Spanish authority in the colony was too weak to do anything.

Pinckney's Treaty also allowed American forces to cross the border into Florida if they were in "hot pursuit" of Indians. In early 1818, President Monroe ordered Jackson to eliminate the Indian menace and hinted rather broadly that he might enter Florida in the process. The Seminoles, learning that Jackson was on the move, scampered for home, but Jackson barged across the frontier anyway, captured two Spanish forts, St. Marks and Pensacola, and executed two British civilians for trafficking with the Indians. He then shipped the Spanish governor off to Cuba, ran up the American flag, and headed for home, leaving the future of the colony to the diplomats.

Deeply embarrassed, President Monroe prepared to disavow his impulsive general, but Adams persuaded him that there might be an advantage in the incident. When Britain protested the execution of its citizens by an American army on Spanish soil, Adams, in effect, told the ministry to keep its gunrunners at home. In response to Madrid's outcry, he hinted that if Spain could not keep its Indians under control, he might have to unleash Jackson again. He also pointed out that the entire problem could be solved by the sale of Florida to the United States. Spanish authorities agreed, and instructed their minister in Washington, Luis de Onis, to come to terms on both Florida and the Texas boundary. Silver-laden Mexico was far more valuable to Spain than Florida, and Madrid authorities were anxious to secure a clearly defined boundary between Louisiana and Texas to prevent future American intrusion.

Adams and Onis quickly reached agreement, and in February 1819, they signed a treaty that involved both the transfer of Florida and the drawing of a transcontinental boundary line. In return for Florida,

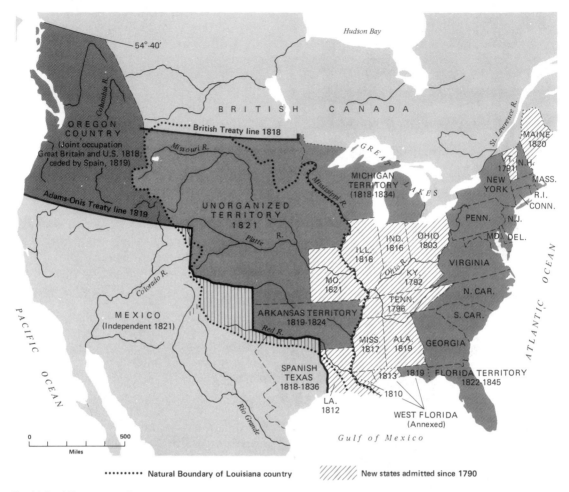

The United States in 1821.

the United States assumed $5 million worth of claims American citizens had against Spain. In the West, the transcontinental line followed the Sabine, Red, and Arkansas rivers to the Continental Divide; it followed the Divide north to the forty-second parallel and followed that to the Pacific. Viewed in conjunction with the Oregon Convention signed with Britain in the previous year, the Transcontinental Treaty gave the United States a diplomatic foothold on the Pacific Coast. Far ahead of his time, Adams envisioned a republic that extended across the continent from sea to sea.

Territorial expansion was only one aspect of John Quincy Adams's vigorous pursuit of American national interests. He was also concerned about developing America's existing trade and finding new markets for American goods. The breakup of the Spanish empire in Latin America offered a prime opportunity for expanding both. Revolutions broke out in Latin America, inspired in part by French revolutionary ideals. Spain was too distracted by the war in Europe to put up much of a fight for its empire. By 1821, when Mexico won its independence, there were a number of independent republics in South America. The end of Spain's monopoly presented enormous commercial opportunities to the United States and to Great Britain. After Spain ratified the Transcontinental Treaty in 1821, the United States opened missions in the United Provinces of the Rio de la Plata (Argentina), Colombia, Chile, Peru, and Mexico.

Monroe and Adams were not deeply concerned that Spain might attempt to recover Latin America, but they were anxious about other European powers. After the Napoleonic wars, leading European powers formed a Holy Alliance of monarchies to preserve the status quo. When a revolution broke out in Spain in 1823, France, acting as an agent of the Holy Alliance, intervened to restore the Bourbon monarchy. There was instant concern in both Britain and the United States that France might also have designs on Latin America. British Foreign Minister George Canning invited the United States to join in a warning to the French, but Secretary Adams was leery of a British embrace. He felt that the British presence in Oregon and the Russian colonization of Alaska posed a far greater threat to American interests than anything anyone might do to Latin America. Adams therefore suggested that the administration issue an independent statement of American policy rather than "come in as a cockboat in the wake of a British man-of-war." Monroe agreed and inserted a statement of American policy in his annual message to Congress, December 2, 1823.

The message opened with a reference to the British overture and noted that it presented an occasion to assert a principle "that the American Continents, by the free and independent condition which they have assumed and maintained, are henceforth not to be considered as subjects for

future colonization by any European power." This concept of noncolonization was drafted by John Quincy Adams and placed in Monroe's message at his insistence. It was aimed at Britain and Russia, and it had to do primarily with Oregon and Alaska. Turning to the Latin American crisis, Monroe reiterated the doctrine of the spheres, a staple of American global thinking since Washington's farewell address. The halves of the earth, said Monroe, are separated by more than geography; they have different political systems. Thus, while they might exchange goods and observe one another as "interested spectators," neither hemisphere has a right to interfere with the other. "In the wars of the European powers," Monroe continued, "in matters relating to themselves, we have never taken any part, nor does it comport with our policy to do so." Similarly, "we could not view any interposition for the purpose of oppressing [the Latin American republics] . . . in any other light than as the manifestation of an unfriendly disposition toward the United States."

The statesmen of Europe dismissed Monroe's message as simple "blustering," and since Monroe had no navy to enforce it, the doctrine was more a pious hope than an ultimatum. Britain's George Canning, on the other hand, reacted with anger, as well he might, for much of the Monroe Doctrine was addressed to Britain, not France or Spain. Even the shield thrown across the New World was an indirect warning that Britain could not monopolize the trade of Latin America. The United States had plans of its own for the Latin American market.

Congress followed this slap at the British with one of its own. In 1824 it increased the tariff duties considerably and extended protection to a vast array of American manufactures. Taken together, the Monroe Doctrine and the tariff of 1824 were a statement of commercial nationalism, a proclamation of political and economic maturity. They were, in a sense, a declaration of economic independence as important as the political declaration issued nearly a half-century before.

⎍Nationalism versus Sectionalism

The Monroe Doctrine and the tariff of 1824 were also evidence of a reversal in Republican philosophy. In place of the states rights agrarianism they had espoused in 1800, Republicans by 1824 were committed to the exercise of federal powers to promote commerce and manufacturing. A shift in regional postures accompanied the ideological switch. The War Hawks of 1812 and the nationalists of 1816 had been anchored in the South and the West. New England in 1816 was

antinational and flirting with states rights. By 1824, the regional postures were reversed. The North generally and New England in particular supported bank, tariff, and other forms of government aid. The South was becoming sectionally minded. In 1825 the South Carolina legislature adopted resolutions denouncing the tariff as unconstitutional. Congress had power to impose duties for revenue, said South Carolina; Congress did not have power to protect or subsidize northern manufactures.

The regional change of position forced some dramatic individual reversals as politicians adjusted to the shifting interests of their constituents. Daniel Webster, as a New Hampshire congressman in 1816, was a New England sectionalist opposed to bank and tariff; as a senator from Massachusetts in the 1820s, he became an ardent

The House of Representatives, 1823. This painting is by Samuel F. B. Morse, who is best known as the inventor of the telegraph and the Morse code. Morse began life as a painter. He was one of the last students of Benjamin West. This painting is in the grand tradition pioneered by West, but it lacks drama.

In the Collection of The Corcoran Gallery of Art.

nationalist. John C. Calhoun went in the opposite direction, becoming by the end of the 1820s an apologist for southern rights.

THE AMERICAN SYSTEM

Henry Clay, on the other hand, suffered no such embarrassment. One of the architects of the postwar nationalism, he was still in the mid-1820s its most zealous proponent. Indeed, he sought to elevate his creed into a theory of political economy he called the American System. The cornerstone of the system was the tariff, a protective shield for American manufacturers that would enable them to expand production until eventually they could supply the nation's needs. The growth of factories would mean more jobs, and the emergence of an urban labor force in turn would provide a home market for American farm products. Thus, in Clay's view, all segments of American society—not just business—would benefit from the tariff. The commercial result was self-sufficiency. Consumers would no longer be dependent on foreign goods, farmers and cotton planters would no longer be at the mercy of European market prices. The political result was national unity through interdependence, as each portion of the country produced what it did best. The North and East would concentrate on manufactures, the South and West would deliver food, cotton, and raw materials.

To facilitate the exchange among sectors, Clay proposed a national network of roads and canals, planned and financed by the federal government. And at the apex of Clay's American System was the Bank of the United States, facilitating the transfer of goods and services by providing a national currency and interstate credit arrangement. Bank, tariff, and internal improvements—Clay had been touting that trio for nearly a decade. But elevated into

New York Public Library Picture Collection.

Henry Clay.

a "system," they made an arresting theory. It was a coherent program for the application of governmental power to the goal of economic development.

Clay, however, could not overcome regional jealousies, and the American System was never given fair trial. Westerners, suspicious of paper money, opposed all banks, and especially the Bank of the United States. New Englanders disliked being taxed for internal improvements that would primarily benefit other regions. And the South opposed all elements of Clay's program. Blessed with a magnificent river system to carry their heavy staples to market, southerners had little need for roads and canals. Planters eyed the Bank of the United States with deep suspicion, and they viewed the tariff as a parasitical drain on their cotton profits. Southerners, moreover, had become wary of ballooning federal power. "If Congress can make canals," muttered one southerner, "they can emancipate [the slaves]." The concern that federal power might be extended into the realm of slavery stemmed from an effort, a few years earlier, on the part of northern congressmen to restrict slavery in the territory of Missouri. The Missouri controversy, during which the first blunt criticism was made of the "peculiar institution" from the floor of Congress, generated a mood of sectional defensiveness.

THE MISSOURI CONTROVERSY, 1819–1821

William Henry Harrison's victory at the Thames coupled with Andrew Jackson's triumph at Horseshoe Bend in the latter stages of the War of 1812 ended effective Indian resistance east of the Mississippi River. The generals extracted huge land cessions from the defeated tribes, and population flowed into the Mississippi Valley after the war. Within four years four new states were added to the Union—Indiana, Illinois, Alabama, and Mississippi (Louisiana had been admitted in 1812).

In February 1819, the House of Representatives had just sealed the admission of Illinois and taken up a routine Missouri enabling bill (enabling Missouri to draft a state constitution) when James Tallmadge, a little-known congressman from Poughkeepsie, New York, rose to offer an amendment. Tallmadge's amendment was twofold: He would prohibit the further introduction of slaves into Missouri, and he would free the children born of slave parents in the state when they reached the age of twenty-five. The proposal was moderate enough. It presented no threat to slavery in those states where it was already established, and as a program of gradual emancipation, it would not even seriously discomfort Missouri slaveholders. Northern congressmen who rose to defend Tallmadge's motion pointed out that Missouri was still a territory and still subject to con-

gressional regulation. Congress had prohibited slavery in the Northwest by the Ordinance of 1787; surely it could do so in new states carved out of the Louisiana Purchase.

Tallmadge's amendment might have been less inflammatory had it been directed at a territory with little or no slave population. But Missouri in 1820 already had 10,000 slaves in a total population of 66,000; so southerners viewed the amendment as an attack on slavery. In defense of their institution, southerners fell back on the constitutional argument. Congress did not have power to limit slavery, they argued, because slaves were property; the government could not deprive people of their property unless they committed a crime. Moreover, Missouri was applying for statehood. As a sovereign state, Missouri could have any social system it wanted, including slavery. If Congress imposed conditions on the admission of Missouri, it would reduce Missouri, in effect, to a second-class state. Thus strict construction, states rights, and slavery were wedded from the very inception of the forty-year controversy that led ultimately to secession and civil war.

Votes counted more than arguments, however, and in the House of Representatives the populous North had a majority. The House attached the Tallmadge Amendment to the Missouri bill and sent it to the Senate. In the Senate in 1819, by a quirk of history, there happened to be an equal number of free and slave states. In addition, several free-state senators were impressed with the South's constitutional argument. As a result, the Senate deleted the amendment. The House refused to yield, however, and Congress adjourned in stalemate.

When Congress reassembled in December 1819, Missouri was again knocking on the door. But there was also another applicant for statehood: Maine, which wanted to separate itself from Massachusetts. Sens-

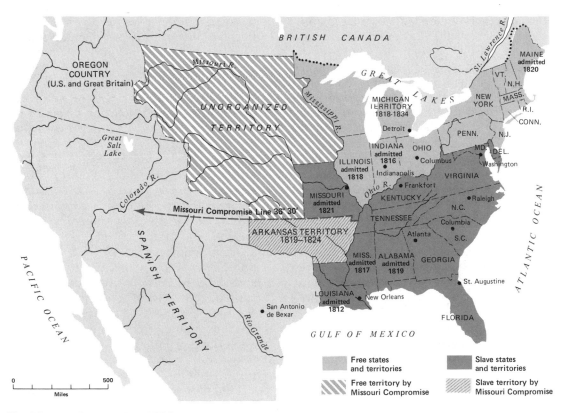

The Missouri Compromise, 1820.

ing a possible bargain, the Senate attached a Maine enabling bill to Missouri's, thereby coupling a free state with a slave state. Northerners in the House rejected the overture. Maine would enter as a free state in any case; they wanted Missouri free too. Debate resumed and dragged on for the next three months. The acrimony reverberated through the nation. At Monticello, Thomas Jefferson reflected the common apprehension. "This momentous question," he wrote, "like a fire-bell in the night, awakened and filled me with terror."

Backstairs negotiations, in which Speaker of the House Henry Clay figured prominently, resulted in an additional concession to antislavery northerners in the House, and the compromise was passed into law in March 1820. Maine would be

admitted as a free state, Missouri would be allowed to draft a constitution without restrictions on slavery, and slavery would be prohibited in the remainder of the Louisiana Purchase north of latitude 36° 30'. The latter restriction meant that only one more slave state, Arkansas, would be carved from the Louisiana Purchase (Oklahoma was shortly thereafter declared Indian Territory), and the remainder of the Great Plains would be free soil.

Southerners emerged from the controversy in a state of shock, for it brought home the fact that they had become a minority in the Union. Southerners were slow in realizing this because ever since the federal ship of state had been launched, they had been at the helm. With the exception of John Adams, every president had been a southerner—indeed, a Virginian. Southerners controlled the committee structure of Congress; a Virginian presided over the Supreme Court. This political dominance masked the fact that the South had fallen steadily behind the North in population, industry, and wealth. The Missouri controversy exposed the South's position; worse, it revealed that the northern majority was a potential enemy. Southerners listened in stunned horror as northerners denounced slavery as an evil and condemned southerners as sinners. Faced with a hostile phalanx of free states, southerners retreated into a defensive sectionalism. They self-consciously sought to emphasize the regional traits that bound them together—plantation agriculture, easygoing gentility, and a slave labor force. That fewer than a third of all southern families owned slaves did not matter. Slavery conferred status on southern poor whites, for it established a class of persons lower on the social ladder than they. Moreover, if the slaves were freed, they would compete with the white poor for jobs and land.

BIRTH OF THE SECOND PARTY SYSTEM

The criticism of slavery that reverberated through Congress in the heat of the Missouri controversy was by no means a reflection of northern public opinion. The vast majority of northerners were, and would remain until the very eve of the Civil War, utterly indifferent to the plight of the black slave in the South. Thus the slavery controversy subsided quickly after the Missouri Compromise, and little more was heard about the "peculiar institution" for almost a decade. Sectional animosity continued to run high, however, in part because southerners felt they had other grievances.

The beginning of the Missouri debate coincided with a financial panic in the spring of 1819. Most banks and manu-

facturing enterprises recovered rather quickly, but farm prices remained low for some years because exports dwindled as European agriculture recovered from its wartime devastation. Cotton remained depressed for a time because the South was growing more fiber than the mills of England could absorb. Westerners blamed the depression on banks generally and the Bank of the United States in particular. Others looked elsewhere. South Carolina focused on the tariff; Georgia concentrated on expelling its Indians. The Cherokees and Creeks were in possession of large portions of the state's prime cotton lands. Georgia politicians asked the federal government to relieve the Indians of their lands, and when it failed to do so, Georgians plotted means of their own. Whatever the grievance, the common scapegoat was the national government, something it had done or failed to do. In the process, states rights won new converts; sectionalism was reinforced.

The postwar years—the Era of Good Feelings—were spotted with ill temper: controversies over banks, internal improvements, and slavery, as well as discontent stemming from financial panic and rural depression. These were also years of rapid social and economic change, as we will see in the following chapter. People were changing positions, seizing new opportunities or finding themselves replaced. That too stirred unrest and ill-will. Inevitably, these social stresses had a political impact. The Republican party weathered the early controversies over internal improvements and slavery, but by the mid-1820s it was showing signs of strain. Its breakup began with the presidential election of 1824.

There was no obvious successor to Monroe, who followed precedent and retired at the end of his second term, but Adams and Clay were among the possibilities. So too was Andrew Jackson, hero of New Orleans. Jackson was particularly trouble-

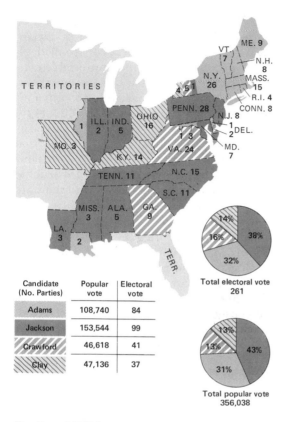

Candidate (No. Parties)	Popular vote	Electoral vote
Adams	108,740	84
Jackson	153,544	99
Crawford	46,618	41
Clay	47,136	37

Total electoral vote 261

Total popular vote 356,038

Election of 1824.

electoral vote. Thus for the second and last time in American history the election went to the House of Representatives. Henry Clay had been eliminated as a candidate, but as Speaker of the House he had the opportunity to play kingmaker. Clay's choice was Adams, and with the help of Daniel Webster, who had some influence in the divided New York delegation, Clay swung enough states behind Adams to secure his election. Adams thereupon named Clay secretary of state and, by implication, his successor in the White House. There was no bargain between the two, for none was necessary. Their political views were virtually identical, and neither could abide Jackson.

Jackson understandably thought he had been robbed, and his friends instantly accused Adams of making a "corrupt bargain" to secure the presidency. The slogan "bargain and corruption" was hardly a ringing battlecry, but it touched a political nerve. It enabled the Jacksonians to portray Adams and Clay as eastern aristocrats conniving to keep themselves in power against the will of the people. Jackson, who had never demonstrated much interest in the "common man," was suddenly the champion of democracy. The "corrupt bargain" was the first nail in the coffin of John Quincy Adams's troubled presidency.

John Quincy Adams was a brilliant man and a creative statesman, but like his father, he was no politician. Unable to appreciate the function of parties, he ignored them. He made little effort to reward his friends and no attempt to remove his enemies from the administration. He sought to lecture Congress rather than lead it. Isolated and friendless, Adams seemed curiously out of tune with his time. His first annual message contained a "shopping list" of federal projects. He recommended to Congress the founding of a national university, the financing of scientific expeditions, construction of an astronomical observatory, creation of a department of the

some because no one knew what his political ideas were. He was a southerner and a slaveowner, and he was hostile to banks. But that is all that was known of him. Yet Jackson was not to be regarded lightly. He was well known and widely admired, and he was a skilled politician. When asked for his views on the tariff—the litmus of ideological orientation—Jackson replied simply that he favored a "judicious" tariff. He made no promises (campaign speeches were not yet in vogue), but to the discontented he somehow stood for change.

Jackson won the election in the sense that he obtained more popular and electoral votes than any other candidate. But because of the surplus of candidates in the field, no one obtained a majority of the interior, and federal appropriations for the advancement of science, literature, and fine arts. It was a grand vision, but it was also a century ahead of its time. The message evoked ridicule in the North and dread in the South.

While Adams's oratory previewed the twentieth century, his behavior was reminiscent of the eighteenth. He was brought up in the genteel tradition of New England federalism. In his youth the political game was practiced by gentlemen; appeals to the people were few and modest. The gentlemanly style was out of place in the 1820s because the electorate was changing. After the War of 1812, many states revised the constitutions that had been drafted during the revolution. The revisions usually involved removal of property qualifications for voting, and by the end of the 1820s nearly all adult white males had the vote. In addition, in nearly all states presidential electors were chosen by popular vote instead of by state legislatures. This vast increase in the electorate was not immediately apparent because turnout at election time was low. Politics, to many people, seemed distant and remote, their own participation ineffectual. And the chilly presence of John Quincy Adams did nothing to excite them.

Jackson, by contrast, seemed warm and human. Although the same age as Adams, he seemed a generation younger. He exuded strength and vitality; he was a doer, not a thinker. The scourge of Britons, Spaniards, and Indians, he appealed to Americans' pride—and their prejudices. He was a man of will who cared little for protocol. He was how Americans saw themselves—impulsive, belligerent, candid, sometimes in error, but never weak. Jackson had the qualities that would bring men to the polls; what he needed was party organization. That was supplied him by a relative newcomer to the political scene, Martin Van Buren, senator from New York.

Van Buren was the exact opposite of John Quincy Adams. He was a politician, heart and soul. Without a coherent ideology, without, in fact, any appreciable concern for the interests of the average voter, Van Buren knew instinctively how to manage, manipulate, and organize. While serving in the New York assembly in the postwar years, he had politicized the Irish social club that met at Tammany Hall* in New York City and turned it into a formidable political machine. His followers in the state government were so thoroughly disciplined and so successful that opponents called them The Regency. Party, to Van Buren, was an end in itself. Its object was power, and the purpose of power was to reward the party faithful. Party competition, in turn, assured that power would not be abused. The "ins," Van Buren believed, remained honest because they were under the watchful eye of the "outs."

Van Buren began his effort by wooing Randolph and other "old Republicans." His object, he told them, was to restore the old Jeffersonian alliance of "the planters of the South and the plain Republicans of the North." In 1827 he toured the South to talk to the architects of the new sectionalism. Van Buren's running critique of Adams, Clay, and the American System appealed to them. By the end of that year Calhoun himself, though he was Adams's vice president, was in the Jacksonian camp. There was little of common interest to hold planters and "plain" northerners together

---

* The Society of Saint Tammany, named after the legendary Delaware chief Tamanend, was founded in 1789 as a patriotic, fraternal society with elaborate Indian rituals. In 1812 it moved into the first Tammany Hall, at the corner of Frankfurt and Nassau streets in New York. The society was Jeffersonian in politics, and after the War of 1812 it allied with Van Buren and the Jacksonian Democrats. By mobilizing Irish immigrants who poured into the city in the mid-nineteenth century, Tammany obtained a grip on New York City that lasted until Fiorello La Guardia became mayor in 1933.

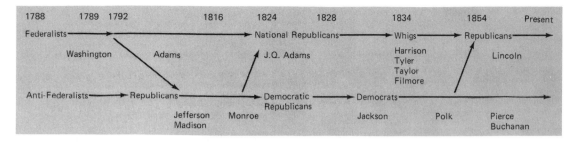

Evolution of American political parties.

except an attachment to Jackson. Jackson was popular enough to be elected and enigmatic enough to have few enemies. Calhoun and Van Buren no doubt also hoped he was malleable enough to be led. That was their only miscalculation.

By 1827, the Jacksonian opposition christened itself the Democratic Republicans, although the only thing democratic about them was their rhetoric. That left the Adams-Clay supporters with the somewhat more accurate name National Republicans. After Jackson's election, his party shortened its name to Democrats, and so they have remained. From the split emerged a second two-party system.

SOCIAL TURBULENCE

The 1820s were a turbulent decade; change was in the air. Much of the change was that associated with modernization. Factories sprouted in the North, cities mushroomed, and so did tenement districts, smoke, filth, and foul water. Trade unions had been in evidence since the beginning of the century, but the first citywide strikes occurred in the 1820s. In 1828 a workers' political party was formed and began publishing a newspaper called *The Workingman's Advocate*. Shopkeepers and artisans rather than factory workers were the backbone of this movement, and their goals were decidedly middle class—free

public education, cheaper land, abolition of imprisonment for debt, and elimination of chartered monopolies. Nevertheless, it was a call for change, and Jackson represented change, a dissolution of the status quo.

Van Buren and his allies in Congress did not fully understand the apprehensions and ambitions of the common man, but they did know how to make President Adams into his own worst enemy. And that, in the end, accomplished the change. An example of Van Buren's handiwork is the tariff of 1828. Adams did not regard the tariff as central to national development, but Clay and most nationalist Republicans did. Southerners, on the other hand, verged on apoplexy whenever the subject came up. Van Buren could go either way. He once made a two-hour speech on the subject, and when he was through one of his listeners, who said he knew a great speech when he heard one, asked Van Buren whether he was for or against the tariff.

In Van Buren's mind, the critical factor was that New York and Pennsylvania favored the tariff, and the Jacksonians needed those states if they were to win the White House in 1828. Van Buren was also aware that the South would never vote for Adams no matter what the Jacksonians did with the tariff. So it was that a political ally of Van Buren's drafted a new tariff bill for the House of Representatives in the spring of 1828. The increase quickly

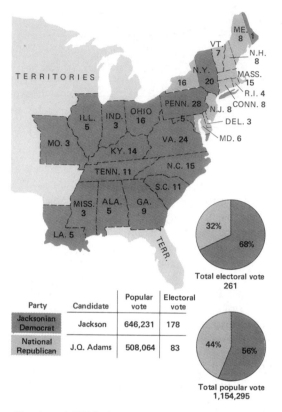

Party	Candidate	Popular vote	Electoral vote
Jacksonian Democrat	Jackson	646,231	178
National Republican	J.Q. Adams	508,064	83

Election of 1828.

have been what Van Buren intended; there were some at the time who said he expected the bill to be defeated, so he could take credit for having tried but without hurting the South. Van Buren nevertheless boldly voted in its favor. He also saw to it that the Jacksonians got credit for the measure in New York and Pennsylvania, while silently letting the administration take the blame in the South. President Adams had not liked the measure, but he could think of no sound constitutional reason for vetoing it. Capers such as this earned Van Buren the nickname Little Magician, and they earned Andrew Jackson the White House in the election of 1828.

The "bargain and corruption" cry set up by the Jacksonians after the election of 1824 was a preview of the election of 1828. Neither party discussed the issues; the election was fought on personalities, and each man was more symbol than person. Adams *vs.* Jackson was aristocrat *vs.* democrat, East *vs.* West, city *vs.* country.

Jackson won handily—178 to 83 in the electoral vote and 647,276 to 508,604 in the popular vote. There was some increase in voter turnout over 1824, but not the massive popular participation that Jackson's presidency later stimulated. The country was still not sure what Jackson would do, and there was as much apprehension in the land as hope. The measure of the man would be his presidency.

got out of control as congressmen scrambled to secure favors for their constituents. The result was the highest tariff rate level of the pre–Civil War period. It may not

SUMMARY

The Jeffersonians, when out of power, had talked loudly of states rights and limited government. Once in office after 1801, however, they made full use of their governmental powers, especially in the realm of foreign affairs. Jefferson and Madison were no more willing than John Adams

had been to suffer at the hands of foreign powers. Early in his presidency, Jefferson conducted a successful war with the pirates of the Barbary Coast to end the payment of tribute. In similar fashion, when he learned that Spain had retroceded Louisiana to France, Jefferson threatened to ally himself with Great Britain if France occupied New Orleans. By combining threats with money, Jefferson obtained the purchase of Louisiana from France. He then precipitated a dispute with Spain over the ownership of the Gulf Coast east of New Orleans, which lasted until the United States seized West Florida in 1810. National honor and national expansion went hand in hand.

A sensitivity to American honor also helped bring on the War of 1812. Angered by British provocations on the high seas—impressment, paper blockades, ship seizures—the United States retaliated with trade restrictions, and when these failed it declared war in June 1812.

The young Republicans Henry Clay and John C. Calhoun, who led the country to war in 1812, sought to use national power in a new way after the war ended—to promote economic development. Together they ushered through Congress a charter for a new Bank of the United States and a tariff with rates high enough to encourage American manufactures. These programs, together with a scheme for federal construction of roads and canals, Henry Clay wove into his American System, a philosophy of national development he championed for the next thirty years.

John Quincy Adams, as secretary of state (1817–1825), brought together the strands of commercial and territorial nationalism. He negotiated agreements with Britain and Spain that gave the United States a foothold in the Pacific Northwest and then warned the British and Russians that the Northwest was not to be considered a field for future European colonization. With eyes on the Latin American market, President Monroe and Secretary Adams collaborated in 1823 on an announcement—the Monroe Doctrine—restating the noncolonization principle and warning Europe to keep "hands off" the New World.

Adams's election as president in 1824 might have been the capstone of Jeffersonian nationalism, but it was not. By the mid-1820s the public mood had changed. Hard times, especially in the South and West, had turned the government from savior into scapegoat, its use of power more a threat than a promise. Southerners, smarting from the congressional assault on slavery in the Missouri controversy (1819–1820), worried that a government that could charter banks and build roads might as easily free slaves. Out of this national distemper emerged a new party system and a new sort of politician—Andrew Jackson.

READING SUGGESTIONS

Marshall Smelser, *The Democratic Republic, 1801–1815* (1968), offers a good overview of Jeffersonian foreign relations. The most detailed treatment of the Louisiana Purchase is to be found in George Dangerfield, *Chancellor Robert R. Livingston of New York* (1960).

The most recent study of the War of 1812 is J. C. A. Stagg's *Mr. Madison's War: Politics, Diplomacy and Warfare in the Early American Republic* (1983). Another viewpoint is offered by Clifford L. Egan, in *Neither Peace nor War:*

Franco-American Relations, 1803–1812 (1983). Glen Tucker's *Tecumseh: Vision of Glory* (1956) makes splendid reading.

The best general studies of the postwar period are the two delightfully written works of George Dangerfield, *The Era of Good Feelings* (1952) and *The Awakening of American Nationalism, 1815–1828* (1965). Harry Ammon's *James Monroe: The Quest for National Identity* (1971) is also a fine piece of work. The diplomacy of the period is chronicled in lavish detail by Samuel F. Bemis, *John Quincy Adams and the Foundations of American Foreign Policy* (1949) and by Bradford Perkins, *Castlereagh and Adams* (1964). Ernest R. May's *The Making of the Monroe Doctrine* (1975) is the latest scholarship on that topic.

Glyndon G. Van Deusen's *Life of Henry Clay* (1937) and Robert Remini's *Andrew Jackson, 1767–1823* (1978) are the best biographies of the dominant political figures of the 1820s.

Charles Sydnor, *The Development of Southern Sectionalism, 1819–1848* (1948), traces that phenomenon, and Robert Remini, *Martin Van Buren and the Making of the Democratic Party* (1959), explores the birth of the second party system. Ralph Ketcham, *Presidents Above Party: The First American Presidency, 1789–1829* (1984) is an important new assessment of the Jeffersonian presidents.

10

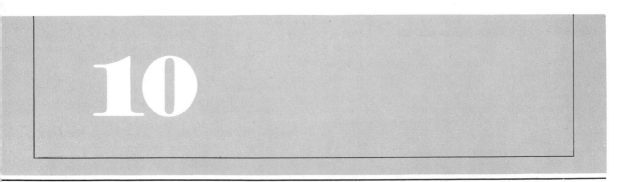

THE AGE OF JACKSON:
1829–1844

ever had a presidential inauguration generated such excitement. For days, thousands of well-wishers converged on Washington, overflowing the inns and roominghouses, jamming the streets. "A monstrous crowd of people is in this city," wrote Daniel Webster in awe. "I never saw anything like it before. Persons have come 500 miles to see General Jackson, and they really seem to think that the country is rescued from some dreadful danger." Even the weather cooperated. Inauguration day, March 4, 1829, dawned clear and balmy after a winter so brutal that some of the poor had frozen to death in the nation's capital. At noon a vast throng congregated in front of the Capitol to hear the new president, garbed in black out of reverence for his late wife Rachel,* deliver his inaugural address.

After his speech, Andrew Jackson proceeded down Pennsylvania Avenue to the executive mansion, where a reception had been prepared. The mob traipsed after him, crowding into the reception chamber in a rush to get a glimpse of the hero and a share of the cake and punch. Glass and china were broken in the melee, ladies fainted, and men bloodied noses in the pushing and shoving. Jackson himself had to be rescued by friends and whisked out the back door to his rooms at Gadsby's Tavern. Servants lured the guests out of the house by moving the refreshments onto the lawn. Justice Joseph Story, a fixture on the Supreme Court since Madison's day, thought that the scene marked the beginning of "the reign of King 'Mob.'"

---

* She died, probably of heart disease, a few weeks after the election. Such was Jackson's grief, so observers said, that his hair turned white in a single night.

⊔ The Meaning of Jacksonian Democracy

The horde of well-wishers and office-seekers who attended Jackson's inauguration were a sort new to American democracy. By 1829, most states had abolished the wealth requirements for voting and officeholdings. For white males, democracy had arrived, insofar as it could be legislated. Yet voter turnout was low during the "era of good feelings," and a small elite of officeholders managed the federal government with little change from one administration to another. The scene at Jackson's inauguration signaled a shift in popular mood. The new regime seemed more sympathetic to popular concerns, more open and receptive. The Jacksonians had created an image that struck a responsive chord among the people, and the result was increased popular participation in government. It was another step in the long evolution of American democracy.

The Jacksonian image was not a conscious creation; rather, it evolved from Jackson's own personality and background. Jackson was not simply a military hero; he was popular because he represented values that Americans admired, virtues they saw in themselves. Jackson was rugged, determined, and self-reliant. He was a man of action rather than reflection. His was a Romantic age, an age that placed will above reason, preferred the raw and unfinished, an age that worshipped nature and its child, the "noble savage." It was no accident that novelist James Fenimore Cooper, creator of Natty Bumppo and Chingachook, simple but worthy inhabitants of a virgin wilderness, was an ardent Jacksonian. Nor was it an accident that Jackson's most influential advisers were westerners who looked to America's rural past as a simpler, more virtuous time.

(*Chapter opening photo*) "The County Election," oil painting by George Caleb Bingham.

Jackson professed the same objective. He wanted to restore the Jeffersonian system. That meant cutting the cost of government, eliminating unnecessary offices, and paying off the national debt. The program was scarcely new, but when contrasted with the grand schemes of Henry Clay, it took on new meaning. Clay's American System could be seen as "logrolling"* on a massive scale (the term was Jackson's), and Americans had come to view such political brokerage as corrupt.

THE SPOILS SYSTEM

In his first annual message, the president demonstrated the link between corruption and oppression on the one hand, and popular rule on the other. The discovery that one of the Treasury auditors who had served Monroe and Adams had embezzled public funds presented Jackson with the opportunity. With veiled reference to the European practice of making offices heritable or salable, Jackson declared that rotation in office was "a leading principle in the republican creed." Longevity in office, he was saying, bred villainy and sloth; rotation encouraged honesty and alertness. He also believed that rotation gave people a sense of sharing in their own government. Jackson wished to encourage this attitude by filling the government with common people. The duties of federal office, he stated, were so "plain and simple that men of intelligence may readily qualify themselves for their performance."

Jackson did not fulfill either his threat of wholesale dismissal or his promise of equal opportunity. His intent initially was to remove only the demonstrably corrupt, and although this included most of the fol-

lowers of John Quincy Adams, it did not amount to wholesale firing. In his eight years in office Jackson replaced only about 15 percent of federal officeholders. His appointments also exceeded in quality his simple criteria of honesty and intelligence. Most were college-trained men, some of considerable wealth, and a few even were of distinguished lineage. In terms of social status, there was little to distinguish Jacksonian officialdom from that of its predecessors. Indeed, the entire business of appointments might have passed unnoticed had not the opposition loudly protested the dismissal of officeholders on political grounds, a protest that called forth Senator William L. Marcy's defense of the practice on the grounds that "To the victor belongs the spoils of the enemy." The "spoils system" would in later years become both the trademark and the despair of American politics, but Jackson was no spoilsman. He regarded rotation in office as fair, clean, and democratic; that it was more image than substance did not matter, and many voters agreed with him.

JACKSON VERSUS CALHOUN

Jackson talked the language of states rights and limited government, but he believed strongly in preserving the American Union and the integrity of the federal government. A sectional crisis that dominated his early years in office gave him a chance to demonstrate both his nationalism and his capacity for presidential leadership.

In the decade since the controversy over slavery in Missouri, South Carolina had emerged as the leader of southern sectionalism. As early as 1825, the South Carolina legislature had passed resolutions denouncing the protective tariff as unconstitutional. Beneath the opposition to the tariff was a deeper fear of federal power, a fear that a strong, active federal govern-

---

* *Logrolling* originally meant the cooperation among neighbors in helping a new settler erect his log cabin. In politics it came to denote the practice among legislators of supporting one another's pet projects.

ment might one day set out to free the slaves. Nowhere in the South was emancipation more dreaded than in South Carolina, where the slave population was nearly equal to the white population. In some parts of the rice-growing low country, blacks outnumbered whites by a substantial margin. The population ratio also made white South Carolinians fearful of slave revolt. To prevent rebellious notions from spreading among its slave population, South Carolina even prohibited black seamen serving on northern merchant vessels from coming ashore in the port of Charleston. The regulation kept the state at odds with the federal government for much of the 1820s, because in many cases the seamen were northern citizens, with a citizen's right to travel from state to state.

No South Carolinian could articulate these fears or even admit that they existed. So instead they focused on the tariff, a ready symbol of federal power and northern oppression. In December 1828, the South Carolina legislature published an *Exposition and Protest* directed against the "tariff of abominations." Though unsigned, the *Exposition* was widely known to be the work of Vice President John C. Calhoun. It showed, in fact, Calhoun's complete turnaround from nationalist to sectionalist. Calhoun repeated the familiar South Carolina argument that the encouragement of one economic interest (manufacturers) at the expense of others (farmers) was not within the constitutional powers of Congress. Broadening the argument, Calhoun went on to discuss the whole problem of protecting minority rights in a democracy. He found such protection against the "despotism of the many" in the concept of state sovereignty. Borrowing from the Jefferson-Madison resolutions of 1798, Calhoun contended that a state had the right to move against unconstitutional acts of the federal government. Specifically—and here he entered conceptual terrain that Jefferson and Madison had avoided—a

In the Collection of The Corcoran Gallery of Art.

John C. Calhoun, about 1830. The English traveler, Harriet Martineau, described him as "the cast iron man who looks as though he had never been born."

state had a right to declare an act of the national government null and void. Calhoun, in contrast to John Marshall, believed that the Constitution was a compact among sovereign states, and one not involving the American people.

Calhoun's *Exposition* was intended as a warning to the new administration. Jackson was not impressed; he thought the tariff ought to be lowered, but not abolished. A series of incidents over the next two years brought the differences between Jackson and Calhoun from the theoretical to the personal. In the spring of 1830, the Senate got into a squabble over the price of western lands, an issue in which the sectional rift, for a change, was East-West rather than North-South. Hoping to disengage the West from its traditional alliance with the South, Daniel Webster pointed out that the true issue was not land prices but national development, in which the West would be a principal beneficiary. Robert Y. Hayne of South Carolina rose to the bait and responded with a ringing defense of states rights and nullification. Land prices were forgotten as Webster summoned his oratorical powers in a "Reply to Hayne" that ended in a patriotic appeal for "Liberty and union, now and forever, one and inseparable."

States rights southerners planned to use the traditional celebration of Jefferson's birthday, April 13, to restore their alliance with the West and broaden their support. They even invited the president to the dinner. Jackson accepted, though he was aware that the affair could become a propaganda forum for nullification. He prepared accordingly, and when invited to present the first after-dinner toast, he said: "Our *Federal* Union. It *must* be preserved." Calhoun desperately tried to salvage the situation by following it with "The Union—next to our liberty, most dear." But the president had served notice; there was no doubt where he stood on nullification.

Washington tongues were still clacking over the incident when, in May 1830, Jackson learned from former Treasury Secretary William H. Crawford that Calhoun, as secretary of war in Monroe's cabinet, had urged that Jackson be censured for his invasion of Florida in 1818. Jackson demanded an explanation from Calhoun; and when Calhoun failed to provide a satisfactory one, the estrangement of the two men was complete. It remained only to purge the Calhoun influence from the administration. Several members of the cabinet were friends of Calhoun, so Jackson demanded the resignation of the entire cabinet and appointed men loyal only to himself. Martin Van Buren, who resigned as secretary of state, was named minister to Great Britain. Van Buren's influence in the administration had risen as Calhoun's had declined.

Furious at the purge of his friends, Cal-

houn formed an alliance with the leaders of the opposition, Webster and Clay. It was obviously a marriage of convenience, but it lasted as long as Jackson was president. The first fruit of the alliance was the Senate's rejection in January 1832 of Van Buren's appointment as minister to Great Britain. The vote was rigged to end in a tie, allowing Calhoun, as vice president, to cast the deciding vote. Certain that Van Buren was the cause of his fall from grace, Calhoun savored his revenge. "It will kill him, sir," he exulted, "kill him dead. He will never kick, sir, never kick." It did nothing of the kind: Instead it made Van Buren a martyr to the Democratic cause. If he had not been previously, he was now the natural choice as Jackson's vice president in 1832 and his successor in 1836.

THE NULLIFICATION CRISIS

The comic opera presented by the Jackson circle was played before a backdrop of mounting sectional tension. After its initial blast against the tariff in 1828, South Carolina had adopted a wait-and-see attitude. Jackson's failure to lower the tariff and his break with Calhoun rekindled the state's anger. Then, in August 1831, came the most serious rebellion in the history of North American slavery. Led by Nat Turner, slaves in Virginia slaughtered some sixty whites. Nowhere was the shock felt more deeply than in low-country South Carolina, where slaves substantially outnumbered whites. Feeling surrounded by enemies, South Carolina planters were prepared for any extreme as 1831 came to a close.

Jackson had maintained the tariff because its revenue enabled him to retire the national debt. In December 1831, he announced that the debt was nearly eliminated and recommended a reduction in the tariff. Congressman John Quincy Adams introduced a bill containing fewer reductions than Jackson wanted, but he endorsed it anyway. The measure sailed through Congress with bipartisan support. Nullifiers found the tariff of 1832 completely unsatisfactory. It failed to reduce the rates sufficiently; worse, it was portrayed by its backers as a compromise. The South, in short, was to be saddled permanently with a tariff. In the fall election that year, the nullifiers won control of the South Carolina assembly and issued a call for a state convention to put Calhoun's theory into practice. The convention met and passed an ordinance declaring the tariffs of 1828 and 1832 null and void in South Carolina. Beginning February 1, 1833, customs duties could not be collected within the limits of the state. The delay in enforcing nullification was to give Congress time to reduce the duties to the 12 percent level South Carolina wanted.

Jackson reacted to the challenge with a shrewd blend of compromise and coercion. In December he issued a proclamation denouncing nullification as "incompatible with the existence of the Union." The United States, he said, is "a *government*, not a league," and when the states joined to form "a single nation," each gave up a part of its sovereignty. Hence the states had no right to nullify or to secede, and "disunion by armed force is treason." Treason, of course, was punishable by death. Jackson backed the threat by sending reinforcements to the federal military posts in the state. In January he sent to Congress a force bill that gave him the authority to use the army to enforce collection of the customs duties.

Dangling a carrot next to his stick, Jackson threw his support to a new tariff bill in the House of Representatives that promised to cut the tariff in half by 1834. The president's moves inspired others to action. Henry Clay recognized that some sort of reduction in his cherished tariff was inevitable, but he felt the administration's bill went too far. Besides, if a compromise was

in the works, he wanted the credit. He found a ready ally in Calhoun, who now occupied one of South Carolina's seats in the Senate. Calhoun was anxious to avoid an armed confrontation between state and federal governments, for he had long maintained that nullification was a peaceful means of preserving the Union. And he, as well as Clay, did not want Jackson to have the credit for resolving the crisis.

The result was a compromise calling for biennial reductions in the tariff rates over a period of ten years, after which the top-level duty would stand at 20 percent. For his part of the bargain, Calhoun induced South Carolina to extend its deadline and summon a new nullification convention in March 1833. Congress approved both the compromise tariff and the force bill, and both measures landed on Jackson's desk on March 2. The president pointedly signed the Force Act first. South Carolina got its symbolic revenge by repealing the ordinance that had nullified the tariff and passing a new ordinance nullifying the Force Act. The tension subsided, and Clay enhanced his reputation as a compromiser. Jackson, who had preserved federal authority without resorting to force, received little credit and in fact lost support in the South.

⊔ The Indians, Internal Improvements, and the Bank

The nullification crisis was not of Jackson's doing. He handled it with more dexterity than anyone might have expected, but it was in fact a distraction that drew his attention from more worthy causes. Jackson's political ideology— some would have called it a set of biases, for it lacked intellectual depth—was antimonopolistic, essentially negative, and instinctively egalitarian. His ideas had been shaped by the political environment of the West. He favored a modest tariff and improvement projects of a local nature. He wanted to eliminate, or at least shackle, the Bank of the United States, and he wanted eastern Indians removed to lands west of the Mississippi River. To implement this program, Jackson relied not on his cabinet, but on a collection of informal advisers, most important of whom were a pair of westerners who shared his views, Amos Kendall and Francis Preston Blair.

Kendall was a New Englander by birth and a graduate of Dartmouth College who had migrated to Kentucky in search of fortune. He found fame instead as the leader of a debtor-relief party in Kentucky in the 1820s. As editor of the Lexington *Argus of Western America*, he sympathized with artisans and land-poor farmers, and he blasted the state's Bluegrass elite for refusing to help the common person. He blamed the depression on the policies of the Bank of the United States, and he demanded the use of metal currency with stable value.

When Jackson was elected, Kendall joined the well-wishers and office-seekers who descended on Washington to attend the inauguration. He was rewarded with the post of fourth auditor in the Treasury, where he uncovered the first and only important instance of corruption in the Adams administration. Finding Kendall a kindred soul, Jackson soon came to rely on him for counsel and occasional speechwriting.

At Kendall's suggestion, Jackson invited Kendall's Kentucky friend, Francis Preston Blair, to Washington to found a newspaper that would reflect the political views of the administration. Blair was a Virginia-born lawyer who had been drawn into politics by Kentucky's debtor-relief war. When Kendall departed for Washington, he left Blair in charge of the Lexington *Argus*, to which Blair had been a frequent contributor. When Blair went to Washington in De-

cember 1830, he founded *The Globe*, to which Kendall was part-time contributor. Blair was a natural propagandist who sensed the needs and apprehensions of middle-class Americans. He made the editorial a prominent feature of *The Globe*, often splashing it across the front page, and he kept in contact with Jacksonian papers throughout the country, reprinting their editorials as samples of popular opinion. *The Globe* played a key role in the fabrication of the Jacksonian image.

Van Buren was also among the circle of informal advisers, though he did not reflect Jackson's own thinking as accurately as Kendall and Blair. Jackson's opponents jokingly called the advisory circle the "Kitchen Cabinet," but they failed to realize that, by relying on men utterly loyal to him, men (except for Van Buren) who had no political clientele of their own, Jackson kept a tight rein on policy formation.

REMOVAL OF THE INDIANS

Indian removal was the first item on Jackson's agenda when he took office. President Adams had conducted a running feud with the state of Georgia over the Creek and Cherokee tribes who were still in possession of millions of acres of prime farmland. Neither tribe wished to cede any more land, and Adams was unwilling to force them. In 1827, the Cherokees adopted a constitution and proclaimed themselves an independent nation with total sovereignty over their lands. Georgia officials countered by declaring the state to have sovereign authority over the lands and inhabitants within its boundaries. Adams bequeathed this impasse to his successor.

Jackson outlined his policy in his first annual message, drafted with the aid of Kendall. He proposed to set aside a tract of land west of the Mississippi to be given to the eastern tribes in exchange for their eastern holdings. In addition to opening new lands for white pioneers, the exchange would help the Indians, Jackson believed, by removing them from the corrupting influences of white civilization. Those Indians who refused to remove to the West would be subject to state laws and could expect ultimately to "become merged in the mass of our population." Congress responded with the Indian Removal Act of 1830. During Jackson's eight years in office, the United States signed some seventy

Symptoms of a Locked Jaw. This 1834 cartoon by David Claypoole Johnston is a breakthrough in the craft of political cartoon drawing. While most cartoonists of the day cluttered their pictures with stiff-legged characters and wordy balloons, Johnston made his point with a simple, yet dramatic piece of action. No one at the time would have missed the reference to the years-long contest of power and personality between Jackson and Clay. In 1834, Clay induced the Senate to censure Jackson for having removed the government's deposits from the Bank of the United States. Jackson sent a protest, which he demanded be placed in the Senate journal. Clay persuaded the Senate not to publish the protest, thereby sewing up Jackson's mouth.

"SYMPTOMS OF A LOCKED JAW"

American Antiquarian Society

treaties and acquired about 100 million acres of Indian land at a cost of $68 million and 32 million acres in Oklahoma, Kansas, and Nebraska.

Jackson's stance on Indian removal at the beginning of his administration was a forecast of his ideological bent. The removal policy was especially popular in the West and South, where Indian holdings were regarded as an obstacle to progress. And, although implementation involved the use of federal power, it was done in the name of states rights, for Jackson specifically endorsed Georgia's position that Indians who remained within state limits were subject to state laws. In 1832, a series of cases brought by or on behalf of the Cherokees against the state of Georgia came before the United States Supreme Court. Chief Justice John Marshall held that the Indian tribes were "dependent domestic nations" and that only the federal government could deal with them. Georgia's effort to exercise authority over the Cherokees was illegal. Unfortunately for the Cherokees, Marshall's opinion was a hollow legalism, given the political temper of both the administration and the state of Georgia. Jackson's alleged response was: "John Marshall has made his decision. Now let him enforce it."

INTERNAL IMPROVEMENTS

Jackson applied the same logic to internal improvements, an issue that had tormented politicians since it first appeared in 1817. Though he made few public pronouncements on the subject prior to becoming president, Jackson was suspicious of federal improvements. He opposed national projects of the sort advocated by Henry Clay because they inevitably benefited a few at the expense of many. He also objected to spending tax revenue on construction projects while the government was still in debt. Van Buren shared the president's views. New York had completed the Erie Canal at its own expense; the Empire State had no desire to see its tax dollars poured into competitive projects in Pennsylvania or Virginia.

Presidents Madison and Monroe had also opposed undefined appropriations for internal improvements. As a result, the only project Congress had consistently financed over the years was the National Road, which wound west from Cumberland, Maryland, through Wheeling, Virginia, and into Ohio. Under President Adams, however, numerous appropriations for local projects slipped through Congress and were signed by the president.

Casting about for a congressional appropriation on which Jackson could take a stand in the spring of 1830, Van Buren hit upon a bill that authorized the government to buy stock in a corporation that planned to construct a turnpike from Maysville, Kentucky, on the Ohio River, to Lexington. Proponents of the measure ushered it through Congress on the theory that it was an extension of the National Road, though in fact it had no connection. For Van Buren's purposes, the Maysville Road was ideal. It was essentially a local project, since it was confined to one state (Henry Clay's at that!), and it involved an alliance between government and a private corporation of a sort Jackson was known to oppose.

Jackson's veto message was a masterpiece of constitutional pragmatism. It endorsed in theory the Madisonian principle that Congress had no power to build roads and canals and affirmed as policy the idea that Congress could appropriate money for projects that contributed to national defense or otherwise were "of general, not local, national, not state, benefit." The compromise reaffirmed Jackson's Jeffersonian orthodoxy while leaving him free to sign into law more internal improvement measures in the course of his presidency than all his predecessors combined.

DUEL WITH A MONSTER

A similar combination of ideology and tough-minded politics characterized the administration's fight with the Bank of the United States. The bank war climaxed Jackson's presidency and, more than any other issue of the time, shaped the tenets, the rhetoric, and the popular support of the new Democratic party.

Andrew Jackson's views concerning the Bank of the United States reflected his western background. People of the rural South and West distrusted banks because, in those credit-shy regions, banks were unreliable. In times of financial stress they commonly refused to let depositors withdraw their money, suspended payments to noteholders, and sometimes closed down altogether. Farmers particularly distrusted banks of issue—that is, banks whose charters authorized them to issue notes. The notes, which represented gold or silver coin in the bank's vaults, circulated as money, their acceptability depending upon the amount of faith people had in the bank that issued them. Because the notes passed from hand to hand, rather than reappearing at the bank, a bank normally issued more notes than it could redeem. Among conservatively run banks, the ratio of paper money to coin was about five to one, but "wildcat" banks, which were common in the South and West, issued ten or one hundred times more paper than they could redeem. When they collapsed, their money instantly became worthless. On the frontier there were even "saddlebag" banks, which consisted of a horseman and a printing press. The "banker" settled into a town, ran off notes, made loans, and collected interest until townspeople got suspicious and tried to redeem the notes in coin; then he rode on. Developers and land-jobbers often approved such practices because they provided capital for their schemes. Planters and farmers, on the other hand, generally preferred metal currency of known and

Philadelphia Convention and Visitors Bureau.

The Old Lady of Chestnut Street. The Second Bank of the United States, designed by William Strickland, was the first example of Greek Revival architecture in America (1817).

stable value. Their spokesman in Congress was Missouri Senator Thomas Hart Benton, whose hard-money rhetoric earned him the nickname "Old Bullion" Benton.

Although the Bank of the United States was generally popular in the North and East, there were pockets of opposition. Artisans of the sort who founded the Workingmen's party in the late 1820s preferred hard money and mistrusted banks. They wanted their wages paid in coin, just as western farmers wanted hard money for their crops. Neither group had any direct contact with the Bank of the United States, but that mattered little. The president's attack on the federal institution struck a responsive chord.

Finally, among the federal bank's potential enemies were the hundreds of state-chartered banks. As a result of interstate trade or the payment of federal taxes, the notes issued by these banks drifted into the vaults of the Bank of the United States. That enabled the Bank of the United States to regulate the activities of the state banks. Should a "wildcat" bank issue too many notes, the federal bank could send around an agent with a few basketsful and demand instant redemption in coin. The Bank of the United States thus worked as a conservative brake on the nation's banking system. But in an age that worshipped laissez faire and limited government, such paternalism was resented. There is no evidence that state banks started the bank war—indeed, most refused to take sides for fear of retaliation—but they certainly benefited from the destruction of the Bank of the United States. Whether the nation's economy benefited is another question.

Jackson criticized the bank in his first annual message of 1829, and the following year, with the help of Kendall and Blair, he outlined what he considered a good alternative. He suggested the creation of a national bank as a virtual arm of the Treasury, with strict limitations on its note issues to ensure a currency that would be the equivalent of coin. The idea was worth pursuing, but Jackson went no further, perhaps because little could be done until the bank's charter expired in 1836.

The bank war was in fact begun by the Bank of the United States itself. In January 1832, Nicholas Biddle, president of the bank, applied to Congress for a new charter, even though his franchise had four years to run. Biddle's motive was purely political. The bank had strong support in Congress, counting among its friends a number of eastern Democrats as well as National Republicans, and Biddle feared that his support might erode if he waited until 1836. Clay and Webster, moreover, assured him that the bank stood a better chance in a presidential election year. Clay, the candidate of the National Republicans, also saw the bank as an election issue. Whether Jackson signed the charter or vetoed it, Clay stood to gain. If Jackson signed the bill, Clay, who had championed the bank for twenty years, could take credit for its recharter in states such as New York and Pennsylvania, where the bank was popular. If Jackson vetoed it, Clay had an election issue.

The bill renewing the bank's charter glided easily through Congress in the spring of 1832. The voting in each house was sectional rather than partisan. The most intense controversy was within the administration, where several members of the cabinet, including Treasury Secretary Louis McLane, favored the bank. Jackson, however, was determined. It was not in his nature to flinch before a challenge such as this. Van Buren, newly returned from his mission to England, found the president, drawn and pale, stretched on a White House sofa. "The bank is trying to kill me," he said in a hoarse whisper, "but I will kill it."

Amos Kendall drafted the veto message, and it glistened with the rhetoric of the Kentucky relief wars. Jackson called on "the humble members of society—the farmers, mechanics, and laborers" to support his crusade against privileged institutions dominated by "the rich and powerful." The rhetoric was that of class appeal, but Jackson's concern was not inequality, but special privilege and monopoly, the use of governmental powers to benefit a few. It was an argument that appealed to the middle class as much as the "lower orders."

Election of 1832.

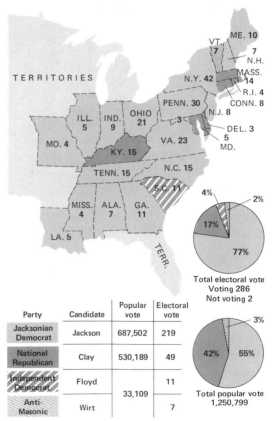

Party	Candidate	Popular vote	Electoral vote
Jacksonian Democrat	Jackson	687,502	219
National Republican	Clay	530,189	49
Independent Democrat	Floyd	33,109	11
Anti-Masonic	Wirt		7

The true extent of the argument's appeal is difficult to gauge, however. The bank veto was only one of several issues in the election of 1832, and its impact was mixed. It clearly hurt Jackson in Pennsylvania, where the bank was popular, but it reinforced his grip on the South and West. Jackson won 56 percent of the popular vote in 1832, almost exactly the same margin by which he was elected in 1828. Yet turnout among eligible voters was a bit lower. The Jacksonian rhetoric had not yet seeped through to the grassroots.

Jackson's reelection sealed the fate of the Bank of the United States. Though Jackson could do nothing about the bank's existing charter, he did have one important weapon—government deposits. By removing these, Jackson could effectively sever the connection between bank and Treasury, cut the bank's lending power, and reduce the bank to the status of a private corporation. To do so, Jackson had to dismiss Secretary of the Treasury McLane, and McLane's successor as well, before he found a willing agent in Roger B. Taney, who had previously served as attorney general. In the summer of 1833, Amos Kendall toured the country to select a dozen properly managed state banks as repositories for the federal funds. Taney then deposited his Treasury receipts in these "pet banks," while making government disbursements from the funds remaining in the Bank of the United States.

As the federal monies on deposit dwindled, Nicholas Biddle tightened his lines of credit. The action was not unreasonable, since he had fewer funds at his disposal, but he consolidated more than necessary. Indeed, he squeezed so hard that by the end of 1833 the nation was in a mild depression. By creating distress, Biddle hoped to arouse public anger against the president. Instead, he proved only what the Jacksonians had been saying all along— that the bank represented too much power in irresponsible hands.

THE BANK WAR AND THE JACKSONIAN PERSUASION

During the election campaign of 1832, Amos Kendall published an "Address" in which he attempted to explain the Jacksonian ideology. "The function of government," said Kendall, "is to *keep off evil*. We do not want its assistance in seeking after good." The Jacksonians believed, as did the theorists of the revolutionary era, that republican government rested on a virtuous citizenry. The proper role of government, then, was an essentially negative one of maintaining law and order, for any positive program, implemented by tax policy or subsidy, would corrupt the virtuous and reward the few. Kendall appealed for support to "honest and upright" men, who asked "for no advantage over others" while insisting "that others shall have no advantage" over them.

Kendall's address was a reaffirmation of Jeffersonian liberalism, yet it had a peculiar relevance for his own time. Jacksonian America was a patchwork of divergent interests—regional, economic, ethnic, and religious. Some areas were experiencing revolutionary changes in industry and communication; others were stagnant backwaters, forlorn and forgotten. The Jacksonian philosophy of decentralization, with its tolerance of diversity, suited this society. Southern planters and northern merchants alike could rally to the slogan of "laissez faire." The Jacksonian hostility to monopoly and privilege, moreover, appealed to certain ethnic groups, such as Irish Catholics, and it appealed to artisans and shopkeepers. The workingmen's political movement that had blossomed in the 1820s did not give wholesale support to Jackson's election, but in the course of his term its membership aligned itself with the Democrats. Those hard-money, anticorporation egalitarians—this American *petit bourgeoisie*—gave a decidedly reformist cast

Courtesy of The New-York Historical Society, New York City.

Jackson slaying the many-headed monster. The unlabeled head at the center of the monster is Nicholas Biddle. Each head is labeled with the name of a state, an apparent reference to the many branches of the Bank of the United States.

to the Democratic party in several northern states. In New York they were given the name Locofocos* after they lit matches in an 1835 Tammany Hall meeting which conservative Democrats sought to disrupt by turning off the lights. The bank war thus helped to focus the Democratic party's ideology and drew into its ranks people who until now had been politically silent.

Destruction of the Bank of the United States (it carried on as a state-chartered bank until 1841) did not, however, create the austere, pay-as-you-go financial system

desired by the Jacksonians. Indeed, quite the opposite. State banks, filling the vacuum, multiplied in number and expanded their note issues. "I did not join in putting down the Bank of the United States, to put up a wilderness of local banks!" wailed Thomas Hart Benton. A speculative mania gripped the country. Southern cotton growers, emboldened by high cotton prices in Europe, rushed to plant the lands formerly occupied by Creeks and Cherokees. Midwestern states began ambitious canal- and road-building projects. Alarmed at the trend, Jackson sought at least to put the government on a hard-money foundation. In 1836 he issued a Specie Circular that ordered Treasury officials to accept noth-

---

* *Locofoco*, literally meaning "self-fire," or "self-igniting," was the popular term for the first matches that could be ignited by friction.

1800

1820

1840

1860

Manhood suffrage

Light property or tax qualifications

Heavy property qualifications

Growth of democracy, 1800–1860.

ing but gold or silver in payment for public lands. That too had an unintended result, for it forced the transfer of specie to the West to conduct land transactions. The removal left eastern banks with fewer reserves to back their notes and, therefore, more susceptible to panic. When the "bust" came—beginning with a European financial upheaval and a collapse in cotton prices in the spring of 1837—it resulted in a prolonged depression. The hard times, as if to round out the circle of irony, in turn clouded the administration of Jackson's friend, confidant, and successor, Martin Van Buren.

⊔ Rise of the Whigs

Henry Clay had almost singlehandedly welded the anti-Jackson forces into a political party. A New York newspaper referred to the opposition as Whigs in 1834, and the name stuck. Since Whigs were the traditional foes of royal authority, Clay and his allies symbolically placed themselves in opposition to "King Andrew" and his heavyhanded use of executive powers. Claiming to be the true heirs of Jefferson, the Whigs stood for legislative rather than executive control of policy.

The Whig party was a coalition of National Republicans, southerners who had deserted Jackson as a result of the nullification or bank controversies, and Anti-Masons. The latter were a bloc of reform-minded egalitarians who appeared in western New York in the late 1820s. Their enemy was the Order of Freemasons, a secret, ritualistic European transplant that had come to occupy a special place in rural America. It was an organization of the small-town elite, commonly including the village physician, lawyer, judge, innkeeper, and land-jobber. By being both elitist and secretive, Freemasonry provoked criticism in an age of rising democratic awareness. When a man who had threatened to expose

the secrets of the Masons mysteriously disappeared in western New York in 1826, a protest movement blazed across the state. Two opponents of the Van Buren organization in New York, William H. Seward and Thurlow Weed, saw political potential in the uproar. They helped organize an Anti-Mason party, which ran a candidate for president in 1832, and in 1834 they brought the Anti-Masons into the Whig party.

The Whigs in general attracted the developers and the businessmen, people who desired government aid and investment, but they also appealed to certain ethnic groups. Transplanted New Englanders, who populated the Great Lakes basin from western New York to Wisconsin, usually voted Whig, as did English and other Protestant immigrants. Whig reformers were less interested in economic problems than were Democrats, and more concerned with social ills, such as liquor and later slavery. The Whigs never achieved the organizational cohesion of the Democrats, and only once in their twenty-year history did they adopt a platform for a presidential election. Their beliefs found expression in the columns of Horace Greeley's New York *Tribune*. Greeley was an ally of Seward and Weed, who helped him to found the *Tribune* in 1841. Though he had never been an Anti-Mason, Greeley shared that group's egalitarian ideas. He admired Henry Clay and the American System, but he also endorsed women's rights, temperance, pacifism, vegetarianism, antislavery, and socialism. Late in life he employed Karl Marx as a European correspondent. Greeley was more reform-minded than most Whigs—so much so that conservatives founded the *New York Times* to rival the *Tribune* in 1850—but Greeley's thought revealed a new dimension of the American System. In addition to encouraging manufactures and building roads and canals, government could be used to promote social change.

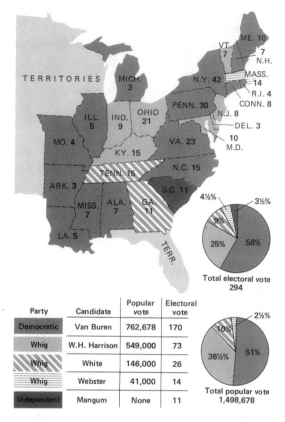

Party	Candidate	Popular vote	Electoral vote
Democratic	Van Buren	762,678	170
Whig	W.H. Harrison	549,000	73
Whig	White	146,000	26
Whig	Webster	41,000	14
Independent	Mangum	None	11

Election of 1836.

Both Democrats and Anti-Masons experimented with national nominating conventions in 1832. In 1836 the Democrats met and adopted a formal set of rules and procedures that made the nominating convention a permanent feature of the party system. Jackson's word was law in the convention, even though he was retiring from office, and the Democrats nominated his choice, Martin Van Buren. The Whigs were not yet sufficiently organized for such a procedure. They developed a strategy of nominating regional candidates in the hope that by dividing the electoral vote, they might throw the contest into the House of Representatives. Daniel Webster, for instance, was the Whig choice in the New England states, and William Henry

Harrison (Old Tippecanoe) stood in the western states. The strategy failed, however, because Van Buren polled enough electoral votes to win a majority. His administration was nonetheless doomed when financial panic struck in May 1837, just two months after his inauguration.

THE PANIC OF 1837

In the summer of 1837, Van Buren summoned a special session of Congress to consider the nation's plight. Banks had suspended specie payments, and the federal government could not even recover the funds deposited in state banks. Whigs recommended the chartering of a third Bank of the United States, or at least the issue of government paper money, but Van Buren rejected both courses. He recommended that the government divorce itself from banks altogether by keeping its money in vaults ("independent treasuries") scattered around the country. The concept was fiscally naive in time of depression, for it meant a reduction in the money supply if the government squirreled away gold and silver for its own needs, thereby aggravating the hard times. Whigs prevented enactment of the independent treasury bill until 1840 and then repealed it at their first opportunity in 1841. The only other achievement of the Van Buren presidency was a presidential order limiting federal employees to a ten-hour day. A reflection of Van Buren's own Locofocism, the order was the first piece of federal labor regulation.

Bound in the intellectual straitjacket of Jacksonian hard-money principles, Van Buren was otherwise unable to respond to the depression. The impression he conveyed, as a result, was one of chilly insensitivity. The Whigs, with an eye on the election of 1840, made the most of Van Buren's problems. "Martin Van Ruin" they called him, or "Sweet Sandy Whiskers,"

CLIO'S FOCUS: The Politician and the Radical

The image of Martin Van Buren—even the one conveyed by his own autobiography—is a study in black and white, tempered by gray. There is no color and little warmth. His early career was an odd combination of Jeffersonian ideology and cynical manipulation, all seemingly directed toward one day securing the presidency. And once he achieved his goal, his shrewdness left him; only his ideology remained. Presiding over the country in a time of economic ruin, he seemed distant, uncompromising, and ultimately unpopular. Yet if we judge the man by his friends—and it seems a fair measure of any politician—the image takes on some character.

One of Van Buren's most ardent admirers was a Scottish-born crusader for social justice named Frances Wright. Radicalism was her birthright. Her father had absorbed the political republicanism of the Scottish *philosophes*, and he financed an English edition of Tom Paine's *Rights of Man*, a bit of heresy that earned him police surveillance until his untimely death in 1810. Brought up by an uncle, a Glasgow professor, Frances Wright educated herself in his extensive library and began writing poems and plays. She came to America in 1819 because a Philadelphia theater had agreed to put on one of her plays. Unfortunately, General Andrew Jackson, on one of his northern rambles, appeared in the city the day the play opened. The theater substituted a play more suitable to the occasion, and Frances Wright went touring. On her return to Britain she published the story of her travels, an unabashedly favorable account of the young republic unique in a time when only British aristocrats with flaring nostrils and curled lips toured and wrote about America.

The travel account brought Wright to the attention of one of Europe's foremost Americaphiles, the Marquis de La Fayette, Washington's best-loved lieutenant in the revolution. La Fayette had been forced to flee France during the Reign of Terror, but he had not lost his republican ardor. He invited Frances and her sister Camille to his French chalet. The women became couriers carrying messages to revolutionary cells in France and Spain with which La Fayette was in contact.

In 1824, when La Fayette at the invitation of President Monroe visited America to help celebrate the republic's fiftieth birthday, he brought the Wright sisters with him. After meeting Robert Owen, a Scottish industrialist who had come to America to found a socialist community in Indiana, Frances Wright left La Fayette's entourage and experimented with a utopian community of her own in Tennessee. Called Nashoba, it was an experiment in emancipation by which slaves would earn their freedom through labor. It failed within a few years, largely because of Wright's lack of managerial skill, and she settled in New York City.

There in the late 1820s she became caught up in a workers' political movement organized by another transplanted Briton, George Henry Evans. In January 1829 she began publishing a newspaper, the *Free Enquirer*, in which she attacked religion, the influence of churches on politics, and social inequality. She had by then come to the conclusion that class and privilege were the root of all social evils. Her solution—as chillingly rational as it was unconventional—was to take all children from their parents at the age of two and raise them in government schools, where they would grow up in an atmosphere free of class consciousness and prejudice.

In 1830 she turned the editorial work of the paper over to Owen's son, Robert Dale Owen, and took to the lecture circuit. There she expanded her crusade against privilege to include equal rights for women. She even suggested that marriage laws, which bound women in a legal straitjacket, be abolished so that marriage unions rested on moral obligations only. This sounded suspiciously like "free love," and she was condemned by press and pulpit. "The Great Red Harlot of Infidelity," one New York paper called her. She was mobbed on several occasions. She was the first woman to appear on a lecture platform in America, and this "unfeminine" behavior counted more than anything she could say. She never joined the women's suffrage movement, though she lived to see it come of age. She perceived inequality in broader terms.

By 1830 the banking system had drawn her attention. The New York Workingmen's party, of which she was the dominant intellect, favored hard money. The artisans and shopkeepers that formed its ranks wanted to be paid in gold or silver, not in bank paper. Frances Wright saw banks as "one of the deepest sources of industrial oppression and national demoralization." As legislative creations that thrived on favoritism, she coupled banks with the "professional aristocracy" of priests, lawyers, and politicians who used their power to cheat the people.

Jackson's bank war brought her into the Democratic fold, though it was some time before she became a party worker. In 1831 she returned to Europe, married, and gave birth to a daughter. Upon her return to the United States, she threw herself into Van Buren's 1836 election campaign. It is a measure of Van Buren that he accepted both her help and her advice. Wright, in turn, tempered her Populist rhetoric. Lecture audiences noted that she confined herself to politics and avoided both education and religion. After Van Buren's election, it was rumored that she might receive a government appointment. Instead she started another newspaper devoted to hard money and the administration. Van Buren's independent Treasury, by divorcing the government from financiers, drew her ecstatic applause. "It is the national independence realized," she declared. "It is the effective, definitive, annulment of this country's vassalage. It is the first practical, efficient, decisive realization of the Declaration of '76."

After Van Buren's defeat in 1840, Frances Wright retired from the public scene. She divorced her husband (who ended up with all her property, even though it had been obtained through her lecture earnings) and moved to Cincinnati, where she died a dozen years later. She was a schoolroom radical who made no lasting imprint on American society, except as a spirit that haunted social conservatives. But her alliance with Van Buren tells us something about both of them. And it adds a new dimension to our concept of Jacksonian democracy.

New York Public Library Picture Collection.
Martin Van Buren: "Sweet Sandy Whiskers."

and they portrayed the president as lolling in silken splendor in the White House.

Henry Clay was as eager as ever for the Whig nomination, but when the party convention met in December 1839, Thurlow Weed maneuvered the nomination of William Henry Harrison instead. A Virginian by birth and a westerner by profession, Harrison was a military hero of the War of 1812 whose career had paralleled Jackson's. Under the tutelage of the wily Weed, the Whigs adopted the Jacksonian prescription for success: rely on a hero. To balance the ticket, the Whigs nominated as vice president John Tyler, a states rights Virginian whose political lineage could be traced back to Jefferson and Madison. Adjourning without forming a platform, the Whigs appealed to the country with the slogan "Tippecanoe and Tyler Too!"

THE ELECTION OF 1840

It was, however, the Democrats who accidentally gave the Whigs the best political symbol of the age. Professing to be pleased with the nomination of "Granny" Harrison ("Ol' Tip" was 67), one Democratic newspaper scornfully represented a friend of Clay as having said that if Harrison was given a pension of $2,000 a year, a barrel of hard cider, and a log cabin to live in, he would give up any thought of the presidency. The Whigs picked up the image and made the log cabin and cider barrel part of their campaign. Never was there a more potent political symbol. The log cabin was western and therefore eminently American, and it represented the promise of American life, the opportunity to get ahead. The rags-to-riches theme was already being ingrained on American schoolchildren in the primers written by William Holmes McGuffey. It was inevitable that politicians would pick up the notion that any young American born in humble circumstances might achieve the highest office in the land (as long as he was white and male).

The log cabin—as much as Andrew Jackson himself—was thus a symbol of the age. That it was first employed by the Whigs demonstrates only the ability of American politicians to take from any and all sources. And it worked! Voter turnout in 1840 was higher by far than in any earlier presidential election. The "common man" came into his own, and he voted Whig. Harrison carried nineteen of twenty-six states and logged Whig majorities in both houses of Congress.

The Whigs, unfortunately, were not equipped for power. A horde of office seekers descended on Washington, and their demands sapped the strength of the elderly president. Henry Clay expected to be the dominant force in the administration, but his imperious manner so annoyed the president that Harrison had to tell him to make further communications in writing. Weak and weary, the president caught cold while shopping in the city markets, without benefit of hat or coat, in search of White House groceries. He died of pneumonia on April 4, 1841, after only a

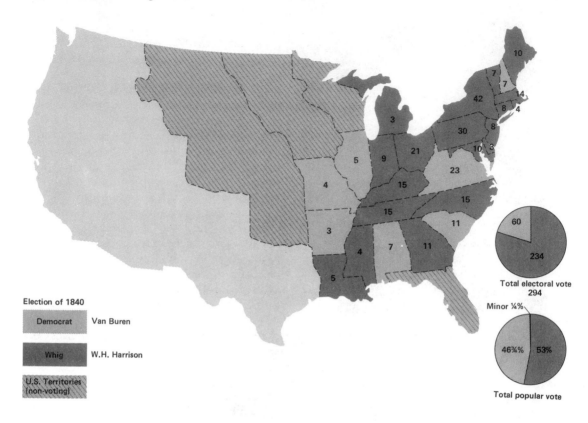

Election of 1840

Democrat   Van Buren

Whig   W.H. Harrison

U.S. Territories (non-voting)

60
234
Total electoral vote
294

Minor ¼%
46¾%   53%
Total popular vote

month in office, and "Tyler Too" was president.

THE LURID YEARS OF "HIS ACCIDENCY"

Two John Tylers—father and son—spanned the political history of Virginia from the revolution to the Civil War. John Tyler, Sr., was an Antifederalist of 1788 and an ally of Patrick Henry. John Tyler, Jr., was an ally of John Randolph and an "Old Republican" of the Monroe era. Fifty-one years old when Harrison died, Tyler was younger than any earlier president, and he lived to preside over the convention that voted Virginia out of the Union in 1861. When he took the oath of office,

Tyler insisted that he was president, not "acting" president. But doubt remained as to whether he could truly lead the government—or even the Whig party. He had been put on the party ticket for tactical purposes, without thought of a presidential succession, and his states rights views were repellent to a majority of Whigs.

The most elementary of Whig beliefs was the superiority of the legislature over the executive, and that suited Henry Clay perfectly in the situation in which he now found himself. He felt he was the true head of the party, and most Whigs agreed. Party ideology and personal ambition combined to make the Whig-dominated Congress the center of policy formation. When Tyler summoned a special session of Congress in the summer of 1841, Clay seized the

New York Public Library Picture Collection.

A Whig parade in the log cabin and cider campaign.

opportunity to outline his program. He planned to repeal the independent Treasury, replace it with a new federal bank, raise the tariff, and distribute the proceeds to the states to help them finance internal improvements. It was the familiar American System; even the idea of distribution was not new. In the course of the 1830s, both parties agreed that distributing federal surpluses among the states was a constitutional and useful way of securing the construction of roads and canals.

The speech got Clay off to a swift start, and he was moving at rhythmic stride when he tripped over the president's veto. Congress repealed the independent Treasury and chartered a new Bank of the United States with unlimited power to establish branches. Tyler vetoed the bank bill, but let it be known he would approve a bank centered in the District of Columbia and empowered to establish branches only with the consent of the states. Clay drove a new bank bill through Congress that met only some of the president's objections, and Tyler vetoed that one too. Tyler was motivated only in part by principle. He wanted to assert his own leadership position in the Whig party. In the wake of Tyler's second bank veto, the cabinet, most of whom were Clay sympathizers, resigned. The one exception was Secretary of State Daniel Webster, who stayed on because he had important negotiations with the British in progress and because he had ambitions of his own for party leadership.

Meanwhile, Clay pushed on with other parts of his program. He secured southern consent to the distribution of funds to the states for internal improvements by promising that tariff rates would not be increased by more than 20 percent, and he appeased the West by supporting a Preemption Act (1841). This act allowed settlers to "squat" on government land, and when the land was opened for purchase, to buy it, free from competitive bids, at the minimum government price of $1.25 per acre. These measures received the president's signature, but the following year, when congressional Whigs sought their reward by raising the tariff to the 1832 level with a provision for distribution, Tyler vetoed it. The president signed a second bill without distribution, but by then the American System was in shambles. The Democrats lowered the tariff to a bare revenue level in 1846, and nothing more was said of the national bank or internal improvements for twenty years.

In the meantime, a Whig convention ousted Tyler and his southern following from the party, and Clay resigned his seat in the Senate to try again for the presidency in 1844. The enmity between president and Congress doomed all action on the domestic front for the remainder of Tyler's term. Tyler did make some important moves in the field of foreign affairs,

New York Public Library Picture Collection.
The inauguration of "Old Tippecanoe."

however. Indeed, his aggressive expansionism ultimately changed the course of American politics with the unintended—but, from the president's view, scarcely unwelcome—result that it ruined Henry Clay's final bid for the presidency.

DIPLOMACY OF THE BORDERLANDS

After twenty years of relative goodwill, Anglo-American relations deteriorated in the late 1830s. The trouble began when a rebellion broke out in Canada in 1837. The British suppressed it with relative ease, but

Americans along the Niagara frontier provided the rebels with arms and sanctuary. In retaliation, Canadian officials crossed the river and burned an American lake steamer, the *Caroline*. The incident revived Americans' latent Anglophobia, and politicians bidding for the Irish vote exploited it to the utmost. The following year the long-standing controversy over the Maine–New Brunswick boundary flared into a "war" between Canadian and American lumberjacks along the Aroostook River. Friction extended onto the high seas; British warships, trying to end the international slave trade, stopped and searched American vessels. In 1841, slaves being sent from Virginia to New Orleans on an American brig, *Creole*, mutinied and sailed the vessel into Nassau in the Bahamas. British officials set the slaves free while southerners screamed with rage.

The British government offered neither apology nor reparations for the *Caroline* and the *Creole*, but it did send to Washington a special envoy, Lord Ashburton, to mend relations. Ashburton was a personal friend of Secretary of State Daniel Webster, and the two quickly came to terms. The Maine boundary was fixed, and so was the previously undefined border of Minnesota between Lake Superior and Lake of the Woods. The United States also agreed to maintain a squadron off the coast of Africa to stop American slavers. The only Anglo-American dispute left unresolved by the Webster-Ashburton Treaty (1842) was Oregon. By restoring an atmosphere of con-

ciliation, the treaty facilitated the resolution of that controversy as well.

Webster had remained in office when the rest of the cabinet resigned to complete the negotiations with Ashburton, and when the treaty was signed he joined the rest of his party in quitting the administration. Webster's resignation, in turn, left President Tyler free to pursue his own pet project, the annexation of Texas. Texas had won independence from Mexico in 1836 and desired admission to the Union, but Presidents Jackson and Van Buren had avoided annexation for fear it would provoke war with Mexico. Tyler had no such concern, and he saw advantage to the South in the admission of a new slave state. He named a fellow Virginian, Abel P. Upshur, to replace Webster, and Upshur immediately opened negotiations with Texas President Sam Houston. An annex-

Webster-Ashburton Treaty, 1842.

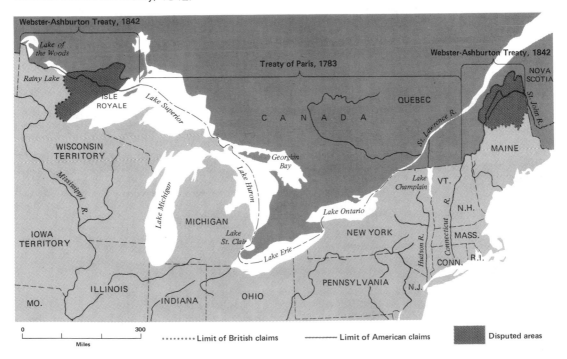

ation treaty was ready for signing when Upshur was killed by the explosion of a cannon on the battleship *Princeton*. Tyler then named Calhoun to head the State Department, knowing that he was an ardent expansionist.

Calhoun quickly completed the negotiations and sent the annexation treaty to the Senate in April 1844. With characteristic lack of finesse, Calhoun also sent to the Senate an exchange of letters with the British ambassador in which he defended the annexation of Texas as necessary for the protection of American slavery. This bombshell landed in the Senate only a few days before the party conventions met to nominate candidates for the presidency. Texas annexation instantly became a political issue and a sectionally divisive one at that. Bank, tariff, and internal improvements, the issues that had dominated presidential elections for a generation, were forgotten as the nation thrilled to the prospect of continental expansion. The real losers were the two men who had dominated American politics for a decade, Clay and Van Buren. A new political age had dawned, and they were not to be part of it.

SUMMARY

Andrew Jackson became president in 1829 without a special commitment or a coherent program. He possessed instead an assortment of attitudes, shaped by his western background and honed by the men with whom he surrounded himself: Martin Van Buren, Amos Kendall, and Francis P. Blair. What emerged from this coalition of intellects was a Jacksonian persuasion, centered on opposition to privilege and the desire to present equal opportunities to all. One corollary was the concept of rotation in office as a means of breaking up entrenched elites and giving more people a chance at governmental decision making. Later in Jackson's term it led to the bank war—a struggle, as the Jacksonians saw it, against corporate monopoly and chartered privilege.

In the meantime, Jackson had to face a challenge from the South. Southern sectionalism, fed by economic hard times and fears of slave uprising, had been growing since the Missouri controversy of 1819–1820. It climaxed with South Carolina's adoption in November 1832 of an ordinance nullifying the federal tariff. Born of John C. Calhoun's theory of states rights, the ordinance directly challenged the authority of the federal government. Jackson responded with a carrot-and-stick approach, asking Congress for authority to use military force while allowing his friends to introduce a compromise tariff bill. Clay and Calhoun, each unwilling to let Jackson take all the credit, worked out the formalities of compromise in January 1833. South Carolina repealed its ordinance of nullification, and Congress approved a bill providing for annual reductions in the tariff over a period of ten years.

The bank war further defined the Jacksonian persuasion. In vetoing the bill rechartering the Bank of the United States in the summer of 1832, Jackson reaffirmed the principle of equal opportunity. Jackson believed, as had the theorists of the revolutionary generation, that republican government depended on a virtuous citizenry. The proper role of government, therefore, was the negative one of maintaining law and order, of providing equal protection to all. Positive government—programs of economic development, such as Henry Clay's American System—inevitably corrupted the virtuous and rewarded the few. This form of Jeffersonian liberalism had a peculiar relevance in Jackson's day. American society in the mid-nineteenth century was a patchwork of divergent interests—regional, economic, ethnic, and religious. A decentralized government, tolerant of diversity, was best suited to it. The Jacksonian persuasion thus appealed to southerners, to ethnocultural groups such as Irish Catholics, and to artisans and shopkeepers, the petit bourgeoisie who made up the workers' parties of the time. These social elements remained broadly associated with the Democratic party for more than a century after Jackson's presidency.

Martin Van Buren, Jackson's successor in 1836, was more committed to the Jacksonian ideology than Jackson himself, but he lacked Jackson's charisma. He also had the misfortune to be president in a time of depression, the most severe the nation had known to that time. The opposition Whigs took advantage of his unpopularity and stormed to victory in 1840 under the banner of Old Tippecanoe, William Henry Harrison.

Harrison died a month after his inauguration, John Tyler inherited the White House, and four years of confusion ensued. Tyler quarreled with his party, which looked to Clay for leadership. The Whigs eventually ousted Tyler altogether, leaving Clay in command as the election of 1844 approached. In the meantime public attention turned to the West; Americans became fascinated by the romance of Texas, Oregon, and California. By 1844, both Henry Clay and his American System seemed all but irrelevant.

READING SUGGESTIONS

Arthur Schlesinger, Jr.'s Pulitzer Prize–winning *Age of Jackson* (1945) is still one of the most entertaining and informative introductions to the period, even though Schlesinger's thesis that Jacksonianism was an eastern, workingman's movement is no longer tenable. Lee Benson, *The Concept of Jacksonian Democracy: New York as a Test Case* (1964), suggests that it is wrong even to associate the Jacksonians with democracy and reform; Edward Pessen, *Jacksonian America: Society, Personality, and Politics* (1969), maintains that social inequality was the norm throughout this period. Both Lee Benson and, more recently, Ronald P. Formisano, in *The Birth of Mass Political Parties: Michigan, 1827–1861* (1971), argue that ethnocultural ties were more important than ideology in determining popular voting behavior.

Despite the doubts cast by these works, attempts to define the Jacksonian ideology and its sources of popular appeal have persisted. Marvin Meyers' *The Jacksonian Persuasion* (1960) is indispensable, and Richard B. Latner, *The Presidency of Andrew Jackson: White House Politics, 1829–1837* (1979), is an important new study. The classic study of the bank war is Bray Hammond, *Banks and Politics in America from the Revolution to the Civil War* (1957), but it should be used in conjunction with more recent works—Peter Temin, *The Jacksonian Economy* (1969), and John McFaul, *The Politics of Jacksonian Finance* (1972).

William Freehling, *Prelude to Civil War: The Nullification Controversy in South Carolina, 1816–1836* (1966), is a masterful analysis of nullification, although Charles Wiltse's three-volume biography of John C. Calhoun is still the best study of the "cast-iron man." For the Whig opposition, Daniel Walker Howe's *The Political Culture of the American Whigs* (1979) is an important new study. Donald B. Cole, *Martin Van Buren and the American Political System* (1984), is the most recent study of the "little magician."

The politics of the 1840s remain murky, despite Joel Silbey's quantitative analysis, *The Shrine of Party: Congressional Voting Behavior 1841–1852* (1967). The most interesting approach is through biography, Clement Eaton's *Henry Clay and the Art of American Politics* (1957) and Irving Bartlett's *Daniel Webster* (1978) being among the best.

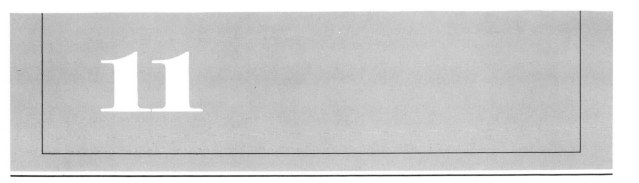

Delaware Water Gap

A PEOPLE IN MOTION

ivilization and savagery—the counterpoint provides one of the great themes of the American story. At no time in our history was the clash of modern and primitive more violent than in the four decades preceding the Civil War. In those years, urban expansion matched westward expansion, and both frontiers challenged the established social order. Fed by immigrants, population grew at a faster pace than ever before, doubling itself every twenty-three years. Cities grew even faster than that, as people moved from farm to factory. New technologies brought new opportunities to some people; others found that their jobs had become irrelevant. And the displacement of people bred social and political tensions. Lawlessness and disorder in the cities were one symptom; a national alcoholic binge was another. It was all part of the process of modernization, but to give it such a slick and comfortable label is to coat with soothing hindsight the discomfort of the age. For those whose values were rooted in a rural past, it was a fearful time. The swift conquest of the frontier was also a source of both pride and apprehension. In 1820 the edge of settlement lay just west of the Mississippi River, about halfway across the continent. By 1860, Anglo-American settlement had reached the Pacific Coast, and miners and cattlemen were encroaching on the mountains and prairies in between. The frontier experience left its own marks on American society, including self-assertiveness and violence. And as the pioneers outran the social and religious rules and restraints of the civilized East, they raised anew the fear of social chaos. Jacksonian America was a paradox of modern and primitive, and the paradox has never been fully resolved.

⊔ The People: Natives and Immigrants

Throughout the nineteenth century, the American population grew at a rate that was more than double that of any European country. In the early decades of the century, the growth was due to natural increase rather than immigration. The high birth rate, in turn, resulted from the usefulness of children in an agricultural society and from a relatively low rate of infant mortality. A decline in the birthrate, however, is one of the signs of modernization, and in the eastern portion of the country this phenomenon was apparent even in the late eighteenth century. By 1840 the decline was so general that the previous rate of population growth was sustained only by an increase in immigration.

Immigration was itself the product of modernization in Europe. New agricultural technology and the replacement of cottage handicrafts by factories created a "surplus" population throughout northwestern Europe. In parts of Germany and Scandinavia, governments encouraged unemployed farmers and artisans to emigrate. In times of political upheaval, such as the year 1848, government repression in Germany and Austria forced thousands to flee. The most important calamity, however, was the Irish potato blight of the mid-1840s, which caused mass starvation and even more massive emigration.

Before the 1840s, immigration to the United States had proceeded at a modest rate, not much different from the emigration to the colonies a half to three quarters of a century earlier. During the Napoleonic Wars, it slowed to about 4,000 persons a year. The flow picked up after 1815, reach-

"Delaware Water Gap," a wash drawing by Augustus Kollinek (1844).

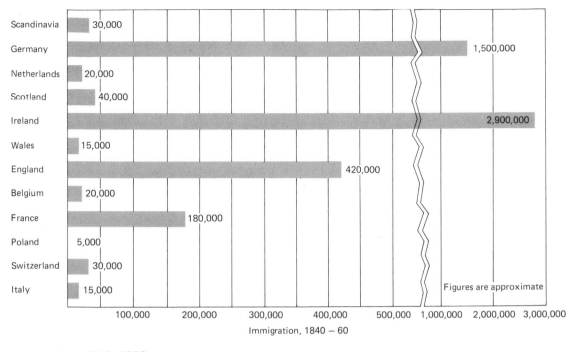

Scandinavia	30,000
Germany	1,500,000
Netherlands	20,000
Scotland	40,000
Ireland	2,900,000
Wales	15,000
England	420,000
Belgium	20,000
France	180,000
Poland	5,000
Switzerland	30,000
Italy	15,000

Figures are approximate

100,000 200,000 300,000 400,000 500,000 1,000,000 2,000,000 3,000,000

Immigration, 1840 — 60

Immigration, 1840–1860.

ing about 6,000 a year in the 1820s. (These are only estimates because until 1819 the U.S. Congress did not even think it important to collect and publish statistics on immigration.) The ethnic mix, too, was similar to the colonial pattern—Scots-Irish and Germans. Immigration numbers remained low in part because the United States had not yet established itself in the European mind as the cornucopia of opportunity. During the 1820s, more Germans went to Brazil than to the United States. Catholic Irish, displaced in their homeland, usually migrated to England to work in the new textile mills. Migrants out of England and Scotland found it cheaper to go to Canada because of British laws regulating passenger traffic with the United States.

During the 1830s, the United States became the principal goal of European emigrants, and it would remain so until it began to restrict immigration nearly a cen-

tury later. It had by then achieved more than a half century of political stability, and it presented a familiar climate, topography, and, for Anglo-Irish emigrants, a familiar language. Its expanding trade was also important, for ships that bore the bulky American staples, cotton and tobacco, eastward had ample room for passengers on the westward journey. The Atlantic passage for persons willing to travel in steerage* was only a few dollars. During the 1830s, the rate of immigration leaped to 50,000 a year.

The flow tripled in the 1840s due in large measure to a famine in Ireland. Since

---

* Originally this term applied to passengers with inferior accommodations below the deck and at the rear of the vessel. Later in the century, when vessels were jammed with people, many of whom lived, slept, and cooked on the open deck, it came to apply to anyone without specific accommodations.

its introduction into Europe from Latin America in the eighteenth century, the "Irish" potato had become a major dietary staple. It was nutritious, easy to grow, and provided a great deal of food on little land. In chronically underfed Ireland, the potato had nourished a population explosion and with it the endless subdivision of farms. A blight which wiped out the potato crop in 1845 wrought instant havoc. The destruction was so general that there was not even a seed crop available the following year. The devastation continued until 1850. In that five-year period, 1 million died of starvation and another 1.5 million emigrated, most of them to the United States.

Toward the end of the 1840s, emigration from Germany also increased dramatically. Germany also felt the ill effects of the potato blight, and a wave of revolutions in central Europe in 1848 sent political refugees scurrying for America. During the 1850s, immigrants flowed into American ports at the rate of 300,000 a year.* By 1860, according to the federal census of that year, Irish men and women made up 39 percent of the foreign-born population, and Germans formed another 31 percent. Natives of England, Scotland, or Wales constituted another 14 percent, and emigres from Canada, 6 percent. Immigration from Scandinavia and other parts of Europe did not become sizable until after 1860.

⊔ The Changing Cities

Many of the Irish spent their last penny on the ocean crossing (a voyage from Liverpool to Boston cost about $20, which included food). Lacking funds to buy farms

---

* This is still a rather modest rate when compared to the peak years of 1900–1905, when immigrants crowded through American ports at the rate of 1 million a year.

or even to move into the interior, they settled in the tenement districts of New York and Boston, and in the factory towns of New England. Poverty and lack of skills drove them to manual labor on the docks or in the public works projects that were transforming the cities. Poor wages and long hours kept them in menial occupations. The Germans, a bit more affluent, moved into the Middle West, where they settled in the bustling lake and river cities— Chicago, Milwaukee, Cincinnati, and St. Louis.

American cities were undergoing a profound change even before the immigrants arrived. The colonial city had been a "walking city," where homes doubled as shops and even wealthy merchants lived near their retail establishments. The poor lived on the periphery of the colonial city, where land was cheap and income could be supplemented with gardens and livestock. The technological invasion changed all that. As artisans' shops grew bigger and employed more workers, they crowded out the family quarters. Dwelling place and workshop became physically separated; family life and work became more psychologically distinct. The advent of the street car widened the gap. Horse-drawn carriages that ran on iron rails enabled middle-class merchants and master craftsmen to move out of the crowded downtown and into pleasant rural surroundings. The coming of the steam railroad in the 1840s enabled the affluent to commute to work from suburbs as far as ten miles from the city center.

Immigrants moved into the void in the city center. The one-time mansions of the wealthy became the multifamily tenements of the poor. Outmoded craft shops were torn down and replaced with inexpensively built tenement houses. The influx of immigrants only hastened the exodus of the middle class from the central city. Land values plummeted, buildings became dilapidated: The slum/ghetto was born, and with it the social evils that commonly attend poverty and hopelessness—crime, drunkenness, and social disorder. Native citizens could not fail to make the connection between immigrants and the numerous maladies that afflicted American society in those years.

NATIVISM

The tendency of immigrants to flock together, as well as their overwhelming numbers (aliens were a majority of the populations of Chicago, Milwaukee, and St. Louis by the 1850s) produced the first significant nativist, or antiforeign, movement in American history. The fact that nearly all the Irish and about half of the Germans were Roman Catholic added to the hostility, for it aroused latent prejudices in a nation founded by Protestants. For generations, Protestant ministers in America and their more devout followers had held a vision of America as a Christian utopia, a grassy Eden in a corrupt and grimy world. The rise of smoke-belching cities, at once profane and corrupt, threatened that vision. The arrival of aliens, who congregated in the cities, spoke in strange dialects, and swore allegiance to a foreign Pope, worried them even more.

The Protestant majority at first hoped that it might redeem the sinners in their slums. During the 1820s, Biblical Tract societies distributed Bibles and religious literature among the poor, hoping that if they more fully understood Christ's work, the poor might adopt His moral standards. Other reformers devised a variety of institutions, from Sunday schools to workhouses, that were aimed at instilling high morals and good work habits among the urban poor. The movement for free public education, which began in the 1820s, was inspired in large part by a middle-class desire to tame the rowdy poor and Americanize the immigrants.

In the 1830s immigration increased, and

so did urban turbulence. Irish Catholics were increasingly singled out for blame. In 1835, Samuel F. B. Morse, who had patented his invention of the telegraph the previous year, published a pamphlet on the *Imminent Dangers to the Free Institutions of the United States through Foreign Immigration.* Morse contended that Jesuits were in control of the transatlantic movement of Catholics and were directing the newcomers to strategic points in the nation in preparation for the overthrow of the government. By the 1840s, antipathy between Catholic immigrants and native Protestants was itself the major source of urban disorder. Riots in working-class sections of the cities and the burning of churches were almost weekly events.

In the early 1850s, when both Irish and German immigration reached a peak, the nativist movement took a political turn. Nativist parties, calling themselves American Republicans, had won some municipal elections in the 1840s, and in 1852 they coalesced into a national American Republican party. Nicknamed "Know-Nothings" by journalist Horace Greeley because of their refusal to divulge information about their secret meetings, the party picked up persons politically orphaned by the major-party schisms of the 1850s. It appealed to shopkeepers and small-town professionals, who felt themselves the cultural guardians of their communities. It also appealed to southerners, who made the movement not only anti-immigrant and anti-Catholic but also anti-black.

The American Republican Party faded as quickly as it had arisen. It ran ex-President Millard Fillmore for President in 1856, and he earned a paltry total of eight electoral votes. Thereafter, white, middle-class Protestants became too preoccupied with the antislavery problem to concern themselves with immigrants and Catholics. Immigration itself declined in the late 1850s as economic and political crises eased in western Europe. Nativism was buried, but not far from the surface. It would rise again.

MOBILITY

The tide of immigrants brought dramatic structural changes in American society and economy. Between 1820 and 1860, cities grew more rapidly than at any other time in their history. In the year of the Missouri Compromise, about 80 percent of the people lived on farms or in rural villages; by the time the Civil War broke out, that proportion had fallen to 55 percent. During the same decades, population exploded onto the "virgin lands" of the West. To European travelers, everyone in America seemed on the move—from farm to city, from town to town, from crowded state to open territory. A common estimate today is that the entire population of the country, on the average, changed its location every ten years. (Those who moved more than once balanced those who stayed put.) Steady population growth made possible the simultaneous development of cities and frontier, and the twin phenomena fed upon one another. The urban East provided the hinterland with capital for machinery and transportation improvements. The rural South and West provided cotton and cereal grains which the cities either consumed or prepared for export.

People moved because they expected to improve themselves, and apparently enough succeeded that others were encouraged to try. The country was built on

The Tremont House, Boston. Inns and lodges for overnight guests had been around for centuries, but the hotel—the multistoried public house with a private room for each guest—was an American invention. The Tremont House in Boston, completed in 1829, was the prototype. Done in the Greek Revival style, it conveyed an instant impression of elegance and public purpose. It symbolized a nation on the move.

Boston Atheneum.

the image of opportunity, and the image persisted through the nineteenth century. People crossed the Atlantic to better their lot, and they crossed the Appalachians and the Great Plains for the same reason. How real the promise was we will never precisely know. We do know that there remained throughout the nineteenth century great inequalities of wealth, and in the eastern cities the gap between rich and poor was actually widening. On the eve of the Civil War, the upper 5 percent of families owned more than half the nation's wealth. In the cities the disparity was much greater. In Philadelphia, by one estimate, the richest 1 percent of taxpayers owned half the

city's property, while the lower 80 percent possessed just 3 percent of the wealth.

In the South, wealth and opportunity were related to slaveholding, and the accumulation of slaves took several generations. Elsewhere, inequalities in wealth were thought to be temporary. The French observer Alexis de Tocqueville expressed the common assumption that in America "most of the rich men were formerly poor" and that "any man's son may become the equal of any other man's son." Despite the inequities in society and the obvious advantages of inherited wealth, there were enough success stories to lend substance to the belief. It is true that most genera-

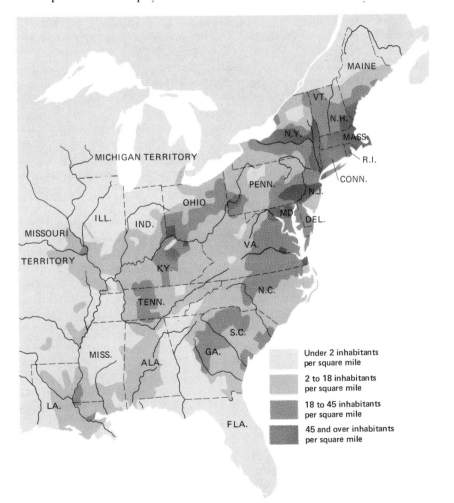

Under 2 inhabitants per square mile

2 to 18 inhabitants per square mile

18 to 45 inhabitants per square mile

45 and over inhabitants per square mile

tional advance, of the sort Tocqueville described, was limited to the next rung on the social ladder. The son of an unskilled manual laborer usually became a semiskilled factory operative. Rarely did a man—and much more rarely did a woman—leap from farm or workshop to a trained profession. Abraham Lincoln, the son of an itinerant land clearer, who became a lawyer, legislator, and president, was rare to the point of unique, but he was the archetype of the "self-made man." Myth or reality, the ideal of the self-made man was reinforced by the freedom to move, the physical pursuit of social happiness.

SOCIAL DISORDER

Those who failed often vented their frustration in violence. The Jacksonian era was a time of almost continuous turbulence among the urban poor. One historian has counted thirty-five major riots in Philadelphia, New York, and Boston between 1830 and 1860, and Baltimore was so turbulent that it earned the nickname "mob city." In the late 1830s, attorney Abraham Lincoln lamented that rioting had become "the everyday news of the time." The violence ranged from the criminal gang wars to fistfights between volunteer fire companies. But most of it was "goal oriented"— that is, planned and organized to express a grievance or punish a foe. Violence was most often directed against immigrants, especially the Irish, blacks, and in the 1830s, abolitionists.

There have been other periods of disorder in our history, notably the 1890s and 1960s, but in no period was rioting so frequent or so uncontrolled. Urban sprawl had far outpaced urban government. Daytime law and order were entrusted to sheriffs and constables elected by the citizens of each ward or precinct. These men derived their income from serving legal papers and collecting debts, and they were reluctant to risk their reelection chances by rushing to the aid of racial and ethnic minorities. Nighttime order was in the hands of watchmen, untrained and often elderly public servants who huddled in their watchhouses for comfort and safety while gangs governed the streets.

MISSIONS AND SUNDAY SCHOOLS

To individuals steeped in the traditional values of rural, Protestant America, the urban challenge was essentially a moral one, and the instruments of religion—Bible and meetinghouse—were the best weapons to combat it. Evangelical revivals had swept the country periodically since 1800, and the cities were an inviting target for the evangelists. Charles Grandison Finney, greatest of the revivalists, campaigned in Philadelphia and New York as early as 1827–1828. Three years later he led a revival in the bustling lake port of Rochester, New York, that allegedly closed the city's taverns, converted the theater into a livery stable, and placed a soap and candle factory in the former circus arena. In 1832, Finney set up a permanent revival center in a rented theater near Five Points, the worst of New York City's slums. Missions, designed to make urbanites regular churchgoers, became an important weapon in the struggle to tame the city. New York City had sixty-five of them by the time of the Civil War.

The mission was directed at adults; the Sunday School took care of the slum children. Moralists concentrated on children because they represented the future. Vice-ridden parents could be written off if the children were saved. Founded in England in the 1780s, the Sunday School spread quickly to America. By 1824, when the American Sunday School Union was founded, there were some 700 Sunday

Schools enrolling some 50,000 children. By the end of that decade, national enrollment was 350,000. Where evangelists and Bible tracts evoked through words and pictures the values of America's Protestant past, the Sunday School actually recreated the idyllic past. The urban child was given a weekly exposure to the orderly regimen of the village. Every lesson, every aspect of the program was designed to instill habits of industry, thrift, and law-abiding restraint.

And all of it failed. The city and its dwellers proved remarkably resistant to the overtures of the reformers. The Irish viewed them as a threat to their identity and to their church; cynics regarded them simply with derision. There were only two lasting results of the monumental effort to tame the cities. One was legislation regulating drinking, Sunday amusements, and school attendance. The other was the creation of modern police departments with trained and uniformed officers. But at mid-century the cities were still turbulent, crime-ridden, hotbeds of "popery" in the view of America's rural Protestant majority.

⊔ The Transportation and Communication Revolution

Improvements in transportation and communication encouraged mobility and promoted economic growth. The period from 1790 to 1820 is commonly called the Turnpike era. In colonial times, roads had been built and maintained by local authorities. Except for the post road from Boston to

"The Old Stage Coach." The painter, Eastman Johnson (1824–1906), was a sentimental New Englander who enjoyed rendering childhood memories and bucolic scenes. By the time Johnson painted this (1871), the Concord coach was a memory of the past, having surrendered to the railroads.

Milwaukee Art Center, Layton Art Gallery Collection.

Charleston, there was no interstate system. Most roads were bumpy swaths through the forest; bridges were virtually nonexistent, ferries unreliable. The Lancaster Pike, from Philadelphia to Lancaster, Pennsylvania, laid out in the early 1790s, was built and maintained by a private corporation that charged a toll for use. Its success inspired other states to build toll roads, either with their own funds or by chartering corporations. The turnpikes benefited primarily passenger traffic, however. Even with improved roads, freight charges remained high, so it was not feasible to transport bulky farm products, such as flour or tobacco, on land for long distances.

Rivers were the principal arteries of American commerce from the earliest times, but traffic for the most part was downstream by flatboat (a raft with a deck and tiller), which was broken up for lumber at its destination. Keelboats could travel upstream pushed by pole or sail, but their freight charges were high. Robert Fulton demonstrated the first commercially operable steamboat, the *Clermont*, on the Hudson River in 1807. Four years later, a steamboat made its first appearance on western waters, completing a successful voyage from Pittsburgh to New Orleans, and in 1819 a steamboat, *Walk-on-the-Water*, was launched on the Great Lakes. Because steamboats could go upstream or down with almost equal facility, they revolutionized freight shipment, especially in the West. By 1840 more than 500 steamboats were plying the nation's waterways. The steamboat, however, was confined to natural waterways. Access to other parts of the country required canals and, ultimately, railroads.

THE CANAL ERA

Canals were a familiar feature of many European cities, and Britain began cutting canals through the countryside in the years following the American Revolution. In the United States, several states began canal projects before 1800, but most were short and important only to certain localities. The construction of New York's Erie Canal (1817–1825) inaugurated the canal era. The Erie Canal stretched from the Hudson River to Lake Erie, giving the Northwest direct access to the port of New York and world markets.

The canal reduced the cost per mile of freight transportation between Buffalo and New York City from 20 to 2 cents. Western New York was the initial beneficiary as farms were cleared in the fertile Genessee Valley and cities sprouted along the canal route—Rochester, Syracuse, Utica, and Lockport. In the 1840s, Ohio, traditionally dependent on the downriver traffic to New Orleans, diverted its cereal surpluses to the Erie Canal, and Cleveland and Toledo blossomed into flour-milling centers. So successful was the Erie Canal that its profits repaid its initial cost of $7 million within twelve years. It was even able to withstand competition from the railroads. Its peak year of traffic was 1880, long after the New York Central spanned the famed "water level route" from New York to Chicago with iron rails.

Success of the Erie encouraged other states to undertake similar projects. Pennsylvania built a Main Line canal from Philadelphia to Pittsburgh; the canal boats were pulled over the mountains on a cog railway. Virginia sought to make contact with the Ohio Valley by means of a James River and Kanawha Canal, but the project barely got past the Blue Ridge. In the 1830s and 1840s the western states, with characteristic optimism, undertook monumental projects linking the Great Lakes and the Ohio River. The Ohio and Erie Canal, completed in 1832, stretched 333 miles from Cleveland, Ohio, to Portsmouth on the Ohio River, fed by waters from the Cuyahoga, Muskingum, and Scioto rivers. Ohio and Indiana cooperated on a canal extend-

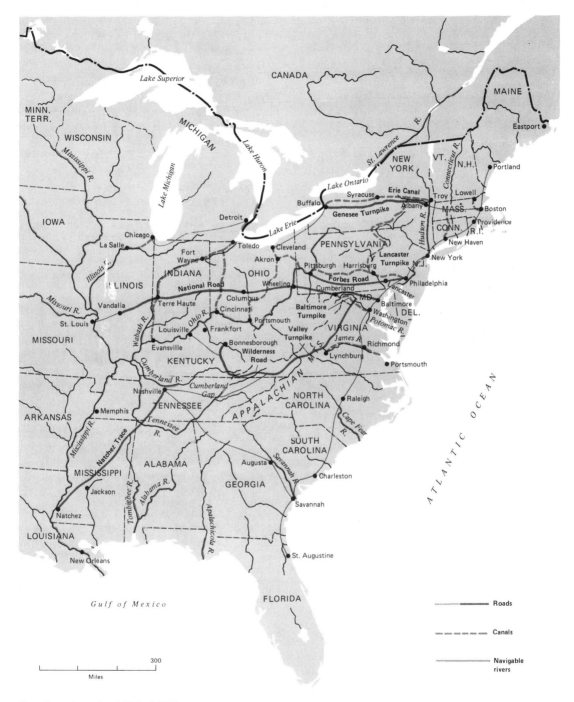

Canals and roads, 1820–1850.

ing from Fort Wayne to Evansville by way of the Maumee, Wabash, and White rivers. The western canals involved an enormous amount of political logrolling as communities vied for the honor of being served. Illinois and Michigan nearly bankrupted themselves by digging ditches in areas that had enough political power to secure legislative appropriations.

Canals came under criticism even while they were being constructed. Not surprisingly, much of it originated with the promoters of railroads. Had the capital and energy been invested in railroads instead of canals, it was suggested, the nation would have had a modern transportation system decades earlier than it did. Sending goods by canals is slow and laborious, and canals were difficult to maintain. They often froze over in the winter, washed out in the spring, and dried up in the summer. An estimate of the worth of canals depends on the accounting system used. None of the canals, except the Erie and some short lines connecting major waterways (such as the Delaware and Chesapeake bays), repaid the costs of construction and maintenance. That is, they failed to show a profit. But that is too simple a criterion. Nearly all the canals promoted economic growth and development. By reducing freight costs, they saved shippers money and improved farm prices. Before the Ohio and Erie Canal opened, for instance, the price of wheat in Akron, Ohio, was 20 to 30 cents a bushel. After Akron obtained water access to Cleveland, the price rose to 75 cents. Improved access to markets increased land prices, encouraged the migration of people, and fostered the growth of cities. Such "social returns" suggest that the canals were, in fact, worth the money.

It should be remembered also that the technology which made the railroads superior to canals was not available, or even easily foreseeable, when the canals were begun. Moreover, the methods by which

the canals were financed—through government loans to private developers, as well as state and federal land grants to finance construction—provided precedents for the building of railroads. Indeed, we can argue that the rapid development of the West, which the canals in part made possible, actually hastened the construction of a railroad network.

THE COMING OF RAILROADS

In the long run, neither steamboats nor canals could compete with railroads. The railroad was faster, nearly as cheap to build and maintain, and could penetrate high country, where much of the nation's forest and mineral resources lay. The British developed both the steam locomotive and the technique of running cars on a track. Construction on the first American railroad, the Baltimore and Ohio, began in 1828 and by 1830 trains were operating on a 13-mile segment of track. Construction of railroads in other states was soon under way, and by 1840 the nation boasted nearly 3,000 miles of track. That figure tripled by 1850 and tripled again to more than 30,000 miles by 1860.

Expansion was accompanied by rapid advances in technology. Construction engineers learned to rest ties on beds of crushed rock to provide a cushion for the pounding of wheels on rails, substituted iron T rails for wooden rails capped with iron straps, and vastly improved the power of locomotives. Even so, when the Civil War began the railroad had barely begun to show its potential. There were no national trunk main lines; most railroads ran from some rural outpost to a city. Track widths were fairly standardized in the North, but a variety of gauges were used in the South, requiring cars to be lifted from one set of wheels to another when two lines met. There were no railroad bridges across the Ohio or the Mississippi rivers until the eve of the Civil War.

The homeward journey of Congressman Abraham Lincoln in 1849 illustrates the difficulties of long-distance travel. After attending the inauguration of President Zachary Taylor, Lincoln left Washington on March 20, 1849, for his home in Springfield, Illinois. An all-day train trip on the Baltimore and Ohio Railroad carried him up the Potomac Valley as far as Cumberland, Maryland. That town was the end of track for the B&O. The journey cost the forty-year-old congressman $8.60. At Cumberland he transferred to a nine-passenger stagecoach, which followed the National Road across the Appalachian ridges to Wheeling on the Ohio River. The 130-mile stage journey took twenty-four hours and cost about $4. At Wheeling, Lincoln boarded a steamboat for a journey down the Ohio River and up the Mississippi to St. Louis, a trip of 1,100 miles that took about four days. At St. Louis he had to wait a day or so for the stage that crossed the Illinois prairies, but by the end of the month he was in Springfield.

Steamboats and stagecoaches still competed with railroads at mid-century, but the potential for the "iron horse" was already evident. During the 1850s railroad construction averaged 1,300 miles a year. By 1860 railroads were a billion-dollar industry—the nation's first. And they were the nation's first "public" corporation, in the sense that they had to offer stock on the open market to multitudes of investors in order to secure enough development capital. In 1850, with a grant to the Illinois Central railroad via the state of Illinois, Congress began the practice of subsidizing railroad construction through gifts of land. All this anticipated the post–Civil War era when the railroads, gulping huge quantities of coal and steel, led America's Industrial Revolution.

OCEAN COMMERCE AND WORLD TRADE

Although the American economy matured rapidly through the middle decades of the nineteenth century, it failed to change its status in international trade. It supplied Europe with raw materials, food, and fiber, like any colonial economy, and it relied on Europe for finished products. As late as 1860, manufactures accounted for only 10 percent of United States exports, but nearly half its imports.

Ironically, this seemingly servile role was made possible by farm mechanization. By the 1860s, the American farmer could feed not only his own war-torn country, but a good portion of the world. British public policy encouraged this interdependence. In the 1820s, Britain began moving toward free trade, and in 1846, pressured by famine in Ireland, Parliament repealed the last of the trade restrictions, the Corn Laws, thereby opening the British Isles to American wheat. That same year Congress passed the Walker tariff, which lowered the duties to a bare revenue level and opened the United States to European manufactures. The Atlantic exchange increased accordingly, and the Irish famine, with tragic irony, made it more profitable than ever. Vessels made the eastward crossing stuffed with wheat and cotton and returned westward jammed with Irish immigrants. It was a heyday for sailors and merchants.

The boom in world trade in the 1840s and 1850s encouraged improvements in ship design. Ever since the War of 1812, when privateers built in Baltimore and Philadelphia shipyards proved to be the fastest vessels on the seas, Americans had experimented with the contours of the wooden sailing ship. The *Rainbow*, designed by John W. Griffiths and launched in 1845, incorporated the innovations of several decades. Its hull was five times as long as it was wide (versus the 3 to 1 ratio established by the Spanish galleon of Elizabethan times). It was narrow at the bow, high at the stern, and its masts were raked (tilted backward) so the slender wooden poles could support more canvas. Griffiths piled sail upon sail—mainsail, royal, topgallant, topsail, skysail—the last reaching so high that it was called a "moonraker," a nickname that became synonymous with the clipper ship.

Clippers were first used in the transAtlantic packet trade, a mail and passenger service founded on speed. But the China trade, involving a round-the-world cruise, was their glory. Britain waged a series of wars in the early 1840s (the Opium Wars) to force the Chinese to trade with the world. Americans followed the British into the port of Canton, China's window on the world, and the westerners soon developed a flourishing trade in tea. The merchandising of tea placed a premium on sailing speed, for the vessel that reached London, New York, or Boston with the first of the year's crop commanded the highest prices for its cargo. In that sort of competition, the American clippers excelled. One, the *Sovereign of the Seas*, designed by Donald McKay of Newburyport, Massachusetts, made a single day's run of 495 miles; another of McKay's masterpieces, the *Flying Cloud*, raced from New York around Cape Horn to San Francisco in 89 days, 8 hours. Both are sailing records that stand to this day.

The California gold rush of 1849 generated new demands for the clippers, which vied with one another to carry "fortyniners" around the Cape to San Francisco. But their days were numbered. Like the Pony Express, the century's other monument to the craze for speed, the clippers were expensive to operate and short-lived. By the end of the 1850s they were yielding to steam-driven ironclads, and within another decade the moonrakers, one of the most graceful of human inventions, were gone forever.

THE TELEGRAPH AND THE PONY EXPRESS

Paralleling these far-reaching changes in transportation was a revolution in communications. Samuel F. B. Morse developed the electromagnetic telegraph in the 1830s and demonstrated its commercial possibilities in 1844 when he wired the outcome of the Democratic nominating convention from Baltimore to Washington. Morse offered to sell his invention to the federal government, and when Congress turned him down, he proceeded with private capital (much of it supplied by newspapers, who could foresee its use to them) to string telegraph wires across the country.

In the 1850s, attention centered on the need for a communications link with California. Projects for a transcontinental railroad became bogged in sectional rivalries, and in the meantime two freight companies, the Butterfield Overland Mail Company and Russell, Majors & Waddell, provided passenger and mail service between western Missouri and California. Butterfield used the southern route via El Paso and the Mojave Desert, while Russell, Majors & Waddell followed the central route from St. Joseph, Missouri, through Salt Lake City to San Francisco. To prove the superiority of the central route and win a government mail contract, in the spring of 1860 Russell and his partners organized the Pony Express—relays of horsemen, galloping at full speed and changing mounts every ten miles, carried the mail from St. Joseph to San Francisco in ten days.

The romantic experiment caught the fancy of the nation, but it lasted only sixteen months. In 1861 the Western Union Telegraph Company (archrival to Morse's Magnetic Telegraph) organized two construction companies—one building west from Nebraska, the other coming east from California—to bridge the continent by wire. Congress offered financial help. The first pole was set on July 4, 1861, and the line was completed on October 24. The Pony Express continued to operate in the gap between the two projects, but it was finished when the lines met. The triumph of technology over the horse symbolized the revolution that had taken place.

⊔ Mechanizing Farm and Factory

The term *revolution* has also been applied—with less justice—to the changes in agricultural and industrial technology in the first half of the nineteenth century. The Industrial Revolution had neither the speed nor the impact of electronic communications. It was a slow, evolutionary process with no clear beginning or end. In Britain the process began in the eighteenth century with a series of innovations in the spinning and weaving operations of the textile industry. By the time of the American Revolution, the textile machines were too large for the household, where spinning and weaving had previously been done. They had to be propelled by water power in "houses" of their own—that is, in factories. Instead of raw materials being farmed out to people, as in the household, or "cottage," system, both workers and raw materials were brought to the factory. And so the mill town developed. At about the same time (1769–1782), James Watt devised a steam engine that could be used to drive machinery, eliminating the factory's dependence on water power. Coal, steam, and iron heralded the new age.

BEGINNINGS OF INDUSTRIALIZATION

In America, the Northeast was the first region to follow Britain's industrial lead. Social and economic conditions there were similar to those in Britain. Profits from trade provided surplus capital for investment in machines and mills. The labor force was free of such impediments as tightly organized guilds, was mobile, and was fairly well educated. Cities provided a market for factory products; canals and turnpikes made the flow of raw materials and finished goods easy.

The factory system in the United States had its beginnings in 1790 when Samuel Slater, an English immigrant, reproduced from memory a model of the latest English spinning machine. With financing from Moses Brown, a Rhode Island entrepreneur with a fortune made in whale oil and candles, Slater set up a textile mill at Pawtucket, Rhode Island. Shielded by Jefferson's embargo and the War of 1812, textile manufacturing slowly spread across southern New England. In 1814 a consortium called Boston Associates established the first integrated factory at Lowell, Massachusetts. It brought all stages of textile manufacture, from raw fiber to finished cloth, under one roof. Protected by tariffs after the war, the textile industry continued to expand. By 1840, domestic manufacturers consumed 270,000 bales of cotton annually, which was about 20 percent of the South's crop.

Textiles set the pace for the Industrial Revolution, but for a long time it was the only industry making significant progress. As late as 1850, in both Britain and America, "factory" meant "textile mill." For all the progress in transportation and communication, the centers of manufacturing in 1850 remained the home and the workshop. Capitalists purchased the raw materials, "put out" the goods to workers who finished them in their homes, and then marketed the finished product. Shoemaking at Lynn, Massachusetts, observed an English visitor, "is carried on almost entirely in private dwellings, from the circumstance that the people who do it are almost all farmers or fishermen likewise. . . . The whole family works . . . during the winter;

Yale University Art Gallery.

The Whitney arms factory and its surrounding mill town.

and in summer the father and sons turn out into the fields, or go fishing." Work thus moved in irregular rhythms, dictated by task rather than time. Manufacturing in 1850 was still an extension of the rural economy, in which each family had long been accustomed to meeting its own needs.

THE LOWELL GIRLS

Even Lowell, first of the large-scale mill towns, was designed by its founders to blend into the rural environment. Francis Cabot Lowell, who conceived the project, wanted to establish an ideal New England community that would stand not as a sample of urban blight, but as a model of republican purity and prosperity. His water-driven machinery actually dictated the site—the falls of the Merrimac River—but Lowell made a virtue of this isolated loca-

tion. Although labor had to be enticed from the surrounding farms and villages, Lowell and his associates did not want a long-term resident labor force that might become a self-conscious proletariat such as they had seen in the smoky cities of industrial England. So they hired New England farm girls to tend their machines for two or three years while they earned money for a dowry or an education. Women had traditionally been the spinners and weavers in the household economy, so the Lowell system was a mere extension of the earlier "putting out" system. In addition, women could be hired at lower wages than men, so profit blended with social ideal. The women responded enthusiastically at first. The "Lowell girls," one of them later recalled, had "a fresh breezy sociability about them which made many of them seem almost like a different race of beings."

The associates who financed the venture

built boardinghouses for the girls and imposed strict regulations to ensure proper behavior. The girls themselves kept alive intellectually by publishing their own monthly magazine, the *Lowell Offering*. Lowell was the marvel of the nation and an obligatory stop for every foreign traveler.

Many of the girls had been raised in strongly religious homes, and the Puritan ethic served the employers. The regimen of the boardinghouse was carried over into the factory, where the girls were told to "devote themselves assiduously to their duty during working hours." The Lowell women accepted the conditions happily for some years, but by the 1830s grumbling could be heard. In the farms and villages from which they came, they had been accustomed to long hours and grinding tasks, but they had also been accustomed to proceeding at their own pace until a task was finished. In the mills, machinery set the pace, and time was the measure of work. Bells tolled them awake, summoned them to meals, and sent them to their jobs. Lateness at any point was severely punished. Unlike the artisans of their home villages, they had no contact with owner or customers. Their lives were governed by a factory superintendent, who in turn received his orders in once-a-week visits by directors of the company. The adjustment of workers to factory life was a critical component of the process of modernization, and like all great social changes, it exacted its price. The experience of the "Lowell girls" was but one of many.

In 1834, the Lowell operatives conducted their first "turn out," a demonstration and a short-lived strike. The occasion was a 15 percent cut in wages, but the proclamation they issued contained a denunciation of the employers' paternalism, including the observation that such a regimen was contrary to republican liberty. Two years later they went on strike again, this time against an increase in the price of board in the company houses, which amounted to a 12 percent cut in wages. After the panic of 1837, Lowell's mill owners began replacing the women with cheaper and more docile immigrant labor. By the mid-1840s, the "Lowell girls" were no more. By then too, the familial paternalism of the early years had become a form of social control, much like the Sunday Schools of the cities. The argument against higher wages and shorter hours, for instance, was that such concessions would merely give workers more time and money for immoral behavior.

⊔Beginnings of a Labor Consciousness

The meaning of work and the status of workers had begun to change even before the introduction of the factory system. The preindustrial handicraft system, which had evolved in Europe and America over the centuries, gave each worker a certain amount of status and security. In charge of the workshop was the master craftsman, who owed his position to skill and a certain amount of entrepreneurial ability. He was a capitalist who procured the raw materials and sold the finished product, but he was also a laborer who often worked side by side with his employees. Under the master craftsman were journeymen, most of them young men who expected some day to become masters with shops of their own. At the bottom of the workshop's social order were apprentices, young boys who were bonded by contract to the master craftsman. They were provided room and board and training in the craft in return for their unpaid labor.

Because skill in a trade was the road to success, the only difference between masters and journeymen was time. No great social gulf separated them, and the work-

shop was a place of genial masculine camaraderie. The centerpiece of this workingmen's culture was alcohol. The workday
was punctuated with periodic breaks as
masters and journeymen lay aside their
tools and adjourned to a neighborhood saloon for a beer. Drinking rituals were a
bond of unity between owner and worker,
and they enabled journeymen to exert an
informal control over the pace of their
work.

All this began to change after 1800. Master craftsmen found it more profitable to
concentrate on business decisions, the acquisition of materials and sale of products.
They employed more journeymen, enlarged their shops, and subdivided workers' skills. Each journeyman became responsible for only a small part of the
manufacturing operation, repeating over
and over his assigned task as the product
passed from worker to worker. By the
1820s, most journeymen were middle-aged
men with neither the skill nor the money
to become masters themselves. By then,
too, the apprentice system had become another form of child labor. Apprentices
were given odd jobs and sent on errands;
few received any formal training. By the
1820s, it was a rare master who joined his
men in a saloon during the workday. Most
masters were urging sober habits on their
workers to increase productivity.

As the interests of masters and journeymen diverged, so did their perceptions of
one another. What in the eighteenth century had appeared to be isolated instances
of poor wages or ill treatment now appeared to journeymen to be part of the
system, a necessary result of restructured
shops and cheapened skills. Sensing that
they had mutual interests, the journeymen
in the larger cities formed labor organizations. As early as 1808, the cordwainers
of New York City went on strike, seeking
the right to bargain collectively over wages
and working conditions. The following
year, New York's printers banned employers from their meetings and announced
that the interests of employers and journeymen were "in some respects opposite."
In 1817, the printers went on strike, and
two years later the masons struck. The
strikes increased the sense of class consciousness. The civility typical of eighteenth-century labor protests disappeared.
Masters were denounced as "haughty aristocrats" and "merciless tyrants." By the
early 1830s there were thirty trade unions
in New York City; between 20 and 30 percent of the city's labor force were union
members.

The brutal inflation of the mid-1830s,
in the wake of Andrew Jackson's bank war,
occasioned a number of strikes in New
York and Philadelphia. The purpose of
most strikes was not so much higher wages
as the winning of a set rate for specific
tasks that would be uniform throughout
the trade. Without a standard rate, masters
could pay journeymen whatever they
chose, or they could "put out" the product
to women and children for finishing. Most
strikes were unsuccessful, but in 1834–
1835, the New York hatters did succeed
in getting employers to recognize the legitimacy of their union and to cease blacklist-
ing its members. The following year, the
mayor of New York paraded an armed regiment of National Guardsmen as a way of
convincing striking stevedores to return to
work. This was the first time a municipality
had resorted to military force to end a
strike, and it represented a further harden-
ing of the lines of conflict.

The most militant unions were in the
consumer finishing trades, such as tailoring
and shoemaking, where the subdivision of
work assignments and the accompanying
degradation of labor had gone the farthest.
These trades also produced the first wom-
en's labor organizations. Women were usually outworkers who labored in the home,
receiving materials and handing over finished goods to the employer. Working in
isolation and lacking in skills, they were

the most exploited of American workers. But they were not incapable of organization. As early as 1825, New York tailoresses went on strike for better wages. In 1831 they organized a Tailoresses' Society, some 1,600 strong, and mounted a bitter three-month strike against wage reductions.

The journeymen never regarded these efforts as equal to their own, but they did sense a mutual interest. When the female bookbinders went on strike in 1835, the New York Association of Journeymen Bookbinders pledged to use "all honorable means" to help them in their fight. The National Trades' Union, founded in 1834 as a clearinghouse for interstate communication among trades unions, even suggested that all trades affected by women's labor add women's auxiliaries to their unions.

All of this activity proved to be nothing more than a false dawn of a national labor movement. The panic of 1837 and the ensuing depression, in which reportedly one third of New York's workers lost their jobs, crushed the newly formed labor unions. In the next decade, the arrival of unskilled immigrants enabled employers to subdivide crafts even further. By 1850, the making of a single shoe required half a dozen operations, each performed by a different worker. With the advent a decade later of a sewing machine capable of stitching soles to uppers, even those narrow skills vanished. Workers became nothing more than machine tenders. Organization of the unskilled required a new form of labor consciousness.

TOWARD A FREE LABOR IDEOLOGY

While the labor strife of the 1830s heightened journeymen workers' class consciousness, it also sharpened the entrepreneurial ideology of master craftsmen and factory owners. What developed in their thoughts and writings was a blend of the Puritan work ethic, evangelical religion's admonition to "act right," and the temperance movement's warnings against drunkenness and dissipation. Taken together, these elements formed a new ethical creed for the nineteenth century—what some historians have called the gospel of free labor.

The faith that God had called everyone to some productive vocation, to toil there for the common good and his greater glory, is as old as Christianity itself. The Protestant Reformation, however, placed greater emphasis on the dangers of idleness as playing into the hands of the Devil. Reformers also narrowed the list of permissible callings, lopping off beggars at one end of the scale and monks and courtiers at the other end. Protestantism, as one historian has observed, "tried to turn religion out of the cloisters into the world of work, but it emptied the monasteries only to give everyone the ascetic responsibilities of a monk." Puritans, for instance, reformed the English calendar, throwing out the irregular happenings of saints' days and replacing them with the clocklike rhythm of the weekly sabbath, when people were expected to be as determined in their rest as they had been tireless in their work the rest of the week. The Puritans thus demanded not only that everyone work, but that they work in a profoundly new way: regularly, conscientiously, and diligently.

Puritans and Quakers brought this work ethic to America. In the course of time the notion of a "calling" in the service of God faded; instead moralists talked of usefulness. By being useful to society, one was also useful to oneself. Benjamin Franklin distilled the new concept in his memorable aphorism "Time is money." After the revolution, God was pushed out of the equation altogether. Americans were told to work hard and improve themselves for "the prosperity and glory of the Republic." Thus factory owners and master craftsmen of the 1840s viewed themselves as patriots serving society with their miracles of production while incidentally serving themselves. And they saw their workers in the same light. They saw a common bond between master and employee as each worked for the glory of the republic.

The ideological cement for this union of interests between master and employee was the concept of the "self-made man." Master craftsmen pointed to their own success stories as models for their workers to emulate. They constructed a political mythology out of the careers of self-made politicians, such as Jackson and Lincoln, who rose from log cabin to the White House. In the land of opportunity everyone was expected to get ahead, unless he suffered from some defect of character, such as laziness or intemperance. Nothing in this free labor ideology, of course, revealed any acquaintance with the unskilled factory operative or the outworker in the tenement house.

The popular evangelists who traveled the North in the 1830s and 1840s reinforced what masters and employers were saying. Conversion brought freedom in Lord Jesus, but it also demanded the elimination of unseemly habits. The convert was expected to be disciplined, temperate, and a Christian steward to his fellow men. The religious revival added numbers to both the Sabbatarian movement and the temperance movement. Both were middle-class movements aimed at inspiring regular habits and orderly behavior. The missionaries had little direct impact on urban journeymen, who had a tradition of religious rationalism and free thinking. But they helped create a climate in which the twin doctrines of free labor and self-help were a national gospel by mid-century.

CHANGES IN AGRICULTURE

Technology was also changing life on the farm. In 1815, farming methods were little different from those used by the ancient Egyptians five thousand years before. Wooden plows with iron points barely scarred the land; sowing, weeding, and reaping were done with hand, hoe, and scythe. A half-century later, the average American farm was a capitalized food or fiber factory with steel plow, mechanical harvester, and threshing machine.

The agricultural revolution began in the eighteenth century with the discovery of the advantages of lime in reducing soil acidity, crop rotation, deep plowing, and root crops that could keep cattle through the winter. To this scientific data, most of it assembled in Europe, Americans added labor-saving devices. In the 1830s and 1840s, John Deere developed a steel plow able to turn a furrow even in thick midwestern prairie sod. Cyrus Hall McCormick revolutionized grain harvesting with a horse-drawn reaper that could cut in a day as much as a man with a scythe could do in two weeks. McCormick patented his invention in 1831, but he sold few until he moved to Chicago and opened a harvester manufacturing plant in 1847. By using innovative sales techniques, such as free demonstrations and installment purchases, McCormick did much to further farm mechanization. As with labor, farmers found that mechanization had its flaws. As they entered the world market, they found themselves at the mercy of world price trends and increasingly dependent on eastern businessmen for capital and manufactured goods. Farm discontent was allayed by high prices and high demand during the Civil War. But after the war, farmers, like workingmen, would turn to protest and collective action.

⊔ The Machine and the Family

The process of modernization made dramatic changes in both family relationships and the character of the household. In earlier days the household, especially in rural areas, was a self-contained productive unit. Each member contributed to the production of food, clothing, and fuel. Roles, to be sure, were sex-specific—women undertook the cooking, cleaning, spinning, and weaving, while men and boys labored in the fields and woods—but the family was an interdependent unit, with the contribu-

"The Confab." Another painting by Eastman Johnson, "The Confab" represents the changed perception of children, the recognition of childhood as a unique stage of life. Compare with the portrait of the seventeenth century child on page 62.

Courtesy Wadsworth Atheneum, Hartford.

tion of each member understood and valued.

Marketing and manufacturing, even in cities and towns, were likewise home-related activities. The residences of artisans and shopkeepers were usually adjacent to their places of work. No social stigma was attached to women doing manual labor, so wives frequently tended their husband's shops or wore the leather apron of the skilled artisan. Even women who worked for employers outside the household, notably in textiles, did their spinning and weaving at home. The first "manufactories" in America were collection centers established in the major cities in the 1760s to take in yarn and cloth spun and woven by women in their homes.

Power-driven machines, which required buildings to house them, workers to staff them, and people to service the workers—in short, the multiple facets of modernization—changed these traditional family relationships. As commercial farming replaced subsistence and the farmer aimed for the marketplace more than the pantry, the woman's role became that of wife and mother, a role no less demanding but less economically visible than her previous contributions. In the cities, business enterprise became separated from the household. Men left home by day to serve in factories and retail outlets as clerks, machinists, superintendents. Women found work outside the home as schoolteachers and millhands, but they also found the new world of business and professions closed to them. "Women's work," it was commonly felt by the 1830s, was in the home.

These unsettling changes in living patterns were widely perceived but little understood. The rhetoric of Jacksonian Democrats reflected the widespread sense of social malaise, and their political nostrums—hard money, frugal government, separation of government from business—were a tribute to the past, a wistful effort to recover traditional values. Others found the proper antidote for social evil to be the home itself, and its presiding figure, the wife and mother.

THE CULT OF DOMESTICITY

By the 1830s, the Protestant clergy was directing its sermons at women, in part from a tacit realization that a majority of their Sunday morning audience were women. American Protestantism had become feminized over the years, and the clergy responded to that fact. The burden of their message was that women, selfless and sensitive by nature, were the repositories of virtue, and the home, under a woman's governance, was the weighted keel that kept society straight and upright. "It is at home," declared a New Hampshire minister in 1827,

> where man . . . seeks refuge from the vexations and embarrassments of business, an enchanting repose from exertion, a relaxation from care by the interchange of affection: where some of his finest sympathies, tastes, and moral and religious feelings are formed and nourished;—where is the treasury of pure disinterested love, such as is not found in the busy walks of a selfish and calculating world.

Women's magazines, multiplying rapidly, echoed the clergy, creating what historians have called a cult of domesticity. The cult accepted the strange new world wrought by machines and sought to come to terms with it. Its central convention was the contrast between home and world. The male of the family spent his day in the competitive, alien, morally slippery world of business or politics. But he could retire at night to the "shady green lanes of domestic life," where woman soothed his passions and restored his moral fiber. Thus woman and the home sustained traditional values

in a changing world. Care of the household came to be regarded as more than "women's work"; it was a "profession," one crucial to the well-being of society. This identification of sex roles served the interests and desires of men, while giving many women a sense of satisfaction.

Although it offered a satisfying outlet for the intellect and energies of many women, the cult of the home was hardly a liberating force. Indeed, its emphasis on piety and submissiveness left women more confined than ever in a social straitjacket. Nonetheless, within the realm accorded them—the home—the cult of domesticity gave women new recognition and new power. By making women the companions of men, superior to them in some ways, the cult broke the ancient tradition of household patriarchy.

Among the household roles in which the woman was preeminent in the nineteenth century was childrearing. Women had always raised children, but in previous centuries the father was the dominant figure in children's lives. Through the seventeenth century, childrearing manuals were even directed at the father. By the nineteenth century, however, the mother was identified as the primary rearer, and the literature of domesticity extolled the female qualities—piety, tenderness, understanding—that made women better endowed for the task. The new role went hand in hand with a new conception of children. Colonial Americans had viewed children as miniature adults, objects to be shaped for a proper role in society by rigid discipline and physical punishment. In the nineteenth century, sometimes called "the century of the child," children were regarded as precious innocents, to be shielded from the cruel and evil world of adults as long as possible. In this too, the mother was the central figure.

These new responsibilities gave women new decision-making power, though the amount, of course, varied with the individual and the family. Two interesting statistics reflected this new female independence—a falling fertility rate and a rising divorce rate. The fertility rate (which is the average number of children borne by a woman in her childbearing years) and the less accurate but more familiar birth rate (which is the number of births in a year divided by the total population) had both been declining in America since the eighteenth century. The decline began before factories and great cities appeared, so it was not related—as we once supposed—to those deep-seated changes in society, industrialization and urbanization. It was tied instead, it would seem, to the enhanced status of women in the family and the new respect men accorded their wishes. Women had always wished to limit the number of children they bore, since continuous childbirth was both debilitating and dangerous. The cult of domesticity at last enabled them to do it. The number of children borne by the average woman dropped from 7.04 in 1800 to 3.56 in 1900. (These figures apply to white women because there are no comparable data for black women.)

As women's authority within the household increased, so did their control over their own lives. This revealed itself most dramatically in the rising divorce rate, as increasing numbers of women abandoned marriage and family altogether when they found their situation intolerable. Because there were many legal obstacles to divorce in the nineteenth century, the divorce rate was very low when compared to that today. Nevertheless, it rose steadily from the 1840s on. And there was a significant shift in the pattern. At the beginning of the century, most divorces were instituted by men; by the late 1860s, almost two thirds of all divorce actions were begun by women. And of those initiated by husbands, over 80 percent rested on the grounds of their wives' failure to be submissive and subordinate.

Let us summarize these changes in American living patterns:

1. Marriages were based on affection (rather than, say, on a union of wealthy families, as had often been the case in the past), and they endured through mutual respect and friendship.
2. Although family roles continued to be sex-specific (men earned the money, women kept house), within the household there was growing equality of authority, and society perceived women to be morally superior.
3. Both parents increasingly devoted their attention and resources to the rearing of children, and childhood was seen as a special and valuable period in the life of every individual.
4. The family was much smaller in size than it had been in previous centuries. The result, by the end of the nineteenth century, was the "modern" family, the living arrangements we know today.

⊔ Cotton and Slavery

Throughout the period from 1815 to 1860, the nation's principal export and biggest money earner was cotton. Britain's industrial progress created an almost insatiable demand for raw cotton, and the explosion of the American frontier into the rich bottomlands of the Old Southwest answered the need. "Cotton is king!" trumpeted southern patriots in the 1850s, who felt the nation could not live without it. The tiny ball of fluff with its inch-long fiber was not that vital, but it certainly played an important role in American development. And the social system it bred—black slaves, poor whites, and opulent planter-masters—caused political controversy and, ultimately, civil war.

Climate and capitalism stamped cotton on the South, and labor shortage wedded

Courtesy of the New-York Historical Society, New York City

A slave family in the cotton fields.

it to slavery. Because of advances in technology, cotton was the indispensable raw material of the Industrial Revolution. Eli Whitney's invention of the cotton gin in 1793 made it possible for cotton to be grown throughout the South. Whitney's device separated cotton seed from fiber quickly and inexpensively. Cotton required a long growing season, abundant rainfall, and fertile soil, and much of the South, from the Carolinas to Texas, was singularly blessed with all three. Demand for raw cotton kept prices high throughout the pre–Civil War period. By 1840, the American South grew over 60 percent of the world's cotton. Cotton culture, moreover, lent itself to slave labor. It required neither finesse nor special handling. Cotton could be planted, cultivated, and picked by gangs of a hundred or more slaves under the eye of a single overseer.

The southern climate, with its mild winters, also proved conducive to slavery.

Farmers in both North and South found it difficult to find hired help. As long as land was cheap, every man wanted his own farm; few were willing to work for another. In the South, therefore, slavery was the only means by which a planter could expand production and take advantage of rising world demand. In the off season, when the harvest was in, slaves could be used to clear new fields for future expansion. In the North, farmwork stopped through much of the winter, and it was not profitable to maintain an idle labor force. So the North met the labor shortage with machinery and schemes to attract immigrants. Initially, few whites in the North or South considered slavery a moral question.

Reliance on plantation slavery retarded industrialization and the growth of cities. Industrialization required capital; the investment surplus in the South was tied up in land and slaves. Northern capital might have filled the gap, but there was little market for manufactured goods in the South, in any case. The plantations, aided by cheap Yankee shoes and textiles, were nearly self-sufficient. And there was no sizable middle class whose consumer wants might have stimulated local manufacturing. Thus the South bound itself in an economic straitjacket of cotton and slavery.

THE PECULIAR INSTITUTION

Both adaptable and profitable, slavery was a remarkably pliant institution. It was just as efficient to own one slave as one hundred (in terms of output per work hour).

A large slaveowner could produce more cotton or tobacco than a small slaveowner, but he also had more expenses to maintain a labor force. So small slaveowners could compete effectively, though they were sometimes dependent on wealthier neighbors for marketing facilities, such as shipping docks and sales agents. As a result, the vast majority possessed only a few slaves. Throughout the entire South there were only about 10,000 large-scale planters (those who owned fifty or more slaves). And except in the Appalachian highlands, slavery permeated all levels and all regions of the South. It was even adaptable to cities. Slaves worked in iron foundries, in tobacco factories, and in shipyards. Many were

Slavery and southern agriculture.

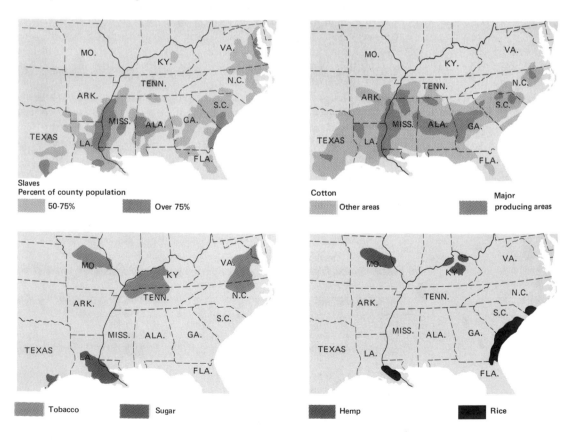

Slaves
Percent of county population
50-75%   Over 75%

Cotton
Other areas   Major producing areas

Tobacco   Sugar

Hemp   Rice

skilled artisans, who were often hired out by their masters to others. Some even worked for wages and earned enough to purchase their freedom.

For the whites, slavery was also a remarkably profitable institution. The price of "prime field hands" rose steadily from the revolution to the Civil War, as did the annual fee for slave rentals. The returns on the South's investment correspond roughly with the returns on the North's investment in capital goods. Slaveholding was frustrating, morally debilitating, and sometimes dangerous, but it was certainly profitable for any planter who paid attention to his fields and his balance sheets.

It was profitable, in part, because of the opening of virgin cotton lands in Mississippi, Louisiana, and Texas. The need for labor in these new regions helped keep slave prices high everywhere. Throughout the pre–Civil War decades, the upper South "exported" slaves to the lower South. Planters in the older states, working depleted soils and facing steadily smaller crop yields, sometimes found it was more profitable to grow slaves than tobacco. (This is not to say that they "bred" slaves by force, as they have sometimes been accused of doing. This would have been impossible, and it was unnecessary because healthy, ad-equately fed people reproduce naturally.) The black birth rate in North America exceeded the death rate as early as 1720, and the natural increase in the black population (slave and free) was roughly equal to the natural increase in whites thereafter. (The white population increased faster than the black between 1790 and 1860, but that was due to immigration.)

The sale and transport of helpless people entailed terrible suffering, as marriages were broken and children separated, but it was part of the westward migration. Whites departed from Virginia and Maryland in about the same proportion as blacks, though the whites left voluntarily.

Although valued for their reproductive abilities, slave women were expected to participate fully in the plantation work force. Older and pregnant women might be assigned some of the less grueling tasks, but all others hoed weeds and picked cotton right along with the men. Indeed, like free working mothers, those with families found themselves with double burdens. After working in the fields all day they had to cook and care for their families at night. New mothers often had to nurse their infants in the fields.

Force was at the root of slavery, and fear. Slaves feared the lash; masters and

---

Black Population of the United States, 1800–1860

	Total Black Population	Percentage of Total U.S. Population	Free People of Color	Free Blacks as a Percentage of Black Population
1800	1,002,000	18.9	108,000	10.8
1810	1,378,000	19.0	186,000	13.5
1820	1,772,000	18.4	234,000	13.2
1830	2,329,000	18.1	320,000	13.7
1840	2,874,000	16.8	386,000	13.4
1850	3,639,000	15.7	435,000	11.9
1860	4,442,000	14.1	488,000	11.0

From Norton et al., *A People and a Nation: A History of the United States,* Copyright © 1982 by Houghton Mifflin Company. Used with permission.

overseers feared rebellion. The institution imprisoned both races, yet somehow they found ways to accommodate. The master's power was limited by state law and his own self-interest. The laws, known as slave codes, prohibited masters from murdering or mutilating their slaves, though "moderate" punishment, such as whipping, was everywhere permitted. There were instances of sadistic cruelty, but most masters treated their slaves with reasonable care. Slaves were valuable property; injuring or maiming them made no sense. The purpose of slavery was profit, and that goal was best achieved by providing slaves with food, clothing, and shelter adequate enough to keep them productive.

Slaves fought the system in subtle and violent ways. They learned how to mock their masters while seeming to flatter them, and they exploited the tensions between the master and overseer or between white overseer and black slavedriver. They were often careless with tools, neglectful of property, and hard on animals—all subtle, perhaps even unconscious, forms of sabotage. And they were masters of deception, because it was essential to survival in a situation where the slightest offense brought a whipping or extra work assignments. One runaway recounted in his memoirs how slaves supplemented their diets on his plantation. A party of men would go into the woods and capture two or three opossums. They skinned these and buried the carcasses. They then stole two or three of the master's pigs, cleaned them, buried the entrails, and put them in a cooking pot. When the master came by and inquired what was in the kettle, he was told "possum" and shown the skins as proof.

THE UNDERGROUND RAILROAD

Running away was the most common form of resistance, and the most futile. As many as one thousand a year, by common esti-mate, escaped to the North. But even there they were not safe, because federal law allowed southerners to pursue their runaways into the North and recapture them. In the North a secret network that called itself the Underground Railroad helped pass runaways on to the safety of Canada. Working by night, "conductors" led parties of runaways from "station" to "station" until they crossed into Canada at Niagara or Detroit.

Brave and romantic though it was, the Underground Railroad was able to aid only a fraction of the runaways, and it hardly affected the slave population at all. Nearly all those who fled to the North came from the border states—Maryland, Virginia, and Kentucky. There was little chance of escaping from the deep South because of the distance to be traveled and the road patrols. Armed slave patrols rode on horseback and were accompanied by dogs. They could punish and even kill any slave caught beyond the boundaries of his plantation without a written pass. The one chance a slave had was that the patrols, manned usually by neighborhood poor whites, could not read or write, so that any sort of document, even the torn fragment of a letter, served as a pass. Even so, few runaways from the lower South made their way to freedom. Most hid in the woods for a few days until cold, hunger, and fear of wild animals drove them back to the plantation.

SLAVE REVOLTS

Slave rebellions were not common, but they occurred with enough regularity to keep the white population in constant apprehension. There are more than one hundred uprisings and conspiracies on record between 1700 and 1860, and there may have been many more. In August of 1800, Virginians uncovered a conspiracy organized by the slave "General" Gabriel Prosser, who planned to seize the Richmond armory, kill all slaveowners in the vicinity, and free their slaves. Gabriel was captured and executed along with about thirty-five of his followers. A similar conspiracy was uncovered in Charleston, South Carolina, in 1822. This one was led by a free black named Denmark Vesey. A carpenter by trade, Vesey had ample opportunity to travel through the South Carolina low country making contacts with potential conspirators on the rice plantations. A house servant betrayed him, however, and Charleston authorities arrested, tried, and hanged him. Some testimony at his trial placed the number of conspirators at 9,000 or more, while others estimated it at about 500.

The most serious slave rebellion was that organized by Nat Turner in southern Virginia in August 1831. A slave preacher known as The Prophet among Southampton County's slaves, Turner had religious visions in which an angry God instructed him to free slaves and punish their guilty masters. Unlike Prosser and Vesey, Turner did not attempt to organize a conspiracy; rather, he expected the uprising to spread spontaneously as he and a few trusted followers moved from plantation to plantation. Starting just after midnight on August 22, Turner cut a swath of destruction across Southampton County, beginning with his own master, who, Turner himself confessed, had treated him kindly. Turner eventually recruited a band of between 60 and 70 insurgents, slaughtered some 60 whites, and sacked 15 homesteads. Armed principally with knives and swords, the rebels were no match for white militia. After a short fight the blacks dispersed, and Turner was captured a few weeks later. Proud and defiant even in custody, Turner was tried and executed along with 21 followers. On a rampage of their own, white militia murdered more than 120 innocent blacks in retribution.

The marvel is that there were not more such acts of violence. The bloody uprisings in the West Indies and in Latin America demonstrated slaves' capacity for organizing revolution. The reason that there were comparatively few revolts lies in numbers. Except for isolated portions of the South, such as the South Carolina low country, slaves were vastly outnumbered by the white population. Among whites, even nonslaveholders had a vested interest in the institution, for it gave them status and a sense of superiority. To southern poor whites, freed blacks meant social and economic competition, so an army of whites could be mustered at the first hint of slave resistance. Rebellions were few for the simple reason that they were hopeless.

THE SLAVE COMMUNITY

The fundamental requirement of survival for most slaves meant an outward acceptance of white domination. "Militants" were whipped until their spirits were broken, and if they could not be broken, they were given a "walking ticket to the south." Those who submitted maintained their self-respect by developing a culture of which whites were largely unaware. The African heritage was an essential part of this subculture—African language, folklore, art, dances, and religion. Slaves communicated with one another in a *patois*, a mixture of English and Africanisms that amounted to a new language. Drivers and house servants who had to deal daily with whites were forced to be bilingual, with English as a second language. In low-country South Carolina, where blacks, being a majority, resisted white acculturalization, the Gullah dialect bore a close resemblance to languages found along the Guinea coast. For transplanted Africans, language was an important link with the "old country," just as it was among Pennsylvania Dutch and other immigrant nationalities.

A communications "grapevine" bound this culture together from plantation to plantation and even from state to state.

Even when the master did not permit any association with slaves of another plantation, his people knew of conditions elsewhere. They encountered one another while running errands for their masters or waiting for corn to be ground at the community mill. They compared experiences, exchanged information. Spirituals were also part of the communications media. When a slave planned to flee, he might bid farewell to his friends by walking through the slave quarters singing,

When dat ar old chariot comes,
I'm gwine to lebe you,
I'm bound for de promised land. . . .

Harriet Tubman, the only Underground Railroad "conductor" who penetrated the South to lead runaways to freedom (nineteen trips between 1849 and 1860), led her charges at night, giving directions, issuing instructions and warnings, all through song.

Slaves who could read were deeply respected in the slave quarters. They often gained access to newspapers from white merchants by passing as free men or agents of their masters. Through these they followed as best they could national politics and the progress of the northern antislavery movement. One escapee recorded in his autobiography that even in Kentucky, where he had been a slave, emancipation in the British West Indies was being discussed in the slave quarters a short time after it occurred. He said the news brought great joy, for Kentucky slaves were sure that they would be next.

The family was the repository of this Afro-American culture; through family relationships, oral traditions were passed from one generation to another. Southern law did not recognize slave marriages, but they existed. Some were entered into with formal ceremony, such as jumping over a broomstick, a custom common in western Africa. Surviving plantation records indi-

cate that the traditional family unit—husband, wife, and children—was the norm among slaves, and marriage ties often survived separation and sale. Slave parents named their own children (rarely was this privilege accorded to a master), and they usually named them after aunts, uncles, or grandparents in a deliberate effort to maintain kinship ties.

Evidence abounds of the deep affection and tenderness within slave families. The following father's lament is but one poignant example:

> I am a father, and have had the same feelings of unspeakable anguish as I have looked upon my precious babes, and have thought of the ignorance, degradation, and woe which they must endure as slaves. The great God who knoweth all the secrets of the earth, and He only, knows the bitter sorrow I now feel, when I think of my four dear children who are slaves, torn from me and consigned to hopeless servitude by the iron hand of ruthless wrong. I love those children with all a father's fondness.*

Religion was also a vital feature of the Afro-American culture. One former slave described the religion of the slave quarters as "Not nearly so complicated as the white man's religion but more closely observed." Slaves accepted Christianity, but they modified it to suit their own needs. Christianity comforted them because it placed a Heavenly Master above the earthly one and thus defined the moral limits of slavery. Even the most harsh of slaveholders was ultimately subject to heavenly judgment. Although certain passages of the Bible seemed to justify slavery, others clearly limited what one human being could do to another. And the slaves were well aware that many faiths viewed slavery as contrary to the teachings of Christ.

Not surprisingly, the slaves ignored reli-

* From *The Experience and Personal Narrative of Uncle Tom Jones: Who Was for Forty Years a Slave* (1858).

CLIO'S FOCUS: Self-Portrait of a Slave

"Typical" and "average" are words that come too easily to the pens of historians. Omar ibn Said was neither: He was extraordinary in many ways. He wrote an autobiography, and not many slaves did that. It was written in Arabic script because, he said, he had forgotten his own language, meaning the language of his West African home. His homeland was Futa Toro, one of the states of the kingdom of Fula. Omar ibn Said was born about 1770 in a village on the bank of the Senegal River. His father was apparently a man of considerable wealth who taught his children genteel manners. Even as a slave, Omar ibn Said commanded respect from those around him. A Presbyterian clergyman who helped convert him to Christianity described him thus: "Meroh's fingers are rather effeminate. They are very well tapered. His whole person and gait bear marks of considerable refinement." Omar Said suffered considerable hardship in his first years as a slave simply because he was not accustomed to manual labor. He was not typical, but his life story still tells us much about what it was like to be a slave.

Omar ibn Said wrote his autobiography in 1831, held it for five years, and then sent it to Paul, or Lahmen Kebby (most slaves had both Christian and African names), a freedman who was in New York at the time awaiting transport to Liberia. He also passed on to Paul a Bible that had been translated into Arabic. Perhaps he intended both documents for the enlightenment of African relatives. Paul instead had the fifteen-page autobiography translated into English for the enlightenment of white Americans.

The manuscript begins with several pages of Muslim prayers, though Omar ibn Said had by then been converted to Christianity. His story follows:

> My name is Omar ibn Seid. My birthplace was Fat Tur, between the two rivers. I sought knowledge under the instruction of a Sheikh called Mohammed Seid, my own brother, and Sheikh Soleiman Kembeh, and Sheikh Gabriel Abdal. I continued my studies twenty-five years, and then returned to my home where I remained six years.

Omar's father, we know from other sources, was killed in war when Omar was only five or six, and an uncle took him to his home in the city of Fula. The sheikhs of whom he speaks were Muslim schoolmasters who taught him Arabic, arithmetical calculation, and science. When he reached adulthood, Omar became a cloth merchant, which may have been a family trade. These details he omitted from his autobiography, which resumes:

> Then there came to our place a large army, who killed many men, and took me, and brought me to the great sea, and sold me into the hands of the Christians, who bound me and sent me on board a great ship and we sailed upon the great sea a month and a half,

when we came to a place called Charleston in the Christian language. There they sold me to a small, weak, and wicked man, called Johnson, a complete infidel, who had no fear of God at all. Now I am a small man and unable to do hard work, so I fled from the hand of Johnson and after a month came to a place called Fayd-il [Fayetteville, North Carolina].

The most remarkable feature of this story is what it does not say. Omar ibn Said does not burden his reader with the horrors of the "middle passage," the mechanics of escape, or the difficulties of surviving in the swamps and pine barrens of eastern Carolina. In the story of his capture there is likewise more between the lines than in them:

On the new moon I went into a church to pray. A lad saw me and rode off to the place of his father and informed him that he had seen a black man in the church. A man named Handah and another man with him on horseback came attended by a troop of dogs. They took me and made me go with them twelve miles to a place called Fayd-il, where they put me into a great house from which I could not go out. I continued in the great house (which in the Christian language they called *jail*) sixteen days and nights.

It is part of North Carolina lore that Omar, who was arrested as a vagrant and advertised for sale as a slave, "astonished the natives" by writing in Arabic on the walls of the jail. "Astonished" is to put it mildly. That a slave could write at all was unusual, since the law prohibited slave literacy. That one might bide his time with extended discourse in an alien script was awesome, even frightening. Fortunately there lived in the vicinity a planter, James Owen, with the sensitivity to appreciate genius. He went to the jail out of curiosity, and after inquiring whether Omar would be willing to go with him, purchased the African and took him to his country home, Milton, in Bladen County, North Carolina. After describing this turn of events, Omar writes of the happy result:

O ye people of North Carolina, O ye People of South Carolina, O ye people of America all of you; have you among you two such men as Jim Owen and John Owen? [John was brother of James, and recently retired governor of North Carolina.] These men are good men. What food they eat they give me to eat. As they clothe themselves they clothe me. They permit me to read the gospel of God, our Lord, and Saviour, and King; who regulates all our circumstances, our health and wealth, and who bestows his mercies willingly, not by constraint. . . .

I continue in the hand of Jim Owen who never beats me, nor scolds me. I neither go hungry or naked, and I have no hard work to do. I am not able to do hard work for I am a small man and feeble. During the last twenty years I have known no want in the hand of Jim Owen.

Omar ibn Said wrote this when he was in his sixties. He lived, according to report, until after the Civil War. He was an unusual man, and so was his master. But the accommodation the two reached, founded on mutual respect and tinted with friendship, was not uncommon.

gious concepts that could be used to justify their degradation, such as original sin, and they had no use for predestination. They preferred the evangelical churches, which emphasized the potential for universal salvation. Slave spirituals were hymns of joy, exploring themes of deliverance and final justice. The sermons of slave preachers, on the other hand, dwelt on the struggles of the ancient Israelites, the prophecies of destruction by fire and pestilence, and the fire and brimstone the Lord visited upon evildoers. One former slave reported that in his part of the South the slaves believed that all slaveholders would be tortured in hell when they passed on, and if any entered heaven it was only by the special sufferance of some saintly slave. Religion, offering both hope and revenge, was the slaves' ultimate escape mechanism.

The African subculture enabled slaves to cope and to survive, but it never reconciled them to their lot. The outward acceptance, however, misled slave owners, who commonly assumed that "their people" were happy, or too ignorant to be otherwise. Nothing illustrated the gulf between black and white better than the angry surprise with which whites, in the last months of the Civil War, learned that their servants, even the most trusted and beloved "mammies," would run away at the first opportunity. The system, whatever face was put on it, was essentially a tyrannical one.

SLAVERY AND SOUTHERN HONOR

Slavery affected the southern mind in a thousand little ways. No matter how loudly they might defend the institution in public, southerners could not escape the private guilt. Guilt, plus anxiety over the implications of miscegenation, led to intense concern among white males with proving their manhood. Sexual liaisons, usually between a white master or overseer and a slave woman, had always been part of the institution, but by the 1850s there appeared to be growing a separate "race" of mulattoes. In 1850, the federal census determined that 7.7 percent of the American population was mulatto (by legal definition, a mulatto could be up to seven-eighths white). In 1860, mulattoes were 10.4 percent of the population, an increase of 35 percent. In compensation for their sexual infidelities and to shore up their manhood, white males loudly and sometimes violently defended the honor of southern white women.

Southerners developed a peculiarly intense form of the cult of domesticity. Southern white women were placed on a pedestal of asexual purity, and black women became associated with degraded promiscuity. As in the northern version of the cult, women were the repositories of virtue and the moral foundation of the republic. But in the South, the source of evil was black. Freeing the slaves, it was assumed, would release a flood of savage passions threatening not only white women but civilization itself. Thus the defense of women became enmeshed with the defense of the South itself. An abolitionist attack on the South became an attack on white womanhood. Honor, both their own and that of their women, required southern whites to rush to the defense of their region and their culture. In defense of honor, southern boys by the tens of thousands, many of whom had never owned a slave, would go off to war—and death.

SUMMARY

Bustling decades, the 1820s, 1830s, and 1840s; each seemed more frantic than the last. Irish and German immigrants poured into the eastern seaports and joined a tide of humanity flowing into the continental heartland. Transportation hubs—Cleveland, Cincinnati, Chicago, St. Louis—doubled in size every decade. Everyone was on the move. But the rootlessness carried a price: Disorder and violence were the hallmarks of the time. The rapid pace of social change, and the disorder, alarmed those who held the traditional values of rural, Protestant America. The challenge of the cities, with their unruly populations holding alien creeds, traditionalists felt to be a moral one. They used the instruments of religion—missions, Bible tracts, and Sunday Schools—to meet it. The results were meager. At mid-century, American cities were still turbulent and crime-ridden, dens of corruption and misgovernment.

A revolution in transportation accelerated the pace of social and economic change. Steamboats began working the western rivers in 1811 and remained the principal carriers of goods and passengers until the Civil War. The Erie Canal, opened in 1825, ushered in the canal era, which was followed soon after by the opening of the railroad era. By 1860, the railroads were a billion-dollar industry, the nation's first, and their demands for coal and steel paced the industrial revolution.

The factory system of production began in New England in the 1790s and prospered behind the protective shield of embargo and war. In 1814 a consortium of Massachusetts investors established at Lowell the first integrated factory, which brought all the stages of textile manufacture under one roof. For a time the Lowell businessmen experimented with using the labor of New England farm girls. The Lowell Girls were well housed, closely supervised, and kept intellectually alive by publishing their own monthly magazine. In the 1830s, they were replaced by Irish immigrants, who were cheaper and more docile. Workers in other mill towns, experiencing similar difficulties, came to feel they were helpless cogs in an implacable economic machine. From this growing consciousness emerged the first labor unions. Court decisions in several states made unions legal enterprises, but without active governmental protection, unions remained weak until the twentieth century.

Modernization also changed family relationships. Business enterprise became separated from the household; men went away by day to work in factories, shipping centers, or retail stores. The spatial gap between home and business soon became a moral gap. The home and its governess, the woman, came to be regarded as the repository of traditional values, the pillar of civilization, restoring at night the moral fiber men lost in the course of the business day. This cult of domesticity stifled women intellectually and economically more than ever. But within the realm accorded them—the household—they had more power and responsibility than before. A falling fertility rate and a rising divorce rate together suggest that women had new decision-making power by the middle of the century.

While factories and machines came to characterize the North, cotton and slavery increasingly characterized the South. Slavery, an institution of uncertain future at the time of the revolution, gained new vitality with the invention of the cotton gin in 1793 and the spread of cotton culture throughout the South. Though frustrating and dangerous, from the standpoint of the slaveholder slavery was undeniably profitable. The price of slaves increased steadily until the Civil War, fed by demand from the new cotton lands opened in the Southwest. Ironically, slavery was again an institution of uncertain future in 1860, Civil War or no. Cotton prices fell in the 1860s due to competition from India and Egypt, and textiles had become less glamorous investments than steel, railroads, and oil.

Slaves battled the system by verbal means, by sabotage and arson, by running away, and occasionally by open rebellion. But rebellion was rare, largely because it was hopeless. Slaves were a minority of the population even in the South. Even if momentarily successful, rebels had no future. As a result, the vast majority of slaves accommodated themselves to the system. They developed an Afro-American subculture within the plantation community, relying heavily on African folklore, art, dance, and religion. The repository of this subculture was the family, which handed oral traditions from one generation to another. Kinship ties, preserved by a child-naming system, extended across plantations and even across state lines. The African subculture enabled slaves to cope and survive, but it never reconciled them to their lot. When the Civil War offered them a chance, they fled to freedom by the tens of thousands.

READING SUGGESTIONS

The phenomenon of modernization needs further scholarly exploration, but a good introduction to the subject is Richard D. Brown, *Modernization: The Transformation of American Life, 1600–1865* (1976). John F. Kasson, *Civilizing the Machine: Technology and Republican Values in America, 1776–1900* (1976), is another slant on the problem. Sam Bass Warner, *The Urban Wilderness: A History of the American City* (1972), is the standard authority on the growth of cities. Anthony F. C. Wallace's *Rockdale: The Growth of an American Village in the Early Industrial Revolution* (1980) is a sensitive and splendidly written account of a Pennsylvania mill town. Merritt Roe Smith, *Harper's Ferry Armory and the New Technology* (1977), chronicles the social impact of the growth of the machine tool industry. A good survey of immigration and the assimilation process is Thomas J. Archdeacon's *Becoming American: An Ethnic History* (1983). Michael Feldberg, *The Turbulent Era: Riot and Disorder in Jacksonian America* (1980), points up the social stresses of the age, and Paul Boyer, *Urban Masses and Moral Order in America 1820–1920* (1978), studies the efforts of traditionalists to control them.

Douglass C. North, *Economic Growth of the United States, 1790–1860* (1961), stresses the importance of cotton exports in the growth of the American economy, while Stuart Bruchey, *The Roots of American Economic Growth, 1607–1861* (1965), sees other factors influencing America's industrial takeoff. Paul Gates, *The Farmer's Age: Agriculture 1815–1860* (1960), and George R. Taylor, *The Transportation Revolution, 1815–1860* (1951), are the standard authorities on those sectors of the economy. More specific studies include Carter Goodrich, *Government Promotion of American Canals and Railroads 1800–1890* (1960), and Albert Fishlow, *American Railroads and the Transformation of the Ante-Bellum Economy* (1965).

For the impact of modernization on women and the family, Carl Degler's superb synthesis, *At Odds: Women and the Family from the Revolution to the Present* (1980), is indispensable. Joseph F. Kett, *Rites of Passage: Adolescence in America, 1790 to the Present* (1977), treats another aspect of the problem. Two pioneering essays are Robert Wells, "Women's Lives Transformed— Demographic Patterns in America, 1600–

1970," in Berkin and Norton, eds., *Women of America: A History* (1979), and Francis Kobrin, "The Fall in Household Size and the Rise of the Primary Individual in the United States," in Gordon, ed., *The American Family in Social-Historical Perspective* (1978). The story of the Lowell Girls is told by Hannah Josephson in *Golden Threads* (1949). Lynn Y. Weiner, *From Working Girl to Working Mother: The Female Labor Force in the United States, 1820–1980* (1985), provides a brief survey of that subject, nicely tied together by a fresh synthesis.

Sean Wilentz's prize-winning work, *Chants Democratic: New York City and the Rise of the American Working Class, 1788–1850* (1984), traces the degradation of work and the rise of labor consciousness even before the advent of industrialization.

Bertram Wyatt-Brown, *Southern Honor: Eth-ics and Behavior in the Old South* (1982), examines the cultural ethos that bound southerners together and ultimately induced them to fight for their way of life. F. N. Boney, in *Southerners All (1984),* sees a bourgeois spirit among antebellum southern whites that was not much different from the capitalistic, aggrandizing spirit of the bourgeois North. Eugene Genovese's brilliant work, *Roll, Jordan, Roll* (1974), is now the fundamental work on slavery, especially useful for the analysis of the interaction of masters and slaves. The Afro-American subculture is the topic of two very important books: John Blassingame's *Slave Community* (1972) and Herbert G. Gutman's *The Black Family in Slavery and Freedom, 1750–1925* (1976). Deborah Gray White, *Ain't I a Woman* (1984), provides a unique look at the lives of female slaves in the plantation South.

12

"THE MILLENNIAL MORNING HAS DAWNED": Religion and Reform

Alexis de Tocqueville, a young Frenchman who toured the United States in the 1830s, concluded that the Christian religion had "a greater influence over the souls of men" in America than in any other country. The root of this influence, Tocqueville shrewdly observed, was the principle of voluntary membership. Unlike Europe, where a state-church affiliation was common, American churches were forced to compete for members and were free of political controversy. As a result, the churches actually strengthened their hold on American society after the revolution. By the time Tocqueville wrote, about three out of four adult Americans had some sort of connection with a church. So much power did the clergy seem to have over the manners and morals of Americans that Tocqueville considered religion "the foremost of the political institutions of the country." Christianity, Americans of all shades of political opinion agreed, was essential to the preservation of the republic. In the form of evangelical Protestantism, it was also a powerful force for social experiment and reform.

⊔ The Second Awakening

Beginning with a huge western revival in 1800, waves of religious enthusiasm swept across the United States in the first half of the nineteenth century. The camp meeting, which was to become a familiar feature of frontier revivals, made its first appearance at Cane Ridge, Kentucky, in the 1800 revival. People came from great distances, sometimes more than a hundred miles, to gather for several days of uninterrupted preaching and prayers. Methodist, Baptist, and Presbyterian evangelists, ignoring the theological niceties that separated their churches, followed one another to the platform in round-the-clock rotation. People

accustomed to rural isolation were susceptible to such an emotional atmosphere. Tormented souls shouted or moaned, jumped uncontrollably, or writhed on the ground.

The camp meeting was a frontier phenomenon, but religious enthusiasm was not confined to the frontier. The next wave appeared in the late 1820s in the "boom towns" along the Erie Canal—Rochester, Utica, Syracuse. The leading evangelist of this awakening, Charles Grandison Finney, was a small-town lawyer before he met Jesus (quite literally, he claimed), became a Presbyterian minister, and took to the road. Finney appealed to the middle classes of these mushrooming cities, who fretted about social disorder and moral decay. As noted in the previous chapter, Finney and other evangelists early turned their attention to the violent and vice-ridden cities of the seaboard, so that by the 1850s, cities, rather than the frontier, were the principal centers of religious enthusiasm.

A DEMOCRATIC RELIGION

The nineteenth-century revivals changed the character of American Protestantism. Evangelists were more concerned with behavior than with fine points of theology. As a result, the revivals fostered a spirit of interdenominational brotherhood. They also encouraged active lay participation. The spirit of democracy, which permeated American society and politics in the Jacksonian era, extended even to Heaven. The bleak Calvinism of the Puritans gave way to a sunny promise of salvation for all who willed it. Even in the eighteenth century, the Methodists had altered the Calvinist doctrine of predestination by preaching that God had given every person the ability to respond to the call of the Gospel, to be sanctified and cleansed.

This blend of free will and universal

(*Chapter opening photo*) "The Whisky War in Ohio," a cartoon satirizing the temperance movement.

atonement became the standard theological fare of nineteenth-century evangelism. Charles G. Finney, for instance, took the view that all men and women possessed a "natural ability" to choose the right path, and that by a combination of human will and God's benevolence, it was possible to sanctify all humankind. When this happened, the earth would experience the millennium predicted by the Bible. Finney was not alone in this belief. Indeed, all the nineteenth-century evangelists believed their mission was to prepare for Christ's second coming by bringing sinners to the Gospel. That he would begin his work in America seemed only natural, for from the earliest Puritans, Americans had commonly assumed it was their mission to serve as a model for the regeneration of humankind.

In 1836, William Miller, a western New York convert with an instinct for precision, published a book claiming that scriptural references to the return of Christ pointed to a Second Coming "about the year 1843." Miller's book and his circuit preaching won him a following. When the year passed and a second, more precise, date in 1844 came and went, Miller's following fell away, but millennialism was not discredited. Two of the churches that emerged from the Second Awakening, the Mormons and the Seventh Day Adventists, made it central to their teaching. The Millerite excitement, in fact, helped spread millennarian ideas among the churches of evangelical leaning—notably Methodist, Baptist, and Presbyterian.

Millennialism, as expounded by Finney or, in mid-century, by Henry Ward Beecher, was also a catalyst for social reform. Preparing the kingdom for the coming of the King required the elimination of social evils, such as taverns and bawdyhouses, war, and even slavery. In fact, the democratization of Heaven and the democratization of society went hand in hand. The millennium described by the evangelists was a tension-free, egalitarian society. When they denounced sin, they specified excessive wealth, luxury, and materialism more often than carnal faults. Aid to the poor was as high on their agenda as temperance. "The loss of interest in benevolent enterprises," growled Charles G. Finney as late as 1868, was usually evidence of a "backslidden heart." Among the enterprises he thought worthy of Christian endeavor were good government, Christian education, temperance reform, the abolition of slavery, and relief for the poor.

The Great Revival was further linked to social reform in its impact on women. Women were far more susceptible than men to the ministrations of the evangelists. During an 1838 Baptist revival in Utica, New York, for instance, women, who made up only half the population, were 72 percent of the converts. The reason, apparently, is that choice of church, along with marital partner, was one of the few decisions that women were allowed. Commitment to a church offered a woman a degree of control, as well as something with which to identify. Ministers came to recognize the preponderance of women in their congregations, and before long their sermons were directed at women, appealing to them to use their new-found faith and innate benevolence to change the world. This in turn gave women a legitimate reason to move out of the home and into the public arena. They came to dominate the many improvement societies that sprang from the religious revival. Temperance, because of the threat presented by alcohol to the security of the home, was an early concern of theirs, and so, before long, was antislavery.

TRANSCENDENTALISM— THE CREED OF RATIONALISTS AND ROMANTICS

Evangelical religion, with its emphasis on free will, divine benevolence, and good works, was a death blow to orthodox Calvinism. The harsh doctrines of the Puritans had been yielding to a more liberal theology since the late seventeenth century. This liberalizing tendency was called Arminianism, after the Dutch theologian Jacobus Arminius, who was executed by Orthodox Calvinists for his teachings in 1609. Arminius had pointed out that Calvinist doctrine, which viewed the vast majority of humankind as depraved and wicked, made God, as creator of man, the author of evil, which is a theological absurdity. Arminius suggested instead that men and women, for all their sins, were fundamentally good and capable, if they so willed, of obtaining salvation. One strain of Arminian thought led, by way of Wesley and the Methodists, to the evangelical creed of Finney and the Beechers. Another strain worked to liberalize the Calvinist churches—Congregational and Presbyterian—from within.

Religious rationalism, or deism, which accompanied the eighteenth-century Enlightenment, hastened the liberalizing process. Deists such as Tom Paine raised doubts about such orthodox doctrines as the Trinity and the divinity of Christ. In England some religious rationalists called themselves Unitarians, and orthodox Congregationalists fastened the label on American liberals after 1800. It was a disparaging label, for it implied that the liberals believed in a single divinity, rather than the Trinity, and therefore were not Christian at all. In 1819, William Ellery Channing, pastor of Boston's Federal Street Church and a leading liberal, accepted the name Unitarian, and in a well-publicized sermon he set forth the position of the new church.

Unitarians, said Channing, viewed God as merciful and loving, not angry and vindictive. Similarly, men and women were fundamentally good, blessed with free will, and capable of pursuing upright lives. There is nothing in Scripture, said Channing, to support the doctrine of predestination. The Bible itself ought to be approached rationally, as a historical document. And Christ, as depicted in the Bible, was certainly a good man, perhaps the best of men, but he was not necessarily divine. The question of Christ's divinity would be up to each individual to decide. Indeed, the essence of Unitarianism was tolerance, a respect for each individual's perception of the truth.

Transcendentalism was a blend of Unitarian rationalism and Romanticism, with

American Romanticism. Horatio Greenough (1805–1852) set up a sculpture studio in Florence, Italy, shortly after he graduated from Harvard. Daniel Webster suggested that Greenough do a monumental statue of George Washington for the Capitol rotunda. Following the neoclassical mode, Greenough clad Washington in a Roman toga. The sculpture was greeted with general derision. One comic suggested that Washington looked like he was waiting for his bath. It is now retired to the Smithsonian Institution in Washington, D.C.

National Museum of American Art, Smithsonian Institution.

a dash of German philosophy. The Romantic movement originated around the turn of the century among the poets and painters of England and Germany. It was a revolt against the eighteenth century's worship of reason. Romantics emphasized the importance of intuition and will. They liked the wild, the primitive, and the unfinished. The Romantic ideal was the natural human, the "noble savage." In American writing, this attitude surfaced in the 1820s in the Leatherstocking tales of James Fenimore Cooper, such as *The Deerslayer* and *The Last of the Mohicans*. Cooper's heroes, frontiersman Natty Bumppo and his Indian friend Chingachook, were untutored and simple beings endowed with marvelous physical skills and a natural morality untainted by contact with civilization. In later years the Romantic mood permeated the writings of Herman Melville, whose *Typee* and *Omoo* were set in the exotic surroundings of the South Pacific, and whose *Moby Dick* depicted with rich symbolism the elemental struggle between man and whale. In American painting, Romanticism influenced the works of the Hudson River School, painters whose landscapes were wild and untamed, virgin, and even a bit ghostly.

The catalyst for the strange compound of rationalism and Romanticism was Ralph Waldo Emerson, a Unitarian minister who resigned his pastorate because he found the church too chill and dispassionate. Emerson came into contact with European thought at Harvard College in the 1820s. He and a circle of like-minded friends living in Boston and Concord, Massachusetts, began calling themselves the Transcendental Club in 1836. The group included Unitarian clergymen Theodore Parker and George Ripley, teachers Margaret Fuller and Bronson Alcott, and writers Henry David Thoreau and Nathaniel Hawthorne. The Transcendentalists believed that God, or "the Oversoul" in Emerson's term, existed in all matter and spirit. So each human being had within himself or herself a spark of divinity. Having this divine quality, each individual knew intuitively what was right and just. Transcendentalists urged each person to follow only the dictates of conscience, even when those dictates were contrary to social rules. Thoreau refused to pay his taxes because he thought the government's war with Mexico in 1846 was unjust. Clapped in jail, he wrote his famous *Essay on Civil Disobedience*. "Must the citizen," Thoreau asked, "ever for a moment, or in the least degree, resign his conscience to the legislator? Why has every man a conscience, then?"

John James Audubon (1785–1851). One of the features of nineteenth-century romanticism was a rediscovery of the wilderness, a reverence for the wild and the primitive. John James Audubon reflected this spirit as he traveled the American backwoods making drawings of its wildlife. His *Birds of America* was published between 1826 and 1838.

Library of Congress.

By its stress on the free individual, Transcendentalism was also a philosophy of reform. Reform, wrote Emerson, was a matter of eliminating evils that fettered human freedom—evils such as liquor, war, slavery. All such change was to be brought about by human conscience. Transcendentalists assigned no positive role to the government; indeed, Emerson agreed with the Jacksonian slogan: "That government is best which governs least."

⊔ Religion and Social Reform

Evangelists and Transcendentalists, though they came to their beliefs by widely separated paths, were agreed on the need for social improvement. They were in general agreement also on the evils that beset society and on the means of eradicating them: individuals working in benevolent associations. Benevolent societies were the emblems of the age. There was one for every conceivable social need—poor relief, care of the deaf and dumb, care of the blind, prison reform, preservation of the Sabbath, one even for the salvation of seamen.

Spreading benevolence fulfilled a number of social and psychological needs. For the religious convert, doing God's work offered additional assurance of attaining his grace. Insofar as they blotted out social evils, good works also promoted law and order, thus creating a more promising environment for the entrepreneurial ambitions of merchants, shopkeepers, and master craftsmen. No one better illustrated the well-to-do missionary at work than the Tappan brothers, Arthur and Lewis, silk merchants of New York City. Converted in the course of the revival to New School Presbyterianism, the Tappans and their friends in 1825 formed the New York Tract Society to distribute Bibles and religious literature to the poor. In the next

few years, they invaded some of New York's most hostile and impious realms to distribute tracts, upbraid the ungodly, and gather lost souls. Their efforts climaxed with the arrival in 1830 of Charles Grandison Finney himself, who set up a mission in the Five Points district, the slimiest of New York's slums.

Neither the Tappans nor Finney, it must be said, had much impact on the mores of New York City, where the steady flow of immigrants kept the city in constant flux. Elsewhere, however, the middle-class missionaries sometimes met with spectacular success. In Rochester, New York, a bustling community of transplanted New Englanders on the Erie Canal, a visit by Finney triggered a momentous revival. Artisans, journeymen, and even day laborers took the temperance pledge and rigorously observed the sabbath. Work habits improved, and with the improvement came a noticeable increase in output and profits. In the phrase of one historian, Rochester was, for at least one heady moment, "a shopkeepers' millennium."

TEMPERANCE

The temperance cause early attracted the attention of reformers because drinking was so blatant a social evil. Americans, especially males, drank morning, noon, and night. The corner saloon or grocery grogshop was part of the workingman's culture. It offered a masculine milieu, free from the responsibilities of home or workshop. Journeymen dropped their tools periodically throughout the day for a visit to the saloon, and invariably congregated there after work. Even at home meals were often washed down with whiskey. The average annual consumption of alcohol per adult in 1820 has been estimated at seven to ten gallons.

Master craftsmen initially joined their journeymen in the camaraderie of the saloon, but as they took on more entrepreneurial responsibilities and ceased their own handiwork, they became more conscious of production loss due to alcohol. Master craftsmen and factory owners were among the earliest and most ardent adherents of the temperance movement; women were not far behind. Women were natural temperance advocates because masculine addiction threatened them and their children. And a male-dominated society, which otherwise frowned upon their appearance on the public stage, tolerated them when they spoke and marched on behalf of family unity. In addition to women and employers, the temperance crusade attracted middle-class reformers, generally because excessive drinking was widely believed to be the cause of most other social ills.

In 1826, a number of local societies formed the American Temperance Union. The early results were disappointing, however, principally because temperance advocates spent most of their time talking to one another. In the 1840s the movement began appealing directly to the drinkers. Washingtonian Societies, made up mostly of reformed alcoholics, utilized the techniques of the revival. "Camp meetings" featured personal testimony in which former alcoholics described in lurid detail the sad effects of excessive drinking. Such testimony was followed by songs that instilled a fear of "demon rum" and by the "salvation" of new recruits. The Washingtonians' message was couched in the familiar tones of evangelical protestantism, but their method was quite different. By bringing in speakers whose recitation of past exploits became transformed into a confes-

Temperance *vs.* T-Total. The temperance crusade, like most reform movements of the day, was divided between moderates and extremists. This poster, entitled "Temperance But No Maine Law," promoted the idea that moderate drinking was neither evil nor socially harmful.

Courtesy of The New-York Historical Society, New York City.

sion, they stood barroom boasting on its head. Instead of prayers, they offered to help people enmeshed in a drinking culture by finding them new jobs and alternative forms of leisure. By 1843, the Washingtonians claimed that more than half the intemperate drinkers in the nation had signed their pledge. How many of these returned to their cups when the excitement died cannot be said, but the society's magazine, the *Cold Water Army*, found enough support to maintain publication for twenty years.

In the meantime, temperance advocates turned from persuasion to force. In enlisting the government in their cause, prohibitionists won support from people concerned about lawlessness and disorder. Indeed, there was much overlap between the temperance societies and the societies devoted to publishing religious tracts or founding Sunday Schools. The crusade against alcohol also received support from Nativists who identified the Irish with drinking and disorder. Political action against drinking took two forms—prohibition and higher taxes on beverages—and it was most successful in New England where the values of rural Yankee Protestantism and immigrant Irish Catholicism stood in dramatic confrontation. In the 1840s states tightened the licensing requirements for liquor retailers, and New England towns began banning taverns altogether. In Maine, Neal Dow, merchant and mayor of Portland, organized a campaign that resulted in the first statewide prohibition act in 1851. "Maine laws" were adopted by several other northern states and one southern state over the next decade, but few survived the Civil War and the amoral era that followed. Taxation proved to have greater long-run impact. Whiskey had become a common feature of the American diet, in part because it was so cheap (a dollar a gallon on the average). New taxes that substantially increased the price, together with other governmental regulations, cut per capita consumption to about two gallons a year after 1840— a level that has been maintained to the present day.

PEACE

A peace crusade was another natural outgrowth of the impulse to reform. Unlike other benevolent causes, this one was entirely new; it had sprouted from the carnage of the Napoleonic wars. (Earlier wars, involving relatively small numbers of professional soldiers, had not generated much moral opposition.) Liberal Calvinists or Unitarians, rather than evangelists, started this movement. As early as 1793, the tireless redeemer Benjamin Rush wrote an essay suggesting that the new federal government ought to establish a Peace Office instead of a War Department. If, however, the War Department were to be maintained, he suggested a variety of signs to be placed over the doors of its subdivisions: "An office for butchering the human species," "a widow- and orphan-making office," and "an office for creating public debts, speculators, stock jobbers, and bankrupts." In 1809, a wealthy Presbyterian merchant of New York, David Low Dodge, published an essay arguing that war was contrary to the teachings of Christ. In 1828, Dodge, with the help of William Ladd, a religious philanthropist from New England, organized the American Peace Society.

The peace crusade never attracted many followers, and early in its progress it stumbled on the rock of defensive war. Like the temperance movement, which divided on the question of whether to countenance beer and wine,* peace advocates divided on the issue of whether it was morally justified to fight when under attack. The move-

---

* An English prohibitionist with an unfortunate stammer gave a speech in favor of "teetoteetoteetotal" abstinence from all alcoholic beverages, thereby introducing a new word to the Anglo-American language.

ment nevertheless laid the theoretical foundation for the condemnation of war, and it explored means of resolving international disputes, including some form of world federation. In the 1840s, leadership of the peace movement fell to Elihu Burritt, whose nickname, The Learned Blacksmith, told his life story. Realizing that a peace movement must be international in scope, Burritt taught himself seven languages and sailed for Europe to carry his message. One result of his travels was the Friendly Address movement, in which British and American cities paired with one another to exchange friendly communications. The other result was the formation of the League of Universal Brotherhood, a sort of temperance society in which members pledged in "the spirit of Christianity" not to enlist in any army or navy or sanc-

tion any sort of war. Even Horace Greeley, a man given to social schemes, found Burritt's league a bit unreal. It was doomed to failure in any case, as war clouds loomed in both Europe and America in the 1850s. The Crimean War, the wars for the unification of Italy and Germany, and the American Civil War ended further serious talk of peace until the early twentieth century.

UTOPIAN COMMUNITIES

War and liquor were two of the most obvious blemishes that would be eliminated in the millennium. Less obvious were two other human imperfections, selfishness and acquisitiveness. It was thought by some that these too would disappear when humanity reached its perfect state. The be-

The Kitchen of the Oneida Community. Even communists evidently regarded cooking as women's work.

New York Public Library Picture Collection.

nevolent societies discouraged self-interest, but an assault on private property itself was beyond their means. Indeed, so revolutionary was the notion that acquisitiveness and profit might be eliminated from society that it required a model, a small-scale utopia to serve as a blueprint for the rebirth of society. A number of small communitarian experiments thus sprang out of the revival movement. Most succumbed to the worldly lure of profit and gain. The longest-lived—and most radical in concept—was the Oneida community founded by John Humphrey Noyes.

Noyes was a New England lawyer who took up the ministry after a session with Charles G. Finney. After several years of study, Yale gave him a license to preach, but the school revoked the license when he began teaching that conversion brought a complete release from sin, a perfect purity of heart. The concept, known as perfectionism, was not new—indeed, Finney himself had reached the same conclusion. Noyes, however, pursued the implications of the idea with the tenacity of a trial attorney. He soon concluded that perfection was not possible in a capitalist, profit-minded society. Self-interest bred selfishness. It followed, then, that the existing social order itself was corrupt and needed to be replaced by a new cooperative system.

Noyes's communalism extended even to the marriage rite, which at that time did involve the dominion of one human being over another. "When the will of God is done on earth as it is in heaven," he wrote to a friend, "there will be no marriage. Exclusiveness, jealousy, quarreling have no place at the marriage supper of the lamb. . . . I call a certain woman my wife. She is yours, she is Christ's, and in him she is the bride of all saints." When his wife, Harriet, experienced a succession of extremely painful stillbirths, Noyes began to question even the justice of man's role in procreation. How could one be perfect and yet cause pain to another? From these two

quests came the twin notions of "complex marriage" and "male continence." The latter, which meant, in effect, sexual satisfaction without ejaculation, made possible the former. No thinker prior to Sigmund Freud penetrated as deeply and as imaginatively in his writings as did John Humphrey Noyes into the tabooed mysteries of sex, marriage, and family.

In 1846 Noyes began his experiment in communism at Oneida in western New York; so often had the area witnessed the fires of religious enthusiasm that it was known as the "burnt-over district." The community of saints lasted for thirty-five years. Ironically, its success rested on its ability to compete in the capitalist world. Rigidly structured and closely supervised to prevent "complex marriage" from degenerating into "free love," the community was made up of deeply religious, highly motivated men and women who worked side by side without special sex-role identities. Its principal source of income was the manufacture of animal traps used in the western fur trade. After the Civil War, the community fell victim to internal bickering and external pressure. Religious puritans ultimately forced Noyes into exile in Canada and broke up the community. The shutdown symbolized the reversal in the social role of American evangelical Protestantism. In the Jacksonian era it was an agency for experiment and social reform; in the Gilded Age it became a stronghold of conservatism.

⊔ Secular Reform

THE ATLANTIC EXCHANGE: UTOPIAN SOCIALISM

The reforming urge was not exclusively religious in inspiration, nor was it confined to the United States. A similar impulse swept Western Europe in the middle decades of the nineteenth century, and there was a good deal of trans-Atlantic interchange. Much of this intellectual cross-pollinization had to do with political economy.

In Europe, as well as in America, smoke-belching factories and shabby, overcrowded tenements led some people to question the "laws" of the classical economists. Adam Smith and his disciples, Thomas Malthus and David Ricardo, had postulated a set of rules they said governed all human exchange: the law of supply and demand, which necessarily governs price, and the "iron law" of wages. The latter applied the supply-demand principle to labor and led to the conclusion that wages must hover at the edge of human subsistence, for any rise above that level would encourage procreation, bring about an increase in the labor supply, and so increase competition and return wages to the subsistence level.

Three elements were necessary for the production of goods, declared the classicists—land, labor, and capital—and each brought its distinctive return—rent, wages, and interest. Reformers who wanted to break the chain of "dismal" logic focused on the latter—the returns on invested capital, which they often mistakenly called "profit." A disproportionate share of the return went to profit, they felt, and as a result working people could not afford to buy all the goods they produced. The result was periodic economic crises ("depressions") characterized by oversupply and unemployment. Moreover, since labor is the principal determinant of value (Ricardo himself had said as much), profits and rents were essentially "unearned" income. The alternative, which soon went by the label "socialism," was to have the instruments of production collectively owned. To show that such a system could work, reformers such as Charles Fourier in France

established model communities in which each participant, contributing to the best of his or her abilities, earned an equal reward.

A number of Fourierist Phalanxes were set up in America, but all were short-lived—victims of cheap land, good wages, and a cultural climate in which money and success were venerated. A few of these model communities are interesting for their imaginative challenge to the status quo. Robert Owen (1771–1858) was a Scot who rose from wage earner to manager of a cotton mill in New Lanark, Scotland. After absorbing the theories of the utopian socialists, he resolved to establish a model community in America, where traditions of democracy and tolerance had created a fertile field for social experimentation. From a religious sect that had failed as a commune he purchased New Harmony, on the banks of the Wabash River in Indiana. His arrival in America in 1824 attracted attention because his was the first experiment in secular communism. In Washington, D.C., he gave two addresses in the House of Representatives that were attended by a throng of government officials, including President Monroe. Some 900 eager colonists followed him to the banks of the Wabash in the summer of 1825. But the aura of hope and expectancy soon faded. The colony functioned tolerably as long as Owen was present to administer it; but when he departed for England, it dissolved into bickering faction.

Owen's lasting imprint, ironically, was not in the advance of socialist theory but in education reform. He had read the theories of the Swiss educator Pestalozzi and sought to implement them at New Harmony. Pestalozzi believed that the function of education was to develop the natural abilities of each human being. The teacher's function was simply to assist nature, not to imprint facts. Owen's school at New Harmony attracted a number of educational reformers, and Pestalozzi's principles were applied in other communities. Educators down to the present have periodically resurrected, experimented with, and reburied Pestalozzi's approach.

Frances Wright was another Scot of humble origins and grandiose schemes. She toured America as soon as she came of age and returned to Britain to write a glowing account of her travels. A rarity in an age when travelers routinely denounced Americans' travel facilities and scorned their manners, Wright's account came to the attention of one of the new nation's first nonresident admirers, the Marquis de Lafayette. When Lafayette returned to the United States in 1824 to help celebrate the republic's fiftieth anniversary, Frances Wright and her sister Camille accompanied him. An interview with Jefferson on her first visit had called Frances Wright's attention to the problem of slavery, and on her next visit, an interview with Robert Owen suggested a solution. With help from some of Owen's associates, she purchased a plantation in Tennessee called Nashoba and attempted to turn it into a utopian community where slaves could work for their freedom. It was a fresh idea, but Frances Wright lacked the administrative skill and perseverance to see it through. She spent much time traveling back and forth across the Atlantic and used up her energies in social protests of all kinds. In 1830 the dozen or so blacks who had worked the colony were resettled in Haiti, which offered them jobs and homes.

Dozens of communities such as New Harmony and Nashoba sprouted in the American countryside during the Jacksonian era, but they had little effect on the society that surrounded them. They failed not simply because they were short-lived, but because they were ignored. And they were ignored in part because their method was to withdraw from the larger community. More effective in promoting change were reformers who were content to work within the system.

EDUCATION

The central impulses of the age—political democracy, middle-class morality, and evangelical fervor—coalesced in the public school movement. "In a republic," intoned Massachusetts educator Horace Mann, "ignorance is a crime." If the "common man" were to be given the vote, he must be educated. Schooling, moreover, was felt to be the great social leavener, the avenue to self-improvement. Education, said Mann, is "the balance wheel of the social machinery. . . . It does better than to disarm the poor of their hostility toward the rich; it prevents being poor."

Such feelings were new to neither Mann nor his time. Thomas Jefferson and other founders of the republic believed that a nation could not long remain ignorant and free. But for Mann and other educators of the Age of Reform, the problem went beyond mere knowledge; America's children also needed moral elevation. "Never will wisdom preside in the halls of legislation," warned Mann, "until common schools . . . create a more far-seeing intelligence and a purer morality than has ever yet existed among communities of men." In the 1820s, Mann absorbed the teachings of Boston evangelist Lyman Beecher, and he believed that schools were a valuable agent in the war against sin. And they could do more even than churches: By combining Protestant morality with patriotism, they could inspire good work habits in the poor and Americanize the immigrants. Public schools were the harbingers of the "shopkeepers' millennium."

To accomplish all this, however, it was essential that the schools be publicly supported, publicly controlled, and open to all. Public tax support ensured that the schools would be available to the poor, who were the people most in need of them. Public control, through state legislatures and local boards of education, ensured that the public would be entrusted with the continuing definition of the proper values to be taught to its children. The movement for free public education was under way before Mann came upon the educational scene. Boston initiated city-wide public schools in the early 1820s. A decade later, Pennsylvania instituted the first state public school system. By the time of the Civil War, all northern and some southern children had an opportunity to attend publicly financed schools.

Equally important was the extension of the principle of tax-supported schools to secondary education. The high school was a new institution (the first was formed in 1820), and it reflected a growing awareness of adolescence as a stage of life. The high school's predecessor, the private academy, was a catchall institution for the postelementary education of boys who ranged in age from ten to mid-twenties. With the high school came a trend toward age grading. Elementary education became confined to those under ten or twelve. Those from eighteen to twenty-two attended college, and high schools concentrated on the teens.

High schools also offered the first postelementary education for females. Indeed, girls soon made up a majority of the students and an even greater majority of the graduates. Boys remained in high school only if they expected to go on to college; otherwise they withdrew and went to work. Less progress was made in opening the public schools to blacks. Until the 1850s, all states maintained segregated school systems. In 1855, Massachusetts became the first state to declare that no applicant to a public school could be denied on account of "race, color, or religious opinions." In this regard, the colleges did somewhat better. By the 1850s, blacks were attending Oberlin, Harvard, and several other private institutions.

Higher education was also the field of greatest advancement for women in this period. With the exception of the tireless Benjamin Rush, no leader of the revolutionary era had given any thought to college training for females. In 1819 Emma Willard published a *Plan for Improving Female Education* and followed it two years later with the founding of a Female Seminary at Troy, New York. Willard's Seminary was devoted primarily to training elementary school teachers and ultimately prepared some 200 women for that profession. The Troy Female Seminary was not, however, on a par with the male colleges of the day. That honor belongs to Mary Lyon's Mount Holyoke, which opened its doors in South Hadley, Massachusetts, in 1837. Although Mount Holyoke's curriculum was comparable to that of most male colleges, the state government was slow to give it recognition. Not until 1888, almost forty years after Lyon's death, was Mount Holyoke granted a state charter as a college.

The democratization of education was only one of the advances of the age. The other push was toward better quality. Teachers in the early nineteenth century were still essentially amateurs. They considered their positions temporary while they prepared themselves for more rewarding careers. Town school boards also had their priorities reversed—they seemed to feel that their principal duty was saving money. Schools were located on the cheapest land; they were unpainted and desolate on the outside, drab and drafty on the inside. The curriculum was sparse, and teaching methods centered on rote memorization enforced by a birch rod.

In an effort to save money, several eastern states began employing female teachers instead of men in the 1820s. They discovered that women, because of a lack of employment opportunities, were willing to

The Saint Louis Art Museum.

"The Country School," oil painting by Winslow Homer (1871).

work for half the pay given men. In New York, where the state financed half of a teacher's salary, school districts found that they could employ a woman to teach full time without bearing any of the cost themselves. By the early 1840s, female teachers in Massachusetts outnumbered males by two to one.

It was Catherine Beecher who made a virtue of this school board parsimony, to the benefit of both schools and women. The eldest daughter of evangelist Lyman Beecher, Catherine and her sister Mary opened a school for women in Hartford, Connecticut, in 1823. In a rented room above a harness shop the two young women taught grammar, geography, philosophy, chemistry, history, mathematics, theology, and Latin. Often they were only a few pages ahead of their students in the textbooks, but that was standard practice for the time. When Lyman Beecher went west to Cincinnati in 1832 to begin a cam-

paign to win the West for Christ, Catherine followed him and organized another school, called the Western Female Institute. While her father organized Bible tract societies and Sunday schools, Catherine saw a similar need for voluntary societies working on behalf of public schools. In *An Essay on the Education of Female Teachers* (1835), she proposed a network of voluntary organizations that would raise money to endow teacher-training seminaries for the express purpose of preparing female teachers for the common schools. Taking advantage of the prevailing view that women were naturally endowed with an extra measure of sympathy, piety, and obedience, Catherine Beecher argued that women were by nature the best teachers. They not only could impart knowledge with sympathy and understanding; they were also better equipped than men to inspire patriotism, good morals, and steady habits—all the things that people expected of their schools. Thus, in Catherine Beecher's millennial view, the female teacher was at the center of a web of interlocking institutions, including the family, the school, and the church.

Beecher also saw in this a new vocational outlet for women, especially for women raised in poverty, whose only opportunity other than marriage was the textile mill. Women would have moved from factories to schoolrooms in any case; what Catherine Beecher did was to ease the transition. And in so doing, she offered new hope to women and new status to the teaching profession.

Horace Mann and other educators endorsed Catherine Beecher's efforts and helped with her fund-raising. After he became secretary to the Massachusetts Board of Education in 1837, Mann went a step further by proposing state-supported teacher-training institutes. Mann expected that most of the students in these institutions would be women. Called "normal schools," these teacher colleges were a clue to another aspect of educational reform—uniformity. Systematization was thought to be the key to excellence. Boston's first public schools, for instance, were modeled on the factory. Raw youths were to be turned into polished citizens in the same way that the Lowell mills turned lint into cloth. The ideal was a uniform, quality product turned out at minimal cost.

As secretary of the Board of Education, Horace Mann had little real power but much room for publicity. His reports to the Board of Education, on which his fame rests, were appeals for legislative action. Sounding throughout the reports is a call for uniformity—uniformity of curricula, textbooks, teaching methods, and discipline. His "normal schools" were designed to train teachers under uniform standards or norms. Mann organized the local school districts into a statewide system managed by a professional bureaucracy, and he established a standard curriculum with regu-

lar procedures for advancing from one grade to another. By the time of the Civil War, these elements of a modern school system had been adopted in most northern and a few southern states.

The notion of state-supported universities was slower to take hold. Colleges were founded at a frantic pace throughout the pre–Civil War years, but most of them were private, church-related schools. In New England, which led the movement for public elementary and secondary schools, only Vermont created a state university before the Civil War. By contrast, the southeastern states—Georgia, the Carolinas, Virginia, and Maryland—all had a state university of some sort by 1825. Yet only North Carolina adopted a comprehensive state school system. In the West, on the other hand, Indiana, Michigan, and Wisconsin developed public school systems that stretched from the primary grades to the state university.

PRISONS AND ASYLUMS

Democratic humanitarianism combined with the search for social order to produce a new awareness of the outcasts of American society—the criminals and the insane—in the Jacksonian era. There were no prisons or asylums in early America. Wrongdoers met with corporal punishment, not incarceration. They were executed for serious crimes; publicly whipped or branded with a hot iron for lesser offenses. Town jails were places of temporary confinement for prisoners awaiting trial or punishment. And they became catchalls for social misfits. The insane, the insolvent, even runaway children were cast into them, side by side with hardened criminals.

Such conditions offended reformers, who found the system untidy, inhumane, and socially disruptive. Assuming that human nature could be reshaped and human flaws corrected, reformers devised special-

New York Public Library Picture Collection.

A New York City prison. Note the individual cells and visitor privileges.

ized places of incarceration—prisons for criminals, asylums for the insane, orphanages for wayward children—where, in a planned environment, social deviants could be cured. The state penitentiaries New York built at Auburn and later at Sing Sing were much admired and imitated. In these institutions, each convict had a cell of his own, where presumably he meditated on his shortcomings by night. During the day the convicts worked in a common shop. The goods they produced were sold to pay the cost of running the prison. The convicts were thus forced to earn a living through honest labor. The prison, in effect, was the moral counterpart of the urban Sunday School—an institution for curing the wayward by inculcating traditional values of industry, sobriety, and regularity. And while the process of reformation went

on, the social deviant was kept apart from and not allowed to disturb or contaminate respectable society.

The establishment of asylums for the insane followed much the same rationale, except that asylums were devoted more to a medical than a moral cure for deviancy. Massachusetts schoolteacher Dorothea Dix led the crusade to get the mentally ill out of jails and into facilities of their own. Asked to give a Sunday School lesson in the Cambridge town jail, she was distressed to find a number of insane persons caged in a cold, dreary room. Her sympathies aroused, she undertook a two-year study of every jail and poorhouse in Massachusetts. Enlisting the support of Horace Mann and other reformers, she got the attention of the legislature with a published report. She documented instances in which she had found the mentally ill incarcerated regardless of age or sex in cold, dark, insanitary facilities, sometimes unclothed or chained to walls, and often whipped. The legislature was moved to enlarge and renovate the Worcester asylum. Dix began a forty-year crusade for the care of the insane, adopting the argument that insanity was a disease susceptible to treatment. Her efforts resulted in the construction of thirty-two new hospitals in the United States and Europe and the restaffing of existing facilities with trained personnel.

THE WOMEN'S MOVEMENT

Dorothea Dix was not the only woman caught up in reform; women were involved in every reform movement of the day. Temperance got their attention early because it related closely to the integrity of the household, the domain social custom accorded to women. They participated in the peace movement, in educational reform, and in antislavery campaigns. Yet their efforts were hampered in an environment where they were branded as inferior.

Women, it was commonly believed, were physically and intellectually unsuited for participation in world affairs. Their place was in the home, where their purity, warmth, and devotion protected and preserved the family, the basic building block of the community. Women who entered the public arena compromised their integrity, diffused their energies, and threatened the entire structure of society. Piety, submissiveness, and purity were the attributes of true womanhood. Ministers and popular magazines bombarded women with this litany from childhood on.

The law reflected and reinforced the social ethic. Women were not allowed to vote or hold public office. Legally, they were treated as minors, wards of their nearest male relatives. They could not even protect themselves from domestic cruelty, for the law did not allow suits between husbands and wives. Divorce was rare, and in those instances where it was granted, the husband invariably received custody of the children. The sharp differentiation between family and the outer world, moreover, fostered a humiliating double standard of morality. Premarital or extramarital sex was taboo for women, but among men it was tolerated—if not condoned—because men, as envoys from the family to the business world, were exposed to sin and hence temptation.

This cult of domesticity was satisfying to many women. But others felt constrained by the role assigned to them. Educated women in particular looked beyond their domestic duties for fulfillment. Beginning with Abigail Adams, who in 1776 had advised her husband John to insert provisions for women's rights in the laws being made for the new American government, women had periodically protested the subordinate position in which they had been placed. Not until the 1840s, however, did they organize, and the cult of domesticity itself was in part responsible for the rise of organized feminism. The cult promoted female education as a necessity if mothers were expected to shape the minds and morals of children, and education in turn widened their intellectual horizons. The cult also gave women a feeling of solidarity, for the idea that women were uniquely sensitive and compassionate led naturally to the notion that only a woman could understand other women. In valuing another female, moreover, a woman confirmed her own value. So women began to communicate with one another, establishing an individuality that was not derived from home and family. And those who felt stifled by their domestic role found sympathetic listeners. To organize on behalf of women's rights was then an easy step.

The founders of the movement, however, were women with little or no domestic experience. Although Frances Wright's interests were too varied to allow her to focus on women's rights, she showed women the way by taking the public stage in the cause of reform. Her appearances on the lecture platform in the 1830s stirred more controversy than her denunciation of banks and businessmen. Following her example were the Grimkè sisters, Sarah and Angelina, young Quaker idealists who left their South Carolina home to join the antislavery lecture circuit. Appearances before hostile male audiences who jeered and rejected their arguments inspired the Grimkès to consider the plight of women, who lived in a form of "domestic slavery." In 1838 Sarah Grimkè published a series of letters she had written to a female friend as *Letters on the Equality of the Sexes and the Condition of Women*. It was America's first feminist tract.

In the following year Margaret Fuller, schoolteacher and friend of Emerson's, set out to revitalize the minds of adult women, whose wits had been dulled by the numbing routine of household duties. Borrowing the method of the Transcendental Club, Fuller began holding "conversations," evening discussion groups that ex-

CLIO'S FOCUS: Amelia Bloomer and Women's Dress Reform

The debate began as something of a joke, but for women the problem was real. Women's fashions in the 1850s were impractical, unhealthy, and sometimes dangerous. Skirts flowed in a "great pyramid" from a tiny waist to a wide, floor-length bottom. To achieve the desired effect, women pinched their waists with corsets, sometimes so tightly that they injured internal organs. The skirt, requiring eighteen to twenty yards of material, was so massive that it was difficult to get through doorways and halls. An accidental brush against fireplace, oven, or lighted candle was a constant danger.

A conservative newspaper editor of upstate New York started the debate when he jokingly suggested that female reformers ought to wear pantaloons in imitation of men. Amelia Jenks Bloomer promptly took up the idea. She had long sponsored a variety of reforms, including temperance and women's rights. Her home was Seneca Falls, New York; both she and her husband had attended the Women's Rights Convention of 1848. She also published *The Lily*, the first newpaper owned and edited by a woman and devoted to the interests of women. In response to the editor's sneer, she took up the cause of dress reform.

So sensational was the Bloomer costume that it even inspired a song. "The New Costume Polka," doubtless a tongue-in-cheek spoof of female dress reform.

Library of Congress.

Amelia Bloomer was not prepared to cut off her own skirts, however. That bold move was made by a friend of hers, Elizabeth Smith Miller, daughter of Gerrit Smith, a philanthropic lawyer who helped finance nearly every reform crusade of the age. On her honeymoon in Switzerland, Mrs. Miller visited a hospital where women were recuperating from the damage done by too-tight corsets. For comfort, the patients were wearing Turkish pantaloons gathered at the ankle and partially covered by a knee-length skirt. Elizabeth Miller brought the costume home to Seneca Falls. Amelia Bloomer adopted it and broadcast its advantages in the columns of *The Lily*. Newspapers around the country quickly picked up the story, and the bloomer became a symbol of the women's rights movement, as well as a source of masculine mirth.

Though a useful idea, the costume was ahead of its time. Women lacked the social and economic leverage to win such a revolutionary change in custom, and the controversy over clothing obscured more important issues, such as legal rights. Amelia Bloomer herself recognized this and abandoned the costume after a short time, though it remained forever associated with her name. Instead, she devoted the rest of her long life to the temperance movement and women's suffrage. She died in 1894, a quarter of a century before women got the vote. She would have applauded, we can be sure, the revolution in women's apparel that came in the 1920s after the suffrage amendment was passed.

plored for a period of weeks some branch of knowledge—history, literature, painting, or music. More than 200 Boston women participated in Fuller's seminars, and many became active participants in the feminist movement of the following decade. In 1845 Fuller published *Woman in the Nineteenth Century*, which was to become the Bible of the women's rights movement. Fuller mustered an array of evidence indicating that men and women were intellectually equal, and she blamed women themselves for submitting meekly to a repressive system.

Three years later, in 1848, Elizabeth Cady Stanton and Lucretia Mott organized a women's rights convention that met at Seneca Falls, New York. Stanton, far in advance of her time in her advocacy of liberal divorce laws and birth control, drafted the convention's statement of grievances. Paraphrasing the Declaration of Independence and substituting "Man" or "He" for Jefferson's indictment of King George, the docu-

ment listed the legal, social, and economic usurpations of males. It demanded for women "immediate admission to all the rights and privileges which belong to them as citizens of the United States."

The feminist movement could claim a few victories. Oberlin College admitted a woman to its all-male undergraduate ranks in 1837, and in 1856 the University of Iowa became the first coeducational public institution. The legal barricades against women also showed some cracks. In the 1850s several states gave married women control over their own property, and unmarried women won the right to sue in court.

New York was by far the most advanced of these states, because of a formidable alliance between Elizabeth Cady Stanton and Susan B. Anthony. Anthony, like Stanton, came to women's rights by way of the temperance movement. When, in 1852, she was prohibited from taking the floor in a temperance convention because it was deemed "unseemly," she joined with Stan-

National Archives.

Elizabeth Cady Stanton.

ton to form a separate New York State Women's Temperance Society. Thereafter the pair branched out into a broad feminist crusade. In 1854 they flooded the New York legislature with petitions listing women's basic demands: the vote, control of their own earnings, and custody of children in divorce cases. Such was the attention they aroused that Elizabeth Cady Stanton was invited to address the assembly on legal reforms. Their campaign paid off six years later when New York adopted the most advanced feminist code in the nation, granting women the right to sue, to keep their own wages, and to take control of a husband's property at his death. After the Civil War the women's movement languished, but the inexhaustible team of Stanton and Anthony gave it leadership until the end of the century.

Feminist leaders were involved in several movements, such as temperance, peace, and antislavery. Whether women might have accomplished more for themselves had they concentrated on women's issues is a question. They were no less affected than men by the vision of an ideal. Nor was theirs the only movement to be caught up in the antislavery crusade. Human bondage, after all, was the most obvious cancer in American society. By 1850 it had become the focal point for the whole reform impulse.

⊔ The Crusade against Slavery

Like other movements for social betterment, antislavery was born of the marriage of evangelical Protestantism and secular humanitarianism. The earliest criticism of slavery was religious. Throughout the eighteenth century, Quakers, Moravians, and other Pietists opposed human bondage. Quakers founded the first antislavery society in Philadelphia in 1775. The revolution, with its rhetoric of freedom, added a new motive for opposing slavery. John Jay, Alexander Hamilton, and others who founded the first nonreligious antislavery society in New York in 1785 argued simply that the institution was incompatible with the spirit of liberty.

During and after the revolution, slavery was eliminated in the northern states and in the Northwest Territory, but little other progress was made until the Second Awakening revitalized the religious aspect of antislavery. Whites, in the North as well as South, assumed that blacks were an inferior race, and all states restricted their liberties. Jim Crow laws prohibited racial intermarriage and required segregation of races in all public facilities—schools, railroad cars, parks, even cemeteries. Several western states even prohibited the immigration of free blacks. When John Randolph of Roanoke left a will that freed his 300 slaves on condition they leave Virginia, the state of Ohio turned them back at the Ohio River when they tried to emigrate.

Thomas Jefferson, who reflected some of the more liberal attitudes of southerners of the revolutionary generation, admitted that slavery was an evil but could see no quick end to it. If slaves were suddenly emancipated, he believed, some might seek retribution for past injuries. The only alternative Jefferson could see was to relocate the blacks in the West Indies or Africa. This concept was put into practice in 1817, when the American Colonization Society was formed in Washington, D.C. Among its charter members were such enlightened slaveowners as James Madison, John Marshall, and Henry Clay. The society grew rapidly, though most of its local chapters were in the South.

The Monroe administration cooperated by giving $100,000 to the society and helping to establish the republic of Liberia in Africa to receive repatriated blacks. To make a significant dent in the slave population, however, required expenditures far beyond the means of either the society or the government. For the first ten years of the society's existence, it transported to Africa only free blacks. It did not begin buying slaves for repatriation until 1827, and though the society continued its work through the nineteenth century, it had no impact on slavery or the black population. (Most of those who populated Liberia were freedmen who went to Africa after the Civil War.)

Whether antislavery or simply antiblack, the colonization movement was the last echo of revolutionary idealism. Stung by congressional criticism of slavery during the Missouri controversy, southerners grew defensive on the subject. They ceased their own criticism of slavery and came to resent what they considered northern interference with their "peculiar institution." In 1831–1832, the Virginia assembly debated a bill for the gradual elimination of slavery in the state, a measure prompted by Nat Turner's rebellion the previous summer. Its defeat marked the end of any further discussion of slavery in the pre–Civil War South.

Following the legislative debate, Thomas R. Dew, president of the College of William and Mary, published a proslavery argument that became a bulwark of the southern defense. Far from being a necessary evil, said Dew, slavery is a positive good. It benefits the planter, who profits from slave labor, and it benefits the slave, who is better off than he was in Africa. Slavery is sanctioned by the Bible, Dew continued, and endorsed by a multitude of peoples over the centuries. Now it was clear that any further criticism of slavery would have to come from the North.

A few people in the North had already grasped the torch. In 1829, David Walker, a former slave living in Boston, published an *Appeal to the Colored Citizens of the World* in which he denounced colonization as a hoax, upbraided blacks for submitting to slavery at all, and suggested that they resist it by force of arms. In Boston and elsewhere in New England, the religious revival brought calls for immediate emancipation. Inspired by the evangelists' vision of a society reborn in Christian brotherhood, converts rejected the old notions of gradual emancipation (employed by some states after the revolution) and colonization. Slavery was contrary to Christian conscience, they said; it must be eradicated immediately and without compromise.

BEGINNINGS OF ABOLITIONISM

William Lloyd Garrison, a printer from Newburyport, Massachusetts, was among the converts burning with evangelical zeal. In 1829 he became an associate editor of the *Genius of Universal Emancipation*, the leading antislavery paper of the time. The *Genius*, published in Baltimore, was owned by Quaker Benjamin Lundy, an advocate of colonization. Finding Lundy's views too tame, and in trouble with Baltimore authorities for his writings, Garrison left after six months and moved north to Boston to found a paper of his own. *The Liberator* appeared on January 1, 1831, and in the first issue Garrison announced his editorial policy:

> I will be as harsh as truth and as uncompromising as justice. On this subject I do not wish to think, or speak, or write with moderation. No! No! Tell a man whose house is on fire to give a moderate alarm; tell him to moderately rescue his wife from the hands of the ravisher; tell the mother to gradually extricate her babe from the fire into which it has fallen;—but urge me not to use moderation in a cause like the present. I am in earnest—I will not equivocate—I will not excuse—I will not retreat a single inch—AND I WILL BE HEARD.

Garrison, like others of his day, felt that reform meant the elimination of some evil, and that it was best achieved by a form of religious conversion—that is, a realization by the wrongdoer of the error of his ways and a voluntary compulsion to do good. Garrison called it "moral suasion," but it was not as naive as it sounds. As a recent scholar has pointed out, the abolitionists "were not expecting some sudden Day of Jubilee when, with a collective shudder of remorse, the entire planter class would abruptly strike the shackles from all two million slaves and beg their forgiveness." They realized that persuasion was a gradual process, like the progress of religious conversion. They asked only that it be begun and that alternatives such as colonization or compensated emancipation be rejected because they served as cover for those who would do nothing at all.

The Liberator had little immediate impact except in the South, where Garrison was blamed for inciting Nat Turner's rebellion in August of 1831 (unjustly, it would seem; there is no evidence that Turner had seen the paper). Garrison's subscription list in the first year numbered only fifty, most of them free blacks residing in Boston and

vicinity. Other whites, however, had traveled routes parallel to Garrison's, from conversion to reform to abolitionism. Among these were Theodore Dwight Weld, a schoolmaster from western New York and a disciple of Finney; Lewis and Arthur Tappan, wealthy New York drygoods merchants; Quaker poet John Greenleaf Whittier; and former slaveowner James Gillespie Birney.

The trans-Atlantic exchange of ideas was important in abolitionism, as it was in other reform movements. In 1833 the British Parliament, responding to mounting pressure from British evangelicals, passed an act emancipating the slaves in the British West Indies. This example inspired American abolitionists, and at the instigation of the Tappan brothers sixty-two activists gathered in Philadelphia in December 1833, to form the American Antislavery Society. Twenty-one were Quakers. There were four women in attendance (all Quakers) and three free blacks. Garrison and his New England contingent dominated the proceedings; Garrison drafted the Society's Declaration of Sentiments, which committed the society to immediate, uncompensated abolition.

The society grew rapidly, boasting within a couple of years more than a hundred local organizations sprinkled throughout the North and East. One of its most spectacular successes was an 1834 student rebellion at Cincinnati's Lane Seminary. The seminary had been founded by the Tappans as an outpost of evangelical religion. They had even persuaded the great Boston evangelist Lyman Beecher (a colonizationist on the slavery issue) to assume Lane's presidency. In 1834 they decided to make Lane into a center of abolitionism as well, and they sent Theodore Weld to Cincinnati. Within three weeks Weld had the campus in an uproar and a solid block of students on his side. Among his converts was the president's daughter, Harriet Beecher (who later married the school's professor of biblical literature, Calvin Stowe). When the school's trustees, under pressure from the citizenry, ordered the antislavery group to disband, forty students renounced their affiliation with the seminary and followed Weld north to the more congenial atmosphere of Oberlin, Ohio, where another recently founded evangelical college was under the presidency of that preeminent evangelist, Charles Grandison Finney himself. Oberlin soon became a hotbed of western abolitionism, as well as one of the first American colleges to admit blacks.

The spread of abolitionist societies was in some sense deceptive, for abolitionists remained a tiny fragment of the population until near the end of the Civil War. They also encountered fierce resistance in both North and South. Southerners blamed the Nat Turner insurrection on the abolitionists, and village meetings throughout the South put up rewards for the arrest of persons distributing abolitionist literature. The state of Georgia offered $5,000 to anyone who would kidnap Garrison and bring him south for trial. Far from pricking southern consciences, the abolitionist assault made southerners more defensive than ever. The abolitionists also met violent resistance in the North. The vast majority of northerners felt little sympathy for the slaves, and the abolitionists' insistence on uncompensated emancipation ran counter to Americans' regard for property rights. Their millennialist vision, moreover, seemed to invite anarchy. The mobs that attacked abolitionist speakers were often composed of lawyers, doctors, judges, and state legislators, town elites that felt threatened by radical change. In 1834 a New York City mob broke into Lewis Tappan's house and smashed the furnishings. The following year, a Boston mob dragged Garrison through the streets until authorities intervened and placed him in jail for his own protection. The violence reached a climax at Alton, Illinois, in 1837, when a mob surrounded a building that housed the printing press of antislavery editor Elijah Lovejoy, set fire to it, and shot Lovejoy dead when he came running out.

Persecution brought new converts, as religious cults so often discover. Wendell Phillips, a Boston lawyer and one of the few abolitionists who could boast pedigree, wealth, and education, found his sympathies aroused by the sight of Garrison being dragged through the streets, and when he learned of Lovejoy's murder, he joined the cause. A persuasive speaker and penetrating thinker, Phillips may have been the ablest of the abolitionists. He was one of the few who remained close to Garrison throughout, and when Garrison shut down his newspaper and retired at the end of the Civil War, thinking his job was done, Phillips continued battling for black suffrage and women's rights.

Through it all, the abolitionists managed to remain on the offensive. Speakers financed by the American Antislavery Society trouped through the countryside like itinerant evangelists. Former slaves were among the society's most effective platform speakers because they could describe the system in detail. Among the more prominent black orators were Samuel Ringgold Ward, a runaway from Maryland; Lunsford Lane, who had purchased his freedom and moved north from North Carolina; and Sojourner Truth, a New York woman who had been freed by the state's emancipation act. The best-known of the black orators was Frederick Douglass, a slave-laborer in the Baltimore shipyards who escaped and made his way to New England. Garrison heard Douglass recounting his experiences as a slave at an antislavery meeting and employed him as a traveling lecturer for the New England Antislavery Society. After some years of that, Douglass shook himself free of Garrison's intellectual stranglehold and moved to Rochester, New York, where in 1847 he founded a liberation paper of his own, *The North Star*.

Library of Congress.

Frederick Douglass.

The title referred to the heavenly beacon that guided runaways to freedom.

THE GAG RULE

In 1835, the American Antislavery Society undertook a mailing campaign whose object was to flood every village post office in the country with abolitionist propaganda. Within three years, the society sent out over a million antislavery tracts. The South exploded anew with rage. President Jackson, in his annual message, decried the postal campaign and asked Congress to ban antislavery literature from the mails. Pending such legislation, Postmaster General Amos Kendall informed southern postmasters that if they did not want to deliver objectionable mail, he would not force them to. If nothing else, the administration's action demonstrated what the abo-

litionists had been saying all along, that the canker of slavery infected every segment of American society and government.

Paralleling the postal campaign was a nationwide petition campaign, masterminded by the society and carried out by its mounting number of local branches. Petitions had been a principal means for pressuring legislatures into enacting emancipation laws in the revolutionary era. Now the society's target was Congress, and it had a willing helper in Massachusetts Representative John Quincy Adams. By 1837 thousands of petitions were deluging Congress, and Adams was turning the House into a public forum for abolitionism. In that year embarrassed southerners pushed through the House a rule that all such petitions were to be automatically tabled without being read or discussed. Claiming that his rights as a congressman were being violated, Adams refused to be silenced. When fellow congressmen pushed the old man down into his seat, he shouted, "Am I to be gagged or not?" So began Adams's long, lonely crusade against the "gag rule," a one-man war for the right of free expression. By the time he won its repeal in 1844, abolitionism was no longer a moral protest by a conscience-stricken few; it was a political movement that threatened to split both the major parties.

The petition movement and the attempt to stifle it had two important repercussions. First, it brought local initiative and community involvement to an extent that abolitionists had not previously achieved with their preachings and slave testimonials. Petitions were carried from door to door by known members of the community, and the mere act of signing involved a commitment. Most of the petitions involved slavery in the District of Columbia and the western territories, places that were under the jurisdiction of Congress. These could be signed by almost anyone suspicious of the South and its institutions.

Second, the southern effort to suppress antislavery expression, whether in the mails or in Congress, involved much more than slavery's moral balance sheet; it involved a fundamental right of free speech. It meant that the perverted values of the slaveowners were being forced upon the country as a whole. Slavery was not simply the oppression of a race; it was a threat to all. Gerrit Smith, wealthy philanthropist converted to antislavery after watching an anti-abolitionist mob in Utica, New York, declared in 1836 that northerners must oppose slavery "in self defense." "If it not be overthrown," he warned, slaveholders would continue their "aggression . . . and effectually prepare the way for reducing northern laborers into a herd of slaves." Some twenty-two years later, Abraham Lincoln, in his famous "House Divided" speech, would bear the same message.

Thus, despite fierce opposition and despite the fact that they were still a tiny minority of the northern population, the abolitionists had, by the end of the 1830s, broken what Garrison had called "the conspiracy of silence." They had made slavery the central issue of American politics.

POLITICAL ABOLITIONISM

This very success helped precipitate a schism in abolitionist ranks. The split reflected the fundamental difference between pragmatists and millennialists evident in the reform movement as a whole. Garrison in the late 1830s became perfectionist in outlook (even befriending John Humphrey Noyes); he proclaimed that American society itself was hopelessly corrupt and that a moral revolution must precede any meaningful or lasting reform. Like Noyes, Garrison declined to participate in any sort of political activity, refusing even to vote. By the early 1840s, *The Liberator* was bearing on its masthead the inscription "No Union With Slaveholders"; Garrison advocated secession as the solution to the slavery problem.

At the same time other abolitionists, such as Theodore Weld and James G. Birney, came to feel that "moral suasion" was too easily ignored by the irreligious and the indifferent. They also feared that Garrison, in his insistence on moral revolution, was frittering away abolitionist energies and confusing antislavery with other causes. The petition campaign had taught them the value of piecemeal conversion; it opened the possibility of building an antislavery political bloc, operating within the system, using the traditional partisan methods to forge what victories it could.

By 1840 these fundamental differences in strategy were too fervently held for compromise. Both sides recognized that a showdown was inevitable at the July 1840 meeting of the American Antislavery Society. Both factions tried to pack the meeting in hopes of controlling the proceedings.

The critical moment came when Garrison proposed adding feminist Abby Kelley to the society's executive committee. The gesture symbolized the differences between the two blocs, and when Garrison won by a vote of 557 to 451, the political abolitionists—the Tappans, Weld, and Birney—withdrew from the society. The influence of both Garrison and the Antislavery Society declined thereafter, their approach dismissed as too "exotic" for American acceptance, though Garrison's popularity rebounded in the 1850s.

The political abolitionists, with a presidential election approaching in 1840, created the Liberty party and nominated James G. Birney, thus presenting the voters with an antislavery alternative to Harrison and Van Buren. Garrison had predicted that entry into politics inevitably meant compromise of principle, and the Liberty party's platform, in some sense, bore him out. The platform endorsed the principle of immediate abolition, but it also admitted that under the Constitution the federal government had no power to abolish slavery in those states where it existed. It called only for the end to slavery in the District of Columbia and a bar to the admission of new slave states. Even with this moderate position, Birney polled a mere 6,000 votes in the election.

Liberty party leaders nevertheless came to exercise an influence far in excess of their electoral strength. By running candidates in state and congressional elections, they forced the candidates of the major parties to take a stand on antislavery. Joshua R. Giddings, for example, was elected to Congress as a Whig in 1840 from the Western Reserve district of Ohio. Because his district was populated by transplanted Yankees and subject to antislavery sentiment radiating from Oberlin, Giddings was vulnerable to Liberty party pressure. To counteract it, he moved steadily closer to the position of the political abolitionists. In similar fashion, a group of "Conscience Whigs" appeared in the Massachusetts legislature, and the number of antislavery Whigs and Democrats in Congress grew steadily. By 1844 they were numerous enough to secure repeal of the Gag Rule.

By that date also, political abolitionists had a new concern—the annexation of Texas. Texas had secured its independence from Mexico in 1836 and requested admission to the Union. Presidents Jackson and Van Buren had denied the Texas claim for fear of provoking a war with Mexico, but President Tyler was openly friendly, regardless of the risk. The admission of Texas was an open challenge not just to abolitionists, but to northerners of many political hues, whether mildly antislavery or simply antisouthern. Expansionism and antislavery were the principal issues in the presidential election of 1844, and their fiery conjunction touched off the chain of political explosions that led to the Civil War.

SUMMARY

An intense religious revival, sometimes called the Second Great Awakening, swept the northern states in the 1820s and 1830s. The evangelists, best-known of whom was Charles Grandison Finney, preached a democratic theology that offered salvation to all who opened their hearts to Christ. At the opposite end of the Protestant spectrum were the rationalists—Unitarians and Transcendentalists—who developed a humanistic creed that emphasized free will and human responsibility for ethical behavior.

Both evangelists and rationalists, however, agreed on the need for social reform. They also agreed generally that the best means of eradicating the evils of society was through individuals involving themselves in benevolent associations. Americans were a nation of joiners; they formed societies for every conceivable social need—prison reform, preservation of the Sabbath, temperance, peace, care of the blind and the insane. They also formed utopian communities designed to serve as models for a new society free of selfishness and acquisitiveness.

There were secular as well as religious motives for reform. Traditionalists worried about the disorder in the cities, the rootlessness of youth, and the alien ways of immigrants. Many thought public education was the cure-all for society's ills. Education acquainted the young and the foreign-born with traditional values; as well, it was the avenue to self-improvement and financial success. There were two facets to educational reform—public financing and professionalization. Tax-supported, tuition-free schools reflected the democratic impulse of the age; they also had the practical objective of reaching those elements of society most in need of value and vocational training. Horace Mann in Massachusetts led the way in the professionalization of education through teacher training and the standardization of the curriculum.

Humanitarianism and concern for social order combined to produce a new awareness of the outcasts of American society—

criminals and the insane. The asylum as a place for social misfits, who had previously been allowed to roam free, was one of the key discoveries of the age. Prisons for criminals and hospitals for the insane answered the needs of both conservatives and reformers. Dorothea Dix, the leading crusader for asylums for the mentally ill, exemplified the importance of women in the reform movement. Women, who constituted a majority of church congregations, played a prominent role in the benevolent societies, many of which were affiliated with churches. Their early reform efforts—such as the temperance and peace crusades—were related to preservation of the home and family. But they soon developed a concern for their own social and legal standing. The demand for legal rights, such as more liberal property and divorce laws, led directly to a demand for political rights. The movement climaxed with a women's rights convention at Seneca Falls, New York, in 1848, but it accomplished little in the way of change.

By 1850 the crusade against slavery was absorbing the energies of women and most other reformers. The movement for the immediate, uncompensated emancipation of slaves had begun in 1831 with the publication of William Lloyd Garrison's *Liberator*, but it had little impact until political abolitionists broke with Garrison to form the Liberty party in 1840. The move into politics meant compromises—symbolized by the Liberty party's slogan, "Gradual emancipation immediately begun"—but it also forced politicians to take a stand on the issue. Except for annual bouts over the gag rule, however, congressional leaders kept the slavery issue in the background until the Mexican War thrust it center stage.

READING SUGGESTIONS

An excellent introduction to the social and intellectual history of this period is Russel B. Nye, *Society and Culture in America, 1830–1860* (1974). On Protestant evangelism, the preeminent scholar is William G. McLoughlin. He explores the Second Great Awakening in *Modern Revivalism: Charles Grandison Finney to Billy Graham* (1959) and the connection between religion and reform in *Revivals, Awakenings, and Reform: An Essay on Religion and Social Change in America, 1607–1977* (1978). The benevolent associations are the subject of C. S. Griffin's *Their Brother's Keepers, Moral Stewardship in the United States 1800–1865* (1960).

R. G. Walters, *American Reformers, 1815–1860* (1978), provides a good overview. W. J. Rorabaugh, *The Alcoholic Republic* (1979), suggests that there was good reason for the temperance movement. Lawrence Cremin, *American Education: The National Experience 1783–1876* (1980), is the most recent and balanced treatment of that subject. David J. Rothman, *The Discovery of the Asylum: Social Order and Disorder in the New Republic* (1971), presents what is now the accepted view on prison and asylum reform.

The current state of the art in women's history in this period is Catherine Clinton, *The Other Civil War: American Women in the Nineteenth Century* (1984). Catherine Clinton has also described the unique position of southern women in *The Plantation Mistress: Woman's World in the Old South* (1982). For women in the West, see Julie R. Jeffrey, *Frontier Women, 1840–1880* (1979). Biographies remain some of the best studies of women's attitudes; among them are Kathryn Kish Sklar's *Catharine Beecher: A Study in American Domesticity* (1973), and K. Lumpkin, *The Emancipation of Angelina Grimke* (1974).

The best introduction to the antislavery movement is James B. Stewart, *Holy Warriors: Abolitionists and American Slavery* (1976). Lewis Perry and Michael Fellman, *Antislavery Reconsidered: New Perspectives on the Abolitionists* (1979), summarizes the most recent scholarship. Lawrence J. Friedman, *Gregarious Saints: Self and Community in American Abolitionism, 1830–1870* (1982), offers another perspective. R. J. M. Blackett explores a long-neglected contribution to the antislavery movement in *Building an Antislavery Wall: Black Americans in the Atlantic Abolitionist Movement* (1983). John L. Thomas's *The Liberator* (1963) is a comprehensive but critical biography of Garrison, and Robert H. Abzug, *Passionate Liberator* (1980), offers a new and imaginative interpretation of the career of Theodore Dwight Weld. Waldo E. Martin, Jr., *The Mind of Frederick Douglass* (1984), is a good analysis of Douglass's ideas on a broad spectrum of reforms. For the political abolitionists, the standard treatment is Richard Sewell, *Ballots for Freedom* (1976); the question of black civil rights in the North is discussed by Leon Litwack in *North of Slavery: The Negro in the Free States, 1790–1860* (1961).

13

BUILDING AN "EMPIRE FOR LIBERTY"

mericans had always considered themselves different, unusual, and somehow better than anyone else. It was their destiny, they felt, to serve as a model for the rest of humankind, a standard that deserved emulation. By being copied they would change the pattern of history. "We shall be as a city upon a hill," was the way Governor John Winthrop expressed the notion in 1630. The Puritan model was of course a religious one, a Bible Commonwealth, with which New England did experiment for a time. The revolution transformed the model from a religious to a political one— a federated republic founded on the consent of the governed. And Americans looked on proudly as first France and then Latin America threw off the twin yokes of monarchy and empire and borrowed liberally from the American Constitution and Bill of Rights.

That the American republic was also an empire seemed to trouble no one. Americans came upon their empire initially by inheritance, and they formed a unique system by which "colonies" could join "mother country" as equals when they reached a certain population level. Moreover, expansion of the republic extended its blessings. President Jefferson, on purchasing Louisiana in 1803, called it "an empire for liberty."

To that point, Americans did not have to force their values on anyone. Other people borrowed American institutions because of their quality; no promotion was needed. The empire expanded by purchase or agreement, not by force, and the lands acquired were "empty" but for Indians. With the West Florida revolution of 1810 Americans began to give destiny a helping hand. In this instance the empire of liberty was extended by force. Yet it was assumed that the revolutionaries represented a majority view, and if the residents of that Spanish province wished to cast off the imperial harness and join the American republic, they had every right to do so. A generation later there were similar uprisings in Texas and California, and the rationale was the same. If the people of California, wrote Secretary of State James Buchanan in 1845, "wish to unite their destiny with ours, they will be received as brethren." Unfortunately, it was not that simple, for a majority of the population of both Texas and California was Mexican by nationality, Spanish-speaking, and Roman Catholic in religion, and few of them had any desire to unite their destiny with that of the United States.

Racial bias blinded Americans to this critical fact. The feeling of superiority, so fundamental to the sense of mission, had become by the 1840s a notion of "Anglo-Saxon" superiority. "Imbecile and distracted, Mexico can never exert any real governmental authority" over California, wrote an American journalist in 1845. "The Anglo-Saxon foot is already on its borders. Already the advance guard of the irresistible army of Anglo-Saxon emigration has begun to pour down upon it, armed with the plough and the rifle, and marking its trail with schools and colleges, courts and representative halls, mills and meetinghouses. A population will soon be in actual occupation of California, over which it will be idle for Mexico to dream of dominion." Therein is the classic argument of the empire builder—so superior are his ways that others must submit to them whether they want to or not. At that point the religious mission of the Puritans and the republican mission of the revolutionary generation degenerated into imperialism.

(*Chapter opening photo*) "The Trail of Tears."

⊔ The Middle Border and the Mountain Men

The national sense of mission did not include the Indians. Few whites talked of receiving them as brethren and assimilating them into American society. Instead, they were pushed westward and then "removed" to the inhospitable grasslands of the Plains. Yet the brutal treatment of the Indians, over centuries of time, helped condition white American attitudes toward other peoples—Mexicans, Hawaiians, Filipinos—in the course of the nineteenth century.

The Middle Border was an intellectual as well as geographical dividing line in the rise of imperialism, for it marked a switch from haphazard, piecemeal dispossession of the Indians to a deliberate policy of colonization. In 1824 Secretary of War John C. Calhoun drew an imaginary line along the longitude of the Red River and the Missouri (the line would later form the western boundaries of Minnesota, Iowa, Missouri, and Arkansas). The land west of this border, declared Calhoun, was to be reserved permanently for the Indians. In view of the fragile nature of earlier Indian boundaries, Calhoun's proposition might seem cynical or naive, yet the Monroe administration had fair reason to believe that this one might indeed be permanent. In 1819–1820, Major Stephen Long explored the Dakota landscape between the Red River and the upper Missouri and judged the region to be unfit for white American habitation. This information, coupled with the earlier intelligence gathered by Lieutenant Zebulon Pike on the country south and west of the Arkansas River, was already leading cartographers to dismiss the Plains as the Great American Desert. That it might make a permanent Indian reservation was a natural conclusion.

INDIAN REMOVAL

The government began moving the remnants of the Great Lakes tribes, already weakened by war and disease, to the Nebraska country in the 1820s. The Indian Removal Act of 1830 hastened the process. The act authorized the president to exchange government lands west of the Middle Border for Indian holdings in the East. The concept of removal was not inherently wrong—President Jackson actually thought he was doing the Indians a favor. But the government's methods brought much unnecessary suffering. Bowing to southern states rights feelings, Jackson withdrew federal military protection from the Indians. That allowed rapacious whites to invade the homes of Indians who were being resettled and seize their furnishings. Many families were allowed to take to the West only what they could carry on their backs.

Choctaws and Creeks, the first of the southern tribes to go, were carried by steamboat in 1832–1833 up the Mississippi and Arkansas rivers to the Indian Territory (Oklahoma). The government turned the job of transporting the Indians over to private contractors, who overloaded the steamboats in order to make a profit. Cholera—a world epidemic had begun in Russia in 1830—swept through the crowded boats, killing hundreds. The Cherokee, an agricultural people with a constitutional government, a written language,* and even a newspaper, managed to resist removal until 1837. Finally, the government sent in troops to evict the Cherokee forcibly.

---

* No Indian tribe had a written language until a Cherokee silversmith named Sequoyah devised characters for each of the 85 basic syllables in spoken Cherokee (on the same principle as Chinese or Japanese writing). The project took him twelve years and was completed in 1821.

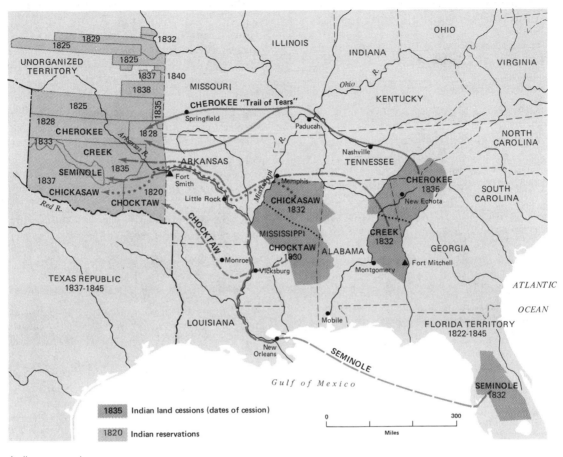

Indian removal.

Too numerous to be sent by steamboat, the 14,000 Cherokees were forced to walk to the Indian Territory across Tennessee, Arkansas, and Missouri—the infamous "trail of tears," on which some 4,000 died.

Although most Indian tribes submitted peacefully to removal, there were instances of resistance. In 1832 a band of Sac and Fox Indians, led by Blackhawk, returned from Iowa to their Illinois homeland, causing panic along the frontier. The governor of Illinois summoned the army and a running fight ensued until the Indians were finally trapped and butchered by gunfire as they tried to recross the Mississippi River. (Blackhawk escaped and lived to tell the story in his autobiography.) In the South the Seminole, led by Osceola, conducted a lengthy guerrilla war in the swamps of Florida to avoid removal. The U.S. army finally captured Osceola by trickery and shipped to the West all the Seminole it could capture, but a proud remnant of the tribe remains in Florida today.*

THE MOUNTAIN MEN

The concept of a vast Indian reservation in the trans-Missouri West was outdated when Calhoun announced it. Trappers and fur traders had already penetrated into the branches of the upper Missouri River in pursuit of beaver. When Indians who lived on the river objected, the army intervened. The following advertisement, inserted in the St. Louis *Gazette* on February 13, 1822, transformed the Indian domain into a business empire:

> To Enterprising Young Men. The Subscriber wishes to engage one hundred men to ascend the river Missouri to its source, there to be employed for one, two, or three years.
>
> . . . William H. Ashley

Ashley was a St. Louis promoter who had made, lost, and remade a fortune in lead and saltpeter mines in the Ozark Mountains. His advertisement revolutionized the fur trade. Unlike independent traders who penetrated the wilderness for a trapping season and returned to market their catch, Ashley's men would stay in the mountains year-round, meeting at some designated rendezvous annually to sell Ashley their pelts and buy supplies. Thus organized and supplied, the Mountain Men fanned out across the West, all but exterminating the beaver. In the process, they uncovered the remaining topographical features that had escaped earlier explorers. In 1824 Jim Bridger discovered the Great Salt Lake, and Jedediah Smith pursued the sources

---

* The Seminole is the only Indian tribe that has never signed a peace treaty with the United States government and never officially recognized its authority. During World War II, the tribe issued its own declaration of war against Germany and Japan.

of the North Platte River to the South Pass across the Continental Divide. In 1826 Smith made the first overland trek to California, crossing in the process the bleak Mohave Desert and the Nevada basin. The information garnered by the Mountain Men in their brief heyday (virtually all the beaver in the West were trapped by 1830), proved that the trans-Missouri empire, with all its forbidding terrain, was a cornucopia of natural riches. The great Indian reservation stretching from the Dakotas to Oklahoma could not last long. The ensuing half-century of conflict on the Great Plains and the desert Southwest was simply another war for empire.

⊔ The Texas Revolution

To the south and west of John Quincy Adams's Transcontinental Line, the lands that beckoned America's empire builders were not "vacant," as they were along the Middle Border; they were the possession of foreign governments, first Spain and then Mexico. And they were populated by a people of Spanish language and culture. Spain, ever fearful of American subversion, kept the border tightly closed. American traders who ventured into Santa Fe, the northernmost of the Spanish missions and a governing center, found themselves in jail and their goods confiscated. In 1821 William Becknell, a merchant of Franklin, Missouri, led a party across the Kansas prairie from Westport Landing on the Missouri River, followed the Arkansas River into the mountains, and crossed the treacherous Raton Pass leading to Santa Fe. His intentions were unclear, since he was aware of the fate of earlier traders, but to his surprise, he was welcomed by local authorities. Mexico that very year had won its independence, and it welcomed Americans and their goods. Becknell led a second and larger expedition to Santa Fe the following year, blazing a cutoff south of the Arkansas

Walters Art Gallery, Baltimore.
The Interior of Fort Laramie, 1837.

River across the Cimarron Desert that avoided the Raton Pass. Other traders followed, Santa Fe merchants sent caravans of their own north to Missouri, and the Santa Fe Trail was soon a major artery of trade.

In Texas, the Spanish barricades against Americans began to crumble even before Mexican independence. In 1819, Moses Austin, a long-time resident of the Spanish borderlands, obtained permission from Spanish authorities to settle 300 American colonists in Texas. When Moses died shortly thereafter, his son, Stephen F. Austin, obtained a confirmation of the grant from Mexican officials, and in 1823 he established a settlement on the lower Colorado River. Other proprietors, or *empressarios*, won similar grants and soon the whole American South was ablaze with "Texas fever." By 1835 there were 30,000 Americans in Texas, outnumbering the native Mexican population by ten to one.

Americans moved into Texas for the same reason they had moved into West Florida a quarter century before—rich land. Many brought their slaves with them and set up cotton plantations. They soon became disenchanted with alien rule, however, just as they had in Florida. Texas did not have its own government; it was part of the state of Coahuila, which was dominated by Mexicans. The Americans, moreover, were suspicious of Mexican land titles

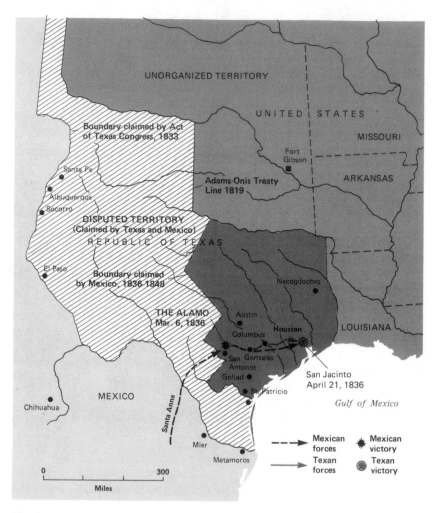

The Texas Revolution.

and of periodic rumors that Mexico planned to free its slaves. When General Antonio Lopez de Santa Anna made himself military dictator in Mexico City in 1834 and reneged on a promise to give Texas state government, the Americans felt their liberties were threatened. Armed settlers clashed with Mexican troops. In 1835 Santa Anna started north with an army to restore order and that caused open rebellion. In March 1836, the American settlers declared their independence from Mexico,

approved a constitution for the independent republic of Texas, and named Samuel Houston president. Santa Anna, in the meantime, laid siege to the Alamo, a mission in San Antonio defended by 187 courageous but foolish Texans (Houston warned them that their fort could become a trap), among them former Whig congressman David Crockett. Santa Anna captured the mission and slaughtered its defenders, but it cost him 1,544 men.

Santa Anna then headed for the sea and

Courtesy of The New-York Historical Society, New York City.
An artist's conception of the storming of the Alamo.

General Houston, who made his stand at the San Jacinto River, just above Galveston Bay. In the ensuing battle, April 21, 1836, 630 Mexicans were killed. The rest, including Santa Anna, were captured. At gunpoint, Santa Anna agreed to Texan independence. Houston and most other Americans in Texas wanted to join the American union, but President Jackson declined, fearing it would provoke a war with Mexico. Texas remained an independent republic, under a banner bearing a single star, for nearly ten years. The Lone Star Republic became a state in 1845.

⊔ Westward to the Pacific

Protestant missionaries were the heralds of empire in the Pacific Northwest. They began the pilgrimage in the 1830s, along a trail marked by Mountain Men. It followed the Platte River across present-day Ne-

braska and Wyoming to the South Pass over the Continental Divide, then wound north across all but impassable mountains to the Snake River and followed its narrow, rocky canyon to the Columbia River and finally to the Pacific.

OREGON FEVER

As a result of the Convention of 1818, the United States and Great Britain jointly occupied the country west of the Continental Divide and north of the 42nd parallel. The real authority in the area, however, was the British-owned Hudson's Bay Company, which maintained an outpost—Fort Vancouver—at the point where the Willamette River flows into the Columbia. In charge of the fort was Dr. John McLoughlin, an artful Scot. Though soon outnumbered by the Americans in his midst, McLoughlin outsmarted them for many years.

McLoughlin persuaded the first missionaries who arrived in the Oregon country to settle in the Willamette Valley. He could keep an eye on them there, and his London employers had no territorial interest in the country to the south of the Columbia. Jason Lee, a Methodist missionary, was the first to establish a station in the Willamette. Lee found few prospects for salvation, the Indians of the valley having been decimated by an epidemic some time before, but his mission became a landmark, the end of the Oregon trail. Oregon attracted other missionaries, among them a Presbyterian minister, the Rev. Marcus Whitman, who arrived in 1836. Whitman was not one to be lulled into planting a mission under McLoughlin's watchful eye and chose instead a site near the junction of the Snake River and the Columbia, in the heart of Nez Percé Indian country. Whitman had no better luck than Lee in securing converts, but his errand into the wilderness was not in vain.

In 1839 Whitman returned east to seek recruits for the Oregon enterprise. He toured the rural hamlets of the Mississippi Valley, portraying Oregon as an earthly Eden. Hard times stemming from the panic of 1837 were an additional inducement, and across the Middle West farmer after farmer caught the "Oregon fever." The trickle of covered wagons winding across the western plains mounted steadily until 1843, when a caravan of nearly a thousand people rumbled into the Willamette Valley.

CALIFORNIA FEVER

The coastal lands south of the forty-second parallel, Mexican-governed California, also lured American emigrants. Seafarers had been familiar with California since the 1790s, and over the years had developed a profitable trade in cattle hides and tallow. Carried by ship around Cape Horn (an od-

yssey made famous by Richard Henry Dana's novel *Two Years Before the Mast*), the hides were used in the New England shoe industry; the tallow went into soap and candles. Shipping agents, responsible for purchasing hides and storing them, settled in California in the 1830s. Their letters home, full of glowing descriptions of the land of sunshine, stimulated a new wanderlust in the Middle West. Guided by Mountain Men, pioneers bound for California split off from the Oregon Trail north of the Great Salt Lake and followed the Humboldt River across the arid Nevada Basin. The Sierras were the most formidable obstacle on this trail until 1844, when a party guided by an Indian nicknamed Truckee discovered a pass (which they named after the guide) that led to the Sacramento Valley. The end point of the California Trail was the ranch of Johann Sutter, a Swiss who had made his way to California by way of Oregon and Hawaii. By a mixture of charm and enterprise, Sutter had acquired a large domain along the American River, a tributary of the Sacramento, and he provided the overland pioneers with food, shelter, and employment.

By the end of 1844, there were one thousand or more Americans in California, and they were already looking to the day when that land might become part of the United States. Of the Mexican population, one emigrant wrote: "They are only a grade above the aborigines, and like them will be compelled by the very nature of things, to yield to the swelling tide of Anglo-Saxon adventure." Thomas O. Larkin, a wealthy merchant who had been named American consul in Monterey in 1843, did his best to keep the rambunctious immigrants under control, but as caravan after caravan came bumping down the Truckee Pass an uprising, on the order of those in Texas and West Florida, became only a matter of time.

The Oregon pioneers, as their number multiplied, also became restless under for-

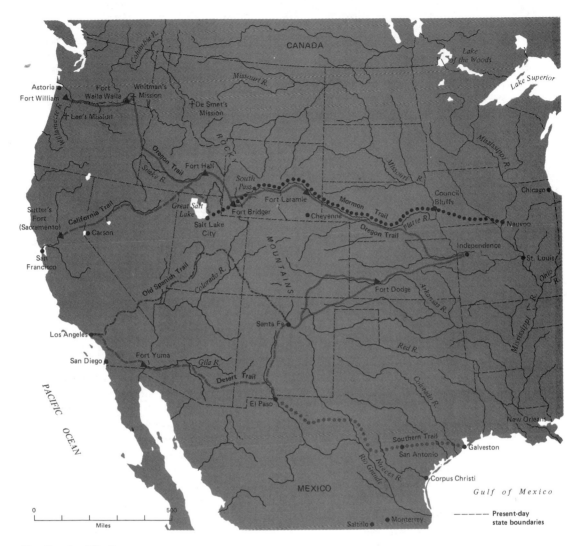

The Overland Trails.

eign rule. McLoughlin and the Hudson's Bay Company steadfastly refused to allow the Americans to form even a local government until 1843. During the summer of that year, the Americans called a popular meeting, outvoted the British, and named a committee to draw up a frame of government. This "First Organic Law," as the settlers called it, provided some rudimentary machinery until "such time as the United States of America extend their jurisdiction over us." As in California, that moment was not long in coming.

MANIFEST DESTINY

The overland migration seized the public imagination. Indians, buffalo, oceans of grass, craggy mountain peaks, and thundering gorges—it had the romance of a storybook. The travel accounts of the pioneers were devoured by easterners; they were, perhaps, the first form of "wild west" literature. And no one doubted that the colonies on the Pacific Coast would one day become part of the republic. Expansion had come to seem a natural course of events, and it mattered not that other countries might have claims to the land. Under the caption "Oregon and War," a New York journalist wrote: "There is in fact no such thing as title to the wild lands of the new world, except that which actual possession gives. They belong to whoever will redeem them from the Indian and the desert, and subjugate them to the use of man." The doctrine of use, initially formulated to justify depriving the Indians of their lands, had become a foundation for imperial expansion.

Politicians echoed these ideas, and the efforts of President Tyler and Secretary of State Calhoun to annex Texas injected expansionism into the presidential election of 1844. Tyler, a political maverick after the Whigs threw him out of the party, desired reelection in 1844, and he seized on Texas annexation as a popular issue. Texas President Sam Houston was willing, and the two governments signed a treaty of annexation in the spring of 1844. In submitting the treaty to the U.S. Senate for approval, however, Secretary of State Calhoun candidly admitted that one purpose of annexation was to add slave territory to the Union. Northerners instantly objected, and the treaty failed to win the necessary two-thirds majority. The result of the furor, however, was that the issues of slavery and expansionism were bound together, and would remain so until the Civil War.

TEXAS AND OREGON

Henry Clay, the Whig candidate in the election of 1844, was on record as opposing the annexation of Texas lest it provoke war with Mexico, and former President Van Buren, the Democratic party leader, took a similar stand. Sensing a popular issue, the Democratic party convention, meeting in May 1844, skipped over Van Buren and nominated instead James K. Polk,* an outspoken expansionist from Tennessee. To paper over the sectional antagonism aroused by Calhoun's injection of the slavery issue into the Texas question, the Democratic platform linked Texas with Oregon, the one slave and the other free, calling for the annexation of each at the earliest possible moment. To focus attention on Oregon, the Democrats demanded not simply the territory south of the Columbia River (which Britain was quite happy to give up), but the entire Pacific Coast as far as Russian-owned Alaska, 54° 40' north latitude. Their slogan, as alliterative as it was fanciful, promised "Fifty-four Forty or Fight."

The outcome was not the mandate for expansion that Polk might have wished, for he defeated Clay by the rather narrow electoral margin of 170 to 105. Lame-duck President Tyler nonetheless saw it as sufficient evidence of the popular will, and he urged Congress to adopt a joint resolution annexing Texas (a device that needed only a majority for approval, instead of the two-thirds required for Senate ratification of a treaty). A hurriedly drafted resolution slipped through both Houses, and President Tyler signed the measure on March 1, 1845, three days before leaving office. The Texas Congress agreed by unanimous vote, and in December 1845, one more slave state joined the Union.

That same month John L. O'Sullivan,

---

* The convention met in Baltimore, and Samuel F. B. Morse, who had received a grant from Congress to string the nation's first telegraph line between Washington and Baltimore, wired the news of Polk's nomination to Washington. Congress refused to believe it and sent a delegation by horseback to have the news confirmed.

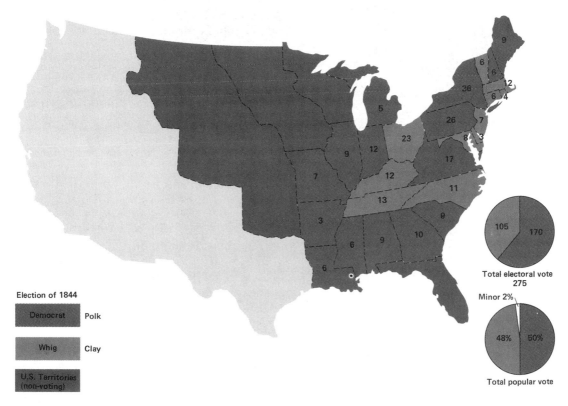

Election of 1844

Democrat — Polk

Whig — Clay

U.S. Territories (non-voting)

105   170

Total electoral vote
275

Minor 2%

48%   50%

Total popular vote

Election of 1844.

Democratic editor of the New York *Morning News*, enriched the American vocabulary with the spine-tingling phrase "manifest destiny." The words encapsulated the age-old sense of mission. It was America's destiny, wrote O'Sullivan, "to possess the whole of the continent which Providence has given us for the development of the great experiment of liberty and federated self-government entrusted to us." The "empire for liberty," it seemed, had nothing less than divine sanction. Those who stood in the way of this unfolding of destiny would be brushed aside or "removed," just as the Indians had been.

President Polk was not content to let Providence take its natural course. In December 1845, he asked Congress for authority to terminate the treaty of joint occu-

pation of Oregon signed with Britain in 1818. He was not willing to risk war, however, despite his party's commitment to "Fifty-four Forty or Fight." Polk privately informed the British ambassador that he was prepared to compromise on an extension of the 49th parallel from the Continental Divide to the straits of Juan de Fuca. In London, British Foreign Minister Lord Aberdeen had trouble enough with famine in Ireland and had no desire for an American war. Besides, he thought of Oregon as "a pine swamp." During the winter of 1845 he ordered McLoughlin to shift the operations of the Hudson's Bay Company to Fort Victoria on Vancouver Island, and in the spring of 1846 he sent the American government a draft treaty marking the boundary at the forty-ninth parallel. Polk

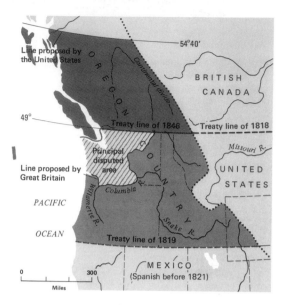

The Oregon controversy.

camped at Sutter's Fort. California was probably his destination all along. The administration no doubt expected that his presence there would cause trouble, and it did. Tension between American settlers and Mexican authorities reached a new height. The Mexican governor ordered him to leave. After some blustering he did, though his steps were so slow that it was May 1846 before he crossed the border into Oregon.

In the meantime the president made some moves of his own. In the autumn of 1845, Polk sent an emissary, John Slidell, to Mexico City with an offer to purchase New Mexico and California. Expecting that mission to fail (as it did), he also sent a messenger with secret dispatches for his consul in Monterey, California, Thomas O. Larkin. The dispatch-bearer, Archibald Gillespie, was a Marine lieutenant who spoke fluent Spanish. Traveling across Mexico disguised as a merchant, Gillespie appeared in Monterey in April 1846. Among the letters he gave Larkin was one from Secretary of State James Buchanan inviting the Californians to "unite their destiny with ours." Gillespie then started after Frémont, catching up with him on May 9. Frémont was more impressed with Gillespie's news than with his dispatches, for Gillespie reported that war between the United States and Mexico was imminent. Frémont wheeled and dashed for California.

By the time Frémont arrived at Sutter's Fort in mid-June, the Americans had taken matters into their own hands. A band of them seized the Spanish outpost at Sonoma, making a prisoner of the general in command, and there on June 15 they raised their grizzly bear flag. Frémont proceeded to Sonoma, took command, and led the rebels to the capital city of Monterey. He found in the harbor seven ships of the American Pacific Fleet, and from the squadron commander he learned that the Bear Flag Revolt had become merged in

agreed to the compromise, and the Senate approved the treaty on June 15, 1846. On that same day, a band of American settlers in California raised a homemade flag bearing an emblem of a grizzly bear (cut from a red flannel shirt), and proclaimed their independence from Mexico. By that date also, the United States was at war with Mexico.

THE BEAR FLAG REVOLT

President Polk resolved the Oregon question with diplomatic bravado; California, he seemed to feel, required more finesse. In April 1845, the War Department, no doubt with the president's knowledge, sent John C. Frémont, former army captain who had earlier mapped the Oregon Trail, and sixty men to explore and map the Nevada basin. Frémont moved swiftly along the California Trail, making little effort to gather data, and by December he was a larger war between the United States and Mexico.

TO THE HALLS OF MONTEZUMA

On January 12, 1846, President Polk received word from Slidell in Mexico City that Mexico refused even to discuss a Texas settlement or the sale of territory. That same day the president ordered General Zachary Taylor, with 1,500 troops, to occupy the territory in Texas between the Nueces River and the Rio Grande. Ownership of this hundred-mile-wide swath of real estate had been disputed while Texas was an independent republic. As part of the Mexican state of Coahuila, Texas's boundary was the Nueces. After winning independence, Texas claimed the Rio Grande. The United States inherited the dispute when Texas joined the Union, and Polk was too much of an empire builder to back down.

Mexico, it must be said, was eager for a fight. The Mexican army was five times larger than the American army and more experienced, having long been engaged in intermittent warfare with Texans and Indians. The American army on its most recent exercise (the War of 1812) had been unable even to mount an invasion of Canada, and an invasion of Mexico with a supply line stretching across mountains and deserts was far more difficult. A victory over the United States was a distinct possibility, many Mexicans felt. In any case, there was no need to suffer further humiliation.

Mexico, accordingly, responded to Taylor's advance by sending an army of its own to Matamoros, across the Rio Grande from Fort Brown. On April 24, 1846, a detachment of Mexican cavalry crossed to the north bank of the river and engaged an American company that was sent to investigate. General Taylor viewed the incident as an act of war and said as much in a

dispatch to the president. The Mexican commander evidently took the same view, because he moved his army to the north side of the Rio Grande on May 1. A week later the two sides met at Resaca de la Palma in a battle that sent the Mexicans retreating back across the river.

News of the skirmish of April 24 arrived in Washington on May 9. Polk was already preparing a war message when he received the news, and he sent it to Congress the next day. He asked for war on the grounds that "After repeated menaces Mexico has passed the boundary of the United States, has invaded our territory, and shed American blood upon the American soil." Congress approved a declaration of war the next day by a vote of 174 to 14 in the House and 40 to 2 in the Senate. The lopsided margins reflected the overwhelming popularity of the war. Nevertheless, there were many in the North who suspected that Polk had deliberately provoked the fight in order to seize Mexican territory for the extension of slavery. One young congressman with a troubled conscience achieved momentary fame by introducing a series of "spot resolutions" asking the president to name the spot where American blood had been shed on American soil. His name was Abraham Lincoln.

The Polk administration, Senator Thomas Hart Benton later reflected, "wanted a small war, just large enough to require a treaty of peace, and not large enough to make military reputations, dangerous for the presidency." It was critical for Polk that the war be brief. Army enlistments went well in the South and West, where the war was popular, but even there people would tire quickly of a drawn-out conflict. And in the Northeast, where only one man in 2,000 volunteered for service, a lengthy war would produce a dangerous political backlash. It risked also the possibility of creating a military hero whose popularity exceeded that of the president. The approaching election of 1848 weighed

Henry Thoreau on Civil Disobedience

Henry David Thoreau, transcendentalist reformer and nature lover, objected to the Mexican War because he thought it was being fought for the extension of slavery. In a gesture of resistance to an unjust government, he refused to pay his taxes. Massachusetts authorities jailed him, but he was released after only one night because a relative paid his taxes. Still boiling with indignation, he wrote an essay justifying his stance, from which the following is excerpted. The essay was perhaps the most widely read and influential piece of writing produced by an American in the nineteenth century.

> The mass of men serve the state thus, not as men mainly, but as machines, with their bodies. They are the standing army, and the militia, jailors, constables, posse comitatus, etc. In most cases there is no free exercise whatever of the judgment or of the moral sense; but they put themselves on a level with wood and earth and stones; and wooden men can perhaps be manufactured that will serve the purpose as well. Such command no more respect than men of straw or a lump of dirt. They have the same sort of worth only as horses and dogs. Yet such as these even are commonly esteemed good citizens. Others— as most legislators, politicians, lawyers, ministers and officeholders—serve the state chiefly with their heads; and, as they rarely make any moral distinctions, they are as likely to serve the Devil, without intending it, as God. A very few, as heroes, patriots, martyrs, reformers in the great sense, and *men*, serve the state with their consciences also, and so necessarily resist it for the most part; and they are commonly treated as enemies by it.

Henry David Thoreau, "Resistance to Civil Government," 1849

heavily in the president's strategic thinking.

General Zachary Taylor was in fact a Whig, and the press made much of his early victories despite his failure to pursue the Mexican army across the Rio Grande. Politicians and public demanded that "Old Rough and Ready" be made supreme commander for the conquest of Mexico. Polk agreed—Taylor was sixty-one, overweight, slow-moving, and inarticulate, a man ill-fitted to be a hero. Yet, although he promoted Taylor to the rank of major general with overall command, Polk also divided the responsibility—and hence the glory— for the conquest of Mexico. The president planned a triple thrust—an Army of the West to seize New Mexico and California, an Army of the Center to occupy northern Mexico, and an Army of Occupation to penetrate to Mexico City and dictate the terms of peace.

Only an Army of the West materialized from this grand strategy. Commanded by Stephen Watts Kearny, an Indian fighter with a solid reputation among Missouri frontiersmen, in June this force moved out of Fort Leavenworth along the Santa Fe Trail. The governor of New Mexico made a pretense of defending the Raton Pass but dispersed his army when Kearny approached, and the Americans entered Santa Fe without firing a shot. Kearny then divided his force. A third was left to occupy Santa Fe; another third, under General Alexander Doniphan, was sent into northern Mexico; Kearny led the remainder west to California.

Each of the three had adventures aplenty. Halfway to California Kearny en-

Bettmann Archive.

"Men of the Granite State!" This 1847 handbill from New Hamsphire calls for volunteers to fight against Mexico. Congress offered as compensation both money and land.

countered Kit Carson—Mountain Man, scout, and friend of Frémont—riding east with news of the Bear Flag Revolt. Kearny hurried on to California to take command, and he arrived in time to help Frémont and Pacific fleet commander Robert Stockton suppress a major Mexican uprising. The garrison left in Sante Fe meantime had their hands full with a rebellion of Mexicans in the city of Taos, which took several hundred lives before it was over.

General Doniphan started from Santa Fe in November 1846 with the third force, an army of 856 Missouri backwoodsmen. They had little training, less discipline, and no uniforms, but as one scholar has ob-

scrved, they "could ride like Comanche, shoot like Mountain Men, and were as full of fight as gamecocks." Doniphan's leadership style suited the informality of his army. In battle hc would sit on his horse and whittle while offering occasional words of encouragement to his men. Marching south along the Rio Grande, Doniphan's "ring-tailed roarers" defeated a Mexican army of 1,200 near El Paso and pushed on into Mexico. The Taos rebellion cut off his supply line, but Doniphan moved on, living somehow on a countryside where the wildlife consisted mostly of lizards and scorpions. Outside the city of Chihuahua he defeated another Mexican army, this one numbering 3,700. After resting for some weeks, he started east in search of Taylor, making his rendezvous with the main American force at Monterey in May 1847. In six months Doniphan had marched 6,000 miles and defeated two enemy forces of vastly superior size without instructions, pay, or supplies.

Nor had the supreme commander, General Taylor, been idle. In August 1846 he moved south from the Rio Grande with an army of 6,000. After a brief siege, he forced the surrender of a Mexican army in Monterey. As part of the surrender terms, Taylor foolishly agreed that he would advance no farther into Mexico for a period of two months. The respite allowed the government in Mexico City to reorganize, and General Santa Anna headed north with a new army. The two forces met at Buena Vista in February 1847, in the biggest battle of the war. Santa Anna hammered at Taylor's defenses in the city for two days, and then retired south in defeat. The road to Mexico City was open, but it was a road 800 miles long through some of the most forbidding terrain on the continent.

President Polk was keenly aware of that. He was aware as well that Buena Vista had made "Old Rough and Ready" Taylor a national hero. So Polk decided to send an-

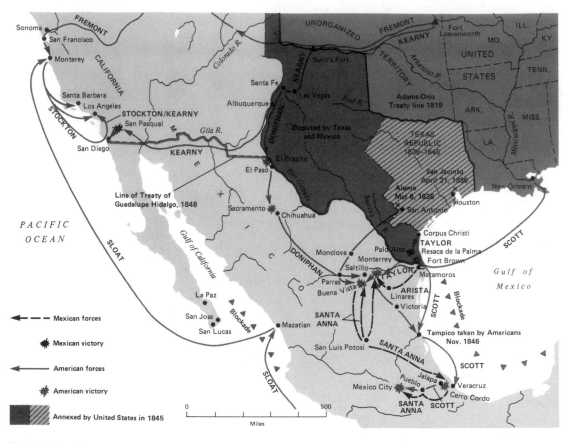

The Mexican War.

other army to make an amphibious landing in the vicinity of Vera Cruz, from which an assault could be made on the Mexican capital with a better line of supply. Polk placed in command Winfield Scott, the army's other major general. Scott, like Taylor, was a Whig, and he was known to have political ambitions. But he too was old (sixty-one), and his military nickname, Old Fuss and Feathers, suggested limited potential for popularity.

Scott's army of 10,000 landed near Vera Cruz in March 1847 and captured the fortress after an eighteen-day siege. The road from there to Mexico City led upward through narrow canyons to the central plateau of Mexico. Santa Anna positioned his army on the steepest of these, Cerro

Gordo, but Scott outflanked him by using New England mountain climbers. A series of small but bloody skirmishes ensued, climaxing with the storming of heavily fortified Chapultepec Hill, which guarded the main causeway into the city. American marines fought their way through the narrow streets in fierce hand-to-hand combat and planted the Stars and Stripes on the National Palace. Santa Anna surrendered on September 17, 1847.

ALL MEXICO

Accompanying General Scott's invasion force was a diplomat, Nicholas Trist, to whom the president had given full powers

CLIO'S FOCUS: The Mormon Exodus

Joseph Smith lived in that portion of western New York known as the burnt-over district because it was so often swept by the fires of religious revival. He came of a poor, ill-educated family and early in his life began having mystical visions. In 1830 he published *The Book of Mormon*, which he had translated, so he said, from golden plates he had found with the help of an angel. The theology that underlay the book and the revelations that accompanied it were alluring to some and alarming to others. To converts it promised salvation on the Day of Judgment, while nonbelievers stood condemned. The "saved," moreover, would inherit the earth.

Such a promise understandably appealed to the have-nots, for it promised both worldly treasure and otherworldly redemption. Mormon missionaries, for instance, had great success in parts of Europe—England and Scandinavia—where rapid economic change made traditional crafts obsolete and displaced their practitioners. Highly motivated and energetic, Mormon immigrants frequently prospered in the American environment, and they took their improved circumstances as a sign of the approaching millennium. An English convert who settled in a Mormon community in America wrote home: "In this place there is a prospect of receiving every good thing both of this world and that which is to come."

A romantic conception of the Mormon emigrants pushing their handcarts through a storm.

Courtesy of the New-York Historical Society, New York City.

The concept of a chosen people—Latter-Day Saints—however, aroused suspicion and hostility among non-Mormons (gentiles) of the sort Jews had experienced for centuries. In his home town, Palmyra, New York, Smith managed to attract only a few relatives and neighbors into his Church of Jesus Christ of Latter-Day Saints, so he led his converts to the village of Kirtland, in northern Ohio. There his movement prospered for a time. But then hard times, stemming from the panic of 1837, brought distrust, especially when a bank Smith sponsored went under. He moved again; the new Zion was in western Missouri (later the site of Independence), but neighborhood hostility soon forced Smith to move once more.

Throughout this odyssey, Smith's followers multiplied in number and in wealth, and the Mormon practice of voting as a bloc gave them enormous political power. Smith looked east to Illinois for his next location. He was able to wring substantial concessions from the state legislature, as both Whigs and Democrats vied for his support. Smith picked a site on the Mississippi River, naming it Nauvoo, and the charter issued by the legislature allowed the Mormons to govern themselves. In effect, Smith was absolute sovereign—although God, through revelations, frequently took a hand in the community's affairs. Numbering 12,000 people in 1840, Nauvoo from its inception was easily the largest city in Illinois (Chicago then had only 4,000). An influx of European converts increased its population at the rate of about a thousand a year.

Trouble began in 1843 when Smith announced that God, through revelation, sanctioned polygamy. Smith and other Mormon elders had practiced polygamy secretly for some years (he had twelve wives by 1843), but formalization of the concept caused dissent. The following year Smith announced plans to run for the presidency, and the dissenters within found allies without. When Smith sent the Nauvoo marshal to destroy a printing press established by his opponents, he was arrested and jailed in the nearby town of Carthage. There a lynch mob shot him to death on June 27, 1844.

Brigham Young, who had led the hugely successful European mission, became president of the council that assumed leadership of the church. Having faced nothing but hostility in the settled parts of the continent, Young decided to lead his flock to the unsettled West, where they could practice their unique form of Christianity in peace. A pioneer band of 2,000 started west across Iowa in the spring of 1846. At Council Bluffs on the Missouri River they paused for the summer to plant crops. Some of the harvest was preserved for the trek across the plains; the remainder was left for the second wave of emigrants.

In the spring of 1847, Young, with an advance party of 148, set out to find a suitable spot for settlement. Guided by mountain man Jim Bridger, they followed the Oregon Trail across the South Pass and then turned south to the Great Salt Lake. That landmark may have been Young's objective from the beginning, for there were few other sites that could meet his curious needs. The place had to be remote and uninhabited, yet productive enough to support a sizable community. Young was in bed with fever when his wagon train mounted the final ridge and stood gazing at the valley below. Carried to the head of the column for a look, Young said simply: "It is enough. This is the right place. Drive on."

While the advance guard fenced in some acreage and planted crops, Young returned to Council Bluffs to prepare the main party. During the winter, the council elected Young successor to Joseph Smith, with the title Prophet, Seer, and Revelator. God's visitations with Young were less frequent than with Smith and seem to have been reserved for critical occasions. In general, God and Young were inclined to let the Mormons take care of themselves. The hegira began in May 1848, when 2,400 started up the trail along the Platte River. In succeeding months and years, smaller wagon trains plodded the same dusty route, and the Salt Lake settlement grew steadily. Within a decade, it numbered more than 25,000 souls.

The Mormon economy was communal in the early years, not from any religious commitment, but from necessity. Irrigation was necessary, and the nearest water supply was in the Wasatch Mountains, some twenty miles away. Under Young's direction, the Mormons built the first large-scale irrigation system in the country and devised a means for sharing the supply. During the gold rush of 1849, the community prospered by selling supplies to emigrants setting forth on the California Trail. When Utah became a federal territory the following year, the president appointed Young territorial governor.

Suspicion and hostility continued to shadow the Mormons, however. Visitors noticed and commented on the practice of polygamy, and the stories became exaggerated as they sifted eastward. In an effort to quell rumors, Young in 1852 publicly explained the concept (Smith's revelation had been a church secret), but the announcement failed to allay suspicion. In the presidential election of 1856, the Republican party platform denounced "those twin relics of barbarism—polygamy and slavery." The following year, President Buchanan sent an army detachment to bring Utah under closer federal control. The army's approach brought tensions within the Mormon community to the breaking point. The result was one of the most grisly tragedies in the bloody history of the West. A band of Mormons, operating without official sanction, descended on a wagon train of pioneers from Missouri, among whom were rumored to be the assassins of Joseph Smith, and at a place called Mountain Meadows they massacred 136 men, women, and children.

In 1861 President Lincoln replaced Young with a non-Mormon territorial governor, and Young turned his energies to building a commercial empire out of merchandising, cattle, and lumber. When he died in 1877, he left a fortune of $2 million to the seventeen wives and fifty-six children who survived him. The Mormon community also prospered as telegraph and railroad linked it with the national economy, and external criticism subsided with the gradual abandonment of polygamy (the church officially renounced the practice in 1896). The success of the Latter-Day Saints on the Day of Judgment is a matter of belief; their success as empire builders is a matter of record.

to negotiate a peace settlement. Polk's instructions to Trist were essentially those he had offered Mexico before the war—Mexican agreement to the admission of Texas to the American Union, and the sale of the remaining territory from New Mexico to California for $15 million. Trist met with Mexican officials at the village of Guadalupe Hidalgo, just outside the Mexican capital, and there on February 2, 1848, the two sides agreed to a treaty that ended the war. The treaty was drafted according to Trist's instructions. The new boundary between the two countries would be the Rio Grande, a surveyed parallel west of El Paso, the Gila River, and another surveyed line below San Diego in California.

Given the extent of the American conquests and the position of its occupying forces, Trist's settlement was a modest one. Too modest, in fact, to suit Polk. Even though Trist had carried out his instructions, Polk was not happy. The war had begun in a blaze of patriotic expansionism; the military victories fanned the fires. As American armies climbed farther into the mountains of Mexico, wrote New Englander James Russell Lowell with heavy sarcasm, "our Destiny higher an' higher kep' mountin'." Southern congressmen were demanding the cession of the Mexican provinces of Coahuila and Chihuahua. Within the president's cabinet, Secretary of State James Buchanan and Secretary of the Treasury Robert J. Walker believed that the Mexican people as a whole ought to be "benevolently assimilated" into the United States.

The All Mexico movement that swept the United States in the fall of 1847 had little popular support outside the South. It was largely political bombast. But it did show the extent to which America's "mission" had become confused, even perverted. President Polk sympathized with the All Mexico principle but could see no good reason to repudiate the treaty. He was also alarmed by the growing antiwar sentiment in the North and feared that more fighting would split his party in an election year. So he submitted the treaty to the Senate, which approved it by a vote of 38 to 14.

Nevertheless, the peace settlement of 1848 placed some 75,000 Spanish-speaking people under the jurisdiction of the United States, and the bloody uprisings in New Mexico and California during the war indicated that many were not at all happy with the transfer. Politicians spoke glibly of "benevolent assimilation," but what they meant was the imposition of an English-speaking, North European, predominantly Protestant culture on the Southwest. Whether destiny willed that is doubtful; that it was a form of imperialism is certain. Of more immediate concern to the victorious "Anglo-Saxons" of the North was the disposition of this vast empire. Many in New England and elsewhere assumed that the war was the product of a "conspiracy" among southerners to add territory for the expansion of slavery. The region west of Texas had been free soil under Mexican rule. The United States had seized it to extend the "area of freedom," as Andrew Jackson had put it; how ironic if it were subjected to slavery. Was the West, in short, to be slave or free? In the answer to that question lay the germ of civil war.

SUMMARY

Long before the term *manifest destiny* was coined in 1845, Americans had felt that one day their republic would stretch from the Atlantic to the Pacific. As early as 1792, the Washington administration laid the basis for a claim to the Pacific Northwest by sending a warship to find the mouth of the Columbia River. Lewis and Clark's overland trek in 1804–1806 reinforced the claim, as did John Jacob Astor's outpost on the Columbia in 1811. In 1818–1819, Secretary of State John Quincy Adams reached agreements with Britain and Spain that provided for the joint Anglo-American occupation of Oregon and restricted the Spanish to the area south of the forty-second parallel (California).

In the 1820s and 1830s, mountain men spread across the West in search of beaver pelts, and in the process they learned the best routes across the continent. In the 1840s, pioneers followed the trails blazed by mountain men to Oregon and California. Peaceful settlement was followed by political unrest and then revolution. Texas set the pattern in the 1830s with a successful revolution against Mexican rule. It emerged an independent republic, and in 1844 it agreed to annexation by the United States. Oregon settlers were by then agitating for annexation as well, and the Democratic party in that election year shrewdly coupled the two to avoid sectional jealousy. James K. Polk's election in 1844 on the promise of "Texas and Oregon" was a triumph for expansionism—or, as one journalist phrased it, for manifest destiny.

Texas was admitted in the wake of Polk's election victory, but it brought with it a boundary dispute with Mexico. The dispute involved a hundred-mile swath of territory between the Nueces River and the Rio Grande. Polk accepted the Texas claim to the Rio Grande and sent General Zachary Taylor to occupy the disputed territory. While thus risking war with Mexico, Polk also risked war with Britain by terminating the treaty of joint occupation and ordering the British out of Oregon.

In April 1846, Taylor's army clashed with a Mexican force on the north side of the Rio Grande, and Polk used the incident as an excuse to ask Congress for a declaration of war, on the grounds that "American blood has been shed upon the American soil." Meanwhile, the British had removed their fur trading company from Oregon, and in June they offered Polk a treaty compromising the American-Canadian boundary at the forty-ninth parallel. Polk accepted. That same month, the Bear Flag Revolt placed northern California in American hands. By August, American armies occupied New Mexico and California. In twelve weeks, Polk had achieved his war aims.

It remained only to convince Mexico. Taylor marched into Mexico and won a hard-fought victory at Buena Vista in February 1847. He was still, however, 800 miles from Mexico City. Opting against a long and risky overland march, Polk sent another army, commanded by General Winfield Scott, on an amphibious landing at Vera Cruz. Scott fought his way up through the mountain passes to Mexico City, which he occupied in September 1847. Nicholas Trist, a diplomat who accompanied Scott's army, negotiated a peace settlement signed at Guadalupe Hidalgo in February 1848.

By the treaty, Mexico ceded the Southwest from Texas to California to the United States, and with it the area's Mexican inhabitants. Differing from North Americans in language, culture, and religion, the Mexican population was not at all happy at being annexed to the United States, as bloody uprisings at Taos, New Mexico, and in southern California showed. The annexation also revealed that manifest destiny was only a form of imperialism: The republic had become an empire.

READING SUGGESTIONS

The best introduction to the westward movement is Ray Billington's *The Far Western Frontier, 1830–1860* (1956). In *Virgin Land* (1950), Henry Nash Smith analyzes Americans' perceptions of the West as revealed by popular literature. Daniel Boorstin's *The Americans: The National Experience* (1965) is a sophisticated update of the thesis that the frontier experience helped shape the American character. D. Morgan, *Jedidiah Smith and the Opening of the West* (1964), tells the exciting story of the mountain men. Connoisseurs of exploration should try Allan Nevins' biography of John C. Frémont, *Pathmarker of the West* (1944). A fascinating look at the personal experiences of people who traversed the overland trails is J. R. Jeffrey, *Frontier Women: The Trans-Mississippi West, 1840–1880* (1979). Norman Graebner's *Empire on the Pacific* (1955) points to Americans' interest in Pacific seaports.

Manifest destiny has been looked at from every conceivable angle. Frederick Merk, *Manifest Destiny and Mission in American History* (1966), relates it to the larger concept of mission and finds parallels between the Mexican War and the Spanish-American War. Gene M. Brack views it from south of the border in *Mexico Views Manifest Destiny, 1821–1846* (1975), and Reginald Horsman, *Race and Manifest Destiny: The Origins of American Racial Anglo-Saxonism* (1981), is the most recent treatment.

For the war against Mexico, Charles G. Sellers' splendid biography *James K. Polk: Continentalist, 1843–1846* (1966) is a good place to start. Bernard De Voto's *The Year of Decision, 1846* (1943) does justice to that dramatic year. Otis Singletary, *The Mexican War* (1960), is a good brief summary of the military engagements.

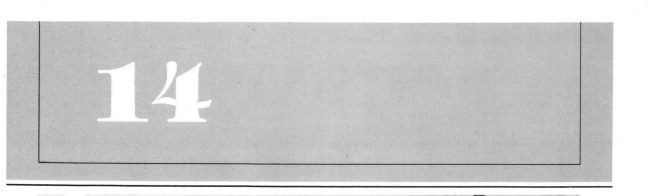

14

Library of Congress.

THE GATHERING STORM:
1846–1860

he din over Texas and Oregon —"Fifty-four Forty or Fight!" —momentarily drowned out the quarrel over slavery. But the sudden expansion of the national frontier added a new dimension to the slave controversy. The South's blunt admission that it wanted Texas for the sake of slavery placed the forces of expansion and antislavery on a collision course. The result was civil war.

The war with Mexico was barely three months old when the collision began. The House of Representatives was debating a routine appropriation bill when David Wilmot, a Democrat from western Pennsylvania, offered an amendment to bar slavery in any territory acquired from Mexico because of the war. The language was deliberately copied from the Northwest Ordinance of 1787, and Wilmot's obvious purpose was to extend the principle of restricting slavery, which Jefferson had first stated, to the new empire in the Southwest.

⊔ From Abolition to Free Soil

The Wilmot Proviso marked a switch in tactics for the antislavery movement. In the decade and a half since the founding of Garrison's *Liberator* in 1831, the abolitionists had pricked the nation's conscience, but had won no constituency. Few people in the North were truly concerned about the plight of the blacks. And legalists worried about the implications of depriving southern whites of their property without compensation.

FREE SOIL

Wilmot's proposal, by contrast, was something most people could accept, no matter what their position—antislave, antiblack,

or antisouthern. "Free soil" was the shorthand term for it. Free soil appeared to accept slavery in places where it was already established and sought only to prevent its extension into new territories. It was, as one scholar has called it, "the lowest common denominator" of antislavery feeling, and that made it a powerful political weapon. For the next fourteen years, free soil was the central issue of American politics.

Wilmot's Proviso started a bitter debate in Congress that divided both parties along sectional lines. John C. Calhoun, back in the Senate after a brief and tempestuous stand in the State Department, claimed that Congress lacked the constitutional power to exclude slavery from western lands. Prior to the formation of territorial governments in the region, he maintained, all the states held the new land in common. Congress had no right to deprive some states of their interests by restricting the movement of slaves. Northerners retorted that the Constitution gave Congress power to prescribe all needed regulations for the territories, including the power to regulate slavery. Besides, they argued, Congress had repeatedly exercised that power, beginning with the Northwest Ordinance of 1787.

Constitutional arguments, however, swayed few on either side of the congressional aisle, and the southern bloc, with the aid of a few administration Democrats, voted down the Wilmot Proviso in 1846 and twice more in succeeding years. Northern congressmen similarly rejected a compromise proposal that would have extended the 36° 30′ line west to the Pacific, because this would have imposed slavery on New Mexico and southern California. As a result, the Wilmot Proviso was never enacted into law. But it raised questions both parties had to answer in the presidential election of 1848.

(*Chapter opening photo*) "The Black Moses," Harriet Tubman was a conductor on the underground railroad. On her tombstone is inscribed: "She never ran her train off the track and never lost a passenger."

THE ELECTION OF 1848

Few southern slaveholders actually expected to move west. Most, in fact, knew that neither cotton nor slavery could survive in the arid plains. To southerners, the issue of the Wilmot Proviso was not one of economics, but one of rights. It was a matter of equality. If southerners could not carry their possessions—and their slaves—into the West, then southerners were not equal to northerners. To southerners, free soil was a symbol of northern aggression. By the end of 1847, as the war with Mexico came to a close, northern Democrats were searching for a compromise that would satisfy the South. The Wilmot Proviso, they feared, might prevent the United States from winning any territory from Mexico by uniting anti-expansionist Whigs and insulted southerners. Their solution was to let the people of the West themselves decide whether they wished to be slave or free. Known as "popular sovereignty," the idea was eminently democratic because it would submit the question to popular vote. It had the added virtue of removing the controversy from Congress, where impassioned rhetoric fuddled more than it clarified. It also assured southerners an equal opportunity to carry their institutions into the western territories until settlers determined otherwise.

Popular sovereignty was the Democrats' rallying cry in the election of 1848, and they nominated one of its champions, Lewis Cass, an elderly Jacksonian from Michigan. Polk had regarded himself as a one-term president and did not seek renomination. It may have been just as well, for his appointment policies had alienated an important segment of the party, notably the Van Buren element in New York. But there was principle, as well as patronage, involved in the Van Buren defection. Free soil was popular in New York, especially in the "burnt-over district," where the Liberty party had garnered nearly half its votes in 1844. When the Free Soil party, a new and expanded edition of the Liberty party, offered Van Buren its nomination in 1848, he accepted.

The Whigs too had their troubles. In New England and New York, the party was badly divided by the slavery issue. In Massachusetts, the party was split between "cotton" and "conscience" wings, the former reflecting the bond of economic interest between planter and millowner. In New York, the triumvirate of Horace Greeley, Thurlow Weed, and William H. Seward, founders of the Whig party in that state, were committed to antislavery by 1848. Greeley's *Tribune* dosed its readers with a daily ration of abolitionism, along with women's rights, phrenology, and socialism.* So radical, in fact, had the *Tribune* become that alarmed conservatives were already plotting the founding of a rival paper, *The New York Times*. Southern Whigs were more united, but they were also a dwindling minority. They might be eliminated altogether if the party selected a northern candidate with strong views.

Faced with these problems, the Whigs resorted to the tactic that had worked eight years before—nominating a military hero. Their choice, as Polk had anticipated, was Old Rough and Ready, General Zachary Taylor. As a native of Louisiana and a slaveowner, Taylor had substantial support in the South; and as a professional soldier, he was free of enemies (he didn't even admit to being a Whig until a month before the convention). To balance the ticket geographically, the Whigs selected Millard Fillmore of New York as Taylor's running mate. The convention then adjourned without drafting a platform. The Taylor campaign was not to be embarrassed by ideas.

---

* Greeley's London correspondent was Karl Marx, who earned world fame that year with the publication of his *Communist Manifesto*.

A light vote on election day gave Taylor and Cass each fifteen states, but Taylor won the larger ones, including New York, Massachusetts, and Pennsylvania. Van Buren polled 300,000 votes but failed to carry a single state, though the Free Soilers did elect nine congressmen. They also gained a voice in the Senate when the Ohio legislature selected a Democrat turned Free Soiler, Salmon P. Chase. Both North and South were divided evenly in the election, proving that both parties had successfully obscured the slavery issue. A solution to that problem seemed more remote than ever.

⊔ The Compromise of 1850

Though it never became law, the Wilmot Proviso effectively prevented any decision on the lands acquired from Mexico. By the end of 1848, the most that quarreling congressmen could agree upon was the establishment of a territorial government in Oregon, a region even southerners admitted was unfit for slavery. The region south of the forty-second parallel remained unorganized and ungoverned. So long as no one lived there except warlike Indians, sullen Mexicans, and a handful of Mormons, it mattered little. But the discovery of gold in California and the rush of '49 forced a decision.

THE GOLD RUSH OF '49

Gold was discovered in a millstream belonging to Johann Sutter in the summer of 1848. By December the news had filtered to the East; President Polk even referred to it in his annual message to Congress. In the course of 1849 some 80,000 goldseekers raced for California by land and sea; population enough, in fact, to qualify the place for immediate statehood. In October 1849 a convention of miners drafted a constitution. The voters ratified it a month later. The military, which had governed California since the war, happily turned over authority to the newly elected state officials. But statehood was not to be won so easily. The constitution prohibited slavery; California sought admission as a free state.

President Taylor gave his blessing to California's request; he saw it as a simple solution to the controversy provoked by the Wilmot Proviso. With the same reasoning, he endorsed statehood for New Mexico. If the territory acquired from Mexico were formed into states, he felt, they could resolve the slavery question for themselves. There would be no need for Congress to act, and the Wilmot Proviso, so offensive to the South, would become irrelevant. Unfortunately, the president's solution was too simple. Southerners screamed in anguish, feeling betrayed by one of their own. If California were admitted as a free state, it would upset the sectional balance in the Senate that had been maintained ever since Maine and Missouri were paired in the Compromise of 1820. By subdividing Texas, whose western claims reached to the Rio Grande and included the old Spanish capital of Santa Fe, southerners might have obtained a slave state to pair with California. But statehood for New Mexico, endorsed by the president, prevented that. Populated by Mexicans who had long since rid themselves of slaves, New Mexico too would be a free state.

Outnumbered in the House of Representatives and outvoted in the electoral college, the South regarded equal representation in the Senate as the last bastion for the defense of its rights. And increasingly it felt under attack. Political abolitionists were gaining public support for their demand that slavery be abolished in the nation's capital. Northern states had begun enacting laws that made it difficult for

Courtesy of the New-York Historical Society, New York City.
San Francisco, about 1850.

southerners to recover runaway slaves. To some southerners, the only solution was to leave the Union altogether. In January 1850, the Mississippi legislature issued a call for a southern convention to meet at Nashville in June. No one doubted that secession would be the principal item on the agenda. California's knock at the door had precipitated the most serious sectional crisis since nullification.

THE GREAT COMPROMISE

At that critical point, Henry Clay, now in his seventy-third year and near the end of a dazzling political career, took command. On January 20, 1850, he took the floor of the Senate with a package of resolutions designed to solve all the outstanding sectional disputes in one gigantic bargain. His proposals were as follows: (1) California would enter the Union as a free state. (2) Territorial governments without any restrictions on slavery would be created in the rest of the land acquired from Mexico. (3) Texas would relinquish its claims to New Mexico (the Rio Grande valley north of El Paso) in exchange for federal assumption of part of its debt. (4) Slaveowners in the District of Columbia could keep their slaves, but the slave trade would be abolished there. (5) Congress would declare that it lacked the power otherwise to interfere in the interstate slave trade. (6) Congress would enact a new fugitive slave law making it easier for southerners to recover their runaways.

Southerners were still unsatisfied. Clay's package still allowed the admission of California and possibly New Mexico as free states without any compensation for the South. On March 4, John C. Calhoun, too ill to stand, was carried into the Senate to

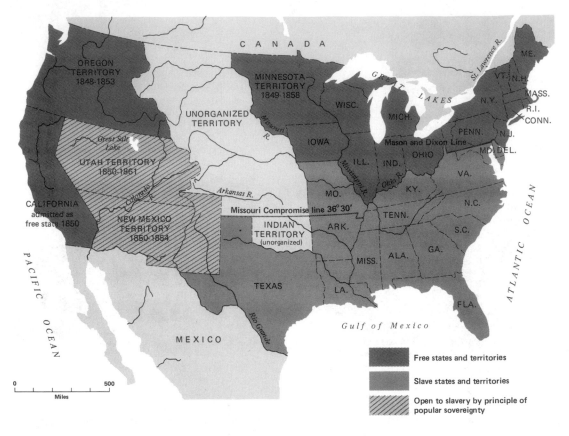

The United States in 1850.

listen while a colleague read his last address, an unbending defense of southern rights. The godfather of sectionalism would die before the session ended. As a further concession to southerners, Stephen A. Douglas of Illinois, leader of the western Democrats, proposed that two territories in addition to California be created out of the Mexican Cession: Utah and New Mexico. The territorial governments of each should be given the power to determine the slavery question. That, in effect, added popular sovereignty to the compromise and gave southerners the right, if they so wished, to take their slaves into the West.

President Taylor continued to insist that California ought to be admitted without

concessions to the South, but in July 1850 he caught a fever and died. His successor, Millard Fillmore, a moderate who wished to build a following of his own in the Whig party, supported the compromise. Douglas took charge and steered the various bills through Congress, and on September 17, Fillmore signed the last of them. The Great Compromise was in place.

THE FUGITIVE SLAVE LAW

Far from being the conclusive settlement Clay and Douglas desired, the Compromise of 1850 was only a truce, a temporary suspension of sectional hostilities. The call for secession in the South was momentarily stilled, but the South's agreement to the compromise depended on northern acceptance of it. Unfortunately, from the southern point of view the North violated its end of the bargain. The snag was the fugitive slave law. Like the question of slavery in the territories, the fugitive slave question was more symbolic than real in importance. Southern losses in runaways numbered fewer than a thousand a year. Nevertheless, an act making it easier to recover fugitives was the South's principal reward in the compromise—indeed, almost its only one. The law permitted a slave catcher, many of whom made a business of tracking down fugitives, to seize an alleged slave simply by appearing before a commissioner appointed by a court. The accused black was not allowed a jury trial. The commissioners earned 10 dollars for every fugitive reclaimed, and only 5 dollars in cases in which the accused was set free.

The law thus threatened the safety not only of runaways, but of blacks who had been living in the North for some years. In early 1851, for instance, an Indiana black was taken from his wife and children on the word of a slave catcher who claimed he had escaped nineteen years before. Panic rippled through the free black community, and several thousand fled to Canada for safety. But most of them prepared to resist the threat. Frederick Douglass, a runaway himself, put it bluntly: "The only way to make the Fugitive Slave Law a dead letter," said he, "is to make a half dozen or more dead kidnappers."

Among northern whites, the most inflammatory feature of the law was a provision that empowered federal marshals to summon citizens to aid in its enforcement.

A runaway slave being helped from wagon to daytime hideaway on the underground railroad.

That not only put the federal government in the business of manhunting, it threatened to make manhunters of everyone. Slavery was no longer a remote, ill-defined evil. It was at the back door of every northern household in the form of a runaway pleading for help. Mobs of angry whites occasionally intervened to save a fugitive, and though instances of mob action were relatively few, they received extensive publicity. In Detroit and Boston, military force had to be used to prevent the rescue of fugitives. In Wisconsin, after a band of Milwaukee vigilantes set free an accused black,

the state supreme court declared the law unconstitutional, thereby sanctioning resistance to it. The uproar over the fugitive slave law kept sectional tensions alive and lent weight to the arguments of southern extremists, or "fire eaters," that the North was the enemy.

UNCLE TOM'S CABIN

In June 1851, the *National Era*, an abolitionist sheet published in Washington, D.C., began printing weekly installments

Slavery and the Underground Railroad.

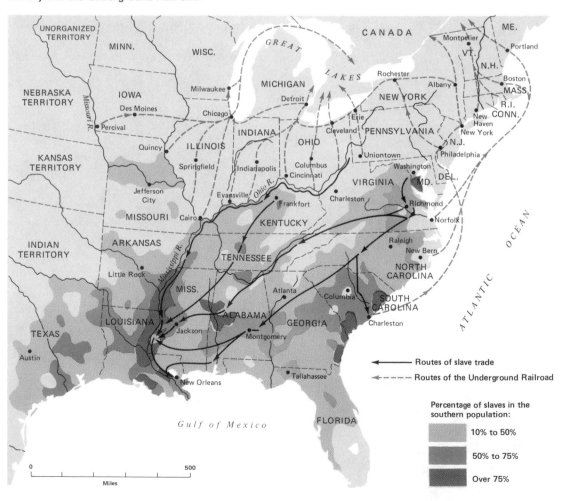

UNCLE TOM'S CABIN;

OR,

LIFE AMONG THE LOWLY.

BY

HARRIET BEECHER STOWE.

VOL. I.

BOSTON:
JOHN P. JEWETT & COMPANY.
CLEVELAND, OHIO:
JEWETT, PROCTOR & WORTHINGTON.
1852.

Harriet Beecher Stowe.
Library of Congress.

of a fictional account of slavery written by a little-known Cincinnatian, Harriet Beecher Stowe. The daughter of evangelist Lyman Beecher and wife of a Lane Seminary professor, Stowe was in perfect tune with northern views on slavery. And her timing was exquisite. Published as a book in March 1852, *Uncle Tom's Cabin, or Life Among the Lowly*, was an instant success. It took eight power presses, running simultaneously, to keep up with popular demand in its first year. The book ultimately sold 3 million copies in the United States and 3.5 million elsewhere in the world, making it the best-selling piece of American fiction ever produced.

Stowe's critics pointed out that she had never visited a plantation or even ventured into the South, but it mattered not. She provided symbols and stereotypes that simplified a complex institution. *Uncle Tom's Cabin* contained all the standard accusations against slavery—broken Negro families, brutal and often unjustified punishment, and harrowing escapes to freedom. Northern readers wept over the fate of Uncle Tom, the perfect Christian who even loved his oppressors, and anxiously followed Eliza Harris as she fled across the icy Ohio River to uncertain freedom. Stowe may not have been the little lady who started the Civil War, as Lincoln is alleged to have said, but she certainly dramatized the nation's moral dilemma. The northern view of slavery was never quite the same after *Uncle Tom's Cabin*.

Equally important was the book's impact on the South. Coinciding with northern resistance to the fugitive slave law, *Uncle Tom's Cabin* seemed to slaveowners one more example of northern aggression. Already a self-conscious minority, southerners became more defensive—and, accordingly, more combative—than ever. Southern assertiveness, in turn, provoked fears in the North that there was a vast conspiracy afoot to extend the limits of slavery. The prosouthern policies of Franklin Pierce, who was elected president in 1852, seemed to bear this out.

⊔ A Doughface Administration

The Democrats recaptured the White House in 1852, and before long it appeared that southerners had captured the Democrats. The new president, Franklin Pierce, was a New Englander, but he owed his nomination to southerners in his party.* It was soon clear why. In his inaugural address he promised to revive the expansionist policies of Polk, and the only direction that could go was south. As if to clear up any doubts, he named southern expansionists to the key diplomatic posts of Mexico and Spain. Mexico and Spanish-owned

Cuba were the most obvious targets for American land hunger.

The Gadsden Purchase. Pierce's envoy to Mexico, James Gadsden of South Carolina, was a railroad president who had labored for years in behalf of a transcontinental railroad to California. He naturally favored a southern route, with a terminus in Memphis or New Orleans. Such a route not only favored southern commerce, it meant a southern influence in California. West of El Paso, the best route for a railroad would cross Mexican territory south of the Gila River, so Gadsden carried instructions to purchase whatever Mexico was willing to sell. General Santa Anna, an old hand at dealing with money-laden American envoys, refused to part with anything more than a strip of land along the Gila River. Gadsden accepted this and returned with a treaty in January 1854. The Gadsden Purchase was the United States' last contiguous territorial acquisition, the last gasp of Manifest Destiny.

Gadsden's limited success in Mexico only whetted the administration's appetite for Cuba. Southern expansionists had eyed Cuba for years because it had a large slave population and profitable export staple, sugar. To Cuba's parent country, Spain, President Pierce sent Pierre Soulé of Louisiana, a flamboyant French immigrant known in the U.S. Senate for his flowery eulogies of Cuban rebels. Secretary of State William L. Marcy did restrain Soulé somewhat by forbidding him to enter into purchase negotiations. The administration's view was that Cuba would "release itself" from Spanish control, meaning of course by revolution on the pattern of Texas and California. A small group of would-be rebels maintained an office in New York, and the administration, through Secretary of War Jefferson Davis, a Mississippi "fire eater," gave them secret encouragement. Privately organized military expeditions were against the law, but Secretary Davis

---

* "Doughface" was the nickname given to northerners who sympathized with the South.

assured the Cubans that the United States would not obstruct a landing.

The Ostend Manifesto. When the "revolution" failed to materialize, Secretary of State Marcy suggested that the key American ambassadors in Europe—Soulé in Madrid, James Buchanan in London, and John Y. Mason in Paris—hold a meeting to coordinate American policy. The trio met in Ostend, Belgium, and sent the State Department a confidential memorandum that was published at the insistence of Congress as the Ostend Manifesto. Reflecting Soulé's penchant for diplomatic fireworks, the manifesto proposed that the United States make an earnest effort to purchase Cuba. Should Spain refuse to sell, then "by every law, human and Divine, we shall be justified in wresting it from Spain if we possess the power."

Secretary Marcy repudiated the manifesto, but the damage was done. The moral bankruptcy of the administration's foreign policy was laid bare. American diplomacy, sermonized the London *Times*, was given to "the habitual pursuit of dishonorable objectives by clandestine means." Manifest Destiny seemed nothing more than a cloak for aggression. Americans themselves were disillusioned, and expansionism evaporated, not to be revived for half a century. The demise of Manifest Destiny was not immediately apparent, however; indeed, American adventurers continued to prowl the West Indies and Central America for the rest of the decade. What did seem apparent to many northerners was that the Pierce administration was being manipulated by a secret cabal. "The *government* has fallen into the hands of the slave power *completely*," wailed Boston abolitionist Wendell Phillips. "So far as *national* politics are concerned, we are beaten—there's no hope. We shall have Cuba in a year or two, Mexico in five." By the time Phillips wrote those words in August 1854, the controversy over slavery in the western territories had burst forth anew, affording northerners fresh evidence that they were victims of a slave power conspiracy.

⊔ The Kansas– Nebraska Fight

Slavery was not the only political issue on the American scene in the 1850s. Tariffs, land policy, and internal improvements stirred intermittent discussion, but they always became embroiled in the sectional rivalry that stemmed from the slavery question. This was especially true of the project for a transcontinental railroad, which, nearly all agreed, was the nation's most needed investment now that its frontier extended to the Pacific. The question was not whether but where, for it was also clear that the route chosen—northern or southern—would give one section or the other a dominant influence over the economy and perhaps the politics of California.

Southerners wanted a route that originated in Memphis or New Orleans, skirted the Rocky Mountains via the Rio Grande and Gila rivers, and ended in Los Angeles or San Diego. Gadsden's Purchase in 1853 signified the Pierce administration's unofficial blessing for this path to the Pacific. The purchase also forced those who favored a northerly route originating in St. Louis or Chicago to redouble their efforts. This route would logically follow the Oregon and California Trails via the South Pass, and terminate in Sacramento or San Francisco. The central route passed through the Indian country west of the Missouri River, which had never been organized. The idea of a vast Indian reservation had been abandoned, though the government had made no offer to purchase the land, and a few settlers had gone to the Platte and Caw River valleys. Settlers, railroad interests, and northern sectionalists joined in a call for territorial government in the Great Plains.

REPEAL OF THE MISSOURI COMPROMISE

These various interests came to bear on Stephen A. Douglas, chairman of the Senate Committee on Territories. Douglas took credit for organizing much of the West, and the Nebraska country was a patch of unfinished business. In addition, Douglas had railroad investments of his own, and he saw political profit in the wishes of Chicago and St. Louis promoters. Thus it was, on January 4, 1854, that

Douglas reported from his committee a bill to organize the Nebraska Territory. Following the language of the Utah and New Mexico acts of 1850, the bill provided simply that the territory would ultimately be received into the Union with or without slavery, as its constitution prescribed at the time of admission. This provision was deceptive, if not illegal, because by the Missouri Compromise of 1820, the country north of 36° 30′ was free soil.

Pressed for clarification, Douglas on January 10 had printed an additional sec-

---

Sojourner Truth: "And A'n't I a Woman?"

Blacks, many of them former slaves, were among the most effective of antislavery orators. One of the most popular was Sojourner Truth, although, sadly, we have few specimens of her oratorical powers. A rare recording of one of her speeches was made by Frances D. Gage, who chaired a large women's rights meeting in Akron, Ohio, in May 1851. Sojourner Truth had already won fame as an abolitionist speaker, but she never hesitated to speak out for women's rights as well when the occasion demanded. Despite her support for their cause, the women of Akron clearly regarded her as an extremist when she rose to speak.

There were very few women in those days who dared to "speak in meeting"; and the august teachers of the people were seemingly getting the better of us, while the boys in the galleries, and the sneerers among the pews, were hugely enjoying the discomfiture, as they supposed, of the "strong-minded." Some of the tender-skinned friends were on the point of losing dignity, and the atmosphere betokened a storm. When, slowly from her seat in the corner rose Sojourner Truth, who, till now, had scarcely lifted her head. "Don't let her speak!" gasped half a dozen in my ear. She moved slowly and solemnly to the front, laid her old bonnet at her feet, and turned her great speaking eyes to me. There was a hissing sound of disapprobation above and below. I rose and announced "Sojourner Truth," and begged the audience to keep silence for a few moments.

The tumult subsided at once, and every eye was fixed on this almost Amazon form, which stood nearly six feet high, head erect, and eyes piercing the upper air like one in a dream. At her first word there was a profound hush. She spoke in deep tones, which, though not loud, reached every ear in the house, and away through the throng at the doors and windows.

"Wall, chilern, whar dar is so much racket dar must be somethin' out o' kilter. I tink dat 'twixt de niggers of de Souf and de womin at de Norf, all talkin' 'bout rights, de white men will be in a fix pretty soon. But what's all dis here talkin' 'bout?

"Dat man ober dar say dat womin needs to be helped into carriages, and lifted ober ditches, and to hab de best place everywhar. Nobody eber helps me into carriages, or ober mud-puddles, or gibs me any best place!" And raising herself to her full height, and her voice to a pitch like rolling thunder, she asked, "And a'n't I a woman? Look at me! Look at my arm! (and she bared her right arm to the shoulder, showing her tremendous muscular power). I have ploughed, and planted, and gathered into barns, and no man could head

Courtesy of the New-York Historical Society, New York City.

Sojourner Truth. After being set free, she took the surname of her "master," God's Truth.

me! And a'n't I a woman? I could work as much and eat as much as a man—when I could get it—and bear de lash as well! And a'n't I a woman? I have borne thirteen chilern, and seen 'em mos' all sold off to slavery, and when I cried out with my mother's grief, none but Jesus heard me! And a'n't I a woman?

"Den dey talks 'bout dis ting in de head; what dis dey call it?" ("Intellect," whispered some one near.) "Dat's it, honey. What's dat got to do wid womin's rights or nigger's rights? If my cup won't hold but a pint, and yourn holds a quart, wouldn't ye be mean not to let me have my little half-measure full?" And she pointed her significant finger, and sent a keen glance at the minister who had made the argument. The cheering was long and loud.

"Den dat little man in black dar, he say women can't have as much rights as men, 'cause Christ wan't a woman! Whar did your Christ come from?" Rolling thunder couldn't have stilled that crowd, as did those deep, wonderful tones, as she stood there with out-stretched arms and eyes of fire. Raising her voice still louder, she repeated, "Whar did your Christ come from? From God and a woman! Man had nothin' to do with Him." Oh, what a rebuke that was to that little man.

Turning again to another objector, she took up the defense of Mother Eve. I can not follow her through it all. It was pointed, and witty, and solemn; eliciting at almost every sentence deafening applause; and she ended by asserting: "If de fust woman God ever made was strong enough to turn de world upside down all alone, dese women togedder (and she glanced her eye over the platform) ought to be able to turn it back, and get it right side up again! And now dey is asking to do it, de men better let 'em." Long-continued cheering greeted this. "'Bleeged to ye for hearin' on me, and now ole Sojourner hasn't got nothin' more to say."

Amid roars of applause, she returned to her corner, leaving more than one of us with streaming eyes, and hearts beating with gratitude. She had taken us up in her strong arms and carried us safely over the slough of difficulty turning the whole tide in our favor.

Excerpted from Frances D. Gage, Reminiscences of Sojourner Truth in *History of Woman Suffrage*, edited by Elizabeth Cady Stanton, Susan B. Anthony, and Matilda Joslyn Gage, vol. 1 (New York: Fowler & Wells, 1881), pp. 115–117.

tion of the bill that referred all questions concerning slavery to the residents of the territory. This popular sovereignty provision, said Douglas, had been omitted from the original through a clerical error. Southerners pointed out, correctly, that popular sovereignty was meaningless as long as the Missouri Compromise remained in effect because before the territory became a state, the residents could not vote in favor of slavery even if they wanted to. Douglas agreed with this logic, and in the course of the following week he accepted two fateful amendments to the bill. One explicitly repealed the 36° 30' feature of the Missouri Compromise, and the other split the region

into two territories, Kansas and Nebraska. The first amendment in effect threw the entire region open to slavery; the second implied that one territory would be a slave state and the other free. In the view of many northerners, Douglas had handed the South one more slave state—Kansas. This possibility was brought immediately to the public by the issuing on January 24 of an *Appeal of the Independent Democrats*, an exposé drafted by Senator Salmon P. Chase, with help from Massachusetts Senator Charles Sumner and Free Soilers Joshua R. Giddings and Gerrit Smith. What had begun as a railroad question had become, like every issue, a slavery question.

The Kansas-Nebraska Act.

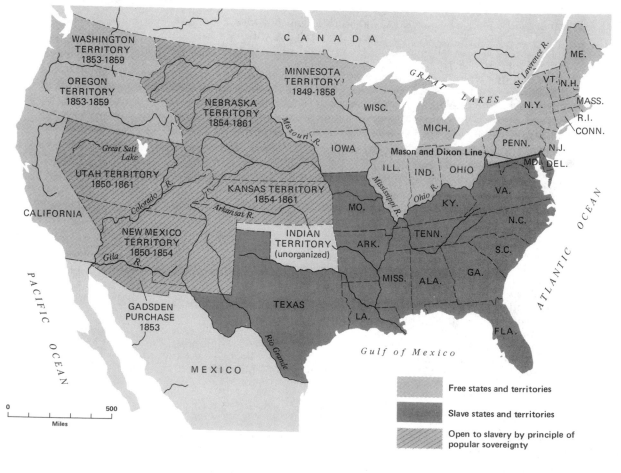

Why Douglas reopened the Pandora's box of slavery controversy remains a mystery. There were those who accused him of catering to the South out of presidential ambition. Southerners—so runs this line of reasoning—had vetoed his candidacy in 1852, and he needed their support to win the Democratic nomination in 1856. Douglas certainly had presidential ambitions, and he obviously welcomed southern support. But there is no evidence that the price of this support was the repeal of the Missouri Compromise. Indeed, southerners were generally indifferent to the Kansas-Nebraska bill until the northern uproar called their attention to it. The South joined Douglas only after Chase's *Appeal* pointed out that he deserved its support.

Douglas was driven more by the logic of his own position. He had maintained for years that popular sovereignty would resolve the slavery issue; this was his opportunity to give it a try. Yet it could not receive an honest trial so long as the Missouri Compromise mandated a vote in favor of free soil. At the same time, Douglas did not believe he was opening the Great Plains to slavery. The repeal of the Missouri Compromise, he told a New Hampshire newspaper, was a "matter of no practical importance," because "all candid men who understand the subject admit that the laws of climate, and of production, and of physical geography have excluded slavery from that country." There were natural limits to the expansion of slavery, Douglas was saying. The institution could not survive on the plains. Regardless of what position Congress took, Kansas would ultimately vote itself free.

Douglas's position was realistic enough, but it ignored the basic moral issue. To men like Chase and Sumner and Seward, slavery violated national values, and it was too important to be left to local option. Douglas's bill, moreover, involved a break with tradition, a rejection of the Founding Fathers. The founders of the republic, though many of them were slaveowners themselves, had taken the position that slavery was an evil. They had abolished it in some states, and through the Ordinance of 1787, had slowed its spread into the West. At the same time, for the sake of the Union, they had been willing to compromise, writing certain protections for slavery into the Constitution. This compromising spirit, which had resurfaced in 1820, in 1833, and as recently as 1850, had fallen victim—so northerners felt—to the slave power and its defender, Douglas.

The entire West was to be thrown open to slavery, and maybe the rest of the continent as well. The "slave power conspiracy," a land-hungry monster that spread its greedy tentacles from the Caribbean to the Great Plains, had already taken charge of the White House. As an unperturbed Douglas steered his bill through Congress, the conspiracy seemed to have spread to that body as well. By the time President Pierce signed the bill in May 1854, the uproar in the North was deafening.

In the ensuing chaos, the Whig party disappeared from view, and the Democrats split wide open. On June 15, Horace Greeley ran an editorial in the *Tribune* calling for the formation of a new antislavery party and even suggested the name "Republican." Spontaneous meetings all over the North that summer brought together "conscience" Whigs, Free Soilers, and anti-Nebraska Democrats. The name Republican for the new party was a logical choice, for it brought to mind the idealism of Jefferson, Madison, and other Founding Fathers. In the fall elections of 1854, the new party, sometimes in alliance with Know-Nothings, captured the legislatures of seven northern states and elected a number of congressmen. Though almost instantly a force in the nation's councils, the Republicans remained a sectionally oriented party possessed, for the moment, of a single issue—free soil. Their appearance, moreover, quickened the slide of the Democrats into the arms of the South. Before long, the party system itself had become sectionalized.

The tidal wave of feeling stirred up by the Kansas-Nebraska Act also swept away both Douglas and his cause, popular sovereignty. Northerners accused Douglas of being a servant of the slave power; southerners regarded him as excessively ambitious. Nor did the Kansas-Nebraska Act prove that popular sovereignty was workable. Rather, it exposed the vagueness in the doctrine that made it difficult to put into practice. If the immediate result of the Kansas-Nebraska Act was the birth of the Republican party, the long-term effect was Bleeding Kansas.

BLEEDING KANSAS

The fatal defect in popular sovereignty was ambiguity. No one was quite sure when the rule would come into play. Were the people to vote on the critical question of slavery or free soil at the time of admission to the Union, on organization of a territorial legislature, or earlier? How many residents would constitute a quorum—60,000, 5,000, or 100? Whatever the answer, popular sovereignty seemed to involve a race. "Come on then, Gentlemen of the Slave States," William H. Seward told the Senate shortly after the act was passed, "since there is no escaping your challenge, I accept it in behalf of the cause of freedom. We will engage in competition for the virgin soil of Kansas, and God give the victory to the side which is stronger in numbers as it is in right."

A month earlier, in April 1854, the Massachusetts legislature had incorporated the Massachusetts Emigrant Aid Company to assist the settlement of antislavery Yankees in Kansas. The company actually dispatched relatively few emigrants—750 in 1854, 900 in the following year—but its efforts were attended by an enormous propaganda barrage. When the pioneers of western Missouri read an account of the company's plans in Greeley's *Tribune*, they got the impression, as one put it, that they were "being made the unwilling receptacle of the filth, scum, and offscourings of the East" who come "to preach abolitionism and dig underground Rail-roads." Missourians, prosouthern although few of them actually owned slaves, organized "emigration committees" of their own to cross the border at election time.

In the fall of 1854, a territorial governor, Andrew Reeder, arrived in Kansas. Reeder ordered a census and scheduled the election of a territorial legislature. The census revealed a total of 2,905 eligible voters. In the election, which took place on March 30, 1855, a total of 6,307 votes were cast, with a heavy proslavery majority. Missouri "border ruffians," who had crossed into Kansas just long enough to vote, gave the South a victory in the first leg of the Kansas relay.

Governor Reeder called for new elections in certain districts where the results were contested, but otherwise he felt obliged to let the results stand. When the legislature met, it expelled the handful of free soilers who had been elected, imposed slavery, and made abolitionism a capital offense. Expelling the Free Soilers was a blunder, for it allowed this group to deny the validity of the territorial government and erect a "government" of their own. In the fall of 1855, the free state legislature met at Topeka, elected a governor, and began the steps toward statehood.

The rival governments deepened the divisions among Kansas settlers and encouraged violence. In May 1856, a posse sent by the proslavery government descended on the free soil town of Lawrence, bombarded the village's lone hotel with a cannon, and burned several buildings. The "sack of Lawrence," as the papers phrased

Courtesy of The New-York Historical Society, New York City.

"Desperate conflict in a barn." Runaway slaves battle their pursuers.

it, invited retaliation. The Massachusetts Emigrant Aid Company began sending rifles to leaders of the Topeka government. The shipments became known as "Beecher's Bibles" after evangelist Henry Ward Beecher declared that the rifle was a greater moral force in Kansas than the Bible.

THE SUMNER–BROOKS AFFAIR

Violence in the nation's capital echoed the violence in Kansas. Congress by the spring of 1856 was paralyzed by the sectional conflict. It took weeks simply to elect a Speaker of the House; some members carried pistols for self-defense. On May 22, the day after the sack of Lawrence, Congressman Preston Brooks went into the Senate in search of Senator Charles Sumner. Two days earlier, Sumner had delivered a tirade against the South entitled "The Crime against Kansas," in which he had referred insultingly to several senators, among them South Carolina's Andrew Pickens Butler, a cousin of Brooks. Determined to avenge the family name, Brooks found Sumner seated at his desk and beat him senseless with a cane. Sumner suffered severe shock and did not return to his seat for more than three years. In the interim, his vacant seat was silent witness to northern outrage at the brutal methods of the "slave power."

Just two days after the Sumner-Brooks affair, the violence in Kansas reached a climax. John Brown was a fifty-six-year-old emigrant who had come to Kansas from Ohio the previous year. A deeply religious man who believed himself to be an agent of God's wrath, he set out to avenge the sack of Lawrence. At the head of a party of seven, including four sons and a son-in-law, Brown descended on a cluster of proslavery settlers on Pottawatomie Creek. They broke into three cabins and killed five men, hacking their bodies with broadswords, and then rode off with the settlers' horses. It is tempting to dismiss Brown as a lunatic, or simply an ultraviolent horse-thief, but neither assessment does justice to an incredibly complex individual. No lunatic could have conceived the plan or inspired the loyalty that made possible the raid on Harpers Ferry three and a half years later. On the other hand, the maiming and the horse stealing was puzzling behavior for an agent of the Lord. In any case, the incident, called the Pottawatomie Massacre, sent a new shock through a nation already in trauma.

⊔A House Dividing

Against this background of violence, both in Kansas and in Washington, party conventions met in June 1856 to select candidates for the presidency. Under more normal circumstances, Douglas would have been the obvious choice when the Democrats assembled in Cincinnati. He was the most able, attractive candidate the party possessed. But the Kansas-Nebraska Act had weakened his standing in the North without winning him friends in the South. President Pierce was also under suspicion in the North for his "doughface" policies. So the party turned to James Buchanan, an old Jacksonian with a strong political organization in Pennsylvania. An ardent

expansionist, Buchanan also had support in the South, reinforced by his participation in the Ostend Manifesto. After shunting Douglas aside, the Democrats adopted Douglas's platform because popular sovereignty, despite its flaws, was the one program on which both wings of the party could agree. It was the only solution for the slavery problem in sight.

The young Republican party settled on a candidate even before its first convention opened in Philadelphia. John C. Frémont, leader of California's Bear Flag revolt, fitted the mold of Whig military heroes. But he was also a moderate free soiler who had made no statements that could antagonize the South. The party's more forceful leaders—Seward, Sumner, Chase—were pushed into the background as the party dressed itself in the garb of benign moderation. Its platform was summarized in the slogan, "Free men, Free soil, Free speech, and Frémont."

ELECTION OF 1856

Youth and the lack of a grassroots organization hurt the Republicans, and Buchanan won the election with 174 electoral votes to Frémont's 114. Millard Fillmore, a candidate of both the nativist American party and the remnant of the Whigs, picked up 8 electoral votes. The significance of the election, however, lay in its geographic bias. Frémont's support was confined to New England and the Northwest; Buchanan's lay principally in the South. The Democrats' success hinged on the votes of four states—New Jersey, Pennsylvania, Indiana, and Illinois. Only by their tenuous hold on those four states could the Democratic party claim to be a national organization. And it was almost the only national institution the country possessed.

By 1856 the nation was almost completely divided, socially as well as politi-

Election of 1856

American Know-Nothing — Fillmore

Democrat — Buchanan

Republican — Fremont

U.S. Territories (non-voting)

8

114   174

Total electoral vote
296

22%   45%

33%

Total popular vote

1850

1860

cally. Lacking such unifying institutions as a national university or a state church, the country was held together more by habit than interest. Even the major Protestant churches had divided on the slavery issue; Presbyterians, Baptists, and Methodists split during the 1840s into northern and southern wings. Nor were there solid economic ties to reinforce the semblance of federalism. The nation's railroads ran generally east and west, and different gauges of track were used in North and South. This meant that freight cars had to be reloaded at the Mason-Dixon line. No bridge was constructed over the Ohio River until the eve of the Civil War, and the Mississippi River, a bond of union in Jefferson's time, had been overshadowed as a trade artery by the Great Lakes and the Erie Canal.

In politics, one great national organization—the Whig party—had succumbed to the sectional conflict and been replaced by a sectionally based antislavery party. The Democratic party, though dominated by the South, was in 1856 the one institution that could claim popular support in both North and South. The politics of the next four years is largely the story of the disruption of the Democratic party, climaxing in the convention walkouts of 1860. At that point, a disruption of the Union itself no longer seemed an unthinkable calamity.

DRED SCOTT VS. POPULAR SOVEREIGNTY

In his inaugural address on March 4, 1857, President Buchanan predicted that the Supreme Court would shortly be able to resolve the question of slavery in the territories. This forecast indicated that one or more members of the Supreme Court had discussed with the president the implications of a case pending before the court, a move that was unusual if not downright injudicious. The case of *Scott* v. *Sanford* was well known, and its implications had been

freely discussed in the press. Anticipating that the Court's ruling would favor the South, Republican papers had already begun to challenge the Court's authority.

Scott was the personal servant of an army officer who had lived for several years at a post in the Wisconsin Territory (present-day Minnesota), from which slavery had been banned by the Missouri Compromise. After returning to Missouri in the late 1840s, Scott sued for his freedom on grounds that he had resided in free territory. Missouri courts ruled that, having returned to Missouri, he was a slave. His legal efforts, however, attracted the attention of abolitionists, who wanted to test whether a slave automatically became free when he touched free soil. Such a proposition had profound implications for the enforcement of the fugitive slave law. In the meantime, Scott had passed by inheritance to a new master, John A. Sanford, a resident of New York. Scott sued again, this time in federal court. Losing again, he appealed to the Supreme Court of the United States.

The Supreme Court might have ruled narrowly that Missouri law governed this matter, and that Scott was still a slave. Instead, Chief Justice Roger B. Taney, with President Buchanan's encouragement, sought to resolve the entire question of slavery in the territories. Delivering the opinion of the Court majority on March 6, 1857, just two days after Buchanan's inauguration, Taney took up first the question of whether Scott had ever resided on free soil. Taney held that a restriction on slaveowners that prevented them from moving into a federal territory with their slave property in effect deprived them of the use of their property without due process of law, in violation of the Fifth Amendment to the Constitution. Congress therefore had no power to prohibit slavery in the territories, and the provision of the Missouri Compromise restricting slavery in the Louisiana Purchase north of 36° 30′ was unconstitutional. The Minnesota coun-

Library of Congress.
Dred Scott.

try, therefore, had never been free soil, and Scott was not free by virtue of having resided there. Being a slave, he had no legal rights. Taney dismissed the suit for lack of jurisdiction.

Politically motivated, the decision was a weak one from almost any legal point of view. Its principal flaw was that it misread the intentions of the men who had drafted the Constitution and its amendments. The same year they drafted the Constitution, the Founding Fathers prohibited slavery in the Old Northwest. To conclude, as Taney did, that they intended by the Fifth Amendment (which was drafted only two years later) to prevent Congress from regulating slavery in the territories in the future was to violate both history and legal logic.

Even in its political purposes, the Dred Scott decision failed. Instead of quieting the sectional strife, it further inflamed the North because it completely negated the whole free soil argument. By ruling that

Congress had no power to restrict the expansion of slavery, Taney adopted the position the South had been advocating for a decade. In fact, Taney made slavery a national institution. Since the revolution, the nation had been committed to freedom, with slavery considered an abnormality preserved in some parts of the Union by local law and custom. With the Dred Scott decision, the nation was committed to slavery, and the area of freedom was confined by local law and custom to a few northern states. To northerners, this dramatic reversal was further evidence of the existence of a conspiracy—one that ruled Congress, manipulated presidents like puppets, and now had even infiltrated the Supreme Court.

Perhaps worst of all, by limiting Congress's power over slavery, the Dred Scott decision impaired Congress's ability to settle sectional conflict. It left no middle ground. The decision even dealt a fatal

New York Public Library Picture Collection.

"The Bear Garden." By 1858, passions ran so high that members of Congress were carrying pistols into the debates. This scene depicts a brawl that broke out in the House of Representatives during the debate on the Kansas statehood bill.

blow to popular sovereignty, the one avenue that promised escape. If Congress could not prohibit slavery in a territory, how could it authorize a territorial legislature to do so? This consequence was not immediately evident, however. Douglas and others continued to maintain that a territory might exclude slavery if it wished. The requiem on popular sovereignty was pronounced not at the bench of the Supreme Court, but on the prairies of Kansas.

THE LECOMPTON CONSTITUTION

By the summer of 1857, the population of Kansas approached the number that would qualify the territory for statehood.

Proslavery forces called for a constitutional convention, and the governor obliged. Free state men refused to participate in the election, however, and the convention that assembled at Lecompton, Kansas, in November was solidly proslavery. Realizing that their handiwork had to be submitted to the voters, the southern element compromised. The constitution protected slave property already in the state, but left to the voters the question of admitting or excluding more slaves. This was hardly the choice between "slavery" and "freedom" popular sovereignty had promised, and free staters in Kansas promptly objected. The territorial legislature, where free staters had at last achieved a majority, proposed that the entire Lecompton constitution, and not just the slave provision, be submitted to the voters.

The governor agreed, and two referendums were held. In the first, the one arranged by the Lecompton convention, there were 6,226 votes for the Lecompton constitution with slavery and 569 for it without slavery. In the second vote, authorized by the legislature, with the proslavery group abstaining, there were 10,226 votes against the constitution and 162 in favor of it. Combining the returns, it is evident that a clear majority of the eligible voters of Kansas opposed both slavery and the Lecompton constitution.

Buchanan nevertheless plunged grimly ahead. He announced his support for the constitution and submitted it to Congress for approval. He instantly ran into a snag when Douglas, disenchanted by the fraud in the Kansas elections, announced he could not support the Lecompton document. A combination of southerners and Buchanan loyalists secured approval of the constitution in the Senate, but an alliance of Douglas Democrats and Republicans prevailed in the House. After weeks of the most bitter wrangling the nation had witnessed since Kansas became an issue in 1854, the two houses agreed to a compromise. Taking advantage of a technicality that allowed the administration and the South to save face, Congress sent the constitution back to Kansas for a new referendum. Kansas trooped to the polls once again, and this time they rejected the Lecompton constitution flatly, 11,300 to 1,788. The territory was not admitted to the Union until after the South departed in 1861. But the uproar itself had discouraged slaveowners and helped determine that Kansas would be free. In the census of 1860, there were only two slaves in the entire territory.

The fight over the Lecompton constitution cost the Democrats dearly. The disagreement between Buchanan and Douglas split the party and boded ill for the presidential contest of 1860. The party, moreover, was steadily losing popularity in the North. When Franklin Pierce came into office in 1853, there had been 92 free state Democrats in the House of Representatives and 67 from slave states. When Buchanan entered office in 1857, there were 53 free state Democrats and 75 slave state Democrats. The election of 1858 reduced the number of free state Democrats to 32, and 12 of those had preserved their popularity with the voters by deserting the administration and opposing the Lecompton constitution. Among the Democrats up for reelection in 1858 was Douglas himself. Douglas had to retain his Illinois Senate seat; otherwise he had no chance of getting control of the party in 1860.

THE IDEOLOGICAL CONFLICT

In 1854, the year of the Kansas-Nebraska Act, slavery apologist George Fitzhugh published a work entitled *Sociology for the South*, and in the year of the Dred Scott decision he followed it with another, entitled *Cannibals All!* Fitzhugh's work was an elaboration of a theme developed some years earlier by John C. Calhoun. In a system of so-called free enterprise, wrote Fitzhugh, the rule is "every man for himself, and the devil take the hindmost." The ablest or the most ruthless rise to the top and maintain their position by exploiting the mass of propertyless workers at the bottom. Factory "wage slaves," argued Fitzhugh, were no more free than southern plantation workers; indeed, their living conditions were probably worse. Slavery, Fitzhugh concluded, was not a racial institution at all; it was a natural outgrowth of capitalism. Thus, if the southern form of it were extended to the whole country, white laborers would in fact benefit from the care and security it offered.

This notion, that slavery was or ought

THE LITTLE GIANT IN THE CHARACTER OF THE GLADIATOR.

New York Public Library, Aston, Lenox, and Tilden Foundation.

Stephen A. Douglas, the "little giant," seen as a Roman gladiator by a cartoonist.

to be a national institution, absurd though it seems today, mirrored what many in the North were coming to fear—that there was a conspiracy afoot for the expansion of slavery. On this fear the Republicans capitalized. They could not hope to win elections simply by promising to limit the spread of black slavery; northern racial biases ran too deep. So they gave a new and broader meaning to the word *slavery*. In Republican rhetoric, slavery meant yielding to tyranny, the loss of liberty and equality—in short, the overthrow of the republic. This they accused the South of trying to do. By promising to ward off *that* slavery, they appealed to northern workers and shopkeepers, people who otherwise had little or no interest in the fate of blacks.

No one phrased this ideology better than Abraham Lincoln, whom Illinois Republicans nominated to oppose Douglas in the state senatorial election. Addressing the Republican state convention in 1858, Lincoln began with a quotation from St. Paul that was popular among politicians in the 1850s: "A house divided against itself cannot stand." He then proceeded:

> I believe this government cannot endure, permanently half *slave* and half *free*.
> I do not expect the Union to be dissolved—I do not expect the house to *fall*—but I do expect it will cease to be divided.
> It will become *all* one thing, or *all* the other.

Nothing surprised Lincoln more than the conclusion, reached by many of those who heard or read the speech, that he was predicting civil war. "I said no such thing," he later insisted. What he did predict was a southern takeover, with the connivance of Douglas and other northern Democrats. Slavery was knocking at the door of every farmer and wage earner. To protect themselves, they must vote for people who promise to "arrest the further spread of it" and place the institution on a "course of ultimate extinction." The House Divided speech was the opening salvo in the battle to unseat Douglas. It was also a bid to reestablish for the Republicans the old Jacksonian alliance of small farmers and workers.

Although the choice of senator lay with the legislature, Lincoln and Douglas agreed to hold a series of joint debates, one in each of the state's congressional districts. Lincoln's principal aim was to expose to public view the rift in the Democratic party by probing the inconsistency between the Dred Scott decision and popular sovereignty. How, he asked Douglas, in the light of Dred Scott, could people of a territory prohibit slavery? If Congress could not prohibit slavery, how could it give a territory power to do so? Douglas had been answering the question ever since the Dred Scott decision was published. His answer to Lincoln at Freeport, thereafter dubbed the Freeport Doctrine, was only the best-remembered of his responses. The people of a territory could bar slavery, in effect, said Douglas, simply by refusing to enact a slave code. Without laws regulating slave crimes and punishments, imposing curfews, and authorizing slave patrols, the "peculiar institution" could not exist, even if it were legally permitted.

The effort to reconcile the Dred Scott decision with popular sovereignty was satisfactory to most Illinois voters, who returned a Democratic majority to the legislature and thus assured Douglas's reelection to the Senate. Yet, like so many of Douglas's victories, this was a costly one. The Freeport Doctrine confused and alienated southerners, already suspicious because of his opposition to the Lecompton constitution. It boded ill for Douglas's chances in the presidential election of 1860.

Courtesy of the New-York Historical Society, New York City.

John Brown.

⊔ Impending Crisis: The Election of 1860

America's presidential elections are not noted for their calmness or rationality. Even in the most placid of times, politicians manage to convey a sense of urgency, a feeling that the nation stands at some important crossroad. In 1860 this character portrayal was set against the backdrop of sectional hypertension, as North and South each considered itself the victim of aggression. An incident at Harpers Ferry, Virginia, in October 1859 deepened the atmosphere of conspiracy and intrigue.

JOHN BROWN'S RAID

John Brown, whose contribution to the free soil movement in Kansas had done more harm than good, returned east after the Pottawatomie Massacre, encouraged by Kansas free staters. With the aid and financing of a handful of Boston abolitionists, several of them Unitarian clergymen, he concocted a scheme to seize the federal arsenal at Harpers Ferry, where the Shenandoah River joined the Potomac, and make it a center for a slave uprising. Brown assumed, as did many abolitionists, that the South was a powderkeg. Slaves would revolt, or at least escape to freedom, if given an opportunity.

Even if Brown's assessment had been accurate, there was no time for an uprising. He descended on the village on the morning of October 17, 1859, with twenty-two men. Within hours the local militia had him cornered in the engine house of the Baltimore and Ohio Railroad, which ran through the town. No more than a handful of slaves heard his call for an uprising, and those who did obviously discounted its chances of success. A federal army detach-

CLIO'S FOCUS: John Brown Resurrected and Reconstructed

Historians reflect the time in which they write, and nowhere is this more evident than in the changing perceptions of John Brown. The details of John Brown's remarkable career have long been known. Much of his life story was elicited at his trial; friends and relatives published further details shortly after his execution. What has changed over time is not the factual record, but the judgment of historians, who have labeled him variously a misguided fanatic, a dangerous rebel, a madman, and a hero. John Brown's odyssey through the history books has a history of its own.

Throughout the Civil War and for some time after, John Brown was more symbol than man—a martyred saint to northerners, a murderous madman to southerners. James Ford Rhodes was one of the first to undertake a scholarly assessment of the man in his *History of the United States from the Compromise of 1850* (1893). After describing the Pottawatomie massacre, Rhodes quoted an exchange between Brown and one of his sons in which Brown admitted only to having approved the act. The son replied: "Whoever did it, the act was uncalled for and wicked." Brown then said: "God is my judge. The people of Kansas will yet justify my course." And Rhodes commented:

> In passing judgment at this day, we must emphasize the reproach of the son; yet we should hesitate before measuring the same condemnation to the doer and to the deed. John Brown's God was the God of Joshua and Gideon. To him, as to them, seemed to come the word to go out and slay the enemies of his cause. He had no remorse. It was said that on the next morning when the old man raised his hands to Heaven to ask a blessing, they were still stained with the dried blood of his victims. What the world called murder was for him the execution of a decree of God. But of the sincerity of the man there can be no question.

Despite Rhodes's determined effort at scholarly detachment, his view was essentially a northern one. Historians after 1900 became more sympathetic to the South, especially in their view of reconstruction, and more inclined to criticize the prewar abolitionists. James Truslow Adams distilled the scholarship of his day in his *Epic of America* (1931), the most widely used secondary school textbook of the 1930s and 1940s. Wrote Adams of the raid on Harpers Ferry:

> The old man's striking physical dignity and impressiveness, as well as his courage when captured and hung, won him admiration among those in the North whose hearts were stronger than their heads. The conflict was coming to the country rapidly enough without such melodrama, and the South could not fail to be yet more embittered by the sight of arms being put into the hands of negroes. The possibility of a slave uprising and of a massacre of the whites, such as had occurred in Hayti, was ever in the minds of the slaveowners, responsible for the lives of their women and children on widely separated plantations, and Brown's armed advance into the South with blacks in his party was as cruelly insensate as it was childish. Perhaps no man in American history less deserves the pedestal of heroism on which he has been raised. . . .

Adams, though a New Englander, clearly empathized more with southern whites than with their slaves. Nor was he alone in his judgment; such subtle bias also permeates the writings of the "repressible conflict" school of the 1930s.

World War II reawakened historians to the moral issues in war. They ceased condemning Brown and instead dismissed him as an emotionally unbalanced fanatic. Allan Nevins, in his monumental study *Ordeal of the Union* (2 vols., 1947) and *The Emergence of Lincoln* (2 vols., 1950), resurrected the evidence of insanity that had been introduced at Brown's trial. On the subject of slavery, Nevins concluded that Brown's "monomania . . . or his paranoia as a modern [psychoanalyst] would define it, rendered him irresponsible." In 1966 John Garraty, in a widely used college textbook, *The American Nation*, declared flatly that Brown was "deranged." Rather than hang him, wrote Garraty, "It would have been far wiser and more just to have committed Brown to an asylum. Then his escapade could have been seen in proper perspective."

Even as Garraty wrote, the civil rights movement was helping to bring a reappraisal of the motives and methods of the abolitionists. In his 1970 biography of John Brown, *To Purge This Land with Blood,* Stephen Oates reminded readers that to call John Brown insane "is to ignore the tremendous sympathy he felt for the black man in America," and "to label him a 'maniac' out of touch with 'reality' is to ignore the piercing insight he had into what his raid—whether it succeeded or whether it failed—would do to sectional tensions."

The appearance of four full-scale biographies in the 1970s testified to the new relevance of John Brown. While admitting that Brown was in no sense "normal," recent writers have pointed to the number of wholly reasonable people who supported his activities. The black abolitionist Frederick Douglass, for instance, objected to the plan for raiding Harpers Ferry only because he thought it would not work. Harriet Tubman not only approved the idea but tried to join Brown; only an accident of timing prevented her from doing so. Howard Zinn, in his avowedly liberal *People's History of the United States* (1980), cites both Douglass and Tubman in arguing that Brown's activities were both reasonable and just:

> It would take either a full-scale slave rebellion or a full-scale war to end such a deeply entrenched system. If a rebellion, it might get out of hand, and turn its ferocity beyond slavery to the most successful system of capitalist enrichment in the world. If a war, those who made the war would organize its consequences. Hence, it was Abraham Lincoln who freed the slaves, not John Brown. In 1859 Brown was hanged, with federal complicity, for attempting to do by small-scale violence what Lincoln would do by large-scale violence several years later—end slavery.

John Brown's truth goes marching on. And so does his reputation.

ment, commanded by Lieutenant Colonel Robert E. Lee, took him prisoner, and the state of Virginia put him on trial before he even recovered from his wounds. He was convicted of treason against Virginia and hanged in December, 1859.

Brown thought his execution would be his final triumph, and for once he was right. Thousands in the North made him a martyr. It capped a decade of popular emotionalism. As events cascaded one upon another, the mood of the North had shifted from a sentimental reverence for the Union, with tolerance for the South's peculiarities, to an abiding dislike for anything southern. Nothing revealed the isolation of the South more than the northern hero worship of John Brown. The feeling of oppression, combined with the never-distant fear of slave uprising, also hardened southern attitudes, just as it had in the nullification crisis almost thirty years before. And now another presidential election loomed. Events seemed to be taking on a momentum of their own.

THE DEMOCRATS SPLIT

The Democrats' initial mistake in 1860 was selecting Charleston, South Carolina, for a convention site. The city was a hotbed of secessionism, and local fire eaters crowded the convention hall and interrupted the proceedings with stomps and shouts. The convention sat for ten days in heat and humidity unusual even for that area in April. Nerves frayed under the tension, and tempers grew short.

Compromise may not have been possible even if conditions had been better. Southerners, suspicious of Douglas and alarmed by his Freeport Doctrine, came to the convention with a virtual ultimatum: The platform must promise a congressional guarantee for slavery in the territories—even to the extent of a federal slave code—and the party must nominate a southern candidate. Some delegations were instructed to walk out if these demands were not met. Several southerners wanted the nomination, as did President Buchanan, but the only Democrat with a shadow of a chance of defeating the Republicans was Douglas. And Douglas was just as rigid as the southerners. He insisted on popular sovereignty because it was the one solution with appeal in the North. Douglas controlled about half of the convention votes, but his support was far short of the two-thirds majority needed for nomination under the party's rules. When the "clan Douglas" won the vote on the platform, the Deep South delegates, led by William Lowndes Yancey of Alabama, filed out of the convention. There followed a farce with overtones of tragedy. The southerners assembled in a building across the street and waited for an olive branch that never came. Inside the hall, the convention chairman ruled that two thirds of the original number of delegates was required to nominate. When no candidate achieved that total in several ballots, the convention decided to adjourn and meet again in Baltimore in June.

When the Democrats met in Baltimore, a number of delegates who had walked out at Charleston appeared to take their seats. The Douglas forces, taking the position that the walkout at Charleston amounted to resignation from the convention, refused to seat them. This tactic brought a new walkout, this time by most of the delegates from the Upper South, joined by a handful of Buchanan Democrats from the North and West. What was left of the convention proceeded to nominate Douglas and endorse popular sovereignty. The seceders assembled a few blocks away and nominated John C. Breckinridge of Kentucky on a platform that promised federal protection of slavery in the territories. The party schism was now complete.

THE REPUBLICANS NOMINATE LINCOLN

The Republican party, which met in Chicago that spring, had matured substantially in both leadership and program over the past four years. Though Seward was its best-known leader, some delegates doubted he could carry the "lower North" (Pennsylvania to Iowa). So on the third ballot the convention turned to Lincoln, a moderate on slavery who came from a state the Republicans needed. The Republican platform reflected the maturing Republican ideology. It endorsed free soil, of course, but it also favored a protective tariff and a Pacific railroad (proposals that revealed its Whig ancestry), and as a gesture to farmers and workers, promised free homesteads in the West.

As if three candidates were not enough,

there was a fourth party in the field. The old Whig party never really disappeared in the border states of the Upper South. It united in 1856 with remnants of the Know-Nothing movement to form the American party in support of Millard Fillmore. As the sectional crisis deepened, the "opposition" elements in the Upper South began calling themselves the Union party. In May 1860, these various elements formed the Constitutional Union party and nominated John Bell of Tennessee, formerly a Cotton Whig. The platform was a collection of vague generalities that presented the party as the only alternative to disunion and civil war.

In splitting the Democratic party, the best the South could hope for was to throw the election into the House of Representatives, where it could bargain for its program. The Republican strategy—to avoid

"The political rail splitter." A cartoonist, drawing on the legend that Lincoln started out as a rail splitter, portrays Lincoln using William H. Seward's phrase "irrepressible conflict" as a wedge to divide the union.

New York Public Library, Aston, Lenox and Tilden Foundation.

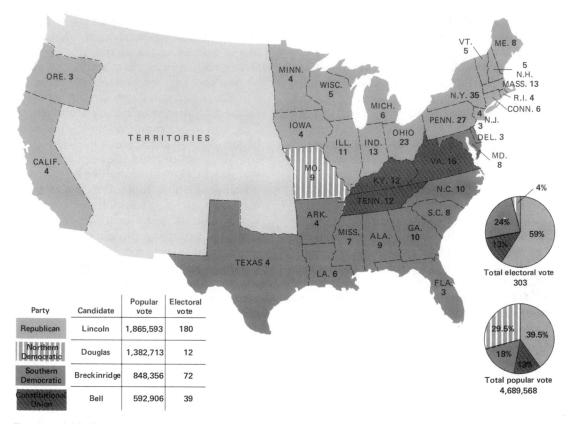

Party	Candidate	Popular vote	Electoral vote
Republican	Lincoln	1,865,593	180
Northern Democratic	Douglas	1,382,713	12
Southern Democratic	Breckinridge	848,356	72
Constitutional Union	Bell	592,906	39

Election of 1860.

any such contest by carrying every single northern state—proved better. Lincoln carried the entire North, plus Oregon and California, thus winning an absolute majority of the electoral college votes. Though a "minority" president in the sense that his popular vote was less than the combined vote of his opponents, Lincoln would have won even if the Democratic party had been united. Douglas, though second in popular vote, carried only Missouri and half of New Jersey, while Breckinridge swept the Deep South. The Unionist candidate, Bell, won the electoral votes of Virginia, Kentucky, and Tennessee.

Six weeks after the election results were

known, South Carolina seceded from the Union, followed within another six weeks by all the states in the Deep South. Southern politicians and journalists had threatened secession if the results of the election were adverse to their interests. Republicans ignored the warning because they had heard such threats before. Now that it was a fact, they were not sure what stance to take. When Lincoln invoked the "house divided" metaphor, he did not refer to secession or civil war. But others did. "If a house be divided against itself, it will fall," Daniel Webster had declared in 1851. And, he added, "crush everybody in it." Talk of secession in the 1850s had often led to talk of war. Concepts that had once seemed too terrible to be broached in public were now commonplace. Leaders in both North and South had failed to keep the house together; it remained to be seen whether they could avoid civil war.

SUMMARY

The Wilmot Proviso, which sought to bar slavery from the territory acquired from Mexico, reflected the suspicion of many in the North that the Mexican War was a southern conspiracy to add slave territory. It was also an expression of a moderate form of antislavery called free soil. Adherents of this concept would leave slavery alone where it already existed; they sought only to prevent its expansion into the West. As a moderate approach, which appealed also to those northerners who were more antiblack than antislavery, free soil was a powerful political engine.

Although never put into law, the Wilmot Proviso divided both political parties. The Democrats mended their differences with an idea; the Whigs mended theirs with a man. The Democrats' idea was popular sovereignty, letting the inhabitants of the West themselves decide whether they wanted slavery or free soil. The Whigs' man was General Zachary Taylor, who won them the White House in the election of 1848.

The controversy over the Wilmot Proviso prevented Congress from organizing territorial governments in the Mexican cession. It mattered little until the gold rush of 1849 carried enough people to California to warrant statehood for the area. California's application for admission as a free state brought a crisis because there was no slave state to pair with it. Ever since the compromise of 1820, the balance of free and slave states in the Senate had been maintained by pairing northern and southern states on admission. Fearful of losing their last line of defense, equality in the Senate, southerners threatened to secede if California were admitted.

A compromise was eventually worked out, though not until after the death of President Taylor in the summer of 1850. The principal features of the Great Compromise were the admission of California and compensation to the South in the form of a new and more effective fugitive slave law. The remainder of the Mexican cession was divided into the Utah and New Mexico territories, with the issue of slavery to be decided by popular vote.

Northern resistance to the Fugitive Slave Act, which threatened the freedom of blacks who had resided in the North for years, kept the political pot boiling. Southerners, alarmed by the constant controversy, felt they were victims of northern aggression. Northerners felt victimized by the pro-southern policies of the government. Franklin Pierce, elected president in 1852, was a weak man who yielded to the influence of southerners in his cabinet. The result was a revival of expansionism, as the government more or less openly sought new slave territory in the Caribbean and Central America. In 1853, the administration gave its blessing to a southern route for a transcontinental railroad by sending South Carolina railroad promoter James Gadsden to purchase a tract of land in southern Arizona from Mexico.

In 1854, Stephen A. Douglas's effort to organize the Kansas and Nebraska territories raised the sectional conflict to a new level of ferocity. In order to give popular sovereignty an honest test, he accepted an amendment to the bill that repealed the 36° 30' feature of the Missouri Compromise. The effect was to throw open the Great Plains to slavery if southerners wished to move there. Douglas thought that they would not and that popular sovereignty would be vindicated. Northerners saw it as a betrayal of an earlier agreement and an attempt to make Kansas a slave state. Amid the uproar, the Whig party disintegrated and the Republican party was born.

Bleeding Kansas was the long-term result as pro- and antislavery forces battled on the prairie frontier. President Pierce recognized as legitimate a proslavery territorial legislature in Kansas that had been elected by Missouri border crossers.

In 1857, the Supreme Court took a hand in the sectional controversy, ruling in the Dred Scott case that Congress lacked the constitutional power to prohibit slavery in the West. The North saw the decision as further evidence of a southern conspiracy, for the decision effectively opened the nation to slavery except where it was prohibited by state law. In the Lincoln-Douglas debates (1858), Douglas sought to reconcile the Dred Scott decision with popular sovereignty by suggesting that westerners could effectively block slavery, even though they could not prohibit it, by refusing to enact slave codes.

This evasion, known as the Freeport Doctrine, alarmed southerners, who went to the Democratic convention in 1860 insisting on a southern candidate for president and a federal slave code for the territories. The party split: The northern wing nominated Douglas and the southerners nominated John C. Breckinridge. Lincoln, the Republican candidate, won the election. In December 1860, South Carolina seceded from the union, triggering a chain reaction of secessions by the Deep South states. In February 1861, the southerners formed the Confederate States of America, and civil war began in April.

READING SUGGESTIONS

The best brief overview of the coming of the Civil War is David Potter's *The Impending Crisis, 1848–1861* (1976). Also good, and mercifully brief, is Michael Holt's *The Political Crisis of the 1850s* (1980). Eric Foner's *Free Soil, Free Labor, Free Men* (1970) is an interesting and imaginative interpretation of the formation of the Republican party. George Forgie, *Patricide of the Founding Fathers* (1981), offers an interesting explanation for the North's emotional reaction to the Kansas-Nebraska Act.

The period can also be approached through biography. The best works on the leading figures are Glyndon G. Van Deusen, *William Henry Seward* (1967); David Donald, *Charles Sumner and the Coming of the Civil War* (1950); Robert W. Johannsen, *Stephen A. Douglas* (1973); and Stephen Oates, *With Malice Toward None: The Life of Abraham Lincoln* (1977). For Lincoln in the 1850s, Don Fehrenbacher's highly interpretive collection of essays, *Prelude to Greatness, Lincoln in the 1850s* (1962), is indispensable.

The Making of a Southern Nationalist (1983), by William B. McCash, a biography of Thomas R. R. Cobb, affords a glimpse of the southern mind in this period. The most recent analysis of the motives of John Brown and those who backed him financially is Jeffrey Rossbach, *Ambivalent Conspirators: John Brown, The Secret Six, and a Theory of Slave Violence* (1982).

On the secession crisis and the outbreak of war, Stephen Channing, *Crisis of Fear: Secession in South Carolina* (1970), is a dramatic account of events in that state. Kenneth Stampp, *And the War Came: The North and Secession Crisis,* *1860–1861* (1950), tells the story from the northern viewpoint; Richard N. Current, *Lincoln and the First Shot* (1963), examines the role played by Lincoln.

15

STORM
OVER THE LAND:
1861–1865

o, erring sisters," Horace Greeley said to the South; "Depart in peace." For years secession had been linked with the prospect of civil war, yet the vast majority of Americans in the winter of 1860–1861 desired a peaceful solution to the crisis. Seceding southerners certainly had no wish to start a fight. They left the Union because they felt the political system was no longer capable of protecting their immense investment in slaves. But most southerners also realized that war was a greater threat to that investment than abolition. Secessionists wanted peaceful independence, or a reunion on their own terms. Those terms amounted to a guarantee that they could carry slaves into the western territories, and that guarantee Lincoln and the Republicans simply could not make. Such a concession would have meant repudiating the platform on which they had been elected. More to the point, it meant submission to minority rule. Secession, in short, presented Republicans with a moral cause more appealing even than free soil—the preservation of democracy itself. To yield on any point was to surrender the whole. "The tug has come," declared Lincoln, "and better now than any time hereafter."

In this context, the efforts of compromisers in Congress, such as Stephen A. Douglas, were foredoomed. Yet the compromise movement, backed by northern Democrats and the border slave states, did slow the momentum of secession. On February 1, 1861, Texas became the seventh state to leave the Union, and it was the last to go before the war came. In the eight slave states that remained in the Union, attention focused on efforts at reconciliation.

⊔ The Twisting Path to Fort Sumter

In December 1860, Kentucky Senator John J. Crittenden laid before a select Senate Committee of Thirteen a package of compromise proposals designed to hold the Union together. The package consisted of six proposed amendments to the federal Constitution and four supplementary resolutions. Crittenden's "omnibus" was in fact less a compromise than a bundle of concessions aimed at appeasing the South. The critical item was an amendment restoring the Missouri Compromise line and extending it to the Pacific. In the territory south of 36° 30', slavery was not only to be tolerated, it was to be protected by the federal government. Another amendment provided for compensation to owners of runaway slaves, and one of the resolutions called upon northern states to repeal their personal liberty laws. The last of Crittenden's six amendments was the oddest of all—it provided that the other five could never be altered or repealed by any future amendment, and it forbade any amendment from ever interfering with slavery. The notion that future generations could be bound by promises on paper was illusory; it revealed only how barren was the ground for compromise.

Republicans lined up solidly against the Crittenden proposal. It violated the fundamental principles of their party, and it would have placed the incoming administration in a political straitjacket. "Inauguration first—adjustment afterwards," insisted Salmon P. Chase, soon to become Lincoln's secretary of the treasury. Toward the end of February 1861, the House rejected Crittenden's plan 113 to 80, and on March 3

(*Chapter opening photo*) Abraham Lincoln in 1861. The photograph is by Matthew Brady.

the Senate defeated it 20 to 19. At peace conferences and Unionist meetings plans for reconciliation were discussed throughout the spring, but nothing came of them. Compromise failed, in essence, because a majority in both North and South felt that to yield a part of their position was to surrender the whole.

BIRTH
OF THE CONFEDERACY

Brushing aside the compromisers, delegates from six of the seceded states met in Montgomery, Alabama, on February 4, 1861, to form a southern confederation. They drafted a frame of government, modeled on the federal Constitution, and elected a president and vice president. Jefferson Davis of Mississippi (a former Democrat) and Alexander H. Stephens of Georgia (a former Whig) were inaugurated on

February 18, while Abraham Lincoln was making his own journey from Springfield to Washington. Federal authority in the South disappeared quickly as state officials seized customs houses, post offices, and other federal property. At Pensacola, Florida, officials reached an agreement with the army commander of Fort Pickens allowing the federal army to retain control as long as it received no reinforcements.

By the time Lincoln was inaugurated, the only remnant of federal authority in the Deep South was a garrison of 100 men in Fort Sumter, nestled on a tiny island in Charleston harbor. In December, after South Carolina seceded, the garrison's commander, Major Robert Anderson, had moved his men from Fort Moultrie on the mainland to the newer and more easily defended Sumter. Southerners viewed the move as preparation for a fight and reacted angrily, but President Buchanan refused

"The National Game," a Currier and Ives cartoon in which the election of 1860 is portrayed as a baseball game. Lincoln wins by using a split rail for a bat and hitting a "fair ball." Note the number of baseball terms—"short stop," "put-out," "foul ball"—that had entered the language by 1860.

New York Public Library, Aston, Lenox, and Tilden foundation.

to order the fort evacuated. In January the federal army sent an unarmed steamship loaded with supplies and reinforcements into Charleston harbor. Confederate shore batteries turned the vessel back. A tense stalemate ensued, and as the days passed Fort Sumter became the symbol of the conflict between state and national sovereignty.

THE FIRST SHOT

Lincoln, who viewed secession as a conspiracy among a small group of southern extremists bent on blackmail rather than independence, stood firm on Fort Sumter.

In December, when he heard a rumor that Buchanan planned to surrender the outpost, Lincoln exclaimed: "If that is true, they ought to hang him!" In his inaugural address on March 4, 1861, Lincoln promised to "hold, occupy, and possess" federal property in the South, notably forts Sumter and Pickens, but his tone was otherwise conciliatory. He would collect federal import duties, but from ships stationed offshore. Mail would be delivered "unless repelled," and if no local residents could be found to fill federal offices, the president would not impose "obnoxious strangers" on the people. Lincoln's posture thus did not differ much from the wait-and-see strategy pursued by Buchanan.

The United States on the eve of the Civil War.

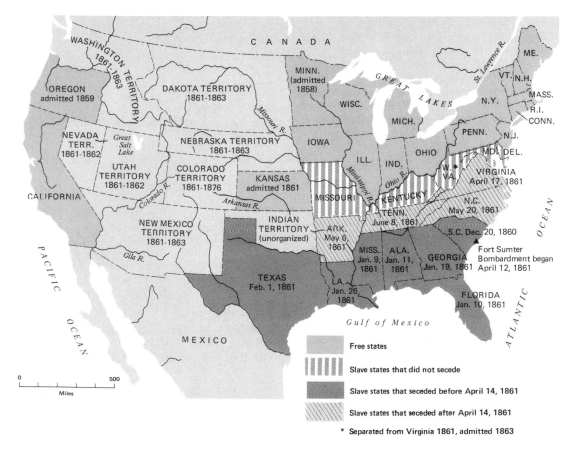

The day after his inaugural, however, a dispatch from Major Anderson forced Lincoln's hand. The Confederate buildup was such, declared Anderson, that a relief force of 20,000 men would be required to save Fort Sumter. And it had to be assembled quickly—supplies would run out in four to six weeks. Still threading the fine line between war and disunion, Lincoln decided to send supplies but not reinforcements. In early April he so notified the governor of South Carolina. Confederate officials took the message as a challenge to their new nation's integrity. Jefferson Davis himself ordered an attack. Confederate guns opened up on the fort on the morning of April 12, and Anderson surrendered the next day.

War had come, a war no one wanted and no one knew how to prevent. Decades of sectional hostility had led to deep mistrust, and mistrust had caused miscalculation. Jefferson Davis and his cabinet utterly misjudged northern attitudes. They expected the North to yield Sumter peacefully, if not gracefully, and then separation would be complete. Instead, their aggression aroused and unified the North. The firing on Fort Sumter not only started a long and bloody war; it spelled ultimate southern defeat.

⊔North vs. South:
The Balance Sheet

The South's one chance for success lay in a series of quick victories that would destroy the North's morale. In a prolonged contest the South was certain to be crushed. There were twenty-three states in the North (counting the border slave states that remained in the Union) to the South's eleven (Virginia, North Carolina, Tennessee, and Arkansas seceded after the Fort Sumter battle). The North's population was nearly 21 million compared to the South's 9 million, 3.5 million of whom were slaves of uncertain loyalty. In manufacturing, transportation, and credit facilities, the disparity was greater still.

RESOURCES

Nearly all the nation's factories were in the North. A single county in Connecticut alone produced more firearms annually than the entire Confederacy. Confederate armies were continually hampered by shortages of weapons, ammunition, clothing, medicines, and shelter. The South possessed less than a third of the nation's railroad mileage, and most of its lines were short and local. Only one railroad spanned the entire South, and that was severed when Union armies captured Chattanooga midway through the war. Northern gunboats controlled the western rivers, and when the North seized Vicksburg on the Mississippi in 1863, the South was cut in two. Vegetables and grain rotted in Texas fields while General Lee's troops starved in Virginia.

The North also possessed most of the nation's banks, and the government mobilized them effectively. The Treasury initially sought to finance the war as it had in the past—by issuing paper money. When these greenbacks depreciated in value, Treasury Secretary Salmon P. Chase tried an experiment. In 1862, Chase made the Philadelphia firm of Jay Cooke & Company the government's sole financial agent. Cooke purchased the government's bonds and resold them, at a tidy profit, to people all over the nation. Through an immense publicity campaign, Cooke induced farmers and laborers to put their savings into government bonds. Most of the issues, of course, were purchased by banks, but Cooke's experiment changed the history of wartime finance. Over four years of war, the federal government managed to borrow the stupendous sum of $2.5 billion.

Congress also reformed the federal tax

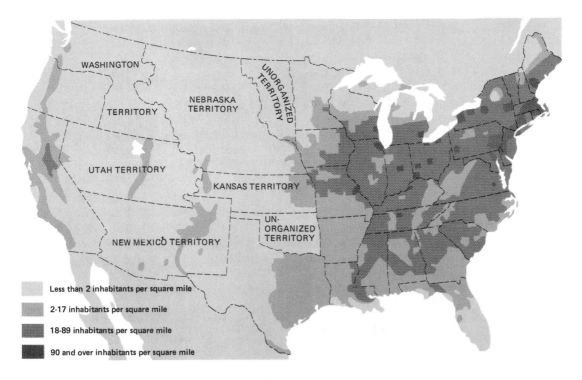

WASHINGTON

UNORGANIZED TERRITORY

NEBRASKA TERRITORY

TERRITORY

UTAH TERRITORY

KANSAS TERRITORY

UN-ORGANIZED TERRITORY

NEW MEXICO TERRITORY

Less than 2 inhabitants per square mile

2-17 inhabitants per square mile

18-89 inhabitants per square mile

90 and over inhabitants per square mile

structure. Since Jefferson's day, the federal government had existed on the income from customs duties and land sales. In 1861 Congress raised the tariff and imposed excise taxes on goods produced within the country. It also experimented with an income tax, ultimately making it graduated to extract more money from the wealthy. The income tax was too low to yield any significant amount of revenue, but it was an interesting, and prophetic, experiment in public finance. Congress considered it temporary, however, and it was allowed to expire after the war.

The South, in contrast, suffered chronic fiscal chaos. Possessing few banks and little hard money, the Confederacy financed the war with paper money. Patriotism kept the money afloat for a time, but its long-term value depended on the government's ability to develop tax resources. And the Con-

federate Congress never fully overcame its bias against government levies. Not until 1863 did it levy a tariff on imports, and by then there were none because of the federal blockade. As a result, the Confederate dollar declined from 90 cents (in terms of gold) in 1861 to less than 2 cents by early 1865. And the inflation produced economic chaos.

CONTRASTS IN LEADERSHIP

The final—and possibly decisive—advantage of the North was that it possessed an existing government and an experienced bureaucracy. This enabled the North to mobilize in orderly fashion and gave it standing in the eyes of the world. Southerners had to create a government in the midst of war, and from the foreign point of view, they were rebels. Defects in leadership and provincialism further hampered their efforts. Many of their prewar leaders proved useless. Vice President Stephens, unable to cooperate with Jefferson Davis, spent most of the war at home. Howell Cobb, a power in Buchanan's cabinet, sought the Confederate vice presidency, and when he failed to get it, he retired sullenly to his Georgia plantation. Davis found competent men to staff his cabinet, but frequent changes disrupted administration. The first secretary of state, Robert Toombs of Georgia, resigned to become a general, and the State Department ultimately went to Judah P. Benjamin. This Louisianan was a first-rate administrator, but as a Jew he encountered latent hostility. The War Department had five successive secretaries, and the Treasury had two.

Jefferson Davis, poor in health and half-blind, lacked the charisma so essential for a wartime leader. He did little to court popularity and bickered constantly with politicians and generals. Developing a personal distaste for two of his most able commanders, Joseph E. Johnston and P. T. Beauregard, he kept them in subordinate positions. At the end, some southerners were ready to say that the Confederacy "died of Davis." This may have been too harsh a judgment, for despite his flaws, Davis displayed energy and devotion. Given the splenetic provincialism of most southern leaders, he had perhaps fewer weaknesses than any other.

THE CONFEDERACY AS A NATION

Davis and his cabinet were also hampered by the political philosophy on which the Confederacy was founded. States rights is a useful defense mechanism, and it had been central to southern thinking at least since the nullification movement. But it is hardly a foundation for a government at war. The South, if anything, "died" of the disruptive forces inherent in its own ideology. Many state governors considered the Confederacy a mere military alliance of sovereign states. Governor Joseph E. Brown of Georgia, impelled by personal dislike for Davis and with political ambitions of his own, obstructed the Confederate government at every turn. At the beginning of the war he sent his own diplomatic mission to Europe, confined Georgia troops to the state, and refused to allow the Confederate government to collect taxes. When the southern Congress enacted a military conscription law, he refused to enforce it until it was adopted by the Georgia legislature, and toward the end of the war he opened his own peace negotiations with the North.

The wonder is that the Confederacy survived as long as it did. Much of its strength lay in its defensive posture. The North had to suppress the "insurrection," and that gave southerners the moral advantage of fighting for their lands and homes. It also gave them the advantage of interior lines of supply—existing roads—compensating in large measure for the deficiencies in the rail system. Military offense, moreover, required far more troops than defense, and in the later stages of the war the North had to use valuable manpower garrisoning conquered territory. Southern women and slaves were another compensating factor, for they made up the major part of the civilian work force, at least until the later stages of the war, when blacks deserted the plantations in droves.

The South, moreover, had a strong military tradition. Many of the most competent and experienced officers in the American army were southerners who resigned to serve the Confederacy. Even before he finally settled on Robert E. Lee, President Davis had a flock of able commanders in Thomas Jonathan (Stonewall) Jackson, P. T. Beauregard, Albert Sidney Johnston, James Longstreet, and Joseph E. Johnston.

Lincoln, by contrast, searched for two years for a suitable commander before he finally discovered Ulysses S. Grant. A martial spirit and brilliant military leadership won the South a series of early victories that foretold a long and bloody war.

VOLUNTEER ARMIES

Young men in both North and South went off to war because they wanted to. The war was fought by volunteers, not conscripts. As casualties mounted, both sides found it necessary to offer bounties to spur enlistments, and each ultimately resorted to a draft. Even so, for the war as a whole about 94 percent of the Union forces and 82 percent of the Confederate forces were volunteers. No one expected a long war, so few volunteers felt they were putting themselves in serious danger. But their youth was also a clue. Some 40 percent of all soldiers were 21 years old or younger when they enlisted. They were responding to both community pressure and individual need. Going off to war was a rite of passage, a symbolic entry into manhood. Manhood meant doing one's duty, and on both sides duty was crystal clear in 1861. Among northern youth it was the moral obligation to preserve the Union; among southerners it was the preservation of honor and the virtue of mother, wife, or sister.

Young men responded to such calls partly because of their own insecurity. Adolescence, defined as a social role, was prolonged in the nineteenth century, often extending from the age of twelve to the mid-twenties. During these years, young men often postponed decisions about leaving home, launching a career, or starting a family. The role of college education in setting a career was as yet unclear, and commercial opportunities in an economy that was slowly transforming itself were no more certain. In the South, the sons of planters faced an even more serious crisis of identity. Their fathers were accustomed to obedience—from slaves, from wives, from children. Young men were kept at home through a promise of future inheritance and the honor of perpetuating the family name, but they were given few tasks and were allowed no decisions. Thus, in both North and South, volunteering removed the ambiguities of extended adolescence and opened the gates to adult self-identity.

The motivation of these young men was soon severely tested by the incompetence or callousness of commanders who threw them into futile assaults against murderous gunfire. The combat record of Civil War regiments on both sides, their ability to withstand staggering losses that would break a modern regiment, was testimony both to their self-motivation and to their sense of community. At the beginning of the war, entire communities of young men volunteered for service by forming companies and choosing their leaders. They thus fought alongside one another as friends and neighbors, and they fought under men they knew and trusted. Later in the war, when communities had been dissolved by death and injury, veteran units were held together by self-discipline. "Our officers, as usual, were nowhere, and the men commanded themselves," wrote one New York sergeant of the Battle of Petersburg in June 1864.

Not all the volunteers were men. Every army camp had a female element. Some were "camp followers," or prostitutes, but others worked as cooks and laundresses. Not all were content to perform familiar domestic chores. In the course of the war, more than 400 women served as soldiers—disguised as men. The reasons for dressing as men varied. Many were simply following husbands or fiancés. Amy Clark continued to serve as a soldier even after her husband was killed in battle; her ruse was finally discovered when she was wounded at

Vicksburg. Indeed, most of the imposters were "found out" only when they were wounded or captured. Some women were driven by the same sense of duty and patriotism that inspired the men. Sarah Edmonds joined the Union army as Franklin Thompson in order to serve as a nurse in the days before women were permitted on the battlefield. At the end of the war she published a book of her exploits as nurse, spy, courier, and soldier. In 1884 the government gave her a pension of 12 dollars a month in recognition of her services. Southern women also served in the army, though in fewer numbers, and usually in an effort to accompany their husbands.

Women on both sides served as spies, sometimes with enduring notoriety. The most famous Confederate spy was Belle Boyd, who left her home in the Shenandoah Valley of Virginia to join the Confederate army as a nurse. Though only a teenager, her riding ability and courage soon led her into a career as a spy. Northern newspapers described her as a "village courtesan," implying that she used sexual favors to obtain her information. More likely, she was just a good listener as soldiers in inns and taverns boasted loudly of their plans and deeds. On one occasion she rode thirty miles in a single night to give plans of an impending attack to a Confederate officer. She was betrayed and arrested in July 1862.

The Union had equally colorful heroines, among them southern-born Pauline Cushman. She was a popular actress in New Orleans who hid her espionage activities under a cover of loudly proclaimed southern sympathies. While on theatrical tours of the border states, she secretly passed information to Union officers. The Confederates caught her in 1864 with plans she had stolen from an army engineer and sentenced her to death. She was rescued at the last minute by federal troops and lived to resume her acting career after the war.

⊔ From Bull Run to Antietam, 1861–1862

Everyone expected a short fight. President Lincoln, the day after Fort Sumter fell, issued a call for volunteers. The War Department, instead of using its 13,000 regulars for training and leading the new recruits, kept its professional units intact. That meant the volunteers would be trained on the battlefield, a prescription for disaster. The Confederacy put itself in the role of aggressor by attacking Fort Sumter, but thereafter it adopted a defensive posture. Davis felt the North lacked the will to engage in a war of conquest. In May, Thomas Jonathan Jackson seized the federal arsenal at Harpers Ferry, Virginia, dislodging a Union force under George McClellan. This allowed Jackson to menace Washington whenever federal armies marched into Virginia.

BULL RUN

By midsummer, a Union army of raw recruits under General Irwin McDowell guarded Washington, while a Confederate army commanded by P. T. Beauregard was encamped a few miles south of the Potomac near Manassas Junction. Prodded by Lincoln, McDowell led his troops across the river and advanced on the southern army, which deployed for battle along the waters of Bull Run. Just as the Union force mounted its attack, Beauregard received reinforcements from the Shenandoah Valley. The Confederates repulsed the attack, McDowell ordered his men to retire, and the retreat turned into a rout. The northern army fled in panic through the capital, carrying with it government officials, congressmen, and ladies who had driven out to watch the show.

The Battle of Bull Run (Manassas), July 21, 1861, boosted southern morale, but of-

Library of Congress.

Billy Yank.

Library of Congress.

Johnny Reb.

fered no particular military advantage. It succeeded only in persuading the North of the need to prepare itself for serious warfare. Lincoln replaced McDowell with George B. McClellan, a methodical professional who spent the next six months organizing and training an effective fighting force. In the meantime, the only important military engagements were in the West.

WAR IN THE WEST

Kentucky was the subject of an ardent courtship by both sides. If it joined the South, the battle lines would be drawn at the Ohio River. If it sided with the North, federal armies could quickly penetrate the southern heartland. Its people were hopelessly divided, southern in affection yet unwilling to leave the Union. The state gov-

ernment managed nothing more than a helpless neutrality.

Missouri was similarly divided and equally strategic. The key to western operations was control of the rivers—the Mississippi, the Ohio, and its tributaries, the Cumberland and the Tennessee. Northern gunboats held the crucial Ohio–Mississippi junction at the outset of the war, but any advance depended on Missouri. In August 1861, General John C. Frémont, commanding in St. Louis, issued a proclamation ordering the freeing of slaves who belonged to masters disloyal to the Union. The move—the first hint of a new Union war aim—proved popular among the German population of St. Louis. Lincoln, however, ordered Frémont to retract the order, and subsequently removed him from command. Thereafter the conflict in Missouri degenerated into partisan raids.

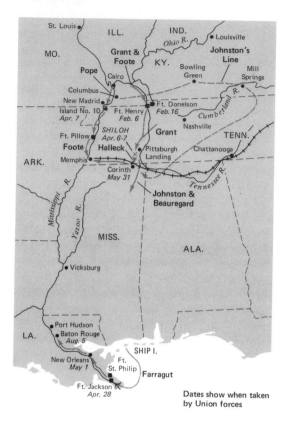

War in the West, 1862.

Early in 1862, Union troops drove the Confederates out of Kentucky and opened the way for the invasion of Tennessee. Albert Sidney Johnston, Confederate commander in the West, organized the defense of Tennessee along the western river system, with strongholds at Fort Henry on the Tennessee River and Fort Donelson on the Cumberland. Direction of the Union effort fell to a collection of isolated generals who proceeded on their own initiative. The most energetic of these, Ulysses S. Grant, aged thirty-nine, seized forts Henry and Donelson in February with an ingenious combination of land forces and river gunboats. Grant pushed on across Tennessee, and in April he fought Johnston again at Pittsburgh Landing (Shiloh),

a few miles from the Mississippi border. Each side suffered heavy losses (13,000 Union casualties and 10,000 Confederate), but the standoff left Grant entrenched in the heart of the Confederacy. Later that month a Union naval squadron, under Flag Officer David Farragut, seized New Orleans, and in June a fleet of federal gunboats captured Memphis. By the end of 1862, Union forces controlled the western rivers except for a small stretch of the Mississippi between Vicksburg and Port Hudson, Louisiana.

THE PENINSULA CAMPAIGN

While Grant was carrying the war into Jefferson Davis's homeland, McClellan had spent the winter shaping the Army of the Potomac into a disciplined fighting force. By spring he was ready to move on Richmond, the Confederate capital. He persuaded Lincoln that the best route was by water. He wanted to utilize northern naval superiority to land an army on the James River, a few miles below Richmond. It was a good strategy, but speed was essential and McClellan was slow of foot.

On May 1, 1862, McClellan landed an army of 112,000 on the north bank of the James not far from Williamsburg. Though his troops vastly outnumbered the Confederate army of Joseph E. Johnston, McClellan, instead of pushing on toward Richmond, frittered away weeks in siege operations around Williamsburg. In the course of these Johnston was wounded, and command of the Confederate army fell to Robert E. Lee. Lee withdrew slowly toward Richmond, fighting a series of battles that sapped northern morale. When McClellan called for help, Lee ordered Stonewall Jackson to step up activities in the Shenandoah Valley. Fearing that Jackson might attack the federal capital, Lincoln kept McClellan's reinforcements at home. Jackson then dashed for Richmond to join Lee, and together they stopped the federal advance in a series of bloody engagements known as the Seven Days Battle (June 25–July 1, 1862). That one week cost the North 15,000 dead and wounded, and the South, which could afford them less, 20,000. While Congress and the northern press shrieked, Lincoln appointed John Pope commander of the Army of the Potomac and ordered McClellan back to Washington.

McClellan ferried his army back up Chesapeake Bay, and Lee and Jackson disposed of Pope. The two forces met at Bull Run on August 28–29. Pope, with superior numbers, ordered an attack; when it was repulsed, he ordered a retreat. Lee pounced on his rear and turned the retreat into a rout. Lincoln removed Pope and placed McClellan in charge of the defense of Washington.

BLOODY ANTIETAM

By brilliant generalship, Lee had shifted the theater of operations from Richmond to the Potomac, and now he pressed his advantage. On September 5 he crossed the Potomac and occupied Frederick, Maryland, a position that menaced both Washington and Baltimore. McClellan moved up the Potomac, hoping to trap Lee between his own army and a large federal force at Harpers Ferry. To avoid ensnarement, Lee sent Jackson to capture Harpers Ferry. Jackson occupied the heights surrounding the town, and the federal force of 11,000 promptly surrendered (the largest surrender in the history of American warfare until Bataan in 1942). With his rear protected, Lee met McClellan at Antietam Creek, a few miles to the east of Harpers Ferry, on September 17. The battle was a costly standoff, with losses so heavy it has been described as a defeat for both sides. McClellan claimed a technical victory, however, when Lee retired south across the Potomac, his first invasion of the

North frustrated. Lincoln was nonetheless distressed that McClellan had let Lee escape and went in search of another general.

⊔ The War at Sea

The gory chess game of feint and counterfeint between Washington and Richmond kept the attention of the nation riveted on Virginia. It can be argued with some conviction, however, that the war was won not in the piney woods of Virginia, but in the hills of Tennessee—and on the ocean. Dominating the sea from the beginning of the war, the Union navy effectively blockaded the South, ran southern cruisers off the ocean, and with amphibious landings, captured the major southern seaports.

On April 19, four days after the surrender of Fort Sumter, President Lincoln proclaimed a naval blockade of the Confederacy. The blockade was largely a paper one because the government had few ships, and those it had were obsolete. The United States had not been affected by the technological revolution that altered Europe's navies in the 1850s—steam, screw propellers, and armor plating. Of the ninety vessels in the American navy in 1861, more than half were wooden sailing ships. This was good enough for a start, however, since the South had none at all. In November 1861, the federal navy seized Port Royal, South Carolina, one of the sea islands between Charleston and Savannah. Its sheltered waters served as blockade headquarters for the duration of the war, a move that shortened the navy's supply lines and enabled it to keep more ships on station.

BATTLE OF THE IRONCLADS

The only threat to the northern blockade came in the spring of 1862 when Virginians resurrected the steam frigate *Merrimac*—scuttled by federal forces when they evacuated the Norfolk navy yard—covered its sides with armor plate, and rechristened it the *Virginia*. On March 8 this curious craft steamed out of the Elizabeth River into Hampton Roads and attacked the wooden ships blockading the mouth of Chesapeake Bay. One northern ship was sunk by ramming and another by cannon fire before the *Virginia* returned to port for repairs.

Emerging the following day for a second assault, the *Virginia* was suddenly accosted by a northern ironclad, the *Monitor*. The first of several ironclads commissioned by the Lincoln administration at the beginning of the war and designed by a Swedish engineer, John Ericsson, the *Monitor* was steaming south from New York when the *Virginia* made its first appearance. The *Monitor* consisted simply of a low, flat hull on which was placed a revolving gun turret. Witnesses described it as "a tin can on a shingle." The two ungainly contrivances grappled for several hours, with neither inflicting much damage. The commander of the *Monitor*, partially blinded by a shell fragment, broke off the battle, and the *Virginia* returned to port. The first battle of the ironclads thus ended in a draw. In succeeding days, the commander of the *Virginia* repeatedly offered battle, but the *Monitor*, to inventor Ericsson's disgust, refused. The long-run advantage lay with the North, however, for the blockade remained intact.

Throughout the war, the South received a trickle of medical and military supplies through blockade runners that sailed to Havana, the Bahamas, or Bermuda. The typical runner was a long, low steamer with side wheels. Rising only a few feet out of the water, painted gray, and burning hard coal so as to leave no smoke, the runners easily blended into the sea. Though many were captured or destroyed, it was a profitable business for the owners, since two or three runs usually were sufficient to pay for the cost of the ship.

CONFEDERATE RAIDERS

Since the South possessed no warships at the beginning of the conflict, it tried to purchase some in Europe. The most famous of these Confederate "raiders" was a steam frigate bought in England and christened the *Alabama*. Commanded by a seafaring cavalier named Raphael Semmes, the *Alabama* ranged over the world preying on northern merchant shipping. Since he had no port to which he would send prizes, Semmes had to burn and sink most of his captures. His vessel was finally caught at Cherbourg, France, in June 1864 and sent to the bottom by a Union cruiser. After similar records of destruction, other Confederate "raiders" like the *Shenandoah, Florida, Tallahassee,* and *Georgia* were either sunk or confined to British ports by northern diplomatic intervention.

The easiest way to enforce the blockade was to seize the most important southern ports. Gradually, as the Union armies moved relentlessly into the Upper South, the federal navy closed in from the rear. The seizure of Port Royal as a blockade headquarters was only the beginning. During 1862, the navy seized Norfolk, St. Augustine, and New Orleans, and it effectively bottled Savannah by capturing the fort at the mouth of the Savannah River. In August 1864, Admiral David Farragut led a squadron of wooden sailing ships through a watery minefield in Mobile Bay to capture the key port of Alabama. With the fall of Wilmington, North Carolina, in January 1865, every major southern port was in federal hands or effectively neutralized.

SEABORNE DIPLOMACY

The existence of civil war in the United States posed peculiar problems for the diplomats of Europe. Whatever they did— even if they did nothing—was certain to be resented by one side or the other. The northern attitude was that the war was a domestic insurrection and that the South was not entitled to any sort of official recognition from Europe. On the other hand, there was a Confederate government with a solid claim to rule a substantial portion of the American continent. A few weeks after it was formed, the Confederacy sent agents to Europe to secure diplomatic recognition. European governments hesitated to take such a step lest the United States resent interference in its domestic affairs.

Europeans looked to London for guidance on the "American question," for Britain had the strongest economic and social ties with the United States. British opinion seemed at first to side with the South. Textile manufacturers were dependent on the South for supplies of raw cotton, and many aristocrats, including Prime Minister Lord Palmerston, felt that a victory for the southern gentry would help to check the worldwide drift toward democracy. The North, however, had its own connections among British merchants, and it had the sympathy of political radicals and economic liberals. It might also have attracted support from evangelical reformers and humanitarians had not Secretary of State Seward committed the error of assuring Britain that slavery was not an issue in the war. The voices of sympathy for the Union cause, however, were slow in making themselves heard. For many months, the North's only advantage was its capable ambassador, Charles Francis Adams, son of John Quincy Adams.

On the day Adams landed in London, May 13, 1861, he was greeted by Queen Victoria's proclamation of neutrality. This was a major victory for the South because it gave the South certain rights as a belligerent and hence meant a tacit recognition of the Confederate government. Adams met with Foreign Secretary Lord John Russell to protest this interference in a domestic rebellion. Russell, in reply, pointed out that the northern blockade itself implied belligerent status for the Confederacy. Moreover, Britain was required under international law to proclaim its status in order to preserve its neutral rights under the blockade. The most Adams could wring from Russell was a promise to hold no further meetings with the Confederate commissioner, William L. Yancey.

In the fall of 1861, the Confederate government sought to replace Yancey with a permanent minister in London, James M. Mason of Virginia. Mason sailed to Havana in company with John Slidell, who was destined for the Paris ministry. In Havana, the two southerners took passage on a British mail packet, the *Trent,* which was intercepted by a Union warship the day after it left port. The Confederate emissaries were arrested and imprisoned in Boston. The commander of the American vessel acted on his own initiative, but the deed was generally approved in the North.

England was understandably outraged at this violation of its neutral rights and national honor. In a cabinet meeting, Lord Palmerston fumed: "You may stand for this but damned if I will!" And the cabinet accordingly authorized sending 8,000 troops to Canada and the mobilization of a steam squadron. Minister Adams felt England intended war. Fortunately reason prevailed, and the British government, rejecting the idea of an ultimatum, agreed to settle for assurances that the ship captain's action was unauthorized. Secretary of State Seward sent a note disavowing the American action, and the crisis eased.

The peaceful resolution of the *Trent* affair demonstrated that the British government, for all the bluster of Lord Palmerston, did not want war. By mid-1862 Adams sensed this, and it strengthened his hand. When he discovered that the Confederacy had secretly purchased two ironclad vessels, equipped with rams, that were being built in British shipyards, he threatened war if the ships were delivered. The government accommodated him and seized the vessels. The change in the attitude of the British government from chilly neutrality to at least half-hearted cooperation reflected a subtle shift in British public opinion. As the war dragged on, the initial British sympathy for the South yielded to a realization that the North was on the side of progress and humanity. The biggest single factor in this change of attitude was Lincoln's Emancipation Proclamation.

⊔ A War to Eradicate Slavery

In his inaugural address, Lincoln stated: "I have no purpose, directly or indirectly, to interfere with the institution of slavery in the States where it exists." To Lincoln and most of the Republican party, slavery was a "domestic institution" controlled by the states. The issue of the military conflict was preservation of the Union. There was realism in this view. For strategic reasons, Lincoln could not afford to alienate the border slave states by making abolition a war aim. Nor could he afford to alienate antiblack northerners. Preservation of the Union was the common denominator that ensured maximum support for the war effort. And this involved no compromise of Lincoln's own principles; he entered the presidency a free soiler, not an emancipator.

There were flaws in this policy, which Lincoln in time came to see. The labor of black millions freed whites in the South for military service. Any sort of antislavery

Black recruits in 1862.

New York Public Library Picture Collection.

pronouncement by the federal administration was certain to cause disruption in the South, though Lincoln shied away from any stance that might bring about a slave rebellion. Making antislavery a Union war aim also had appeal abroad—a crucial point in view of the Confederacy's struggle for diplomatic recognition. Black leaders such as Frederick Douglass forced these considerations on Lincoln, but with little immediate effect.

THE CONFISCATION ACTS

Slaves themselves opened the first crack in administration policy. In May 1861, three runaways knocked at the gate of Union-held Fort Monroe, at the mouth of the James River in Virginia. Learning that the slaves had been forced to build Confederate fortifications across the river, the Union commander, Benjamin F. Butler, declared them "contraband" of war—that is, property with military value and hence subject to seizure. News of this action spread among the neighboring counties of southern Virginia, and within a few months over 900 fugitives arrived at the fortress, where Butler put them to work unloading vessels, storing provisions, and repairing fortifications. In August 1861, Congress sanctioned the policy with a Confiscation Act that announced the forfeit of slaveowners' property rights in any slaves used on Confederate fortifications.

When the federal navy captured Port Royal, South Carolina, the following November, the government found itself in the embarrassing position of possessing slaves. Plantation owners fled with their families when the attack began, but the island's slaves remained. While the navy floundered, New England missionaries helped the blacks restore cotton production. Although not formally granted freedom, the blacks organized themselves militarily as the First South Carolina Volunteers. In

1863, the Unitarian minister Thomas Wentworth Higginson arrived to take command of this regiment. The first black regiment recruited in the North, the 54th Massachusetts, arrived soon after. This all-black army was laying waste low-country South Carolina a year before William Tecumseh Sherman's destructive march from Atlanta to the sea.

While blacks pressed Lincoln from one side, Congress pushed from the other. Republicans were in a majority after the southerners departed, and as the war dragged on and casualties mounted, the radical antislavery wing of the party grew stronger. In July of 1862, Congress passed a second Confiscation Act that offered freedom to any slaves who escaped to Union lines, emancipated the slaves belonging to persons engaged in "rebellion" against the United States, and authorized the president to employ black soldiers. General Benjamin F. Butler, now commanding in occupied New Orleans, was the first to use the law by activating the historic New Orleans Native Guards, a black militia regiment that had fought with Andrew Jackson in 1815.

By the summer of 1862, President Lincoln was yielding. He had always been troubled by slavery; its end was a matter of tactics and timing. The same month that Congress passed the Confiscation Act, Lincoln informed members of his cabinet that he had "about come to the conclusion" that a proclamation of emancipation was "absolutely essential for the salvation of the Union." He disapproved of the Confiscation Act, but not out of principle. Lincoln felt that emancipation was an executive function, not a legislative one. Under the Constitution, Congress did not have power to free slaves. But the president, as commander-in-chief, did, if the move could be justified by military necessity.

Military necessity, in the end, was the decisive factor. Confederate resistance to Union advances was far more effective than he had thought possible, resulting in a seemingly endless war. But the Confederates were vulnerable at one major point: Their economy was dependent on slave labor. By offering freedom, or at least by encouraging the slaves to free themselves, the President could undermine the social and economic foundations of the Confederate war effort. In July 1862, Lincoln told his Secretary of the Navy that a proclamation of emancipation "was a military necessity absolutely essential for the salvation of the Union, that we must free the slaves or be ourselves subdued."

THE EMANCIPATION PROCLAMATION

Timing, nevertheless, was vital. Secretary of State Seward persuaded Lincoln to wait for a military victory. The battle of Antietam, halting Lee's invasion of the North, offered the opportunity, and on September 23 Lincoln declared that, beginning January 1, 1863, slaves in rebellious states or parts of states would be "thenceforward, and forever free." Because it applied only to regions over which the administration had no control, the Emancipation Proclamation in actuality did not free a single slave. As one English journalist complained, "The principle is not that a human being cannot justly own another, but that he cannot own him unless he is loyal to the United States."

The proclamation nevertheless ended any possibility of British intervention. It also added a moral tone to the conflict, though that was not always appreciated by racially biased Americans. The legislatures of Illinois and New Jersey denounced the proclamation, and Democrats accused Lincoln of planning to "Africanize" the country.

In the South, the proclamation meant that territory occupied by federal troops after January 1, 1863, would be free soil;

the Union army became an army of liberation. Slaves recognized this and "voted with their feet" whenever Union armies moved into their vicinity. While thousands of blacks streamed into Union army camps, others stayed on the plantations, drove off the overseers, and claimed the land for their own. Slavery was slowly disintegrating even before the announcement of Lincoln's emancipation policy. The proclamation turned the flight to freedom into a flood. One Union commander in northern Mississippi predicted that the slaves would not wait until the first of January. "I do not know what we shall do with them," he wailed.

Recruiting the adult males for the Union army was one obvious solution. It was also a politically risky one, for it had the potential to create a backlash among northern whites and a drop in troop morale. Lincoln nonetheless took the step in the late summer of 1862, reversing previous policy and ordering the active recruitment of black troops. Northern blacks and abolitionists, who had been recommending such a move for months, were delighted, and so were army commanders, whose manpower needs were all but insatiable. In the course of the war, some 200,000 Afro-Americans served in the Union military forces, four fifths of them recruited in the slave states. By the end of the war, nearly two thirds of the Union troops in the Mississippi Valley were black.

Military recruitment also had an impact on slavery in the four slave states that had remained in the Union. The Emancipation Proclamation did not touch slavery in these states, but the promise of freedom as a reward for military enlistment certainly did. An English traveler on the eastern shore of Maryland in the autumn of 1863 noted, "The government is revolutionizing this district by recruiting all negroes who will go, slave or free." Union naval vessels picked up runaways on the shores of Chesapeake Bay and transported them to army camps in Baltimore. Slavery had virtually disintegrated in the loyal states by the time it was abolished by constitutional amendment in 1865.

Recruitment promised freedom, but not an end to discrimination. Black soldiers were not given enlistment bonuses, and they were paid less than whites. Black regiments were placed under white officers who sometimes used them in battle with little thought for life. The fighting ability of black troops impressed everyone, but their incredible death toll—more than 68,000, about 37 percent of their total number—was testimony both to battle action and to abuse.

⊔ The Civilian War

Southerners, whose homeland quickly became a battleground, suffered severely in the war. Food shortages became the norm as Union armies slashed and burned their way across the South's breadbasket regions, such as the Shenandoah Valley of Virginia. The destruction of breeding stock in cattle and hogs by hungry soldiers of both sides left the South destitute for decades after the war ended. One resident of Richmond, Virginia, recorded with wry humor in 1864 that the city was cleaner than it had ever been because all the refuse was scavenged and consumed.

Northerners too felt the burdens of war. The initial excitement and moral fervor evaporated quickly before the reality of battlefield casualties. Men who joined the army for glory soon found that their duties ranged from the tedious to the terrifying. Most of those who stayed at home saw a steady erosion of their living standards as prices rose faster than wages. Some who worked for the government even suffered wage cuts. At the Philadelphia plant where army uniforms were made, the government paid seamstresses 17 cents for a shirt in 1861 and cut the price to 15 cents in

1864. Unprepared for such a long and costly conflict, northerners became increasingly critical of the administration's conduct of the war. Advocates of peace, though always a minority, became louder and more numerous as the war dragged on.

Even so, the North handled the greatest crisis that has ever faced the American people with a composure that commands admiration. The pursuit of science, art, and learning went on amid the battlefield carnage. The following calendar of random events attests to the vitality of northern society in the war years.

1861. Flushed with patriotism, volunteers answered President Lincoln's call to arms in greater numbers than the army could handle. Thousands were turned away because the army lacked arms and equipment for them. In the Far West, where labor was always in short supply, army enlistments created a critical shortage. The Central Pacific Railroad, chartered by California to build the western section of a projected transcontinental railroad (it got federal financial help in 1863), had to recruit workers at 35 dollars a head from China. It ultimately employed 9,000 Chinese in carving a railroad bed across the Sierra Nevada Mountains into the Nevada-Utah basin. In the Midwest, the labor shortage forced farmers to mechanize. Cyrus Hall McCormick, whose grain harvester could do the work of four or five men, was marketing 20,000 reapers a year on the eve of the war. In the course of the war he sold 165,000. Chicago, the site of McCormick's reaper plant, exported 50 million bushels of wheat to drought-stricken Europe in 1861, up more than 50 percent over the previous year's shipment. Mechanization enabled northern farmers to feed the Union, its armies, and a good part of the world as well.

Military contracts also stimulated the development of new food products, notably

Borden's condensed milk and Van Camp's pork and beans. The technique of preserving food in tin cans had been developed in Britain, principally for use on ships. Gilbert C. Van Camp, an Indianapolis tinsmith turned grocer, pioneered the art in America. His cans, however, had to be opened with hammer and chisel until the can opener was invented in 1865.

While their students went off to war, American educators looked to the future. Among colleges founded in that first year of the war were the Massachusetts Institute of Technology (MIT), Vassar Female College, and the universities of Colorado and Washington.

1862. A. T. Stewart, who had made a fortune in dry goods before the war by placing a price tag on each item in his store (prices previously had been a matter of haggling between proprietor and customer)—a system that enabled him to employ unskilled, low-paid female salesclerks—erected the world's largest department store (eight stories), complete with Elisha Otis's newly patented elevators. The John Hancock Life Insurance Company was founded in Boston as changes in state law, together with a war-inspired awareness of life's jeopardies, encouraged the development of the life insurance industry. The Travelers Insurance Company, founded the following year in Hartford, Connecticut, would be the first American accident insurance company.

Congress, amid military appropriations, tax bills, and discussions of slavery, found time to promote science and technology. It created the cabinet-level Department of

The confederate prison at Andersonville, Georgia. Thirty thousand prisoners were jammed into a 16½ acre stockade without sufficient food or sanitary facilities. Over 13,000 died.

The Bettmann Archive.

Agriculture and passed the Morrill Land-Grant Act, giving states 11 million acres of federal lands for the support of colleges devoted to agriculture and mechanics. In addition to subsidizing the founding of A &M colleges, the proceeds from the land sales would be used to benefit established institutions such as the universities of Michigan, Wisconsin, and Iowa.

1863. The early enthusiasm for the war had all but vanished. After the carnage at Bull Run and Antietam, enlistments virtually ceased. The Confederacy resorted to the draft as early as 1862; the Union Congress passed a conscription law in March 1863. It declared all able-bodied males between the ages of twenty and forty-five, with certain exceptions for the sons of widows and infirm parents, liable for military service. Selection was to be by lottery. Ensuring that the war would be "a poor man's fight," the act allowed men to hire substitutes. In an effort to keep the price of substitutes from escalating, it permitted a man to buy exemption from the draft for $300. The rate for substitutes ranged from about $500 to $800.

Even so, the attempt to conscript men into the army provoked open resistance in several parts of the North. The worst instance of violence occurred in New York City in July, where the drawing of names by federal officers triggered three days of rioting. It was at first a class war as the mob of predominantly Irish workingmen looted the homes of the rich, and then a race war as the mob went after blacks. White workers resented blacks, who competed with them for jobs, and whites blamed them for causing the war. The mob first sacked the Colored Orphan Asylum on Fifth Avenue (the 200 children fortunately had been evacuated), and then pursued and killed blacks indiscriminately throughout the city. Federal troops were finally required to restore order.

In Washington, D.C., frequently menaced by southern armies, President Lincoln ordered work continued on enlarging the capitol dome. The dome was finally capped on December 2, marking the completion of an edifice begun in Washington's day. The first major American racetrack, with leveled ground and grandstand, was opened at Saratoga Springs, New York. Among inventions patented that year were four-wheeled roller skates; among new products, cold breakfast cereal (called Granula). A new college was founded—Massachusetts Agricultural College, later renamed the University of Massachusetts.

1864. Immigrants had been arriving in ever-increasing numbers since the beginning of the war, attracted by the labor shortage and abetted by the Cunard Line's low rates on its new screw-propelled vessels. Congress gave further encouragement to the human tide in 1864 by enacting a contract labor law that authorized American businesses to import laborers by paying the costs of their transportation and recovering the costs from future wages (a version of the colonial system of indentured servitude). A gold rush in the northern Rockies attracted immigrants as well as the native-born, and Congress provided a government for the boomtowns of Virginia City, Helena, and Butte by forming the Montana Territory. Nevada, site of an 1859 gold rush, was admitted to the Union as a state.

George Perkins Marsh, veteran of the U.S. Foreign Service, initiated the science of ecology (though the word was not coined until 1869) with a book entitled *Man and Nature,* in which he described humankind's destruction of the environment in such places as Greece, Italy, and Africa. Marsh might also have cited his native Vermont, which was turning itself into a vast sheep pasture in response to the wartime demand for wool. Congress, at the urging of another environmentalist, Frederick Law Olmstead, set aside California's Yosemite

Valley as the first national scenic and recreational reserve.

Among new inventions was George M. Pullman's railway sleeping car with folding upper berths; among new products, Pabst beer. New colleges and universities were Swarthmore, Bates, Kansas, and Denver.

1865. On May 5, the first U.S. train robbery was committed when bandits derailed a passenger train bound from Cincinnati to St. Louis and swarmed through the cars lifting money and valuables from passengers. Cincinnati and St. Louis stagnated throughout the war because the downriver traffic to New Orleans was interrupted by the fighting on the lower Mississippi. Chicago, which had committed itself to railroads in the 1850s, replaced the river cities as the nation's meatpacking center. Chicago's Union Stockyards, the world's largest, with a daily capacity of 10,000 head of cattle and 100,000 hogs, opened on Christmas Day.

John B. Stetson, Philadelphia hatmaker who went west seeking a cure for tuberculosis and found himself in the Pike's Peak gold rush of 1863, returned home and opened a factory to produce a high-crowned, wide-brim "ten-gallon hat" for use on the hot and shadeless western plains. A modification of the Mexican sombrero, the hat was decorated with ten "galions" (ribbons) in a leather hatband. Stetson's contribution completed the cowboy costume just as the era of the great cattle drives was beginning. Other new products that year were the Yale lock, baking powder, and Hamm's beer. New universities were Kentucky, Maine, Lehigh, and Fisk, the last a college for blacks founded by northerners in Nashville, Tennessee.

The Civil War was a national trauma, but it neither sapped Americans' energies nor dulled their inventiveness.

Wartime demands on the economy and the jobs it created were particularly beneficial to women. In 1860 there were 270,000

females working in northern factories, mainly in the clothing industries. The war added 100,000 more women to the industrial work force. The shortage of manpower also enabled women to move into government service. The federal government had employed a few women on a temporary basis during the 1850s. The permanent employment of women began in 1861 when Francis Spinner, treasurer of the United States, recruited women as clerks, copyists, and currency counters. Administrators in other offices viewed these "government girls" as temporary employees, but many held their jobs after the war. Although they were paid less than half what their male coworkers earned, women eagerly sought government jobs because they were safe, clean, and not physically demanding—conditions that would later impel them to take up secretarial positions in private businesses.

Another outlet for the energies of women was the Freedmen's Bureau, created during the war to help freed blacks find food and shelter. It soon added to its responsibilities the task of educating the ex-slaves and protecting their civil rights. Josephine Griffin had persuaded Lincoln to fund this effort, and she marshalled female volunteers to work for the bureau. By 1869 there were 9,000 teachers in the Freedmen's Bureau, and half of them were women. Many women stayed on in the South as teachers even after the Union armies departed.

⊔ The Road to Appomattox, 1862–1865

On November 5, 1862, Lincoln named General Ambrose E. Burnside to command the Army of the Potomac. Burnside's previous contribution to the war effort had been a day-long assault on an unneeded bridge while the rest of the army fought at Antie-

General Ambrose Burnside posing with his sideburns.

tam. He soon demonstrated that that was the outer limit of his imagination. In December he flung his army against an entrenched Confederate position near the village of Fredericksburg and saw 12,600 of his blue-coated veterans fall before he ordered a retreat. Deciding next on a flanking maneuver, Burnside marched his army west, hoping to cross the Rappahannock upriver from Lee. January rains turned the Virginia clay into a copper-colored glue, and Burnside's strategy sank into the ooze along with his army. After the "mud march" Burnside departed, consigning to history nothing but his novel method of whisker trimming, which came to be known as "sideburns."

CHANCELLORSVILLE

Burnside's successor, "Fighting Joe" Hooker, also enriched the language (the camp followers of his army were called

"Hooker's girls," or simply "hookers"), and he was only slightly more effective than Burnside. On May 1, 1863, he crossed the Rappahannock River near the village of Chancellorsville with an army numbering 130,000 to Lee's 60,000. Undaunted by this numerical superiority, Lee divided his army and sent Stonewall Jackson with 30,000 men on a long flanking movement. After an all-night march, Jackson's force descended on the Union flank on the morning of May 2, taking Hooker by surprise and reducing his army to confusion. Hooker repulsed the Confederate attack, but three days later he retired back across the Rappahannock. Chancellorsville was undoubtedly Lee's most brilliant victory, but he suffered an irreparable loss in the death of Stonewall Jackson, killed accidentally by his own men in the confusion of battle.

After the victory, Lee himself confessed: "We had really accomplished nothing; we had not gained a foot of ground, and I knew the enemy could easily replace the men he had lost." The South, too, felt the frustrations of the Virginia campaigns. Lee's victories were costing men the South could not afford to lose, while the North seemed to have an inexhaustible stock of humanity to throw into the conflict. Jefferson Davis agreed that what Lee needed most was a political victory, one that would break northern morale and end the war before the South was crushed under the weight of northern resources. With his encouragement, Lee undertook his second invasion of the North.

GETTYSBURG

Swinging to the west to avoid Hooker, Lee marched northward along the edge of the mountains across Maryland and into southern Pennsylvania. Hooker followed, cautiously keeping his army interposed between Lee and the seaboard cities. On July

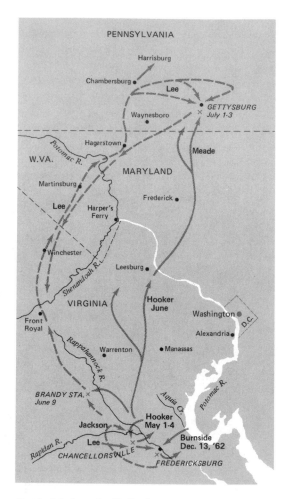

Fredericksburg to Gettysburg, 1862–1863.

1, 1863, a Confederate patrol, searching for boots and clothing in the village of Gettysburg, encountered Union troops. A brief skirmish resulted, and the two armies deployed for battle. On the eve of the battle, President Lincoln juggled his general staff once more, replacing Hooker with George G. Meade. The change was not popular with the army, which had hoped for the return of McClellan, but Meade had shown substantial competence as a corps commander. Besides, neither imagination nor initiative was immediately required. With a superior army, numbering 88,000 to Lee's 75,000, the task of any northern commander was merely to find a favorable position and force the enemy to attack.

In choosing battle, Lee abandoned the defensive posture he had used so successfully in the earlier campaigns and risked his irreplaceable troops in an assault on a well-entrenched, numerically superior foe. It might suggest that Lee's chain of victories made him overconfident, but the Virginian really had no choice. He could hardly proceed farther into the North with a strong federal army at his rear, and to retire without giving battle would have damaged his own prestige as well as southern morale.

Meade chose an excellent defensive position atop a long ridge flanked by hills. Lee spent a day probing the Union flanks and then in desperation sent a charge straight up the center. A brigade of 15,000 men commanded by George Pickett reached the "bloody angle" at the crest of the ridge but then fell back, its ranks decimated. The following day Lee retired toward Virginia, admitting: "The army did all it could. I fear I required of it impossibilities." What Winston Churchill eighty years later would call "the hinge of fate" had turned against the Confederacy. That same day, July 4, 1863, Grant took Vicksburg.

THE WAR IN THE WEST, 1862–1863

Perhaps the biggest mistake Lee made in the Gettysburg campaign was his initial decision to invade the North. A sounder strategy might have called for a holding action in Virginia, with reinforcements going to hard-pressed Confederate forces in the West. A follower of outmoded European tactics that focused attention on the capture of the enemy's capital, Lee failed to recognize that the war would be won or lost in the West. Possession of Tennessee gave the North access to the heart of the Confederacy, enabling Union armies to cut the South in two along the Mississippi and then sever it again by marching across Georgia to the sea. These were the morale-crushing campaigns that broke the South.

By the end of 1862, the North, using its naval superiority, was in possession of New Orleans, and Union gunboats controlled the Mississippi except for a short stretch of river in the vicinity of Vicksburg. The strategy thereafter was simple enough—strike at Chattanooga in the east, sever the South's most important rail line, and seize Vicksburg in the west, thereby winning control of the Mississippi and isolating Arkansas and Texas from the rest of the Confederacy.

General Ulysses S. Grant, commanding the Army of the Tennessee, undertook the Vicksburg campaign, and the strategy he devised matched Lee's Chancellorsville operation for daring and resourcefulness. To avoid fighting his way to Vicksburg, he crossed over to the west bank of the Mississippi, though the move cut him off from his supply base at Memphis and forced his troops to live off the countryside. Northern riverboats then ran the guns of Vicksburg and ferried Grant back across the river south of the city. By the middle of May 1863, Grant had Vicksburg surrounded. The garrison and townsfolk scraped along for seven weeks before surrendering on July 4. Grant had split the Confederacy.

The union strategy was equally successful in eastern Tennessee, where General William S. Rosecrans outmaneuvered his southern foe and slipped into Chattanooga in September. Rosecrans made a tentative probe into Georgia but was turned back at Chickamaugua (September 19, 1863). In November, Grant, having been made supreme commander in the West, appeared in Chattanooga. With bold frontal assaults, he cleared the southerners from the heights that menaced the city, Lookout Mountain and Missionary Ridge (November 23–25). From the top of the heights, he and the commander who had led the assault force, William Tecumseh Sherman, could peer down on the placid Georgia countryside toward Atlanta and the sea.

GRANT IN THE WILDERNESS

On March 9, 1864, President Lincoln appointed Grant supreme commander of all northern armies, informing him: "The particulars of your plan I neither know nor seek to know. . . . I wish not to obtrude any constraints or restraints upon you." Af-

Library of Congress.
General Ulysses S. Grant.

Virginia campaigns, 1864.

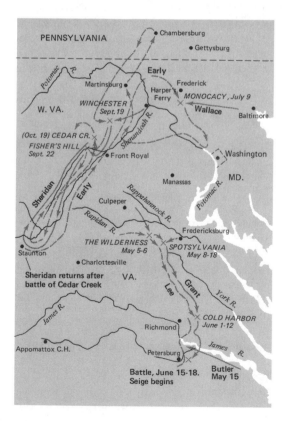

ter years of interference in military affairs and strategy, Lincoln at last appeared to recognize that he had found a competent general. Grant's reply was typical: "I am determined to hammer continually against the armed forces of the enemy and his resources until by mere attrition if in no other way there should be nothing left for him but submission." Herein lay a new concept of warfare. No longer would war be a gentleman's game, characterized by deft maneuvers rather than pitched battles and designed to secure bargaining advantages in the peace negotiations.

Grant's object was nothing less than total victory. He would wear down the enemy's resources and break its will to fight. The strategy was simple, if unimaginative. Grant, with his vastly superior army, would push relentlessly toward Richmond, losing large numbers of men but wearing down the Confederacy. William T. Sherman, Grant's replacement in Tennessee, would

CLIO'S FOCUS: The Medical War

The battlefield carnage of the Civil War leaves the impression at times of a people bent on national suicide. Ghastly though the casualty statistics are, however, there is another statistic that is even more pathetic: For every battlefield death, two soldiers died of disease. Typhoid, dysentery, and malaria decimated both armies because medicine was still a primitive art. The germ theory of disease, though formulated, was far from accepted; the relationship between health and sanitation was poorly understood. Charles Francis Adams, Jr., described a Civil War army as "a city without sewage, and policing only makes piles of offal to be buried or burned." Every encampment exuded a stench that poisoned the air for miles.

Disease not only cost lives, it broke morale and encouraged desertion. At any given moment, the effective strength of a Civil War army was only one third to one half its paper strength. "Our armies disappear before our eyes," General Sherman wrote to his wife; "They are merely paper armies."

Adding to the problem was a chronic shortage of doctors. When the war began, the Union Army's entire staff of physicians numbered 98, headed by an eighty-year-old veteran of the War of 1812. To make up the shortage, the government offered a commission to anyone who could claim some medical knowledge. Many who volunteered were competent and well trained, but many others were not. And even the best trained struggled with poor working conditions. Until the government created a hospital system late in the war, the wounded were cared for in makeshift tent camps, and when those became overcrowded, they were placed in farmhouses, barns, and chickencoops.

Time and experience brought some improvement. Generals learned the value of sanitation. The government attracted physicians to the army by offering higher rank and pay. And, perhaps most important, the field of nursing was revolutionized. At the outset of the war, army nurses were men, and few had any training. Some were convalescent invalids barely able to care for themselves; others were misfits willingly loaned to the medical corps by harried commanders.

So disorganized were the Union Army's medical facilities at the first Battle of Bull Run that wounded were left lying on the battlefield for days. Horrified by this, Clara Barton quit her job at the U.S. Patent Office and headed for the battlefield to organize field nurses and stretcher bearers. Her action marked the entry of women into the field of military nursing. Later in 1861, Dorothea Dix, pioneer in the treatment of mental illness, was appointed government superintendent of nurses. Realizing that the moralistic northern public would be shocked by reports of young women nursing soldiers in crude field hospitals and army camps, Dix took care to avoid scandal. Her directives set the minimum age for a nurse at thirty, and only women "plain in appearance" were invited to apply. Their clothing was to be of somber color, without

National Archives.
Clara Barton.

hoops, and unadorned with bows or lace. Dr. Elizabeth Blackwell, the first woman to graduate from a medical college in the United States, was put in charge of a training program for nurses.

Although no more than 20 percent of army nurses were women—and the proportion was even lower in the South—they proved their worth on every battlefield. Mary Ann Bickerdyke, a Quaker of dynamic personality and rough speech, covered nineteen battlefields in the course of the war. Through her efforts and those of others, the sick and wounded received steadily improved care. Even so, the best prescription for an army's health was peace.

simultaneously cut a swath through the heart of the South, destroying everything as he went, to break southern morale. The Civil War, some have said, was the first modern war.

On May 4, Grant started moving south from the Rappahannock River west of Fredericksburg. His army was twice the size of Lee's, but in the dense Virginia woods, a morass of pine and honeysuckle, the difference in numbers meant little. Both armies became disorganized, and combat was occasionally hand to hand. By May 12, Grant had suffered 26,000 casualties, but he informed Lincoln of his resolve to fight it out "on this line if it . . . takes all summer." With a smaller force, Lee suffered proportionately, even higher losses, and his battered army retired slowly toward Richmond.

Grant pressed on. At Cold Harbor on June 3, just a few miles north of the Confederate capital, he ordered a frontal attack against an entrenched position and lost 12,000 men in eight minutes. It was the bloodiest moment of the war. Northern newspapers labeled Grant a "butcher," and the peace movement took new heart. But Lincoln stood by his general: "I can't spare this man—he fights," said the president. Cold Harbor, however, forced Grant to rethink his strategy. On June 12 he under-

took the sort of "end run" that had worked so well at Vicksburg. Moving around to the east of Lee's army, he suddenly turned south across swampy terrain, forded the Chickahominy and the James, and three days later appeared outside Petersburg. He hoped to take the city by surprise and then move into Richmond by its undefended back door. The tactic failed when four days of frontal assaults failed to breach the Confederate lines. On June 18 Lee arrived with reinforcements, and Grant settled down to a siege. Petersburg held out until April 2, 1865.

ELECTION OF 1864

Grant's casualty figures gave new ammunition to Lincoln's political foes, who were already looking toward the presidential election. His own party was divided, with radicals, who felt he was moving too slowly in abolishing slavery, flirting with the possibility of an alternative candidate. The Democrats were also a threat despite their prewar southern connection. They had actually gained seats in Congress in the off-year election of 1862, and in 1864 they nominated a Lincoln critic with impeccable credentials, General George B. McClellan. Lincoln's supporters tried to broaden their

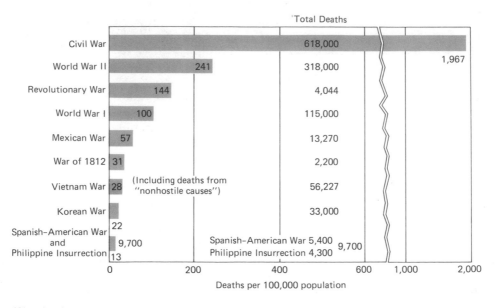

War deaths.

appeal by reconstituting themselves as the Union party and naming a war Democrat, Andrew Johnson of Tennessee, as Lincoln's running mate.

Northern military achievements, as slow in coming as they were inevitable, decided the election. In September, General Sherman captured Atlanta, Georgia, after a five-week siege and then burned the city to the ground. In August, Rear Admiral David Farragut, bellowing to his ship commander, "Damn the torpedoes! Four bells, Captain Drayton, go ahead!" steamed into Mobile Bay and captured the last of the southern seaports. And in September and October, General Phillip Sheridan cleared southern troops out of Virginia's Shenandoah Valley and burned the valley's fertile croplands. Buoyed by this steady stream of good news, Lincoln won with 55 percent of the popular vote and carried the electoral college 212 to 21. The president, visibly aged by four years of tension, turned back to the war.

SURRENDER IN VIRGINIA

Sherman's march to the sea. With Grant bogged down in front of Petersburg, attention centered on Sherman in Georgia. On November 16, 1864, Sherman began the march from Atlanta to the sea. His army advanced along four parallel roads, 15 miles a day, destroying everything as it went. Though Sherman issued strict orders against trespass on private property and the abuse of civilians, the army, with no enemy to face, was not easy to control, and much wanton destruction resulted. Discipline was generally maintained, however, and despite the passions aroused by civil war, little injury was inflicted on southern civilians. Sherman's object was to break southern morale, and if he shortened the war by as much as a week, his march was justified.

On December 22, Sherman's army reached Savannah. He rested his troops for a month and then struck north into the

Lee's Farewell to His Army

One of the most poignant moments of the Civil War came when General Robert E. Lee had to bid farewell to the men who had fought and suffered with him for almost three years.

Headquarters, Army of Northern Virginia, April 10, 1865

After four years of arduous service, marked by unsurpassed courage and fortitude, the Army of Northern Virginia has been compelled to yield to overwhelming numbers and resources. I need not tell the survivors of so many hard-fought battles, who have remained steadfast to the last, that I have consented to this result from no distrust of them; but, feeling that valour and devotion could accomplish nothing that could compensate for the loss that would have attended the continuation of the contest, I have determined to avoid the useless sacrifice of those whose past services have endeared them to your countrymen. By the terms of the agreement, officers and men can return to their homes and remain there until exchanged. You will take with you the satisfaction that proceeds from the consciousness of duty faithfully performed; and I earnestly pray that a merciful God will extend to you His blessing and protection. With an increasing admiration for your constancy and devotion to your country, and a grateful remembrance of your kind and generous consideration of myself, I bid you an affectionate farewell.

R. E. Lee, General

Carolinas. In South Carolina the devastation was worse, for his soldiers blamed that state for the war. Most towns, including the capital city of Columbia, were burned to the ground. On March 10, 1865, Sherman occupied Fayetteville, North Carolina, and brought his long march to a temporary halt, awaiting developments in the Richmond theater.

Lee's army at Petersburg starved through the winter, short of clothing and shoes, its lines thinned by disease and desertion. On April 1, Grant opened his new offensive and swept through the Confederate lines. Richmond and Petersburg could no longer be held, and on April 2 Lee retreated west toward Lynchburg. Fearing Lee might escape into North Carolina, Grant moved to cut him off. Unwilling to press his tired and hungry troops further, Lee asked for surrender terms. The two generals met at Appomattox Courthouse, and Grant's terms were generous enough.

The southern army was allowed to return home on parole, surrendering only its arms and artillery. Privately owned horses and officers' sidearms were retained. Grant did not ask for Lee's sword; Lee did not offer it. The agreement was signed on April 9, 1865.

The war was over for everybody except Jefferson Davis. On April 2, the Confederate president fled from his capital to Danville, Virginia, where he issued an address urging the southern people to continue the fight. But Joseph E. Johnston, facing Sherman in North Carolina, replied simply that the southern people were tired of war. On April 26 Johnston surrendered to Sherman at Durham, and a month later General Kirby Smith surrendered the Confederate forces west of the Mississippi. Secession was dead, slavery was dead, and so were 620,000 Americans. More Americans died in this war than in all other American wars combined.

SUMMARY

On the day after the South fired on Fort Sumter, President Lincoln issued a call for 75,000 volunteers. They were to serve only for a few weeks and be discharged by mid-summer 1861. No one expected a lengthy war, yet no one knew how to stop the fighting. Efforts at reaching a new sectional compromise had failed earlier that spring when the South demanded federal guarantees for slavery in at least part of the West and a constitutional amendment forbidding future interference with slavery. The South assumed the North lacked the will to fight over such an abstract principle as free soil. Bloodshed bolstered the North's will. And the more blood that was shed, the more firm became the need for victory.

On paper, a northern victory seemed assured. It outnumbered the South in population, 21 million to 9 million, twenty-three states to eleven. Nearly all the nation's factories and most of its banks and railroads were in the North. Perhaps most important, the North possessed an existing government and an experienced bureaucracy; the South had to create a government while fighting a war. Jefferson Davis's flaws of personality, frequent changes in cabinet, and poor cooperation from state governors also hampered the Confederate cause.

The Confederacy survived as long as it did because for the most part it was militarily on the defensive. Defense requires far fewer men and resources than offense. It also gave southerners the moral advantage of fighting for their lands and homes. They probably could have held out longer than they did if Robert E. Lee had not wasted resources on invasions of the North.

The war went badly for the North at first, in part because the Union army insisted on keeping its regiments of professionals intact, instead of using them for training and leadership. That meant enlistees had to learn the art of war on the battlefield with inexperienced officers. In May 1861, Thomas Jonathan ("Stonewall") Jackson seized the federal arsenal at Harpers Ferry, a position that enabled him to menace the federal capital whenever northern armies marched into Virginia. In July, General P. T. Beauregard turned back a federal advance at Bull Run, and the inexperienced Union troops fled from the battlefield in panic.

The first Union victories came in the West. Early in 1862, Union troops drove the Confederates out of Kentucky, and General Ulysses S. Grant invaded Tennessee. The key to the West was naval control of the great river systems—the Mississippi, the Cumberland, and the Tennessee. Grant seized the key Confederate forts on the Tennessee River and fought a bloody but inconclusive battle at Pittsburgh Landing (Shiloh), a few miles from the Mississippi border. After a Union naval force occupied New Orleans, gaining control of the mouth of the Mississippi, Grant in 1863 marched into Mississippi and laid siege to Vicksburg, last confederate stronghold on the Mississippi. With its fall (July 4, 1863), the South was cut in two.

In the East, General George B. McClellan spent the winter of 1861–1862 training and organizing the Army of the Potomac. In May 1862 he used northern naval superiority to make a landing on the James River, a few miles below Richmond. Jefferson Davis placed Robert E. Lee in command of the Army of Northern Virginia, and Lee stopped McClellan's advance in a series of bloody engagements on the outskirts of Richmond. Lincoln, losing heart, summoned McClellan back to Washington to protect the federal capital and replaced him with John Pope. Lee dispatched Pope at the second Battle of Bull Run (August 1862) and then invaded Maryland. But the invasion of the North ended in a bloody draw at Antietam (September 17, 1862).

Antietam, which the North claimed as a victory after Lee retired to Virginia, enabled Lincoln to issue the Emancipation Proclamation. Blacks and radical Republicans had pressured Lincoln from the beginning of the fight to do something about the slaves, but Lincoln had stalled, fearing that northern opinion was not prepared to make the war anything but a war to preserve the union. The proclamation, effective January 1, 1863, was put forth as a war measure, and it freed the slave property of those persons who were making war against the United States. Limited though it was, the proclamation made emancipation a war aim, and it ended any possibility of British intervention. After issuing the proclamation, Lincoln moved more decisively. In 1863 he ordered the army to begin accepting black enlistees, and in 1864 he endorsed a constitutional amendment, the thirteenth, that declared all slaves free.

After turning back another union advance at Chancellorsville, Virginia (May 1863), Lee mounted his second invasion of the North. This one ended in the titanic battle of Gettysburg (July 1–3, 1863). Defeated and exhausted, Lee retired to Virginia; he would not take the offensive again. In the spring of 1864, Lincoln named Grant commander of the Army of the Potomac. Grant marched through the Virginia wilderness (May–June, 1864), taking enormous casualties but moving relentlessly toward Richmond. After suffering great losses at Cold Harbor, Grant changed tactics, slipped around Lee's army, and tried to come on Richmond from the south. Lee wheeled in time to occupy Petersburg, and Grant settled down to a nine-month siege.

While Grant besieged Richmond and Petersburg, General William T. Sherman burst out of Tennessee in the fall of 1864 and cut a swath of destruction across Georgia from Atlanta to the sea. Reaching the coast at Savannah, he turned north in January 1865 and carried his destructive march into the Carolinas. Sherman's object was to break southern morale and will to fight. Lee tried to escape Grant's encirclement in April 1865; failing, he surrendered at Appomattox Court House in Virginia. Within a month, the Confederate armies in the West had laid down their arms. The war, the bloodiest in the nation's history, had cost 620,000 lives. Among the dead was President Lincoln, the victim of an assassin's bullet.

READING SUGGESTIONS

A recent synthesis of the Civil War era is James M. McPherson's *Ordeal by Fire: The Civil War and Reconstruction* (1982). Those who enjoy military history should try Allan Nevins's *The War for the Union*, four vols. (1959–1972), or the many splendid works of Bruce Catton: *Mr. Lincoln's Army* (1951), *Glory Road* (1952), *A Stillness at Appomatox* (1954), and *This Hallowed Ground* (1956). A fresh synthesis of the enormous military literature on the war is Herman Hattaway and Archer Jones, *How the North Won* (1983). The southern strategy of offensive warfare is explored by Grady McWhiney and Perry D. Jamison, *Attack and Die* (1982).

The life of the common soldier is nicely recreated in Bell I. Wiley's *The Life of Johnny Reb* (1943) and *The Life of Billy Yank* (1952). Michael Barton's *Good Men: The Character of Civil War*

Soldiers (1981) is an imaginative exploration of the values and motives of the soldiers.

The role of blacks in the war is discussed in Benjamin Quarles, *The Negro in the Civil War* (1953); in D. T. Cornish, *The Sable Arm: Negro Troops in the Union Army, 1861–1865* (1958); and by J. M. McPherson in *The Negro's Civil War* (1965). Lincoln's policy toward slavery has recently been examined by LaWanda Cox in *Lincoln and Black Freedom* (1981).

David Donald, *Lincoln Reconsidered* (1956), offers some fresh insights on the war president. Allan G. Bogue's *The Earnest Men: Republicans of the Civil War Senate* (1981) is a brilliant quantitative analysis of the divisions within the Republican party. J. B. Hyman's *Stanton: The Life and Times of Lincoln's Secretary of War* (1962) offers a fascinating peek into Lincoln's cabinet. The Democratic opposition is surveyed in Joel Silbey, *A Respectable Minority: The Democratic Party in the Civil War Era* (1977). For the strains the war placed on Anglo-American diplomacy, one will not do better than Martin Duberman's biography of Lincoln's minister to Britain, *Charles Francis Adams* (1961). R. S. West, Jr., *Mr. Lincoln's Navy* (1957), is a good account of the war at sea.

The home front has received much less attention than the military events. A. Cook, *The Armies of the Streets: The New York City Draft Riots of 1863* (1974), is an account of one of the North's major problems. The diary of Mary Boykin Chestnut, most recently edited by C. Vann Woodward and titled *Mary Chestnut's Civil War* (1979), reveals much of life and attitudes in the South. For a survey of the Confederate homefront, see Emory M. Thomas, *The Confederate Nation, 1861–1865* (1979).

16

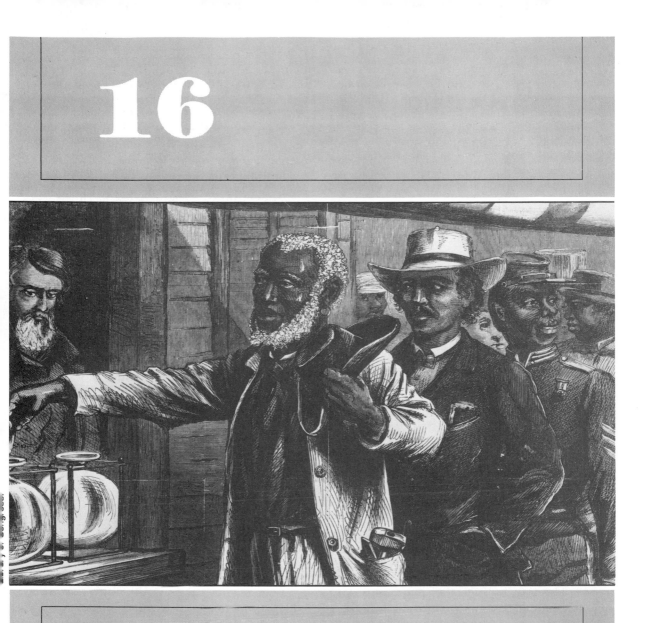

BITTER REUNION:
1865–1877

harles A. Beard, the most influential historian of the twentieth century, once described the Civil War as "the second American Revolution." The war, in Beard's view, ushered in the triumph of industrial capitalism. It shifted the focus of the economy from farm to factory, the focus of politics from state to national government. The Civil War, in short, created modern America.

Such a broad interpretation leaves many gaps, but it remains a useful framework for exploring the meaning of the Civil War and its aftermath, Reconstruction. The Civil War, for a start, did not bring about industrial growth. In fact, the effort diverted to military service probably slowed economic development. The growth rate of the economy—one measure of industrialization—began to accelerate as early as 1840. The rate of growth in commodity production was about 60 percent in the 1850s, and that rate was reached again in the 1870s. But in the 1860s, increase in manufacturing output was only 23 percent. The North experienced an economic boom during the war, but it was due in part to government deficit spending and in part to inflation. The textile mills of New England were idle much of the time for lack of cotton fiber; it was high prices that maintained high profits. The railroads prospered. They had been built for future demand; not until the Civil War did they use their full carrying capacity.

The war, on the other hand, did bring some important changes. Contrary to what Beard supposed, the war probably changed agriculture more than industry. Before, southerners had always boasted that "Cotton is king!" The war demonstrated that the true king was in fact wheat. Britain found it could do nicely without American cotton because of alternative sources in India and Egypt, but it could not do without

American foodstuffs. Despite losing sons and hired hands to the army, the northern farmer was able to feed the city population, the army, and part of Europe as well. He did it by mechanization. The technology for agricultural revolution was available before the war—the steel plow with interchangeable parts, for instance, and the mechanical grain harvester. High food prices and a labor shortage encouraged farmers to buy them. Between 1861 and 1865, the number of machines on northern farms tripled.

War-related industries also grew rapidly. Stimulated by the demand for uniforms, clothing and shoe manufacturers purchased sewing machines. The new devices quickened the shift in both industries from small shops to large-scale factories. The canning industry came of age during the war, largely through military contracts. Borden's condensed milk and Van Camp's pork and beans became standard features of army field rations, and the new tastes acquired by soldiers permanently altered the diets of thousands of families after the war.

⊔ The Political Revolution

Beard's phrase "second American Revolution" refers more to political than economic change. Before the war, government policy catered to rural interests and to the South. Ever since the Polk administration, the federal government had adhered to hard money and a low tariff. In 1857 Congress reduced further the already low rates prevailing since the Walker Tariff of 1846, putting the nation virtually on free trade. Congress left internal improvement projects to the states, though it did provide

---

a federal land grant to the Illinois Central Railroad (via the state of Illinois) in 1850. A Homestead Act, designed to benefit the working classes by offering them free farms in the West, fell victim to Buchanan's veto. *States' rights* and *laissez faire* had been watchwords since the time of Jackson. Except for antislavery, southern planters had had no reason to complain. Secession, on the other hand, allowed the North to pass the economic legislation it had long desired. The result was the enactment of something very like the American System of Henry Clay, tailored to meet the needs of a new generation.

ECONOMIC LEGISLATION

The tariff was the first item on the Republican agenda. In February 1861, while the Confederacy was taking form in Montgomery, Alabama, Congress approved a bill introduced by Justin S. Morrill of Vermont that raised tariff rates to the 1846 level. After the war began, military expenses brought further increases, and by the end of the war the average level of rates was 47 percent, more than double the average of 1857. The wall of tariff protection was of particular benefit to the iron and steel industry, which previously had not been able to compete with British products. For the better part of the next century, the United States remained a high-tariff nation.

Internal improvements meant, by 1860, federal support for a Pacific railroad. Republicans committed themselves to the project in the presidential election that year, and secession left them free to choose the central route. In 1862 Congress chartered two corporations, the Union Pacific Railroad, with authority to build westward from Omaha, and the Central Pacific, authorized to lay track eastward from California until the two lines met somewhere in the Great Basin. By the terms of the charters, the government underwrote railroad construction militarily and financially. It guaranteed the right of way, extinguished the Indian land titles, and ordered the army to protect construction workers from Indians. In addition, for each mile of track laid the railroads were to receive a grant of 6,400 acres of public land. This amounted to a swath of alternate sections extending 20 miles on each side of the track (40 miles in the mountains) from the Missouri River to the Pacific. Also, millions of dollars in government bonds were made available to railroad promoters in need of ready cash.

Government generosity, ultimately extended to four transcontinental railroads before subsidies were stopped in 1873, seemed justified at the time. The railroads plunged through terrain inhabited only by Indians and buffalo. It would be some time before the railroads developed enough traffic to make a profit, but in the meantime they served a national need by uniting East and West. As it turned out, the railroads made a good profit from the beginning by selling their land and mineral assets. Government ownership and operation of railroads—a modern alternative—was beyond the realm of nineteenth-century thinking.

Banking and currency also commanded Republican attention in 1862. Since 1846, the government had accepted only gold and silver in receipt of taxes or the sale of public lands, and this hard currency was stored in various subtreasuries. Besides being cumbersome, the system meant that badly needed investment capital was squirreled away in public vaults. Private financial transactions were performed with notes issued by state-chartered banks. Those issued by the larger banks achieved wide circulation, but most were unreliable or circulated only in their own localities. Watching over this unwieldy system was the ghost of Andrew Jackson, who had destroyed the central bank thirty years before.

The U.S. Treasury financed the war in the time-honored way—by issuing paper money. Its notes were called "greenbacks" because of their distinctive color, and they depreciated, as paper money had in every earlier war. The Treasury also issued long-term bonds, but the war proved so fantastically expensive that by 1862 the resources of the financial community were dry. In December of that year, Treasury Secretary Salmon P. Chase outlined a plan for solving in one stroke both the currency question and the banking problem, while at the same time creating a new market for federal bonds. The plan blended private interest with national need in a way that Alexander Hamilton would almost surely have approved. Chase's proposals formed the basis of the National Banking Act passed in February 1863 and amended substantially a year later. By these acts Congress created a system of national banks with federal charters and under the general supervision of the Treasury. Each bank that joined the system was required to purchase at least $30,000 in government bonds, which were then deposited in the U.S. Treasury. These deposited bonds were the security for notes issued by the national banks, and those notes provided the nation with a stable, uniform currency.

The system started slowly, due largely to the huge amount of capital needed to form a national bank, but in 1865, when Congress levied a 10 percent tax on state bank notes, most of the state-chartered banks joined the new program. The national bank system, which remained the nation's primary banking system until the Federal Reserve Act of 1913, was decentralized and privately controlled, thus avoiding the accusations of monopoly and irresponsible power that had destroyed the Bank of the United States. Yet it provided a reasonably stable financial system and a uniform national currency.

Banks, tariff, and Pacific railroad were all designed to appeal primarily to the interests of businessmen and manufacturers. The Republican party, however, did not forget its promises to farmers and workingmen, whose demands since Jackson's time, had focused on cheap land. Even labor unions and workingmen's parties felt their members would have increased bargaining power in the East if workers possessed the alternative of cheap farms in the West. The idea proved to be false, since the average urban laborer was ill-equipped for farming, but it was a politically powerful myth.

The Homestead Act, passed in May 1862, granted 160 acres of public land to any adult male or head of family on the sole condition that he or she live on it for five years. By the end of the war, 1.5 million acres were occupied under the act, and the postwar decades witnessed a rush of homesteaders into the West. There were flaws in the law, to be sure. Many homesteaders failed in trying to farm the arid plains, and the chief beneficiaries often appeared to be lumber and mining companies who used various loopholes to help themselves to huge tracts of land. But the act did answer a long-felt popular demand.

Of even greater long-term social benefit was the Morrill Land Grant Act of 1862, which offered public lands to the states for the support of higher education. Representative Justin Morrill of Vermont had conducted a long crusade in Congress for the bill, but the measure was delayed by the opposition of southerners who feared federal influence in education. The act passed in 1862 was based on population: The states were offered 30,000 acres of public lands for each senator and representative. The eastern states should have benefited as much as the West. In practice, however, the main effect of the law was to stimulate state interest in higher education. This was most pronounced in the West, where public universities financed by land grants were promoted as state enterprises.

Confined at first to "loyal" states, the act was extended to the South after the war. The result was a major stride for higher education, and a sprinkling of land grant colleges that specialized in practical agricultural and industrial arts.

THE FREE LABOR IDEOLOGY

The Homestead Act and the Morrill Land-Grant Act are important clues to Republican thinking. Beginning with Lincoln's "house divided" appeal to northern factory workers, the Republicans claimed to speak for all Americans regardless of social or economic standing. If some of their programs spoke directly to the interests of industrial tycoons and railroad promoters, the Republicans justified them on the grounds that everyone benefited from modern factories and transportation facilities. Free farms and educational opportunity had been the twin goals of the labor movement from its inception, and Republicans responded as soon as they were in power. When labor revised its goals and began aiming for an eight-hour day, most Republicans accepted that idea too. They passed a law establishing an eight-hour day for federal government employees in 1868. Gradually, however, businessmen gained the upper hand in party councils. The contract labor law of 1864, for instance, was passed at the insistence of factory owners who wanted a steady supply of cheap foreign labor. The labor movement's complaint that immigrants undermined domestic wage levels was met by the creation of an Immigration Bureau to encourage still more immigrants.

Actions such as this suggested that the ideology of free labor, on which Republicans had grounded their opposition to slavery and on which they had appealed to businessmen and working people alike, had its limitations. Free labor meant just that. Individuals were expected to rely on

their own resources, not on government programs. Freedom meant the elimination of some evils, such as slavery or liquor, not the imposition of some well-intended public policy. In time this view of the role of government in society forced the Republicans to abandon two of their earliest constituencies—factory workers and freed blacks. By the end of the war, workers were beginning to discover that in the competitive jungle of free enterprise, they lacked the strength to bargain effectively with the corporate giants the war and Republican policy had helped to create. It was not long before the newly freed blacks in the South, bereft of government aid and at the mercy of their former masters, made a similar discovery.

⊔Lincoln, Johnson, and the Radicals

Throughout the war the Republican party was divided over the question of postwar reconstruction. Reconstruction involved two things: the return of the South to the Union with representation in Congress, and the restoration of civil governments in southern states that were occupied by federal armies. Both involved another, even more sensitive, issue— securing civil, and perhaps political, rights for the freed blacks.

The Republican party had never been united in its attitude toward slavery and secession. Abolitionists were not happy with the party's selection of Lincoln, and their suspicions were confirmed by his procrastination on the question of emancipation. As the war progressed, these radical Republicans grew in numbers and volubility, though they never formed a majority. Led by Benjamin F. Wade of Ohio, Charles Sumner of Massachusetts, and Thaddeus Stevens of Pennsylvania, the radicals drafted the wartime confiscation acts and hoped to restructure southern society when the conflict ended. Accepting secession as a fact, they argued that the southern states were "conquered provinces" at the mercy of Congress. Before letting the South return to the Union, the radicals planned to purge it of slavery, secure civil rights for former slaves, and destroy the planter elite that had caused all the trouble.

Moderate Republicans, by contrast, adhered to law and tradition. They worried that some of the wartime measures, such as the confiscation acts, might be unconstitutional. In company with Democrats (who occupied about a third of the seats in Congress), moderates were more aware than radicals of states rights and the interests of loyal whites in the border slave states. Less vindictive than radicals in their attitudes toward the South, moderates were also less confident of the intellectual potential of the freed slaves and less concerned for ensuring their civil liberties. In this the moderates reflected the racial bias that continued to prevail in the North.

LINCOLN AND RECONSTRUCTION

Lincoln, distinctly a moderate when he took office, grew more radical as the war went on. By 1864 he was prepared to throw the weight of his presidential authority behind a constitutional amendment (the thirteenth) freeing the slaves. And by early 1865, he was even suggesting privately that free black men who could read and write be given the right to vote. The president's reconstruction program, however, was more lenient than that of the radicals because it was influenced by military considerations. By being generous rather than vindictive, Lincoln hoped to attract southerners to his cause and further weaken the Confederacy. In contrast to the radicals, who viewed reconstruction as a matter for legislation, Lincoln felt that restoration of

the South could be accomplished by executive orders under the president's war powers. Utilizing loyal minorities that existed in every southern state, Lincoln hoped to create provisional civil governments in the South in the wake of the advancing Union army.

Virginia presented Lincoln with the first opportunity to implement this policy. The mountain counties of western Virginia, populated by small farmers who owned few slaves, had voted against secession. In August 1861, delegates from counties along the Ohio River met at Wheeling to form a legislature of their own and elected Francis H. Pierpont governor. Western delegates subsequently drew up a state constitution, and in 1863 Congress admitted West Virginia to the Union after adding to it the counties around strategic Harpers Ferry. In the meantime, Pierpont transferred his administration to Alexandria, and Lincoln named him provisional governor of Virginia. By the end of 1863, Lincoln had appointed provisional governors to rule the parts of Tennessee, Louisiana, and Texas that were in Union hands.

In an amnesty proclamation, December 8, 1863, Lincoln outlined his program for the reconstruction of the South. He offered to pardon any southerner (except Confederate government officials and high-ranking army officers) willing to take an oath of loyalty to the Constitution. Once the southerner promised loyalty to the Union, he would be granted full citizenship and restoration of his property. When, in any southern state, the nucleus of citizens willing to take the loyalty oath numbered 10 percent of the votes cast in the election of 1860, that state could elect a government. Once the new civil regime abolished slavery, Lincoln promised to recognize it as the legitimate authority in the state.

It was hardly a revolutionary program. The electorate would be that of 1860, which meant a probable restoration of the prewar regimes on the promise only of future loyalty. Freed slaves would have no civil or political rights except those the southern governments might be willing to confer. Arkansas and Louisiana, both in Union hands, promptly accepted Lincoln's terms, formed loyal regimes satisfactory to the president, and elected representatives to Congress. Congress refused to seat them. The radicals had other plans for the South, and Lincoln's failure to consult Congress pushed some moderates to their side.

The radical response to Lincoln's plan was the Wade-Davis bill of July 1864. It proposed to place the southern states under military rule, with northern generals serving as governors. The governor was to enroll all white males, and when a majority of these in any state submitted to a loyalty oath, that state could draw up a constitution and form a civil government. In order to participate in the constitutional convention, either as voter or officeholder, a citizen had to take another "ironclad" oath. The person had to swear by this oath that he had never voluntarily supported the Confederacy or borne arms against the United States. The only persons who could take such an oath were northern "carpet-baggers,"* who had drifted south on the heels of the Union army, and southern unionists, or "scalawags." Some of the southerners were planters and businessmen, but most were poor whites and mountaineers who had nothing in common with the planter-gentry that had engineered secession. By requiring a majority of all white males to take the oath, the Wade-Davis bill ensured a prolonged period of military

rule. By disenfranchising former Confederates, it sought to remake the South into a land of small farmers, black and white.

Lincoln gave the Wade-Davis Bill a pocket veto,** which enabled him to pursue his own program while avoiding a confrontation with Congress. Though it never went into effect, the Wade-Davis bill was a blueprint for the congressional version of reconstruction that was enacted in 1867. In the meantime, Lincoln went ahead with his own version of reconstruction. By the time of his death in April 1865, Virginia, Arkansas, Tennessee, and Louisiana had working governments under it.

Despite occasional disagreements with the radicals, who even toyed with the idea of replacing him with another candidate in the election of 1864, Lincoln moved steadily toward their position in the last months of the war. When Congress took up a constitutional amendment to free the slaves in January 1865, Lincoln used his patronage powers to secure passage. The president's support was vital, for the Thirteenth Amendment squeaked through the House of Representatives by a mere three votes. (This was evidence of the North's continuing racial bias, despite four years of a war in which one of the aims had become the freeing of slaves.) But that was his last great achievement. On Good Friday, April 14, 1865, the president attended a play at Ford's Theater in Washington. John Wilkes Booth, a southern sympathizer, climbed the stairway to the president's box, where the door was unaccountably left unguarded, and shot the president from behind at close range. The nation lost more than a wartime leader; it lost a voice that spoke for compassion and understanding.

It is tempting to speculate what might have happened had Lincoln lived out his term. His reconstruction program would almost certainly have been altered by Congress. Few northerners could see much point in restoring the prewar southern re-

---

* Southerners regarded these northern transients as fortunehunters and scornfully claimed they could put everything they owned into a cheap cloth handbag.

** An act of Congress requires a president's signature in order to become law. If, toward the end of a congressional session, a president delays signing a bill—figuratively stuffing it in his pocket and forgetting it—the measure dies when Congress adjourns.

Library of Congress.

Lincoln's funeral procession down Pennsylvania Avenue.

gimes, and there was a conviction that the South ought to be punished for its rebellion. Even so, it is unlikely, had Lincoln survived, that relations between executive and Congress would have broken down so completely as they did under Johnson, to the point where Johnson became the only president in our history to suffer impeachment. Lincoln resisted the radicals without resorting to name calling, and he kept open his lines of communication. Radical congressmen who detested his policies enjoyed his private company. Lincoln's drift toward abolition during the war, moreover, showed that he was flexible. After the Thirteenth Amendment was passed, it is quite likely that Lincoln would have cooperated with further efforts to confer civil rights on freed blacks. And cooperation between president and Congress might have resulted in a more successful plan of reconstruction than the one eventually enacted.

JOHNSON AND THE RADICALS

Johnson differed from Lincoln in politics and personality. Hailing from the Tennessee hill country, where farms were small and slaves were few, Johnson's political ideology was a states rights agrarianism derived from Jefferson and Jackson. A foe of the southern gentry, Johnson sympathized with the radical view that the South ought to be remade into a land of small farmers. But his attachment to limited government prevented him from using presidential powers to enforce such a social revolution. The new president was also stubborn, thin-skinned under criticism, and spiteful in political combat. In public appearances he often adopted the rough speech and crude manners of a frontier stump speaker, evoking mockery and anger rather than sympathetic attention.

Johnson's antipathy toward southern planters encouraged the radicals to think that he might be one of their own. When Senator Benjamin F. Wade, one of the authors of the Wade-Davis bill, suggested to the president in April 1865 the execution of a dozen leading southerners as an example, Johnson raised no objection. He only wondered how, out of several million "traitors," ten or twelve might be selected. The reconstruction plan he announced in May, however, dismayed the radicals. Congress had adjourned and would not reconvene until December 1865. By refusing to summon Congress into special session and proceeding on his own, Johnson indicated that

Andrew Johnson.

Library of Congress.

he considered reconstruction a presidential function, as Lincoln had. Radicals were unhappy also because Johnson's amnesty proclamation was similar to Lincoln's. He retained Lincoln's 10 percent plan, except that he proposed to exempt from amnesty, in addition to political and military leaders, persons whose property exceeded $20,000 in value. This provision would have excluded the planter elite from participating in the restored governments, but Johnson nullified it by granting individual pardons to all who applied.

Johnson detested the planter gentry, but once those grandees had been humbled by military defeat and came to him, caps in hand, for pardons, he felt justice had been done. He also had the southern, poor white's disdain for blacks. He was willing that they be free, but he saw no need for further government efforts in their behalf. Thus, his program for reconstruction, while it recognized the end of slavery, seemed in other respects to turn the clock back to 1860.

Johnson recognized the governments Lincoln had established in Virginia, Tennessee, Arkansas, and Louisiana, and in the course of the summer and fall of 1865 he extended recognition to civil governments in the remaining southern states. By the time Congress assembled in December, the South was "restored," a term Johnson preferred to "reconstructed." The new civil governments embarrassed the president in two ways, however—by enacting black codes regulating the former slaves and by electing to office many of the same men who had governed the Confederacy.

Some sort of legislation was necessary, for the South was in ruins. In addition to Sherman's march through Georgia from Atlanta to the sea, northern armies had cut swaths of destruction through Alabama, Mississippi, and Louisiana. Cities were desolate piles of rubble. In many places, schools and churches had ceased to function. Many white families thought

The Louisiana Black Code

There was wide concern among southern legislators in 1865 that blacks might not be willing to work once they were no longer under the discipline of the lash. Thus the black codes all contained laws regulating labor contracts and prohibiting vagrancy. The following excerpts from Louisiana's Act to Provide for and Regulate Labor Contracts suggest why northerners considered the black codes slavery by another name.

Sec. 1. Be it enacted by the Senate and House of Representatives of the State of Louisiana in general assembly convened, that all persons employed as laborers in agricultural pursuits shall be required, during the first ten days of the month of January of each year, to make contracts for labor for the then ensuing year. . . .

Sec. 2. Every laborer shall have full and perfect liberty to choose his employer, but, when once chosen, he shall not be allowed to leave his place of employment until the fulfillment of his contract. . . .

Sec. 8. Be it further enacted etc. that in case of sickness of the laborer, wages for the time lost shall be deducted, and where the sickness is feigned for purposes of idleness, and also on refusing to work according to contract, double the amount of wages shall be deducted for the time lost. . . .

Sec. 9. Be it further enacted, etc. that, when in health, the laborer shall work ten hours during the day in summer, and nine hours during the day in winter, unless otherwise stipulated in the labor contract. . . .

Sec. 10. Be it further enacted, etc. that for gross misconduct on the part of the laborer, such as insubordination, habitual laziness, frequent acts of violation of his contract, or the laws of the State, he may be dismissed by his employer. . . .

Acts of the General Assembly Regulating Labor, 1865

only of survival. Blacks viewed their sudden change in status from slavery to freedom with a mixture of exhilaration and uncertainty. The first instinct of many of them was simply to move about, to visit distant relatives and friends, to breathe the air of freedom. "They are just a swarm of bees," one observer noted, "all buzzing about and not knowing where to settle." To whites who had lived for generations in dread of slave rebellion, this mass of vagrants was a threat to public order.

The laws concerning freed slaves, known as black codes, did spell out their legal rights. The laws legitimized marriages, gave blacks access to courts, and allowed them to possess property. But, reflecting the fears of whites, the laws also contained vagrancy clauses by which unemployed blacks could be placed under the control of white employers. Some states enacted curfews or required blacks to have passes in order to leave their places of employment. Other laws imposed fines on blacks for trespassing, preaching without a license, possessing firearms, or using alcoholic beverages. Even in the laws that conferred rights, there was racial discrimination. Blacks could marry, but only a member of their own race; they could testify in court, but only if one party to the suit was black. Taken as a whole, the black codes made of the freed slaves second-class citizens.

Such regulations ran counter to the free labor ideology of the Republicans. The freed slaves were tied to their plantations by the authority of the state, given only the freedom to work as a landless peasantry under labor terms set by their former owners. By denying any pretense of equality, the black codes also challenged the Republicans' sense of loyalty. Black people had died in the Union cause; the Union was obliged to protect them from their former masters. "Loyal negroes must not be put down, while disloyal white men are put up," was one moderate Republican's view of it.

The election of former Confederate leaders further weakened the president's position. Some who were elected did not qualify even under Johnson's lenient requirements. Among those elected to Congress was Alexander H. Stephens, vice president of the Confederacy. Such conduct by voters was perhaps to be expected. A proud people convinced of the righteousness of their cause, southerners naturally tried to minimize the effects of the war and preserve as much of their culture as possible. What southerners did not realize was that by rejecting the role of the vanquished, they invited further punishment. By refusing even the pretense of contrition, the South deprived the North of its victory. If nothing was to be changed, the bloodshed was meaningless. That realization gave the radicals in Congress the upper hand.

⊔ The Critical Year: 1866

The extent to which the president and his southern clients had alienated northern opinion was evident when Congress convened in December 1865. Moderate Republicans agreed with radicals that Congress ought to have a hand in reconstruction and that something had to be done to protect the blacks. Congress re-fused to seat the senators and representatives elected by the Lincoln-Johnson governments and appointed instead a Joint Committee on Reconstruction to investigate conditions in the South. The chairman of the committee, Senator William P. Fessenden of Maine, was a moderate, but Thaddeus Stevens, the radical from Gettysburg, Pennsylvania, who headed the House delegation on the committee, had a powerful voice.

While the joint committee interviewed generals and journalists, former Confederates and freed blacks, building up a file of southern intransigence, the Senate Judiciary Committee drafted the first fragments of reconstruction legislation—a Freedmen's Bureau bill and a civil rights bill. The guiding hand behind these measures was Senator Lyman Trumbull of Illinois, a moderate who, in the previous year, had introduced and floor-managed the Thirteenth Amendment. Distressed by reports of racial oppression in the South, Trumbull decided that Congress had the power to preserve the freedom the amendment promised.

FREEDMEN'S BUREAU AND CIVIL RIGHTS ACTS

The Freedmen's Bureau had been added to the War Department in March 1865 to feed and care for the thousands of refugees drifting into Union army camps. Trumbull's bill, introduced in January 1866, enlarged the bureau's authority, making it the guardian of the rights of the freedmen. The bill also authorized the president to rent 40-acre tracts of unoccupied public land to freed slaves, with the right of future purchase. A companion measure, the civil rights bill, made free blacks citizens of the United States and promised them the "full and equal benefit of all laws and proceedings for the security of persons and property as is enjoyed by white citizens." In the

Senate debate, Trumbull explained that the purpose of this measure was to negate the southern black codes.

Although both measures passed Congress by substantial margins, Johnson vetoed them. He considered both to be special interest legislation, benefiting blacks at the expense of everyone else, and beyond the power of Congress. Literally and even historically, Johnson was right, but politically his veto was disastrous. It meant that he was prepared to leave blacks at the mercy of their former masters. He even rejected Secretary of State Seward's advice that he at least appear less rigid. A furious Congress overrode the veto of the Civil Rights Act (the first time ever for a major piece of legislation) and proceeded to draft an amendment designed to enshrine civil rights in the Constitution. The task fell to the Joint Committee on Reconstruction, which by March of 1866 had completed its investigation of conditions in the South. Drafting an amendment was not easy, for the language had to be broad enough to serve as a platform for congressional reconstruction, yet moderate enough to secure ratification. The committee skirted the issue of black suffrage, for instance, because the North was not yet ready for so bold a stroke. Even so, the Fourteenth Amendment dramatically altered the constitutional history of the United States.

Thaddeus Stevens introduced the committee's handiwork and explained its rationale. The amendment began by defining citizenship in such a way as to make blacks citizens of the nation and of the states in which they resided. It then prohibited the states from abridging the privileges and immunities of citizens, from depriving any person of life, liberty, or property without "due process of law," or denying to any person "the equal protection of the laws." These limitations, explained Stevens, were designed to cure a deficiency in the federal Constitution, which had limited (through the Bill of Rights) only the actions of Congress and not those of the states. The amendment, said Stevens, would allow "Congress to correct the unjust legislation of the States, so far that the law which operates upon one man shall operate equally upon all."

The amendment also encouraged southern states to give blacks the vote by threatening to reduce their representation in Congress if they failed to do so. Stevens considered this the most important feature of the amendment, though he recognized that much more was needed to ensure true independence for the former slave. "Forty acres of land and a hut," he declared, "would be more valuable to him than the immediate right to vote. Unless we give him this we shall receive the censure of mankind and the curse of Heaven."

The most politically important section of the amendment, from the standpoint of the Republicans, was the third. It addressed age-old northern fears of southern political power dating back to the three-fifths compromise in the Constitution which had given southerners a disproportionate vote in Congress and the electoral college. This section barred from political office any southerner who had violated his oath to uphold the Constitution by aiding the rebellion. In effect, it disqualified the old ruling class of the South.

The Amendment passed Congress by partisan votes, with Republicans in favor and Democrats against. The amendment was not a victory for Republican radicals. It was, rather, a distillation of the minimum terms which Republicans, momentarily reunited by Johnson's intransigence, demanded of the South. It did not require black suffrage, disenfranchise former Confederates, or break up the plantations. It demanded only that blacks be given equal rights as citizens and that the South be governed by men loyal to the Union. It was a potential bridge between North and South, between victor and vanquished, that the President might have utilized. Had he done so, the story of reconstruction might have been very different.

JOHNSON'S RESPONSE

Although the Fourteenth Amendment answered some of the constitutional misgivings expressed by the president in his veto of the civil rights bill, Johnson nevertheless objected to it, principally because of the disabilities placed on former Confederates. He thus severed himself completely from the Republicans and placed his political future in the hands of those who were constitutionally deprived of the vote. Taking the cue, the Johnson regimes in the South refused to ratify the amendment—except for Tennessee, which Congress rewarded by seating its representatives.

In August, Johnson's supporters organized a National Union convention in Philadelphia in hopes of launching a new political party. Off-year congressional elections that autumn seemed to present an opportunity for a referendum on Reconstruction policy. The third party movement fizzled, and in desperation the president decided to enter the campaign personally. On August 28 he embarked on a "Swing around the Circle," traveling by railroad and steamboat west to Chicago and returning by way of St. Louis, Indianapolis, and Pittsburgh. Never before had an incumbent president embarked on a partisan tour, and the novelty of the occasion dramatized the president's eccentricity. Losing all sense of proportion, he harangued his audiences, engaged in verbal duels with hecklers, and denounced his radical opponents as "a subsidized gang of hirelings and traducers." Toward the end of the journey, city and state officials openly avoided the president's appearances. He returned to Washington more isolated than ever.

In the fall elections, the voters pronounced judgment: The Republicans car-

ried every northern state. Democrats retained a majority of the congressional delegations only of Delaware, Maryland, and Kentucky. Equally important, the distinction between radical and moderate largely vanished. The Republican party was reunited; it would reconstruct the South in its own way, with or without presidential support.

The lame duck Congress also read the election returns, and that winter it prepared for the new order that would begin on March 4, 1867. First, it moved to take control of its own sessions. To prevent the nine-month gap that had allowed the president a free hand over reconstruction in 1865, Congress passed an act decreeing that the new Congress would begin its session on Inauguration Day, March 4, instead of waiting until the following December. It then moved to restrict the president's power and authority. A Tenure of Office Act (March 2, 1867) prohibited the president from dismissing members of his own cabinet without the consent of the Senate. That same day, by an amendment to an army appropriation act, Congress prescribed that all military orders issued by the president had to be funneled through the Office of General of the Army (Ulysses S. Grant), whose headquarters were to be in Washington, D.C., and who could not be removed or reassigned without the consent of the Senate.

The radicals thus ensured themselves some control over the army, a significant move when one recalls that their blueprint for reconstruction involved a period of military rule. Doubts concerning that intent were instantly resolved when, that same day, March 2, 1867, the outgoing Congress enacted the first of four reconstruction acts. Congress now had control over reconstruction. The president vetoed each of these bills and then watched as Congress overrode his vetoes. The president had become irrelevant; within a year, Congress would seek to remove him altogether.

⊔ Congress on the March

The four reconstruction acts Congress passed involved two main principles. Ignoring the existing governments created by presidential order, the acts divided the Confederate states (except for Tennessee) into five military districts, each governed by an army general. Second, the acts outlined the procedure for the restoration of civil government and readmission to the Union (which meant, in effect, having representatives seated in Congress). The district commanders were to enroll all voters, including blacks (but excluding former Confederates who were barred by the Fourteenth Amendment); and they were to hold elections for delegates to state constitutional conventions. The new state constitutions had to include a provision for black suffrage. When a civil government was established, the first legislature elected under it was to ratify the Fourteenth Amendment. When all these conditions were met, the state would be entitled to representation in Congress.

In 1868, six states had complied with these requirements and were readmitted. All had Republican governments, and their readmission was hastened by the Republican desire to have them participate in the presidential election that year. Readmission of the remaining four—Virginia, Georgia, Mississippi, and Texas—was delayed by white efforts to evade the congressional requirements. While whites procrastinated, Congress in 1869 approved the Fifteenth Amendment, which prohibited any state from denying the vote "on account of race, color, or previous condi-

Reconstruction of the South, 1865–1877.

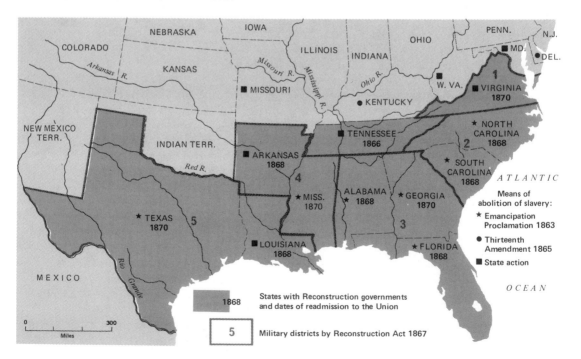

Library of Congress.

A mixed jury of blacks and whites, 1867.

tion of servitude." These four states were required to ratify the Fifteenth Amendment as well, a process completed by 1870.

RADICAL RULE IN THE SOUTH

Thus began a period of Black Reconstruction—military-radical Republican rule—that lasted in some states for ten years, in others less than two. Though seemingly harsh, the radical program was not as severe as it might have been. No civil war in history has ever ended with so few reprisals. There was only one postwar execution—Henry Wirz, Swiss-born commander of the infamous Andersonville prisoner camp, was hanged for "war crimes."* Con-

---

* More than 12,000 Union prisoners of war died at Andersonville in the last year of the war, out of a total of 30,218 who died in all Confederate prison camps. Less well known is the fact that 25,976 "Rebels" died in Union POW camps.

federate president Jefferson Davis was imprisoned for only two years, and Robert E. Lee was allowed to retreat into the unsung captivity of a college presidency.

The military rule was both brief and light-handed. The federal occupying force numbered only 20,000 men, spread over ten states. The army rarely intervened in civilian affairs; indeed, it cooperated with the Lincoln-Johnson governments until Congress declared them no longer viable. In fact, it can be argued that the army did not exert itself enough. In the summer of 1866 it allowed hideous race riots in Memphis and New Orleans to go on for days. Later, when whites formed vigilante clubs to intimidate blacks, the army stood by helplessly until the president ordered it to act. From the standpoint of the blacks, the tragedy of Reconstruction was that Congress and the army did not go far enough.

Whether Congress had the constitutional authority to impose military rule on the South is, of course, another question. The war had been fought to prevent the

South from leaving the Union—if they were sovereign states and members of the Union, what right did Congress have to evict their governors and install army generals? Cowed by the radicals, the Supreme Court never directly confronted the issue. In 1866 the Court declared in *Ex Parte Milligan* that military courts could not try civilians in areas where the civil courts were open and operating. The case originated in the war, but it seemed to threaten the system of military government the radicals had in mind for the South. Congress promptly retaliated by reducing the number of justices on the Supreme Court and limiting the Court's jurisdiction. Some radicals proposed abolishing the Supreme Court altogether. The Court got the message. In 1867, when two southern states, Georgia and Mississippi, challenged the constitutionality of Reconstruction by asking the court to issue injunctions preventing the president and his secretary of war from enforcing the acts, the Court refused to hear the cases.

JOHNSON'S IMPEACHMENT

The president showed no such discretion. Challenged by the radicals, he planted his feet and fought back. In the summer of 1867, he curtailed the powers of the army commanders in the South and replaced those who were sympathetic to the radical program. In August 1867, he dismissed Secretary of War Edwin M. Stanton. Stanton had worked closely with the radicals in Congress, and as head of the War Department he was the central figure in military reconstruction. Johnson's dismissal did not actually violate the Tenure of Office Act, since Stanton was a Lincoln appointee, but it was certainly a challenge

Johnson's impeachment trial in the Senate.

New York Public Library Picture Collection.

CLIO'S FOCUS: The Captain of the Planter

Captain F. J. Nickols of the *Onward*, the inside ship of the Union fleet blockading Charleston, South Carolina, stared disbelievingly at the vessel steaming out of the heavily fortified port. The craft was flying the stars and bars of the Confederacy as well as the Palmetto flag of South Carolina. As it steered boldly toward the blockading squadron, the name *Planter* could be discerned on its bow. Just as Captain Nickols ordered his gunners at ready, the Confederate vessel raised yet another emblem—a white bedsheet signaling surrender. The *Planter* drew alongside and sixteen ragged fugitives (eight men, five women, and three children) climbed aboard the Union warship.

In charge of the party was Robert Smalls, a slave who had been trained as a river pilot. When the Confederate government chartered the cotton steamer *Planter* to use as a dispatch boat, Smalls, a slave hired by the vessel's owner, went with the ship. He had spent the early months of the war piloting the *Planter* on various missions through the web of waterways between Charleston and Port Royal. He knew by heart the location of the Confederate batteries and the signals used in passing. When the Union Navy seized Port Royal Sound in November 1861, he began to think of escape. From Beaufort, his birthplace, Smalls's mother wrote that the Federals, though they called the Port Royal blacks "contrabands," treated them well and allowed them to work their fields as free people.

The opportunity to escape came on May 13, 1862, when the white officers of the *Planter* went into town, leaving the crew of eight blacks on board. The previous day the *Planter* had taken on two hundred pounds of ammunition and four cannons, a cargo Smalls judged might be of considerable value to the soldiers in blue. Following a prearranged plan, the crew put the vessel under steam, picked up their families at the city's North Atlantic wharf, and sailed into the harbor. With Smalls dressed in the captain's uniform and giving all the proper signals, the *Planter* cleared the Confederate batteries at Forts Sumter and Moultrie and joined the Union squadron. Captain Nickols passed his happy fugitives on to the flag officer at Port Royal, and by nightfall Smalls had delivered his cargo of munitions to the Union depot at Hilton Head.

The abduction of the *Planter* caused a sensation in the North. The Lincoln administration's emphasis on preserving the Union had pushed slavery into the background. Smalls's exploit was evidence that the slaves, at least, understood what the war was about. The antislavery press pounced on the incident with glee. Smalls was the war's first black hero, his deed a clear demonstration that southern blacks had the skill and enterprise to survive in freedom. The abduction had material as well as symbolic value. Loss of the *Planter* deprived the Confederacy of a badly needed supply ship. General Lee himself took note of the loss and issued orders to prevent a recurrence of the "misfortune."

Smalls, commissioned as a second lieutenant, United States Colored Troops, spent the remainder of the war piloting the *Planter* and other Union vessels through the shallow sea island waters. After the war, he and other black veterans formed a cooperative that pooled the meager assets of Port Royal freedmen to purchase a coastal steamer. In command of this vessel, Smalls developed a lucrative trade, profits from which he invested in real estate. By 1868 he was one of the wealthiest men in Beaufort, landlord to much of the town and proud possessor of a stable of racehorses and an elegant carriage.

The regulations adopted by the postwar regime set up under President Johnson and its candid admission that it meant to keep South Carolina a white man's country taught Smalls how fragile a blessing freedom was. In March 1867, while Congress wrote a new reconstruction program, Smalls organized a Beaufort Republican Club, the first in South Carolina. The club, consisting of thirty-eight blacks and three whites, issued a call for a convention to organize a state Republican party. Smalls served as a delegate to that convention and to the convention summoned the following year to draft a state constitution. Smalls's most important contribution to the Reconstruction constitution was a provision for state-supported public education. The article he drafted prohibited racial segregation in the schools and made attendance compulsory for children between the ages of seven and fourteen. On paper at least, South Carolina had the most progressive educational system in the South.

Smalls was a hero to sea island residents not only because of his war record, which he never tired of recounting, but also because he symbolized self-made success. His loyal and predominantly black constituency sent him successively to the assembly (1868–1870), to the state senate (1870–1874), and finally to Congress (1874–1886). Yet he emerged from this lengthy service with little to show. He campaigned for land grants to freedmen, state-support for black business cooperatives, and state and federal protection of civil rights. But neither the white radicals who governed South Carolina in the 1870s nor Republicans in Congress were prepared for such reforms. He managed to hold his seat in Congress after white Democrats won control of the state in 1877, but even there he was an anomaly. In a scandalously fraudulent election in which black votes were thrown out by the boxful, the Democrats finally unseated him in 1886.

Robert Smalls lived until 1915, loyal to the end to the party of Abraham Lincoln, a party that long before had cynically called itself "lily white." It is sad that his party and his country could do no more for such a competent, farsighted leader.

to the radicals. The Senate, however, was not then in session, so Johnson had time to maneuver. In a rare display of political cunning, he persuaded General Grant to accept the post.

When Congress returned in December, the Senate refused to approve Stanton's removal. Grant promptly resigned. Johnson angrily denounced Grant for this "treachery," thereby driving the bewildered general into the arms of the radicals. Johnson then selected General Lorenzo Thomas, a braggart with a fondness for the bottle. A rare comedy ensued. Stanton, encouraged by the radicals, barricaded himself in the War Department, refusing to allow Thomas entry. When Thomas, at a Washington social function, announced his intent to take the building by force, Stanton had him arrested. In the midst of this, the House of Representatives voted that the president "be impeached of high crimes and misdemeanors in office." The House subsequently adopted eleven articles of impeachment, the first nine of which related in one way or another to the attempted removal of Stanton. The tenth

article, though it did not allege a crime, was actually the heart of the Radicals' case. It accused the president of attempting, through "intemperate, inflammatory, and scandalous harangues" to bring into "disgrace, ridicule, hatred, contempt, and reproach the Congress of the United States." The eleventh article repeated the charges of the previous ten.

The trial opened in the Senate on March 5, 1868, with Chief Justice Salmon P. Chase presiding. The argument developed by the impeachment managers appointed by the House was that the president was guilty of high crimes and misdemeanors within the meaning of the Constitution. Alternatively, if he could not be convicted of a

Election of 1868.

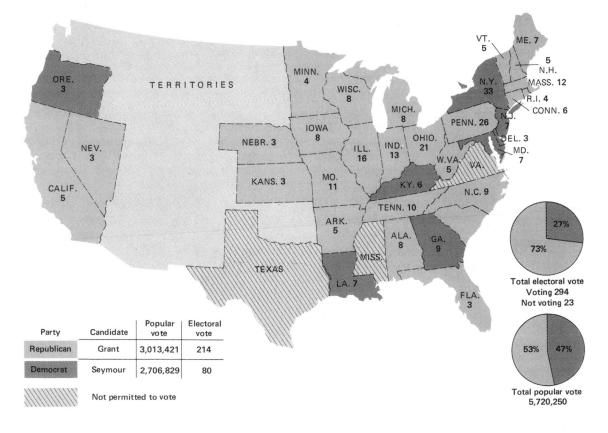

Party	Candidate	Popular vote	Electoral vote
Republican	Grant	3,013,421	214
Democrat	Seymour	2,706,829	80

Not permitted to vote

Total electoral vote
Voting 294
Not voting 23

Total popular vote
5,720,250

crime through judicial procedure, the Senate needed only to decide whether Johnson was "fit to retain the Office of. President." The latter argument worried some senators, for it implied that impeachment was a political weapon which might be used against any president who faced a hostile majority in Congress. Republican moderates also worried about the presidential succession. Benjamin F. Wade, president pro tem of the Senate, was next in line if Johnson were removed, and the crusty Ohioan was the most radical of radicals.

On May 16, the Senate voted on the eleventh article, which was the broadest in scope. The vote was 35 in favor of conviction and 19 against—1 vote short of the two-thirds majority required to find the president guilty. The division held firm on two other articles, and the Senate adjourned without bothering with the remainder. The minority that had saved the president consisted of twelve Democrats and seven Republicans. Criticism of the Republican dissenters was harsh but short-

lived, as public opinion swung around rather quickly to their point of view.

While the Senate pondered the fate of one president, a Republican convention met in Chicago to nominate another; for 1868 was an election year. The Republican choice was Ulysses S. Grant, a hero in the North and, since midwinter, the darling of the radicals. The general, devoid of political experience, was not eager for the office. Nor was he sure he wanted a Republican nomination, having been a prewar Democrat. He accepted, however, and in the election he swamped the hapless Democratic candidate Horatio Seymour, governor of New York, by an electoral vote of 214 to 80.

Six southern states were readmitted in the summer of 1868, and throughout much of the South the radical program was in place. The new president's task was simply to make it work. That proved a formidable one because the Republican regimes in the South began to crumble almost as soon as they were installed. Radicalism was

"Reconstruction or 'A White Man's Government.'" A Currier & Ives cartoon which depicts a drowning southerner rejecting the helping hand of a freed man, while President Grant advises him to accept the help.

New York Public Library, Aston, Lenox, and Tilden Foundation.

on the wane by 1869, both in Congress and in the reconstructed South.

⨆ Gray Reconstruction

Slavery had locked the black and white races in a love-hate relationship of mutual dependence. Emancipation changed the form of that relationship, but not its substance. Whites, in possession of most of the land and investment capital, were dependent on blacks for labor, and labor was all blacks had to offer. Master became employer; former slave became wage earner or tenant farmer. Freedom, however, did give blacks some mobility and hence some leverage. At the end of the war there was an enormous amount of movement. Even after the wanderlust subsided, black workers did not hesitate to desert an employer if they felt themselves mistreated. For several years after the war, the end of every growing season meant a general rearrangement of population. Some blacks moved into the cities, and others joined the white exodus to the West. But the vast majority stayed in neighborhoods with which they were familiar. Within a couple of years the movement declined and employment relationships became firm. A traveler in South Carolina in 1870 noticed that there was "little or no disparagement of the negro as a labourer among respectable countrymen, who need his services and employ him. On the contrary, there is much appreciation of his good qualities, and much greater satisfaction with what he has done, and may yet be trained to do, as a free labourer, than one might be prepared to find."

THE SHARECROPPER SYSTEM

Although blacks remained in a position of economic dependence after the war, the relationship was more complex than that of employer and employee. Few planters had the ready cash to pay wages, and few blacks were willing to become wage slaves. They hungered for land, even if they could not own it. Sharecropping met the needs of planters and freed blacks. Plantations were divided into rental plots, and the rent was a share of the tenant's crop. That share varied from half to three quarters, depending on the amount of tools and livestock the owner supplied in addition to the land. The system offered a small amount of independence for the tenant, but it also bound him in perpetual poverty. Only by rare good fortune and extraordinary effort could the sharecropper ever save enough money to purchase land of his own.

And ill fortune dogged the southern economy for a decade and more after the war. Cotton was the South's principal market crop, and cotton was no longer king. Cotton had become important in the world economy because textile technology led the Western World's industrial revolution. After 1860 other industries, notably steel and railroads, paced American and European economic growth. Textile manufacture, and cotton consumption, continued at the same level as before. But the South was no longer the key to the world economy. And the South's role in world trade would have been smaller even if there had been no Civil War; the war simply speeded the decline. Small white farmers thus became locked in the same circle of poverty in which the freed blacks found themselves. By 1880, one third of all white farmers in the cotton states were tenants or sharecroppers.

The one thing the Civil War did not change was the concentration of land ownership in the hands of a relatively small number of white planters. The central failure of reconstruction is that the federal government failed to provide land for the freed blacks, a redistribution that would almost surely have benefited poor white farmers as well. Redistribution of wealth was not, to be sure, within the realm of mid–nineteenth-century American thought, but a certain amount might have been accomplished by indirect means. During the war, Congress had already ordered the confiscation of slaves belonging to Confederates. The confiscation of plantations was but a small extension, one in fact advocated by Thaddeus Stevens and other radical Republicans.

In January 1865, General William Tecumseh Sherman, after a conference in Savannah with Secretary of War Stanton, issued Special Field Order Number 15. This military directive set aside for settlement by freed blacks the islands and seacoast from Charleston south to the St. Johns River of Florida and for a distance of 30 miles inland. Each black head of family was to be allowed to have up to 40 acres of land, though ultimate title was left unclear. Sherman and Stanton may have hoped that the lands would be given to the freed blacks, but more likely they expected Congress to set up a program for selling the preempted lands to blacks at low prices. But President Johnson, when the fighting ended, allowed the former white owners to repossess their lands, and a potential model for reconstruction was lost. Congress, even after the radicals won control, made no effort to provide cheap lands for the freed blacks other than those available in the western plains under the Homestead Act.

The failure to provide land for any substantial number of blacks was part of a larger flaw in congressional Reconstruction—that, while it was labeled radical, it was in fact so conservative that it failed to

Black members of Congress, 1869–1873. At left is Senator Hiram R. Revels of Mississippi. The others are members of the House of Representatives, three from South Carolina, and one each from Georgia, Florida, and Alabama.

New York Public Library Picture Collection.

alter the pattern of human relationships in the South. Black suffrage was undeniably a bold step, but otherwise congressional Republicans stood bound in the straitjacket of tradition. They accepted without question the Jeffersonian concept of states' rights (rejecting only its extreme form, secession), reverence for private property, and individualism. The Fourteenth Amendment offered paper guarantees for the rights of the freed blacks, but its enforcement depended on the realities of political power within the southern states. The Reconstruction Acts, far from bringing about any changes in the South, simply shifted the scene of battle from Congress to the states. Black voters and their allies there were left with the burden of determining the ultimate results of the Civil War.

FREED BLACKS AND THE BALLOT

Blacks understood the challenge before them, and they made as much use as their numbers permitted of the opportunities presented by the Reconstruction Acts. In South Carolina, the first statewide meeting of the predominantly black Republican party adopted a platform calling for free public education, "the division of unoccupied lands among the poorer classes," reorganization of the state's judicial system, and public support for "the poor and destitute." When elections were held in November 1867 for delegates to a constitutional convention, 85 percent of the eligible blacks turned out to vote, and they selected quality leadership. Of the seventy-four blacks elected to the convention, only about half were former slaves. Fourteen were northerners who went to South Carolina after the war in search of political and economic opportunity, and several of these were well educated. Robert Brown Elliott, who would later become a member of Con-

gress, was a graduate of Eton and the Massachusetts School of Law. Among the former slaves chosen to the convention, the majority were ministers or tradesmen, such as the steamboat pilot Robert Smalls, another future congressman.

When the South Carolina constitution was submitted to a popular referendum in the spring of 1868, turnout among eligible blacks was again about 85 percent, whereas less than 60 percent of the registered white voters bothered to participate. Similar enthusiasm enabled blacks to win a majority in the legislature in the elections of 1870 and 1872. In the other southern states, however, the freed blacks, no matter how well motivated, did not have the numerical strength to dominate either the constitutional conventions or the Reconstruction governments. They were dependent on their white allies—northern carpetbaggers and southern scalawags. White Republicans drafted the Reconstruction constitutions and monopolized the top executive and judicial offices in the new governments. The results were as varied as the political mixture—a record of social progress marred by violence, venality, and betrayal.

The state constitutions required by the Reconstruction Acts brought some needed reforms. In addition to extending the suffrage through the addition of black and poor white voters to the poll lists, they reapportioned the legislatures to reflect population changes. Several states, where local officials had been appointed by the governor, made county offices elective. Some expanded the legal rights of women and liberalized penal codes. All provided for a uniform system of free public schools, though only South Carolina and Louisiana prohibited racially segregated school systems. In short, the Reconstruction constitutions brought to the South some of the social and political reforms that had engaged the North in the prewar decades. Next to the constitutional amendments that conferred civil and political rights on freed blacks, they were the main achievement of Reconstruction.

REDEMPTION OF THE SOUTH

The period of radical Republican rule endured in the memories of southern whites for a century afterward. The radical governments were denounced as unconstitutional, fraudulently elected, and hopelessly corrupt. Much of this poor historical image was the work of the white conservatives (Redeemers, they called themselves) who succeeded the radicals. Racially biased and appealing to an all-white constituency, the Redeemers had no difficulty convincing their listeners (and posterity) that radical Reconstruction was a dark day for the South. They drew pictures of governors and legislators making private fortunes through graft and fraud. Corruption was certainly present, but it was no more prevalent than in the North—or in the federal government under Grant.

The debts of the southern states did increase dramatically during the Reconstruction years, but graft was not entirely the cause. The South needed business investment to rebuild, and some states were too generous in their encouragement of business. Alabama purchased the bonds of the Alabama and Chattanooga Railroad in order to encourage construction, and when the railroad defaulted on its debt, the state lost millions. The fiasco was biracial and bipartisan, as both Republicans and Democrats cooperated in the scheme.

The financial problems faced by all southern governments, regardless of who controlled them, were staggering. The total wealth of the South, independent of the loss of slave property, declined by some 40 percent between 1860 and 1870. Emancipation eliminated the major source of state revenue—the tax on slaves—which

had provided the prewar states with nearly half their income. Emancipation also increased tremendously the social services required of the state governments. In South Carolina, for example, a total of 20,000 children, all white, were enrolled in public schools in 1860. The state's reconstruction constitution expanded the state's commitment to public education, and by 1870 there were 120,000 children (50,000 whites and 70,000 blacks) in the public educational system. The resulting taxes, five to ten times the prewar rates, added to the fury of southern whites, who equated taxes with tyranny in the revolutionary tradition.

A depression, beginning with the panic of 1873, was a further cause of debt. In the hard times that ensued, people were unable to pay taxes, and state after state went into debt. Yet in Mississippi, where radical Republicans did not win control until 1874, it was the radicals who introduced the reforms designed to reduce government expenditures. In South Carolina, Republicans exposed and cleaned out their own corruption long before the state was "redeemed" by white Democrats. And in Virginia, where charges of corruption flew as wildly as anywhere, the state not only incurred no Reconstruction debt, but even managed to pay off part of its prewar indebtedness.

The Reconstruction experience varied with each state, and so did the manner and timing of "redemption" by white conservative Democrats. Virginia never did experience Republican rule. In 1868 Virginia Democrats and former Whigs formed the Conservative party, which quickly gained a majority in the legislature and controlled the convention that drafted the Reconstruction constitution. The key to the Conservative success was electoral strength in the predominantly white mountain counties. In North Carolina and Tennessee, the small farmers of the Appalachian highlands generally voted Republican. Some states had a valid two-party system during the Reconstruction years. In Alabama the Democrats won in 1870, yielded to the Republicans in 1872, and returned in 1874. In North Carolina, where blacks numbered only a third of the population, the Republicans held the executive branch of government and the Democrats the legislature from 1870 to 1876. In Florida, on the other hand, Republicans kept themselves in power until 1877 by catering to white interests. Segregation prevailed, no effort was made to secure black civil rights, and only one black, a congressman, was elected to high office throughout the era of Florida's "reconstruction."

Because Reconstruction depended principally on black votes, it was doomed to fail. Freed blacks, even with white allies, were a minority everywhere in the South. After Congress passed an Amnesty Act in 1871, which removed virtually all the political disabilities imposed on former Confederates, "redemption" to white conservative rule was only a matter of time. White violence only hastened the process. Night-riding vigilantes adorned with mystical titles such as Ku Klux Klan or Knights of the White Camellia began intimidating black voters as soon as Reconstruction governments were established. The night riders were most active in those states with a large black voting population, and the violence was directed at the most politically active blacks and their closest white allies. Four predominantly black and solidly Republican counties in Alabama were the scene of almost nightly mayhem in 1869 and 1870. In 1870 all four voted Democratic and gave the Democrats the election.

Not all the violence was secret or organized. The worst riots occurred in South Carolina in 1870–1871, when the state's radical governor organized and armed a black militia. Whites, still shuddering at the memory of John Brown and Harpers Ferry, raided black homes in search of weapons, plundering and beating their occupants. The governor ultimately had to

New York Public Library Picture Collection.
Hooded members of the Ku Klux Klan.

summon help from President Grant and the U.S. Army to restore order, though by the time the army arrived, the weapons had vanished and the rioting had subsided.

Except in Arkansas, where the Republican governor effectively suppressed terrorism with arrests and executions, the Ku Klux Klan was a potent agent of the Redeemers. Alabama, Texas, and Mississippi returned to white conservative rule in 1874–1875 after an extensive campaign of intimidation that frightened blacks away from the polls. It was clear by then that only strong action by the federal government could preserve the social and political gains made by the freed blacks. In 1875 Congress passed a civil rights act guaranteeing blacks equal access to schools and other public facilities and banning their exclusion from jury duty. But enforcement of such guarantees would have taken an army of federal marshals, and the Grant administration was not prepared to take on such a burden.

THE END
OF RECONSTRUCTION

The fact is that northern idealism had largely evaporated. The failure to give land to blacks showed that there were limits to northern idealism; the abolition of the Freedmen's Bureau in 1869 signaled its decline. The North never wanted to impose a social and economic revolution on the South, and it soon lost whatever will it had to impose a political revolution. The Republican alliance with the "lower orders," in factory or farm, North and South, had been founded on the free labor gospel—a Christian promise of future reward through hard work and self-discipline in a free environment. In the new age that dawned with the Civil War, the self-help gospel served best those who already had status and wealth, for it justified their success. By the early 1870s, the northern middle class had come to fear the immigrant factory worker and the black field hand as part of the faceless mob of poor who threatened law, order, and property rights. The Republicans, ever the party of the northern middle class, whatever their gestures to factory and field hands, shifted with the groundswell of opinion. The party of political reform under Lincoln was transformed into the party of corporate capitalism under Grant. In the process it abandoned both southern blacks and northern factory workers.

In the South, the Redeemers, with their talk of a New South remade in the urban, industrialized image of the North, appealed to Republican leaders. Republicans of the 1870s felt far more comfortable in the company of wealthy businessmen than in the company of black tenant farmers. And the blacks lost out, because "redemption" brought racial segregation, the denial of civil rights, and the gradual loss of political privileges. Florida in 1885 adopted a new state constitution that specifically disenfranchised blacks, and by 1900 blacks were excluded from the polls everywhere in the South, regardless of the Fifteenth Amendment.

By 1876, when the radical governor of Mississippi fled the state rather than face impeachment by a hostile Democratic legislature, only three southern states remained under Republican rule. The "redemption" of those three—South Carolina, Louisiana, and Florida—by the infamous Compromise of 1877 is part of another story. The Reconstruction era by then had passed.

SUMMARY

Southern secession gave congressional Republicans an opportunity to pass legislation the North had long desired, proposals for economic development once embodied in Henry Clay's American System. The passage of this legislation symbolized the shift in the economy from farm to factory, and it shifted the focus of politics from state to national government. The principal items on the Republican agenda were a protective tariff to foster manufactures, federal aid for the construction of the transcontinental railroad, a national bank system with power to issue money, and a Homestead Act that offered free land to the nation's toilers, both urban and rural. The burst of legislative activity also set the political agenda for the future. Tariffs, banks, and railroads were the central issues of American politics for the remainder of the century.

Although its commitment to economic growth eventually allied the Republican party with big business, its constituency in the 1860s was composed of the northern middle class and the working people. And Republicans remained concerned, at least through the 1860s, about the fate of blacks in the South. Through the early years of the war, radical Republicans pressured Lincoln to move faster toward emancipation. After the Emancipation Proclamation they quarreled with the president over reconstruction—what to do about the South after the war. Lincoln's approach, set forth in his Amnesty Proclamation of December 1863, was to allow southerners to hold elections for civil governments as soon as 10 percent of the voters in any state were willing to take a loyalty oath. The radical plan, embodied in the Wade-Davis Bill of July 1864, was to impose military rule on the postwar South, disenfranchise the planter-gentry that had caused all the trouble, and build new governments based on middle- and lower-class whites.

After Lincoln's death, Johnson adopted his Reconstruction policy with only minor changes and proceeded to establish civil governments in the South in the course of 1865. The new governments embarrassed the president in two ways, however: They contained a number of ex-Confederate officeholders, and they enacted black codes for the regulation of the former slaves. To many in the North, it seemed as if the war had accomplished very little. Johnson nevertheless adhered to his policy, and the effect was to throw Republican radicals and moderates together. In the spring of 1866, Congress struck at the black codes with a Civil Rights Act, and it reinforced that with the Fourteenth Amendment, which prohibited a state from denying to

its citizens the equal protection of the laws. Johnson's refusal to accept these moderate and obviously needed laws alienated the public, and the radicals won a majority of Congress in the off-year 1866 election.

In the course of 1867, the Congress passed, over Johnson's vetoes, four Reconstruction Acts. These imposed military rule on the South, forced the South to draft new state constitutions that gave blacks the vote, and required the southern states to ratify the fourteenth, and ultimately the fifteenth, amendments as a condition of reentry to the Union. Johnson's obstruction of the reconstruction acts, notably by removing from office his secretary of war, Edwin Stanton, led to his impeachment, though he was not convicted. Shortly after this, in 1868, six states complied with the reconstruction acts (Tennessee having been admitted earlier), and the remaining four were admitted in 1870.

Although it seemed harsh to southern whites, radical Reconstruction benefited blacks but little. They needed more than legal rights; they needed land if they were to have a chance at social and legal equality. But a breakup of the great plantations was beyond the realm of Republican liberalism. Republicans, like most pre–Civil War reformers, felt that freedom meant the elimination of some evil, such as liquor or slavery, not the imposition of some well-intentioned government program. As a result, having freed the slaves and guaranteed their legal rights, the Republicans were inclined to let them fend for themselves. Since blacks were a minority in every southern state, that meant they had to rely on white allies for political survival. After Congress in 1871 restored the vote to whites who had served the Confederacy, blacks were doomed. The radical regimes collapsed one by one, despite sporadic efforts by the Grant administration to shore them up. The last of them were "redeemed" to white conservative Democratic rule in 1877. The white "redeemers" whittled away at black rights, imposed segregation in public facilities, and eventually found ways of depriving blacks of the vote. Civil rights for blacks would have to await the second reconstruction a century later.

READING SUGGESTIONS

Kenneth Stampp's *The Era of Reconstruction, 1865–1877* (1965) is the best introduction to the field. The different approaches to Reconstruction by Lincoln and the radicals during the war are examined by Herman Belz, *Reconstructing the Union: Theory and Policy during the Civil War* (1969); and Hans Trefousse gives a sympathetic portrait of the radicals in *The Radical Republicans: Lincoln's Vanguard for Racial Justice* (1969). Leonard P. Curry's *Blueprint for Modern America* (1968) describes the sweeping legislative program of the Republicans that transformed the nation's political economy.

Dan T. Carter, *When the War Was Over* (1985), examines conditions in the South at the end of the war and the efforts of the Lincoln-Johnson governments. Eric L. McKitrick's *Andrew Johnson and Reconstruction* (1960) is a critical portrait of Lincoln's successor. LaWanda Cox and John H. Cox also examine Johnson's "critical year" in *Politics, Principle, and Prejudice, 1865–1866* (1963). The radical constitutional amendments are the subject of J. B. James, *The Framing of the Fourteenth Amendment* (1956), and William Gillette, *The Right to Vote: Politics and the Passage of the Fifteenth Amendment* (1965). Gillette presents the interesting thesis that the Fifteenth Amendment was passed for the benefit of northern rather than southern blacks.

Michael Les Benedict's *A Compromise of Principle: Congressional Republicans and Reconstruction, 1863–1869* (1974) is a detailed study of the evolution of Radical Reconstruction. Interesting aspects of the story are explored in Robert C. Morris's *Reading, 'Ritin, and Reconstruction: The Education of Freedmen in the South, 1861–1870* (1982) and in Claude F. Oubre's *Forty Acres and a Mule: The Freedmen's Bureau and Black Land Ownership* (1978).

The experience of the southern states under Reconstruction has been drastically revised in the past twenty years. The best survey of the new scholarship is an anthology edited by Otto Olsen, *The Reconstruction and Redemption of the South* (1979), which contains a chapter on each of six states. A particularly good case study, and one that stresses black initiative, is Joel Williamson, *After Slavery: The Negro in South Carolina during Reconstruction, 1861–1877* (1965). Robert Cruden's *The Negro in Reconstruction* (1969) describes black efforts to exercise power throughout the South. The best and most recent study of the black experience in Reconstruction is Leon Litwack's Pulitzer Prize–winning study, *Been in the Storm So Long* (1979). Mark W. Summers, *Railroads, Reconstruction, and the Gospel of Prosperity* (1984), describes railroad politics in the era and the efforts of northern Republicans to spread their version of progress.

THE DECLARATION OF INDEPENDENCE

When in the Course of human events, it becomes necessary for one people to dissolve the political bands which have connected them with another, and to assume among the Powers of the earth, the separate and equal station to which the Laws of Nature and of Nature's God entitle them, a decent respect to the opinions of mankind requires that they should declare the causes which impel them to the separation.

We hold these truths to be self-evident, that all men are created equal, that they are endowed by their Creator with certain unalienable Rights, that among these are Life, Liberty and the pursuit of Happiness. That to secure these rights, Governments are instituted among Men, deriving their just powers from the consent of the governed, That whenever any Form of Government becomes destructive of these ends, it is the Right of the people to alter or to abolish it, and to institute new Government, laying its foundation on such principles and organizing its powers in such form, as to them shall seem most likely to effect their Safety and Happiness. Prudence, indeed, will dictate that Governments long established should not be changed for light and transient causes; and accordingly all experience hath shown, that mankind are more disposed to suffer, while evils are sufferable, than to right themselves by abolishing the forms to which they are accustomed. But when a long train of abuses and usurpations, pursuing invariably the same Object evinces a design to reduce them under absolute Despotism, it is their right, it is their duty, to throw off such Government, and to provide new Guards for their future security.—Such has been the patient sufferance of these Colonies; and such is now the necessity which constrains them to alter their former Systems of Government. The history of the present King of Great Britain is a history of repeated injuries and usurpations, all having in direct object the establishment of an absolute Tyranny over these States. To prove this, let Facts be summitted to a candid world.

He has refused his Assent to Laws, the most wholesome and necessary for the public good.

He has forbidden his Governors to pass Laws of immediate and pressing importance, unless suspended in their operation till his Assent should be obtained; and when so suspended, he has utterly neglected to attend to them.

He has refused to pass other Laws for the accommodation of large districts of people, unless those people would relinquish the right of Representation in the Legislature, a right inestimable to them and formidable to tyrants only.

He has called together legislative bodies at places unusual, uncomfortable, and distant from the depository of their public Records, for the sole purpose of fatiguing them into compliance with his measures.

He has dissolved Representative Houses repeatedly, for opposing with manly firmness his invasions on the rights of the people.

He has refused for a long time, after such dissolutions, to cause others to be elected; whereby the Legislative Powers, incapable of Annihilation, have returned to the People at large for their exercise; the State remaining in the mean time exposed to all the dangers of invasion from without, and convulsions within.

He has endeavoured to prevent the population of these States; for that purpose obstructing the Laws of Naturalization of Foreigners; refusing to pass others to encourage their migration hither, and raising the conditions of new Appropriations of Lands.

He has obstructed the Administration of Justice, by refusing his Assent to Laws for establishing Judiciary powers.

He has made Judges dependent on his Will alone, for the tenure of their offices, and the amount and payment of their salaries.

He has erected a multitude of New Offices, and sent hither swarms of Officers to harass our People, and eat out their substance.

He has kept among us in times of peace, Standing Armies without the Consent of our legislature.

He has affected to render the Military independent of and superior to the Civil power.

He has combined with others to subject us to a jurisdiction foreign to our constitution, and unacknowledged by our laws; giving his Assent to their acts of pretended Legislation:

For quartering large bodies of armed troops among us:

For protecting them, by a mock Trial, from punishment for any Murders which they should commit on the Inhabitants of these States:

For cutting off our Trade with all parts of the world:

For imposing taxes on us without our Consent:

For depriving us in many cases, of the benefits of Trial by Jury:

For transporting us beyond Seas to be tried for pretended offences:

For abolishing the free System of English Laws in a neighbouring Province, establishing therein an Arbitrary government, and enlarging its Boundaries so as to render it at once an example and fit instrument for introducing the same absolute rule into these Colonies:

For taking away our Charters, abolishing our most valuable Laws, and altering fundamentally the Forms of our Governments:

For suspending our own Legislature, and declaring themselves invested with Power to legislate for us in all cases whatsoever.

He has abdicated Government here, by declaring us out of his Protection and waging War against us.

He has plundered our seas, ravaged our Coasts, burnt our towns, and destroyed the lives of our people.

He is at this time transporting large Armies of foreign Mercenaries to compleat the works of death, desolation and tyranny, already begun with circumstances of Cruelty & perfidy scarcely paralleled in the most barbarous ages, and totally unworthy the Head of a civilized nation.

He has constrained our fellow Citizens taken Captive on the high Seas to bear Arms against their Country, to become the executioners of their friends and Brethren, or to fall themselves by their Hands.

He has excited domestic insurrections amongst us, and has endeavoured to bring on the inhabitants of our frontiers, the merciless Indian Savages, whose known rule of warfare, is an undistinguished destruction of all ages, sexes and conditions.

In every stage of these Oppressions We have Petitioned for Redress in the most humble terms: Our repeated Petitions have been answered only by repeated injury. A Prince, whose character is thus marked by every act which may define a Tyrant, is unfit to be the ruler of a free People.

Nor have We been wanting in attention to our British brethren. We have warned them from time to time of attempts by their legislature to extend an unwarrantable jurisdiction over us. We have reminded them of the circumstances of our emigration and settlement here. We have appealed to their native justice and magnanimity, and we have conjured them by the ties of our common kindred to disavow these usurpations, which, would inevitably interrupt our connections and correspondence. They too have been deaf to the voice of justice and of consanguinity. We must, therefore, acquiesce in the necessity, which denounces our Separation, and hold them, as we hold the rest of mankind, Enemies in War, in Peace Friends.

We, therefore, the Representatives of the United States of America, in General Congress, Assembled, appealing to the Supreme Judge of the world for the rectitude of our intentions, do, in the Name, and by Authority of the good People of these Colonies, solemnly publish and declare, That these United Colonies are, and of Right ought to be Free and Independent States; that they are Absolved from all Allegiance to the British Crown, and that all political connection between them and the State of Great Britain, is and ought to be totally dissolved; and that as Free and Independent States, they have full Power to levy War, conclude Peace, contract Alliances, establish Commerce, and to do all other Acts and Things which Independent States may of right do. And for the support of this Declaration, with a firm reliance on the protection of divine Providence, we mutually pledge to each other our Lives, our Fortunes and our sacred Honor.

THE CONSTITUTION OF THE UNITED STATES,
And What It Means Today

The Preamble. Chief Justice John Marshall pointed out in 1803 that the Preamble begins "We the people," and not "We the states." Thus the federal government derives its authority directly from the people and not from the states.

We the people of the United States, in Order to form a more perfect Union, establish Justice, insure domestic Tranquility, provide for the common defense, promote the general Welfare, and secure the Blessings of Liberty to ourselves and our Posterity, do ordain and establish this CONSTITUTION for the United States of America.

ARTICLE I

Section 1. All legislative powers herein granted shall be vested in a Congress of the United States, which shall consist of a Senate and House of Representatives.

Section 2. The House of Representatives shall be composed of Members chosen every second Year by the People of the several States, and the Electors in each State shall have the Qualifications requisite for Electors of the most numerous Branch of the State Legislature.

No Person shall be a Representative who shall not have attained to the Age of twenty-five Years, and been seven Years a Citizen of the United States, and who shall not, when elected, be an Inhabitant of that State in which he shall be chosen.

Direct taxes. This provision was altered by the Sixteenth Amendment, which allows the federal government to levy an income tax directly on the people.

Apportionment of representation. In 1929 Congress limited the House of Representatives to 435 members, who are allotted among the states on the basis of population. Each ten-year census thus requires a rearrangement of the House of Representatives. "Three fifths of all other persons" referred to slaves, and it was among the several sectional compromises in the Constitution.

Representatives and direct Taxes shall be apportioned among the several States which may be included within this Union, according to their respective Numbers, which shall be determined by adding to the whole Number of Free Persons, including those bound to Service for a Term of Years, and excluding Indians not taxed, three fifths of all other Persons. The actual Enumeration shall be made within three Years after the first Meeting of the Congress of the United States, and within every subsequent Term of ten Years, in such Manner as they shall by Law direct. The number of Representatives shall not exceed one for every thirty Thousand, but each State shall have at Least one Representative; and until such enumeration shall be made, the State of New Hampshire shall be entitled to chuse three, Massachusetts eight, Rhode Island and Providence Plantations one, Connecticut five, New York six, New Jersey four, Pennsylvania eight, Delaware one, Maryland six, Virginia ten, North Carolina five, South Carolina five, and Georgia three.

Selection of senators. By the provisions of the Seventeenth Amendment, senators are chosen by the voters rather than by the state legislatures.

The vice president's "casting vote." John Adams cast the first tie-breaking vote in 1789 on a rule that allowed the president to remove important executive officers without the "advice and consent" of the Senate.

Impeachments. The persons subject to impeachment are "civil officers of the United States," which does not include members of Congress. *Impeachment* means an accusation of misconduct, which must first be voted by the House of Representatives. The misconduct must amount to a charge of "treason, bribery, or other high crimes and misdemeanors" (Article II, Section 4). The Senate tries all impeachments, with members of the House serving as the prosecution. A two-thirds majority is required for conviction. It has never been determined whether a person has to be convicted of a crime or simply of "misbehavior." Judges are appointed for life during good behavior (Article III, Section 1), but they can be removed only by impeachment. In all, three persons, all judges, have been convicted and removed under this article.

When vacancies happen in the Representation from any State, the Executive Authority thereof shall issue Writs of Election to fill such Vacancies.

The House of Representatives shall chuse their Speaker and other Officers; and shall have the sole Power of Impeachment.

Section 3. The Senate of the United States shall be composed of two Senators from each State, chosen by the Legislature thereof, for six Years; and each Senator shall have one Vote.

Immediately after they shall be assembled in Consequence of the first Election, they shall be divided as equally as may be into three Classes. The Seats of the Senators of the first Class shall be vacated at the Expiration of the second Year, of the second Class at the Expiration of the fourth Year, and of the third Class at the Expiration of the sixth Year, so that one-third may be chosen every second Year; and if Vacancies happen by Resignation, or otherwise during the Recess of the Legislature of any State, the Executive thereof may make temporary Appointments until the next Meeting of the Legislature, which shall then fill such Vacancies.

No Person shall be a Senator who shall not have attained to the Age of thirty Years, and been nine Years a Citizen of the United States, and who shall not, when elected, be an Inhabitant of that State in which he shall be chosen.

The Vice President of the United States shall be President of the Senate, but shall have no vote, unless they be equally divided.

The Senate shall choose their Officers, and also a President pro tempore, in the absence of the Vice President, or when he shall exercise the Office of the President of the United States.

The Senate shall have the sole Power to try all Impeachments. When sitting for that purpose, they shall be on Oath or Affirmation. When the President of the United States is tried, the Chief Justice shall preside: And no person shall be convicted without the Concurrence of two thirds of the Members present.

Judgment in Cases of Impeachment shall not extend further than to removal from Office, and disqualification to hold and enjoy any Office of honor, Trust, or Profit under the United States: but the Party convicted shall nevertheless be liable and subject to Indictment, Trial, Judgment, and Punishment, according to Law.

Section 4. The Times, Places and Manner of holding Elections for Senators and Representatives, shall be prescribed in each state by the Legislature thereof; but the Congress may at any time by Law make or alter such Regulations, except as to the Places of Chusing Senators.

The Congress shall assemble at least once in every Year, and such Meeting shall be on the first Monday in December, unless they shall by Law appoint a different Day.

Qualifications of members. Control over seating was one of the early privileges claimed by the English Parliament, and American legislatures have uniformly claimed the same power. Congress has usually used the power to purge itself of undesirable elements. In 1900 the House refused to seat a representative from Utah because he was guilty of polygamy. In 1919 it refused to seat a Wisconsin congressman because he was a Socialist.

Journal of proceedings. The requirement that each house keep a journal and record roll-call votes was intended to ensure that the voters could keep track of the conduct of their representatives and senators.

Immunity. Immunity from arrest while attending sessions and freedom of speech in debate were rights claimed by the English Parliament to protect itself against interference from the crown. In America they have served little purpose other than to protect legislators from libel suits.

Revenue bills. The provision that taxation measures must originate in the House of Representatives was intended to make that house more important. It was part of the large state–small state compromise that based representation in the House by population and in the Senate by states.

The veto. The requirement that the president must sign a bill before it becomes law, and the requirement that each house of Congress must muster a two-thirds vote to override a president's veto, are among the "checks and balances" of the Constitution. The ten-day rule allows a president to give a bill a "pocket veto" simply by withholding his signature until Congress adjourns, if the bill has been sent to him within ten days of the end of the session.

Section 5. Each House shall be the Judge of the Elections, Returns and Qualifications of its own Members, and a Majority of each shall constitute a Quorum to do Business; but a smaller number may adjourn from day to day, and may be authorized to compel the Attendance of absent Members, in such Manner, and under such Penalties, as each House may provide.

Each House may determine the Rules of its Proceedings, punish its Members for disorderly Behaviour, and, with the Concurrence of two thirds, expel a Member.

Each House shall keep a Journal of its Proceedings, and from time to time publish the same, excepting such Parts as may in their Judgment require Secrecy; and the Yeas and Nays of the Members of either House on any question shall, at the Desire of one fifth of those Present, be entered on the Journal.

Neither House, during the Session of Congress, shall, without the Consent of the other, adjourn for more than three days, nor to any other Place than that in which the two Houses shall be sitting.

Section 6. The Senators and Representatives shall receive a Compensation for their Services, to be ascertained by Law, and paid out of the Treasury of the United States. They shall in all Cases, except Treason, Felony, and Breach of the Peace, be privileged from Arrest during their Attendance at the Session of their respective Houses, and in going to and returning from the same; and for any Speech or Debate in either House, they shall not be questioned in any other Place.

No Senator or Representative shall, during the Time for which he was elected, be appointed to any civil Office under the Authority of the United States, which shall have been created, or the Emoluments whereof shall have been increased, during such time; and no Person holding any Office under the United States shall be a Member of either House during his continuance in Office.

Section 7. All Bills for raising Revenue shall originate in the House of Representatives; but the Senate may propose or concur with Amendments as on other Bills.

Every Bill which shall have passed the House of Representatives and the Senate, shall, before it become a Law, be presented to the President of the United States; If he approve he shall sign it, but if not he shall return it, with his Objections, to that House in which it shall have originated, who shall enter the Objections at large on their Journal, and proceed to reconsider it. If after such Reconsideration two thirds of that House shall agree to pass the Bill, it shall be sent, together with the Objections, to the other House, by which it shall likewise be reconsidered, and if approved by two thirds of that House, it shall become a Law. But in all such Cases the Votes of both Houses shall be determined by Yeas and Nays, and the Names of the Persons voting for and against the Bill shall be entered on the Journal of each House respectively. If any Bill shall not be returned by the President within ten Days (Sundays excepted) after it shall have been represented to him, the Same shall be a Law, in like Manner as if he had signed it, unless the Congress by their Adjournment prevent its Return, in which Case it shall not be a Law.

Every Order, Resolution, or Vote to which the Concurrence of the Senate and House of Representatives may be necessary (except on a question of Adjournment) shall be presented to the President of the United States; and before the Same shall take Effect, shall be approved by him, or being disapproved by him, shall be repassed by two thirds of the Senate and House of Representatives, according to the Rules and Limitations prescribed in the Case of a Bill.

Section 8. The Congress shall have Power To lay and collect Taxes, Duties, Imposts and Excises, to pay the Debts and provide for the common Defense and general Welfare of the United States; but all Duties, Imposts and Excises shall be uniform throughout the United States;

To borrow money on the credit of the United States;

To regulate Commerce with foreign Nations, and among the several States, and with the Indian Tribes;

To establish an uniform Rule of Naturalization, and uniform Laws on the subject of Bankruptcies throughout the United States;

To coin Money, regulate the Value thereof, and of foreign Coin, and fix the Standard of Weights and Measures;

To provide for the Punishment of counterfeiting the Securities and current Coin of the United States;

To establish Post Offices and post Roads;

To promote the Progress of Science and useful Arts, by securing for limited Times to Authors and Inventors the exclusive Right to their respective Writings and Discoveries;

To constitute Tribunals inferior to the Supreme Court;

To define and punish Piracies and Felonies committed on the high Seas, and Offenses against the Law of Nations;

To declare War, grant Letters of Marque and Reprisal, and make Rules concerning Captures on Land and Water;

To raise and support Armies, but no Appropriation of Money to that Use shall be for a longer Term than two Years;

To provide and maintain a Navy;

To make Rules for the Government and Regulation of the land and naval forces;

To provide for calling forth the Militia to execute the Laws of the Union, suppress Insurrections and repel Invasions;

To provide for organizing, arming, and disciplining the Militia, and for governing such Part of them as may be employed in the Service of the United States, reserving to the States respectively, the Appointment of the Officers,

The powers of Congress. The phrase "general welfare" in the first paragraph of Section 8 is a limitation on what Congress can do with tax revenue; it does not add to the powers of Congress. The framers of the Constitution intended the powers of Congress to be specific, not general. However, the courts over the years have found within these specifically enumerated powers various "implied powers." For instance, the power to regulate interstate commerce has been interpreted to include social security, Medicare, labor legislation, and civil rights acts. The power to "raise and support armies" includes the power to build interstate highways to facilitate army movements.

Necessary and proper. The advocates of "implied powers," beginning with Alexander Hamilton, have always pointed to the final clause of Article I, Section 8, as a catchall intended to give Congress broad legislative authority. John Marshall interpreted the clause thus in 1819: "Let the end be legitimate, let it be within the scope of the Constitution, and all means which are appropriate, which are plainly adapted to that end, which are not prohibited, but consist with the letter and spirit of the Constitution, are constitutional."

Importation of persons. This phrase referred to the importing of slaves from Africa. The requirement that Congress could not prohibit the import until 1808 was one of the sectional compromises in the Constitution. Congress did prohibit the import in 1808, although the government did not seriously enforce the law until the 1840s.

Habeas corpus. This has been called "the most important single safeguard of personal liberty known to Anglo-American law." It means that a person who has been arrested is entitled to have a court inquiry into the cause of his or her detention, and if she or he is not detained for good cause, is entitled to be freed.

Limits on the states. No state shall. . . . This list of restrictions on state powers was intended by the framers to rectify some of the problems that had arisen during and after the revolution. The stricture on bills of credit or making anything but gold or silver legal tender was designed to prevent the states from printing paper money and to prevent them from making tobacco, whiskey, or deerskins a medium of exchange. The stricture on laws "impairing the obliga-

and the Authority of training the Militia according to the discipline prescribed by Congress;

To exercise exclusive Legislation in all Cases whatsoever, over such District (not exceeding ten Miles square) as may, by Cession of particular States, and the acceptance of Congress, become the Seat of Government of the United States, and to exercise like Authority over all Places purchased by the Consent of the Legislature of the State in which the Same shall be, for the Erection of Forts, Magazines, Arsenals, dock-Yards, and other needful Buildings;—And

To make all Laws which shall be necessary and proper for carrying into Execution the foregoing Powers, and all other Powers vested by this Constitution in the Government of the United States, or in any Department or Officer thereof.

Section 9. The Migration or Importation of such Persons as any of the States now existing shall think proper to admit, shall not be prohibited by the Congress prior to the Year one thousand eight hundred and eight, but a tax or duty may be imposed on such Importation, not exceeding ten dollars for each Person.

The privilege of the Writ of Habeas Corpus shall not be suspended, unless when in Cases of Rebellion or Invasion the public Safety may require it.

No Bill of Attainder or ex post facto Law shall be passed.

No Capitation, or other direct, Tax shall be laid unless in Proportion to the Census or Enumeration herein before directed to be taken.

No Tax or Duty shall be laid on Articles exported from any State.

No Preference shall be given by any Regulation of Revenue to the Ports of one State over those of another: nor shall Vessels bound to, or from, one State, be obliged to enter, clear, or pay Duties in another.

No Money shall be drawn from the Treasury, but in Consequence of Appropriations made by Law; and a regular Statement and Account of the Receipts and Expenditures of all public Money shall be published from time to time.

No title of Nobility shall be granted by the United States: And no Person holding any Office of Profit or Trust under them, shall, without the Consent of the Congress, accept of any present, Emolument, Office, or Title, of any kind whatever, from any King, Prince, or foreign State.

Section 10. No State shall enter into any Treaty Alliance, or Confederation; grant Letters of Marque and Reprisal; coin Money; emit Bills of Credit; make any Thing but gold and silver Coin a Tender in Payment of Debts; pass any Bill of Attainder, ex post facto Law, or Law impairing the Obligation of Contracts, or grant any Title of Nobility.

No State shall, without the Consent of the Congress, lay any Imposts or Duties on Imports or Exports, except what may be absolutely necessary for exercising its inspections of contracts" was intended to prevent the states from enacting debtor-relief laws. In 1933, however, the Supreme Court held that a state could, in time of depression, enable debtors to postpone meeting their obligations for a "reasonable" period of time.

The electoral college. This cumbersome method of selecting an executive is unique to the American system of government. The only model of it available at the time the Constitution was drafted was in Maryland, where the upper house was indirectly elected. The original purpose of the electoral college was to ensure qualified leadership (since electors experienced in government were assumed to be better judges of a candidate's qualifications than the voters) and to insulate the executive from popular pressures.

The arrangement that the person with the most electoral votes would be president and the one who came in second would be vice president was altered by the Twelfth Amendment (1804), which established the procedure of nomination by ticket.

The Constitution originally made no provision regarding the reelection of a president. George Washington established a tradition of serving no more than two terms. After Franklin Roosevelt violated the tradition by running for office four times, Congress passed the Twenty-second Amendment, which limits a president to two terms.

tion Laws: and the net Produce of all Duties and Imposts, laid by any State on Imports or Exports, shall be for the Use of the Treasury of the United States; and all such Laws shall be subject to the Revision and Control of the Congress.

No State shall, without the Consent of Congress, lay any duty of Tonnage, keep Troops, or Ships of War in time of Peace, enter into any Agreement or Compact with another State, or with a foreign Power, or engage in War, unless actually invaded, or in such imminent Danger as will not admit of delay.

ARTICLE II

Section 1. The executive Power shall be vested in a President of the United States of America. He shall hold his Office during the Term of four Years, and, together with the Vice President, chosen for the same term, be elected, as follows:

Each State shall appoint, in such Manner as the Legislature thereof may direct, a Number of Electors, equal to the whole Number of Senators and Representatives to which the State may be entitled in the Congress: but no Senator or Representative, or Person holding an Office of Trust or Profit under the United States, shall be appointed an Elector.

The Electors shall meet in their respective States, and vote by Ballot for two Persons, of whom one at least shall not be an Inhabitant of the same State with themselves. And they shall make a list of all the Persons voted for, and of the Number of Votes for each; which List they shall sign and certify, and transmit sealed to the Seat of the Government of the United States, directed to the President of the Senate. The President of the Senate shall, in the Presence of the Senate and House of Representatives, open all the Certificates, and the Votes shall then be counted. The Person having the greatest Number of Votes shall be the President, if such Number be a Majority of the whole Number of Electors appointed; and if there be more than one who have such Majority, and have an equal Number of Votes, then the House of Representatives shall immediately chuse by Ballot one of them for President; and if no Person have a Majority, then from the five highest on the List the said House shall in like Manner chuse the President. But in chusing the President, the Votes shall be taken by States, the Representation from each State having one Vote; a quorum for this Purpose shall consist of a Member or Members from two-thirds of the States, and a Majority of all the States shall be necessary to a Choice. In every Case, after the Choice of the President, the Person having the greatest Number of Votes of the Electors shall be the Vice President. But if there should remain two or more who have equal votes, the Senate shall chuse from them by Ballot the Vice President.

The Congress may determine the Time of chusing

Removal, death, resignation of the president. The first vice president to succeed to the presidency was John Tyler (1841), who established the precedent, since followed, that he was president in fact, rather than merely an "acting president."

Gerald Ford was the only president who was never elected to the office, having been appointed by Richard Nixon as vice president (after Spiro Agnew resigned under criminal indictment) and having succeeded to the presidency on Nixon's resignation.

Congress has established the presidential succession in the event of the death or resignation of both president and vice president as follows: Speaker of the House, president pro-tem of the Senate, and then the members of the cabinet, beginning with the secretary of state.

The powers of the president. The powers given to the executive are fewer than those granted to Congress, but they are less specific. The president is made commander-in-chief of the armed forces, thereby ensuring civilian control of the military. He conducts foreign relations, appoints officials (both with the advice and consent of the Senate), executes the laws, and that's it.

Executive power was much feared at the time the Constitution was drafted, and the framers had no desire to make enemies for their document by endowing the president with visible authority to affect the lives of citizens. Yet in the Constitution's vagueness alone lies enough expandable power to create what has been called the "imperial presidency." The rubbery injunction to "take care that the laws be faithfully executed" alone includes the power to spend money, create bureaus, appoint task forces, mediate labor disputes, set aside forest reserves, ban pesticides, and eavesdrop on suspected subversives.

the Electors, and the Day on which they shall give their Votes; which Day shall be the same throughout the United States.

No person except a natural-born citizen, or a Citizen of the United States, at the time of the adoption of this Constitution, shall be eligible to the Office of President; neither shall any Person be eligible to that Office who shall not have attained to the Age of thirty-five Years, and been fourteen Years a Resident within the United States.

In case of the Removal of the President from Office, or of his Death, Resignation, or Inability to discharge the Powers and Duties of the said Office, the same shall devolve on the Vice President, and the Congress may by Law provide for the Case of Removal, Death, Resignation, or Inability, both of the President and Vice President, declaring what Officer shall then act as President, and such Officer shall act accordingly, until the Disability be removed, or a President shall be elected.

The President shall, at stated Times, receive for his Services a Compensation, which shall neither be increased nor diminished during the Period for which he shall have been elected, and he shall not receive within that Period any other Emolument from the United States, or any of them.

Before he enters on the Execution of his Office, he shall take the following Oath or Affirmation:—"I do solemnly swear (or affirm) that I will faithfully execute the Office of President of the United States, and will, to the best of my Ability, preserve, protect, and defend the Constitution of the United States."

Section 2. The President shall be Commander in Chief of the Army and Navy of the United States, and of the Militia of the several States, when called into the actual Service of the United States; he may require the Opinion, in writing, of the principal Officer in each of the executive Departments, upon any subject relating to the Duties of their respective Offices, and he shall have Power to Grant Reprieves and Pardons for Offenses against the United States, except in Cases of Impeachment.

He shall have Power, by and with the Advice and Consent of the Senate, to make Treaties, provided two thirds of the Senators present concur; and he shall nominate, and by and with the Advice and Consent of the Senate, shall appoint Ambassadors, other public Ministers and Consuls, Judges of the supreme Court, and all other Officers of the United States, whose Appointments are not herein otherwise provided for, and which shall be established by Law: but the Congress may by Law vest the Appointment of such inferior Officers, as they think proper, in the President alone, in the Courts of Law, or in the Heads of Departments.

The President shall have Power to fill up all Vacancies that may happen during the Recess of the Senate, by granting Commissions which shall expire at the end of their next Session.

Section 3. He shall from time to time give to the Congress Information of the State of the Union, and recommend to their Consideration such Measures as he shall judge necessary and expedient; he may, on extraordinary occasions, convene both Houses, or either of them, and in Case of Disagreement between them, with respect to the Time of Adjournment, he may adjourn them to such Time as he shall think proper; he shall receive Ambassadors and other public Ministers; he shall take Care that the Laws be faithfully executed, and shall Commission all the Officers of the United States.

Section 4. The President, Vice President and all civil Officers of the United States, shall be removed from Office on Impeachment for, and Conviction of, Treason, Bribery, or other high Crimes and Misdemeanors.

ARTICLE III

Section 1. The judicial Power of the United States, shall be vested in one supreme Court, and in such inferior Courts as the Congress may from time to time ordain and establish. The Judges, both of the supreme and inferior Courts shall hold their Offices during good Behaviour, and shall, at stated Times, receive for their Services, a Compensation, which shall not be diminished during their Continuance in Office.

Section 2. The judicial Power shall extend to all Cases, in Law and Equity, arising under this Constitution, the Laws of the United States, and Treaties made, or which shall be made, under their Authority;—to all Cases affecting Ambassadors, other public Ministers and Consuls;—to all Cases of admiralty and maritime Jurisdiction;—to Controversies to which the United States shall be a Party;—to Controversies between two or more States;—between a State and Citizens of another State;—between Citizens of the same State claiming Lands under Grants of different States, and between a State, or the Citizens thereof, and foreign States, Citizens or Subjects.

In all Cases affecting Ambassadors, other public Ministers and Consuls, and those in which a State shall be Party, the supreme Court shall have original Jurisdiction. In all the other Cases before mentioned, the supreme Court shall have appellate Jurisdiction, both as to Law and Fact, with such Exceptions, and under such Regulations as the Congress shall make.

The trial of all Crimes, except in Cases of Impeachment, shall be by Jury; and such Trial shall be held in the State where the said Crimes shall have been committed; but when not committed within any State, the Trial shall be at such Place or Places as the Congress may by Law have directed.

Section 3. Treason against the United States, shall consist only in levying War against them, or in adhering to their Enemies, giving them Aid and Comfort. No Person

The judicial power. Courts, judges, and lawyers were as suspect in the United States of the 1780s as kings and ministers. The poor looked upon law courts as agents of the rich, using the power of the state to collect debts and enforce contracts. Article III, which establishes the third branch of government—"the judicial power of the United States"—is therefore deliberately vague. The framers had no desire to stir up a hornet's nest of controversy by outlining a hierarchy of courts staffed by learned judges. Article III specifies only a Supreme Court, and it leaves to Congress the thorny questions concerning the number of "inferior courts" and the extent of their powers.

Congress in 1789 did establish a hierarchy of circuit and district courts—which, expanded in number, remain today—but it cautiously confined their jurisdiction to the "Constitution, laws, and treaties of the United States." Ordinary civil and criminal jurisdiction is left to the state courts. A federal court can take jurisdiction only when a suit involves a federal issue, such as the interpretation of an act of Congress, or when the parties to the suit reside in different states ("diversity of citizenship"). Even then, the Supreme Court declared in 1938 in the case of *Erie Railroad* v. *Tompkins*, federal courts are obliged to apply the law of the forum state. There is no federal common law.

shall be convicted of Treason unless on the Testimony of two Witnesses to the same overt Act, or on Confession in open Court.

The Congress shall have power to declare the Punishment of Treason, but no Attainder of Treason shall work Corruption of Blood, or Forfeiture except during the Life of the Person attainted.

ARTICLE IV

Section 1. Full Faith and Credit shall be given in each State to the public Acts, Records, and judicial Proceedings of every other State. And the Congress may by general Laws prescribe the Manner in which such Acts, Records and Proceedings shall be proved, and the Effect thereof.

Section 2. The Citizens of each State shall be entitled to all Privileges and Immunities of Citizens in the several States.

A Person charged in any State with Treason, Felony, or other Crime, who shall flee from Justice, and be found in another State, shall on demand of the executive Authority of the State from which he fled, be delivered up, to be removed to the State having Jurisdiction of the crime.

No Person held to Service or Labour in one State, under the Laws thereof, escaping into another, shall, in Consequence of any Law or Regulation therein, be discharged from such Service or Labour, but shall be delivered up on Claim of the Party to whom such Service or Labour may be due.

Section 3. New States may be admitted by the Congress into this Union; but no new State shall be formed or erected within the Jurisdiction of any other State; nor any State be formed by the Junction of two or more States, or parts of States, without the Consent of the Legislatures of the States concerned as well as of the Congress.

The Congress shall have Power to dispose of and make all needful Rules and Regulations respecting the Territory or other Property belonging to the United States; and nothing in this Constitution shall be so construed as to Prejudice any Claims of the United States, or of any particular State.

Section 4. The United States shall guarantee to every State in this Union a Republican Form of Government, and shall protect each of them against Invasion; and on Application of the Legislature, or of the Executive (when the Legislature cannot be convened) against domestic Violence.

ARTICLE V

The Congress, whenever two thirds of both Houses shall deem it necessary, shall propose Amendments to this Constitution, or, on the Application of the Legislatures of

Full faith and credit. The intent of this provision is to ensure cooperation and mutual respect among the states. In the twentieth century it has been commonly invoked by people who travel to another state, such as Nevada or Florida, in order to obtain a quick divorce.

New states. The framers of the Constitution contemplated the indefinite expansion of the American union. The organism they created was both a republic and an empire, but it was a unique empire in that the colonies (territories) were expected, upon maturity, to join the Union on a par with the original thirteen states.

Amendments. The framers of the Constitution, with commendable foresight and humility, anticipated that posterity might want to make some changes in their handiwork. But they deliberately made the amendment procedure cumbersome, so that the Constitution would not be subject to popular whim. Amendments must be approved by a two-thirds vote in each house of Congress, and then they have to be ratified by legislatures or conventions in three fourths of the states. The only amendment ratified by specially summoned conventions was the Twenty-first, which repealed prohibition. The first ten amendments (the Bill of Rights) were drafted and approved only four years after the Constitution was written. Since then, only sixteen have been added.

two thirds of the several States, shall call a Convention for proposing Amendments, which, in either Case, shall be valid to all Intents and Purposes, as part of this Constitution, when ratified by the Legislatures of three fourths of the several States, or by Conventions in three fourths thereof, as the one or the other Mode of Ratification may be proposed by the Congress; Provided that no Amendment which may be made prior to the Year One thousand eight hundred and eight shall in any Manner affect the first and fourth Clauses in the Ninth Section of the first Article; and that no State, without its Consent, shall be deprived of its equal Suffrage in the Senate.

ARTICLE VI

All Debts contracted and Engagements entered into, before the Adoption of this Constitution, shall be as valid against the United States under this Constitution, as under the Confederation.

This Constitution, and the Laws of the United States which shall be made in Pursuance thereof: and all Treaties made, or which shall be made, under the Authority of the United States, shall be the supreme Law of the Land; and the Judges in every State shall be bound thereby, any Thing in the Constitution or laws of any State to the Contrary notwithstanding.

The Senators and Representatives before mentioned, and the Members of the several State Legislatures, and all executive and judicial Officers, both of the United States and of the several States, shall be bound by Oath or Affirmation to support this Constitution; but no religious Test shall ever be required as a qualification to any Office or public Trust under the United States.

Ratification. Mindful of the difficulties that had attended efforts to alter the Articles of Confederation in the 1780s, the framers of the Constitution provided that the document would go into effect when only nine of the thirteen states gave their approval. They also bypassed potentially jealous and divided state legislatures by providing that the Constitution was to be approved by specially elected conventions.

ARTICLE VII

The Ratification of the Conventions of nine States shall be sufficient for the Establishment of this Constitution between the States so ratifying the same.

Done in Convention by the Unanimous Consent of the States present the Seventeenth Day of September in the Year of our Lord one thousand seven hundred and Eighty seven and of the Independence of the United States of America the Twelfth. In Witness whereof We have hereunto subscribed our Names.

Articles in Addition to, and Amendment of, the Constitution of the United States of America, Proposed by Congress, and Ratified by the Legislatures of the Several States, Pursuant to the Fifth Article of the Original Constitution.

The Bill of Rights. The first ten amendments were intended as restraints on the power of the federal government. Since 1931, the Supreme Court has progressively applied them to the states under the theory that they are embodied in the "due process" clause of the Fourteenth Amendment.

The First Amendment, which protects the freedom of speech, press, and belief, is clearly the most important. In recognition of this, the Supreme Court places the burden of proof on the government where freedom of speech is in question; that is, the government must demonstrate, when a citizen complains, that its action does *not* inhibit freedom of speech, press, or religion.

The Second and Third amendments are the product of English tradition and American colonial experience. The Fourth through the Eighth amendments are judicial safeguards intended to ensure fair court procedure. The Ninth Amendment is a catchall intended to overcome the misgivings, expressed by James Madison among others, that a listing of human rights would be restrictive—that is, imply that these are the *only* rights people have. The Ninth Amendment has been invoked by the Supreme Court most recently in a decision that overturned a state law restricting the use of contraceptives.

The Tenth Amendment, though drafted and approved with the rest of the Bill of Rights, addresses itself to power, not rights. It is a reminder that the government established by the Constitution is one of specifically delegated powers, and that all other powers reside in the states. This residual power is usually described as the "police power": the power to legislate for the health, safety, welfare, and morals of the people. The Tenth Amendment was long relied on by the advocates of states' rights, but in 1941 the Supreme Court declared the amendment a mere truism that expressed the distribution of power between the federal government and the states without, of itself, restricting the authority of either.

The Eleventh Amendment was the product of a fleeting political controversy involving the efforts of Loyalists to recover property that states had confiscated during the revolution.

The Twelfth Amendment resulted from the tie in the electoral college between Thomas Jefferson and Aaron Burr in 1800. By requiring a "distinct list" of persons running as president and another for those running as vice president, the amendment, to be workable, requires a nominating procedure. It is therefore an indirect recognition of the function of political parties.

AMENDMENT I [1791]

Congress shall make no law respecting an establishment of religion, or prohibiting the free exercise thereof; or abridging the freedom of speech, or of the press; or the right of the people peaceably to assemble, and to petition the Government for a redress of grievances.

AMENDMENT II [1791]

A well regulated Militia, being necessary to the security of a free State, the right of the people to keep and bear Arms, shall not be infringed.

AMENDMENT III [1791]

No Soldier shall, in time of peace, be quartered in any house, without the consent of the Owner, nor in time of war, but in a manner to be prescribed by law.

AMENDMENT IV [1791]

The right of the people to be secure in their persons, houses, papers, and effects, against unreasonable searches and seizures, shall not be violated, and no Warrants shall issue, but upon probable cause, supported by Oath or affirmation, and particularly describing the place to be searched, and the persons or things to be seized.

AMENDMENT V [1791]

No person shall be held to answer for a capital or otherwise infamous crime, unless on a presentment or indictment of a Grand Jury, except in cases arising in the land or naval forces, or in the Militia, when in actual service in time of War or public danger; nor shall any person be subject for the same offence to be twice put in jeopardy of life or limb; nor shall be compelled in any criminal case to be a witness against himself, nor be deprived of life, liberty, or property, without due process of law; nor shall private property be taken for public use, without just compensation.

AMENDMENT VI [1791]

In all criminal prosecutions, the accused shall enjoy the right to a speedy and public trial, by an impartial jury of the State and district wherein the crime shall have been committed, which district shall have been previously ascertained by law, and to be informed of the nature and cause of the accusation, to be confronted with the witnesses against him; to have compulsory process for obtaining witnesses in his favor, and to have the Assistance of Counsel for his defence.

AMENDMENT VII [1791]

In Suits at common law, where the value in controversy shall exceed twenty dollars, the right of trial by jury shall be preserved, and no fact tried by a jury, shall be otherwise re-examined in any Court of the United States, than according to the rules of the common law.

AMENDMENT VIII [1791]

Excessive bail shall not be required, nor excessive fines imposed, nor cruel and unusual punishments inflicted.

AMENDMENT IX [1791]

The enumeration in the Constitution, of certain rights, shall not be construed to deny or disparage others retained by the people.

AMENDMENT X [1791]

The powers not delegated to the United States by the Constitution, nor prohibited by it to the States, are reserved to the States respectively, or to the people.

AMENDMENT XI [1798]

The Judicial power of the United States shall not be construed to extend to any suit in law or equity, commenced or prosecuted against one of the United States by Citizens of another State, or by citizens or Subjects of any Foreign State.

AMENDMENT XII [1804]

The Electors shall meet in their respective States and vote by ballot for President and Vice President, one of whom, at least, shall not be an inhabitant of the same State with themselves; they shall name in their ballots the person voted for as President, and in distinct ballots the person voted for as Vice-President, and they shall make distinct lists of all persons voted for as President, and of all persons voted for as Vice-President, and of the number of votes for each, which lists they shall sign and certify, and transmit sealed to the seat of the government of the United States, directed to the President of the Senate;—The President of the Senate shall, in the presence of the Senate and House of Representatives, open all the certificates and the votes shall then be counted;—The person having the greatest number of votes for President, shall be the President, if such number be a majority of the whole number of Electors appointed; and if no person have such majority, then from the persons having the highest numbers not exceeding three on the list of those voted for as President, the House of Representatives shall choose immediately, by ballot, the President. But in choosing the President, the votes shall be taken by states, the representation from each state having one vote; a quorum for this purpose shall consist of a member or members from two-thirds of the states, and a majority of all the states shall be necessary to a choice. And if the House of Representatives shall not choose a President whenever the right of choice shall devolve upon them, before the fourth day of March next following, then the Vice-President shall act as President, as in the case of the death or other constitutional disability of the President.—The person having the greatest number of votes as Vice-President, shall be the Vice-President, if such number be a majority of the whole number of Electors appointed, and if no person have a majority, then from the two highest numbers on the list, the Senate shall choose the Vice-President; a quorum for the purpose shall consist of two-thirds of the whole number of Senators, and a majority of the whole number shall be necessary to a choice. But no person constitutionally ineligible to the office of the President shall be eligible to that of Vice-President of the United States.

The war amendments. Adopted after the Civil War, the Thirteenth Amendment freed the slaves, the Fourteenth sought to protect their civil rights, and the Fifteenth prevented the states from denying the right to vote on the basis of race.

AMENDMENT XIII [1865]

Section 1. Neither slavery nor involuntary servitude, except as a punishment for crime wherof the party shall have been duly convicted, shall exist within the United States, or any place subject to their jurisdiction.

Section 2. Congress shall have the power to enforce this article by appropriate legislation.

AMENDMENT XIV [1868]

Due process. The Fourteenth Amendment has, through the years, been the most controversial of the war amendments. The phrase "due process" has been held to include the whole panoply of rights outlined in the first ten amendments. The phrase "equal protection of the laws" has been held to exclude racially segregated facilities and to require periodic reapportionment of state legislatures to ensure that all ballots are of equal weight.

Section 1. All persons born or naturalized in the United States, and subject to the jurisdiction thereof, are citizens of the United States and of the State wherein they reside. No state shall make or enforce any law which shall abridge the privileges or immunities of citizens of the United States; nor shall any State deprive any person of life, liberty, or property, without due process of law; nor deny to any person within its jurisdiction the equal protection of the laws.

Section 2. Representatives shall be apportioned among the several States according to their respective numbers, counting the whole number of persons in each State, excluding Indians not taxed. But when the right to vote at any election for the choice of electors for President and Vice President of the United States, Representatives in Congress, the Executive and Judicial officers of a State, or the members of the Legislature thereof, is denied to any of the male inhabitants of such State, being twenty-one years of age, and citizens of the United States, or in any way abridged, except for participation in rebellion, or other crime, the basis of representation therein shall be reduced in the proportion which the number of such male citizens shall bear to the whole number of male citizens twenty-one years of age in such State.

Section 3. No person shall be a Senator or Representative in Congress, or elector of President and Vice President, or hold any office, civil or military, under the United States, or under any State, who, having previously taken an oath, as a member of Congress, or as an officer of the United States, or as a member of any State legislature, or as an executive or judicial officer of any State, to support the Constitution of the United States, shall have engaged in insurrection or rebellion against the same, or given aid or comfort to the enemies thereof. But Congress may by a vote of two-thirds of each House, remove such disability.

Section 4. The validity of the public debt of the United States, authorized by law, including debts incurred for payment of pensions and bounties for services in suppressing insurrection or rebellion, shall not be questioned. But neither the United States nor any State shall assume or pay any debt or obligation incurred in aid of insurrection or rebellion against the United States, or any claim for the loss or emancipation of any slave; but all such debts, obligations, and claims shall be held illegal and void.

Section 5. The Congress shall have the power to enforce, by appropriate legislation, the provisions of this article.

AMENDMENT XV [1870]

Section 1. The right of citizens of the United States to vote shall not be denied or abridged by the United States or by any State on account of race, color, or previous condition of servitude—

Section 2. The Congress shall have the power to enforce this article by appropriate legislation.

AMENDMENT XVI [1913]

The Congress shall have power to lay and collect taxes on incomes, from whatever source derived, without apportionment among the several States, and without regard to any census or enumeration.

Civil rights. Section 5 of the Fourteenth Amendment was clearly intended to give Congress power to pass laws for the protection of civil rights. This Congress attempted to do in 1875 by passing a law forbidding inns, railroads, and theaters from discriminating among persons on the grounds of race. In 1883 the Supreme Court struck down the law on the grounds that the Fourteenth Amendment prohibited only official discrimination, not the private acts of individuals. As a result, modern civil rights legislation, notably the Equal Opportunity Act of 1964, rests on Congress's power to regulate interstate commerce, rather than on the Fourteenth Amendment.

The Fifteenth Amendment. For nearly a century after it was drafted, the Fifteenth Amendment was evaded by various devices that hindered blacks from registering and voting. The Voting Rights Act of 1965 is the most recent attempt to enforce the amendment by providing federal supervision of voter registration in localities with a history of discrimination.

The Progressive amendments. The Sixteenth through Nineteenth amendments were the product of the Progressive movement. The Sixteenth was necessitated by a Supreme Court decision in the 1890s that a federal income tax violated the constitutional requirement that direct taxes (as opposed to excises) had to be apportioned among the states, which in turn would collect from the people. The Seventeenth Amendment was intended to democratize the "millionaires' club," the U.S. Senate, by requiring that its members be elected directly by the people. The Eighteenth Amendment authorized prohibition, and the Nineteenth women's suffrage.

The lame duck amendment. The Twentieth Amendment did away with an anomaly created by Article I of the Constitution, the requirement that elections would be held in November but inaugurations delayed until March. This resulted in a "lame duck" session of Congress, lasting from December until March in even-numbered years, when members, many of whom had failed to be

AMENDMENT XVII [1916]

The Senate of the United States shall be composed of two Senators from each State, elected by the people thereof, for six years; and each Senator shall have one vote. The electors in each State shall have the qualifications requisite for electors of the most numerous branch of the State legislatures.

When vacancies happen in the representation of any State in the Senate, the executive authority of such State shall issue writs of election to fill such vacancies: *Provided*, That the legislature of any State may empower the executive thereof to make temporary appointments until the people fill the vacancies by election as the legislature may direct.

This amendment shall not be so construed as to affect the election or term of any Senator chosen before it becomes valid as part of the Constitution.

AMENDMENT XVIII [1919]

Section 1. After one year from the ratification of this article the manufacture, sale, or transportation of intoxicating liquors within, the importation thereof into, or the exportation thereof from the United States and all territory subject to the jurisdiction thereof for beverage purposes is hereby prohibited.

Section 2. The Congress and the several States shall have concurrent power to enforce this article by appropriate legislation.

Section 3. This article shall be inoperative unless it shall have been ratified as an amendment to the Constitution by the legislatures of the several States, as provided in the Constitution, within seven years from the date of the submission hereof to the States by the Congress.

AMENDMENT XIX [1920]

The right of citizens of the United States to vote shall not be denied or abridged by the United States or by any State on account of sex.

Congress shall have power to enforce this article by appropriate legislation.

AMENDMENT XX [1933]

Section 1. The terms of the President and Vice President shall end at noon on the 20th day of January, and the terms of Senators and Representatives at noon on the 3rd day of January, of the years in which such terms would have ended if this article had not been ratified; and the terms of their successors shall then begin.

reelected and were on their way to private life, were voting on matters of national importance. By moving inauguration day back from March 4 to January 20, the amendment shortens the interval between popular selection and the exercise of presidential and legislative power.

Section 2. The Congress shall assemble at least once in every year, and such meeting shall begin at noon on the 3d day of January, unless they shall by law appoint a different day.

Section 3. If, at the time fixed for the beginning of the term of the President, the President elect shall have died, the Vice President elect shall become President. If a President shall not have been chosen before the time fixed for the beginning of his term, or if the President elect shall have failed to qualify, then the Vice President elect shall act as President until a President shall have qualified; and the Congress may by law provide for the case wherein neither a President elect nor a Vice President elect shall have qualified, declaring who shall then act as President, or the manner in which one who is to act shall be selected, and such person shall act accordingly until a President or Vice President shall have qualified.

Section 4. The Congress may by law provide for the case of the death of any of the persons from whom the House of Representatives may choose a President whenever the right of choice shall have devolved upon them, and for the case of the death of any of the persons from whom the Senate may choose a Vice President whenever the right of choice shall have devolved upon them.

Section 5. Sections 1 and 2 shall take effect on the 15th day of October following the ratification of this article.

Section 6. The article shall be inoperative unless it shall have been ratified as an amendment to the Constitution by the legislatures of three-fourths of the several States within seven years from the date of its submission.

The Twenty-first Amendment. The Twenty-first Amendment repealed the Eighteenth, and thereby repealed prohibition. It is the only amendment that provides for its ratification by specially selected conventions, and it is the only one that has been approved in this way.

AMENDMENT XXI [1933]

Section 1. The eighteenth article of amendment to the Constitution of the United States is hereby repealed.

Section 2. The transportation or importation into any State, Territory, or possession of the United States for delivery or use therein of intoxicating liquors, in violation of the laws thereof, is hereby prohibited.

Section 3. This article shall be inoperative unless it shall have been ratified as an amendment to the Constitution by conventions in the several States, as provided in the Constitution, within seven years from the date of the submission hereof to the States by the Congress.

The Twenty-second Amendment. The Twenty-second Amendment, a belated slap at Roosevelt by a Republican-dominated Congress, limits the president to two terms in office. Ironically, the first president to which it applied was a Republican, Dwight D. Eisenhower.

AMENDMENT XXII [1951]

No person shall be elected to the office of the President more than twice, and no person who has held the office of President, or acted as President, for more than two years of a term to which some other person was elected President shall be elected to the office of the President more than once.

But this Article shall not apply to any person holding the office of President when this Article was proposed by the Congress, and shall not prevent any person who may be holding the office of President, or acting as President, during the term within which this Article becomes operative from holding the office of President or acting as President during the remainder of such term.

AMENDMENT XXIII [1961]

Section 1. The District constituting the seat of Government of the United States shall appoint in such manner as the Congress may direct:

A number of electors of President and Vice President equal to the whole number of Senators and Representatives in Congress to which the District would be entitled if it were a State, but in no event more than the least populous State; they shall be in addition to those appointed by the States, but they shall be considered, for the purposes of the election of President and Vice President, to be electors appointed by a State; and they shall meet in the District and perform such duties as provided by the twelfth article of amendment.

Section 2. The Congress shall have the power to enforce this article by appropriate legislation.

AMENDMENT XXIV [1964]

Section 1. The right of citizens of the United States to vote in any primary or other election for President or Vice President, for electors for President or Vice President, or for Senator or Representative in Congress, shall not be denied or abridged by the United States or any State by reason of failure to pay any poll tax or other tax.

Section 2. The Congress shall have the power to enforce this article by appropriate legislation.

AMENDMENT XXV [1967]

Section 1. In case of the removal of the President from office or his death or resignation, the Vice President shall become President.

Section 2. Whenever there is a vacancy in the office of the Vice President, the President shall nominate a Vice President who shall take the office upon confirmation by a majority vote of both houses of Congress.

Section 3. Whenever the President transmits to the President pro tempore of the Senate and the Speaker of the House of Representatives his written declaration that he is unable to discharge the powers and duties of his office, and until he transmits to them a written declaration to the

The Twenty-third Amendment. The Twenty-third Amendment allows residents of the District of Columbia to vote in presidential elections.

The poll tax amendment. The Twenty-fourth Amendment prevents the states from making payment of a poll tax a condition for voting. Common at the time among southern states, the poll tax was a capitation (poll, or head) tax on individuals. A poll tax receipt was often required in order to vote. It was designed to prevent uneducated people, especially blacks, who were unaccustomed to saving receipts, from voting.

The Twenty-fifth Amendment. The Twenty-fifth Amendment, inspired by President Eisenhower's heart attack and President Johnson's abdominal surgery, provides for the temporary replacement of a president who is unable to discharge the duties of the office.

contrary, such powers and duties shall be discharged by the Vice President as Acting President.

Section 4.   Whenever the Vice President and a majority of either the principal officers of the executive departments, or of such other body as Congress may by law provide, transmit to the President pro tempore of the Senate and the Speaker of the House of Representatives their written declaration that the President is unable to discharge the powers and duties of his office, the Vice President shall immediately assume the powers and duties of the office as Acting President.

Thereafter, when the President transmits to the President pro tempore of the Senate and the Speaker of the House of Representatives his written declaration that no inability exists, he shall resume the powers and duties of his office unless the Vice President and a majority of either the principal officers of the executive departments, or of such other body as Congress may by law provide, transmit within four days to the President pro tempore of the Senate and the speaker of the House of Representatives their written declaration that the President is unable to discharge the powers and duties of his office. Thereupon Congress shall decide the issue, assembling within 48 hours for that purpose if not in session. If the Congress, within 21 days after receipt of the latter written declaration, or, if Congress is not in session, within 21 days after Congress is required to assemble, determines by two-thirds vote of both houses that the President is unable to discharge the powers and duties of his office, the Vice President shall continue to discharge the same as Acting President; otherwise, the President shall resume the powers and duties of his office.

The Twenty-sixth Amendment. The Twenty-sixth Amendment corrected the anomaly that young men could be drafted and sent to war at the age of eighteen, but not allowed to participate in the nation's democratic processes until they were twenty-one. It extended the vote to eighteen-year-olds.

AMENDMENT XXVI [1971]

Section 1.   The rights of citizens of the United States, who are 18 years of age or older, to vote shall not be denied or abridged by the United States or any state on account of age.

Section 2.   The Congress shall have the power to enforce this article by appropriate legislation.

PRESIDENTIAL ELECTIONS

YEAR	CANDIDATES	PARTY	POPULAR VOTE	ELECTORAL VOTE
1789	**George Washington**			69
	John Adams			34
	Others			35
1792	**George Washington**			132
	John Adams			77
	George Clinton			50
	Others			5
1796	**John Adams**	Federalist		71
	Thomas Jefferson	Republican		68
	Thomas Pinckney	Federalist		59
	Aaron Burr	Republican		30
	Others			48
1800	**Thomas Jefferson**	Republican		73
	Aaron Burr	Republican		73
	John Adams	Federalist		65
	Charles C. Pinckney	Federalist		64
1804	**Thomas Jefferson**	Republican		162
	Charles C. Pinckney	Federalist		14
1808	**James Madison**	Republican		122
	Charles C. Pinckney	Federalist		47
	George Clinton	Independent-Republican		6
1812	**James Madison**	Republican		128
	DeWitt Clinton	Federalist		89
1816	**James Monroe**	Republican		183
	Rufus King	Federalist		34
1820	**James Monroe**	Democratic-Republican		231
	John Quincy Adams	Independent-Republican		1
1824	**John Quincy Adams**	Republican	108,740	84 (elected by the House of Representatives)
	Andrew Jackson	Republican	153,544	99
	Henry Clay	Republican	47,136	37
	William H. Crawford	Republican	46,618	41
1828	**Andrew Jackson**	Democratic	647,286	178
	John Quincy Adams	National Republican	508,064	83

YEAR	CANDIDATES	PARTY	POPULAR VOTE	ELECTORAL VOTE
1832	**Andrew Jackson**	Democratic	688,000	219
	Henry Clay	National Republican	530,000	49
	William Wirt	Anti-Masonic	255,000	7
	John Floyd	National Republican		11
1836	**Martin Van Buren**	Democratic	762,678	170
	William H. Harrison	Whig	549,000	73
	Hugh L. White	Whig	146,000	26
	Daniel Webster	Whig	41,000	14
1840	**William H. Harrison**	Whig	1,275,017	234
	Martin Van Buren	Democratic	1,128,702	60
1844	**James K. Polk**	Democratic	1,337,243	170
	Henry Clay	Whig	1,299,068	105
	James G. Birney	Liberty	62,300	
1848	**Zachary Taylor**	Whig	1,360,101	163
	Lewis Cass	Democratic	1,220,544	127
	Martin Van Buren	Free-Soil	291,263	
1852	**Franklin Pierce**	Democratic	1,601,274	254
	Winfield Scott	Whig	1,386,580	42
1856	**James Buchanan**	Democratic	1,838,169	174
	John C. Frémont	Republican	1,335,264	114
	Millard Fillmore	American	874,534	8
1860	**Abraham Lincoln**	Republican	1,866,452	180
	Stephen A. Douglas	Democratic	1,375,157	12
	John C. Breckinridge	Democratic	847,953	72
	John Bell	Constitutional Union	592,631	39
1864	**Abraham Lincoln**	Republican	2,213,665	212
	George B. McClellan	Democratic	1,805,237	21
1868	**Ulysses S. Grant**	Republican	3,012,833	214
	Horatio Seymour	Democratic	2,703,249	80
1872	**Ulysses S. Grant**	Republican	3,596,745	286
	Horace Greeley	Democratic	2,843,446	66
1876	**Rutherford B. Hayes**	Republican	4,036,572	185
	Samuel J. Tilden	Democratic	4,284,020	184
1880	**James A. Garfield**	Republican	4,449,053	214
	Winfield S. Hancock	Democratic	4,442,032	155
	James B. Weaver	Greenback-Labor	308,578	
1884	**Grover Cleveland**	Democratic	4,874,986	219
	James G. Blaine	Republican	4,851,981	182
	Benjamin F. Butler	Greenback-Labor	175,370	
1888	**Benjamin Harrison**	Republican	5,444,337	233
	Grover Cleveland	Democratic	5,540,050	168
1892	**Grover Cleveland**	Democratic	5,554,414	277
	Benjamin Harrison	Republican	5,190,802	145
	James B. Weaver	People's	1,027,329	22

YEAR	CANDIDATES	PARTY	POPULAR VOTE	ELECTORAL VOTE
1896	**William McKinley**	Republican	7,104,779	271
	William J. Bryan	Democratic; Populist	6,502,925	176
1900	**William McKinley**	Republican	7,219,530	292
	William J. Bryan	Democratic; Populist	6,356,734	155
1904	**Theodore Roosevelt**	Republican	7,628,834	336
	Alton B. Parker	Democratic	5,084,401	140
	Eugene V. Debs	Socialist	402,460	
1908	**William H. Taft**	Republican	7,679,006	321
	William J. Bryan	Democratic	6,409,106	162
	Eugene V. Debs	Socialist	420,820	
1912	**Woodrow Wilson**	Democratic	6,293,454	435
	Theodore Roosevelt	Progressive	4,119,538	88
	William H. Taft	Republican	3,484,980	8
	Eugene V. Debs	Socialist	897,011	
1916	**Woodrow Wilson**	Democratic	9,129,606	277
	Charles E. Hughes	Republican	8,538,221	254
1920	**Warren G. Harding**	Republican	16,152,200	404
	James M. Cox	Democratic	9,147,353	127
	Eugene V. Debs	Socialist	919,799	
1924	**Calvin Coolidge**	Republican	15,725,016	382
	John W. Davis	Democratic	8,385,586	136
	Robert M. LaFollette	Progressive	4,822,856	13
1928	**Herbert C. Hoover**	Republican	21,392,190	444
	Alfred E. Smith	Democratic	15,016,443	87
1932	**Franklin D. Roosevelt**	Democratic	22,809,638	472
	Herbert C. Hoover	Republican	15,758,901	59
	Norman Thomas	Socialist	881,951	
1936	**Franklin D. Roosevelt**	Democratic	27,751,612	523
	Alfred M. Landon	Republican	16,618,913	8
	William Lemke	Union	891,858	
1940	**Franklin D. Roosevelt**	Democratic	27,243,466	449
	Wendell L. Willkie	Republican	22,304,755	82
1944	**Franklin D. Roosevelt**	Democratic	25,602,505	432
	Thomas E. Dewey	Republican	22,006,278	99
1948	**Harry S. Truman**	Democratic	24,105,812	303
	Thomas E. Dewey	Republican	21,970,065	189
	J. Strom Thurmond	States' Rights	1,169,063	39
	Henry A. Wallace	Progressive	1,157,172	
1952	**Dwight D. Eisenhower**	Republican	33,936,234	442
	Adlai E. Stevenson	Democratic	27,314,992	89
1956	**Dwight D. Eisenhower**	Republican	35,590,472	457
	Adlai E. Stevenson	Democratic	26,022,752	73
1960	**John F. Kennedy**	Democratic	34,227,096	303
	Richard M. Nixon	Republican	34,108,546	219

YEAR	CANDIDATES	PARTY	POPULAR VOTE	ELECTORAL VOTE
1964	**Lyndon B. Johnson**	Democratic	43,126,233	486
	Barry M. Goldwater	Republican	27,174,989	53
1968	**Richard M. Nixon**	Republican	31,783,783	301
	Hubert H. Humphrey	Democratic	31,271,839	191
	George C. Wallace	Amer. Independent	9,899,557	46
1972	**Richard M. Nixon**	Republican	47,168,963	520
	George S. McGovern	Democratic	29,169,615	17
	John Hospers	Republican (noncandidate)		1
1976	**Jimmy Carter**	Democratic	40,827,292	297
	Gerald R. Ford	Republican	39,146,157	240
	Ronald Reagan	Republican (noncandidate)		1
1980	**Ronald Reagan**	Republican	43,899,248	489
	Jimmy Carter	Democratic	35,481,435	49
	John Anderson	Independent	5,719,437	
1984	**Ronald Reagan**	Republican	53,428,357	525
	Walter Mondale	Democratic	36,930,923	13

INDEX